Welcome to
Teaching Reading in the 21st Century *Fourth Edition!*

Rooted in the extensive research of its well-known author team, this comprehensive, balanced approach to reading instruction includes two full chapters on comprehension and emphasizes the need for students to learn how to read critically as well as fluently.

 Not only does [*Teaching Reading in the 21st Century*] comprehensively cover certain aspects such as the history of the field, the needs of ELL, and the aggressive political influences in the field, but it covers those things and more in an even, balanced way and in a friendly, accessible voice.
—Christine Woodcock, *Massachusetts College of Liberal Arts*

Teaching Reading in the 21st Century also acknowledges the integral role of ongoing assessment in reading instruction through marginal assessment notes throughout, as well as a full chapter and a supplementary booklet filled with assessment instruments, both co-written by assessment expert Robert Calfee.

 The primary strength of [*Teaching Reading in the 21st Century*] is its careful merger of theory and practice. The features are woven into the narrative in a way that encourages readers to get engaged, [and] the diversity components are highly appropriate for our students. I appreciate that diversity issues are presented throughout rather than solely in a separate chapter.
—Jeanne Shay Schumm, *University of Miami*

And this new edition continues to be informed by authentic classroom practice, with a wealth of In the Classroom anecdotes and Instructional Routines that transfer the strategies and guidelines from the page into the classroom and three in-depth Classroom Portraits that follow real teachers through the complex processes of planning, instructional implementation, and ongoing assessment.

 [*Teaching Reading in the 21st Century* is] sound in theory, updated in content, and comprehensive in scope. The authors should be congratulated on the thorough, accurate content they present.
—Donna Rhinesmith, *Truman State University*

Teaching Reading
in the 21st Century

Teaching Reading in the 21st Century

FOURTH EDITION

Michael F. Graves
University of Minnesota

Connie Juel
Stanford University

Bonnie B. Graves
Children's Author

PEARSON

Boston | New York | San Francisco
Mexico City | Montreal | Toronto | London | Madrid | Munich | Paris
Hong Kong | Singapore | Tokyo | Cape Town | Sydney

Executive Editor: Aurora Martínez Ramos
Editorial Assistant: Lynda Giles
Senior Development Editor: Virginia Blanford
Executive Marketing Manager: Krista Clark
Production Editor: Janet Domingo
Editorial Production Service: Lifland et al., Bookmakers
Composition Buyer: Linda Cox
Manufacturing Buyer: Megan Cochran
Electronic Composition: Omegatype Typography, Inc.
Interior Design: Carol Somberg
Photo Researcher: Sarah K. Evertson/Image Quest
Cover Administrator: Kristina Mose-Libon

For related titles and support materials, visit our online catalog at
www.ablongman.com.

Between the time website information is gathered and then published, it is not unusual
for some sites to have closed. Also, the transcription of URLs can result in
typographical errors. The publisher would appreciate notification where these errors
occur so that they may be corrected in subsequent editions.

Library of Congress Cataloging-in-Publication Data

Graves, Michael F.
    Teaching reading in the 21st century / Michael F. Graves, Connie Juel, Bonnie B.
Graves.—4th ed.
        p. cm.
    Includes bibliographical references and index.
    ISBN 0-205-49264-9
    1. Reading (Elementary) I. Juel, Connie. II. Graves, Bonnie B. III. Title. IV. Title:
Teaching reading in the twenty-first century.

LB1573.G656 2006
372.4—dc22

                                                                    2006044778

Photo credits appear on pages 503–504, which should be considered an extension of
this copyright page.

Printed in the United States of America

10 9 8 7 6 5 4 3 2 1   RRD-OH   10   09   08   07   06

*A*s was the case with past editions, this edition is dedicated to Susan Jones, Mike's sister, who in her 35 years of teaching led well over a thousand second-graders toward the high level of literacy they needed to succeed in the 21st century.

It is also dedicated to the more than 3 million other elementary and middle-school teachers who each day nurture over 50 million students toward this same goal.

Brief Contents

Contents

Cookie knocked a plant
off the windowsill.

Classroom Portrait   A Day in the Life of Jenna LeBlanc and Her First-Grade Students

list of Features

in the Classroom

All the In the Classroom features reflect what happens when various reading strategies are used in today's classrooms. Those marked with an asterisk (*) on this list provide step-by-step **instructional routines** that may be transferred directly into their classrooms by new teachers.

(continued)

in the Classroom *(continued)*

the Reading Corner

Classroom Portrait

Strengths and Challenges of DIVERSITY

Preface

Like its predecessors, *Teaching Reading in the 21st Century*, Fourth Edition, has but one goal: to provide you with the knowledge and skills necessary to carry out the most challenging and rewarding task ahead of you—teaching young children the literacy skills they will need to lead happy, productive, and rewarding lives. With this goal in mind, we have considered recent national reports on reading instruction, including the National Research Council's *Preventing Reading Difficulties in Young Children* (Snow, Burns, & Griffin, 1998), the National Reading Panel's *Teaching Children to Read* (2000), and the RAND Reading Study Group's *Reading for Understanding* (2002). We have also considered the No Child Left Behind Act of 2001 (2002) and the curriculum advanced by Reading First. As a result, this book directly addresses each of the "Five Pillars of Reading Instruction" that make up the Reading First curriculum: Chapter 4 considers phonemic awareness and other aspects of emergent literacy; Chapter 5, phonics and word recognition; Chapter 6, fluency; Chapter 7, vocabulary; and Chapters 8 and 9, comprehension.

While we recognize the importance of the five-part Reading First curriculum, we, like many of our colleagues (for example, Allington, 2005; NCTE Commission on Reading, 2004; Pressley, 2006), also recognize that the Reading First curriculum does not constitute a comprehensive and balanced approach to reading instruction. For this reason, in addition to the above-mentioned chapters, this book includes chapters on encouraging independent reading and reader response (Chapter 10), fostering higher-order thinking and deep understanding (Chapter 11), the reading-writing connection (Chapter 12), reading instruction for English-language learners (Chapter 13), and classroom assessment (Chapter 14). Also, to provide the background necessary to gain a deep understanding of reading instruction, the book begins with information about reading theories, students' proficiency in reading, and the reading curriculum (Chapter 1) and continues with information about instructional principles that undergird effective reading instruction and past and present-day approaches to reading instruction (Chapter 2). Finally, prompted by both recent research on motivation and recent recognition of the importance of motivation (see, for example, National Research Council, 2004; Pressley, 2006; Wigfield & Eccles, 2002), we have included in this edition of the book a separate chapter on motivation and engagement (Chapter 3).

In sum, this book presents a multifaceted, comprehensive, and balanced approach to reading instruction designed to help children achieve the high level of literacy essential for the 21st century. In the curriculum described here, students receive instruction, practice, encouragement, and ongoing support in the full range of knowledge, skills, and attitudes necessary for them to become competent and committed readers—children and later adults who both can read and choose to read. It is our hope as well as our very strong belief that *Teaching Reading in the 21st Century,* Fourth Edition, will equip you with the knowledge and skills you need to begin your journey toward becoming the very best teacher of literacy you can be.

New to the Fourth Edition

We have made a number of changes in this edition to ensure that everything you read here is current and accurate. Additionally, we have written two new chapters covering areas that are critical to literacy instruction: motivation and fluency.

Chapter 3, Motivation and Engagement, addresses perhaps the most difficult challenge that teachers face in 21st-century classrooms. Unique in reading methods textbooks, this chapter encourages you to make motivation a top priority and provides clear, concrete strategies for creating a literate environment, setting appropriate challenges, and ensuring student success. An extended discussion of a master teacher in the classroom concludes the chapter.

Chapter 6, Fluency, brings together a variety of classroom-proven, research-based strategies for building fluency in young learners.

Other major changes include greatly expanding the *Assessments and Lesson Plans* booklet that accompanies this text, including more information on assessment throughout the text, and adding a number of practical suggestions to Chapter 13, Reading Instruction for English-Language Learners.

We have, of course, also updated all the chapters, incorporating the latest information on topics ranging from the findings of the National Assessment of Educational Progress to research-based approaches to vocabulary instruction. And references have been added to some of the best of the newest children's literature.

Special Features

This edition uses a rich variety of special features to emphasize the ways in which reading instruction and learning play out in contemporary classrooms.

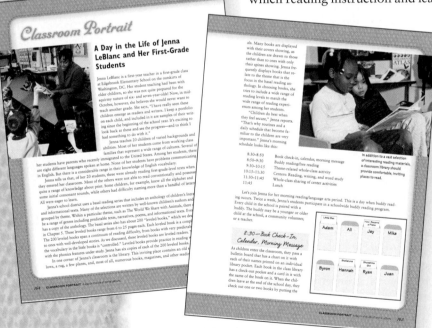

■ **Classroom Portraits** are in-depth models that show how real teachers—one in a first-grade classroom, another in a third-/fourth-grade classroom, and one in a fifth-/sixth-grade classroom—teach real lessons. These step-by-step, day-in-the-life portraits begin with planning and move through the actual lessons, with illustrations, time charts, and instructional notes. We have tried in this unique feature to show you the reality of a lesson—not just the actual instructional moment, but the preparation that leads up to it and the reflection that follows it.

■ **In the Classroom** boxes model dialogues, interactions, and vignettes that reflect exemplary literacy instruction. Those marked "Instructional Routines" provide ready-to-use lessons and activities that can be transferred directly to your own classroom.

■ **Reading Corner** boxes offer annotated lists of useful and relevant children's literature. An additional list of children's literature appears at the end of every chapter.

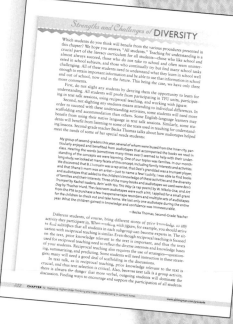

■ **Reflect and Apply** questions at the end of major sections invite you to think critically about what you have read and try out some of the central ideas presented.

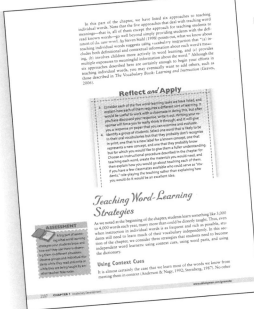

■ A **Strengths and Challenges of Diversity** section at the end of most chapters addresses the issues and opportunities in today's diversity-rich classrooms.

Three kinds of **marginal notes** provide strategies and cross-references to other resources.

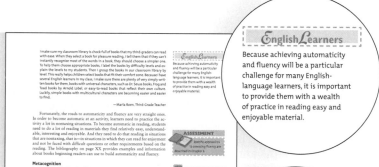

■ **English Learners** marginal notes offer appropriate strategies for working with students whose first language is not English.

English Learners

Because achieving automaticity and fluency will be a particular challenge for many English-language learners, it is important to provide them with a wealth of practice in reading easy and enjoyable material.

■ **Assessment** notes offer assessment tips and strategies, as well as references to additional instruments and resources available in the *Assessments and Lesson Plans* booklet, which is packaged with every new copy of this text.

ASSESSMENT

Specific approaches to assessing fluency are described in Chapter 6.

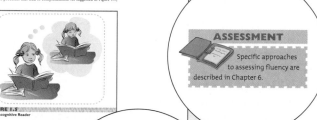

CW 1.4 links to more information on metacognition and how important it is to your students' success.

■ **Companion Website** notes direct you to additional appropriate content on the Website for this book (www.ablongman.com/graves4e).

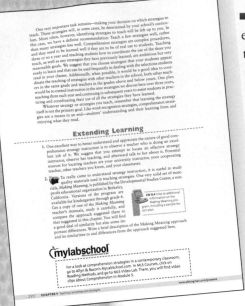

■ **Extending Learning** activities at the end of each chapter focus on observing classrooms, talking with parents and teachers, or investigating topics further. At least one activity in each chapter encourages you to create an artifact to be included in your teaching portfolio and is indicated by the following icon:

■ **Additional end-of-chapter resources** include listings of children's literature selections and cross-references to rich video models included in Allyn & Bacon's MyLabSchool.

Supplements

For Students

The *Assessments and Lesson Plans* booklet, packaged with every new copy of this text, provides a wide range of ready-to-use assessment instruments to evaluate proficiency in areas critical to student success in reading, including emergent literacy, phonics and other word-recognition skills, vocabulary, fluency, and comprehension. Written by assessment experts Robert Calfee and Kathleen Wilson, the booklet also includes detailed lesson plans authored by Michael Graves. These detailed plans show you just how to present effective lessons that assist students in understanding and enjoying the books and other materials they read, teach useful strategies for learning vocabulary, and teach powerful comprehension strategies.

The **Companion Website** (www.ablongman.com/graves4e) provides a wealth of objectives, review questions, key concepts, and links to useful Websites for each chapter.

MyLabSchool is Allyn & Bacon's unique resource for preservice teachers. Discover where the classroom comes to life! From videoclips of teachers and students interacting to sample lessons, portfolio templates, and standards integration, Allyn & Bacon brings you the tools you'll need to succeed in the classroom. If your text is not packaged with a MyLabSchool access code, go to www.ablongman.com to find out how to access MyLabSchool's powerful insights into how real classrooms work and a rich array of tools that will support you as you strive to be the very best teacher you can be.

For Instructors

Instructor's Manual with Test Items offers teaching suggestions and test items for every chapter.

PowerPoint Presentations will enhance your teaching of each chapter.

MyLabSchool is Allyn & Bacon's unique resource for preservice teachers. From videoclips of teachers and students interacting to sample lessons, portfolio templates, and standards integration, Allyn & Bacon brings your students the tools they'll need to succeed in the classroom. Available through a passcode-protected Website, MyLabSchool gives preservice teachers powerful insights into how real classrooms work and a rich array of tools that will support them on their journey from their first education class to their first classroom. MyLabSchool is also available in WebCT, Blackboard, and CourseCompass, Allyn & Bacon's private-label course management system.

Acknowledgments

Clearly, *Teaching Reading in the 21st Century* continues to change and evolve. With each new edition, we have built on the combined expertise of many colleagues throughout the country who are dedicated to literacy education. To you, we extend a special thank-you for your valuable feedback and assistance.

- Our editors, Aurora Martínez Ramos and Virginia Blanford, who assisted us throughout the revision process; our production editor, Janet Domingo, who helped make the finished book what it is; Carol Somberg, who did the outstanding interior design; Sarah K. Evertson, who supplied the excellent photos; and our book packaging and copyediting experts, Sally Lifland and Jeanne Yost, who finalized and polished the book.
- The many people who granted us permission to cite their work and reproduce their materials in this text.
- The reviewers for the Fourth Edition: James Barton, Rhode Island College; Donna Rhinesmith, Truman State University; Patsy Self, Florida International University; Jeanne Shay Schumm, University of Miami; and Christine Woodcock, Massachusetts College of Liberal Arts.
- The reviewers of previous editions, who have been so helpful in shaping this text.
- The teachers, researchers, and teacher-educators whose names you will see mentioned on nearly every page of this text, especially Cheri Cooke, Lauren Liang, and Cheryl Peterson, who wrote outstanding lesson plans; Maureen Prenn, who created much of the initial *Instructor's Manual*; Kathleen Clark, who assisted us with the emergent literacy and word-recognition chapters; Raymond Philippot, who assisted us with many of the other chapters; as well as Mark Aulls, Ann Beecher, Barbara Brunetti, Jerry Brunetti, David Carberry, Jim Hoffman, Susan Jones, Stephen Koziol, Anita Meinbach, Judy Peacock, Lynn Richards, Randall Ryder, Wayne Slater, Margo Sorenson, Kelly Spies, and Diann Stone. All lent their time and very special talents to this project.
- Our colleagues at the University of Minnesota and Stanford University, with special thanks to Lee Galda, Jay Samuels, Barbara Taylor, and Susan Watts, whose scholarship and dedication to the profession are without equal.
- Our colleague and Mike's mentor at Stanford, Robert Calfee, and Kathleen Wilson, of the University of Nebraska, for their outstanding chapter on assessment and their work on the *Assessments and Lesson Plans* booklet.
- Our students and teachers from kindergarten through graduate school, who over the years have inspired our thinking and contributed significantly to the ideas you will read about in this text.
- Our friends and family, who listened, encouraged, and sustained us throughout this lengthy and, at times, exhausting endeavor, especially our accomplished, supportive daughters, Julie and Erin.

About the Authors

In writing and revising this book, each of us brought to the task his or her experiences and expertise, and we would like to briefly introduce ourselves.

Michael F. Graves is Professor of Literacy Education at the University of Minnesota and a member of the IRA Reading Hall of Fame. Mike taught in the upper grades, and his research and writing focus on such matters as vocabulary, comprehension, and higher-order thinking. His current major research effort is an IES-funded research and development project on teaching comprehension strategies.

Connie Juel is Professor of Education at Stanford University and a member of the IRA Reading Hall of Fame. Connie taught in the primary grades, and her research and writing focus on such matters as phonemic awareness, phonics, and word study. Her current research centers on the effects of early elementary school instruction and specific interventions on literacy and language growth.

Bonnie B. Graves is a full-time education writer and the author of 15 books for children. Bonnie taught in third and fourth grades, and her major interests are making literature enticing and accessible to beginning and middle-grade learners. In addition to writing, Bonnie currently spends time working with children, teachers, and other educators on children's writing.

Added to our own experiences are those of the authors of the assessment chapter and of the *Assessments and Lesson Plans* booklet that accompanies this text—Robert Calfee, Professor Emeritus at Stanford University and a member of the IRA Reading Hall of Fame, and Kathleen Wilson, Assistant Professor at the University of Nebraska. Both Bob and Kathy have extensive experience in reading assessment.

Together, we have done everything possible to make *Teaching Reading in the 21st Century,* Fourth Edition, the very best book we could create, one that is truly comprehensive and balanced and that addresses the needs of all students, including children of color, students from low-income families, those with disabilities, and those of limited English proficiency.

Teaching Reading
in the 21st Century

Reading and
Learning to Read

chapter outline

CLASSROOM VIGNETTE

*I*t was the first day of summer vacation, and ten-year-old Carmella couldn't wait to meet up with her best friend Amber at the community pool. Just as she was considering which bathing suit to wear, she heard the patter of rain on the roof and looked out the window. "Daaang," she muttered. "No pool today." She flopped back on her bed and reached for Kate DiCamillo's *Because of Winn-Dixie* on her nightstand. Within minutes, she was deep into India Opal Buloni's new life in Florida, thoughts of the pool temporarily forgotten.

On the other side of town, when Carmella's friend Amber woke up and saw that rain had spoiled their plans for the community pool, she never thought of picking up a book. Unlike Carmella, she had not mastered the complex process of reading. Reading wasn't much fun for her, and she didn't do it often. Amber will probably spend most of the rainy day watching TV.

For some children, like Carmella, mastering the complex process of reading comes easily, and by fourth grade they are quite accomplished readers. For others, like Amber, this is not the case. As Carmella and Amber progress in school, they both will face increasingly challenging reading tasks, and both will need help in meeting those challenges. Amber—and other students who struggle in reading—will, of course, need more assistance than Carmella and other accomplished readers; but all your students will need the very best instruction and encouragement you can provide if they are to become the sort of readers the 21st century demands.

The Reading Process

Why should you care about the reading process? Why is it vital to develop a deep understanding of it? The answer is straightforward. Regardless of what you learn about the specifics of teaching reading from this text, your university courses, in-service sessions, conferences, and discussions with other teachers, much of what you do in the classroom will result from your personal understanding of the reading process. The number of teaching options you have is so great, the needs of different students so diverse, and the specifics of a particular teaching situation so unique that it is impossible to anticipate all of the decisions about literacy instruction that you will make each day. But understanding the mental processes involved as a reader actually reads can prepare you to make wise choices. Though not a simple task, developing an understanding of the reading process is vital to becoming an effective reading teacher and well worth the time and effort you will spend on it.

Although different authorities view the reading process somewhat differently, over the past 40 years, a widely accepted, balanced, and strongly supported view of the process has emerged. Here, we call this the cognitive-constructivist view of reading. This construct forms the foundation of the approach to reading presented in this book. In the following section—which includes subsections on the cognitive orientation, schema, constructivism, reader-response theory, and sociocultural theory—we define this concept. In the next section, we explain several theories that elaborate, complement, and supplement this concept.

The Cognitive-Constructivist View of Reading

The cognitive-constructivist view of reading emphasizes that reading is a process in which the reader actively searches for meaning in what she reads. This search for meaning depends very heavily on the reader's having an existing store of knowledge, or schemata, that she draws on in that search for meaning. In fact, the active contribution of the reader is significant enough to justify the assertion that she actually constructs much of the meaning she arrives at in reading.

For example, as she reads *Because of Winn-Dixie,* Carmella learns that India Opal is sad because her mother recently walked out on her and her father. Later in the book, when Carmella learns that Amanda Wilkinson, a girl India Opal does not at first get along with, is sad because her younger brother recently died, Carmella can construct the inference that Opal and Amanda may become friends. Nothing in the text tells Carmella this; the inference comes from her knowledge that people who have things in common often become friends and from her active processing of the text. Notice how teacher Martin Cummings highlights this use of background knowledge and encourages active processing with his sixth-graders in In the Classroom 1.1.

Using Background Knowledge

Martin Cummings wrote the first paragraph from Sharon Flake's novel *The Skin I'm In* on the board:

> The first time I seen her, I got a bad feeling inside. Not like I was in danger or nothing. Just like she was somebody I should stay clear of. To tell the truth, she was a freak like me. The kind of person folks can't help but tease. That's bad if you're a kid like me. It's worse for a new teacher like her.

He read the paragraph aloud to his sixth-graders and then said, "What does this paragraph tell us? What meaning do you get from it?"

Chris: The narrator's someone young, maybe our age.

Mr. Cummings: What makes you think so?

Chris: 'Cause it says "a kid like me" and sounds like the way kids talk.

Lateisha: Yeah, Black kids, not White kids. I think the person talking is Black.

Mr. Cummings: So you think the narrator's Black. What else do we know about the narrator from this paragraph?

Kyle: She has a low opinion of herself.

Mr. Cummings: How do you know that?

Kyle: 'Cause she calls herself a freak.

in the Classroom 1.1

As the preceding dialogue illustrates, Mr. Cummings is helping his students realize that readers actively search for meaning in what they read, and that the meaning they construct from a text depends on their own knowledge about the world and its conventions.

The Cognitive Orientation

The earliest influence behind this view comes from cognitive psychology, the psychological orientation that became the main perspective of American psychology beginning in the 1960s (Gardner, 1985).

Cognitive psychologists view the learner and her background knowledge as central to learning and the study of learners' thought processes as a central focus of their work. They also view learners as active participants, who act on, rather than simply respond to, their external environment as they learn. In the

CW 1.1 links to the American Educational Research Association's *Research Points,* where you can download a copy of "English-Language Learners: Boosting Academic Achievement" for a brief overview of a cognitive approach to instruction of English learners.

cognitive view, reading is very much an active process in which the meaning the reader gleans from a text is heavily influenced by the cognitive work that she puts into the reading process. Both the beginning reader—whom we might observe carefully sounding out words as she reads orally—and the accomplished reader such as Carmella—who appears to be effortlessly absorbing *Because of Winn-Dixie*—are in fact actively engaged in making meaning from the text.

Schema

The concept of schema, the second influence on the view of the reading process we are describing, is closely related to the cognitive orientation. Schema theory is concerned with knowledge, particularly with the way knowledge is represented in our minds and the importance of prior knowledge to learning something new. According to the theory, knowledge is packaged in organized structures termed *schemata*. David Rumelhart (1980) states that schemata constitute our knowledge about "objects, situations, events, sequences of events, actions, and sequences of actions." We have schemata for objects such as a house, for situations such as being in a class, for events such as going to a football game, and for sequences of events such as getting up, eating, showering, and going to work. We interpret our experiences—whether direct encounters with the world or vicarious experiences gained through reading—by comparing and, in most cases, matching those experiences to existing schemata.

Figure 1.1 suggests the wealth of knowledge that a youngster we'll call Maggie, and every human being, internalizes. However, although the figure suggests the huge number of schemata Maggie has internalized, it does not capture another crucial feature of schemata. Our schemata are related to each other and constitute a vast and elaborate network of interrelationships. For example, Maggie's schema for *house* is related to her schema for *neighborhood*, in that her house is part of her neighborhood; and it is also related to her schema for

ASSESSMENT

Using an interest inventory such as the one described in Chapter 6 will help you find out about students' interests and their background knowledge.

English Learners

For some English-language learners, knowledge of the culture depicted in the reading you do and the culture of the classroom will be a significant challenge. Make every effort to find out what schemata your students do and do not have, and teach accordingly.

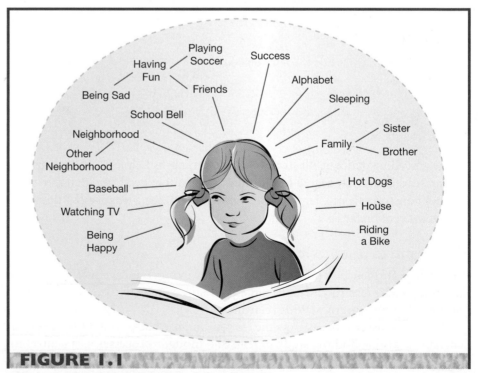

FIGURE 1.1

A Few of Maggie's Schemata

Today's students bring a host of different schemata to today's classrooms.

family, in that her family lives in her house. At the same time, her schema for *house* is related to her schema for *tepee* because both houses and tepees are dwellings. These networks of *organized* knowledge are virtually endless and constitute much of the intellectual capital that human beings have to work with.

One very important consequence of readers having these rich, internalized networks of schemata is that, once a particular schema is evoked, a huge store of knowledge becomes instantly available. Suppose a student is reading a story and comes across the sentence "Mark stopped at McDonald's on the way home." Immediately, her schema for fast-food restaurants provides her with a wealth of information: Mark ordered and picked up his food at the counter; he ordered something like a burger or fries or a soda—not steak or lobster; he had to pay for his food, but not too much; he seated himself in the restaurant or perhaps took his food somewhere else to eat it; and he probably ate it fairly rapidly. Information such as this, and often richer bundles of information, becomes available to us as soon as we evoke a schema for something we are reading or hearing or viewing.

Right now, you are building a schema for schemata; the more you learn about schemata, the easier it will be for you to learn even more about them. Both what we learn and the ease or difficulty of learning it are heavily influenced by our schemata. The more we know about something, the easier it will be to deal with that topic and learn more about it. Schemata assist the reader in initially making sense of what she reads, relating newly acquired information to prior knowledge, determining the relative importance of information in a text, making inferences, and remembering (Anderson & Pearson, 1984).

Constructivism

Constructivism, the third influence on the view of the reading process we are describing here, has many roots and many branches (Phillips, 2000), being in fact a philosophical (von Glaserfeld, 1984), political (Searle, 1993), and social (Gergen, 1985) construct as well as a psychological one. Here, we use the term in its psychological sense. Used in this sense, constructivism serves to emphasize a point already made and to introduce an additional point.

ASSESSMENT

It is vital that you know as much as possible about the background knowledge of both your English-language learners and your native-English speakers. One of the most practical ways to access that knowledge is to frequently talk to individual students about topics you're dealing with.

> **Kaiya:** Mei-Mei wanted a bear for Christmas.
>
> **Lawrence:** Mei-Mei wanted her mother to be happy.
>
> **Ali:** Mei-Mei wanted to be warm most of all.

FIGURE 1.2

Three Students' Responses to the Same Question About a Story They Read

CW 1.2 links to descriptions and discussions of constructivism and several related concepts.

Constructivism emphasizes the fact that comprehending a text is very much an active, constructive process. In addition to emphasizing the active nature of reading, constructivism holds that the meaning one constructs from a text is subjective—the result of one particular reader's processing of the text. Just as no two builders will construct exactly the same house from a blueprint, so no two readers will construct exactly the same meaning from a text. Each reader is influenced by the sum total of her experience as well as by her unique intellectual makeup. Because of this, each reader constructs a somewhat different interpretation of the text, the text as she conceptualizes it (von Glaserfeld, 1984). The three student journal entries listed in Figure 1.2 illustrate this concept. All three students were given the same prompt for the picture book *Mama Bear* by Chyng Feng Sun. The story tells of a girl who bakes and sells almond cookies in order to earn enough money to buy a large, expensive stuffed bear for Christmas because she thinks it will help keep her and her mother warm. The students were asked to respond to this question: "What did Mei-Mei want most for Christmas?" Each answer is, of course, correct yet points up a different perspective on the story.

Having noted that constructivism emphasizes the subjectivity of meaning, we want to also note that different texts differ dramatically in how much they constrain it (Stanovich, 1994). An abstract poem may prompt many appropriate interpretations, but a manual on how to install new software should prompt only one. In between these two extremes lies a range of texts that invite various degrees of individual interpretation. However, when reading straightforward stories and a good deal of informational material, most readers will construct quite similar meanings for what they read.

As we noted in beginning this section, constructivism is a social construct as well as a psychological one. Most constructivists emphasize that the social world in which we live heavily influences the meaning that we derive from our experiences, including our experiences with text. Thus, constructivism strongly supports the inclusion of a variety of sorts of discussion and group work as part of reading and learning (Calfee & Patrick, 1995).

Reader-Response Theory

Reader-response theory, the fourth influence on the cognitive-constructivist view of reading, has much in common with constructivism. Over the past 30 years, it has become a very prominent influence on literature instruction (Beach, 1993; Galda & Graves, 2007; Marshall, 2000). Reader-response theory puts a good deal of emphasis on the reader. It stresses that the meaning one gains from text is the result of a transaction between the reader and the text and that readers will have a range of responses to literary works (Rosenblatt, 1938/1995, 1978). When reading complex literary texts, students will derive a variety of interpretations. Many literary texts simply do not have a single correct interpretation, and readers should be allowed and encouraged to construct a variety of interpretations—if they can support them.

One important fact to keep in mind when considering reader-response theory is that it applies primarily to certain types of texts and certain purposes for reading. As part of explaining when and where reader-response theory applies, Rosenblatt (1978) points out that there are two primary types of reading—*efferent*, or informational, reading and *aesthetic* reading. In efferent reading, the reader's attention is focused primarily on what she will take from the reading—what information will be learned. Much of the reading that both students and adults do is done for the sake of learning new information, answering questions, discovering how to complete a procedure, or gleaning knowledge that can be used in solving a particular problem. Much of the reading done in such subjects as health, science, math, and geography is informational reading. These texts, unlike many literary texts, often constrain meaning substantially, do not invite a variety of interpretations, and should yield quite similar interpretations for various readers (Stanovich, 1994).

The other sort of reading Rosenblatt considers, aesthetic reading, is quite different. In aesthetic reading, the primary concern is not with what students remember about a text after they have read it but with what happens to them as they are reading. The primary purpose when reading aesthetically is not to gain information but to experience the text. Although the aesthetic reader, like the reader whose goal is gaining information, must understand the text, she must "also pay attention to associations, feelings, attitudes, and ideas" that the text arouses (Rosenblatt, 1978). For the most part, literature is written to provide an aesthetic experience. Most adults read literature for enjoyment; they do not read literature to learn it. And students need to be given opportunities to do the same.

Sociocultural Theory

Sociocultural theory, the last influence on the cognitive-constructivist view we will describe, includes both differences from and similarities to the influences discussed thus far. It differs most notably from the cognitive orientation, in that learning is viewed as primarily a social matter rather than an individual matter. This theory is most similar to constructivism, in that learning is viewed as an active and constructive task and what is learned is viewed as subjective. As described by its originator, Vygotsky (1978), or by Vygotskian scholars such as James Wertsch (1998), sociocultural theory is complex. However, its implications for the view of reading and learning described here can be succinctly listed.

First, the social and cultural backgrounds of students have a huge and undeniable effect on their learning. Unless we as teachers take students' social backgrounds and modes of learning and thinking into account, little learning is likely to occur. Second, since learning is quintessentially social, much learning—particularly much of the best and most lasting learning—will take place as groups of learners work together. Dialogue—give-and-take, face-to-face

English Learners

In order to give English-language learners opportunities to make personal responses to literature, we need to give them literature that touches their lives and their feelings. Finding literature that will engage your English-language learners should be a continuing goal.

discussion in which students strive to make themselves understood and to understand others—is a mainstay of learning. Third, the classroom, the school, and the various communities of students in a classroom are social contexts that have strong influences on what is or is not learned in the classroom. Each of these contexts must be carefully considered in planning and carrying out instruction.

Reflect *and* Apply

As we have just explained, a central tenet of the view of the reading process that underlies this book is that comprehension is an active, constructive process. What that means is that, if you are to understand the ideas we present, remember them, and use them in your teaching, you must mentally manipulate them in some way. To help you do this, we include Reflect and Apply sections periodically throughout the text. Ideally, as constructivist and sociocultural principles suggest, you will discuss your responses with others—a study group, your class, or your course instructor.

1. Suppose that one teacher taught the word *relax* by simply saying, "*Relax* means to loosen up," while another taught it by having students view several pictures of people relaxing, having them assume relaxing positions themselves, and then having them talk about situations in which they have felt comfortable and relaxed. Explain how the second teacher is demonstrating a cognitive perspective.

2. Identify a schema that both inner-city students and suburban students are likely to have, one that inner-city students are likely to have but suburban students might lack, and one that suburban students are likely to have but inner-city students might lack. Why do certain groups of students share some schemata but not others? What does sociocultural theory say about the importance of students having different schemata?

Concepts That Elaborate and Complement the Cognitive-Constructivist View

Here, we consider several concepts that extend the cognitive-constructivist view of the reading process and that underlie the instructional procedures we will present throughout this book. These are the interactive model of reading, automaticity, fluency, and metacognition.

The Interactive Model of Reading

Schema theory emphasizes the importance of the reader's knowledge in understanding a text. The interactive model of reading, on the other hand, reminds us that both the reader and the text play important roles in reading. In the interactive model of reading set forth by Rumelhart (1977), processing is neither exclusively text based nor exclusively reader based. Instead, the reader arrives at her understanding of a text by simultaneously synthesizing information from a variety of sources. These include word-level knowledge, syntactic knowledge, and various sorts of schemata she has internalized.

SITUATION	RESULT
Selection with an unfamiliar topic and difficult vocabulary	The reader will give too much attention to individual words and neglect to use prior knowledge to help in understanding the text.
Too much oral reading with an emphasis on being correct and a penalty for being incorrect	The reader will focus on individual words and letters, rather than on sentences, paragraphs, and ideas.
A less-able student reading orally in front of peers	The reader will focus attention on correctly pronouncing individual words and give little attention to meaning.
Only silent reading with no postreading follow-up discussion	The reader will pay too little attention to the ideas in the text and guess at the meaning with little use of the text to confirm guesses.

FIGURE 1.3

Situations That Encourage Too Much or Too Little Attention to the Text

Good readers simultaneously rely on the text and on their background knowledge as they construct meaning. We as teachers need to provide students with the sorts of texts and tasks that promote this interplay of text and background knowledge. Figure 1.3 depicts situations that encourage too much or too little attention to the text and that should be avoided.

In concluding this section on the interactive model, it is worth pointing out that although the interactive model was developed nearly 30 years ago, it is fully consistent with the model of reading comprehension developed by the RAND Reading Study Group (2002), a group much more recently commissioned by the U.S. Department of Education to review the research on reading comprehension: "We define reading comprehension as the process of simultaneously extracting and constructing meaning through interaction and involvement with written language." The RAND group goes on to note that comprehension entails three elements:

- the *reader* who is doing the comprehending
- the *text* that is to be comprehended
- the *activity* in which comprehension is a part

Furthermore, the RAND group notes, these three elements operate within and are heavily influenced by a *sociocultural context,* a situation depicted in Figure 1.4.

We have reproduced this summary of the RAND group's orientation here because, in addition to being consistent with the interactive model, it is consistent with the view of the reading process we have just discussed and with the program of reading instruction we recommend throughout this book.

Automaticity

The concept of automaticity is both crucial and straightforward. An automatic activity is one that we can perform instantly and with very little attention. As David LaBerge and S. Jay Samuels (1974) pointed

CW 1.3 links to the complete RAND Reading Study Group Report— *Reading for Understanding.* This is just one example of a host of timely and useful full-text documents available on the Web without charge.

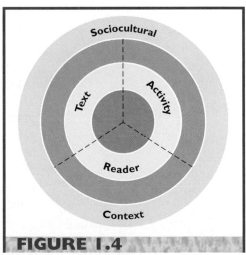

FIGURE 1.4

RAND Study Heuristic for Thinking About Reading Comprehension

Source: RAND Reading Study Group. (2002). *Reading for Understanding: Toward an R&D Program in Reading Comprehension,* MR-1465-OERI. Santa Monica, CA: RAND Education. Copyright 2002. Reprinted with permission.

out in their pioneering work on automaticity in reading, the mind's attentional capacity is severely limited; in fact, we can attend to only about one thing at a time. If we are faced with a task in which we are forced to attend to too many things at once, we will fail. For example, a number of people have reached a level of automaticity in driving a stick shift car. They can automatically push in the clutch, let up on the accelerator, shift gears, let out the clutch, and press on the accelerator—and they can do all this while driving in rush hour traffic. Beginning drivers cannot do all of this at once; they have not yet automated the various subprocesses, and it would be foolish and dangerous for them to attempt to drive a stick shift car in an attention-demanding situation such as rush hour traffic.

Reading includes a number of subprocesses that need to take place at the same time—processes such as recognizing words, assigning meanings to words, constructing the meanings of sentences and larger units, and relating the information gleaned from the text to information we already have. Unless some of these processes are automated, readers simply cannot do all of this at once. Specifically, readers need to perform two processes automatically: They need to recognize words automatically, and they need to assign meanings to words automatically. For example, if a student is reading and comes across the word *imperative*, she needs to automatically recognize the word and automatically—immediately and without conscious attention—know that it means "absolutely necessary." If the student needs to pause often and struggle to recognize and assign meanings to words, reading will be difficult and laborious, and the student will not understand much of what she is reading.

Fluency

Achieving automaticity is vitally important because automaticity is a prerequisite for fluency, a closely related skill. Fluency is the ability to "read a text orally with speed, accuracy, expression, and comprehension" (Samuels, 2002a). It is also important to recognize the need for fluency in silent reading—to read at an appropriate rate, smoothly, and with good comprehension. Fluent readers decode text automatically. Because they can decode a text automatically, they are able to decode it and comprehend it at the same time. In turn, being able to simultaneously decode and comprehend a text results in oral reading that is accurate, smooth, and fairly rapid, and that shows proper expression.

To become fluent silent readers, students need to do a lot of silent reading in materials that are interesting, enjoyable, and relatively easy. To become fluent oral readers, students can engage in a variety of different oral reading activities such as paired reading, echoic reading, and repeated reading (Rasinski, 2003). These and many other techniques for creating fluent readers, as well as the many prerequisite skills that underlie fluent reading (Pikulski & Chard, 2005), are discussed in Chapter 6.

Achieving automaticity and fluency is often a particular challenge for students for whom English is a second language. In addition to going through the processes that native speakers do, nonnative speakers may need to translate English words into their own language in the process of arriving at meaning. Thus, becoming automatic in processing words and fluent in reading texts is extremely important for English-language learners. Teacher Marla Roen understands the importance of providing students with plenty of easy reading material to help them gain automaticity:

Because achieving automaticity and fluency will be a particular challenge for many English-language learners, it is important to provide them with a wealth of practice in reading easy and enjoyable material.

I make sure my classroom library is chock-full of books that my third-graders can read with ease. When they select a book for pleasure reading, I tell them that if they can't instantly recognize most of the words in a book, they should choose a simpler one. To help them choose appropriate books, I label the books by difficulty levels and explain the levels to my students. Then I group the books in our classroom library by level. This really helps children select books that fit their comfort zone. Because I have several English learners in my class, I make sure there are plenty of very simply written books for them, books with universal characters, such as Dr. Seuss books, Frog and Toad books by Arnold Lobel, or easy-to-read books that reflect their own culture. Luckily, simple books with multicultural characters are becoming easier and easier to find.

—Marla Roen, Third-Grade Teacher

Fortunately, the roads to automaticity and fluency are very straight ones. In order to become automatic at an activity, learners need to practice the activity a lot in nontaxing situations. To become automatic in reading, students need to do a lot of reading in materials they find relatively easy, understandable, interesting, and enjoyable. And they need to do that reading in situations that are nontaxing—that is, in situations in which they can read for enjoyment and not be faced with difficult questions or other requirements based on the reading. The bibliography on page 12 provides examples of and information about books beginning readers can use to build automaticity and fluency.

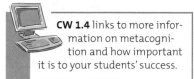

ASSESSMENT

Specific approaches to assessing fluency are described in Chapter 6.

Metacognition

As defined by John Flavel (1976), "metacognition refers to one's knowledge concerning one's own cognitive processes and products or anything related to them." With respect to reading, metacognition refers to the reader's awareness of her comprehension of a text as she is reading it and to the reader's regulation of the processes that lead to comprehension. As suggested in Figure 1.5,

CW 1.4 links to more information on metacognition and how important it is to your students' success.

FIGURE 1.5
The Metacognitive Reader

metacognitive readers have the ability to mentally step outside of themselves and view themselves as learners faced with particular learning tasks. By stepping outside of themselves, they can become self-regulated learners, learners who generate thoughts, feelings, strategies, and behaviors that help them attain their learning goals (Schunk & Zimmerman, 1998).

Accomplished readers have metacognitive knowledge about themselves, the reading tasks they face, and the strategies they can employ in completing these tasks. For example, as you began to read this section, you might have realized that you have no prior knowledge about metacognition (self-knowledge), noticed that the section is brief (task knowledge), and decided that the strategy of reading the section through several times would be fruitful (strategy knowledge). Thus, you exhibited metacognitive knowledge prior to beginning reading.

the *Reading Corner*

Books to Help Build Automaticity and Fluency in Young Readers

As we just said, to become automatic in reading, students need a lot of practice reading things they find easy, understandable, and enjoyable. For children who are just beginning to read—typically first-graders—books that include frequently repeated common words (for example, *run* and *book*) and common word parts (for example, phonograms such as *-ick* and *-ake*) are ideal. Here we list some books from series specifically designed to be easy to read and thus to build beginning readers' automaticity and fluency, as well as several sources of information on easy-to-read books.

Easy-to-Read Series Books

Norman Bidwell. *Clifford Goes to Dog School.* Scholastic, 2002. Clifford proves to be quite a challenge for dog school. Just one of dozens of books in the Clifford series. 32 pages.

Denys Cazet. *Minnie and Moo: The Attack of the Easter Bunnies* (I Can Read Book 3). HarperCollins, 2005. In this Minnie and Moo adventure, these unconventional cows try to find an Easter bunny for Mr. and Mrs. Farmer's traditional Easter egg hunt. 48 pages.

Lillian Hoban. *Arthur's Birthday Party.* Harper-Trophy, 1999. At his gymnastics birthday party, Arthur the chimp is determined to be the best. 48 pages.

Arnold Lobel. *Frog and Toad Are Friends.* Harper & Row, 1970. The earliest adventures of these two friends. 64 pages.

Cynthia Rylant. *Henry and Mudge and the Tall Tree House.* Simon and Schuster Books for Young Readers, 2002. Henry gets a new tree house but worries that his dog Mudge won't be able to share it with him. One of the newest books in this popular series. 40 pages.

Jean Van Leeuwen. *Oliver and Amanda's Halloween.* Dial Press, 1992. Oliver and Amanda scramble to get just the right costume for Halloween. 48 pages.

Information on Easy-to-Read Books

R. L. Allington. *What Really Matters for Struggling Readers: Designing Research-Based Programs.* Longman, 2001. Chapter 3, "Kids Need Books They Can Read," provides a number of suggestions for choosing books young readers can read.

I. C. Fountas & G. S. Pinnell. *Leveled Books (K–8): Matching Texts to Readers for Effective Teaching.* Heinemann, 2005. Lists thousands of books leveled for grades K to 8.

M. F. Graves & B. B. Graves. *Scaffolding Reading Experiences: Designs for Student Success* (2nd ed.). Christopher Gordon, 2003. Chapter 10, "Assessing Text Difficulty and Accessibility," discusses features that make books easy or difficult.

Readers can also make use of metacognitive knowledge as they are reading; in fact, most metacognitive behavior probably takes place as one is reading. For example, if a reader comes across an unknown word as she is reading, one very reasonable response would be to read ahead a little to see if the context suggests a meaning. If it does, she can return to processing the text as a whole. If it does not, she has the choice of continuing to read even though the meaning of the word is unclear or seeking outside help with the word—perhaps asking the teacher or a classmate or checking the dictionary.

Readers can also make use of metacognitive knowledge after reading. For example, if a fifth-grader finished a section of a science chapter and realized she had gotten virtually nothing from it, it would probably be a good idea to read it again. And if she reread and still learned nothing, it would make good sense to ask the teacher or a classmate for help before struggling further with the text.

Active awareness of one's comprehension while reading and the ability to use effective fix-up strategies when comprehension breaks down are absolutely essential tools for becoming an effective reader, and lack of such metacognitive skills is a particularly debilitating characteristic of poor readers. But metacognition is not just a matter of *skill*; it is very much a matter of *will*. Students need to care whether or not they are comprehending and be motivated to use appropriate fix-up strategies if they are not. The goal is to bring all students to the point where they can and will make the effort to be as metacognitive as possible.

Reflect *and* Apply

3. One excellent way to check your understanding of a concept is to consider its opposite—what it is not. With this in mind, describe the sorts of reading you would assign, the after-reading requirements you would have, and the amount of reading you would have students do if your goal were that they *not* develop automaticity and fluency.

4. As we noted, a reader can be metacognitive before reading, during reading, or after reading. Now that you have read this section of the chapter, exercise your metacognitive skills by characterizing your understanding of it and noting some of the steps you could take to better understand it.

The Reading Proficiency of U.S. Students

Critics of the U.S. educational system have frequently lashed out at what they perceive as the inability of U.S. schools to educate students as well as they once did, the poor performance of U.S. students compared to that of students in other countries, and the general failure of U.S. schools to effectively teach reading. However, as David Berliner and Bruce Biddle demonstrate in *The Manufactured Crisis* (1995), many of these claims are "myths, half-truths, and . . . outright lies."

Here, we respond to such criticism and go beyond it to note the sorts of reading skills U.S. students can and must acquire. We begin by presenting solid evidence to dispel the myth that U.S. students read less well than they used to. Next, we present evidence to dispel the myth that they read less well than students in most other countries. After that, we briefly characterize U.S. students' reading proficiency. Finally, and most importantly, we consider the sorts of reading proficiency required in today's and tomorrow's world. This, of course, is the proficiency you want to help all students to achieve.

A Response to Current Criticisms

Our main purpose in this section is to respond to the frequently heard charge that U.S. students' reading skills are abysmal, that they are far worse than they were in this country in the past, and that they are pathetic when compared to those of students in other nations. We base our response primarily on two sources that provide the most reliable large-scale assessments data available—the National Assessment of Educational Progress (NAEP) and the International Association for the Evaluation of Education (IEA). The NAEP was established by the federal government 35 years ago to provide a periodic report card on U.S. students' achievements in reading and other academic areas. In other words, it was established to do exactly the job we are trying to do here—communicate about how U.S. students are doing in school. The NAEP tests for long-term trends about every four years and reports data for ages 9, 13, and 17. Figure 1.6 shows the results of eight administrations of these tests (Perie, Moran, Lutkus, & Tirre, 2005). The trend lines for ages 13 and 17 are basically flat, indicating that there has been little or no change in reading performance at these grade levels since 1971. The trend line for age 9 goes up very slightly from 1971 to 1999 and then just a bit more steeply from 1999 to 2004, indicating a small improvement in reading for this age level. Thus, over the past 35 years, the reading performance of 9-year-old U.S. students may have gone up just a bit, while those of 13- and 17-year-olds have remained very much

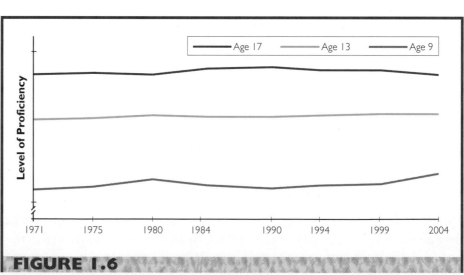

FIGURE 1.6

U.S. Students' Reading Proficiency 1971–2004

Source: Perie, M., Moran, R., Lutkus, A. D., & Tirre, W. (2005). NAEP 2004 trends in academic progress: Three decades of student performance in reading and mathematics. Washington, DC: U.S. Department of Education.

the same. Comparisons with reading levels of earlier times, though difficult to make because comparable data are in short supply, show very similar results (Anderson, Hiebert, Scott, & Wilkinson, 1985).

The IEA was established in the late 1950s to conduct international studies. The most recent IEA study of reading achievement was conducted during the 2001 school year in 35 countries (Mullis, Martin, Gonzales, & Kennedy, 2003). Figure 1.7 shows the results of this study, which gathered data from over 150,000 fourth-graders. As you can see, the United States ranked ninth among the 35 countries. While U.S. students did not score quite as well as Swedish students and students in seven other countries, they scored 41 points above the international average of 500. This is a very respectable showing indeed.

In summary, the best data available indicate that U.S. students' reading proficiency has not declined in recent years and is about like that of students in other industrialized nations. However, there is still cause for concern. Our interpretation of the NAEP data over the past 35 years suggests the following pattern of performance among U.S. students: By fourth grade, the vast majority of students can read easy material and answer simple questions on it. However, once the texts become slightly more difficult—the sorts of things middle-grade students are expected to deal with—a large percentage of middle-grade students cannot read and understand the material and neither can a sizable percentage of high school

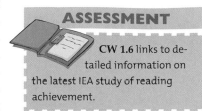

ASSESSMENT

CW 1.6 links to detailed information on the latest IEA study of reading achievement.

COUNTRIES	AVERAGE SCALE SCORE	COUNTRIES	AVERAGE SCALE SCORE
Sweden	561	Greece	524
Netherlands	554	Slovak Republic	518
England	553	Iceland	512
Bulgaria	550	Romania	512
Larivia	545	Israel	509
Canada (O, Q)	544	Slovenia	502
Lithuania	543	**International Avg.**	**500**
Hungary	543	Norway	499
United States	542	Cyprus	494
Italy	541	Moldova, Rep. of	492
Germany	539	Turkey	449
Czech Republic	537	Macedonia, Rep. of	442
New Zealand	529	Colombia	422
Scotland	528	Argentina	420
Singapore	528	Iran, Islamic Rep. of	414
Russian Federation	528	Kuwait	396
Hong Kong, SAR	528	Morocco	350
France	525	Belize	327

FIGURE 1.7

Reading Scores of the 35 Countries Participating in the IEA International Study of Reading Achievement

Source: An International Perspective on Fostering Reading Development–PIRLS 2001 Highlights. Available at http://pirls.bc.edu.

seniors. And once both texts and questions become demanding—the sorts of material one would need to read to understand political and social issues or enjoy relatively sophisticated literature—very few students, even those about to graduate from high school, can deal with them. Additionally, the data indicate that many children raised in poverty and many Black, Hispanic, and American Indian students score lower than their middle-class and White counterparts. The United States still has a long way to go to ensure that all students become proficient readers.

Literacy for Today's and Tomorrow's World

As important as it is to understand how well U.S. students read, it is even more important to understand present-day literacy requirements and the way in which those requirements are growing. At one time, literacy was defined as the ability to sign your name. At another time, it was defined as the ability to read aloud a simple text with which you were already familiar—typically a passage from the Bible. Today, although there is no single definition of literacy, there is universal agreement that everyone needs a far higher level of literacy than at any time in our past, and this requirement will continue to grow. Irwin Kirsch and Ann Jungeblut (1986) define present-day literacy as "using printed and written information to function in society, to achieve one's goals, and to develop one's knowledge." Lauren Resnick (1987) views present-day literacy as a "higher-order skill" and notes that it requires thinking that is complex, that yields multiple solutions, that involves multiple criteria, and that demands nuanced judgments. David Perkins (1992) notes that contemporary education must go beyond simply presenting students with information and must ensure that students retain important information, understand topics deeply, and actively use the knowledge they gain. A truly literate person will be able to achieve these goals from reading because she consciously seeks understanding and uses for the knowledge she gains through reading. Finally, the RAND Reading Study Group (2002) notes that the United States today "demands a universally higher level of literacy achievement

Literacy for the 21st century requires much more than passively absorbing what is on the printed page. It requires that readers be able to do something as a result of reading, not merely know something.

than at any time in history" and goes on to say that "it is reasonable to believe that the demand for a literate populace will increase in the future."

Although various authorities describe the specifics of present-day literacy somewhat differently, their general message is very clear and tremendously important: Present-day literacy requires much more than passively absorbing what is on the printed page. It requires attaining a deep understanding of what is read, remembering important information, linking newly learned information to existing schemata, knowing when and where to use that information, using it appropriately in varied contexts in and out of school, and communicating effectively with others. Literacy for today's world requires that readers be able to *do* something as a result of reading, not merely know something. Moreover, literacy for today's world requires that readers be able to do something with a variety of different texts—not just short stories, novels, poetry, and history texts, but also tax forms, computer manuals, complex directions for operating even more complex machines, and technical documents related to business, economics, agriculture, the military, and a huge variety of other enterprises. Many of these texts are extremely complex, and both the number of complex texts and their level of complexity continue to grow each year.

To be sure, students do not read all of these types of complex texts in elementary school, but their early reading experiences should provide a foundation for dealing with complex material in the future. Today's elementary students must become considerably more competent, flexible, and sophisticated readers than their predecessors. Moreover, given the lower level of reading proficiency demonstrated by many children raised in poverty and many Black, Hispanic, and American Indian students, we need to work especially hard to dramatically improve the reading of these students. We particularly need to improve all children's higher-order skills. We need to guide as many students as we possibly can to a level of literacy that enables them to read challenging material, to analyze it closely, to learn from it, to reason from it, and to problem solve. We need to nurture and encourage students to become competent readers in today's increasingly complex and demanding world.

In the Classroom 1.2, which comes from *Standards for the English Language Arts* (National Council of Teachers of English and International Reading Association, 1996), provides a glimpse into a sixth-grade classroom and exemplifies a reading experience that promotes the kind of literacy we are talking about.

ASSESSMENT

See the read-write cycle assessments, an example of an assessment that fosters higher-order thinking, in the *Assessments and Lesson Plans* supplement.

Developing Present-Day Literacy in the Sixth Grade

Sometimes visual aids are helpful in fostering high levels of literacy. Here, the teacher makes use of the following learning web on grizzly bears. A group of sixth-grade students are reading and studying science texts, such as primary sources, magazine articles, textbooks, and essays on scientific and environmental topics. As part of a thematic exploration of large mammals, the students read a number of magazine articles on endangered animals and work in small groups to practice using study strategies, such as underlining, annotation, and summarizing information through visual diagrams. Their teacher models study strategies in explicit class demonstrations.

instructional routines in the Classroom 1.2

One day, before reading an article on grizzly bears, the students talk about the specific ways of learning and remembering important ideas and information encountered during reading. The teacher models strategies she uses as she reads, such as underlining and note taking, "thinking aloud" for the class as she sifts through information to highlight and organize important points. She shows students a way in which to transform key ideas and details that support them into a learning web on grizzly bears that helps show the relationships among key concepts.

The students gather in small groups to read articles about large animals. Working together, they decide which points are important enough to underline or annotate. Each group then organizes the information it has found, using a learning web. Each group displays its diagram to the class as an overhead transparency, explaining the process used to produce it.

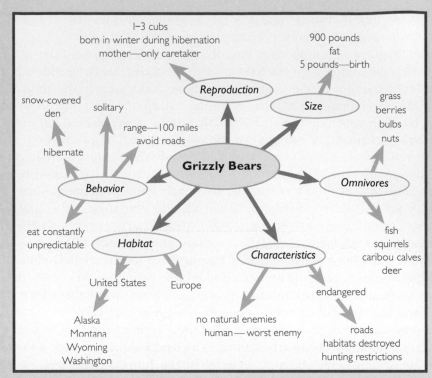

Source: From IRA and NCTE. (1996). *Standards for the English Language Arts.* Newark, DE: International Reading Association; and Urbana, IL: National Council of Teachers of English. Reprinted with permission.

The next day, the students write summaries of the articles they have read and work together to prepare for an oral presentation to the class, using their notes and diagrams to help them plan.

Reflect *and* Apply

5. Suppose you are sitting with a small group of parents at a school open house when one woman abruptly demands to know why today's students read so poorly compared to those in her day. A man picks up her prompt and with similar abruptness wants to know why American kids can't read as well as those in other countries. Compose a response in which you cite data to reassure these parents that U.S. students are certainly holding their own.

6. The concept of present-day literacy is a complex one. At this point, describe your understanding of the concept in a paragraph or two. Keep your description, and add to it as you gain a broader knowledge of this concept in later chapters.

A Literacy Curriculum for Today's and Tomorrow's World

We now turn to a description of the components of a program to lead students to the high level of literacy required in the 21st century.

Before continuing, we should point out that the focus in this book is reading; therefore, some aspects of a comprehensive literacy curriculum are not discussed. These topics include spelling and handwriting. Also, although we consider writing as it relates to reading, we do not present a comprehensive writing program. Finally, we do not present curricula for specific subjects such as history, science, and the like.

That said, the reading curriculum we describe in this book is both broad and deep. In recent years, the federal government has taken an increasingly active role in influencing reading instruction. The federally sponsored report of the National Reading Panel (2000) and the Reading First provisions of the No Child Left Behind Act of 2001 (2002) identified five curricular components as having strong support from research and being key to effective reading instruction—phonemic awareness, phonics, fluency, vocabulary, and comprehension. Reading First—the massive federal program designed to ensure that the curriculum endorsed by the National Reading Panel (NRP) is implemented in kindergarten through third-grade classrooms throughout the United States—has already had and will continue to have a substantial effect on reading instruction in the primary grades. We believe that the curricular components identified by the NRP and Reading First are vital and should definitely be included in the present-day literacy curriculum. However, like most literacy educators (for example, Allington, 2002; Krashen, 2004; Pressley, 2002; Routman, 2002; Taylor, Pearson, Peterson, & Rodriguez, 2003, 2005), we believe that a comprehensive and balanced literacy curriculum that addresses the needs of primary-grade students, upper-elementary students, and middle-grade students includes considerably more than the components endorsed by the NRP and Reading First. The literacy curriculum outlined on the next several pages and elaborated on in this book includes all of the components endorsed by the NRP and Reading First, as well as a number of additional components. In this section, we describe nine components that we believe are vital to help all students achieve the sort of literacy required for full participation and success in today's world (see Figure 1.8).

Phonemic Awareness and Other Aspects of Emergent Literacy

As part of learning to read, students need to internalize a substantial body of knowledge about print and about the relationship between print and speech. One very important component of such knowledge is phonemic awareness—the insight that spoken words are composed of somewhat separable sounds. But there are many other aspects of emergent literacy. For example, students must recognize that the written language they are just beginning to learn about is in many ways similar to the oral language with which they are already quite proficient, that words are closely grouped sets of letters with white space at either end of them, and that when reading they track from left to right and

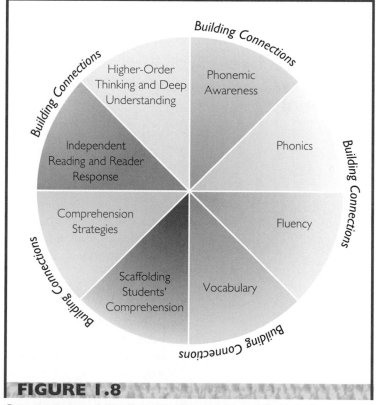

FIGURE 1.8

Components of the Present-Day Literacy Curriculum

from the top of the page to the bottom. Additionally, as part of emergent literacy, children need to develop positive attitudes about reading and about their ability to learn to read. We deal with phonemic awareness and emergent literacy in Chapter 4.

Phonics and Other Word-Recognition Skills

Phonics is the area of reading instruction that deals with the relationships between letters and sounds. Children use their knowledge of phonics to sound out written words they do not immediately recognize. If an adept reader comes to the word *bike* and doesn't immediately recognize it, she can follow a series of steps to arrive at its pronunciation. She might, for example, proceed through the following steps:

- identify the sound of *b* as /b/,
- identify the sound of *k* as /k/,
- identify the sound of *i* as /ai/ (using her knowledge that the *e* at the end of the word signals the long vowel sound),
- blend these sounds to arrive at the pronunciation /baik/,
- realize that the word is *bike,* a word she knows perfectly well when she hears it.

Phonic skills help children become independent readers. Other word-recognition skills—for example, identifying syllables, blending sounds to form syllables and words, and dealing with word parts such as prefixes and suffixes—also assist children in becoming independent readers. We deal with phonics and other word-recognition skills in Chapter 5.

Fluency and Matching Students with Appropriate Texts

In Chapter 3, we give special attention to assisting English learners in building fluency.

Fluency, as we have already noted, is the ability to "read a text orally with speed, accuracy, expression, and comprehension" (Samuels, 2002a). Additionally, it is important that students become fluent in their silent reading (Pikulski & Chard, 2005). When reading silently, students need to read smoothly, at an appropriate pace, and with good comprehension. This means that as students mature as readers they need to use their word-recognition skills sparingly, for the most part automatically and instantaneously recognizing words. There are a number of effective practices for building students' fluency. Additionally, in order to become fluent readers, students need to do a lot of reading in appropriate texts, texts that are not too difficult and that they readily comprehend, learn from, and enjoy. We deal with fluency and matching students with appropriate texts in Chapter 6.

Vocabulary Learning and Instruction

A huge amount of research has been conducted on students' vocabulary knowledge, and reliable estimates indicate that many students have acquired reading vocabularies of something like 5,000 words by the end of the first grade and something like 50,000 words by the time they graduate from high school (Graves, 2006). Obviously, vocabulary learning represents a significant task throughout children's years in school, and effectively fostering students' vo-

One hugely important factor in learning to read is reading a lot in material that is understandable and enjoyable.

cabularies requires a multifaceted and long-term program. Such a program includes rich and varied language experiences, teaching individual words, teaching word learning strategies, and fostering word consciousness. We describe such a program in Chapter 7.

Scaffolding Students' Comprehension of Text

Comprehension is both a complex process and the ultimate goal of reading, and as a consequence comprehension instruction needs to be powerful, long term, and multifaceted. As one facet of comprehension instruction, we need to do everything possible to ensure that students comprehend and learn from each and every text they read—to scaffold their efforts with both narrative texts such as short stories and plays and expository texts such the chapters in their science and social studies texts. We describe our approaches to scaffolding students' comprehension of text in Chapter 8.

Teaching Comprehension Strategies

As Pearson, Roehler, Dole, and Duffy noted well over a decade ago (1992), comprehension strategies are "conscious and flexible plans that readers apply and adapt to a variety of texts and tasks." Although many strategies have been identified, a handful of them have been repeatedly singled out as particularly useful. These include establishing a purpose for reading, using prior knowledge, asking and answering questions, making inferences, determining what is important, summarizing, dealing with graphic information, imaging and creating graphic representations, and monitoring comprehension (Sales & Graves, 2005). In Chapter 9, we discuss a very powerful approach to teaching comprehension strategies.

Encouraging Independent Reading and Reader Response

It is not enough for students to read and comprehend texts they are assigned. Students need to become independent readers who voluntarily choose to read both narrative and expository texts for the pleasure, knowledge, and satisfaction that only reading can provide. Additionally, with literary texts, students need to respond to what they read in a variety of different ways. Only by doing a great deal of reading in different types of materials will students really master the skill of reading. Only by doing a lot of reading in material they find interesting and enjoyable will students realize the joy of reading. And only by gaining in-depth knowledge on topics they find particularly important or intriguing will students gain the deep and lasting knowledge needed in today's world. Thus, we strongly advocate truly varied and extensive reading—sensitive and moving fiction such as Patricia Reilly Giff's *A House of Tailors*, revealing non-fiction such as Lori Dolphin's *Our Journey from Tibet*, and light fiction such as Lemony Snicket's *The Carnivorous Carnival*. We focus specifically on independent reading and reader response in Chapter 10, but the whole of this book is devoted to assisting all students in becoming independent and avid readers.

Fostering Higher-Order Thinking and Deep Understanding

As we move firmly into the 21st century, two goals have become increasingly important—fostering higher-order thinking and promoting deep and lasting understanding. Fostering higher-order thinking—assisting students in mastering such complex tasks as analyzing, synthesizing, and evaluating—requires a clear conception of the nature of higher-order thinking, knowledge about the various question types that prompt higher-order thinking, and understanding of what constitutes higher-order responses. Promoting deep and lasting understanding—teaching in such a way that students understand topics deeply, retain important information, actively use the knowledge they gain in a variety of tasks in and out of school—requires a clear conception of the nature of un-

Helping students understand that the things they learn in school have purposes outside the classroom is an important component of any literacy curriculum.

derstanding and instructional techniques that lead students to deep understanding. Both the nature of higher-order thinking and deep understanding and ways to teach for higher-order thinking and deep understanding are described in Chapter 11.

Building Connections

The final component of the critical literacy curriculum cuts across all of the others. Building connections—establishing links among the vast array of schemata that students internalize—is important whether students are involved in decoding, in higher-order thinking, or in the other components of the curriculum.

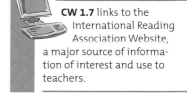

CW 1.7 links to the International Reading Association Website, a major source of information of interest and use to teachers.

Students need to build connections in several directions. First, we want students to realize that what they bring to school—the wealth of out-of-school experiences that they bring when they enter first grade and that are constantly enriched each year—is relevant to what they are learning in school. For example, the pride they felt when they were first allowed to go to the grocery store alone can provide insight into a story character's feelings when she successfully meets a challenge. Second, we want students to realize that the various subjects they study in school are interrelated in many ways. For example, the understanding of the Revolutionary period they gained in social studies can help them understand the motives of Johnny in Esther Forbes's *Johnny Tremain*. Third, we want students to realize that ideas and concepts learned in school are relevant to their lives outside of school. For example, a character's discovery that persistence paid off in meeting her goal may suggest to a student that similar persistence may lead to success as she tries to help a younger brother develop the habit of putting his toys away neatly. All chapters of this book address the matter of building connections.

Reflect *and* Apply

7. Although almost all schools now make phonics an important part of beginning reading instruction, this was not always the case. Think back to the instruction you received in the primary grades, and jot down a statement about how much phonics instruction you received. If possible, compare your experiences with phonics with those of some of your classmates.

8. Almost all authorities believe that doing a substantial amount of independent reading is an essential part of becoming a good reader. Consider how much independent reading you have done since you entered first grade, or perhaps even before that. Brainstorm some approaches you might use to encourage today's students, many of whom do not do much independent reading, to do more of it.

An Overview of This Book

Here, we first briefly note the contents of each chapter. Then, we explain the common components and organization of the chapters. Internalizing the organization of the book will be a great aid in understanding and remembering what you learn.

Chapter-by-Chapter Overview

This book is divided into 14 chapters. Chapters 1, 2, and 3—Reading and Learning to Read, Reading Instruction, and Motivation and Engagement—deal with general concepts and principles that are applied throughout the book. Chapters 4, 5, and 6—Emergent Literacy, Word Recognition, and Fluency—deal with topics that are particularly important in the early grades. Chapters 7 through 11—Vocabulary Development, Scaffolding Students' Comprehension of Text, Teaching Comprehension Strategies, Encouraging Independent Reading and Reader Response, and Fostering Higher-Order Thinking and Deep Understanding in Content Areas—discuss topics that are crucial at all grade levels. Chapters 12 through 14 deal with the special topics of Writing and Reading, Reading Instruction for English-Language Learners, and Classroom Assessment. Additionally, classroom vignettes following Chapters 5, 10, and 14 present in-depth scenarios at three grade levels.

The Components and Organization of the Chapters

We have designed each chapter to facilitate your reading and learning as effectively and efficiently as possible, and most chapters have the same components and the same organization.

Each chapter begins with a photo and an outline of the major sections of the chapter. Next comes a brief personal statement or scenario in which we convey our interest in the topic of the chapter and suggest one or more of the major themes of the chapter. Following the scenario is the body of the chapter, usually consisting of two to four main sections and a number of subsections. This is by far the longest part of the chapter. After this comes a section titled Strengths and Challenges of Diversity. Here we look back at the chapter and ask if there is more that can be done to ensure that all students—those whose experiences and schemata differ from those of many of their peers, those who move more quickly than their peers, and those who move less quickly than their peers—achieve in the area covered in the chapter. Finally, the last regular section in the chapter is titled Concluding Remarks; this includes a summary and several comments on the chapter.

In addition to these regular sections, chapters include a number of additional features. Samples of children's work illustrate their growth toward present-day literacy. Reading Corner boxes provide annotated lists of children's literature useful in teaching particular literacy skills and topics. Frequent interjections of teachers' "voices" give you a feel for the classroom. In the Classroom features offer a variety of examples of classroom interaction—student-teacher dialogues, vignettes, and the like—designed to nurture students toward literacy. Marginal notes on English-language learners, assessment, and technology provide important information on these vital topics. And Reflect and Apply sections are embedded at the ends of major sections to give you an opportunity to review and try out some of the central ideas presented.

Chapters end with two standard features. A section titled Extending Learning invites you to apply and elaborate on some of the major ideas presented by observing classrooms, talking with parents and teachers, or investigating a particular topic further. Some of these activities are specifically designed to provide material to put in a portfolio and have a portfolio icon next to them. Following this, a section titled Children's Literature provides citations and brief annotations

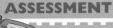

ASSESSMENT

CW 1.8 links to the National Reading Conference Website, which includes an important position paper on high stakes testing.

of the selections mentioned in the chapter and occasional citations of other sources of children's literature.

Strengths and Challenges of DIVERSITY

In this section of each chapter, we ask if there is more that can be done to ensure that all students—the diverse groups of children present in almost all classrooms today, those for whom school is easy and those for whom it's a challenge—achieve at their highest potential. In this chapter, we emphasize four points.

Different children will arrive at kindergarten, first grade, and every other grade with dramatically different schemata—varied knowledge about the world, about different types of text, about the content of specific subjects, and about school and how it functions. For example, many children who come from the East Coast will have little knowledge of the Southwest desert, children who come from other cultures may lack the American cultural knowledge assumed by some narratives, and children from affluent suburbs may have little understanding of inner-city issues. If all children are to succeed, we must take advantage of the varied schemata that different students have, accommodate students' differing schemata, and do everything possible to make school relevant to the lives of all children.

Because most teachers come from mainstream, middle-class backgrounds, recognizing and understanding the differing prior knowledge of students who come from non-mainstream and non-middle-class cultures is particularly problematic and particularly important. Even small differences in background knowledge can sometimes interfere with learning. But many cultural differences are not small. For example, Shirley Brice Heath (1983) compared communication patterns in two working-class communities in the Piedmont Carolinas—an African American community and a White community—to communication patterns in the middle-class school the children attended and found significant differences. One finding was that at home children from both of these working-class communities were used to direct commands such as "Put the book on the shelf." In the middle-class school, on the other hand, children often received indirect commands such as "Is this where the book belongs?" when they left a book unshelved. Because students from working-class communities were not used to such indirect requests, they did not understand the implied command and seemed to be disobeying the teacher by leaving their books where they were. Kathryn Au (1993), Lisa Delpit (1995), and other scholars have documented many cultural differences of this sort. Of course, substantial cultural differences and substantial linguistic differences exist for many English-language learners. To be effective in the diverse classrooms of today's schools, teachers must recognize, understand, and build on the cultural background and practices that children with different backgrounds bring to school.

All students at all grade levels need and deserve the opportunity to participate in all components of the literacy curriculum that they have not yet mastered—to have rich and varied literacy activities. This means that all students should be involved with learning vocabulary, learning from text, working with comprehension strategies, reading independently, doing

English Learners

CW 1.9 links to the Baharona Center for the Study of Books in Spanish and books in English for Latinos, a terrific source of books for Hispanic students.

higher-order thinking, and building connections. It will not do, for example, to have some beginning readers—those who are not achieving as rapidly as their peers—spend virtually all of their time on phonemic awareness, phonics, and fluency and wait forever for the "good stuff."

Concluding Remarks

In this chapter, we have done four things. First, we described the concept of the reading process underlying this book—the cognitive-constructivist view. We also described several concepts that elaborate and complement this view—the interactive model of reading, automaticity, fluency, and metacognition. Second, we briefly characterized U.S. students' proficiency in reading, contrasted their proficiency today to what it was in the past and to the proficiency of students in other industrialized countries, and described the sort of literacy necessary in today's and tomorrow's world. Third, we listed the components of the present-day literacy curriculum that serve as the foundation for the book. Fourth, we gave a brief chapter-by-chapter overview and explained the common organization that all chapters share.

The topics in this chapter are particularly important to internalize because they underlie the remainder of the book. As we have said several times, the richer your background knowledge relevant to the book—the more you know about the view of the reading process that informs it, the level of present-day literacy it is designed to help you achieve for your students, the components of the curriculum, and the organization of the book and each chapter—the easier it will be for you to learn, remember, and use the information and procedures presented. We therefore strongly encourage you to review the chapter, take some notes, respond again to some of the prompts in the Reflect and Apply sections, make use of some of our suggestions in the Extending Learning section, and perhaps search out and read some works listed in the references.

Extending Learning

Here we suggest several activities that take you beyond this book—to schools, students, teachers, parents, libraries, and others sources of information—to help you more fully understand and appreciate your role in nurturing children toward present-day literacy.

1. One way to increase your understanding of new and complex concepts is to examine several perspectives on them. The concepts about the reading process that we have discussed have all been described in a variety of other texts, and all of them are complex enough to warrant further study. Pick two or three concepts that you would like to further explore, and read more about them either in the references that we have supplied or in a general text on psychology or educational psychology.

2. Develop a set of questions about U.S. students' current level of reading proficiency, the proficiency of previous generations of U.S. students, the proficiency of students in other countries, and the proficiency needed in today's

world. Then use the questions to conduct interviews with half a dozen or so adults. Solicit and record their answers to your questions, and compare their answers to the characterization of students' proficiency presented in the chapter. Write up your comparison. As the portfolio icon suggests, this would make a good portfolio item.

3. List the components of the present-day literacy curriculum we have outlined and interview some elementary school teachers to find out which components they deal with, which they don't, and the literacy activities they engage in that are not part of the curriculum presented in this chapter. Try to include teachers from primary, middle-elementary, and upper-elementary grades. Once you have completed your interviews, sum up what you have discovered and comment on (1) the extent to which the teachers you interviewed employ the curriculum we have outlined and (2) any components of the literacy curriculum that are not among the components we consider but that you probably want to include in your classroom.

mylabschool
Where the classroom comes to life!

For a look at literacy instruction in a contemporary classroom, go to Allyn & Bacon's MyLabSchool.com. In MLS Courses, click on Reading Methods. There, you will find a wealth of resources, including video clips and case studies about a range of literacy topics.

Children's Literature

DiCamillo, K. (2000). *Because of Winn-Dixie*. Cambridge, MA: Candlewick Press. A poignant and well-told story of a young girl's building a new life after her mother left and she and her father moved to Florida—with, of course, a little help from her dog Winn-Dixie. 182 pages.

Dolphin, L. (1997). *Our Journey from Tibet*. New York: Dutton. A true story based on interviews with a nine-year-old Tibetan girl, Sonam. Includes dramatic and stunning photos. 40 pages.

Flake, S. G. (1998). *The Skin I'm In*. New York: Jump at the Sun/Hyperion. Thirteen-year-old Maleeka, uncomfortable because her skin is extremely dark, meets a new teacher with a facial birthmark and makes some discoveries about how to love who she is and what she looks like. 171 pages.

Forbes, E. (1998). *Johnny Tremain*. New York: Houghton Mifflin. Johnny Tremain, apprentice silversmith, takes on the cause of freedom as a message carrier for the Sons of Liberty in pre-Revolution Boston. Audiotape available. 293 pages.

Giff, P. R. (2004). *A House of Tailors*. New York: Wendy Lamb Books. Set in the late 19th century, this novel for intermediate readers tells the story of how 13-year-old Dina adjusts to her new life in the United States after being sent from Germany to live in Brooklyn with her tailor uncle. 149 pages.

Lord, B. B. (1984). *In the Year of the Boar & Jackie Robinson*. New York: Harper and Row. In 1947, a Chinese girl comes to Brooklyn where she becomes Americanized at school, in her apartment building, and by her love for baseball. Illustrated. 169 pages.

Snicket, L. (2002). *The Carnivorous Carnival: Book the ninth*. The continued adventures and misadventures of the Baudelaire orphans in the Series of Unfortunate Events series. New York: HarperCollins. 286 pages.

Sun, C. F. (1994). *Mama Bear*. Boston: Houghton Mifflin. Young Mei-Mei bakes and sells cookies in order to earn enough money to buy a large and expensive stuffed bear for Christmas. Illustrated. 28 pages.

Reading Instruction

chapter outline

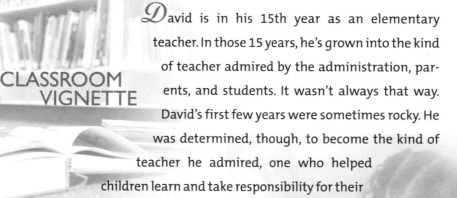

CLASSROOM VIGNETTE

$\mathcal{D}$avid is in his 15th year as an elementary teacher. In those 15 years, he's grown into the kind of teacher admired by the administration, parents, and students. It wasn't always that way. David's first few years were sometimes rocky. He was determined, though, to become the kind of teacher he admired, one who helped children learn and take responsibility for their own learning. And he did.

What David has learned in his 15 years of teaching is that we know a tremendous amount about effective teaching and learning and this knowledge can be tremendously valuable in planning classroom instruction. Of course, David has had to take this knowledge, make it his own, and tailor it to his students and his teaching style. Over the years, he has done just that, and his classroom is now an exemplary model.

The atmosphere David has created and the activities and opportunities he has provided make it clear that the classroom is both a place for learning and a place where he and his students take genuine satisfaction and pleasure from learning. David is enthusiastic about his class, and his enthusiasm is contagious. The students respond to his explanations of new concepts or assignments with animation and excitement. Whether students are working in groups or alone, they clearly view the classroom as an interesting and rewarding place. They value their pursuit of learning. They are actively and purposely engaged in learning, and they thrive on the success their efforts bring them.

Not every effective classroom looks like David's, and not every teacher will have the same sort of success he does. But the large and constantly increasing body of information on reading instruction can help all of us become successful beginning teachers and create increasingly successful classrooms throughout our years of teaching.

Instructional Principles

Although providing effective instruction has always been a concern of teachers, researchers, and policy makers, a huge proportion of the most productive research and theorizing on the topic has occurred in the past four decades. This chapter focuses on this body of knowledge. First, we discuss traditional instructional principles, most of which were validated in the 1960s and 1970s. Next, we consider constructivist and sociocultural perspectives, which for the most part emerged in the 1980s, the 1990s, and the early years of this century and which refined and modified earlier thinking.

Traditional Instructional Principles

In this section of the chapter, we discuss traditional instructional principles, and in the next section, constructivist and sociocultural perspectives on instruction. Unfortunately, orientations toward instruction come into favor and fall out of favor all too often. Most of these can be placed on a continuum, with more open, student-centered, and indirect approaches at one end and more structured, teacher-centered, and direct approaches at the other end. Sometimes, educators endorse one or another of these approaches, largely to the exclusion of others. We believe quite differently. In keeping with current theory and research (for example, Pressley, 2006; Taylor, Pearson, Peterson, & Rodriguez, 2003), we believe that in order to become fully literate, children need to develop a wide array of talents and attitudes and that only a wide array of instructional approaches can help them achieve this goal.

In the period from about 1960 to about 1980, educators and researchers produced a rich body of basic information about effective instruction. Here, we briefly discuss six of the most important traditional principles established during that time:

- Focusing on academically relevant tasks
- Employing active teaching

- Fostering active learning
- Distinguishing between instruction and practice
- Providing sufficient and timely feedback
- Teaching for transfer

For more information on these principles, Tom Good and Jere Brophy's *Looking into Classrooms* (2003) is an excellent source.

the *Reading Corner*

Informational Books That Give Students Opportunities to Make Critical Responses

One extremely relevant academic task is that of making critical responses to informational texts. The books listed here—science and social studies tradebooks about the world we live in—are interesting and involving and provide extended opportunities for students to make critical responses while reading books representing this important genre.

Deborah Chandra & Madeleine Comora. Illustrated by Brock Cole. *George Washington's Teeth*. Farrar, Straus and Giroux, 2003. This light-hearted account of the tooth problems that plagued Washington all his adult life provides a unique focus for a detailed timeline of Washington's life and accomplishments. 40 pages.

Rick Chrustowski. *Bright Beetle*. Holt, 2000. This colorful book, illustrated from a bug's eye view, describes the life cycle of a ladybug. The bright colors and accessible text make it a fun read-aloud, share-aloud book. Unpaged.

Bonnie Graves. *The Whooping Crane*. Perfection Learning, 1997. This informational book begins with a narrative relating a true, potentially fatal incident in 1967 involving a whooping crane chick, then one of 55 remaining of a seriously endangered species; it ends with factual information about the whoopers and efforts to save the species. 54 pages.

Linda Lowery. *Cinco de Mayo*. Carolrhoda Books, 2005. This addition to the On My Own Holidays series, which encourages understanding of diverse cultures, features full-page illustrations by Barbara Knutson and describes the colorful holiday that honors Mexico's victory over the French army at the Battle of Pueblo in 1862. 48 pages.

Sandra Markle. *Inside and Outside Killer Bees*. Walker, 2004. One of the many books in Markle's Outside and Inside series, this addition, with striking photos and accessible text, focuses not only on factual information about bees, such as their anatomy, social behavior, and honey production, but also on the ecological impact of invasive species. 40 pages.

Wendy Pfeffer. *Dolphin Talk: Whistles, Clicks, and Clapping Jaws*. HarperCollins, 2003. From the Let's-Read-and-Find-Out series, this book focuses on dolphin communication while also revealing the basics of dolphin anatomy, behavior, and life cycle. 40 pages.

Laurence Pringle. *Snakes! Strange and Wonderful*. Boyds Mills, 2004. This book, by well-known nonfiction author Laurence Pringle and illustrated in watercolor paintings by Meryl Henderson, presents a wide variety of snakes and explains the unusual behaviors that characterize the various types. 32 pages.

Ken Robbins. *Seeds*. Atheneum, 2005. Through text and photos by the author, this book reveals the basic facts about seeds—their different shapes and sizes and the connections between a seed's structure and function in terms of its transport. 32 pages.

Pamela Turner. *Gorilla Doctors: Saving Endangered Great Apes*. Houghton Mifflin, 2005. This book in the Scientists in the Field series takes a look at mountain gorillas, one of the most endangered species in the world, and reveals through text and photos how veterinarians in Rwanda and Uganda are working to save them.

Carole Boston Weatherford. *Freedom on the Menu: The Greensboro Sit-Ins*. Dial, 2004. As seen through the eyes of a young Southern Black girl, this book offers a unique perspective on the 1960 civil rights sit-ins at the Woolworth's lunch counter in Greensboro, North Carolina. Unpaged.

Focusing on Academically Relevant Tasks

If you are going to get really good at something, you need to do a lot of it. You need to have a lot of what educational researchers have termed "opportunity to learn," chances to learn about and practice whatever it is you are trying to get good at (Berliner, 1979). If students are going to become proficient readers, they need to do a lot of reading. Certainly, doing a lot of reading is the central academically relevant task in learning to read. But it is by no means the only academically relevant task.

In addition to reading itself, several subtasks are important. If students are going to become proficient decoders—readers who can use their knowledge of letter-sound correspondences, spelling patterns, and the like to decode unfamiliar words and eventually to process them automatically—they need to be actively engaged in decoding tasks. If students are to become proficient at responding to literature orally and in writing, they need many opportunities to discuss their reading and to write about what they have read. And if students are to become critical readers and writers of informational prose, they need abundant opportunities to read and to write informational material and to make critical responses to it. These are only some of the reading-related areas in which students must become proficient, but we think we have made our point: Curriculum—what students study—matters!

To be sure, students will learn many things we do not teach in school, and they will not learn everything we do teach. But if we have things we really want students to learn, it is sheer folly not to give them the opportunity to actively engage in learning them!

Employing Active Teaching

The term *active teaching* refers to a set of principles and teaching behaviors that research has shown to be particularly effective, especially in teaching basic skills. As noted by Brophy (1986), teachers who engage in active teaching are the instructional leaders of their classrooms; they are fully knowledgeable about the content and purposes of the instruction they present and about the instructional goals they wish to accomplish. Active teachers do a lot of teach-

English Learners

CW 2.1 links to the SIOP Model of Sheltered Instruction for English-language learners, a model that includes a good deal of active teaching and active learning.

Teachers must actively engage students and help them internalize the knowledge and strategies they are learning.

ing. Although they use discovery learning for some purposes, they do not generally rely on students to discover what it is they are supposed to learn, particularly when the learning deals with basic skills. Similarly, although they use a variety of materials as part of their teaching, they do not rely on the materials to do the teaching. They directly carry to students the content to be learned in short presentations, discussions, and demonstrations.

Fostering Active Learning

Just as it is vital that the teacher be actively involved in teaching, it is also crucial that the learner be actively involved in learning (Good & Brophy, 2003). As we explained in our discussion of the cognitive-constructivist orientation in Chapter 1, the learner must do something with the material he is studying if he is to learn much from it. Fourth-grade teacher John Fitzhugh puts it well in In the Classroom 2.1.

Actively Engaging Students in Reading and Responding to a Text

Students *must* be actively involved in order for any sort of learning to take place. That's simply a fact. But there are a number of ways this can happen. Say, for instance, a student is reading a trade book on sharks, perhaps Seymour Simon's *Sharks.* As he reads, the student can

- think about the new things he is learning about sharks,
- discuss new insights with others,
- make outlines or sketches that depict his new knowledge,
- write a brief story about how he might respond if he were in the water and saw a shark fin nearby,
- draw relationships between the new knowledge and his existing knowledge of sharks, and/or
- attempt to implement the new knowledge (for example, simulate an underwater environment by making a diorama of sharks and their habitat, as one of my students did).

Or the student can undertake many other activities that cause him to grapple with the new knowledge and integrate it into his existing schema. As we all know, precious little new knowledge will be absorbed passively.

in the
Classroom
2.1

Distinguishing Between Instruction and Practice

Effective teaching requires both instruction and practice, but the two need to be clearly distinguished. Practice involves asking students to do something they already know how to do. Instruction involves showing or telling students how to do something that they do not yet know how to do. Simply asking students to do something does not constitute teaching them how to do it. Practice is appropriate *after* students have learned whatever it is they are to practice.

Emphasizing this distinction, Gerry Duffy and Laura Roehler (1982) coined the terms "proactive teaching" and "reactive teaching." *Proactive teaching* consists of deliberately showing students how to do something before expecting them to do it themselves. *Reactive teaching* consists of first asking students to do something and then showing them how to do it only if they fail. Proactive teaching sets students up for success, whereas reactive teaching sets them up for failure. Reactive teaching is inefficient because it often leaves the teacher trying to clarify matters after the fact for students who became confused while working at something they did not know how to do; the confusion could have been avoided by providing instructions at the outset. Reactive teaching is especially demoralizing for students who repeatedly fail.

Thus, before asking students to explain the conflict in a particular story, check to see that they understand the concept of *conflict* as used in literature. If they do not, teach the concept before asking them to deal with it. Note that with a difficult concept such as *conflict,* instruction could take some time.

Providing Sufficient and Timely Feedback

Feedback is perhaps the most long-standing principle in this section on traditional principles. It's also an integral part of current conceptions of learning (see, for example, Bransford, Brown, & Cocking, 2000). From the dialogues of Socrates to the answers included in programmed instruction to the beep our word processor makes when we key in an inappropriate command, feedback has long been a central component of instruction. In the years before school, young children get a great deal of immediate, positive feedback—fussing brings a bottle; a smile, a lot of attention; saying "ball," a round object to play with. During these same years, young children also receive a good deal of immediate, negative feedback—too much fussing may bring only a closed door, a smile at the television set produces no response, and "bla" spoken in an attempt to get a round object to play with may instead bring a blanket.

Once in school, students continue to get feedback, although with one teacher working with perhaps 30 students, individual feedback is not as readily available as it was at home. But such feedback is every bit as necessary. There is no way for a learner to know whether he is on the right track unless he receives some sort of response. And this rule applies whether newly learned material is the sound represented by the letter *m,* the pronunciation of the word *rabbit,* or the identification of the central theme in a story. Sometimes feedback can be imbedded in the learning situation and does not require a response from another person. For example, when the child reads, "The rabbit really liked the carrots," his understanding of the sentence as a whole is established by his correct pronunciation of "rabbit"; the pronunciation brings the meaning to mind. At other times, other students can provide the feedback; for example, a group of fifth-graders read a novel and agree that the theme is the importance of friendships. But much of the time, such as in learning letter-sound correspondences, the feedback must come from the teacher. Figuring out how to provide timely, telling, and kind feedback for 30 or so students is a major task for a classroom teacher.

Teaching for Transfer

Transfer is the use of knowledge or skills learned in one context in another context. The well-known Chinese proverb—"Give a man a fish, and you feed him for a day. Teach a man to fish, and you feed him for a lifetime"—emphasizes the tremendous value of transfer. Knowledge and skills that transfer become tools that students can use throughout their lives. In a very real sense, transfer is the central purpose of schooling. Schools are future oriented. Students attend school today so that they can use what they learn tomorrow. We want students to apply what they learn in the early grades to their learning in later grades; even more important, we want them to apply what they learn in school to the world outside of school.

Given the obvious centrality of transfer to schooling, it may shock you to learn that schools have often been unsuccessful in promoting transfer. Transfer is one of the oldest topics of educational research, and the repeated finding has been that students very frequently fail to use what they learn in school out of school. The student who adds and subtracts quite competently during math class fails when he tries to calculate how much allowance he has left. The student who writes a competent letter of complaint as a class exercise never thinks of writing the distributor when his magazine fails to arrive two months in a row. As British philosopher Alfred North Whitehead (1929) aptly put it over 70 years ago, the knowledge students gained in school has all too frequently been *inert*—fragile, tip-of-the-iceberg knowledge that might enable them to choose a correct answer on a multiple-choice test but is not lasting and does not serve much purpose in the real world.

On a more positive note, John Bransford and Daniel Schwartz (1999) have noted that many of the tests that have been used to assess transfer have not been sufficiently sensitive. We concur with their interpretation, and thus we believe that transfer is both possible and more frequent than the literature sometimes suggests. But it is not easy! Maximizing your students' success in applying what they learn in your classroom in other classrooms, as they continue through school, and in their lives beyond school will require direct and substantial efforts on your part. Throughout this book, we suggest what those efforts might look like.

Reflect *and* Apply

1. Think back as far as you can in your schooling—to elementary school, if possible, or to secondary school—and jot down a list of tasks you completed that you think were academically relevant and a list of tasks you completed that you think were not academically relevant. Then write about what does and does not constitute an academically relevant task.
2. Get together with a few classmates, review the descriptions of proactive and reactive teaching we have provided, and create and present two scenarios—one of proactive teaching and one of reactive teaching.
3. Think of a teacher you have had who has been particularly effective in his or her use of one of the traditional principles we have discussed, and describe what he or she did that was so effective.

Constructivist and Sociocultural Perspectives on Instruction

The instructional concepts we discuss here have generally been advanced more recently than those in the previous section and are more closely related to the cognitive-constructivist orientation that underlies this book than are those in the previous section. We view these concepts as absolutely vital in reading instruction.

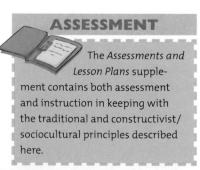

ASSESSMENT

The *Assessments and Lesson Plans* supplement contains both assessment and instruction in keeping with the traditional and constructivist/sociocultural principles described here.

Scaffolding

We believe that the term *scaffolding* was first used in its educational sense by David Wood, Jerome Bruner, and Gail Ross (1976), who used it to characterize mothers' verbal interactions when reading to their young children. In these interactions, mothers gently yet supportively guide their children toward successful literacy experiences. Thus, for example, in sharing a picture book with a child and attempting to assist the child in reading the words that label the pictures, a mother might at first simply page through the book, familiarizing the child with the pictures and the general content of the book. Then she might focus on a single picture and ask the child what it is. After this, she might point to the word below the picture, tell the child that the word names the picture, ask the child what the word is, and provide feedback on the correctness of the answer. The important point to note here is that the mother has neither simply told the child the word nor simply asked him to say it. Instead, she has built an instructional structure, a scaffold, that assists the child in learning. Scaffolding, as Wood and his colleagues have aptly put it, is "a process that enables a child or novice to solve a problem, carry out a task, or achieve a goal which would be beyond his unassisted efforts."

Scaffolding is widely used in the world outside of school, and one particular instance of out-of-school scaffolding—the use of training wheels on children's bicycles—serves as a graphic example of the procedure. Training wheels are supportive; they enable a novice bicycle rider to do something he might not otherwise be able to do—ride a two-wheeler. Equally important, training wheels are temporary, and they can be gradually raised so that the budding cyclist increasingly assumes the task of riding with less and less support from the scaffold.

Scaffolding is also very widely recommended for use in schools; in fact, virtually any list of key components of effective instruction includes scaffolding (see, for example, Bransford et al., 2000; Brophy, 2000; Clark & Graves, 2005). Fortunately, scaffolding is quite frequently used in schools. For example, a teacher is scaffolding students' learning when he sounds out part of a word for them, reads the beginning of a story aloud, or explains the organization of a difficult chapter that they are about to read. A teacher is also providing scaffolding when he models the thought processes he uses in determining what is particularly important in an informational selection students are about to read, and when he suggests a way to begin an essay they are writing. In each of these cases, the teacher is assisting students in doing something that they might not otherwise be able to do. Much of Chapter 8 describes ways to build supportive scaffolds for the many different types of reading students do.

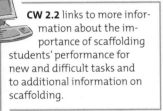

CW 2.2 links to more information about the importance of scaffolding students' performance for new and difficult tasks and to additional information on scaffolding.

The Zone of Proximal Development

The concept of the zone of proximal development was put forth by the Russian psychologist Lev Vygotsky (1978). It emphasizes the social nature of learning and the fact that learning is very much a social phenomenon. We acquire much of what we learn in our social interchanges with others. According to Vygotsky, at any particular point in time, children have a circumscribed zone of development, a range within which they can learn. At one end of this range are learning tasks that they can complete independently; at the other end are learning tasks that they cannot complete, even with assistance. In between these two extremes is the zone most productive for learning, the range of tasks in which children can achieve *if* they are assisted by a more knowledgeable or more competent other.

English Learners

English-language learners' zones of proximal development can often be expanded by letting them read in their native language, giving directions and overviews in their native language, and letting them respond and answer questions in their native language.

If left on their own, for example, many third-graders might learn very little from a *National Geographic World* article on the formation of thunderstorms. Conversely, with your help—getting them interested in the topic, focusing their attention, preteaching some of the critical concepts such as the effects of rising heat, arranging small groups to discuss and answer questions on certain parts of the article—these same students may be able to learn a good deal from the article. However, with other topics and other texts—for example, a chapter on gravity from a high school physics text—no amount of outside help, at least no reasonable amount of outside help, will foster much learning for these third-graders. The topic of gravity and its presentation in the high school text are simply outside their zone of proximal development.

Outside of school, many people can and do serve as more knowledgeable or more competent others—parents and foster parents, brothers and sisters, relatives, friends, and clergy. As a teacher creating scaffolded reading activities, you may occasionally be able to bring in outside resources to assist students. More often, however, you will arrange reading situations so that you serve as the more knowledgeable other who assists students in successfully reading selections they could not read on their own. Additionally, in many cases students will be able to pool their resources and assist one another in dealing with reading selections that they could not successfully work with alone.

ASSESSMENT

During the beginning months of the school year, teach students how to evaluate their own work. Gradually, let students do more and more self-evaluation, continually giving them feedback on how well they are doing. By midyear, students will be able to appraise much of their work for themselves.

The Gradual Release of Responsibility Model

The gradual release of responsibility model depicts a progression in which students gradually assume increased responsibility for their learning. A particularly informative visual representation of the model developed by David Pearson and Margaret Gallagher (1983) is shown in Figure 2.1.

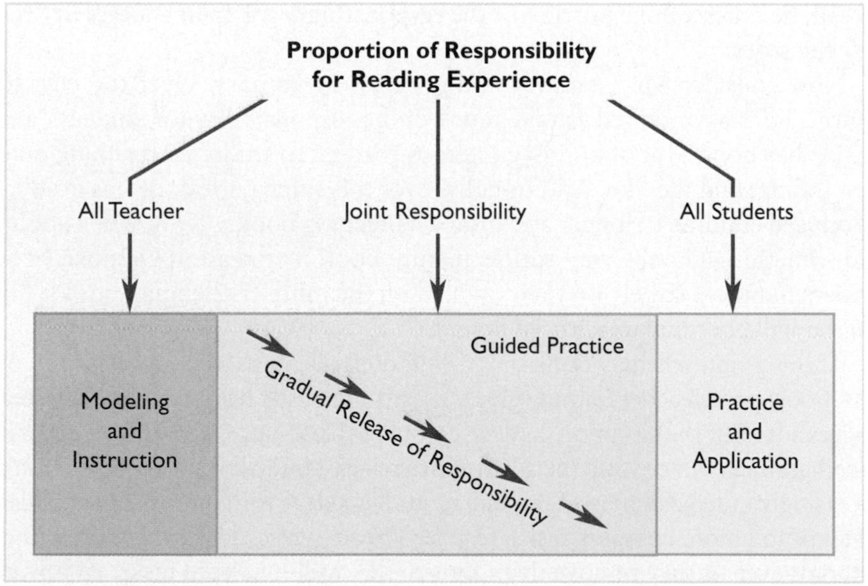

FIGURE 2.1

The Gradual Release of Responsibility Model

Source: Pearson, P. D., & Gallagher, M. C. (1983). "The Instruction of Reading Comprehension." *Contemporary Educational Psychology, 8,* 317–344. Copyright 1983, with permission from Elsevier.

The model depicts a temporal sequence in which students gradually progress from situations in which the teacher takes responsibility for their successful completion of a reading task (in other words, does most of the work for them), to situations in which students assume increasing responsibility for reading tasks, and finally to situations in which students take total or nearly total responsibility for reading tasks. First-grade teacher Richard Gerhardt talks about the nature of gradual release and the part that the text and students' development play in deciding how much responsibility is appropriate for him as the teacher and how much is appropriate for students:

> In early October, you will often find me seated in a circle with a group of children, displaying a picture book such as Christopher Inn's *Help!* or *The Hello, Goodbye Window*, written by Norton Juster and illustrated by Chris Ruschka. First I'll read the title aloud and talk a little bit about what it and the picture on the cover make me think of. Then I'll ask the children what the title and picture make them think of and what the book might be about. After listening to students' responses and trying to emphasize and highlight those that are likely to help them understand the story, I begin reading. Even though there are only a handful of words on each page and the story is very simple, I'll stop every two or three pages, ask students what has happened, summarize the story up to that point if children's responses suggest a summary is necessary, and perhaps ask students what they think will happen next.
>
> After completing the story, I may ask students a few questions to see if they understood it. Or I may get some other sorts of responses from them—how they felt about one of the characters, if they have had similar experiences, or what emotions the story aroused in them. I might also share my understanding of the story and some of my personal responses to it.
>
> —Richard Gerhardt, First-Grade Teacher

Throughout this session, Mr. Gerhardt has done everything possible to ensure that each student gets something from the story and leaves the experience feeling good about it. Appropriately, because these students are just beginning to read, he takes a huge portion of the responsibility for their success in "reading" the story.

Now consider Mr. Gerhardt and his class in January. Over the past four months, he has continued to take much of the responsibility for students' reading. He has done a lot of building interest, reading to students, checking on understanding, and the like. Additionally, over this same period, he has gradually introduced children to longer and more challenging books. Now, when students read something like the very simple picture book they read in October, he will let them handle it largely on their own. With the more challenging books, however, he will continue to scaffold activities.

At this point, you may think that the gradual release model suggests that, over the school years, teachers simply give students increased responsibility in a steady progression. But the situation is more complex than that. Over time, teachers do indeed gradually dismantle the scaffolds they have built so that students become increasingly independent readers. But as students deal with increasingly challenging texts and more complex tasks, teachers create scaffolds for the more difficult materials even as they remove them for simpler, well-mastered tasks. At any particular point in time, learners are likely to be—and should be—dealing with some texts and tasks that are more challenging and some that are less challenging. Many fourth-graders can take full responsibility for reading an easy novel such as *No More Nasty* by Amy McDonald. These same students may need a moderate amount of scaffolding to successfully deal with a somewhat challenging historical novel, such as *Keeper of the Doves* by Betsy Byars, and you may need to assume

Cognitive modeling, thinking aloud as you complete a task, has been shown to be a very powerful instructional approach.

most of the responsibility for their success in reading and understanding a short expository article on acid rain. Many sixth-graders, however, could deal independently with *Keeper of the Doves* and would need only a little assistance from you in tackling the short acid rain article. But these same sixth-graders would need considerably more assistance from you in working through a longer and more technical article on acid rain. Thus, the scaffolding that you provide and the extent to which you release responsibility to students always depend on the particular texts and tasks that they are working with (Brophy, 2000; Graves & Graves, 2003).

Cognitive Modeling

Modeling is another very important tool to use as part of active teaching. When teachers model a task, they actually *do* something, rather than just tell students how to do it. A specific sort of modeling, cognitive modeling, is particularly useful in teaching students difficult concepts and strategies. In cognitive modeling, teachers use explicit instructional talk to reveal their thought processes as they perform the tasks that students will be asked to perform. For example, a teacher might model the mental process of determining the meaning of an unknown word in context, as shown in In the Classroom 2.2.

Cognitive Modeling

Teacher: Suppose I'm reading along and I come to this sentence: "It was raining heavily and water was standing in the street, so before he left for work Mr. Nelson put on his raincoat, buckled on his galoshes over his shoes, and picked up his umbrella." Let me see—*g-a-l-o-s-h-e-s*. I don't think I know that word. Let's see. It's raining, and he picks up his raincoat and umbrella and buckles something over his shoes. *Galoshes* must be some sort of waterproof boots that go over shoes. I can't be certain of that, but it makes sense in the sentence; and I don't think I want to look it up right now.

instructional routines

in the Classroom 2.2

Cognitive modeling provides a window on the teacher's mind and constitutes one of the most powerful tools for showing children how to reason as they seek to understand a text.

Direct Explanation

Direct explanation is an approach to teaching strategies that employs scaffolding, cognitive modeling, and a gradual release of responsibility. It was developed by Gerald Duffy and Laura Roehler and their colleagues two decades ago (for example, Duffy, Roehler, Meloth, Vavrus, Book, Putnam, & Wesselman, 1986), and it continues to be highly recommended (Duffy, 2002; Duke & Pearson, 2002; Graves, 2004b). Although direct explanation has most often been used to teach comprehension strategies, it can also be used to teach word-recognition strategies, such as using word parts or context to learn word meanings, and many other strategies competent readers use. The procedure is straightforward and has repeatedly been proven very effective. As described by Nell Duke and David Pearson (2002), the strategy is composed of these steps:

- An explicit description of the strategy and when, how, and why it should be used
- Teacher cognitive modeling of the strategy and, perhaps, student modeling of it
- Teacher and students collaboratively using the strategy
- Guided practice in which students gradually assume increased responsibility for using the strategy
- Independent use of the strategy by students

In other words, you begin by giving students a good clear explanation of the strategy and why they should use it. After this, you model it and perhaps have some students model it. Next, you and your students use the strategy together, with you scaffolding their efforts. Then, over time, you do less and less scaffolding, and students become increasingly independent. Finally, students become fully independent. The scaffolding, modeling, and gradual release of responsibility all combine to put new and complex strategies within students' zone of proximal development and produce deep and lasting learning. For detailed examples of direct explanation of comprehension strategies, see Chapter 9.

Contextualizing, Reviewing, and Practicing What Is Learned

In our concluding comments on direct explanation, we noted that the procedure produces deep and lasting learning. It certainly does, but only if students use their newly learned strategies in authentic contexts, get many opportunities to practice the strategies and make them their own, are periodically reminded of the strategies, and review them. Although review and practice are traditional instructional activities, the importance of contextualizing students' learning is something we have only recently recognized as absolutely vital to real and lasting learning; and thus we decided to place all three activities in this section on constructivist and sociocultural perspectives on instruction. The concepts are simple ones, but they must be heeded. If, for example, students learn the strategy of summarizing as part of reading instruction, they must be given opportunities and encouragement to use summarizing when they are working with social studies or science material and when they are gathering information in the library or studying at home. Moreover, students need many opportunities to use the strategy in such authentic contexts; they need reminders and prompting to do so; they need review from time to time; and, in many cases, they need additional scaffolding as they try to apply strategies in new and challenging situations.

Teaching for Understanding

As we have noted, over 70 years ago, British philosopher Alfred North Whitehead (1929) railed against schools' fostering what he called *inert knowledge*—fragile, shallow, tip-of-the-iceberg knowledge that is usually soon forgotten and too superficial to be of much use even if remembered. Today, educators are increasingly realizing the value of teaching for understanding—dealing with fewer topics but teaching them in such a way that students not only learn the content itself thoroughly but also appreciate the reasons for learning it and retain it in a form that makes it usable. As Harvard psychologist David Perkins (1992) puts it, teaching for understanding promotes three basic goals of education: understanding of knowledge, retention of knowledge, and active use of knowledge.

We believe that teaching for understanding is terribly important, and much of Chapter 11 is devoted to the topic. In that chapter, which relies heavily on the work of Perkins and his colleagues (Blythe, 1998; Perkins, 1992; Wiske, 1998), we examine this concept in detail. Here, we will note only that the key to teaching for understanding is teaching fewer topics but teaching them well, and that teaching for understanding demands the sort of constructive teaching and learning advocated throughout this section of the chapter.

Cooperative Learning

David and Roger Johnson (Johnson, Johnson, & Holubec, 1994) define cooperative learning as "the instructional use of small groups so that students work together to maximize their own and each other's learning," and Robert Slavin (1987) defines it as "instructional methods in which students of all performance levels work together toward a group goal." As the Johnsons repeatedly said, "None of us is as smart as all of us." Groups of students working together have the potential to achieve well beyond what a student working by himself can do. Moreover, working in cooperative groups can produce multiple benefits. Cooperative learning can improve students' achievement, their effort to succeed, their critical thinking, their attitudes toward the subjects studied, their psychological adjustment, and their self-esteem. Cooperative learning can also foster students' interpersonal relationships, improving their ability to work with others and build relationships among diverse racial, ethnic, and social groups. Additionally, as John Seely Brown and his colleagues note (Brown, Collins, & Duguid, 1989), group learning offers learners opportunities for displaying and recognizing the multiple roles that are often required to solve real-world problems and to recognize and confront their own and others' ineffective strategies and misconceptions.

Cooperative learning is consistent with many constructivist and sociocultural principles that we have mentioned. It relies on the belief that the best learning is often social, gives students an opportunity to scaffold one another's work, and puts students in a position to respond to and elaborate on one another's thinking. Because of its great potential, throughout this book we frequently

As with all students, we need to ensure that English-language learners receive the instruction and practice they need to develop deep and lasting understanding of important topics.

Cooperative learning is particularly recommended as a powerful instructional activity for many English-language learners.

Working in small groups helps students maximize their own and each other's learning.

suggest group activities for elementary students, and many of the Reflect and Apply sections suggest that you engage in group work. Also, because of its effectiveness in fostering understanding, we have included Jigsaw (Aronson & Patnoe, 1997; Tierney & Readence, 2005), a particular form of cooperative learning, as one of the teaching-for-understanding approaches we describe in detail in Chapter 11.

Reflect *and* Apply

4. Each of the instructional concepts in this section is tremendously important. Define each of them in your own words. Next, check your understanding against that of a classmate, and see if you can come up with a common definition of each concept. Finally, team up with this classmate and two others, and together come up with one example of a classroom situation in which instruction is in keeping with each of these concepts and one example of a classroom situation in which instruction runs counter to these concepts.

5. Once you have completed the activities in item 4, select the concept that you think will be the most valuable for you personally, and explain your reasons, preferably in writing.

A Brief History of Reading Instruction in the United States

The history of the United States and of U.S. schools reveals cyclical changes in which alternating political and educational stances would first dominate and in turn be criticized (Cremin, 1990; Graves & Dykstra, 1997; Schlesinger,

1986). To understand the development of contemporary approaches to teaching reading, the history of reading instruction in the United States is best studied against the backdrop of tensions between these competing views. In the brief history that follows—parts of which rely heavily on information taken from Nila Banton Smith's *American Reading Instruction* (2002) and David Pearson's "Reading in the Twentieth Century" (2000)—we focus on these tensions.

The Colonial Period and the 19th Century

The period extending roughly from 1600 to 1840 was relatively free of tensions over instructional approaches. The emphasis was on content. The purpose of reading instruction early in the period was clearly religious, as revealed by this excerpt from the Old Deluder Act passed by the General Court of Massachusetts in 1647:

> It being one chief point of that old deluder, Satan, to keep men from the knowledge of the Scriptures. . . . It is therefore ordered that every township in this jurisdiction, after the Lord hath increased them to the number of fifty households, shall then forthwith appoint one within their town to teach all such children as shall resort to him to write and read. (Quoted in Smith, 2002)

Beginning about the time of the American Revolution and continuing until about 1840, the purpose shifted, and reading series reflected what Smith has termed a "nationalistic-moralistic emphasis," as exemplified in these lines from the preface to Lyman Cobb's *The North American Reader* (1835):

> The pieces in this work are chiefly American. The English Reader so largely used in our country does not contain a single piece or paragraph written by an American citizen. Is this good policy? Is it patriotism? (Cobb, 1835)

However, regardless of whether the reading material focused on religious or patriotic content, the method of instruction throughout the period was much the same—the alphabetic-spelling method. The alphabetic-spelling method was a plodding, step-by-step approach in which students first learned the alphabet, then learned to spell a large number of syllables, spelled words before they read them, memorized sections of text (usually religious, moral, or patriotic in content), and read orally (Smith, 2002). Figure 2.2 shows a page from the *New England Primer,* exemplifying the tediousness of the approach.

Not surprisingly, this approach eventually came under fire, most notably by educational reformer Horace Mann, who advocated instead a focus on whole words and letter sounds. In an 1842 report to the Board of Education in Massachusetts, Mann displays his disdain for the alphabetic-spelling approach and foreshadows the controversy that, though modified, continues today:

> Compare the above method [the more meaningful approach Mann favored] with that of calling up a class of abecedarians—or, what is more common, a single child—and while the teacher holds a book or card before him, with a pointer in his hand,

New England Primer   5

EASY SYLLABLES FOR CHILDREN

Ab	eb	ib	ob	ub
ac	ec	ic	oc	uc
ad	ed	id	od	ud
af	ef	if	of	uf
ag	eg	ig	og	ug
aj	ej	ij	oj	uj
al	el	il	ol	ul
am	em	im	om	um
an	en	in	on	un
ap	ep	ip	op	up
ar	er	ir	or	ur
as	es	is	os	us
at	et	it	ot	ut
av	ev	iv	ov	uv
ax	ex	ix	ox	ux
az	ez	iz	oz	uz

FIGURE 2.2

A Page from the *New England Primer*

Source: Smith, N. B. (2002). *American Reading Instruction,* special edition. Newark, DE: International Reading Association.

says, *a*, and he echoes *a*; then *b*, and he echoes *b*; and so on until the vertical row of lifeless and ill-favored characters is completed, and then of remanding him to his seat, to sit still and look at vacancy. (Mann, 1884/1965)

The Heyday of Basal Readers

Although the exact dates are not important, we will define the heyday of basal readers as running from about 1910 to about 1985. Beginning in the early 1900s, reading programs and reading instruction began to look more like those that you or your parents might have experienced. Teacher's manuals were developed, research on which words appear frequently in English resulted in carefully controlled vocabulary in basal readers, testing was increasingly used, and students were increasingly grouped by ability for reading instruction.

The basal readers themselves consisted of large collections of reading selections, worksheets, teacher's manuals, tests, and supplementary material. The books for the earliest grades employed strictly controlled vocabularies, generally contained very brief narratives, and relied on pictures to convey much of their meaning. The books used in the remainder of the primary grades continued to employ controlled vocabularies and contained largely fiction, which was often quite impoverished. At about the fourth-grade level, selections became longer, vocabulary control eased, the fiction became somewhat stronger, and some expository selections were included. Much of the instruction students received in these programs centered around directed reading lessons—which included preparation for reading, silent reading, and follow-up questions and discussion—on individual selections. These lessons were often punctuated by skills work in decoding, vocabulary, and comprehension; and students spent a good deal of time completing worksheets. Figure 2.3 shows pages from a first-grade reader in a 1950 basal series, typical of the readers of this period.

Oh, Jane.
Look and see.
See Baby go.
See Tim go.
See Spot and Puff go.

Sally said, "Come, Mother.
Come and see Father.
See Father jump and play.
Oh, oh.
Father is funny."

FIGURE 2.3

Pages from a Typical First-Grade Basal Reader of the 1950s

Source: From THE NEW FUN WITH DICK AND JANE. Copyright © 1956 by Scott, Foresman and Company. Reprinted by permission of Pearson Education, Inc.

Although many controversies about reading materials and reading instruction arose during the period, the most persistent and most frequent again involved the tensions between more holistic and more segmented instruction and again centered on letters, sounds, and words. The alphabetic-spelling method had disappeared, but the whole-word method and various approaches emphasizing phonics continued to be in conflict. This conflict reached a crescendo in 1955 when Rudolf Flesch published his best-selling *Why Johnny Can't Read*. Flesch charged that American children were not learning to read because they were not taught phonics. A decade later, in 1967, Harvard University professor Jeanne Chall published a very influential review of research, *Learning to Read: The Great Debate,* in which she concluded that phonics produced at least somewhat better results than the whole-word method. In that same year, the largest study of beginning reading ever conducted, the First Grade Reading Studies (Bond & Dykstra, 1967/1997), produced findings that tended to support Chall's conclusions.

Although these three publications did affect the content of basals, they did not seriously affect the influence and prominence of basals in the schools (Pearson, 2000). Contrary to Flesch's charge, most basals had always included some phonics instruction, and basal publishers responded to criticisms by providing somewhat more phonics. As late as 1985, the vast majority of American children continued to be taught with basal readers, and most teachers, if asked, would have said that they used a basal reading approach.

The Challenge to Basal Readers: Whole-Language and Literature-Based Approaches

When the challenge that ended the dominance of basal readers in their traditional form came, it came not from the advocates of phonics but from the advocates of more holistic approaches—whole-language and literature-based instruction.

The most serious challenge was that from whole language, first widely popularized in the United States in the writings of Kenneth Goodman (1970) and Frank Smith (1971). The basic charge was that basal approaches break up language and learning to read in a way that is unnatural and artificial and actually makes learning to read more difficult. More specific charges were that basals included too much skills instruction, that instruction in phonics and other subskills of reading was not integrated with actual reading, that vocabulary was much too controlled, that stories were banal and not well constructed, that separating students into ability groups had dire results for less-skilled readers, and that teachers were overprogrammed and overscripted. Critics also noted that the selections in basals dealt almost exclusively with White, middle-class characters, themes, and settings and that many of the reading selections were very poor from a literary standpoint. Advocates of literature-based programs had similar criticisms, though they tended not to be as adamantly against basal anthologies and structured programs as their whole-language colleagues. Both groups had a marked effect on basal readers and a huge effect on the reading instruction that takes place in American classrooms. In fact, literature-based basals, such as the one shown in Figure 2.4, were the most common type of basal in the 1990s.

Having outlined what advocates of whole-language and literature-based approaches were against, we now discuss what they favored. Three very general characteristics stand out: the use of authentic children's literature, a child-centered approach, and a focus on learning to read by reading. Authentic children's literature—books written by professional authors to engage and

FIGURE 2.4

Page from a Typical First-Grade Literature-Based Text of the late 1990s

Source: "Lizzie and Harold" by Elizabeth Winthrop, illustrated by Martha Weston.

entertain children—should be the mainstay of reading instruction. Moreover, whole texts should be used; excerpts should be avoided. Students and their needs, desires, and interests are the focus of attention, the primary concern. A preset curriculum is suspect. Student-initiated learning is favored over teacher-initiated instruction. Instruction comes when and as needed, as students are actually engaged in reading, and in quite brief minilessons.

Additional characteristics of whole-language and literature-based instruction include a focus on comprehension (rather than the subparts of reading, such as phonics or vocabulary), use of the process approach to writing (an approach we describe in detail in Chapter 12), and integration of reading with the other language arts and into the curriculum as a whole. For a retrospective look at the thinking of the most prominent proponent of whole language, see Goodman (2005).

Massive Federal Intervention in Reading

The most recent, large-scale movement to affect reading instruction in schools has been massive federal intervention. Here, we will very briefly summarize a lengthy set of events. For some years now, the federal government has sponsored a substantial amount of research on reading through the National Institute of Child Health and Human Development (NICHD), a part of the National Institutes of Health. Most of that research has been on young children, on beginning skills such as phonemic awareness and phonics, and on children who have difficulty learning to read. In 1998, the National Research Council, a prestigious scientific organization, published *Preventing Reading Difficulties in Young Children* (Snow, Burns, & Griffin, 1998), a book that reviewed and brought to prominence much of the research sponsored by the NICHD, as well as other research on early reading. In 2000, the National Reading Panel (NRP), a group of scholars working at the direction of the U.S. Congress, published the *Report of the National Reading Panel: Teaching Children to Read*. In this report, the NRP identified five elements of reading instruction that it saw as strongly supported by research: phonemic awareness, phonics, fluency, vocabulary, and comprehension.

The report has had both very strong supporters and very strong opponents, but both supporters and opponents agree that it has had and is very likely to continue to have huge effects on reading instruction. Most notably, a massive federal funding program titled Reading First is specifically designed to promote instruction in each of the five areas endorsed by the report—that is, in phonemic awareness, phonics, fluency, vocabulary, and comprehension. The program is having a substantial effect (Center for Educational Policy, 2005). Schools and districts are endorsing the federal agenda, and most basal readers now reflect the NRP and Reading First priorities. A page from a first-grade book of one such basal—*Open Court Reading*—is shown in Figure 2.5.

CW 2.3 links to the *Report of the National Reading Panel*, which has had and continues to have huge effects on reading instruction.

Out came the sun
And dried up all the rain,
And the itsy bitsy spider
Climbed up the spout again.

FIGURE 2.5

A Page from *The Itsy Bitsy Spider*

Source: Text and Illustrations copyright © 1993 by Iza Trapani. Used with permission by Charlesbridge Publishing, Inc. All rights reserved.

CW 2.4 links to the Center on Educational Policy Website, an independent advocate for more effective schools and a rich source of information on topics ranging from Democracy & Public Schools to Violence & Crime in Schools.

As we noted in Chapter 1, we believe that phonemic awareness, phonics, fluency, vocabulary, and comprehension are vital parts of a reading program. But as we also noted, we and most other reading educators believe firmly that these five elements constitute only part of a comprehensive and balanced reading program that can lead all students to the sophisticated level of literacy necessary in the 21st century. As we noted in Chapter 1, a comprehensive and powerful reading curriculum includes several types of comprehension—scaffolding students' comprehension of text, teaching comprehension strategies, and fostering higher-order thinking and deep understanding—as well as encouraging independent reading and reader response.

Reading Instruction at Its Best

As our discussion of the current federal intervention in reading suggests, reading instruction is in a period of flux. Whole-language and literature-based programs are being replaced with programs in which instruction is more structured, more skill-oriented, and motivated by the *Report of the National Reading Panel* and the Reading First legislation. Yet whole-language and literature-based programs have not disappeared. Some schools and some teachers continue to employ these approaches or at least significant parts of them. Other schools very closely adhere to the recommendations of the National Reading Panel and the Reading First legislation. This means that when you visit schools, you are apt to see a variety of approaches to reading instruction, some of them much more likely to be effective than others.

Fortunately, recent research has identified a group of schools and classrooms in which students show particularly strong achievement in reading, achievement well beyond that in average schools and classrooms and well beyond what would be predicted of the students in those classrooms. Five studies stand out, three of which deal with instruction generally (Pressley, Allington,

ASSESSMENT

In a weekly newsletter sent home to parents, you can let them know your literacy goals for a certain time period—for example, "Next week we will be working on writing paragraphs. Your child will be learning how to develop a main idea with supporting details."

- The best teachers employ a rich combination of skills instruction (phonemic awareness, phonics, and the like) and more holistic activities (reading quality literature and nonfiction texts, discussing and writing about what they read, and the like), and they focus their instruction on important academic tasks.

- The best teachers teach a lot. They work hard, and their students work hard in turn. In doing so, they employ a combination of well-planned small-group activities and whole-class activities.

- The best teachers scaffold students' efforts so that if students put significant effort into learning, they will be successful.

- The best teachers promote higher-order thinking and give students challenging tasks to complete.

- The best teachers integrate reading instruction with the other language arts and the curriculum more generally.

- The best teachers are masterful classroom managers.

- The best teachers saturate their classrooms with motivation and repeatedly and prominently recognize students' work.

FIGURE 2.6

Characteristics of Teachers Who Produce Outstanding Achievement in Reading

- Strong focus on student learning
- Strong school leadership
- Strong collaboration among teachers
- Consistent use of data on student performance to guide instruction
- Emphasis on professional development for teachers in the school
- Strong links to parents

FIGURE 2.7

Characteristics of Schools That Produce High Achievement in High-Poverty Settings

Wharton-McDonald, Block, & Morrow, 2001; Taylor et al., 2003; Wharton-McDonald, Pressley, & Hampston, 1998) and two of which deal specifically with motivation (Bogner, Raphael, & Pressley, 2002; Dolezal, Welsh, Pressley, & Vincent, 2003). Each of these reports is well worth detailed study, and we encourage you to read them. However, we have summarized the major findings revealed in these studies in Figure 2.6.

In addition to these findings about effective teachers, some of these same studies and others have revealed school-level factors that produce high achievement in high-poverty schools. A summary of these findings reported by Taylor, Pressley, and Pearson (2002) is shown in Figure 2.7. Although these factors are not as directly under your control as are teacher characteristics, they are certainly things you can look for in schools and work toward as a faculty member in a school.

Reflect *and* Apply

6. Consider the four historical periods of reading instruction outlined—the colonial period and the 19th century, the heyday of basal readers, the period of challenges to basal readers, and the period of massive federal intervention—and decide which period you would have chosen to learn to read in and why.

7. Describe the program of reading instruction you received in elementary school. Discuss any characteristics of the four historical periods that you saw in your elementary school. You are not likely to identify any characteristics of the colonial period and the 19th century, but you may well identify characteristics of more than one of the other periods.

8. Try to identify the best elementary teacher you ever had. Then discuss which characteristics of teachers who produce outstanding achievement he or she did and did not have.

Strengths and Challenges of DIVERSITY

As you know, students differ from one another in many ways that we as teachers need to attend to. This section is designed to assist you in accommodating those differences and in capitalizing on the opportunities that this diversity presents. Most of the instructional principles we discuss in the

CW 2.5 links to the ReadWriteThink Website, sponsored by both the International Reading Association and the National Council of Teachers of English. This is a rich source of lessons, standards, and Web resources useful in today's diverse classrooms.

ASSESSMENT

It is important to be candid with students and their parents about both students' strengths and their limitations. The final aim of literacy assessment is to provide the ongoing guidance needed to lead students to the highest possible level of literacy.

chapter hold for virtually all students, and all students must participate in a rich, balanced, and comprehensive literacy curriculum if they are to achieve the level of literacy needed in our society. Still, different students will profit from some different experiences. Here, we consider the matters of differing participation structures, a diverse classroom library and time to read, and high achievement for students of color.

DIFFERING PARTICIPATION STRUCTURES

When working with learners with different cultural and linguistic backgrounds, it is important for the teacher to understand differing participation structures. Participation structures are the tacit arrangements that exist between speakers and listeners as they interact in certain social situations— in this case, in classroom conversations. As Shirley Brice Heath (1983) has pointed out, differences in the conversational patterns of middle-class teachers and of students who are not from the linguistic mainstream can be very debilitating. For example, Kathryn Au and Jana Mason (1983) explain how the mainstream instructional pattern in which teachers direct questions at individual students clashes with the participation structures familiar to native Hawaiian children. Hawaiian children are used to a participation structure in which several people talk at once, and being singled out to individually answer a question can seem uncomfortable and difficult to understand. Somewhat similarly, some African American students respond well to a performer/audience style of teaching. First-grade teacher Debbie Diller (1999) discovered this in her attempts to more successfully connect with the many African American students in her class:

> As I taught students a new concept, I encouraged them to respond chorally or individually at a rather fast, energized pace. "What sounds do you hear at the beginning of *stay*?" I'd ask enthusiastically; "*st st*," the children would respond in rhythm. "Tell your neighbor another word that starts like *stay*," I'd continue. "Tell your neighbor another word that starts with *st*." The children would spontaneously call out words to each other or to me.
>
> —Debbie Diller, First-Grade Teacher

Of course, other linguistic and cultural groups follow other participation structures, and thus teachers need to learn the cultural and linguistic patterns of interaction followed by their students.

A DIVERSE CLASSROOM LIBRARY AND TIME TO READ

As we noted in the section on traditional instructional principles, both focusing on academically relevant tasks and providing ample practice are crucial to learning. No task, of course, could be more academically relevant and provide better practice for learning to read than reading itself. And a well-stocked classroom library is a key to making books easily and readily available, particularly for students who may not have a lot of books in their homes. Every classroom needs a well-stocked library. In order to maximize their effectiveness for diverse classrooms, libraries need to include books that are easy and books that are challenging for *all* students. Thus, the books must span a significant range of difficulty. The library must also include books on topics of interest and relevance to those from various cultures and backgrounds, and it must include informational books as well as narratives. Finally, the classroom must provide an opportunity for independent reading for students who can concentrate on reading for ten minutes as well as for those who can lose themselves in a book for an hour.

CW 2.6 links to the complete American Educational Research Association policy statement "Closing the Gap for Students of Color."

HIGH ACHIEVEMENT FOR STUDENTS OF COLOR

It has now been 50 years since the Supreme Court's landmark Brown versus the Board of Education decision requiring school desegregation. Yet despite a number of strong efforts and the many gains that students of color have made over those 50 years, a large achievement gap continues to exist. By the twelfth-grade, average African American and Hispanic students can read only about as well as White eighth-graders. In a recent policy statement on closing this gap (Gordon, 2004), the American Educational Research Association made two recommendations. First, we must "support programs that engage all students in a rigorous, standards-based curriculum. Provide additional time and instruction as needed, but do not lower expectations." Second, we must "create an environment that provides the necessary social support for learning. It is important for students to be surrounded by peers and family members who value and support academic effort." We very strongly support both recommendations, and we add one of our own: Do everything possible to ensure that students are motivated to succeed in school. Motivation is vital for all students, but it is particularly vital for many students of color. We take up the topic of motivation in depth in Chapter 3.

Concluding Remarks

In this chapter, we discussed three topics: First, we discussed traditional principles of instruction and newer constructivist and sociocultural perspectives on instruction. Second, we gave a brief history of reading instruction in the United States. Third, we described reading instruction at its best, providing characteristics of teachers and schools that produce outstanding achievement in reading.

It is worth summarizing several main points. Both traditional instructional principles, such as fostering active learning and providing sufficient and timely feedback, and constructivist and sociocultural principles, such as scaffolding and cognitive modeling, are important. Instruction is not good simply because it represents an idea that has been around a long time or because it represents a new and different idea. Instruction is good because it is motivated by solid theory, backed by research, and able to be used by real teachers in real classrooms.

The history of reading instruction in the United States indicates that various approaches to reading have come and gone, that we have learned a lot and come to much agreement in recent years, but that tensions continue to exist. The most effective approach to instruction, the one most likely to lead the most children to a high level of literacy, is an eclectic, comprehensive, and balanced approach.

It is also important to realize that effective instruction emphasizes different parts of the curriculum as students become increasingly competent readers. For example, most children will have mastered most of what they need to know about print and most decoding strategies by the end of second grade, and thus these elements constitute a small part of the literacy curriculum after that time. Conversely, all children should receive instruction in vocabulary and various facets of comprehension beginning in kindergarten and continuing throughout their years of school.

Extending Learning

As we noted in Chapter 1, in this section we suggest activities that take you beyond this book to observe and work with schools, teachers, and parents and to access various sources of information that can help you more fully understand and appreciate your role in fostering students' literacy.

1. Identify a simple skill that you have mastered but that many of your classmates probably have not. Choose something specific that can be learned relatively easily, such as tying a square knot. Review the traditional and constructivist/ sociocultural principles of instruction—active teaching, active learning, scaffolding, gradual release, feedback, and the like—and decide which can be incorporated into your instruction. Next, write out a specific plan for teaching your skill—a lesson plan—noting just what you are going to do and indicating which principles you are following at each point. Rehearse your instruction, with a partner if possible; then teach a small group of your classmates the skill. If possible, have a classmate who is not part of the group observe you. Finally, sit down with your classmates—both the learners and the observer—and critique your instruction, being sure to attend to how well people learned the skill, what did and did not go well, how you might improve the lesson, what instructional principles you followed, and what additional instructional principles you might incorporate to improve learning.

2. Identify two really excellent elementary teachers. These could be teachers who have been formally recognized as outstanding, teachers you know of from friends or colleagues, teachers you actually had, or teachers recommended by a principal or one of your professors. Make up some observation sheets listing the seven characteristics of teachers who produce outstanding achievement in reading, as given in Figure 2.6; leave some space below each characteristic for your notes. Then observe the two teachers, and make notes on the extent to which they demonstrate each of the characteristics on the list. Plan on at least three observations, but do more if you can. For each characteristic that the teachers demonstrate, jot down a specific example or two of how they do so. Once you are finished with your observation, write a summary statement on the extent to which the teachers did and did not demonstrate the characteristics and a statement about the extent to which you expect to incorporate the characteristics into your teaching. Finally, discuss your observations and conclusions with a classmate.

Children's Literature

Byars, B. C. (2002). *Keeper of the Doves.* New York: Viking. In this story set in the late 19th century in Kentucky, the precocious Amie McBee searches for her place in the family and discovers a talent of her own, writing poetry. 112 pages.

Inns, C. (2004). *Help!* London: Frances Lincoln. Doctor Hopper (a rabbit) and Nurse Rex Barker (a dog) zoom around to cure sick toys in this witty picture book. 32 pages.

Juster, N. (2005). *The Hello, Goodbye Window.* New York: Hyperion. A little girl visits her grandparents' house and finds a magic gateway in the kitchen window that leads her on a voyage of discovery. 32 pages.

McDonald, A. (2001). *No More Nasty.* New York: Farrar. Fifth grade becomes more than a bit embarrassing and challenging for Simon when his favorite, but eccentric, 74-year-old aunt becomes the substitute teacher in his unruly class. 172 pages.

National Geographic World. Washington, D.C.: National Geographic Society. This richly illustrated, monthly periodical is designed for intermediate-grade students.

Simon, S. (1995). *Sharks.* New York: HarperCollins. With full-colored photos and engaging text that describes fascinating details about 350 different kinds of sharks, Simon demystifies this greatly feared predatory fish. Unpaged.

CHAPTER **3**

Motivation and Engagement

chapter outline

CLASSROOM VIGNETTE

*L*ast year, Cynthia Sanchez switched from teaching first grade to teaching fifth grade, and her first year as a fifth-grade teacher was not an easy one. "What a difference four years make," she sometimes sighed to herself. Of course, she had to learn to teach very different aspects of reading than she had taught in first grade. None of her students needed to work on phonemic awareness, only a few needed help with phonics, and most read fluently. She also had to learn to teach fairly sophisticated lessons in social studies, science, math, and other subjects. What turned out to be much more of a challenge than learning how to teach new material, however, was motivating students. Cynthia's first-graders had come to school enthusiastic about their opportunities, excited about learning, confident that they could learn, and ready to put their best efforts into learning whatever subject they were studying. Some of her fifth-graders displayed very different attitudes. They were not enthusiastic about school or excited about learning. Nor were they confident about learning or prepared to put in their best efforts.

Cynthia soon decided that motivating and engaging students was her number one priority, and throughout the year she read everything she could on motivation, talked to teachers who had reputations for being outstanding motivators and visited their classrooms, tried out a variety of ways of motivating students, and worked very hard not to do anything that undermined students' motivation. Over time, her strategies began to work, and this year's students are much more motivated and engaged than were last year's. Still, motivation is her main priority, and she expects that this will continue to be the case.

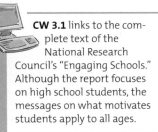

CW 3.1 links to the complete text of the National Research Council's "Engaging Schools." Although the report focuses on high school students, the messages on what motivates students apply to all ages.

Making Motivation a Top Priority

As you will see in this chapter, Cynthia is not alone in realizing that motivation should be a top priority. Other teachers, reading authorities, researchers, and policy makers are increasingly realizing that motivation is essential to learning (Brophy, 2004; National Research Council, 2004; Pressley, 2006). In order for substantive learning to occur, students must have positive attitudes about themselves as learners, about their ability to succeed in school, and about the instructional goals they, their teachers, and their schools set. Students' reading abilities will grow in direct proportion to the extent to which they see reading as a worthwhile and enjoyable activity that they can succeed at. In discussing ways to foster such positive attitudes, we consider the critical importance of success, ways of creating the sort of classroom atmosphere that has come to be called a literate environment, and the importance of positive attributions. We also consider a number of concrete approaches to motivating students, present an extended portrait of a teacher who is a superstar at motivating her students, and discuss ways of grouping students to foster positive attitudes. These building blocks of success are shown in Figure 3.1.

The Critical Importance of Success

A dominant thought underlying not just this section of the chapter but the whole of this book is the overwhelming importance of success. Research has repeatedly verified that if students are going to be motivated and engaged in

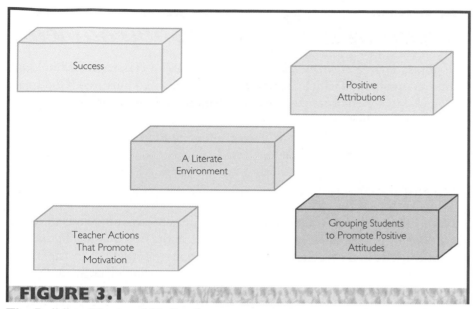

FIGURE 3.1

The Building Blocks of Motivation

school and learn from their schoolwork, they need to succeed at the vast majority of tasks they undertake (Brophy, 1986; Pressley, 2006). This, of course, applies to reading just as it does to other schoolwork. Moreover, if students are to become not only proficient readers but also avid readers—children and later adults who voluntarily seek out reading as a path to information, enjoyment, and personal fulfillment—then successful reading experiences are even more important.

A successful reading experience has at least three features. First, and most importantly, a successful reading experience is one in which the reader understands what she has read. Understanding may take more than one reading, it may require your assistance or that of other students, and it will often require the reader to actively manipulate the ideas in the text. Second, a successful reading experience is one that the reader finds enjoyable, entertaining, informative, or thought provoking. Of course, not every reading experience will yield all of these benefits, but every experience should yield at least one of them. Finally, a successful reading experience is one that prepares the student to complete whatever task follows the reading.

To a great extent, children's success in reading is directly under your control. You can select—and encourage students to select—tasks, materials, and supporting activities that all but guarantee success. For example, suppose you have a group of third-grade students who read at about 150 words a minute and you have a 10-minute period in which they will be reading. Giving these students a selection slightly shorter than 1,500 words will ensure that they at least have time to complete it, while giving them a selection much longer than 1,500 words will leave them frustrated and ensure failure. As another example, suppose you have a group of fifth-grade students who will be reading *Pond & River* by Steve Parker but who have virtually no concept of ecology—they have never even thought about the relationships among organisms and their environment. Preteaching the concept of *ecology* will greatly increase the likelihood that students will understand the selection and not simply flounder in a sea of new ideas.

Creating a Literate Environment

The phrase *literate environment* describes the sort of classroom, school, and home environment in which literacy will be fostered and nurtured (Goodman, 1986). A literate environment includes demonstrations of literacy in action by competent others, time devoted to the practice of literacy, materials that support engagement in literacy, choice about literate activities, and a safe and supportive classroom climate.

Modeling

Probably the most important component of a literate environment is the modeling done by people children respect and love. In the best possible literate environment, children's teachers, principals, parents, brothers and sisters, and friends read a lot and openly display the pleasure reading gives them, the fact that reading opens up a world of information to them, the value they place on reading, and the satisfaction they gain from reading. To be most effective, of course, this modeling should occur not just once but repeatedly—all the time, really. Also, this modeling should include both repeated demonstrations—your reading along with students during a sustained silent reading period, your looking up in a book an answer to a question children have, and your sharing a favorite poem with your class—and direct testimonials—"Wow! What a story." "I never knew what fun river rafting could be till I read this article; I sure wish I'd read it sooner." "Sometimes I think the library is just about my favorite place."

Third-grade teacher Mary Lou Flicker has her own testimonial to the power of modeling.

> I never realized the importance of modeling the kinds of behaviors I would like my students to emulate until one rainy day in March. Normally the kids eat outdoors on picnic tables, but during this unusual California downpour we were forced inside for lunch recess. After the kids finished eating, I told them they could play games together quietly, draw on the chalkboard, read, whatever.
>
> Instead of doing paperwork or watching the kids, I decided to read a book that a young friend had recommended, one of Barbara Park's Junie B. Jones books, *Junie B., First Grader: Shipwrecked*. It turned out to be an extremely funny book that I enjoyed immensely. After I finished, I looked around the room. To my amazement, there in the library corner sat Ramon, one of my least-motivated readers, a kid who hardly ever read by choice, fully absorbed in a Junie B. Jones book. Later in the day, when I told Ramon I was so pleased to see him reading, he said, "Well, you looked like you was having such a great time reading that Junie B. Jones book, I just had to find out why!"
>
> —Mary Lou Flicker, Third-Grade Teacher

Several things about this experience were motivating to students. First, Ms. Flicker modeled engaged reading. Second, she showed students how much she valued reading by spending class time on reading. Third, she praised her student's good behavior.

Time

Developing a literate environment goes beyond demonstrating your own engagement with reading and includes scheduling class time for reading, whether independent or assigned. Regularly scheduled time for independent reading such as sustained silent reading tells students that teachers really care about reading. Providing time in class to read assigned texts also tells students that reading is important. Too often, reading is relegated to homework or serves as a filler when there is time left after the "real" work of school is finished. But reading is the "real" work of the classroom! Time devoted to the pleasure of reading tells students that you value reading and want students to do so as well.

We know that reading independently improves reading fluency and reading achievement more generally (Allington, 1984; Knapp & Associates, 1995; Taylor, Pressley, & Pearson, 2002), but most students do not do enough of it. Most authorities estimate that students spend only about 15 minutes per day doing silent reading in school. It's difficult to become good at something that you do for only 15 minutes a day.

Fifteen minutes a day of in-school reading could, of course, be augmented with independent reading at home; but again, studies demonstrate that children, unless they are already avid readers, simply do not make the time to read at home. Anderson, Wilson, and Fielding (1988) discovered that among the fifth-grade students they studied, 50 percent read 4 minutes a day or less; 30 percent, 2 minutes a day or less, and 10 percent, not at all. They also found that independent reading time in school and time spent listening to books read aloud by the teacher were important factors in motivating students to read. All in all, we believe that students should do at least 30 minutes of in-school reading a day. This figure includes time spent reading in both language arts classes and other content area classes.

Reading aloud to students is another way to demonstrate how much you value reading, and it also becomes an opportunity to teach students about the rewards that reading brings. What you choose to read aloud can serve to entice students to broaden the scope of their reading interests. It allows you to introduce new authors, new genres, and new ideas. It creates a communal experience that students can use to understand new texts that they read, new

Reading independently improves fluency; many children do not do enough of it.

ideas that they consider. Reading aloud offers you the opportunity to talk about writing in a way that is concrete and engaging; students enjoy learning about how writing works when they are engaged with a text.

Reading aloud can also become a way to share engaging fiction and non-fiction with students who might not be able to read it on their own. Students who are struggling readers are often given texts that they can read, but do not enjoy because the books were written for younger readers. One of the reasons to engage in the hard work of becoming a fluent, strategic reader is the joy that books can bring. All readers need to experience the power of a well-written story, poem, or piece of nonfiction so that they can remember the reward that reading can bring. Think of engaging with a text through a teacher read-aloud as a motivational carrot. If you have class sets of texts, it is sometimes worthwhile for students to follow along as you read. At other times, however, letting them just sit back and enjoy the pleasure of listening to a well-read story or informational piece is the best approach.

Time to demonstrate your engagement with texts, time for students to read silently, and time to read aloud are all important components of a literate classroom. Students also need time to talk about what they read with others. Although we often think of reading as an independent, solitary activity, those of us who are avid readers know the joy of talking about what we have read with others. The social nature of reading in the company of others can become a powerful motivating force, encouraging students to read, to read with understanding, and to share their ideas with others. When students have the opportunity to talk with one another about what they read, they come to realize that there are many ways to understand and respond to a text, and they also have the opportunity to enlarge their understanding and repertoire of responses by listening to the responses of others. Providing time for students to talk about texts with others helps them understand the dynamic nature of engaged reading, even as it motivates them to engage in more reading.

The Classroom

Another important component of a literate environment is the physical setting in which children read. In the best possible literate environment, the classroom is filled with books, books that are readily accessible for students to read in school or take home. The walls are covered with colorful posters that advertise books and the treasures they offer and that showcase students' responses to what they have read. There are several inviting places to read—a carpeted corner where students can sit on the floor and read without interruption, bean bags or other comfortable chairs that entice young readers to immerse themselves in a book, places where students can gather in groups to read to each other or discuss their reading, and some tables for students to use to write about what they're reading. An attractive space encourages people to spend time in it, and spending time reading and responding is exactly what you want to encourage. The floor plan in Figure 3.2 shows one way to arrange a classroom to invite literacy.

Materials

The texts that you select for your classroom library are another crucial component of a motivating literate environment. Certainly, some books will be in

English Learners

Reading aloud can be particularly beneficial for English-language learners, whose skills with oral English may be considerably stronger than their skills with written English.

ASSESSMENT

Beginning on the first day of school, be sure to track students' work in and out of class so that you know both how often they do their work and how well they do it. If they are not doing their work or not doing it well, you need to let them know that and then assist them in getting on track.

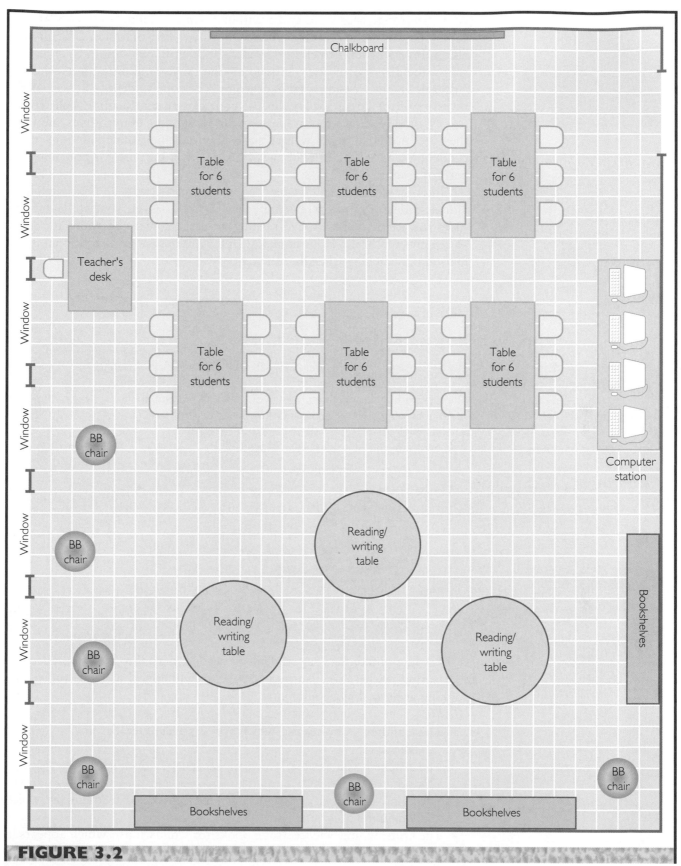

FIGURE 3.2

Floorplan of a Classroom That Invites Literacy

your classroom because they fit within your curriculum. Other materials should be selected so that students have a wide variety of topics, difficulty levels, and types of texts to choose from. Still other books should be chosen to reflect the diversity of your classroom—the range of abilities, interests, and cultural, linguistic, and social backgrounds of your students—as well as the diversity of the larger society outside your classroom. Reading well-written texts should become a tool students use to learn more about topics and ideas they are interested in, as well as supplementing their understanding of the curriculum. This kind of reading gives students a purpose for practicing the craft of reading.

In order to provide all students with appropriate texts and to match individual students with texts, it's important that you assess your students' attitudes toward reading and their reading interests. Some suggestions for doing so are given in In the Classroom 3.1. In Chapter 6, we give additional information on matching students and texts.

Assessing Students' Reading Attitudes and Interests

It's important that you get to know your students as readers early in the academic year. You can find out about their reading habits and preferences by having a one-on-one book conference with each of them, and with primary-grade children that's what you need to do. But with older students, a faster and more efficient way to get the information you need is to have them fill out a brief written survey. You can easily create a set of interview questions or survey that will give you the information you need, with questions such as the following:

in the Classroom 3.1

- Do you like to read? Why or why not?
- Are you reading anything for fun at this time? What is it? Why do you like it?
- Do you have any favorite authors or titles? Why are these your favorites?
- Is there a certain kind of text that you prefer—books, magazines, fiction, nonfiction, etc?
- How do you choose what to read when you go to a library or a book store?
- What do you do if what you are reading is too hard or too easy for you?
- What makes a good reader?

Finding out about your students as readers is vital to being an effective, motivating teacher. You can find books that will appeal to your students by looking at the following annotated lists:

- The Children's Choices list, which appears every October in *The Reading Teacher*
- The Teachers' Choices list, which appears every November in *The Reading Teacher*
- The Notable Children's Trade Books in the Field of Social Studies list, which appears in the May/June issue of *Social Education*
- The Outstanding Science Trade Books for Children list, which appears in the November issue of *Children and Science*

CW 3.2 links to several years of both Children's Choices booklists and Teachers' Choices booklists.

Another effective strategy for identifying books that your students might enjoy is to talk with your school media specialist or the librarians at a local library. These professionals are trained to recognize books that many children will find engaging. They also have access to the American Library Association's resources and can give you lists of books that librarians have identified as being of interest to readers of various ages and levels of proficiency.

As we have noted, the social, linguistic, and cultural backgrounds of your students and of the greater society constitute yet another important factor in selecting books. Readers shape their views of themselves and of the world partly through what they read. Reading about people who are similar to and different from ourselves is important for all students. Recognizing yourself in a book is a powerful affirmation that you are part of the human endeavor—and the world of books. Recognizing the humanity of others who might seem different from ourselves is an important part of becoming a citizen of the world. Good books can act as both a mirror and a window for readers (Galda & Cullinan, in press), reflecting their own lives and offering them a chance to understand the lives of others. Perhaps the best books offer an experience that is similar to looking through a window at twilight. At first you can see through the window into another place, but, as the light gradually fades, you end up seeing yourself (Galda, 1998; Galda & Cullinan, in press). Thinking and talking about experiences like this can help students develop an understanding of themselves and others. And reading books from many cultures exposes students to many wonderful authors.

Since the early 1990s, the publishing industry has responded to the increasing diversity of North America by publishing a slowly growing number of excellent books that reflect this diversity. Unfortunately, the number of books by and about people of color published in any given year hovers around 3 or 4 percent—a far cry from the percentage of students of color who attend school. Books that reflect linguistic diversity (bilingual texts) or those that offer international perspectives are even more scarce. Nevertheless, over the past 15 years there have been a number of excellent books published that can enrich a classroom collection.

Well-written books offer readers authentic glimpses of others' lives. When the portrayal of these lives is situated in a specific cultural context, it's extremely important that it be culturally authentic. Evaluating the cultural authenticity of books about people from a culture different from one's own is a challenge, but there are a number of resources that can help you find culturally diverse literature and that can help you learn how to think about issues surrounding cultural authenticity. Some of these resources are listed in Figure 3.3.

Choice

Scheduling ample time for reading and responding and finding materials that will engage readers are crucial components of a motivating literate environment. Add the element of choice to this mix, and it becomes even more powerful. Simply put, students need to have choices about what they read and what they do to respond to their reading. This does not mean that you never assign selections for students to read or tasks for students to complete after they have read. It does mean that you structure regular opportunities for students to choose their own reading materials and to choose their own response mode. Allowing students some choice often helps motivate them to spend time

Some basic questions to ask yourself as you are selecting culturally diverse literature are these:

- Does the book qualify as good literature?
- Is the culture accurately portrayed, demonstrating diversity within as well as across cultures if appropriate and avoiding stereotypes?
- Is the book a positive contribution to an understanding of the culture portrayed? (Galda & Cullinan, in press)

As you are learning to evaluate literature in terms of literary excellence and cultural authenticity, you may want to rely on published lists of books that have been carefully evaluated by experts in the field. Here are some of the better ones:

- Harris, V. (1997). *Using multiethnic literature in the K–8 classroom.* Norwood, MA: Christopher-Gordon.
- Helbig, A. K., & Perkins, A. R. (2000). *Many peoples, one land: A guide to new multicultural literature for children and young adults.* Westport, CT: Greenwood.
- International Board on Books for Young People. (Quarterly). *Bookbird: A Journal of International Children's Literature.* Basil, Switzerland: Author.
- Miller-Lachmann, L. (1992). *Our family, our friends, our world.* New Providence, NJ: Bowker.
- National Council of Teachers of English. (Multiple editions). *Kaleidoscope: A multicultural booklist for grades K–8.* Urbana, IL: Author.
- Stan, S. (2002). *The world through children's books.* Lanham, MD: Scarecrow.
- Tomlinson, C. M. (1998). *Children's books from other countries.* Lanham, MD: Scarecrow.

You might also consult publication lists from publishers such as Lee and Low, Jump at the Sun/Hyperion, Kane/Miller Book Press, Open Hand, Children's Book Press, Arte Publico, and North-South Books, all of which focus on culturally diverse literature.

And here are some of the major awards given for multicultural books:

- Notable Books for a Global Society (February issue of *The Reading Teacher,* International Reading Association/www.reading.org)
- Coretta Scott King Awards (American Library Association/www.ala.org)
- Pura Belpré Award (ALA)
- Mildred Batchelder Award (ALA)

FIGURE 3.3

Resources for Finding and Evaluating Culturally Diverse Books

reading. We recently talked to reading consultant Peter Dewitz, who had this to say about choice.

> It's absolutely unbelievable the effect that giving students some choice in what they read has on their motivation and interest in what they read. It doesn't have to be a lot of choice. In fact, if we give them their choice among just two or three books, they are much more likely to do the reading and to do it enthusiastically.
>
> —Peter Dewitz, Reading Consultant

Independent reading is one such opportunity. Although students, especially those who are struggling readers and many English-language learners, need support and guidance in selecting books that they can and will want to read, students also ought to be able to choose their own books for independent reading. Some teachers insist that students choose only from the classroom or school library. We suggest that, if reading is the goal, students ought to be able to read

the Reading Corner

Books About Food and Families in Many Cultures

Alma Flor Ada. *Gathering the Sun: An Alphabet in Spanish and English.* HarperCollins, 2001. Dedicated to Cesar Chavez, this alphabet book recounts stories of family farmworkers during that era. For example, "A is for *arboles*" (trees) shows the fruit trees—plum, pear, peach, and orange—that are so much a part of these families' lives. 40 pages.

Debby Atwell. *The Thanksgiving Door.* Houghton Mifflin, 2003. After burning their Thanksgiving dinner, an elderly couple find themselves the guests of honor at the New World Café, a restaurant owned by welcoming Russian immigrants. 32 pages.

Carmen T. Bernier-Grand. *In the Shade of the Nispero Tree.* Orchard, 1999. Because her mother wants her to be part of the world of high society in their native Puerto Rico, 9-year-old Teresa goes to a private school but loses her best friend. 186 pages.

Nora Dooley. *Everybody Cooks Rice.* Carolrhoda, 1991. Young Carrie gets to sample rice recipes from Barbados, Puerto Rico, Vietnam, India, and more when sent out to fetch her little brother at dinnertime. 32 pages.

Ziporah Hildebrandt. *This Is Our Seder.* Holiday House, 1999. This book provides a simple description of the food and activities at a seder, the ritual meal of Passover, including an explanation of its historical and symbolic significance. 32 pages.

Aylette Jenness. *Families: A Celebration of Diversity, Commitment, and Love.* Houghton Mifflin, 1990. Black-and-white photo essays celebrate the lives of 17 children of many cultures, races, and lifestyles. 48 pages.

Angela Johnson. *The Wedding.* Orchard, 1999. An African American wedding is viewed through the eyes of the bride's younger sister. 32 pages.

Dayal Kaur Khalsa. *How Pizza Came to Queens.* Clarkson N. Potter, 1989. When Mrs. Pellegrino comes to visit May's family, she laments that there is no pizza. So May and her friends, with the help of the librarian who defines the word, buy the ingredients and get Mrs. Pellegrino to make pizza. 24 pages.

Susan Kuklin. *How My Family Lives in America.* Bradbury, 1992. Three young children, an African American, Chinese American, and Hispanic American, describe their families, customs, and favorite recipes. Includes nine recipes for rice. 32 pages.

Patricia McMahon. *Chi-hoom: A Korean Girl.* Boyds Mills, 1993. This photo essay depicting a week in the life of an 8-year-old girl in Seoul gives a sense of an individual's place within a Korean family and culture. 48 pages.

Shulamith Levey Oppenheim. *Ali and the Magic Stew.* Boyds Mills Press, 2002. A beggar helps a young Muslim boy save his seriously ill father by telling him how to get the ingredients for a stew with special healing powers. 32 pages.

Lynn Reiser. *Tortillas and Lullabies/Tortillas y concioncitas.* Greenwillow, 1998. A young girl tells about tortilla making, flower gathering, dress laundering, and lullaby singing—activities her great-grandmother, grandmother, and mother all did and that she does with her doll. The text is in English and Spanish and includes a musical score. 40 pages.

Lisa Shulman. *The Matzo Ball Boy.* Dutton, 2005. In this Jewish version of the "Gingerbread Man," a lonely old *bubbe* makes a matzo ball boy in her chicken soup so he can join her for the Passover sedar. 32 pages.

Janet S. Wong. *Apple Pie 4th of July.* Harcourt, 2002. After a young Chinese American girl frets that no one will come to her parents' market to buy Chinese food on the 4th of July, she is happily proven wrong. 32 pages.

Paul Yee. *Roses Sing on New Snow: A Delicious Tale.* Macmillan, 1991. When the governor of South China visits Maylin's home, she creates a new dish in his honor, and her lazy brothers try to take all the credit. However, their attempts to duplicate the recipe only infuriate the emperor, while Maylin triumphs, demonstrating that cooking, like painting, is an art. 32 pages.

all kinds of texts, including newspapers, comic books, and magazines. If we want students to spend time reading, we must allow them to choose what they read as often as possible.

Which of these books would you like to read?

Sometimes teachers are able to offer students limited choice even in the texts they read as a whole class or small group. Offering students a small range of titles, all of which will allow you to meet your curricular goals, helps students feel a part of the instructional environment. So, too, does offering choice about what to do with the texts they have read. By offering students various options for responding to their reading, you increase the likelihood that they will enjoy the task.

Time, materials, and choice all foster engaged reading. In the Classroom 3.2 offers a suggestion for helping students develop an interest in poetry by making use of these motivating elements—including time for browsing through books, something that often looks unproductive but has been found to be important.

Poetry Browsing to Create Interest

Teacher lore has it that it is often difficult to get upper-elementary students engaged in poetry. Whatever the reasons, upper-elementary readers tend to avoid poetry, unless it is humorous verse by authors such as Shel Silverstein and Jack Prelutsky. But this doesn't always have to be the case. Amy McClure and her colleagues (McClure, Harrison, & Reed, 1990) found that, given time and choice, their upper-elementary students came to really enjoy poetry, even selecting books of poetry for independent reading. After assembling a collection of poetry that might interest their students, McClure and her colleagues added it to the classroom library, displaying it so that students were tempted to look at the books. Then they gave students time to browse—to dip in and out of books, finding poems they enjoyed and wanted to read to their buddies and then moving on. Over time, this freedom to simply enjoy and sample a lot of poetry without any task being assigned broke down the negative attitudes that students began with.

in the Classroom 3.2

Classroom Climate

A final and equally important component of a literate environment is the atmosphere in which children read. In the best possible literate environment, everything that happens in the classroom sends the message that reading—including learning from what you read, having personal responses to what you read, talking about what you read, and writing about what you read—is fantastic! In such a classroom, students are given plenty of time to read, they are given ample opportunities to share the information they learn and their responses to what they have read with each other, they are taught to listen to and respect the ideas of others, and they learn that others will listen to and respect their ideas. A literate atmosphere is a thoughtful atmosphere in which values and ideas are respected—values and ideas in texts, one's own values and ideas, and other people's values and ideas.

This kind of climate is developed when teachers, in a positive and supportive manner, help students learn how to engage in discussions and other forms of sharing what they have read. One way students learn to do this is through your modeling how to be positive and supportive as you scaffold students' reading experiences. Modeling and directly teaching students ways to conduct themselves in the classroom, coming up with an agreed-upon set of rules for the classroom, and prominently displaying the rules will also help set the right tone. Trust, respect, and responsibility are important ideas in a safe and supportive classroom, and talking about these concepts and how the successful operation of the class rests on them is crucial, especially at the beginning of the year.

Reflect *and* Apply

1. Describe a successful reading experience you have had and an unsuccessful one you have had. What could you or someone else have done to make the unsuccessful one more successful?
2. Look back at the floor plan in Figure 3.2. Identify a grade level you are familiar with, and sketch an alternative floor plan for a literate environment. The sketch need not be anything fancy, but the plan should clearly be one that lends itself to reading, writing, and discussion.
3. Identify a grade level, and then list the types of reading materials you would have in your classroom library (books, magazines, etc.), along with two or three specific examples of each type.

The Importance of Positive Attributions

Ensuring that students have strong models of competent and engaged readers, providing them with ample time to read, creating a physically attractive classroom, and building a rich classroom library all encourage the development of motivated and engaged readers. So do giving them appropriate choices and creating a supportive classroom climate. However, it is also important to understand some of the internal factors that relate to motivation: how students' perceptions influence their performance.

Educators and psychologists have been studying motivation for many years, and one of the most persistent findings is that the way people view their successes and failures, what has come to be called their "attributions," has a powerful effect on motivation. A closely related finding is that the result of repeatedly failing is learned helplessness. Still another finding is the importance of giving students appropriate challenges. In this section, we discuss each of these important concepts.

Attribution Theory

Attribution theory helps to explain and underscore the importance of success to student motivation and engagement. Attribution theory deals with students' perceptions of the causes of their successes and failures in learning. As Merlin Wittrock (1986) explains, in deciding why they succeed or fail in reading tasks, students can attribute their performance to ability, effort, luck, the difficulty of the reading task, or a variety of other causes. All too often, children who have repeatedly failed in reading attribute their failure to factors that are beyond their control—to an unchangeable factor, such as their innate ability, or to a factor that they can do nothing about, such as luck. Once this happens, children are likely to lose their motivation to learn to read and to doubt their ability to learn. From the children's perspective, there is no reason to try because there is nothing they can do about it. Moreover, as long as they do not try, they cannot fail; you cannot lose a race if you do not enter it.

Learned Helplessness

As Peter Johnston and Peter Winograd (1985) have pointed out, one long-term outcome of children's repeatedly attributing failure in reading to forces that are beyond their control is their falling into a learned-helplessness syndrome. Children who exhibit learned helplessness in reading are apt to be nervous, withdrawn, and discouraged when they are faced with reading tasks. They are unlikely to be actively engaged in reading, to have goals and plans when they read, to monitor themselves when they are reading to see if the reading makes sense, or to check themselves after reading to see if they have accomplished their reading goal.

Obviously, we need to avoid this debilitating cycle of negative attributions and learned helplessness. Second-grade teacher Jerry Costello suggests four approaches:

> The first, and almost certainly the most powerful, way I have found to help students understand that they are in control of their learning is something I hear stressed over and over again by my colleagues and read in the literature: Make students' reading experiences successful ones; make them so frequently successful for students that they will be compelled to realize that it is they themselves and not some outside force that is responsible for their success.
>
> Second, I tell students that their efforts *make a difference*, and when they are successful in a reading task, I talk to them about the activities they engaged in to make them successful. If, for example, after reading an informational piece about dinosaurs, students successfully answer several questions that they generated before reading, we discuss how generating those questions beforehand helped them focus their attention so that they could answer the questions as they read.
>
> Third, I avoid competitive situations in which students compare how well they read a selection to how well others read it and instead focus students' attention on what they personally gained from the selection.

Finally, I try to provide a number of reading activities in which the goal is simply to *enjoy reading,* have fun, and experience something interesting and exciting rather than only offering reading activities that are followed by answering questions or some other sort of external accountability.

—Jerry Costello, Second-Grade Teacher

The Importance of Appropriate Challenges

Although we stress the importance of success, providing appropriate challenges for children is equally essential (Pressley, 2006; Taylor et al., 2002). Saying that students should succeed at the reading tasks you ask them to complete and that you should do everything possible to ensure success does not mean spoon-feeding them. Unless readers undertake some challenging tasks, unless they are willing to take some risks and make some attempts they are not certain of and get feedback on their efforts, there is little room for learning to take place. In order to develop as readers, children need to be given some challenges. As Mihaly Csikszentmihalyi (1990) has learned from three decades of research on what makes people's lives happier and more meaningful, facing and meeting significant challenges is one of the most self-fulfilling and rewarding experiences we can have. However, when we present students with challenges, we need to be certain that they clearly understand the goals toward which they are working, to give them challenges appropriate for their skills, and to provide them with whatever support they need to meet these challenges. This is, of course, true for all students, but it is particularly true for those students who have often found school difficult. In the Classroom 3.3, which is based on an article by Mary Beth Sampson and her colleagues (Sampson, & Linek, 1994/1995), you will see how one teacher creates a successful reading experience that includes providing appropriate challenges and supports for her students.

Providing Both Challenges and Supports

Five students sit at the same table reading about lightning bugs in their science texts. Sarah is reading merely to finish the assignment, daydreaming about what she will do that evening. Carlos, on the other hand, reads with enthusiasm—he had caught lightning bugs the night before, released them in his room, and fallen asleep to their steady blinks. Paul reads with the fascination of a new discovery. He has recently moved from Alaska, where lightning bugs didn't exist. Marinda discovers something she didn't know about lightning bugs and quickly moves from being a passive reader to being an actively involved one. Josh reads as he always does, word by word, with no real interest in the content. Around the room, other groups of five students also sit at tables reading the same text.

in the Classroom 3.3

When they finish reading, Mrs. Tollison tells the class they will be exploring the topic of lightning bugs. They will be working in groups of five using an approach called Circle of Questions. After establishing the groups, she gives the groups three minutes to brainstorm the questions they have about lightning bugs.

After three minutes, Mrs. Tollison calls time, draws a circle on the board, and invites each group to share their questions. She writes the questions around the circle as the students share them. (See Figure 3.4.)

Mrs. Tollison next encourages students to review and examine their questions to see what categories of questions they can find. Using colored chalk, she circles items that belong in specific categories—for example, questions about what makes lightning bugs flash are circled in blue, questions about physical attributes circled in red, and questions about reproduction circled in green. Each group then chooses a category in which to become an expert.

In their groups, students reread the text, searching for answers to the questions in their category. A recorder for each group writes down the answers and where they are found in the text. When all of the groups have finished researching their questions, the class meets as a whole, and the recorder from each group shares the information the group discovered with the class. Mrs. Tollison writes the answers and their sources by the appropriate questions on the Circle of Questions chart.

While Mrs. Tollison records the answers, students discuss whether the text adequately addressed their initial questions or if additional research will be needed to flesh out their knowledge.

FIGURE 3.4

Circle of Questions

Source: Sampson, Mary Beth, Sampson, Michael R., & Linek, Wayne M. (December 1994). Circle of questions. *The Reading Teacher, 48*(4), 364–365. Used by permission.

Can you see how this activity appropriately challenged the readers who were introduced at the beginning of the scenario? Perhaps word-by-word reader Josh began to change his view toward reading that day. As his classmates generated questions they had about the text, he saw that all readers, not just himself, don't understand everything they read. Carlos gained self-esteem because his knowledge of fireflies enabled him to answer many of the group's questions. Paul discovered that an excellent way to clarify the ideas in a text is through group interaction with that text. Sarah, appointed recorder for the group, became an active, interested member of the team. Marinda came to realize that not all questions are answered by a particular text, and sometimes more questions are raised. The entire class was challenged to do what "real" readers do—actively construct their own questions about a topic and find the answers.

Another way for students to be both challenged and supported comes in reading discussion groups. Talking with others about what they have read, what questions they have, and how they reacted to the story, poem, or information they've just processed is a natural part of discussion groups. Successful discussion groups quickly become places where students can say, "I didn't get it when . . ." and their peers can help them.

Concrete Approaches to Motivating Students

Like Jerry Costello, we believe that there are many teaching techniques that can break the cycle of learned helplessness and help our students become motivated and engaged readers. In this section of the chapter, we list some of the most powerful ways of doing so.

Ensuring Student Success

We have already noted that success is critical to student motivation: Ensuring student success is the number one thing you can do to get students motivated and keep them motivated. Here, we repeat that message to emphasize its importance. We also want to emphasize the importance of including a wide selection of materials in your students' reading diet in order to ensure their success during independent reading, in small group work, and when they're reading in content areas like science or social studies. Stocking every classroom library with materials—fiction and nonfiction—that span the reading levels of your students allows every student to select texts with which she can be successful. As students come to know the reading selections in the classroom and their own abilities and interests, they can begin to make appropriate selections. Being free to browse, to read a bit before deciding whether or not they will stick with a text, and to talk with others who have read that text helps students learn which books they can and want to read. This is also a perfect opportunity for students to share their evaluation of what they read with others, as described in In the Classroom 3.4.

ASSESSMENT

Assessing students' attitudes toward school and your classroom is an important step in building a positive classroom climate. One good way to do so is simply to talk to students from time to time about what they think of school and your classroom.

Promoting Academic Values and Goals

Ultimately, motivation and engagement are intrapersonal values, and it is the student herself who must become motivated and engaged—with school and schooling. The fact is that a good deal of schoolwork is just that—work—and we need to find ways to help students truly value that work. One approach to doing so is to reinforce students when they demonstrate that they are valuing and "doing" school—for example, complimenting a student who has been getting her homework in daily. Another is to provide students with role models who express a commitment to education. Teachers are certainly important role models. But in some ways, other students are even more important role models. One of the many reasons that it is important for lower-performing students to be grouped with higher-performing students is that the higher-performing students can serve as academic role models. Another approach is for teachers to directly talk to students about the importance of school and the benefits of doing well in school.

Still another approach to promoting academic values and goals is to offer students choices, something we discussed earlier in the chapter. In fact, a large body of research and practice indicate that "students are more likely to want to do schoolwork when they have some choice in the courses they take, in the material they study, and in the strategies they use to complete tasks" (National Research Council, 2004). Situations that do not provide choices can leave students with a sense of powerlessness, and a sense of powerlessness is more likely to lead to alienation than to engagement. Saying that students should have choices does not, however, mean that they should have no structure and no limits. Students value structure, but it needs to be structure that affords them some opportunities to make choices.

Our final suggestion for promoting academic values and goals is to make learning experiences enjoyable. As Nel Noddings eloquently argues in *Happiness and Education* (2003), happiness should be a major goal of education, but frequently is not. We have already said that a good deal of schoolwork is indeed work, and there is no getting around that. But nothing says that work cannot be made as enjoyable as possible. If, for example, students are learning how to make inferences, the texts teachers find that require inferences can be ones that students will enjoy reading. For example, "getting" jokes often requires inferences, and reading them is wonderful practice. Stories also often require inferences about, for example, a character's motivation for what she is doing. Speculating about why a compelling character is behaving in a particular way is much more interesting than filling out a worksheet designed to test students' ability to make inferences.

Perhaps students are working on their critical thinking skills, learning how to distinguish between fact and opinion or how to differentiate fact, theory, and belief. They can spend time doing uninteresting worksheets, or they can read expository texts about things they are interested in and then discuss those texts, perhaps distinguishing between facts and opinion. Excellent nonfiction that begs to be analyzed in this way includes *Clouds* by Marion Dane Bauer for primary-grade children, *The Secret of the Sphinx* by James Giblin for intermediate-grade students, and *Are We Alone? Scientists Search for Life in Space* by Gloria Skurzynski for middle-grade students.

Finally, we have one suggestion about a widely used practice that very frequently does not promote academic values and goals. That practice is putting too much emphasis on extrinsic rewards. If the primary reason a student reads is to get points, a free pizza, or some free time on Friday afternoon, then she is not likely to do much reading when points, pizza, and free time are not in the offing. We are not suggesting that you can't use some extrinsic rewards, but we are saying that you should use them in moderation. We say more about this later in the chapter.

Fostering Higher-Order Thinking and Deep Understanding

As you may have noticed, Chapter 11 has the same title as this section—Fostering Higher-Order Thinking and Deep Understanding. Our major purpose for devoting an entire chapter to these topics is that we believe they are absolutely crucial to success both in school and outside of school. Lower-order thinking and shallow understanding are not the cognitive tools students need to succeed, thrive, and contribute in the 21st century. Equally importantly—and very fortunately—emphasizing higher-order thinking and deep understanding in your classroom also motivates and engages students (Knapp & Associates, 1995; Taylor, Pearson, Peterson, & Rodriguez, 2003). Completing a worksheet that requires a young reader to answer a set of rote questions on the events in Jerry Spinelli's *Loser* simply is not as engaging as trying to figure what it is about Zinkhof that repeatedly gets him in unfortunate situations. Similarly, learning a little bit about a lot of topics is usually not as interesting as studying a few topics in depth. In fact, almost any topic becomes interesting once we begin to understand it deeply. Several years ago, adult author Mark Kurlansky wrote a book titled *Cod: A History of the Fish That Changed the World*. In researching that book, he became interested in salt (used, of course, in preserving cod) and wrote another book, this one titled *Salt: A World History*. One of us has read them both and found them fascinating. Even topics like cod and salt—as you learn more about them and discover the impact they had on civilization—become interesting. That does not mean we should ask elementary students to develop a deep understanding of cod or salt, but it does suggest that some pretty mundane topics can become interesting when we develop a thorough understanding of them.

Cooperative learning not only encourages reading achievement but also supports better interpersonal relationships among children.

Ensuring Active Participation, Using Cooperative Activities, and Including Variety

As we stressed in Chapters 1 and 2, students learn more when they are engaged in active learning rather than more passive activities. They are also going to be a lot more motivated when engaged in active learning. This is true for elementary students and for college students; if you are using this book as part of a college class, we hope you are engaged in active learning activities as part of that class. Such activities as constructing models, role playing, doing experiments, creating examples, and comparing and contrasting actively involve and interest students. Students in one study (Boaler, 2002), for example, noted that "you learn more by doing something on your own," "you feel more proud of the projects when you've done them yourself," and "because you had to work out for yourself what was going on, you had to use your own ideas."

Cooperative learning is one form of active learning that has become very widely used, and this is fortunate. Importantly, the advantages of cooperative learning have been found to occur in a variety of domains. Students in cooperative groups showed superior performance in academic achievement, displayed more self-esteem, accommodated better to mainstreamed students, showed more positive attitudes toward school, and generally displayed better overall psychological health. Students in cooperative groups displayed better interpersonal relationships; and these improved interpersonal relationships held regardless of differences in ability, sex, ethnicity, or social class (Johnson & Johnson, 1989). Moreover, cooperative learning has been shown to be successful in teaching students how to resolve conflicts (Johnson & Johnson, 2002). Finally, cooperative learning can create a classroom in which students share the responsibility for each other's learning rather than compete with each other—a very positive situation, particularly for students who often do not do well in school and may become alienated in classrooms where they are too often on their own and do not perform as well as their classmates (Cohen, 1994).

A number of authors (Aronson & Patnoe, 1997; Cohen, 1994; Johnson, Johnson, & Holubec, 1994; Slavin, 1987) have described approaches to cooperative learning, and using more than one approach can provide variety and accomplish somewhat different purposes. Moreover, as the title of this section suggests, variety itself tends to be motivating and engaging for students. No one likes to do the same thing in the same way all the time, and sometimes adding variety just to add variety makes good sense. For example, if you typically have independent reading on Fridays, sometimes it might be good to put it on another day for no reason other than varying the schedule. Of course, too much variation is not the goal.

Making Connections to Students' Cultures and Lives Outside of School

It is not at all surprising that students are more engaged and motivated to learn if they feel that what they are learning is related to their out-of-school lives. While not every topic in the curriculum is going to be connected to students' home lives and cultures, many of them certainly should be. One of the easiest ways to do this is to carefully select the reading material for your classroom so that it reflects the issues, concerns, and cultures of your students, as we discussed earlier in this chapter. At the same time, however, we must admit that assuring cultural matches is easier said than done.

Kristen, a teacher who works with Somali immigrants, discovered that there was very little literature available that accurately reflects the lives of her students, so she decided to ask students and their families to create books for their classroom library. She asked students to get family members to tell them stories—stories about life in Somalia, stories about their journey to America, stories about the things that happened to them when they arrived. She then asked students to tell and write stories about their own lives. And she gave her students cameras to take photographs of people and places in their home and neighborhood. Next, she typed up their texts, and the students arranged the photos or drew pictures to illustrate them. Then they put their books together, complete with title page, dedication page, and "publishing" information. The result was a number of books, bound at a local copy center, that had content culturally specific to Kristen's students. Kristen didn't stop there, of course; she found trade books and magazine articles that related to her students' lives in other ways, and she added these to her growing library.

Her students invested in the classroom library by writing some of the books and were motivated and eager to read their own books, those of their peers, and the trade books and magazine articles that Kristen gathered. Her effort to find selections that were culturally relevant to her students became a wonderful opportunity for writing and a strong motivator for reading for these students.

While a culturally diverse library is important no matter whom you teach, it's also important to think about the universals that engage all students. Reading fiction that explores topics such as family, friends, and issues of growing up (such as Lindsay Lee Johnson's middle-grade novel *Worlds Apart*), nonfiction about the wonders of the natural world (such as *Penguin Chick* by Betty Tatham), and inspirational biographies (such as *The Sky's the Limit: Discovery by Women and Girls* by Catherine Thimmesh), can draw your students into the world of reading and help them realize that reading, even the reading they do in school, often relates to their lives outside of school.

English Learners

Recognizing English-language learners' holidays and ways of celebrating them can be a significant boost to their motivation and feeling of belonging in your classroom.

Class projects can also help students connect home and school. Rather than researching and writing about a topic that has little connection to their community, students can choose to pursue a topic that has relevance to their lives. For example, a group of sixth-grade students in the Pacific Northwest spent a year doing research and writing about how pollution had destroyed the salmon stream that ran by their school. They read, discussed, and wrote while they also cleaned up the stream. The result was a cleaner stream, heightened community awareness of issues of pollution, and a book, *Come Back, Salmon!*, that chronicled their project. Eventually, the salmon even came back.

Your students all come from families and communities that have, as Moll (1992) describes it, "funds of knowledge." It's up to you to tap into that knowledge and bring it into your classroom. Connecting school and home is an important part of helping students value what they are learning in school.

Praising Students, Rewarding Them, and Helping Them Set Goals

Praise can be a very effective motivator, and it is certainly a widely used tool. Nevertheless, praise is not without its potential drawbacks. Most importantly, it must be honest, and students must perceive it as honest. According to Guthrie and Wigfield (2000), effective praise is given only in response to students' efforts and achievements, specifies just what students have accomplished to earn the praise, and helps students better appreciate their work. Guthrie and Wigfield also note that effective praise makes it clear to students that they should attribute their success to effort and fosters their understanding of the strategies that they used to accomplish the task for which they are being praised.

Rewards other than praise—points, stars, books, pizzas—can sometimes be effective in the short run. However, one of the most consistent and strongest cautions in the literature on motivation is that extrinsic rewards can undermine motivation in the long run (Guthrie & Wigfield, 2000; National Research Council, 2004; Stipek, 2002). When students become accustomed to getting extrinsic rewards for reading, they may begin reading solely or largely to get the extrinsic reward and actually discontinue reading when the extrinsic rewards are no longer available. Our goal should always be to demonstrate to students that reading is worthwhile for its own sake—for the learning, enjoyment, and satisfaction that it brings. Our greatest tools in accomplishing this goal are giving students good books and other materials to read and scaffolding their efforts so that they can successfully do the reading.

Goal setting is another important component of motivation. Students who set goals to learn certain content or processes—such as understanding a difficult concept or being able to self-check as they read—are more motivated to learn than students who do not. Teachers who help their students set appropriate learning goals are helping to foster students' long-term engagement and learning (Ames, 1992; Maehr & Midgley, 1996)

Factors That Undermine Motivation

In order to understand just what something is, it is often useful to understand what it is not. Although we certainly do not want to dwell on the negative, we do want to list some factors that undermine motivation. Pressley and his colleagues (Bogner, Raphael, & Pressley, 2002; Dolezal, Welsh, Pressley,

CW 3.3 links to Welcome Teachers, a site created by teachers in Contra Costa, California. This site includes tips on creative and appropriate rewards and other approaches to motivation.

ASSESSMENT

For students who read very little English, translating test directions into their native language is sometimes appropriate and can help them avoid a very frustrating and nonproductive experience. Of course, it is important to let others who make use of the test scores know you've done this so that the scores won't be misinterpreted.

Physical Environment

- Few examples of students' work and accomplishments are shown on the walls.
- The room is sparsely decorated, with few posters, pictures, or other elements to make it more attractive and inviting.

Psychological Environment

- The teacher does not have or communicate to students that she has high expectations for their learning.
- The atmosphere fostered by the teacher is not cooperative, and no sense of community and students helping and respecting each other is developed.
- The teacher communicates to students that getting the right answers and high grades are the most important part of school.
- The teacher gives students very little praise.

Classroom Instruction

- The teacher does not check for understanding before moving on.
- The teacher does not use opportunities to connect lessons to other concepts in the curriculum, to previous learning experiences, or to the world outside of school.
- The teacher does not give students time to process questions and think about answers before calling on them.
- The teacher is not fully prepared for the day's lessons.

Classroom Management

- The teacher does not check students' progress as they work and fails to notice students' confusion or off-task behavior.
- The teacher uses negative, punishing techniques to maintain order in the classroom.

FIGURE 3.5

Some Factors That Undermine Motivation

Source: Adapted from Pressley et al. (2003, pp. 45–48).

& Vincent, 2003; Pressley et al., 2003) have identified a number of these factors. A few of them are listed in Figure 3.5. Pressley et al. (2003) provide a much longer list. Most unfortunately, when Pressley and his colleagues (2003) observed primary-grade classrooms, they found many of these factors present.

Reflect *and* Apply

4. Explain two or three things you might do to help a shy second-grader who tends to lack confidence in her ability develop a more positive attitude toward herself as a learner.

5. Now explain two or three things you would not do so that you do not further undermine her attitude toward herself as a learner.

6. Suppose you want to convince your fourth-graders that although schoolwork can be challenging, it is worth doing well and doing their schoolwork well will give them a sense of accomplishment and pride. Jot down what you might say to them.

Nancy Masters, a Superstar at Motivating Students

Nancy Masters is a truly outstanding teacher who was observed by Pressley and his colleagues as part of their in-depth studies of motivation in primary-grade classes (Bogner et al., 2002; Pressley et al., 2003). Here is a description of her efforts taken from "Nancy Masters' Teaching" from © 1996 Michael Pressley (pp. 400–402) and reprinted with permission of The Guilford Press.

On a typical day, Nancy Masters used more than 40 different positive motivational mechanisms to inspire and engage her students. Her classroom was filled to overflowing with motivating activities and positive tone. Cooperation was emphasized consistently during both whole-group and small-group instruction. Thus, when students read books with partners, Ms. Masters reminded them that, "The point is, you're supposed to help your partner." She provided reassurance and interesting scaffolding when students took on challenging activities. Thus, before a test requiring application of phonics skills, Ms. Masters reminded her students of the phonics they had been learning and emphasized that they should apply what they knew about phonics on the upcoming test.

Ms. Masters emphasized depth in her teaching, covering mature and interesting ideas. For example, during Black History Month, students not only completed detailed group book reports about five prominent African Americans, she led a discussion about the Jim Crow laws, one in which the students participated enthusiastically, demonstrating they had learned a great deal about discrimination during the month. During this conversation, Ms. Masters talked about different ways that people can affect social change, covering civil disobedience, disobeying unjust laws, and working within the system to change such laws. She and the first-grade students discussed equality and inequality, with student comments reflecting their grasp of some very difficult concepts.

Nancy Masters' teaching connected across the curriculum and community, between school and home. During the first month of the school year, she took her class to visit the kindergarten room. In doing so, she began to become acquainted with her future students while forging connections across grade levels for the kindergarten and grade-1 students. Her students wrote in their journals about this visit. When they wrote stories a few weeks later, Ms. Masters held out as a carrot another visit to the kindergarten room. She told her grade-1 students, "Maybe we'll show the kindergarten [your stories]." Nancy also pointed out times when students' home experience connected with school. Thus, when a student read the word "little" very quickly, Ms. Masters commented, "Have you been working at home with your Mom? I'm so proud of you!" In doing so, she simultaneously emphasized the importance of effort and homework while connecting to the student's home life. Ms. Masters also hosted a career day during which parents talked about and demonstrated their professional skills. After the visits, the students wrote in journals and did an at-home art project about their favorite profession. This special home assignment complemented the regular homework, which consisted of reading 15 minutes a night, doing a short math worksheet, and practicing spelling words.

Nancy Masters gave many opportunistic mini-lessons. In-class assignments seemed appropriately challenging and engaging (i.e., students could not finish them quickly, and they seemed interested in them). Her emphasis on good literature, the writing process, and comprehension were apparent during every class visit. Also, the class constructed many products, which were tangible evidence of accomplishment, including big books that were displayed prominently in the classroom and discussed often. Ms. Masters promised the class that each one of them would be able to take home one class-constructed book at the end of the year. She made many across-curriculum connections for her students (e.g., having students use the internet and the library to find material about Black History Month, material then used in writing an essay).

Ms. Masters expressively communicated with students. As she read to students, she modeled her interest and enthusiasm and reflected her curiosity about what would happen next in a story, often creating a sense of suspense about the events in a reading. When the class received a new basal reader, she opened it and said, "A brand new book!! It's like a present. I know you want to open it and look inside. Go ahead and look inside. See anything interesting? Anything you've read?"

Ms. Masters provided clear learning objectives and goals. Thus, at the beginning of the school year, she had the students copy stories she had written on the board, explaining they were copying stories so that "You can see what good writing looks like." Similarly, when she taught strategies during writing workshop, Ms. Masters emphasized that use of the strategies would help students write as they needed to write by the end of grade 1.

Nancy Masters emphasized effort attributions. Thus, on the day report cards were distributed to students, she told the students twice that their most important grade was their grade for effort. She and her students often used the term "personal best" to describe how they were doing.

Nancy Masters monitored the students well. She often said, "When I come around, I want to hear you reading or helping your partner or discussing the story." During her walk-arounds, she provided help to students who were struggling.

Of course, Ms. Masters' efforts to motivate her students paid off. There was consistently high engagement in her class. The pace was always quick. The assignments were always interesting. She excited her students about their work. Her students were always engaged in productive work!

Grouping Students for Instruction

One of the most important decisions you make in your classroom, and one that will have a huge effect on motivation and engagement, is that of how to group students. Students can be grouped in a variety of ways for a variety of purposes, yet in all too many cases grouping has not been used effectively and has had a negative effect on many students, specifically those students placed in the low-ability groups. In this section, we discuss some of the reasons for grouping, some of the problems grouping has produced, various types of groups, and some guidelines for grouping.

Reading with a friend can double reading pleasure.

English Learners

English-language learners should generally be grouped with native English speakers. It usually works well to have one native English speaker assigned to work with each English-language learner and assist her in her group work.

A typical class of 25 to 30 students brings with it 25 to 30 different sets of interests, abilities, attention spans, personalities, and reading skills, and it is very difficult to attend to each of these when working with the class as a whole. When teaching the entire class as a single group, teachers tend to teach to an imaginary mean; that is, they gear their instruction to what they perceive to be the middle range of interest, attention span, personality, ability, and so on. Such instruction does not meet the needs of those who are not in this range. Furthermore, in large-group situations, it is tempting for the teacher to do most of the talking, asking only an occasional question and, even then, allowing only one or two students to respond. Thus, most students play a passive role.

Dividing students into smaller groups is often helpful for a number of reasons. First, keeping smaller groups of students on task is generally easier than keeping larger groups on task. Smaller groups tend to facilitate direct instructional engagement for more children and for a longer period of time. Second, smaller groups allow you to provide instruction designed to meet the needs of specific students, thus individualizing your reading program. Finally, smaller groups allow more students to be actively involved in instructional activities. In a group of five, for example, it is possible for each student to respond to a question before you either run out of time or test the patience of the other students.

Given these advantages, it is not surprising that students have often been grouped for reading instruction. However, grouping has typically been based exclusively on reading ability. During much of this century, American students have been grouped homogeneously for reading instruction, with the typical classroom having one high-, one middle-, and one low-ability group (Anderson, Hiebert, Scott, & Wilkinson, 1985). More recently, teachers and researchers have discovered that ability grouping results in a number of disadvantages, particularly for students in low-ability groups. As compared to students in other groups, students in low-ability groups are often given less time to read, spend more time on worksheets and less time being actively instructed, and are asked fewer higher-order questions. Additionally, lower-ability-group students often suffer affective consequences of grouping, including lowered self-esteem, lowered motivation to succeed, and negative attitudes toward reading (Allington, 1983, 1984). Finally, there is much concern about the permanence of group membership; students who are placed in a low-ability group in kindergarten and first grade are all too likely to stay in the low-ability group throughout the elementary school years (Juel, 1990).

These findings have led teachers to develop a variety of grouping options, many of which deliberately include heterogeneous groups of students. Having a variety of reading groups gives children opportunities to learn how to interact with and learn from others who are in some ways different from them. Using a variety of groups also allows you to create appropriate groups for the various goals you have for students. Some of the many useful types of groups include Proficiency Groups (short-term groups of students who share a common strength or a common instructional need), Deliberately Heterogeneous Groups (groups specifically set up to counteract the potentially negative effect of proficiency groups), Formal Cooperative Groups (heterogeneous groups of students specifically taught how to work together as a team), Interest Groups (short-term groups of students sharing a common interest), Literature Groups or Literature Circles (a particular sort of interest group in which students read the same selection and meet to discuss and respond to it), and Project Groups (groups designed to work together on a particular project, such as making a video or preparing a dramatic presentation).

In deciding how to group students, there are many factors to consider. Here are some of the most important ones:

- Your general instructional objectives
- Your specific objectives for individual children
- The material your students will be reading
- Your students' individual strengths
- Students' abilities to work with others in the group
- The number and types of groups you can successfully manage
- The absolute injunction that no student be repeatedly assigned to the low-ability group

Having presented a variety of options for grouping, we obviously believe that students will profit from participating in many types of groups. Still, becoming adept at grouping students is a challenge. We suggest that you meet that challenge by first becoming comfortable with two or three types of grouping and then gradually adding other grouping alternatives as your classroom management and grouping skills become stronger.

We do not mean to suggest that there is no place for whole-class instruction. Whole-class instruction does have a place. Whole-class instruction is useful when you wish to reach all students at once. Spending five or ten minutes with the entire class before students begin working individually or in small groups allows you to touch base with all students, answer their questions, and hear their concerns. However, because lengthy whole-class instruction seldom continues to command students' attention and often invites off-task behavior, whole-class instruction should generally be kept brief and focused. In the Classroom 3.5 is based on a small-group activity found in *Structuring Cooperative Learning: Lesson Plans for Teachers* (Johnson, Johnson, & Holubec, 1987).

Primary-Grade Cooperative Learning to Solve Story Problems

The purpose of this lesson is for students to work together to find the answers to a set of story problems that require mathematical reasoning and the use of addition and subtraction.

Procedure:

- Assign three students of varying abilities to work together as a group—perhaps one high-, one medium-, and one low-achieving math student.

- Tell students you will give each group a set of ten story problems. Their job is to read each story problem, write a math sentence telling what happened in the story, and then figure out the missing number. Next, show them how they are to read and write their answers.

  1. Put a problem on the chalkboard or an overhead projector, and read it aloud. For example: Erika checked out 5 library books. She finished reading 2 and returned these to the library. How many books does she have left?

  2. Model the mental processes you go through to arrive at the mathematical sentence: 5 – 2 =?

  3. Perform the operation: 5 – 2 = 3

- Explain to students that you want *one* set of answers from the whole group, one set that they all helped find and agree upon.

    I expect to see all of you helping and all of you sharing. If you don't understand or agree, ask the others in your group to explain that problem again. If you still think they are wrong, explain your answer to them and see if they agree with you. [Dramatizing, or role-playing, this situation can be helpful in getting students to understand and use this process.]

- Tell students that when they finish the ten story problems, each group member should sign his or her name to the group's paper.

    Signing your name shows me you each helped, shared, and understand. Your group should try to answer all the problems correctly. If your group gets nine or ten correct, that means you have done a super job!

- While students are working in their groups, try to interfere as little as possible. However, occasionally ask individuals to explain one of their group's answers.

- As a group finishes, quickly score the answers. Ask each member of the group if he or she participated and how he or she felt about the task. Praise groups that get nine or ten correct. Try to help groups who got a lower score discern what went wrong and what needs to be done to be more successful with similar tasks in the future.

- After the lesson has been completed, try to determine if students met the conditions you set out. Did all or most of the groups solve the story problems correctly? Do you need to teach more on story problems? Did students demonstrate understanding of the cooperative goal structure? What cooperative skills need to be taught in a future lesson?

instructional routines

in the *Classroom* **3.5**

Reflect *and* Apply

7. Reread the description of Nancy Masters's motivational activities in her first-grade class, and pick out five activities that would work just as well with fourth- or fifth-graders. Now look back at the description, and see if you can find any activities that would be inappropriate for fourth- or fifth-graders. How many did you find? What does this suggest about the extent to which motivational principles are applicable across grade levels?

8. Because grouping can have such a strong effect on students' learning, it is important that you fully understand its possible effects. Toward this end, get together with a small group of your classmates, generate a list of positive and negative effects of grouping, and brainstorm a list of ways in which you can maximize the positive effects of grouping and minimize the negative ones.

Strengths and Challenges of DIVERSITY

All students need and deserve our very best efforts in assisting them in becoming motivated and engaged readers. Here we deal with two topics that are extremely important for all students but absolutely vital for students who face more challenges than do many of their classmates.

SUCCESS

All children need success, but for those children whose preschool experiences have not helped them develop the proficiencies school requires or for those older children who have not met with much success in their first few years of school, fostering success will be both more crucial and more difficult. For these students, success may require a great deal of scaffolding on your part. Perhaps you will read a story to the child several times before she attempts to read along with you, and then you and the child will read the story together several times before she has developed the proficiency and confidence to try reading it by herself. This is particularly true for those students who have repeatedly failed in school, have come to attribute their failure to factors outside of their control, and have fallen into a syndrome of learned helplessness. Not only must these children be led to success; they must also be brought to realize that success is under their control—something they can do something about.

Other students, those whose preschool experiences have served to prepare them for school and who handle routine school tasks competently, will often be able to succeed at typical literacy tasks without a great deal of scaffolding from you and will need sturdy scaffolding only with more challenging tasks. Still other students will succeed independently most of the time and will need significant scaffolding with only the most difficult tasks. Providing appropriate challenges will be your main concern with these students. The youngster who comes to school already reading should not be

ASSESSMENT

Earlier in the chapter, we suggested that talking to students is a good way to assess their motivation. Observing students, "Kid Watching" to use the term that Yetta Goodman (1978) coined, is another excellent way of gleaning information about students' attitudes toward themselves and school.

required to wade thorough a word-study curriculum that she has already mastered or be limited to only very brief and very easy reading materials.

GROUPING

Similar considerations for accommodating diversity exist with grouping. One key, as we have already noted, is flexibility: using several different sorts of grouping. Thus, if you want to group students who are having particular difficulty understanding the concept of plot so that you can review the concept, it is important to also include each of these students in heterogeneous groups or interest groups to avoid the students' stigmatizing themselves or being stigmatized by others. Similarly, it's important to see that both low- and high-performing students are sometimes grouped for instruction and that grouping is often based on a criterion other than reading proficiency. Thus, in addition to pulling aside a group that is having problems with plot, it may be useful to pull aside a group of your most proficient writers and give special attention to a concept such as audience. Or, to take an example of grouping on a different criterion, you might assemble a group of students with particular skills in painting to work on scenery for a class skit.

Finally, when students are grouped heterogeneously, it is important that all believe they are spending their time usefully. In a heterogeneous group of writers, for example, it is important that the less-proficient writers learn something and get opportunities to contribute, but it is equally important that the more-proficient writers learn something and not feel that they have been relegated to helping the less-competent writers and are learning nothing new themselves.

In summary, we readily admit that making adjustments for differences among students is challenging. There are no perfect answers or solutions; many of the choices you make will be compromises, choices that have both advantages and disadvantages. Still, there are some general rules beyond the specific suggestions we have just made here. Remember that each student is an individual with both emotional strengths and weaknesses and cognitive strengths and weaknesses. Over time, all students need and deserve an abundance of success, appropriate challenges, the opportunity to work with others with similar strengths and weaknesses, and the opportunity to work with others with quite different strengths, weaknesses, interests, and concerns.

Concluding Remarks

Creating motivating and engaging classrooms is absolutely essential. Creating motivating and engaging classrooms means creating a literate environment—a place, a space, and an atmosphere—where reading and learning thrive. In motivating and engaging classrooms, students learn to attribute their successes and failures to factors under their control and to avoid learned helplessness. And in motivating and engaging classrooms, teachers employ myriad approaches to motivating students—including but not limited to ensuring student success, fostering higher-order thinking, and making connections to students' cultures and lives outside of school.

We close the chapter with two sets of recommendations, found in Figure 3.6, for motivating students. The first is a set that Pressley and his colleagues (2003) gleaned from the work of Brophy (1986, 1987), recommendations made nearly 20 years ago. The second is a set that one of us (Graves, 2004a) gleaned from the work of Pressley and his colleagues (Bogner et al., 2002; Dolezal et al., 2003; Pressley, in press; Pressley et al., 2003). As you read them, we hope that you will notice two

MOTIVATIONAL STRATEGIES GLEANED FROM BROPHY

- Model interest in learning. . . . Communicate to students that there is good reason to be enthusiastic about what goes on in school. The message should be that what is presented in school deserves intense attention, with the teacher doing all that is possible to focus students' attention on important academic matters.

- What is being taught, in fact, should be worth learning!

- Keep anxiety down in the classroom. Learning should be emphasized rather than testing.

- Induce curiosity and suspense, for example, by having students make predictions about what they are about to learn.

- Make abstract material more concrete and understandable.

- Let students know the learning objectives so that it is very clear what is to be learned.

- Provide informative feedback, especially praise when students deserve it.

- Give assignments that provide feedback (to your students and to yourself).

- Adapt academic tasks to students' interests and provide novel content as much as possible. [Do not cover material students already know just because it is the mandated curriculum.]

- Give students choices between alternative tasks [for example, selecting one of several books to read].

- Allow students as much autonomy as is possible in doing tasks. Thus, to the extent students can do it on their own, let them do it.

- Design tasks to contain an engaging activity [for example, role playing], product [for example, a class-composed book], or game [for example, riddles].

MOTIVATIONAL STRATEGIES GLEANED FROM PRESSLEY AND HIS COLLEAGUES

- Demonstrate your deep concern for students.

- Do everything possible to ensure students' success.

- Scaffold students' learning.

- Present appropriate challenges.

- Support risk taking and help students realize that failures will sometimes occur.

- Encourage students to attribute their successes to their efforts and realize that additional effort can help avoid failures.

- Encourage cooperative learning and discourage competition.

- Favor depth of coverage over breadth of coverage.

- Communicate to students that many academic tasks require and deserve intense attention and effort.

- Make tasks moderately challenging.

FIGURE 3.6

Research-Based Motivational Strategies

Source: Top section from Pressley et al. (2003, pp. 27–28); bottom section from Graves (2004a, p. 448).

points. First, the two sets of recommendations overlap a good deal with each other. Second, both sets overlap a good deal with the recommendations we make in this chapter. Our point is this: We know how to motivate and engage students; our task is to put this knowledge into action.

In the remainder of this book and in our day-to-day teaching in our own classrooms, we keep these recommendations at the center of our thinking. We encourage you to do the same. With motivation and engagement, great things are possible: Students can learn deeply, they can remember important information, and they can use what they learn in school in their lives beyond the classroom. They can do all of this while enjoying the activities in your classroom, enjoying school, and becoming committed lifelong readers.

Extending Learning

1. Spend some time observing a classroom at a grade level you find particularly interesting. Take notes on what you see. What opportunities for engaging in literacy activities are present? How welcoming is the physical setting? What materials are available? Then watch how the teacher and students interact in the classroom. Is the atmosphere safe and supportive? Are students enthusiastic and engaged? Finally, create a list of things to do and a list of things to avoid doing in order to best motivate students.

2. The lists that you created in the above activity represent your judgment based on your observation. There are other sources of information that deserve to be considered. One is the teacher you observed. Talk to the teacher and get his or her perceptions on what motivates students and which specific things he or she does to motivate them. The other source is, of course, students. Talk to a half dozen or so students and get their perceptions of what is and is not motivating in their classrooms. Once you have the teacher's and some students' perspectives, compare them to your lists and revise or fine-tune your lists as seems appropriate.

(mylabschool™
Where the classroom comes to life!

For a look at literacy instruction in a contemporary classroom, go to Allyn & Bacon's MyLabSchool.com. In MLS Courses, click on Reading Methods. There you will find a wealth of resources, including video clips and case studies about a range of literacy topics.

Children's Literature

Bauer, M. D. (2004). *Clouds*. New York: Aladdin. 32 pages.

Giblin, J. C. (2004) *Secrets of the Sphinx*. New York: Scholastic. 48 pages.

Johnson, L. L. (2005). *Worlds Apart*. Ashville, NC: Front Street. 126 pages.

Park, B. (2004). *Junie B., First Grader: Shipwrecked*. New York: Random House. 96 pages.

Parker, S. (2005). *Pond & River* (DK Eyewitness Books). London: Doring Kindersley. 72 pages.

Skurzynski, G. (2004). *Are We Alone? Scientists Search for Life in Space*. Hanover, PA: National Geographic. 92 pages.

Spinelli, J. (2002). *Loser*. New York: Joanna Colter Books. 218 pages.

Tatham, B. (2002). *Penguin Chick*. New York: Harper-Collins. 40 pages.

Thimmesh, C. (2002). *The Sky's the Limit: Discovery by Women and Girls*. Boston: Houghton Mifflin. 73 pages.

CHAPTER 4

Cookie knocked a p-- off the windowsill

Emergent Literacy

CLASSROOM VIGNETTE

*L*ee awakened to find her favorite stuffed animal lying next to her—a teddy bear named Pooh after the character in *Winnie the Pooh*. At breakfast, Lee's mother asked her if she could read the letters on her cereal box to Pooh. After breakfast, Lee scurried off to watch Sesame Street, naming the letters she saw on the screen to Pooh.

Later that morning, Lee went to the grocery store with her mom, showing off her letter knowledge by naming print as they wheeled around the store and by helping her mom check off items on her shopping list.

On the way home, Lee was dropped off at an afternoon kindergarten. She put her gear in a cubby with her name above it. She noticed her name, too, on the list of helpers for the day. After settling in, the children gathered around their teacher to hear her read a folk tale. When Lee's teacher finished, she asked the children to recall all the characters they could. As they named them, she put a picture of each character on a feltboard. Then she had the children help her retell the story, putting up the characters as they appeared in the story. When necessary, she prompted the children with questions such as "Then who came along?" If they weren't sure, she opened up the book and asked them to check.

At home again, Lee was eager to retell the folk tale. She told it first to her older sister and then to her mom and dad. As she snuggled into bed with Pooh, her dad began reading from James Marshall's retelling of *The Three Little Pigs.* "Once upon a time an old sow sent her three little pigs . . . ."

From the time she awoke until the time she was tucked into bed at night, Lee's day was filled with literacy experiences and opportunities to learn about language.

Emergent literacy refers to "the reading and writing behaviors that precede and develop into conventional literacy," and when we talk about emergent literacy, we are ascribing legitimacy to "the earliest literacy concepts and behaviors of children and to the varieties of social context in which children become literate" (Sulzby & Teale, 1996). In other words, emergent readers are children who are in the process of learning what reading and writing are for and how to read and write.

Children enter school with wide differences both in their exposure to text and in what they know about text. Some kindergartners know the alphabet; some know the sounds the letters make and can reproduce letters or even write a few words. Some have been read to extensively, as Lee has, and understand the basic structure of stories, but many have not. Some children enter first grade as readers, but most do not. Most children in preschool, kindergarten, and first-grade classrooms will need considerable help from you to become competent and independent readers.

Emerging Knowledge About Text Structures

The more prior knowledge you have about a topic, the easier it is to comprehend a text about it. This is equally true of text structures. When you read a recipe, for example, you anticipate that it will begin with a list of ingredients and that directions will follow in a step-by-step format. You also know that you should probably read the whole recipe before you begin, so that you can estimate the time it will take and be familiar with the ingredients you will need. You have a *schema* for recipes that allows you not only to comprehend what you are reading but also to write a recipe that others could follow.

Children who have been read to extensively, like Lee, have probably developed a similar schema for how stories like the ones they will encounter in school are put together. They can demonstrate this knowledge if asked. The stories they tell will imitate the stories they heard; they will generally have a central character who must overcome an obstacle of some sort, and the resolution of that problem will generally develop through a chronological sequence of events. They know, for example, that the wolf is hungry and will blow down the houses of the three little pigs to get food—or, if they have been read a different version, that the pigs will succeed in protecting one or more of their houses from the wolf.

But whether or not children have been read to before they arrive at school, you can provide experiences to help them understand the structure of texts and greatly increase their chances of becoming proficient readers. You can read to them in the classroom, and you can provide opportunities, as Mrs. Willey does in In the Classroom 4.1, for them to understand story structure at the same time that they grow in vocabulary, ideas, imagination, and love of language and stories.

Using Wordless Picture Books in a Kindergarten Classroom

in the Classroom 4.1

Seated in a chair, with her kindergartners gathered comfortably around her on the carpeted floor, Mrs. Willey displays a copy of the mostly wordless picture book *Have You Seen My Duckling?* by Nancy Tafuri. Mrs. Willey tells the children that they are going to help make up a story about a mother duck who has lost her ducklings.

Mrs. Willey asks the children to close their eyes. "Think about the baby duck, a duckling we call it, that you just saw. Try to imagine what it feels like to be a duckling, to be so new, so small. What do you see? Now, open your eyes. Tell me, what did you see?"

"Grass!"

"Bugs!"

The children take turns suggesting what the world might look like from the perspective of a baby duck.

Next, Mrs. Willey has the children point to the mother duck on the cover illustration and count her ducklings. She opens the book and has them notice what happens on the opening page.

"There are eight ducklings in a nest. But one of them is climbing out!" Tamara volunteers.

Mrs. Willey smiles and turns the page. "Early one morning . . .," she begins, and then she stops and asks, "What happens?"

Jason replies, "Early one morning, eight baby ducks got up."

"Ducklings!" Tamara corrects him.

"Well, okay, ducklings," Jason says. "They saw a butterfly, and one duckling got into the water and tried to swim after it."

"Then what happens?" asks Mrs. Willey, as she flips the page to uncover new illustrations.

Mrs. Willey continues to call on different children, who add to the story by considering the upcoming illustrations, their own imaginations, and their knowledge of stories, mothers, children, and ducks.

After Mrs. Willey and her kindergartners complete making up a story for *Have You Seen My Duckling?*, the children divide into groups, and each group goes to one of three classroom centers.

In one center, the children have a few additional copies of the book. Here they each get a chance to retell the story to a buddy.

In the art center, there are some black-and-white drawings of a duck and eight ducklings. The children cut out the drawings, color them in, and paste each one on a tongue depressor to serve as a puppet. Then they retell the story to each other, using their puppets to act it out.

In the library center are several wordless picture books, including *Do Not Disturb* and *Early Morning in the Barn*, two other books by Nancy Tafuri. The children take turns making up stories and telling them to each other as they turn the pages.

Making up stories for wordless picture books helps young children understand the structure of text.

Emerging Knowledge About Word Structures

A typical class of entering first-graders, asked what they expect to learn in school that year, will almost always respond that they will learn to read. Despite high motivation and expectations, however, some children will experience considerable difficulty, frustration, and an early loss of self-esteem in the process of learning to read. Why does this happen?

Take a look at the following list of factors that predict children's success as readers (Share, Jorm, Maclean, & Matthews, 1984). Which ones do you think are the most important predictors?

- Phoneme segmentation ability (the ability to tell you the first sound of a spoken word, for example)
- Knowledge of letter names
- Kindergarten teacher's predictions of reading success in first grade
- Performance on the Peabody Picture Vocabulary Test (a measure of oral English vocabulary)
- Parents' occupational status
- Library membership
- Number of books the child owns
- Amount that parents read to the child
- Gender
- Amount that parents read themselves in their spare time
- Whether or not the child attended preschool

You may be surprised to learn that these factors are listed in the exact order in which they predicted the end-of-year reading ability of more than 500

Australian first-graders. The top two predictors (phonemic segmentation ability and knowledge of letter names) were significantly stronger than the others. No matter how much a child has been read to, then, that child must be able to *independently* identify many printed words in order to read on his own.

First-grade teacher Glenna Schwarze knows that reading independence means making sure her students get instruction in decoding skills:

> I am sure any first-grade teacher will tell you the same thing: At the heart of first-grade reading instruction is ensuring that children learn to decode words. Of course, we want children to be able to instantly recognize as many words as possible, but we also need to be sure they are equipped with strategies and skills to use when they don't instantly know a word. The beginning reader, of course, cannot instantly recognize many words. As teachers, however, we can help children identify words they don't know by helping them recognize the letters in the words and how to translate those letters into the sounds they represent.
>
> —Glenna Schwarze, First-Grade Teacher

Children need to acquire two insights about language in order to become successful readers: the alphabetic principle and phonemic awareness (Snow, Burns, & Griffin, 1998). The *alphabetic principle* is the insight that spoken sounds can be represented by written letters. *Phonemic awareness* is the insight that spoken words are made up of a sequence of somewhat separable sounds, called *phonemes*. Children who have been read to have frequently heard the sounds in spoken words linked to printed words and letters, and this has helped them understand the alphabetic principle and phonemic awareness. They may, for example, have attended to the sounds in the rhymes of Dr. Seuss's *There's a Wocket in My Pocket* and laughed at the silly sounds made by a change in the initial phoneme. Children who can take the next step and make this change themselves—transforming *basket* into *wasket*, for example—provide further evidence of phonemic awareness. Alliteration—the repetition of initial consonant sounds used in many nursery rhymes—also focuses attention on phonemes. In In the Classroom 4.2, Mr. Felton helps his kindergartners make phonemic connections.

Kindergartners and the *P* Words

Mr. Felton's kindergartners, sitting in a semicircle on the floor, look quizzically at a large chart he has put on a stand. It is a poem that he has printed in large letters with a black felt pen.

"This is a poem, boys and girls," he tells them. "It's from a favorite book of mine called *Whiskers and Rhymes* by Arnold Lobel." He holds up his copy of the book.

"The poem is about a cat named George, who brushes his teeth!"

The children giggle.

"But guess what George uses for toothpaste? Pickle paste!"

The children roar with laughter as they consider toothpaste made from pickles.

Mr. Felton invites the children to come up and take a look at the book and the three pictures that accompany this poem. First, George squeezes a toothpaste tube labeled "Pickle Paste" onto his toothbrush. Second, he brushes his teeth, and green foam emerges from his mouth. Third, George smiles a big green-teeth smile. When the children sit back down, Mr. Felton reads the poem from the chart, pointing to each word as he reads.

Then Mr. Felton asks the children to find the letter *p* in the words. A child comes up and points to the *p* in *pickle,* and another child points to the *p* in *paste.*

in the **Classroom 4.2**

Mr. Felton asks, "Which letter in *pickle* makes it say /p/?"

The children respond, "*P*."

He asks, "Which letter in *paste* makes it say /p/?"

The children respond, "*P*."

Mr. Felton says, "The letter *p* says /p/," emphasizing the /p/ as he says "pickle paste."

The children can't help giggling as they say "pickle paste" over and over.

Next, Mr. Felton shows the children a large tube of toothpaste cut out of construction paper—just like the one George had. It has "Pickle Paste" printed on the tube.

Mr. Felton asks the children if they can spot some other *p* words in the room to write on the tube. The children glance around at the books on the chalkboard ledge, most of which Mr. Felton has read to them. They find the *p*s in the title of Dr. Seuss's *Hop on Pop*, James Marshall's *The Three Little Pigs*, and Eve Rice's *Peter's Pockets*.

Mr. Felton carefully prints the following words on the tube as he emphasizes and underlines the letter *p*: *pig, Peter, pocket, hop, pop.* He then tells the children he is going to name some colors, and they should say "pickle" if they hear a /p/. He emphasizes putting his lips together as he pronounces the /p/ in this list of words: pink, red, green, purple. Following some discussion, Mr. Felton adds *pink* and *purple* to the tube. He tacks the tube to the wall for future reference and the addition of new words.

Mr. Felton emphasizes phonemic segmentation and alphabetic awareness in this lesson by reading aloud to his class. Mr. Felton realizes, as research suggests, that the potential for predicting success in reading based on a child's ability in phonemic segmentation and alphabetic awareness is not so simple; in fact, these two skills most likely have their origins in having been read to as a young child. So the importance of parents' reading to children, which appears fairly far down the list of predictors, is actually significantly higher than it might seem. In a British study that followed a group of children from ages three to five, researchers found that children's knowledge of nursery rhymes at age three was closely related to their ability to perceive and produce rhyme and alliteration, as well as to recognize letters and some simple words (Maclean, Bryant, & Bradley, 1988). In other words, children who had experienced a lot of nursery rhymes at an early age were better equipped with exactly the knowledge and understanding that enhance learning to read in school.

Phonemic Awareness and Alphabet Recognition

Of the two competencies we discuss here, alphabet recognition is the more straightforward: Students need to recognize letters and their distinguishing features in order to work effectively with print. Learning the names of letters is very useful. We discuss alphabet recognition more thoroughly in Chapter 5.

Phonemic awareness is a more complex matter. Although it is a competency that you mastered long ago, you are probably not familiar with the concept. Yet it is astonishingly important to the process of successfully learning to read. In a longitudinal study of learning to read and write in an elementary school in Austin, Texas, one of us found that development of

ASSESSMENT

Marie Clay developed an assessment called the Concepts of Print Test to determine what young children know about words and books. You can find it in M. Clay (1993), *An Observation Study of Early Literacy Achievement.* (Portsmouth, NH: Heinemann).

phonemic awareness early in first grade was critical to children's successfully learning to read and write in first grade (Juel, 1988, 1994; Juel, Griffith, & Gough, 1986). As children learn to read, they also grow in phonemic awareness, but they have an easier time of learning to read if they rapidly develop this proficiency (Bruck & Treiman, 1992; Ehri & Robbins, 1992; Vandervelden & Siegel, 1995). That is, children need to perceive words as sequences of phonemes and link those phonemes to letters to begin reading words more efficiently. As Snow and colleagues (1998) note, "The theoretical and practical importance of phonemic awareness for the beginning reader relies not only on logic but also on the results of several decades of empirical research."

What Is Phonemic Awareness?

Phonemic awareness is the insight that spoken words are composed of somewhat separable sounds—sounds that can be played with (*dilly dilly silly Willy*), rearranged (*Connie Juel* becomes *Johnny Cool*), alliterated (*teeny tiny Tina*), and even used to create alternative languages (like pig Latin). Phonemic awareness is not synonymous with phonics; it is *not* knowledge about which letters represent particular sounds. Rather, it is an insight about speech—an attention to the sounds (phonemes) that reside within words. These sounds often correspond roughly to letters, but only roughly. For example, there are three phonemes in *cap,* but there are also three phonemes in *cape* and in *shake.* Perceiving words as sequences of phonemes is important in learning to read and write because the link between phonemes and letters is the basis for alphabetic writing systems such as English and Spanish. Keep in mind that a child can be aware of phonemes yet still not recognize a single letter of the alphabet. Phonemic awareness is an awareness of the *sounds of* language; it is not a part of learning to understand or speak oral language.

Phonemic awareness does not come naturally. Achieving it demands that a child attend to the form, rather than the meaning, of speech. This is difficult because our natural inclination is to attend to meaning. Thus, even those children who arrive at school with well-developed oral language may not have developed phonemic awareness. Phonemic awareness is not necessary for speaking or for listening, but it is vital to reading.

Understanding phonemes is complicated by the fact that we rarely say them separately; instead, they run together. In speech, we actually begin forming our mouths to pronounce the upcoming phoneme as we are still saying the previous one. For example, in saying *cat,* we begin saying the /ă/ before we finish the /k/. It is almost impossible to say some phonemes in isolation. That is, it is almost impossible to say either the /k/ or /t/ in *cat* without adding a vowel sound, such as /ə/. It is this overlapping, called *coarticulation,* of phonemes that allows our rapid speech. But it is exactly this coarticulation that makes learning to read words so hard. A letter in a printed word does not map onto one clear, distinct sound.

Teaching phonemic awareness is thus sometimes quite difficult. Some children will need a good deal of assistance in gaining this abstract understanding. Fortunately, however, research very strongly indicates that phonemic awareness can be taught (National Reading Panel, 2000). In the Classroom 4.3 lists standards for phonemic awareness for kindergarten children.

English Learners

Reading poems, stories, and song lyrics aloud as students follow along in a text will promote phonemic awareness in your English-language learners as well as in your other students.

Phonemic Awareness (Segmenting and Blending Sounds)

In kindergarten, teachers should evaluate whether children are developing phonemic awareness. By the end of kindergarten, children should be able to

- produce rhyming words and recognize pairs of rhyming words.
- isolate initial consonants in single-syllable words (for example, /t/ is the first sound in *top*).
- identify the onset (/c/) and rime (*-at*) and begin to fully separate the sounds (/c/-/a/-/t/) by saying each sound aloud when a single-syllable word is pronounced (for example, *cat*).
- blend onsets (/c/) and rimes (*-at*) to form words (*cat*) and slowly blend phonemes to make a word (for example, when the teacher says a word slowly, stretching it out as "mmm—ahhh—mmm," children can recognize that the word being stretched out is *mom*).

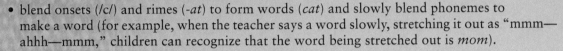

Why Do Phonemic Awareness and Alphabet Recognition So Strongly Predict Success in Reading?

Phonemic awareness and alphabet recognition are highly predictive of success in beginning reading because learning to pronounce words is a primary task for the beginning reader. Children must unlock the relationships between the sounds they use to say words and the letters they use in reading and writing words. In English, consonants are the easiest phonemes to perceive in spoken words. Children often represent consonants before representing vowels when they begin writing English. A child trying to spell *dog*, for example, tries to connect the phonemes he perceives to the actual letters. Initially, *dog* may be represented by just *D*, since the initial consonant is often the easiest for a child to attend to and attach to a letter. Later, this child may spell it *DG* because he feels these two consonants in his mouth as he says the word. Still later, he may spell it *DAG*. These early spellings are called invented or temporary spelling and are perfectly natural for young children. This type of writing goes hand and hand with development of phonemic awareness (Juel, 2006). In stretching out *dog* (for example, *ddawg, dawguh, dawg*), a child notes changes in how much the mouth opens, tongue position, and lip movements as sounds are uttered. This feeling sounds in the mouth is apparent to anyone watching young children as they write unknown words. Children literally move their mouths and exaggerate the sounds as they try to link them to letters. In that parsing of sounds in the mouth, phonemes become more real because they are felt: The tongue pressed on the ridge in the mouth behind the front teeth and the brief holding of air on making the /d/ help children notice the sound of the letter *d*.

At the beginning of first grade, invented spelling plays an important role in Kay Hollenbeck's first-grade classroom, as she explains here:

> Having the freedom to use invented spelling is essential for my first-graders. It allows them to be writers from day one. We call it "sound spelling" because they write words the way they think they sound, using the letters they know. This is a big accomplishment for them, and they are proud that they can "write" any word they can say.
>
> For example, yesterday Mara wrote *Tuda iz mi brda i m 6*. When I read the words back to her—"Today is my birthday; I am six"—her face beamed; she was delighted that I could actually read what she had intended to say. I knew what she had written,

both because she had chosen letters that approximated the sounds in the words she intended and also because I was able to use context clues. I knew it was her birthday, and the picture she had drawn was a give-away, too—a girl and a birthday cake with six candles! Although Mara was thrilled that I knew her exact words, she also was concerned that she hadn't "spelled the words right." So she asked me to "write them the *right* way." Which I did, of course, in her "word book"—a little booklet of pages stapled together that students keep on hand for me to write words they request. There is one page for each letter of the alphabet.

—Kay Hollenbeck, First-Grade Teacher

Of course, children like Mara will need to understand the connections between the approximately 44 phonemes of spoken English and the 26 letters that we use to represent them. This is one of the key tasks of learning to read, and it is not easy. As we all know, the English writing system does not reflect a consistent one-to-one relationship between letters and sounds; this is particularly true with vowel sounds. Letter-sound correspondences in English have their quirks. However—and this is a key point—words contain enough predictable correspondences to at least aid in identification or spelling. In identifying the "irregular" word *come*, for example, the letters *c, m,* and the silent *e* reliably represent certain sounds. A child who can figure out which sounds these letters are likely to represent has a powerful tool for recognizing words, while the child who cannot figure out letter-sound correspondences will often be stumped when he comes to a word he has not previously learned to read.

Reflect *and* Apply

1. Early in the chapter, we noted that having a schema for the structure of narrative texts is very important to children's success in reading. It is also important that *you* understand it. Take a few minutes to jot down that structure in your own words.
2. In her comment about empowering students to become independent readers, first-grade teacher Glenna Schwarze emphasizes that students need both decoding skills and the ability to instantly recognize many words. In your own words, explain why both of these skills are necessary.
3. Suppose you were reading a simple storybook to a kindergarten student and wanted to help him develop phonemic awareness. Describe three things you could do. (You can learn more from this activity if you focus on a particular storybook and give specific examples of things you might point out and questions you might ask.)

Learning to Identify Words

Children learn to identify words both through their own attempts to map sounds coming out of their mouth to letters in printed words and by receiving assistance and instruction from teachers and other knowledgeable adults. Here, we first describe some of children's earlier understandings and then consider how they learn to connect letters and phonemes.

Some Early Understandings About Print

Children begin to read and write before they can identify or write all the letters of the alphabet and before they have developed phonemic awareness. Often, the first word children learn is their own name. Diane, for example, was four years old when her mother, a student in one of our university classes, came in during office hours. To keep Diane busy while she talked, her mom handed her daughter her notebook. Diane slowly and laboriously wrote her name and then wrote the message shown in Figure 4.1.

When Diane was finished, her mother asked her to tell what the message said and to also say the letters in her name. She easily told the message. It was about what she and her mom were going to do after they left the office—though she did not look at her paper as she "read" the message. However, Diane was unable to name any but the first letter, the *D,* in her name.

Diane treated her name as a visual unit, without distinguishing and naming individual letters as components. Quite frequently, the first letters children learn are those in their own names. Certainly, writing your name is an important step in declaring your identity (Bloodgood, 1999). Diane does know a lot about print: She knows that it moves left to right across the page, and there were clearly letterlike forms in her writing. Still, it was real work for her to write her name because she had to remember its visual form without fully understanding that it is composed of individual letters with particular shapes and names. At this point, the letter *d* is not linked to the sound /d/, the letter *i* is not connected to a long *i* sound, and so on.

Fairly frequently, children begin reading by writing. People are natural message-makers. Diane's message is called *invented writing.* Invented writing represents an important level of understanding for a child who is learning to read—that lifeless-looking squiggles can convey real messages.

As children learn letterlike forms, these forms frequently start to creep onto the pages of their drawings. In Figure 4.2 another emergent reader, five-year-old Jake, has drawn himself doing karate. Even an initial inspection of Jake's drawing makes it evident that he has reached a profound milestone in learning. He understands that the sounds that come out of his mouth as he speaks can be linked to letters; he has made an important discovery about the alphabetic principle.

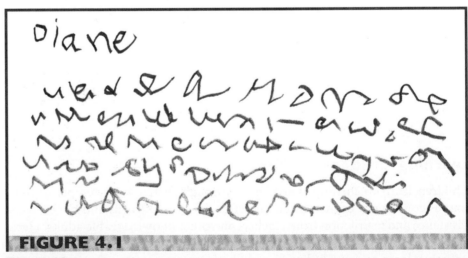

FIGURE 4.1

Diane's Note

Note that Jake's reversal of letters in his name does not indicate a problem; it simply illustrates that Jake perceives his name as a single visual unit. At this stage of development, Jake does not experience directionality as a relevant characteristic of his world. Until children begin working with print, virtually each thing they experience and learn to name retains the same name, regardless of the way it might be facing. Jake is still Jake whether he stands on his head or his feet. His dog is a dog whether he is coming or going. A table may look funny turned upside down, but it is still named a table.

Only in writing is this principle violated. Jake will catch on to the importance of directionality in writing as he writes and reads more. Also, once Jake learns the names of the letters, his task will become easier. When he knows that his name is made of the letter sequence *J, a, k, e,* he will find the spelling of his name easier to recall and to write.

As we mentioned, an extremely important feature of Jake's writing is that it shows an initial understanding that letters can represent sounds. The speech bubble coming out of Jake's mouth contains the letters *a* and *e,* which he says make the sounds he makes as he does a karate chop. Here, he shows some fairly advanced understanding of letters and sounds.

In the Classroom 4.4 describes an activity that will help children like Jake further their understanding of letters and sounds.

FIGURE 4.2

Jake's Drawing

Using Letter Puppets to Help Children Understand the Connection Between Phonemes and Letters

Purpose: To give students practice and feedback in recognizing the initial sound in a word and the letter that represents that sound.

Procedure: Purchase or make a set of puppets with alliterative names such as Pink Pig, Red Rooster, Jumping Jerod, Nice Nora, Mad Mike, and so on.

- Put on one of the hand puppets, such as Pink Pig, which has a big letter *P* on it. Introduce the children to it, saying "Pink Pig only likes things that start with a /p/, like her name, Pink Pig." Emphasize the /p/ as you talk, and point out the letter *P.*

- Walk around the room and ask the children what Pink Pig likes as the puppet touches the object. For example, "Does Pink Pig like pencils? Does Pink Pig like Peter? Does Pink Pig like Pasha? Does Pink Pig like red?" and so on.

- After you have touched several objects and the children have responded, ask, "What do you think is Pink Pig's favorite letter of the alphabet?"

- Students can take turns wearing the puppet and asking the same questions, and other puppets can be used to give practice with additional letters.

instructional routines

in the Classroom 4.4

Connecting Letters and Phonemes

The New Standards Primary Literacy Committee (1999) and most state standards today recommend that children know the letters of the alphabet and the corresponding sounds by the time they leave kindergarten. What is important is not so much how many letters and sounds the child knows, but rather the *idea* of how letters represent sounds.

Once children learn letter names and possess some degree of phonemic awareness, they frequently use the names of letters to help them recall and spell words. They may be particularly dependent on the names of initial consonants for word recall. The name of the letter *b* is the sound of the word *bee,* and the name of the letter *j* is part of the sound of the word *Jake,* for example, and this overlap may help children identify these words when they see them in a text (Ehri & Robbins, 1992).

In writing words, children often use letters whose names represent the sounds that they perceive in the words. At first, they may represent only the initial consonant or the most distinctive sound (for example, *b* written for *bee* or *l* for *elephant*). Even this level of processing represents a remarkable advance in understanding. To do this, children need both some phonemic awareness—to perceive the sounds represented by *b* or *l*—and knowledge of the alphabet. When children use this knowledge to spell, the result is invented or temporary spelling. These terms describe young children's attempts to spell words using their limited knowledge about letters and sounds. In the previous section, Diane engaged in invented writing, as do children who write entirely random strings of letters (for example, *czfdyxsy* for *this is my blue umbrella*). Invented spelling is a more sophisticated accomplishment. As we discuss in Chapter 5, the analysis of a child's invented spelling is a useful diagnostic tool in planning appropriate phonics instruction for him.

Linking Letters and Phonemes: The Alphabetic Principle

Children's writing is very important, because children frequently develop conscious awareness of the phonemes in words as they try to write them. In the following dialogue, five-year-old Paul is trying to write words at his workbench. His questions to his mother, Glenda Bissex (1980), reveal phonemic awareness and more sophisticated skills.

> **Paul:** What makes the /ch/ in *teach*?
>
> **Mother:** *CH.*
>
> **Paul:** What makes the /ə/ sound?
>
> **Mother:** In what word?
>
> **Paul:** *Mumps.*
>
> **Mother:** *U.*

Paul perceives that there is a /ch/ in *teach* and a /ə/ in *mumps*—and that is phonemic awareness. He asks his mother to tell him the letters that make those sounds. With his questions, Paul shows an understanding beyond phonemic awareness. His questions reveal that Paul understands the alphabetic principle, that phonemes can be written down as letters. He wants to know what those letters are in particular words. His mother helps Paul learn the letters used for specific sounds, much as a classroom teacher would do in phonics instruction.

When Paul actually wrote *teach,* he spelled it *TECH.* Not surprisingly, silent letters are not commonly represented in children's early spelling. Paul writes the letters for the sounds he perceives. It will take seeing the word *teach* in print a few times before he learns how to correctly spell it. You will see this same pattern of not writing silent letters in the invented spelling of another young child, Jordan.

The invented spelling of five-year-old Jordan, displayed in Figure 4.3, shows how much this emergent reader has already learned about the code of written English. Jordan has encountered some common words frequently enough to have memorized their correct spelling (for example, *Jordan, and, in,* and *is*). He uses the sounds conveyed in the letter names in his spellings (for example, *im*). He more frequently represents consonants than vowels (for example, *kindrgrdin* and *grd*). He is actively working to link the phonemes he perceives to actual letters. For example, on one occasion he writes *grade* as *GRD*, whereas on another he writes it as *GROD*, adding a letter representing a vowel sound. He will on occasion reverse a letter or number; however, as with Jake, this is not a concern.

Jordan is not yet consistently writing silent letters. To do so requires considerable knowledge of within-word spelling patterns (Henderson, 1990). To acquire such knowledge, a child must have engaged in rather extensive reading. Silent letters must be noticed to be learned. One of the most common within-word spelling patterns is the silent *e* marker, as in *grade*. Another common spelling pattern is *ea,* representing a long *e* (the sound heard in *teach*). As Jordan reads more, he will start to notice these patterns. Jordan is likely to progress from *GRD* to *GRAD* to *GRADE* in writing *grade*.

Notice that Jordan spells the last syllable in *kindergarten* with *IN*. Jordan is from Texas, where *en* is pronounced /ĭn/. In many regions of the United States, both *em* and *en* receive short *i* pronunciations. That is, words like *pin* and *pen, ten* and *tin,* and *Jim* and *gem* have identical pronunciations. Sensitivity to dialect is important as we evaluate children's speech and invented spellings to plan instruction. Unfortunately, sometimes teachers use the word *hen* to represent a short *e* sound when both the teacher and her students pronounce this word as /hĭn/.

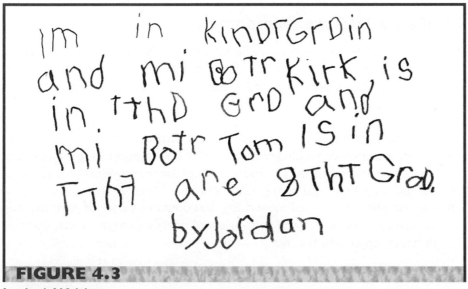

FIGURE 4.3

Jordan's Writing

4. One of us (Juel et al., 1986) once asked some first-grade children to read the word *rain*. Here are the replies of 14 of the children: "ring," "in," "runs," "with," "ride," "art," "are," "on," "reds," "running," "why," "ran," "ran," "ran." We also asked these 14 children to spell the word *rain*, and here are their spellings: *rach, in, yes, uan, ramt, fen rur, Rambl, wetn, wnishire, one drawing of raindrops, Rup, ran, ran*. Consider what understandings are suggested by each spelling and reading of *rain*. Also consider what each child needs to learn to progress.

   Two other first-grade children correctly read the word, but one spelled it *raine* and another spelled it *rane*. What can you say about these two children's understanding of the code of printed English?

5. Explain the progress in perceiving words as sequences of sounds and connecting those sounds to letters, as well as learning common spelling patterns, that a child is making as his spelling of *rain* moves from *R* to *RAN* to *RANE* to *RAIN*.

Instruction That Facilitates Children's Growing Literacy

"Mrs. Cooper, you're going to teach us how to read, aren't you?" six-year-old María asked.

Like María, most youngsters are eager to learn to read. That puts teachers of young children in an enviable position. Fortunately, there are many things you can do to assist these eager learners in understanding the structure of text and the structure of words, developing phonemic awareness, learning to identify words, and all the while nurturing their interest, excitement, and desire to become readers.

Creating a Literate Environment

The starting point in fostering children's emerging literacy is to create a language-rich environment as described in Chapter 3—a classroom that abounds with opportunities to read, write, listen, and talk. A language-rich classroom will include

- walls filled with posters, signs, labels, and student work;
- a reading center with a library chock-full of books, comfortable chairs, pillows, stuffed animals, a rug, and anything else that will make it an enticing and secure spot for young readers; and
- a special area designated for writing that contains paper of various sizes, textures, and colors, as well as a variety of pencils, pens, markers, crayons, alphabet strips, and the like.

In addition to having designated space and materials for reading and writing, children need the time and motivation to read and write. The activities you provide to these children on the threshold of literacy will focus on reading for enjoyment and reading for meaning, as you will see demonstrated in subsequent sections that highlight some of these literacy activities.

Reading Opportunities

Opportunities for children to read in the classroom are almost limitless. Here are some ideas you can try out and expand on in your classroom.

The Morning Meeting

The beginning of each school day is an ideal time to gather your students in a comfortable place and meet with them as a community of learners. The morning meeting can develop and nurture a sense of belonging, community, and purpose, as well as engage students in a variety of literacy experiences. The amount of time you spend, whether it is 10 minutes or 20, will depend on how long your students are able to focus without becoming restless. This time may be relatively short at the beginning of the year and increase as the year progresses.

During this meeting, many activities can take place. Here are some of the possibilities:

- **Attendance count.** Take attendance by showing name cards and having students respond to their names in print. The first word most children learn, because of interest and exposure, is their own name. So students are likely to be successful early on at reading their names.
- **Calendar.** Write the day and date on the board, reminding students of what day came just before and what day will come after (simultaneously teaching and reinforcing children's knowledge of the days of the week and the concepts of *before* and *after*).

The morning meeting is an excellent opportunity to engage students in a variety of literacy experiences.

- **Weather.** Talk with students about the weather, teaching words such as *rainy, sunny, cold,* and *warm.*
- **Current events.** Have students share the events of their lives.
- **Morning message.** Have students read your "morning message." This is a short message you write on the board to your class each day so that when they arrive, they know they will be reading a note from you. This message serves two purposes. First, it reinforces the notion that print conveys meaning. Second, it provides children with practice in tracking print as you read aloud. In fact, it is often worthwhile reading the message several times, drawing attention to the letters or words and having students come up to the board and circle the words they recognize.
- **The daily schedule.** Going over the day's schedule at the beginning of the day gives students a sense of what the day holds and, equally important, illustrates another use of print.

Free "Reading"

Each day, students should have several opportunities to "read" books of their own choosing in any way they like. Some children might wish to share a book with a friend. They might do this by telling a favorite story that they have committed to memory, using the pictures as cues for turning the pages; if you model this activity for them, they will likely find it inviting. Others will silently look at books. Still others will want to be read to or listen to a book that has been put on tape. Whatever their choice, children will be getting experience with books. These sessions need not be long because the attention spans of young children tend to be relatively short, but opportunities for such engagement with books should occur throughout the day.

Selecting Books for Specific Purposes

At the beginning of this chapter, we talked about books as the heart and soul of reading. They also serve a host of specific literacy development purposes. Here, we consider just three of the many purposes books can serve: motivating students, highlighting sounds, and enabling just-beginning readers to read.

Books That Motivate Children to Enter the World of Print. As a teacher of young children, you will want to select books that develop their vocabularies, expand their knowledge of the world, connect to their lives, add to their knowledge of story structures, and increase their desire to read. Such texts can be well-known children's favorites, such as James Marshall's *The Three Little Pigs* (1989), or newer ones, such as Barbara Joosse's *Nikolai, the Only Bear* (2005).

Books That Highlight the Sounds of Language. Because emergent readers need to attend to the form of words, it is important to read texts in which the structure of words is particularly transparent, highlighting the sounds of words in order to foster phonemic awareness. You can choose texts with features such as word play, rhyme, and alliteration to accomplish this goal. One example is Jill Bennett's rendition of *Teeny Tiny* (1997), which Jeff Baptista uses with his kindergartners, as he explains in In the Classroom 4.5.

Here we can list only a limited number of books. Websites for bookstores and libraries, on the other hand, list thousands of them. Use our Companion Website to explore the books Barnes & Noble lists for children ages four through eight.

Developing Phonemic Awareness

I use books such as *Teeny Tiny* with my kindergarten students to help them develop phonemic awareness. After we have enjoyed the story, I will ask them, "What letter in *teeny* makes it say /t/? What letter in *tiny* makes it say /t/? Can you think of other words that start with /t/, like *teeny tiny?*"

Then we might sort pictures or objects that start with /t/ into one column on a pocket chart, and those that start with /s/, like Silly Sally, in another. I will cut pictures from a magazine or create simple line drawings. These pictures can be easily sorted, based on the initial sound of the concept or object they depict. Those that start with a /t/ sound (for example, *table, tail, tiger*) are placed together, while all the /s/ pictures (for example, *sun, salad, soup*) are placed together. Sometimes I will have the children work in pairs or small groups to decide in which column pictures should go. I have also cut a teeny-tiny-woman shape out of construction paper and printed the children's favorite *t* words on it. A word wall works well, too—a large sheet of butcher paper that the children and I fill with *t* words, or whatever letter we are currently focusing on.

in the Classroom 4.5

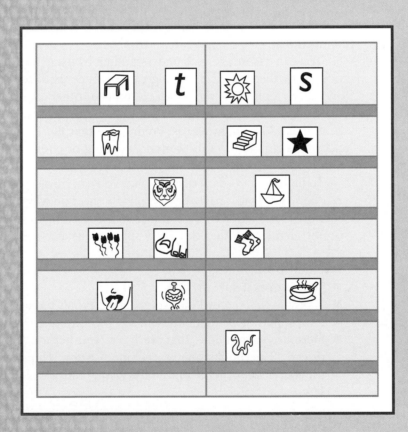

In Chapter 5, such letter-sound activities are described in greater detail.

Word-level instruction begins with a focus on a meaningful text. Then words in that text are highlighted, just as Jeff Baptista did in working with *Teeny Tiny*. The links between meaning, words, and word parts should always be clear.

Books That Children Can Learn to Read on Their Own. The books with predictable patterns that we described earlier in the chapter are purposely written so that children can remember them after hearing them a few times. The overall structure of the books is repetitive, and the picture clues are rich and informative. All in all, these books can make children "instant readers" after only a few readings by the teacher. The children should re-read these books by themselves and with a partner.

Brian Wildsmith's *Cat on the Mat* exemplifies this repetitive structure and strong picture support. In this tale, various animals join a cat on the mat:

> The cat sat on the mat.
> The dog sat on the mat.
> The goat sat on the mat.

As the child re-reads the text and points to the lines and words after hearing it read several times, he can begin to gain insight into the conventions of print, such as the directionality of print from left to right. After re-reading many predictable texts, a child may learn the printed form of some high-frequency words, such as *the,* and some high-interest words, such as *dog;* he may even begin to associate some letters with sounds. The teacher can highlight these connections.

You can encourage such understanding by using big books, which are large enough for the whole class or a group of students to see as you read. They allow you to replicate activities that parents or other caregivers carry out as they read to their children at home: point to the print, track the print as children speak it, and highlight words. Predictable text in big books or on charts can encourage children to follow along, echoing or chorally reading as you point to individual words.

To highlight words, letters, or text, you can frame words in a big book with your hand or cover a page with an acetate sheet on which you underline words, word parts, or letters. You can also ask questions or make comments about specific elements in the text; a few suggestions are listed here:

- Point to where it said *goat.*
- Where does it say *cat?*
- Can you find a word that starts like Devon's name?
- I see some words that end with *at.* What are they?
- Here are some books that we have read before. Can you find *at* in the titles? (The books might include Carle's *Have You Seen My Cat?* the Berenstains' *Old Hat, New Hat,* and Dr. Seuss's *The Cat in the Hat.*)

In the book lists that we include throughout this text, we annotate a number of children's books suitable for reading aloud to emergent readers. A number of these titles are available in a big book format. The following list provides a small sampling of big books.

Writing Opportunities

In order to become increasingly competent readers, children need to become message-makers and authors themselves. For this to happen, you need to create authentic writing opportunities for them. Some tried-and-true approaches are discussed in the following sections.

the Reading Corner

Big Books

Pam Adams. *This Old Man*. Child's Play-International, 1999. Ten old men in colorful outfits are featured in this traditional counting song in big book format. 16 pages.

Doreen Cronin. *Click, Clack, Moo: Cows That Type*. Scholastic, 2004. When Farmer Brown's cows learn to type, they send him a note demanding electric blankets. 32 pages.

Lois Ehlert. *Eating the Alphabet*. Harcourt Brace, 1994. Beginning with apricot and artichoke, this big book takes readers on an alphabetical tour of the world of fruits and vegetables. 32 pages.

Muriel Feelings. *Moja Means One: Swahili Counting Book*. Puffin, 1994. This counting book, which portrays the language and customs of Swahili East Africa, is beautifully illustrated by Tom Feelings. 32 pages.

Lorraine Jean Hopping and Meredith Johnson. *Today's Weather Is . . .: A Book of Experiments*. Mondo Publishing, 2000. Questions suggest various weather experiments students can do, and students can follow instructions to discover the outcomes of these experiments. 32 pages.

Myra Cohn Livingston. *Space Songs*. Scholastic, 1994. This collection of poetry contemplating space is accompanied by bold illustrations. 32 pages.

Bruce McMillan. *Time to . . . .* Scholastic, 1996. This story follows a kindergartner through his day as he learns to tell time. 32 pages.

Ann Morris. *Loving*. Scholastic, 1996. This book about families around the world is richly illustrated with color photos. 32 pages.

David Schwartz. *How Much Is a Million?* Morrow/Mulberry, 1994. Marvelosissimo the Magician uses his magic to help explain the concepts of million, billion, and trillion. 32 pages.

Kate Waters and Madeline Slovenz-Low. *Lion Dancer: Ernie Wan's Chinese New Year*. Scholastic, 1995. In this story, six-year-old Ernie prepares for his first Lion Dance during Chinese New Year. 32 pages.

Audrey Wood. *Silly Sally*. Harcourt, 1994. Sally, the power walker, turns a stroll to the city into a rollicking adventure in this rhyming text. 32 pages.

Journals

When children write, they begin to internalize the notion that ideas can be represented symbolically. We know several kindergarten and first-grade teachers who have students keep journals, beginning on the first day of school. The journal need not be elaborate—several sheets of paper folded over to make a little book is quite sufficient. In the journal, students are encouraged to express themselves in whatever way they choose. They can be given ideas to write about or write without prompts. Like most emergent literacy activities, journal writing should be modeled for children. Modeling should show children many ways to express themselves in writing: drawing pictures, making squiggles, writing letters, and combining several forms of expression. Thus, children can "write" even if they do not yet know the letters of the alphabet. They can then read back what they have written, which is easiest if they can do so right away. Another way for young children to write is to dictate a sentence

ASSESSMENT

Use students' writing journals as a tool to assess areas in which students might benefit from individual or whole-class instruction.

or two that you or a classroom aide writes down. As children experiment with writing, they should be encouraged to get their ideas down in print even if they do not know some letters or spellings; urge them to use invented spelling.

Kindergarten teacher Sid Burns invites each child to work with a special word each day:

> As children are busy illustrating their "word," I circulate around the room and take down dictations. Each child has his or her own journal, made of blank pages stapled between a construction-paper or wallpaper cover. Each student tells me a word that is "on her mind" or special to her that day. (For example, *love* and *heart* were big last week—Valentine's Day fell on Friday.) I write the dictated word in the child's journal. She can then trace or copy it. Sometimes children discuss the word with me or with other children, draw a picture that illustrates the word, and dictate a sentence or two for me to write down regarding the picture. For example, Marta asked me to write, "I love my dog. Her name is Asta." As I wrote the sentences, I used the opportunity to comment on the form of print in a way that was appropriate for Marta. I pointed to the word *dog* and said to her, "dog," emphasizing the initial sound, /d/. "What letter makes that /d/?" Then I asked her to re-read the two sentences and point to the words.
>
> My kindergartners enjoy having an audience for their work and appreciate sharing their journal entries with one another as well as with me.
>
> —Sid Burns, Kindergarten Teacher

Inviting children to read and write what they dictate (whether that dictation be taken by a teacher, a parent helper, or an older student) is only one of the many reading-writing experiences you will want your emergent readers to be engaged in.

Language-Experience Activities

Copying down children's dictation and then having them read their own words, as Sid Burns does, has been termed the *language-experience approach*. With this approach, an adult or older student writes down the words of a story spoken by a student or group of students, using the students' language. When the story is read, students can readily read along. Its vocabulary is familiar because students generated it, and they have prior knowledge related to its content because it is based on their experiences. Because this approach is entirely student-centered, it is particularly useful for meeting the needs of students who vary in ethnic background, English-language competence, and educational needs. In fact, as we point out in Chapter 13, it is an extremely valuable procedure to use with students whose first language is not English.

Shared Reading and Writing Experience

Another opportunity that encourages writing is the shared reading and writing experience, which we discuss again in Chapters 12 and 13. In In the Classroom 4.6, first-grade teacher Connie Martinez combines reading instruction with an opportunity for students to compose a rhyme together. Although the children are not *physically* writing the words, they are participating in the act of composing; their teacher provides a sturdy instructional scaffold.

Reading and Writing Rhymes

Sitting in a large rocking chair, Ms. Martinez holds a big book of Mother Goose nursery rhymes. The children gathered around her can see the words on the first two pages as she begins singing the rhyme:

> Lavender's blue, dilly, dilly,
> lavender's green;
> when I am king, dilly, dilly,
> you shall be Queen;

Ms. Martinez has the children take turns pointing to the color words they know. She helps them with *lavender* and has them tell each other what color this is close to (for example, purple). "Is anyone wearing lavender or blue or green today?" she asks.

Next, she asks them which word in the verse rhymes with *green*.

"Queen!" they chime in unison.

Ms. Martinez stands up and writes *green* and *Queen* directly underneath each other on the portable chalkboard next to her. She asks the children to name the letters in each word and which letters they share.

"*E-E-N!*" a couple of children answer.

Then, Ms. Martinez remarks, "*Dilly* is a silly word!"

So she writes *dilly* on the board, with *silly* right underneath it. She asks them if they can think of some names of boys that sound like *dilly* and *silly*. She helps by saying, "dilly, silly, Billy?"

They shout, "Yes." Then she says, "Dilly, silly, Cassandra?" and they shout, "No."

Ms. Martinez tells the children they are going to write their own rhyme. She puts a large chart pad on a stand. The chart has part of a rhyme already printed on it. The children will suggest words or letters to complete it, and Ms. Martinez will print them on the lines. She begins by asking the children if they want to write about "Silly Billy" or "Silly Willy." They opt for Willy. Ms. Martinez prints *Willy* in the blank on the chart. The children alternate re-reading the rhyme, as Ms. Martinez points to each word, and adding a word in the blank.

At right is the poem they wrote, by filling in the blanks.

Every so often during the week, the children recite this rhyme either as a class or in partner reading, always pointing to the words as they say them.

> Silly ___Willy___
>
> Silly, silly, ___Willy___,
>
> Silly, silly, m_e_,
>
> I fell down and scratched my ___knee___.
>
> I stood up and shook my head.
>
> I stood up and this is what I said:
>
> Silly, silly, ___Willy___,
>
> Silly, silly, m_e_,
>
> I fell down and hurt my head.
>
> I think I should just go to ___bed___.

At the end of our week in Ms. Martinez's class, we were surprised and delighted to hear some of the children on the playground reciting the poem as they jumped rope. *Silly Willy* made a perfect jump-rope jingle. We wouldn't be surprised if the children thought up new verses to add over the days and weeks to come!

Making Books

Children can be encouraged to take their language-experience stories or perhaps write their own stories and make them into small books with illustrations.

This student proudly displays a story that will become part of a classroom book of student-created stories. Student-written and -illustrated books provide a wonderful opportunity to involve children actively in writing and reading.

Bookmaking can be as elaborate or as simple as you wish. Books can be laminated and bound with a plastic spiral or hand-sewn binding or simply stapled together. We recommend saving the more elaborate bindings for class books that can be saved and read over and over again.

Mailboxes

A classroom mailbox system in which students can post one letter a day and have pen pals to correspond with reinforces print awareness and gives students motivation for writing and for reading their own writing (since, early on, they will probably be the only ones who can read their messages).

Play Centers

Many kindergarten teachers include play centers in their classrooms. In these centers, children act out real or imagined situations and events. They might act out what happens at a restaurant or events in a story they have just heard. Literacy activities can easily be included in such play centers. In playing restaurant, for example, a simple pad of paper can be provided for a waitress or waiter to write down orders, or a chart of recipes can be printed for the cook to follow. Similarly, in planning to act out a story, you and the children might together block out the sequence of the story, illustrating it with simple pictures and a few words and phrases.

Listening and Speaking Opportunities

Of course, listening and speaking are normal parts of the kindergarten and first-grade school day. Here, we briefly mention some specific activities that enhance skills in these areas and, as you know by now, promote skills in reading and writing as well.

Reading Aloud

We cannot overemphasize the importance of reading aloud to all children, but it is especially important for emergent readers and doubly so for students who have not had the benefit of being read to at home. When you read to your class, you give students a chance to hear fluent reading and to develop the critical skill of listening comprehension. You also give them the pleasure of hearing a good story and sharing your enjoyment and enthusiasm for it. To create an effective read-aloud experience, it is helpful to keep four suggestions in mind:

CW 4.1 links to Jim Trelease's *Treasure of Read-Alouds*, which includes a list of engaging read-aloud books.

1. Select a story that interests you as well as your students.
2. Practice reading the story, and pick good stopping points for elaborating on the information.
3. Encourage active participation by stopping at appropriate points to ask questions and respond to them. You might, for example, ask students what might happen next or whether they have ever experienced something similar.
4. Whenever possible, invite students to join in! If a word or a phrase is repeated or if you are reading a story students have heard before, encourage them to read along with you. Also, some stories lend themselves to gestures and simple movement.

For more ideas on reading aloud and a host of suggestions on specific books to read aloud, we strongly suggest Jim Trelease's *The New Read-Aloud Handbook* (1995).

Choral Reading

Choral reading simply refers to having children read passages aloud in unison. The passage may be as short as a phrase or as long as a poem or story, but it should definitely be something that is fun to read. Choral reading gives children an opportunity to experience the cadence of oral language, the structure of various forms of text, and the correspondence between print and talk. It also allows them to read aloud in a nonthreatening environment, wherein their voice is one among many. Children enjoy choral reading, and it is a particularly good technique for students whose first language is not English (see Chapter 13).

Choral reading can be both a lot of fun—for you and for children—and very educational. Use our Companion Website to see some additional tips on how to get the most out of choral reading.

Tape Recordings

Tape-recording stories yourself or having a classroom aide or older student do so can provide you with an inexpensive and useful resource. Of course, commercially prepared tapes are also available for many popular trade books, and we have indicated those books that we know are available on tape in the Children's Literature section at the end of each chapter. With tape recordings, a number of children can listen to stories at any time during the day, and you are freed to give attention to other students.

Sing-Alongs

Singing with students encourages listening and speaking development because lyrics are, of course, words. Whenever possible, lyrics should be posted on the wall or put on an overhead projector during singing so that children can follow along.

English Learners

Whether the activity is reading, writing, speaking, or listening, you will increase many English-language learners' success—and therefore their motivation—by letting them sometimes do it in their native language.

A Kindergarten Scenario

To show how a very skillful teacher engages her students in the meaningful literacy experiences we have just described, here we give you a glimpse into a typical day in Ellen Hawkins's afternoon kindergarten class. The location is suburban Virginia. It is February, and the types of literacy activities you will see here have been going on all year.

11:25. Twenty-five children enter the afternoon kindergarten class, shortly after 23 children have left the morning class. The new arrivals put their gear in their cubbies or go straight to a wall chart of library pockets—like those found in library books—one for each child, with the child's name printed on it. As the children file by, they remove the checkout card that they had put in the pocket the day before. The card is from the book they checked out and took home. After they remove the card and put it back in the book, they return the book to the class library.

11:40. All the children gather by the calendar in a front corner of the classroom. Ms. Hawkins asks, "What kind of day is it—lamb or lion?" She has developed this literary vocabulary throughout the course of the year. Voices declare that this roaring, windy day is a "lion" day.

Jamal mentions that they should add the words *lamb* and *lion* to the *L* wall chart that they have been making. Ms. Hawkins is happy to oblige and adds these two words to the list, which already includes *lock, list,* and *library.*

Ms. Hawkins asks for any news. Shawna says her tooth came out. After she smiles to show the space and the class responds, Ms. Hawkins asks her to add this news to the class news record on the chalkboard. As Shawna goes to write her message (in invented spelling), Ms. Hawkins turns to the rest of the class and continues with the calendar. She asks more questions: "How many days have we been in school so far? [They have been keeping track.] How many days are left? What day is it?" As the response of "Thursday" is given, she points to each letter of the word and names it. She remarks that when she says the *th* sound, her tongue is placed between her teeth. The children giggle as they try saying "Thursday" and discover this.

Ms. Hawkins then turns her attention to Shawna, who has written her news on the board. Shawna reads the information. Next, Ms. Hawkins reads her news about what they will do this day. She points to the words, which are clearly printed in neat large print on the board, as she says:

> *Good morning boys and girls!*
> *We get to go to P.E. today.*
> *We can read our books.*
> *Do you see signs of spring?*

Some children chime in as she reads. Ms. Hawkins asks the children to keep a record in their journals of the signs of spring they see. One child volunteers that she saw a robin. This begins a discussion of what other children have seen and will write in their journals. On a page in an oversized journal, Ms. Hawkins writes, "I saw a _____." She will leave this journal on an easel with this page open to serve as a model for students.

11:50. Ms. Hawkins turns to a wall chart that has two columns of words. One is the list of words beginning with *l,* and the other is a list of words that include an *l* somewhere:

leprechaun	yell
list	Emily
Lara	Carlos
library	Melissa
lion	Phillip
lock	Alex
lamb	Michele
love	sell
letter	seal
lost	table
like	
leopard	

Ms. Hawkins asks the children what is the same and what is different about the two lists. The children puzzle over this and start to talk. Most children easily determine that the first column contains words that start with *l.*

There is a lot of discussion about the second list. Some children recognize names, some capital letters; some see that the letter *l* appears in the words. Eventually, they realize that all the words in the second list have *l*s in them. Ms. Hawkins points out that many of the words came from the morning kindergarten class. She asks if they can contribute more words. They add:

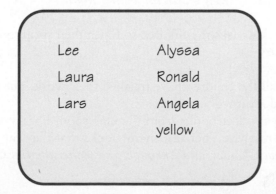

Lee	Alyssa
Laura	Ronald
Lars	Angela
	yellow

Children continue to volunteer words, and Ms. Hawkins says they will add these later. One child says that *later* has an *l*, and Ms. Hawkins adds it to the list—even though she had declared that they were done for now, she can't pass up such a wonderful connection.

12:00. Ms. Hawkins asks the class to stand up and put their hands under their chins, over their heads, and under and over other places. She then asks them to sit down. She says she did that because she is going to read *Over, Under, and Through* by Tana Hoban (a concept book). She reminds the children that they have seen other books with photos by this author, such as the book *Look, Look, Look!*, and a child gleefully notes that *look* starts with *l*, so it is added to the list. As Ms. Hawkins points to pictures in the book, she asks if the child in the photo is over, under, or through the object pictured.

The children discuss a photo that shows a girl standing in the middle of a circle drawn on the ground. The circle is under the girl, but there is some debate about this. In addition, Ryan says, "It's not a circle, it's an oval, and oval has an *l* in it!"

As Ms. Hawkins continues through the book of photos illustrating the concepts of beside, below, against, and behind, the children carefully note which concept each photo represents.

12:05. Ms. Hawkins asks the children to stand and make their bodies into bridges. Then she says:

> Go over the water (the children giggle as they collapse).
> Lie down on your back.
> Make your feet go over your body.
> Sit back down and face the other way.
> Make rain go over your head.

ASSESSMENT

The Tile Test, the first test in the *Assessments and Lesson Plans* supplement, is designed to assess emergent and early reading skills.

After the children settle down, she gives them directions for the project of the day. Each child will get a large sheet of white construction paper. Across the bottom is printed *over and under*. At each table in the room, there are strips of colored paper that children can glue to make over-and-under patterns. Ms. Hawkins reminds them to use only a raindrop of glue and demonstrates how to do this. She demonstrates how to work with the strips of paper, twisting them over and under each other in imaginative ways.

The children go to their seats to make their own over-and-under projects. Tomorrow, Ms. Hawkins will give them an opportunity to use their creations when they read Joy Cowley's *Dan the Flying Man*.

12:25. Ms. Hawkins asks the children to finish their projects and put them in the hallway to dry.

12:30. Almost all the children have finished their work, put their projects in the hallway, and returned to their seats.

Children then select books from the classroom library and read with a buddy or by themselves. There are many books that they can choose, including copies of *Over, Under, and Through and Other Spatial Concepts,* which

Ms. Hawkins just read to the class, as well as trade books (such as *That New Animal* by Emily Jenkins and *What Does Rabbit Say?* by Jacque Hall), books individual children have written, and books the class has written. Some children read together, and some read alone. While the children read, Ms. Hawkins has two children read to her the journals they have been working on. She often does this, and it gives her a chance to focus on individual children. In some journals, she finds rather accomplished writing. Others display much less sophisticated work—some drawings, a few letters, perhaps some invented spelling. Ms. Hawkins knows her individual students' emerging capabilities and is able to praise them or give them a nudge based on where they are in their journey to becoming readers and writers.

12:40. Ms. Hawkins asks the children to finish reading and join the class in the front of the room to share some of their writing. The children bring their personal journals and books. A few children read stories that they have written or dictated to Ms. Hawkins on previous days. Most of the narratives are takeoffs of Ezra Jack Keats's *The Snowy Day*. Ms. Hawkins had read this story aloud the day before. The children had been encouraged to think of another type of "weather" day and what they like to do on such a day. Some had been illustrating and writing their books over the past few days and are now ready to share the finished product. Mostly their books consist of statements that they dictated to Ms. Hawkins and that she neatly printed.

As you will see in the examples, each book includes a page about the author. This gives students more practice in writing, and it personalizes their books.

Here is what Jack reads:

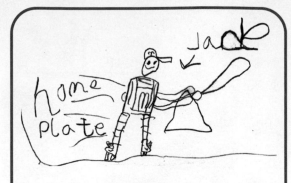

The Warm Day
by Jack
I like to play baseball at the park.
I like to rollerblade at the park.
I like to ride my bike down the street.

About the Author
Hi! I'm Jack Hooper.
I'm 6 years old.
I live in Virginia.
I like the Yankees.

And here is what Sarah reads:

The Sunny Day

by Sarah R.
I would like to jump rope.
I would like to go swimming.
I go in the pool.
I run around the tree.

About the Author

I am 5.
My name is Sarah R.
I am a girl.
I like to swim.

After Jack and Sarah have read, several other children read what they have written. Ms. Hawkins points out that several children wrote the word *like*, and she prints it on the board. Yasem cries, "It starts with *l*." Ms. Hawkins has them feel where their tongues are as they start to say *like*.

Now that's a classroom that fosters emergent literacy! Multiply these types of experiences over a school year, and you can tell how well these children are being guided toward becoming proficient readers and writers who will be prepared to enter first grade.

Reflect *and* Apply

7. Ellen Hawkins is an outstanding teacher, and she does a terrific job nurturing her kindergartners' emerging literacy. Nevertheless, a kindergarten classroom offers almost innumerable options for assisting young learners in their progress toward becoming readers, and it is worthwhile to explore other ways. Go back to two or three of the time slots we have shown, and describe optional or additional activities that you might use.

Strengths and Challenges of DIVERSITY

Some children enter school with considerable experience with print, message-making, books, and exposure to the different places and creatures of our world. These children may need only some help learning the form of words and the content in books. Other children enter our classrooms with very little experience with print, message- making, books, and exposure to the different places and creatures in our world. These children will almost certainly need a good deal of help in learning the form of words and the content in books. It is vital that we assist these children in getting off to a good start and not falling behind in reading (Burns, Griffin, & Snow, 1999; Torgesen, 1998).

For children who come to school with less exposure to print and books or having used primarily a language other than English, one-to-one assistance from older students, such as fourth- through sixth-graders, can be particularly helpful and is also economically and logistically feasible. The task that is easiest to orchestrate is simply having the older students read appropriate books to or with the younger students—predictable books, concept books, alphabet books, and others that foster emergent literacy. As the older students read, they can answer questions the younger students have and talk to the younger students about what they liked about the book, what they would like to read next, and other matters related to fostering their interest in reading.

Older readers do not, of course, have to be students. Parents, senior citizens, or any other readers can be a great asset to emergent readers, particularly to those who need a little extra help and who will profit from the one-to-one relationships that volunteers can offer.

Additionally, as we emphasize in Chapter 13, for children whose primary language is not English, bilingual volunteers who speak the children's first language as well as English can be of tremendous help. The many English-language learners in today's classrooms must, of course, learn to read in English. But they also need to have their own languages recognized and validated. There are a number of ways in which you can contribute to this validation. You can learn a few words in each of your students' languages and introduce them to the class as a whole. You can also sometimes find books that cleverly incorporate several languages. Charlotte Pomerantz's *If I Had a Paka: Poems in Eleven Languages* is a collection of 12 poems that incorporate languages including Dutch, Samoan, Swahili, Vietnamese, and Yiddish. But if you have a class in which students speak a number of languages, you're going to need some help in reading to students in their own languages. This is where volunteers who speak students' first languages can really help. Hearing books read in their native languages in your classroom can be an extremely positive experience for English-language learners as they strive to become literate in English.

Also, although reading to or with children is likely to be the most frequent activity assigned to older children or volunteers from outside the school, they can make other contributions as well. They can take dictation from children, print out the dictation, and then let the children read back their own stories.

All children need different kinds and amounts of instruction to nurture their growing literacy. In Ms. Hawkins's classroom, there were ample opportunities for children who were reading at different levels to select appropriate books to take home. Similarly, all children were involved in writing, but the writing was quite varied, allowing each child to be successful with the knowledge of print conventions he had achieved.

Some children will come to your classroom needing considerable help in the area of phonemic awareness; others won't. There is little point in spending valuable class time "teaching" children something they already know. However, whatever the levels of your students, it is vitally important to remember that the pieces of language and print, such as alphabet knowledge and phonemic awareness, are only building blocks to reading and writing. So, as you plan instruction, you will want to provide activities that have meaning, importance, and relevance to your young students, who are eager to learn the skills that will make them successful communicators.

Concluding Remarks

In this chapter on emergent literacy, we talked about the progression most children follow as they learn to read and the many and varied learning experiences they need in order to become readers and writers.

In learning to read, at first children may rely on distinctive visual cues such as word length, initial or distinctive letters, and illustrations as the primary ways to access printed meaning. As children gain phonemic awareness and letter knowledge, they use their understanding that letters correspond to speech sounds as a means to recognize words. Using letter-sound knowledge is often difficult because reading requires an understanding of the rather abstract concept of phonemes. In fact, learning to read is much harder than learning to speak because reading requires a *conscious* awareness of phonemes that is not needed in speaking. The knowledge and competencies that children need to gain as developing readers include knowledge of stories, phonemic awareness, alphabet knowledge, and a beginning understanding of how letters and sounds relate to make printed words.

The latter part of this chapter described instructional ideas for facilitating and nurturing children's growing literacy in the four modes of language—reading, writing, listening, and speaking. These included creating a literate classroom environment and providing a multitude of reading, writing, listening, and speaking experiences. Some of these literacy activities can revolve around the classroom morning meeting, morning message, and daily schedule. Other important experiences suggested were free reading and engaging students with a variety of books while providing activities that foster knowledge of how printed language works. Writing opportunities, also stressed in this chapter, are crucial to help children learn about the form and function of written language. Some ways to provide these opportunities include student journals, language-experience activities, the shared reading and writing experience, book-making, classroom mailboxes, and play centers. Finally, listening and speaking opportunities for emergent readers were discussed. These included reading aloud, choral reading, tape recordings, and sing-alongs. The chapter concluded with a kindergarten scenario that described the many and varied literacy activities Ms. Hawkins provided for her afternoon kindergartners.

Besides the many practical and concrete ideas we hope you have gleaned from this chapter, what we also hope you will take away is the underlying message that our job as teachers of young children is to provide the kind of literacy experiences that ensure for all children the strongest possible literacy footing on which to build lifelong reading and writing skills and a lifelong love of reading.

Extending Learning

1. Find an adult who reads to a young child at home or in a day care center. Carefully watch and listen to their storybook interactions. How does the adult keep the child's attention? What appears to interest the child? What does the child wonder about in the story? What does the child ask about? What is the child learning about the form or content of books and print in this interaction?

2. The first several chapters of *Starting Out Right: A Guide to Promoting Children's Reading Success* (Burns et al., 1999) contain many ideas for fostering emergent readers' reading-related skills. Identify some of the ideas you see as particularly powerful and discuss them with several preschool teachers or parents of preschoolers.

3. Observe a preschool or kindergarten classroom. Make a list of the kinds of literacy activities you see. Then explain how each of these activities helps children learn about books and print. Alternatively or in addition, observe a preschool or kindergarten child outside of school, and make a list of the literacy activities the child is involved in.

4. In the latter part of the chapter, we mentioned using books with children for three different purposes—to motivate children to expand their knowledge of the world and their imaginations by reading, to highlight the sounds of language in words, and to engage students in reading right from the start by using books with predictable text and helpful illustrations. Go to a library, perhaps a public library, that has a good collection of children's books. Begin an annotated list of books that you think will motivate children to read and to expand their knowledge of the world, books that highlight the sounds of language in words, and books that contain predictable text and helpful illustrations that allow reading right from the start. Include five to ten books in each of these three categories.

5.  Go to a kindergarten class to observe children's writing activities. Jot down the different kinds of activities you see them engaged in. Write a paragraph or so describing which of the four writing opportunities presented in this chapter you would most like to try in your own classroom, and why.

mylabschool
Where the classroom comes to life!

> For a look at emergent literacy in a contemporary classroom, go to Allyn & Bacon's MyLabSchool.com. In MLS Courses, click on Reading Methods, and go to MLS Video Lab. There you will find video clips about Early Literacy in Module 1.

Children's Literature

Bennett, J. (1997). *Teeny Tiny*. New York: Putnam. In this reprint illustrated by Tomi de Paola, a very small woman finds a very small bone and puts it away in her cupboard before she goes to bed. Illustrated. Also available in Spanish. 32 pages.

Berenstain, S., & Berenstain, J. (1970). *Old Hat, New Hat*. New York: Random House. Rhyming text poses the question of whether a new hat can really replace a perfect old one. 32 pages.

Carle, E. (1996). *Have You Seen My Cat?* New York: Simon & Schuster. A boy encounters cats of all sorts while searching for his own lost cat. 24 pages.

Cowley, J. (1990). *Dan the Flying Man*. Bothell, WA: The Wright Group. This book about a flying man is designed for group reading. 16 pages.

Hall, J. (2000). *What Does Rabbit Say?* New York: Doubleday. Rhyming text follows a boy and girl as they ask what sound their pet rabbit makes. 32 pages.

Hoban, T. (1988). *Look, Look, Look*. New York: Greenwillow. In this colorful book, photographs of familiar objects are first viewed through a cut-out peephole, then revealed in their entirety. 42 pages.

Hoban, T. (1973). *Over, Under, and Through and Other Spatial Concepts*. New York: Macmillan. Spatial concepts are illustrated with text and photos. 32 pages.

Jenkins, E. (2005). *That New Animal*. New York: Farrar, Straus, & Giroux. The arrival of a new baby is told from two dogs' point of view. 32 pages.

Joosse, B. (2005). *Nikolai, the Only Bear*. New York: Philomel. Nikolai, the only bear of the 100 orphans at the Russian orphanage, finds the perfect family at last. 32 pages.

Keats, E. J. (1998). *The Snowy Day*. New York: Viking. This 1963 Caldecott Medal classic, about a young city boy enjoying adventures in the snow, is now in board book format. Spanish text and audiotape available. 32 pages.

Lobel, A. (1985). *Whiskers & Rhymes*. New York: Scholastic. This collection contains short, humorous rhymes in the nursery rhyme tradition. 48 pages.

Marshall, J. (1989). *The Three Little Pigs*. New York: Dial. In this version of the familiar tale, one of the three pigs survives the wolf by using its head. 32 pages.

Pomerantz, C. (1993). *If I Had A Paka: Poems in Eleven Languages*. New York: Mulberry Books. A collection of 12 poems incorporates words from 11 languages including Swahili, Samoan, Yiddish, Indonesian, Vietnamese, and Dutch. Unpaged.

Rice, E. (1989). *Peter's Pockets*. New York: Greenwillow. Peter's new pants don't have any pockets, so Uncle Nick lets Peter use his until Peter's mother solves the problem in a clever way. 32 pages.

Seuss, Dr. (1957). *The Cat in the Hat*. New York: Random House. Two children sitting at home on a rainy day are visited by a cat that shows them some tricks and games. Audiotape available. 61 pages.

Seuss, Dr. (1963). *Hop on Pop*. New York: Random House. Pairs of rhyming words are introduced and used in simple sentences. Audio- and videotapes available. 64 pages.

Seuss, Dr. (1974). *There's a Wocket in My Pocket!* This is a good book for developing phonemic awareness. New York: Random House. Audiotape available. 24 pages.

Tafuri, N. (1983). *Early in the Morning in the Barn*. New York: Greenwillow. This almost-wordless picture book depicts farm animals along with some text showing the sounds they make. 32 pages.

Tafuri, N. (1987). *Do Not Disturb*. New York: Greenwillow. On the first day of summer, the forest creatures scurry about and make noise in this wordless picture book. 32 pages

Tafuri, N. (1996). *Have You Seen My Duckling?* New York: Greenwillow. This 1985 Caldecott Honor book, in which a mother duck leads her brood around the pond as she searches for one missing duckling, is now in board book format. 32 pages.

Wildsmith, B. (1982). *Cat on the Mat*. Oxford: Oxford University Press. The cat liked to sit on the mat until the other animals wanted to sit on it too. 16 pages.

Word Recognition

chapter outline

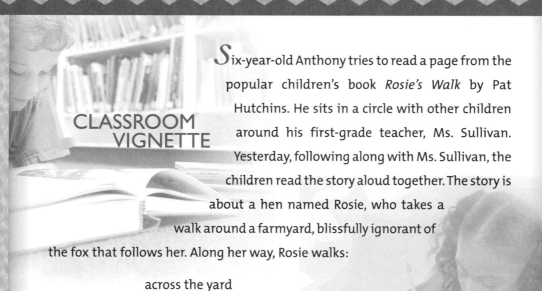

CLASSROOM VIGNETTE

Six-year-old Anthony tries to read a page from the popular children's book *Rosie's Walk* by Pat Hutchins. He sits in a circle with other children around his first-grade teacher, Ms. Sullivan. Yesterday, following along with Ms. Sullivan, the children read the story aloud together. The story is about a hen named Rosie, who takes a walk around a farmyard, blissfully ignorant of the fox that follows her. Along her way, Rosie walks:

across the yard
around the pond
over the haystack
past the mill

Ms. Sullivan has all the children point to the words as they read. Some children are more able to do this than others. Ms. Sullivan either has the entire class read a line aloud, calls on a few children to read, or calls on one child to read. She has just called on Anthony. He points to *around* and slowly says, "around the . . . ," stops, and looks up. Ms. Sullivan suggests that he look at the picture.

Anthony looks at the page and asks, "Tree?"

"Well," says Ms. Sullivan, "it does look as if she might walk around that tree, but what is the tree in front of? What is all this?" (as she points to the pond).

Anthony smiles and says, "Water."

"Yes," agrees Ms. Sullivan. "It is water. Remember, though, it is a special kind of water. Look at the word. What letter does it start with?"

"*P*," replies Anthony.

"*P*, puh—does water start with a puh?" asks Ms. Sullivan.

"No."

"So, it can't be water. Look at the letters. *P*, puh, and the *on* and *d*. You know the letter *d*."

"*D*, duh," volunteers Indigo.

"Yes." Pointing to the letters, Ms. Sullivan slowly says, "It's a puhond."

"*Pond*," declares Anthony.

The Importance of Recognizing Printed Words

To young children like Anthony, who are just beginning to read on their own, recognizing printed words is *the* big challenge to becoming a reader. There are a lot of places Rosie the hen could walk around, and guessing rarely works— rather the reader, like Anthony, must confront the print itself. Anthony is a typical six-year-old native English speaker. He entered first grade with a command of spoken English that is nearly complete in terms of its structure (its underlying grammar and phonological development). He already has a vocabulary and a command of spoken English that would be the envy of any non-native English speaker who, as an adult, is trying to learn English; and his emerging literacy skills are evident in his responses to Ms. Sullivan. Nonetheless, Anthony, like most first-grade children, will work hard at learning to recognize words and acquiring a basic reading vocabulary. Also, like most young children, Anthony will depend on his classroom teacher to help him acquire these reading skills.

Clearly, both spoken and printed English involve the same language. But the reason Anthony can't read, although he is already quite competent at speaking and comprehending oral English, is that *he does not yet know how to translate the printed word into the spoken word*. The printed word forms a barrier between him and the meaning of the text. He needs to learn how to get meaning from this printed form of language. To do this, he must, in a sense, get his eyes to do what his ears currently do for him. When he can do this, the ultimate human language comprehender, the mind, will be able to make sense of printed language.

The goal of both listening and reading is the same—to construct meaning, to understand. But the listener finds the task easier than the reader for several reasons. We will briefly look at six of these reasons and why Anthony's task as a reader is harder than his task as a listener.

Why Listening Is Easier Than Reading

When we look at the features of spoken language that help speakers communicate, we see things that are not as likely to be present in written language. Here are some of the challenging aspects of printed versus spoken language.

Shared Background Knowledge

Conversational partners typically share *background information* about a topic. When you get together with a friend to chat, you most likely share a history of people, places, and events. This means that you as a speaker probably know which words, concepts, and topics are going to be easily comprehended by your friend and which are likely to be difficult. A shared history is much less likely, of course, to exist between an author and a reader. Pat Hutchins, who wrote *Rosie's Walk,* does not know if Anthony has ever seen a pond.

Immediate Feedback

When you are listening to what a friend is saying and don't understand what she says, you can simply tell her so—"Wait a minute. What do you mean when you say to 'caramelize' the onions before I put them in the stew? How do I caramelize them?" On the other hand, when Anthony is reading *Rosie's Walk* and doesn't understand something, he certainly can't directly ask the author, Pat Hutchins, what she meant.

Visual Cues from the Speaker

A listener can see the speaker's features. Lips move as they shape sounds, providing an additional clue to the speech sound being uttered—an especially useful clue in a noisy environment. Additionally, speakers can enhance their message by exaggerating or adding intonation, facial expressions, vocal emphasis, tone of voice, repetition, and gesture. Body language can even override the speaker's words and send a different message than the words do.

More Common Words

We generally converse using words more common than those we employ in writing. In a conversation with a friend, for instance, you might say, "Last night, I just talked on and on about. . . ." In penning your autobiography, however, you might write, "All evening, I chattered incessantly about. . . ." The reader, unlike the listener, is likely to encounter less-common words—such as *chattered, incessantly, beehive, mill, pond*—and less-common words are, of course, less likely to be familiar.

Contextualized Meaning

In a conversation, meaning is almost always *contextualized*. That is, the listener has the benefit of the context provided by the shared background knowledge, the immediate feedback, the visual cues, and the more common vocabulary that are characteristic of spoken language. Conversely, when we read, meaning is typically *decontextualized.* Many of the characteristics that make listening easier are missing, and the reader must construct meaning without these supports (Purcell-Gates, 1989).

No Translation Needed

Most important, the modality of input in listening is primarily aural, whereas the modality of input in reading is visual. Language underlies both listening and reading, of course. But to get to that language in the medium of print requires additional translation: The reader must be able to translate the rather dead-looking printed word into the speech she already knows. Once the text is translated, the reader has access to meaning just as she would in speech. So the child's basic problem in learning to read is learning to translate the printed words into the speech she already understands. But knowing that printed words are often less common than those in ordinary conversation, we want to take every opportunity to build meaningful vocabulary as we build decoding skill.

Skilled Readers Automatically Recognize Words

Although the context of a text occasionally suggests what upcoming words may be, the skilled reader can identify words so quickly that she doesn't need to consider the surrounding context (Adams, 1990; McConkie & Zola, 1981; Stanovich, 1991a, 1991b, 1992). That is, if you are reading "Kevin was walking his . . ." and then come to the word *dog,* you automatically—instantaneously and without conscious attention—process the letters in *dog,* even though in this case the word is fairly predictable. This seemingly obsessive and unnecessary processing of the letters actually makes word recognition faster than trying to predict upcoming words based on context, such as guessing what type of animal Kevin might be walking. Instantaneous word recognition is especially desirable, too, because in many instances context is not that helpful and can even be misleading.

The words that tend to be the most predictable in text are the *function words,* words that express primarily grammatical relationships. They include articles (such as *a* and *the*), prepositions (such as *of* and *in*), and conjunctions (such as *and* and *but*). There are relatively few function words, and the same ones recur frequently—this makes them predictable. The child who is not a good reader can therefore make a good guess about the identity of a function word based on its length and a letter or two. A good guess for a three-letter word that starts with *th* is *the.* In addition, the child's knowledge of grammar helps her identify function words. She knows that a sentence often begins with the word *the,* and that long sentences frequently contain the word *and.*

On the other hand, the *content words,* words that carry much of the specific meaning of what we are reading, are often not very predictable. This is because, as we explain in some detail in Chapter 7, there are an enormous number of content words—nouns, verbs, adjectives, and adverbs—in English.

Because young children cannot quickly recognize many words, we encourage beginning readers to use what they already know about language and the world, as well as the context of the story and its illustrations, to supplement their fledgling skill in word identification. *However, as a child is taught specific ways in which letters relate to sounds, these letter-sound cues to word identification should take precedence over contextual and picture cues. Ultimately, letter-sound cues provide much more reliable information and a more efficient means to word recognition than do contextual cues or illustrations.*

The efficient skilled reader is able to (and with many texts must) spend time thinking about the meaning of what is being read. Efficient word recognition allows the reader to attain this level of reflection and thinking. Your ability to think about, enjoy, and learn from what you read depends on thinking about the content, not thinking about word recognition. Still, efficient word recognition does not ensure good comprehension: A reader may lack the prior knowledge, conceptual knowledge, interest, analytic skill, wit, and other factors required to understand a particular text. Good comprehension, however, is rarely achieved without efficient word recognition.

Although we believe strongly that learning to recognize words involves learning to respond instantly to individual letters and common spelling patterns such as *at, and, ig,* and *ack,* we do not believe that early reading instruction should focus on these parts of words without first placing them in the context of whole words and whole texts. The challenge you will face as a teacher of young children is to help them learn to recognize words without losing sight of the goal of reading—getting meaning. Children must learn how to rapidly pronounce *pond,* but they must also know the meaning of it. Swift and accurate word recognition is the quickest route to finding a text's meaning. Explicit instruction on letter-sound patterns and relationships will be helpful for the vast majority of children.

Finally, learning to read by the end of the first grade, which very definitely means learning to recognize words, is extremely important because the child who flounders at this tender age will have difficulty catching up. Studies in several countries, with different curricula and languages, have found this to be the case (Clay, 1979; Juel, 1994; Lundberg, 1984). It is absolutely critical, then, that teachers of young children be thoroughly competent in teaching beginning reading. To attain this competence, you will need to understand the structure of spoken and written English, the strengths and weaknesses of various approaches to beginning reading instruction, and specific procedures for teaching beginning readers to recognize words. These topics form the remaining parts of this chapter.

The Structure of Spoken and Printed Words

Say your name out loud. You just created speech, using your vocal system to modify the flow of air as you exhaled from your lungs. There are a limited number of things you can do to this exhalation in your throat. You can modify it with your tongue and with your lips, and you can change the direction in which the outgoing breaths are channeled and the length of time it takes the air to pass through the vocal system. Making a speech sound requires several simultaneous manipulations. You can build a puff of air behind your closed lips and let it suddenly burst out to make a /p/ sound; or, as you let out the burst, you can move your tongue up to touch the ridge behind your upper front teeth and make it a /t/ sound.

The Makeup of Spoken and Written English

The speech sounds that are used to distinguish one word from another in a particular language are called *phonemes.* In English, /p/ and /b/ are phonemes.

Individual letter cards make letters and phonemes concrete.

Phonemes represent a rather abstract level of language analysis, and what is perceived as a phoneme differs from one language to another. English employs approximately 44 phonemes, which is about the average number. As you learn to speak a foreign language, you are likely to pronounce the phonemes in that language with the sound patterns of your native language, leading the native speaker to say you have a foreign accent. Thus, the native English speaker will tend not to trill *r*s when speaking Spanish (as would a native speaker of Spanish) but instead pronounce them as English phonemes. The native speaker of Japanese pronounces the *l* in English as an *r* because in Japanese these two sounds are not distinctive phonemes. As we will note in Chapter 13, you can expect that children who are not native English speakers may need particular help in perceiving and pronouncing the phonemes in English that are dissimilar from those in their first language.

Phonemes: Vowels and Consonants

Phonemes are divided into vowel sounds and consonant sounds. *Vowel* sounds are made when the air leaving your lungs is vibrated in the voice box (the larynx or Adam's apple) but then has a clear passage from the voice box to outside your mouth. Different vowel sounds occur depending on how you hold your tongue as the air passes by. *Consonants*, on the other hand, are speech sounds that occur when the airflow is obstructed in some way in your mouth. For example, as we just noted, the consonant sound

/p/ is made by letting air build behind the lips before it is released from your mouth.

Syllables, Onsets, and Rimes

In all languages, the basic phonological unit of speech is the *syllable*. At a minimum, a syllable contains a vowel, and most basic syllables contain an onset and a rime. The *onset* is the initial consonant or consonants, and the *rime* is the vowel and any consonants that follow it. In *sat,* the onset is *s* and the rime is *at.* In *smack,* the onset is *sm* and the rime is *ack.*

In speech, the syllable is the most noticeable unit. It is no coincidence that nursery rhymes and Dr. Seuss books are filled with wordplay involving the onsets and rimes of syllables. Onsets and rimes are naturally compelling sound units, and playing with them typically delights young children. They are likely to repeat lines such as "Jack and Jill went up the hill" literally hundreds of times, just for the fun of it.

A syllable contains one vowel sound. Different languages have different rules about what sounds can precede and follow that core. In English, an onset can be made up of a single consonant (such as *b* in *back* or *s* in *sit*) or a cluster of up to three consonants (*bl* in *black* or *str* in *strike*), and although most English syllables do have an onset, they do not have to. A rime in English must contain a vowel, and a rime usually ends with a consonant or a consonant cluster (*it* in *sit* and *ack* in *back* are examples). In English, the most common syllable structure is consonant-vowel-consonant (or CVC), as in *dog, cat,* or *pig.* CVC syllable units can be strung together to create multisyllabic words, such as *market* or *napkin.* English also allows several modifications of this CVC unit. For instance, two or three consonant sounds can occur together, as in *flat, split, blast,* or *splash.*

There are six common spelling patterns for syllables in English, as shown in Figure 5.1. These are the consonant and vowel spelling patterns that readers usually encounter in words. You have just learned that the most common of these spelling patterns is the CVC group. As you look at Figure 5.1, remember that there can be up to three consonants on either side of a vowel in a syllable.

---

1. Syllable that ends with a consonant: **CVC** (*sat, splat, **napkin***), VC (*at, up*); the vowel is usually short.

2. Syllable that ends with a vowel: **CV** (*me, **spider***), V (*a, **halo, baby***); the vowel is often long.

3. Final *e*: **CVCe** (*take, home, cup**cake***); the vowel is often long while the final *e* is silent.

4. Vowel team (for example, *ai, ee, ea, oa*), as in *team, green, lean, toad, **pea**nut*; in these particular pairs, the first vowel is often long and the second one silent, but that does not apply to many vowel teams.

5. Vowel plus *r: ar, ur, ir, or, er* (for example, *far, fur, fir, for, her*)

6. Consonant plus *le*, as in *little, purple, turtle, tre**ble***

Note: C stands for consonant, V stands for vowel.

FIGURE 5.1

Six Common Spelling Patterns in English Syllables

Word Families and Phonograms

Unfortunately, quite a few terms are used in discussing word study, and they are not always used consistently. Current teacher materials are likely to refer to onsets and rimes. But another term commonly used for rimes that have the same spellings is *phonogram,* and you will sometimes see these two terms used interchangeably. Words that share phonograms are called a *word family.* Thus *cat, bat, hat, flat,* and *mat* share the *at* phonogram (or rime) and belong to the *at* word family. Similarly, *same, game, tame, blame, fame,* and *flame* share the *ame* phonogram (or rime) and belong to the *ame* word family.

Morphemes

All languages use *morphemes* to represent the meaning level of speech. Morphemes are the smallest meaning units into which a word can be divided, and both words and parts of words can be morphemes. *Dog* is a morpheme, and the *-s* in *dogs* is also a morpheme; the *-s* has meaning in that it indicates that the word is plural. Figure 5.2 shows various ways of segmenting words.

	PLANET	CATS
Morphemes	planet	cat s
Syllables	plan et	kats
Onsets and rimes	pl an ət	k ats
Phonemes	p l a n ət	k a t s

FIGURE 5.2
Various Ways of Segmenting Words

Any word can be described at both the morphemic level and the phonological level. *Dog* is a one-syllable word with one morpheme. Its phonological structure is the common CVC syllable pattern: *D* is the onset and *og* is the rime. *Dog* is also called a *root word,* or *root,* because it can both stand alone and be combined with other roots to form new words. *Doghouse* is a *compound word* containing two root words, *dog* and *house. House* consists of the onset *h* and the rime *ouse.*

Affixes: Prefixes and Suffixes

Morphemes that cannot stand alone to form meaningful words are called *affixes.* There are two types of affixes. The first is called a prefix. A *prefix* is placed before a root to form a word with a meaning different from that of the root. Prefixes cannot stand by themselves as words; they must be attached to roots. Thomas White and his colleagues (White, Sowell, & Yanagihara, 1989) have produced a useful list of the most frequently occurring prefixes, shown in Figure 5.3.

The second type of affix is called a suffix. A *suffix* is placed after a root to form a word with a different meaning or a different grammatical function. Like prefixes, suffixes cannot occur by themselves; they must be attached to roots. There are two kinds of suffixes: inflectional and derivational. Inflectional suffixes perform functions such as making a word plural or indicating tense, as do the *-s* in *dogs* and the *-ed* in *snowed.* There are only a few inflectional suffixes, but they occur frequently. Figure 5.4 shows a complete list of inflectional suffixes taken from Lee Ann Rinsky (1993).

Derivational suffixes alter a word's meaning and its grammatical function. A few common suffixes are *-ly* as in *lively, -ive* as in *selective,* and *-ment* as in *excitement.* There are a relatively large number of derivational suffixes, and most of them occur relatively infrequently. Figure 5.5, also taken from Rinsky (1993), shows a few derivational suffixes and illustrates their effects when attached to root words.

As you no doubt realize from reading the last several pages, the structure of spoken and printed words is complex. Words can be analyzed in a number of dif-

PREFIX	WORDS WITH THE PREFIX	PREFIX	WORDS WITH THE PREFIX
un-	782	inter-	77
re-	401	fore-	76
in-, im-, ir-, il- ("not")	313	de-	71
dis-	216	trans-	47
en-, em-	132	super-	43
non-	126	semi-	39
in-, im- ("in" or "into")	105	anti-	33
over- ("too much")	98	mid-	33
mis-	83	under- ("too little")	25
sub-	80	All others	100 (estimated)
pre-	79	Total	2,959

FIGURE 5.3

Most Frequently Occurring Prefixes

Source: White, Thomas G., Sowell, Joanne, & Yanagihara, Alice. (1989, January). Teaching elementary students to use word-part clues. *The Reading Teacher, 42*(4), 302–308. Used by permission.

ferent ways. As Catherine Snow and her colleagues (1998) point out, "Spoken words can be phonologically subdivided at several different levels of analysis. These include the syllable level (in the word *protect*, /pro/ and /tect/); the onset and rime within the syllable (/pr/ and /o/, and /t/ and /ekt/, respectively); and the individual phonemes themselves (/p/, /r/, /o/, /t/, /e/, /k/, and /t/)." And these are only some of the ways words can be analyzed.

As we just explained, words can also be analyzed into morphemes and into roots and affixes. Despite the complexity here—more accurately, *because of* the complexity—you need to be familiar with all of these units—phonemes, syllables, onsets, rimes, morphemes, roots, and affixes—in order to best help children as they learn to identify words.

s (es)	plural	boys, brushes
's, (s')	possessive apostrophe	boy's, boys'
s	third-person singular	sings
ed	past tense	grabbed
ing	present participle	singing
en	past participle	has/have eaten
er	comparative	taller
est	superlative	tallest

FIGURE 5.4

A Complete List of English Inflectional Suffixes

Source: RINSKY, LEE ANN, TEACHING WORD RECOGNITION SKILLS, 5th Edition, © 1993. Reprinted by permission of Pearson Education, Inc., Upper Saddle River, NJ.

ROOT WORD	PART OF SPEECH	SUFFIX	AFFIXED WORD	PART OF SPEECH
base	n.	-ic	basic	adj.
correct	adj.	-ly	correctly	adv.
fool	n.	-ish	foolish	adj.
allow	v.	-ance	allowance	n.
person	n.	-al	personal	adj.
attract	v.	-ive	attractive	adj.
clever	adj.	-ness	cleverness	n.
agree	v.	-ment	agreement	n.

FIGURE 5.5

A Few Derivational Suffixes

Source: RINSKY, LEE ANN, TEACHING WORD RECOGNITION SKILLS, 5th Edition, © 1993. Reprinted by permission of Pearson Education, Inc., Upper Saddle River, NJ.

This kindergartner is having fun naming the letters of the alphabet. Little does she realize that alphabetic writing systems are considered to be one of the most important human inventions.

The Alphabetic Principle

According to the alphabetic principle (the basic principle underlying English writing), the distinctive speech sounds of a particular spoken language, the phonemes, are represented by symbols called letters. The three letters in *mad,* for example, correspond to the three phonemes /m/, /a/, /d/. Of course, as you know, the correspondence between letters and sounds in English is not perfect. In spoken English, there are about 44 phonemes, but we use an alphabet with only 26 letters. Many letters represent more than one sound—for example, *e* represents /ĕ/ in *pet* but /ē/ in *beat.* Two or more letters sometimes represent a single sound—for example, *ea* represents /ĕ/ in *head.* And many sounds can be represented by more than one letter—for example, /o͞o/ is represented by *oo* in *booth* and by *ew* in *threw.* As you know, the vowels are the most troublesome in this regard, but some consonants also represent more than one sound—for example, *c* can represent both /s/ and /k/.

Another difficulty with alphabetic writing systems is that phonemes don't exist as nice, neat, cleanly divisible units. As you say the word *mad,* you actually begin forming your mouth to say the *a* while you are still saying the *m;* likewise, you begin to pronounce the *d* while finishing the *a.* This process is called coarticulation. It allows rapid and seamless speech, but it also makes phonemes less accessible and perceivable in spoken words. Some phonemes are even impossible to say in isolation without adding a vowel sound. If you had to tell a child what sounds (phonemes) the letters *d* and *p* stand for, for instance, you would probably say something like "duh" and "puh." But there is no *duh* in *dad* and no *puh* in *pat.*

Because phonemes don't leap out at listeners, devising a writing system to link letters and phonemes required considerable insight and abstraction, and it appears that an alphabetic writing system was not invented until sometime between 1000 and 700 B.C. (that is, relatively recently). Alphabetic writing systems are often considered to be among the most important human inventions. Their abstract nature is also part of the reason that children have difficulty learning them: Being able to attend to a less-than-concrete individual phoneme in a spoken word, isolate it, and attach it to a letter is quite a mental feat.

The Structure of Printed Words: The Good News

We are thus faced with the fact that the English writing system presents some considerable challenges to children learning to read. The good news, though, is that the words with the strangest spellings tend to be the ones we see most frequently in print. Because of this, we have many opportunities to memorize them. The even better news is that *despite glaring exceptions, there is a lot of predictability in English spelling.* Even words with strange spellings include some letters that provide useful sound cues to their identity. Usually, the most reliable letters are the consonants.

Through years of reading, you have learned a lot about the structure of printed words, such as the common spelling patterns shown in Figure 5.1, even though you may not be able to articulate what you know. You also know intuitively, for example, that some letter sequences are much more likely to occur than others. For instance, you know that words are more likely to start with *pr* or *br* than with *rb* or *rp*—while just the opposite is true at the end of words. You have this tacit knowledge because for years you have carefully looked at individual words as you read. Even as very skilled readers, we do look at almost every word in the text we are reading (Just & Carpenter, 1980). Indeed, we look at the individual letters in most words we encounter (Adams, 1990).

Even multisyllabic words, though they are admittedly difficult, yield to analysis. Multisyllabic words are simply strings of syllables, which themselves are composed of onsets and rimes. Though not perfectly consistent, there is a tendency in English to "chunk" words into syllables by placing at a syllabic division letter sequences that are less likely to occur next to each other within a syllable. In the word *haystack*, for example, we have several clues as to where to divide the word. First, there are two morphemes, *hay* and *stack*. Second, each syllable is a common variant of CVC units and contains common onsets—*h* and *st*—and common rimes—*ay* and *ack*. Third, the letter combination *ys* is not likely to begin a syllable. Double consonants are also a common signal of a syllabic division. Only one consonant is actually pronounced, as you can see in *dinner* or *rabbit*.

A big part of what makes you an efficient recognizer of words is having read a lot. There is a lesson in this for you as a teacher: *Wide reading in and of itself is going to teach children a lot that will speed their word recognition.* And when wide reading is coupled with appropriate instruction, children's word-recognition skills are still further bolstered.

Skilled readers can read many different words because they know a great deal about the structure of printed English words. They have learned the pronunciation of many common words, such as the function words *the* and *that*, and other common words, such as *mom* and *red*. Skilled readers have also learned to respond instantly with the pronunciations of many within-word spelling patterns, such as the onsets *p* and *st* and rimes such as *ick, and,* and *at*. Adults can read nonsense words that contain common spelling patterns and common affixes almost as fast as they can read their own names.

Reflect and Apply

1. Identify the onsets and rimes in *hen, past, back, mill,* and *time.* Then make a list of other words that share one of these rimes and thus belong to the same word family.

2. Identify the function words and the content words in the sentence *Rosie the hen went for a walk across the yard.*

3. What are the morphemes, roots, and affixes in the words *haystack, dinner,* and *beehives?* What are some clues as to how to divide the words into syllables?

4. We just noted that skilled adults can read nonsense words almost as quickly as they can read their own names. See how quickly you can read these nonsense words—*zat, mig, unplick, kip, cleef, fand,* and *bufwixable.* To the extent that you read them quickly, you are proof of the incredible sophistication skilled readers have in analyzing words and coming up with their pronunciations.

Our Position on Phonics Instruction and Related Matters

Phonics is an umbrella term for instruction about letter-sound correspondences. We believe that learning the relationship between letters and sounds—the way in which the written language represents the spoken language—is absolutely crucial to becoming an accomplished and lifelong reader. We further believe that although a small percentage of children learn this relationship on their own without formal instruction, most children stand the best chance of learning it through direct teaching. This position is consistent with the findings of Jeanne Chall, a Harvard professor who reviewed the research on beginning reading instruction in a landmark book titled *Learning to Read: The Great Debate* (1967), and with most interpretations of Guy Bond and Robert Dykstra's *First Grade Study* (1967/1997), the most ambitious study of beginning reading conducted in this country. This position is also consistent with a host of research reports, syntheses of research, and position statements published over the past decade. These include special issues of the *American Educator* published in 1995 and 1998; the International Reading Association's position paper on phonics, *The Role of Phonics in Reading Instruction* (1997); Elfrieda Hiebert and her colleagues' *Every Child a Reader* (Hiebert et al., 1998); Snow and her colleagues' *Preventing Reading Difficulties in Young Children* (1998); Burns and her colleagues' *Starting Out Right* (Burns et al., 1999); the American Federation of Teachers' *Teaching Reading Is Rocket Science* (1999); and the *Report of the National Reading Panel: Teaching Children to Read* (National Reading Panel, 2000a, 2000b). Finally, the position is consistent with the majority of research on beginning reading and with common sense. We are the enormously fortunate inheritors of an alphabetic writing system; we need to teach our children how to take advantage of that fact.

CW5.1 links to both a summary statement of the International Reading Association's position statement on phonics instruction and the IRA site, which contains a .pdf file with the complete position statement.

Some children need less phonics instruction than others, and phonics instruction must always be kept in proper perspective—as a means to an end. Constructing meaning is the main goal of reading, and reading, writing, speaking, listening, and being read to must form the heart of the literacy curriculum. But for readers who have not yet mastered the code of written English, word-recognition instruction—which includes phonics—plays an absolutely essential role. How to provide that instruction is the topic of the rest of this chapter.

Word-Study Instruction

Word study refers to instruction about words. As you are well aware by now, any sort of word-study instruction is a means to a specific end—comprehension of text. We want to empower children with the knowledge and skills to unlock the meaning of the printed word. Word-study instruction can include a focus on the spelling patterns in words (phonics), attention to high-frequency words, and attention to the meaning elements in words (for example, affixes such as -ed and root words such as *play*). Word-study instruction requires the active teaching and active learning we described in Chapter 2. In the remainder of the chapter, we present concrete illustrations of word-study instruction. In the list below, we give examples of the sorts of active teaching and active learning employed in word study:

- Teachers provide explicit instruction concerning which letters represent which onsets, rimes, and phonemes.
- Children sort picture cards on the basis of the onsets, rimes, or phonemes contained in the pictured words.
- Teachers model how to segment words into their constituent sounds and link those sounds to letters.
- Teachers explain and demonstrate how to blend individual phonemes to form words.
- Children sort word cards on the basis of common spelling patterns.
- Children read text with repetitions of both high-frequency words and different words with common spelling patterns.
- Children create word-study journals to record words that share common features of spelling such as phonemes and phonograms or features of meaning such as prefixes, suffixes, and root words.
- Children write dictated words and sentences that contain target spelling patterns or high-frequency words.

Five General Principles of Word-Study Instruction

The word-study instruction we recommend follows five basic principles:

1. Start where the child is.
2. Make word study an active, decision-making process in which children classify words according to the similarity of their sounds and spelling patterns.
3. Base word study on contrasting words with different sounds or spelling patterns.

English Learners

With English-language learners, all of these principles are important. But the first principle—start where the child is—is particularly important to keep in mind because your English-language learners' understandings about words may be very different from those of your native speakers.

4. Help children understand how the writing system works.
5. Keep comprehension as the goal.

First, effective word-study instruction is based on the child's current understandings about words. *Start where the child is,* with the concepts about words the child already understands and the words the child can read. If a child doesn't know many letters but can recognize her name, then learning the names of the letters in her first and last name is a good starting place. Or, if the child writes words primarily as initial consonants (onsets) such as *pig* as a *p, dig* as a *d,* and *big* as a *b* but stops there, then it is time to teach the child rimes such as *ig* and time to help the child perceive and manipulate the letter sounds in *ig.* Of course, it is also in keeping with the tenet of starting where the child is to ensure that the child is not repeatedly "taught" something she already knows. Thus, for example, as we pointed out in Chapter 4, a child who has achieved phonemic awareness should not be subjected to repeated "instruction" on phonemic awareness.

Second, word study is based on the premise that *learning occurs as an active process of classification.* Children learn about words by acting as active decision makers who analyze and classify spoken and written words on the basis of whether or not they share certain features. Words are classified on the basis of features such as whether they have the same or a different phoneme, onset, rime, spelling pattern, affix, or root word.

Third, *effective word-study instruction is based on contrasts.* That is, the child learns to perceive short *i* in words by contrasting short *i* words with words that have another vowel—for example, contrasting *sit* with *sat.* All else being equal, a child will better learn short *i* and its place in CVC words such as *wig* and *pig* by contrasting words that have *i* with words that have a different vowel. By contrasting *sit* with *sat, bit* with *bat, pit* with *pat,* and *slip* with *slap,* the child can begin to perceive which letters represent which sounds. By comparing words that have contrasting patterns, children can focus on which features make which differences.

Words can be contrasted in different ways. Sorting picture cards is one effective way to highlight contrasts in phonemes. A picture card is simply what the name suggests—a card with a picture on it, such as a picture of a pig, rug, wig, or hug. Picture sorting for particular phonemes or rimes is an excellent activity for developing phonemic awareness. For example, the child must determine whether the picture of the hug goes under the picture of the pig or the picture of the rug (hug–pig or hug–rug). Does the word *hug* fit better with the sound /ug/ or the sound /ig/—that is, /ŭ/ or /ĭ/? It requires critical thinking skills rather than drill or memorization to make categorical judgments (Bear, Invernizzi, Templeton, & Johnston, 2004).

Fourth, *children need to understand how the writing system works.* In learning to read and write, children need to understand how speech is written down. They need to perceive units of speech, such as phonemes and rimes. They need to learn which speech units are represented by which letters. As a teacher of emergent readers, you will want to model how to segment spoken words into speech units and how to connect these units to letters. You will also want to help students perceive the units of speech that are represented in writing—words, syllables, and phonemes. And, finally, you will want to help children learn how to represent these units in their own writing. As children learn to write, they are learning the ways words are constructed. As they learn the ways to write, or encode, a word, they are learning what they will need to know to decode a printed word in reading.

ASSESSMENT

Here are two questions to jot down in your teacher logbook at the beginning of the year: What do my students need to know by the end of the year? How will I judge the quality of their accomplishments?

Fifth, *children need to understand that word study is a means to an end—comprehension.* "We are learning what letters make these sounds, so very soon you will be able to read all these wonderful stories yourself! In fact, after what we learn today, you will be able to read this book to a friend!" The goal is for students to learn to decode words until words become automatically identifiable for them. Students must be given many opportunities to read and reread stories so that words can be learned to the point of automaticity. We want to get students to that point as quickly as possible so that all of their attention can be focused on comprehension.

We encourage you to keep the five principles in mind as you plan word-study instruction. These principles will apply whether you are working with initial consonants, phonograms, short vowels, or affixes. They apply to children of any age. And, as we discuss specific word-study activities, we urge you to also keep in mind that word study is but one piece of reading instruction. Children's understanding of how our writing system works and of how to glean meaning from the writing system depends on understanding both that *writing is for communication* and that *speech is related to writing.*

Teaching Children to Recognize Words

So where do you begin? Picture a kindergarten or first-grade classroom. The door opens, and suddenly the room fills with an assortment of bright-eyed children eager to learn. However, these hopeful, energetic children may or may not be able to recognize or produce the letters of the alphabet, may or may not accurately track speech to print by finger-pointing to memorized text, may only be able to scribble letters or intersperse letters and scribbles in their writing, and may not be able to read any words. In other words, children with a wide range of proficiencies relevant to learning to read enter your classroom, and one of your first tasks is to identify what individual children do and do not know and can and cannot do. Following this, your job will be to help all of these children—not just some of them—become competent readers and writers.

We start by discussing sight-word learning, the language-experience approach, and the importance of wide reading. Then, in the next section, we move into word study that involves teaching children letter-sound correspondences—phonics.

Getting Started: Sight Words and Word Banks

Words that children can recognize instantly are often referred to as *sight words*. As we mentioned earlier, there is a small set of words that children encounter frequently in text. These are *high-frequency words*. They are the most common words in printed English and include function words such as *as, the, and,* and *of,* as well as common content words such as *girl, blue,* and *little*. High-frequency words appear often in text, and it is difficult to read very much without knowing them well. Along with phonics instruction, some high-frequency word practice can be helpful in getting beginning readers started.

Many lists of high-frequency words are available, and most reading series that you might use in your classrooms will identify the high-frequency words that appear in their materials. Certainly, you will want to help your emergent readers quickly learn a body of high-frequency words. This will be useful for them in beginning to read right away. Instantaneous word recognition is often referred to as sight-word recognition.

Sight words also serve as examples of how students approach words in word study. It is easier for a child to focus on the parts of a word she knows; familiar letters or patterns may help her recall the whole word. When a child can immediately recognize the word *cat,* it frees her to really focus on which letters relate to the /k/, the /ă/, the /t/, or the /ăt/. She can then compare less-known words, such as other *-at* words (*sat, fat, hat*), to this anchor word. Proceeding from the known to the unknown, our first principle, is always the best direction. You will see this principle at work later in this chapter and throughout this book.

Thus, a good way to teach sight words is to start with words the child already knows. Most children entering first grade can read their names and a few words they learned in kindergarten, such as color words, names of family members, and categories of household pets. A quick individual assessment of the words each child knows might be helpful. Your school or the materials you teach with may provide such an assessment. Or you can construct a list based on that shown in Figure 5.6. In any case, you can easily create a quick assessment by clearly printing a selected set of words on a list or on individual index cards. Then make a duplicate copy of the "test" on which to record what a child says as you ask her to read the list. As you record what a child says, note not only which words she can easily read but also what she does when she can't read a word. Does the child try to use an initial consonant? What does she already know about words that you can build on?

The word list in Figure 5.6 includes both high-frequency function words and common content words. You can modify it by adding words that you are planning to have the child read in books, on charts, around your room, or at home.

the	dog	big	cat	run	is
at	like	see	can	to	dog
he	my	yellow	and	red	get
up	go	she	girl	bus	was

FIGURE 5.6

A List to Use for a Quick Check on Words Children Know

Words that a child already knows can be the initial words to place in word banks. A *word bank* is a child's personal collection of words that she knows well enough to recognize in isolation. The words are printed on small cards and kept in a small plastic bag or other container. It is best if you, rather than the child, print the words unless the child is a good printer, because most emergent readers are still learning how to accurately form letters. New words will be added to the word bank each day. Words can be reviewed in a variety of ways, as well as sorted according to their letter-sound features.

Start a word bank by printing a child's first name on a small card. Then add words the child can already read, such as those she could read on the list in Figure 5.6. Next, you might personalize the word bank by asking the child what other words she can read, writing those on cards, and adding them to the collection. You might also add a few words that the child volunteers she would like to learn. These might include a favorite food, the name of her dog, the name of a favorite friend, a favorite activity, or any other word. Figure 5.7 shows the word bank of Marcos, a beginning first-grader. It includes the words he could read from the list in Figure 5.6, as well as the words his teacher added because Marcos wanted to learn to read them.

A child's word bank should continue to grow until it has about 100 words. At that point, a word bank becomes unwieldy, and the child should have developed enough knowledge about decoding to be able to read more on her own. Words are added to the word bank as they are encountered in books and as they are needed in a child's individual writing. Selection of words to put in the word bank is done by both the child and the teacher. In particular, high-frequency and high-interest words that a teacher knows the child will encounter in books are good word-bank candidates.

Reviewing word-bank words and encountering them frequently in books they are reading will help children continue to recognize the previously learned words as new ones are added. As we explained in Chapter 4, emergent readers frequently have incomplete knowledge of all the letters in a word. They might recognize a word by its initial consonant or by its length. So it is not surprising that as new words are added to the word bank, old words may be "forgotten." For example, the technique of recalling the word *cat* because it starts with the letter *c* fails when the word *can* is introduced. The more times children look at the word-bank words and compare them, the more likely they are to gain full mastery of them. First-grade teacher Gordon Scholander told us how he uses word banks with his emergent readers:

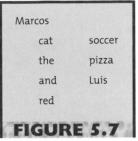

FIGURE 5.7

Marcos's Beginning First-Grade Word Bank

> My young scholars frequently enjoy sharing their word banks. They will sometimes read their word-bank cards to each other or with a buddy sort their cards into categories—such as animals or words that start or end with a particular letter. Sometimes I'll have them spread out ten or so of their individual word-bank cards on their desks, or work with a buddy, to try variants of a "pick-up" game. Here are some prompts I give them for the game:
>
> - Pick up all your animal words. Read your words to a buddy. Do you and your buddy have any of the same animals?
>
> - Pick up all your color words. Hold up the card with your favorite color on it.
>
> - Pick up all your words that start with /sssss/. Read them to a buddy.
>
> - Pick up all your words that start with the letter *s*. Read your *s* words to a buddy.

- Pick up words that rhyme with *cat*. What do you have?
- Pick up all your words that have three letters. Read them to a buddy.
- Pick up your longest word and share it with a buddy.

—Gordon Scholander, First-Grade Teacher

Language Experience

Our focus thus far has been on developing a core set of high-frequency words—words likely to be encountered in many different books—that children can readily identify. Later, we show how to help children gain confidence and ability in identifying unknown words by using letter-sound correspondence strategies. But as we discussed in Chapter 4, children can learn much about how speech and print relate by noting how *their own speech* is linked to letters. Teachers can help children see how speech is written down and develop a more solid concept of words by taking dictation as a child talks. As the teacher writes the child's words, he can explain something about what is being printed. For example, if a child says "sun," the teacher can emphasize the /s/ while printing an *s*. As we mentioned in Chapter 4, this method of instruction has been termed *language experience:* The text is based on the language and experience of the child. Language experience can take various forms. We talked briefly about some of these in Chapter 4. Here we describe a few more:

- Each child has a special book. This can be created with a construction paper cover and filled with plain paper or paper that is plain on top and lined on the bottom. Each day, a child can think about a special word. As children draw pictures of their words, the teacher walks around the class and takes dictation. The teacher carefully prints each child's word while talking about its features, such as saying its letters while printing them. The child then copies the word. Some children may dictate more than a single word, and some children might add additional writing to the page.
- Children dictate a description or story to the teacher, who writes it down on a large pad of lined chart paper. For example, if there is an aquarium in the classroom, children might write a description titled "How to Feed Our Fish." As another activity, children might write their own version of a story with which they are familiar. For example, *Black Cat* by Christopher Myers might become a story titled *White Cat* or perhaps *Black Dog*, and the story's refrain might be changed to "Black dog, black dog, we want to know / where's your home, where do you go?" A first-grade teacher might also use the language-experience approach to create a classroom newspaper; the students report on what is going on in their lives, and the teacher writes down their ideas on a large sheet of paper.
- A large sheet of plain paper (about six feet long), pinned to the wall in the classroom or hallway, can form a bulletin board. Children can dictate various phrases or words for the teacher to write. The teacher begins by writing each child's name, then adds her comments. Children can easily find their names to read back their comments. Words that an individual child dictates are good candidates for addition to that child's word bank.

Read, Read, Read

In this chapter, we look at specific instructional ideas for increasing children's knowledge about how words work and how they are constructed. We emphasize developing phonics skills, but recognize that it is not possible to teach every spelling pattern that children will encounter. The word-study instruction we talk about helps give children insights into how words work. But much of what they learn will come from wide reading.

We want to stress the importance of *applying word-study skills in the context of actual text reading* (Juel & Roper/Schneider, 1985). As a teacher of emergent readers, you will want to make sure children have practice reading words with the common spelling patterns that you teach them in real text. For most teachers we know, this is routine. Georgia Woods talks about one of the books she uses in conjunction with teaching long *a* spelling patterns:

> I like to begin and follow up activities on spelling patterns for long *a* with reading books such as *Who Has a Tail?* (Level G) by Fay Robinson. This text has actual photographs of animals, and many of the words show spelling patterns for long *a*. For example, here are the lines from pages 3 and 4:
>
> Who has a tail that shakes like a rattle?
>
> The snake does.
>
> When this snake shakes its tail, the tail rattles. That way, other animals hear it. They stay away.
>
> As you can see, this book gives students the opportunity to practice reading long *a* word patterns in words such as *tail, shake, stay,* and *away*.
>
> —Georgia Woods, First-Grade Teacher

Teaching Children About Letter-Sound Correspondences

Begin teaching children about letter-sound correspondences by following the first principle of word-study instruction: Start where the child is! Assess what children do and do not know and what they can and cannot do.

We start in Phase 1 with learning the alphabet and recognizing letters—prerequisites to learning letter-sound correspondences—and end with teaching prefixes and suffixes in Phase 3. Figure 5.8 shows a general progression for moving from Phase 1 to Phase 3. But remember that these are general guidelines, not a lockstep description of what you must do. You need to tailor your teaching to students, and research that one of us conducted (Juel & Minden-Cupp, 2000) suggests that different learners will need different emphases.

PHASE 1	PHASE 2	PHASE 3
• Alphabet recognition and production	• Short vowels	• Short vowels
• Beginning word study: onset, rimes, and individual phonemes	• Consonants • Consonant blends • Consonant digraphs	• Long-vowel patterns • Multisyllabic words
• Initial work with blending	• Formal blending instruction	• Prefixes and suffixes

FIGURE 5.8

Three Phases of Word-Study Instruction

Phase 1: Learning the Alphabet, Beginning Word Study, and Initial Blending Instruction

Phase 1 begins with pre-phonics—ideas for helping students recognize and reproduce letters in the alphabet. Next, we move to beginning word study—ideas for introducing the basic speech unit, onset and rime, and how to blend letter sounds in CVC words.

ASSESSMENT

Use the Alphabet Recognition recording sheet from the *IRAS* test in the *Assessments and Lesson Plans* supplement to assess students' knowledge of letter names and their corresponding sounds.

Alphabet Recognition and Production. It is difficult to track print and to attend to printed words as sequences of letters (let alone as individual phonemes) until letters are recognized. Letter recognition can be taught both directly and indirectly. If you discover that some of your students are weak in letter recognition, you can involve them in incidental alphabet activities throughout the day, as well as provide them with direct alphabet instruction during their word-study time. The Reading Corner below lists some possible alphabet books to share with your students or to consider for your classroom library.

You can create incidental alphabet activities as opportunities arise. Keeping a chart of letters that children know is useful for tailoring alphabet work to fit individual students. You can talk about the letters students know when you run across them in your readings. For example, you might say something like

the *Reading Corner*

Alphabet Books

Fortunately, engaging alphabet books are never in short supply. Here is a list of nine of the best of them.

Graeme Base. *Animalia*. Penguin, 1996. Originally published in 1986, this lavishly illustrated ABC book depicts animals with alliterative descriptions. 32 pages.

Chris Demarest. *The Cowboy ABC*. DK Ink, 1999. A cowboy's life and work from *A* to *Z* are detailed in rhyming couplets in this alphabet book. 26 pages.

Stephen T. Johnson. *Alphabet City*. Penguin, 1999. Published first in hardcover in 1995, this 1996 Caldecott Honor book is a sophisticated, artistic, wordless alphabet book presenting letters as objects in the urban environment. For example, the legs of a yellow sawhorse form the letter *A*. 32 pages.

Jean Marzollo. *I Spy Little Letters*. Scholastic, 2000. With photographs of colorful objects by Walter Wick, this rhyming ABC book in the popular I Spy series introduces young children to the alphabet. 26 pages.

Margaret Musgrove. *Ashanti to Zulu: African Traditions*. Dial, 1976. This stunning alphabet book of the African culture, illustrated by Leo and Diane Dillon, won the 1977 Caldecott Medal. 32 pages.

Ann Whitford Paul. *Everything to Spend the Night from A to Z*. DK Ink, 1999. In rollicking, rhyming text, a young girl unpacks her bag filled with items *A* to *Z* for an overnight at her grandparents' home. 32 pages.

Jan Thornhill. *The Wildlife A-B-C: A Nature Alphabet Book*. Firefly Books, 1996. This alphabet book depicts the ABCs of wildlife. 32 pages.

Jane Yolen. *All in the Woodland Early: An ABC Book*. Boyds Mill Press, 1997. Here's an alphabet book that features North American woodland birds, animals, and insects for each letter woven into a story poem that can be sung. 32 pages.

Jane Yolen. *Alphabestiary: Animal Poems from A to Z*. Boyds Mill Press, 1994. This alphabet book is an anthology of more than 70 poems about creatures large and small in alphabetical order. 64 pages.

this: "Look at the title of this book. Can you find the letter *m* in two places?" Or you might say, "I want you to point to all the *p*s on this page."

As you or a child writes, focus on problem letters by using statements such as this one: "You'll need a lowercase *b* to write the word *boy*. Here it is on the alphabet strip" (located on the children's desks). It is also helpful to keep in mind the letters that are problematic for particular children in your classroom.

You will want to engage your students in direct alphabet activities if a child or a group of children have very incomplete alphabet knowledge. In In the Classroom 5.1, we describe some activities that will help students learn the letters in the alphabet.

CW5.2 links to a list of online alphabet books. Although many children learn the alphabet easily, some do not. Online alphabet books—which often include sound, animation, and original ideas—may be useful resources for these children.

Alphabet Activities

instructional routines

in the Classroom 5.1

START WITH THE CHILDREN'S NAMES AND THEIR FAVORITE THINGS

A good starting place for children who do not know many letters is to work on the letters in their names. Names are particularly meaningful to children. When they know the letters in their first names, work on last names or friends' names or the names of their favorite foods, colors, pets, and so forth. Write each letter on a separate card. Lay the cards out in order, and name them as you spell the words. You might use capitals in one row and ask the children to match lowercase letters to them in another row below. Scramble the letter cards and have the children reassemble them, naming them as they point to them. This activity works particularly well when partners team up to name the letters in their names and those of classmates.

ARRANGE THE LETTERS IN ORDER

When students know about half of the letters or more, they can work on putting a set of letters in alphabetical order from *A* to *Z*. Use a set of alphabet flash cards or letter tiles. Use either capital or lowercase letters. You might have children work in pairs and have one child put the capitals in order while another child works to match them with the lowercase letters. Let the children refer to alphabet strips. You might teach children to sing the ABC song. If you do, be sure to have them touch the letters (on their own alphabet strips) as well as sing them.

> Aa Bb Cc Dd Ee Ff Gg Hh Ii Jj Kk Ll Mm
> Nn Oo Pp Qq Rr Ss Tt Uu Vv Ww Xx Yy Zz

USE ALPHABET TRADE BOOKS AND PERSONAL ALPHABET BOOKS

Have children look up the letter they are studying in an alphabet book or picture dictionary to find things that begin with that letter. Create an alphabet book for each child by stapling together blank sheets of paper and assigning a letter to each page. This book can be used in a number of ways with children who need to learn letters:

- Encourage students to practice writing upper- and lowercase forms of the letter.
- Decide on a key picture, the name of which begins with that letter (for example, a picture of a moon for *M* and *m*). You or the child can draw the key picture and paste it on the page. Key pictures for alphabet books can also be computer-generated.
- Write other words that begin with the letter. Look them up in an ABC book or picture dictionary.
- As children begin to acquire word banks, these words can be added to the alphabet book to create a dictionary of known words.

Beginning Word Study: Onsets, Rimes, and Individual Phonemes. After students have a good grasp of the letters in the alphabet and can recognize some high-frequency words, they are ready to begin learning how our alphabetic writing system works. Word-study instruction on letter sounds, or phonics, starts with the sounds of beginning consonants (onsets) and moves to the sounds of rimes (phonograms). Rimes need to be broken down into individual phonemes so that children analyze words at both the onset-rime level and the individual phoneme level.

As we discussed earlier in this chapter, the syllable is the basic speech unit, and the common syllable unit in English is consonant-vowel-consonant (CVC)—or an onset and a rime—as in the word *cat*. There is considerable evidence that children more readily perceive the sounds in syllables as onsets (the beginning consonant units) and rimes (the vowel and what follows) than as sequences of phonemes. Awareness of these intrasyllabic units is easier to develop and occurs before a child is able to attend to the individual phonemes that make up a rime or a complex onset (Treiman, 1992). Thus, a child perceives the onset *k* and the rime ăt in *cat* more readily than she perceives *cat* as containing the three phonemes /k/, /ă/, and /t/. Working with these units early on makes good sense, although students will also need to learn to deal with individual phonemes (Ehri & Robbins, 1992; Gaskins et al., 1996/1997; Juel & Minden-Cupp, 2000).

Using predictable text to foster knowledge of high-frequency words and initial consonants is a good way to begin phonics instruction. In predictable text, there is repetition of structure, rhythm, or some other pattern that, when combined with lots of illustrations, supports the fledgling reader. In the very popular, predictable text *Brown Bear, Brown Bear, What Do You See?* by Bill Martin, Jr. and Eric Carle, colored drawings of animals and a repetitive structure support the emergent reader:

Brown Bear,
Brown Bear,
What do you see?

I see a red bird
looking at me.

Red bird,
red bird,
What do you see?

I see a . . .

The scaffolding provided by predictable text ensures that children will be readers from the start. As we noted in Chapter 4, children often become instant readers after hearing an adult read predictable text just once or twice. Emergent readers can then enjoy, understand, and read text on their own. After your students have enjoyed hearing a predictable story, you can then focus on certain words to study. They might include high-frequency words or words with specific onsets that are being studied in class. These words will make sense to the children, as they have already seen them function in a meaningful text.

The downside, however, of predictable text is that once the text is memorized, children need not look at the words to "read" the text. They can recite the text from memory, getting any help they need from the pictures. So although predictable text can be extremely helpful in early reading instruction, you must phase it out. Also, you can maximize children's attention to onsets or other individual letters in whatever they're reading by including simple procedures such as the one Harriet O'Dell uses with her first-graders:

One method I have found effective in helping children focus on *all* the letters in words is to have them match their word cards to the words in the predictable text. For example, if a child has read *Brown Bear, Brown Bear, What Do You See?* I can be very certain he will have a word card with *brown* written on it in his stack of word cards. He can check that it is *brown* by putting the word card underneath the word in the memorized text that he knows is *brown*. In trying to match the word on the card to the word on the text, that child has to compare all the letters. Children can also use the text to identify a word they aren't certain of on a word card. I have the children review word cards for common words like *brown* and *see*, as well as use the cards in phonics—which one starts with /sss/? I use large zip-lock bags containing a predictable text and some word cards in school and to send home.

—Harriet O'Dell, First-Grade Teacher

In the Classroom 5.2 will help build your schema for helping emergent readers learn onsets. Ms. Campbell and her first-graders have completed the language-experience portion of a lesson.

Beginning Work with Onsets (Initial Consonants)

in the **Classroom** 5.2

After Ms. Campbell's entire class has listened to and discussed the story *What Do You Like?* by Michael Grejniec, she says, "It's center time." Ms. Campbell tells each child which center to go to. She reminds them that they will spend about 20 minutes in each center and that today they will each rotate through all the centers. About a third of the children go to the classroom library center. There they can read with a buddy or read alone a book of their choosing. She has added a copy of *What Do You Like?* to the center. Another third of the children go to the writing center. There they will write and illustrate their "I like" books. And the other third will work at the word center.

Ms. Campbell calls the first seven children to the word center. Here she meets with groups of children who will profit from similar word and phonics instruction. The seven children she sees in this rotation need to review initial consonants. They bring their word banks to the center. Ms. Campbell has seven copies of *What Do You Like?* They each take one. She first has them chorally read the text together as they point to the words. Then she passes out small word cards to each child. The words on the cards are *rainbow, like, love,* and *play.* Three of these words are common ones, and *rainbow* is one that Ms. Campbell knows they would like to learn. She tells them to find the page in their book that has *rainbow* on it. They easily do this. She then says, "Find the word card that says *rainbow.* Check it to see if it is a match by putting it under the word *rainbow.*" She asks the children how they know the word is *rainbow.* Most say because it is long and starts with the letter *r.* Sara mentions that she can also hear an /ā/ in it. Because they have already covered the sound /b/, Ms. Campbell has them point to where it starts saying *bow.*

She next has them put *rainbow* as the heading on their desk and search their word banks for other *r* words. They each line up their *r* words under *rainbow.* Ms. Campbell asks them to read their list to the person sitting next to them. She includes herself, for an even number of participants. Ms. Campbell repeats this procedure with the words *like, love,* and *play.*

The final word center activity is called Writing for Sounds. Ms. Campbell gives the children pencils and blank sheets of paper, and they write their name on the paper. She has them write the letters *p, l,* and *r* across the top of the paper. She then calls out words that start with one of these letters. When she calls out "play," she expects children to write it under the letter *p.* She doesn't expect them to be able to write all of its letters but encourages them to write as many as they can. She emphasizes the initial consonant as she says the word, as this is the phonics element the group has been working on. She will look at these papers later to check on how each child is progressing. Right now, she simply collects them as it is time to rotate the children to another center in the room.

ack	ail	ain	ake	ale	ame	an
ank	ap	ash	at	ate	aw	ay
eat	ell	est	ice	ick	ide	ight
ill	in	ine	ing	ink	ip	ir
ock	oke	op	or	ore	uck	ug
ump	unk					

FIGURE 5.9

Thirty-Seven Rimes That Occur in Nearly 500 Primary-Level Words

We turn now from onsets to rimes. As we discussed earlier in this chapter, the basic syllable is composed of an onset and a rime. Rimes with the same spellings are called phonograms. Words that share a phonogram, such as *hat, mat, cat, sat, chat,* and *fat,* form word families. We have already talked about how to develop children's knowledge of onsets, as well as a corpus of high-frequency words. Once some initial consonants (onsets) are known, we can expand children's reading vocabularies by teaching them short vowels and rimes.

There are many common phonograms whose pronunciations are quite dependable. Richard Wylie and Donald Durrell (1970) developed a list of 37 rimes that are stable and occur in nearly 500 primary-level words. These are listed in Figure 5.9.

Obviously, some word-study instruction should focus on these 37 rimes. Children can make analogies based on these syllable units that will help them read and write new words (Goswami & Bryant, 1992; Goswami & Mead, 1992). That is, once a phonogram such as *at* is known, a child can use her knowledge of initial consonants and the rime to write or read a never-before-seen word, perhaps *rat* or *hat*. However, recent research strongly suggests that working with rimes becomes useful only after the young reader can analyze them into their component phonemes (Ehri & Robbins, 1992; Gaskins et al., 1996/1997; Vandervelden & Siegel, 1995) and that many poor readers cannot do this without explicit instruction (Juel & Minden-Cupp, 2000). Thus, while skilled readers will automatically recognize units like the 37 phonograms as patterns, many children won't become skilled readers by skipping over decoding the components of rimes—the short vowel and final consonant.

It is the vowel in the rime that tends to present children with the most difficulty in learning letter-sound relationships. Initially, this is because consonant sounds tend to be more easily perceived. In *cat,* for example, the /k/ and the /t/ are both distinctive in the mouth as you say the word and distinctive to the ear as you hear the word. Children reflect this distinctiveness by using consonants in their invented spellings more frequently than vowels—for example, spelling *cat* as *k* or *kt* (Henderson, 1981). Children also rely on consonants in their early decoding efforts. Thus, they may recognize *cat* by applying their knowledge that *c* maps to /k/ and *t* to /t/ (Bruck & Treiman, 1992). Later, as we have noted, mapping vowels to spellings is complicated by the fact that, in English, vowels map to various spelling patterns.

Thus, a teacher can anticipate that instruction will need to be extensive to help children (1) perceive short vowels in words (long vowels are more distinctive) and (2) learn the common spelling patterns of both short and long vowels (for example, CVC words like *cat* and *cap* versus CVCE words like *cape* and *Kate* or CVVC words like *pain* and *paid*).

Once some vowel and consonant letter-sounds are learned, knowledge of rimes is likely to help children chunk and decode unknown words (Bruck & Treiman, 1992). But what helps children get to this point is careful analysis of the individual phonemes in known words. So while our goal is to have children instantly recognize the word *cat* and the rime *at,* the way for children to cement these chunks in memory is through a careful analysis of each letter-sound correspondence. We can assist children in doing this by

- encouraging children to look at *all* components of a word, not guess at an unknown word by looking at an illustration or just an initial consonant.
- engaging children in writing activities in which we orally segment words into each of their phonemes and children write the letters representing each phoneme.
- having children compare and contrast the phonemes and letters in words— for example, asking "What do *cat* and *fat* have in common?" or "What do *sat, sit,* and *sad* have in common?"
- helping children blend the sounds of the phonemes together as they try to decode words—for example, elongating the /s/ in *sat* as you blend it with the /a/ and then adding the /t/ to /sa/ in a smooth flow.

It is possible to introduce rimes and vowels at the same time, but the effect of doing so may vary with different children. Research indicates that some children profit more from working with individual letter sounds, while others find making analogies to known rimes in key words easier—decoding *sat* by recognizing the *at* that they already know in the word *cat* (Berninger, 1995; Berninger, Yates, & Lester, 1991; Wise, 1992; Wise, Olson, & Treiman, 1990). You can incorporate both approaches into your teaching and be sensitive to whether a particular child responds better to one or the other, or even responds differently at different times. For example, you are likely to find children who initially need to sound and blend individual phonemes to decode new words but later can decode new words by recognizing rimes the new words share with known words.

In In the Classroom 5.3, we outline a procedure for studying both rimes and their component phonemes.

Working with the Rime *at* and Some Individual Phonemes

- Locate a story with lots of *at* words, such as Alice Cameron's *The Cat Sat on the Mat.* (Note that many reading series include leveled books, based on phonic patterns, that you can choose from.)
- Read the story aloud to students, and then have students read it chorally.
- Have students locate the *at* words in the story, making sure they finger-point to the words as they read them.
- Print the *at* words on an outline drawing of a cat, and post it on a wall. This word wall poster will be a good reference for children to refer to as they decode and encode words. As other stories are read with *at* words, these words can be added to the word wall.

instructional routines in the Classroom 5.3

- Blend the individual sounds in the *at* words; for example, blend /c/, /a/, and /t/ to produce *cat*.
- Dictate *at* words for children to write. For example, say *cat*; then pronounce the individual phonemes /c/, /a/, and /t/ slowly so that children can hear these individual sounds and match them each with a letter as they write.
- Invite children to take the known word *cat* from their word bank or another source and find the *at* in it.

Beginning Word Study: Initial Work with Blending. In describing the procedure for working with the rime *at*, we mentioned your blending individual sounds. But of course it is not enough for *you* to blend individual sounds; children themselves need to learn to blend sounds together to form words. And learning to blend sounds is no easy task for many children. You can model holding the sound of the onset until you add the rime. As much as possible, it is important to not stop saying the onset until the rime is added so that there will be less distortion of the initial consonant. In other words, rather than pausing after the /k/ in *cat* and thus adding an *uh* sound to it, go straight into the *at*, as in /kkkkăăăătttt/. *Because many children have problems with blending, take every opportunity to model this process.* In the Classroom 5.4 shows what you might say about the word *mat* printed on the chalkboard.

Steps in Blending

You can use this approach as a model for helping children learn to blend sounds in words.

instructional routines

in the **Classroom** 5.4

If I don't know what a word is right away, here's how I figure it out. First, I look at the word, and I find any parts I know. So, let's pretend I don't know this word, *mat*.

I know it starts with a /mmmm/ [said as you point to *m*], and then I recognize *at* [said as you point to *at*]. So, I say /mmmm ăăăătttt/ [said as you finger-point to *m* and then to *at*]. *Mat*—that makes sense. I can also go /mmmm ăăăă tttt/ [this time saying each of the three phonemes as you point to each of the three letters].

The following chart gives you a quick overview of the steps in blending for the word *mat:*

YOU POINT TO	YOU SAY
Letter: *m*	Sound: /mmm/
Letter: *a*	Sound: /ăăăă/
Letters: *m-a*	Blend: /măăăă/
(Move your finger from *m* to *a* as you blend sounds.)	
Letter: *t*	Sound: /tttt/
Letters: *m-a-t*	Blend: /măt/
(Move your finger from *m* to *a* to *t* as you blend sounds.)	

Phase 2: Short Vowels, Final Consonants, Consonant Blends, Consonant Digraphs, and Formal Blending Instruction

Phase 2 of the suggested sequence includes additional work with individual phonemes, initial work with consonant blends and consonant digraphs, and more formal work with blending CVC words.

As we have already stressed, in order to become skilled independent decoders, students need to attend to the components of rimes—short vowels and final consonants.

Short Vowels. Short vowels require considerable attention. During the time you are concentrating on the short vowels—/ă/ as in *hat,* /ě/ as in *let,* /ĭ/ as in *bit,* /ŏ/ as in *pot,* and /ŭ/ as in *hut*—it would be useful to put up a prominently labeled short-vowel chart listing each short vowel and a word representing it, as shown in Figure 5.10. If, for example, children come across a sentence such as "The pup sleeps," you could ask students to name the short vowel in *pup* and say the sound it represents. They may use the chart for reference, so the "key" words should be well rehearsed. *Pup* has a *u* like *hut,* /uh/. You might also point out the rime, *up.* Have children join you in blending the three phonemes in *pup* as you point to the letters (see Figure 5.11).

Final Consonants. In addition to learning to isolate short-vowel sounds and recognize their occurrence in words and rimes, children need to internalize these same insights about final consonants. That is, they need to be able to recognize a consonant when it appears in final position at the end of a word or rime, realize that it can be separated from the rest of the word or rime, and recognize and produce its sound. With the *The pup sleeps* sentence we used in discussing short-vowel instruction, this would mean recognizing that *p* is a consonant, recognizing that it represents a separate phoneme in the word *pup,* and recognize that it also represents a separate phoneme in the rime *up.* Much as you did with short vowels, you could instruct and give students practice in dealing with final consonants by asking what the final consonant in a word such as *man* is. When a student says that it is *n,* note that it makes the /n/ sound.

Model Blending. As soon as you have taught some consonants and a couple of short vowels, it is helpful to children if they can handle and move letter cards to make new words. As shown in In the Classroom 5.5, the hands-on activity of moving letter cards accentuates the role each letter plays in the word.

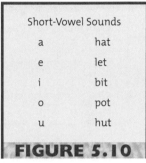

Short-Vowel Sounds	
a	hat
e	let
i	bit
o	pot
u	hut

FIGURE 5.10
Wall Chart Showing Short-Vowel Sounds

YOU POINT TO	YOU SAY
Letter: *p*	Sound: /p/
Letter: *u*	Sound: /u/
Letters: *p-u*	Blend: /pu/
(Move your finger from *p* to *u* as you blend sounds.)	
Letter: *p*	Sound: /p/
Letters: *p-u-p*	Blend: /pup/
(Move your finger from *p* to *u* to *p* as you blend sounds.)	

FIGURE 5.11
Blending Phonemes

Making New Words

To practice segmenting words into phonemes, linking these to letters, and blending consonant and vowel sounds, have children make words with letter cards. Give children a small set of letter cards that match what you have taught. They can work at their desks or on the floor to rearrange the letter cards to make a series of words. You can mirror what you are asking them to do with larger letter cards in a pocket chart.

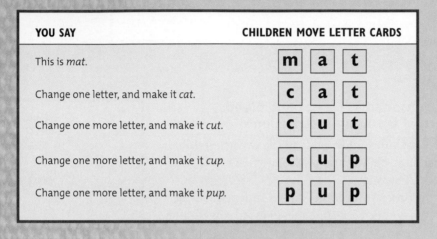

YOU SAY	CHILDREN MOVE LETTER CARDS
This is *mat*.	m a t
Change one letter, and make it *cat*.	c a t
Change one more letter, and make it *cut*.	c u t
Change one more letter, and make it *cup*.	c u p
Change one more letter, and make it *pup*.	p u p

Consonant Blends. As the name implies, a consonant blend is the combined sounds of two or three consonants. *Pl* in *play* and *spr* in *spring* are examples of blends. After short vowels and consonants are known, children's competence with words can be greatly expanded by helping them blend together the phonemes represented by consonant blends. The study of blends can be interwoven with the study of rimes by including blends with short-vowel phonograms. For example, the *at* family, such as *sat, mat, cat,* and so forth, can be expanded to include *flat, scat,* and *brat*.

Again, start with the known. Find the *at* rime in a word like *scat*. Then help children blend together the phonemes represented by the initial consonants. Your modeling of the process might sound like this:

> Here's how I figure out a word I don't know right off. First, I look at the word, and I find any parts I know. So, let's pretend I don't know the word *scat*. I know it starts with a /sss/ [said as you point to *s*], and then I put that together with the letter *c*, so I have /sskk/. I recognize *at* [said as you point to *at*]. So, I say /ssskăăăttt/ [said as you finger-point to each letter as it is pronounced]. *Scat*—that makes sense.

To help children become more aware of consonant blends in words, sorting picture cards is again useful. Words with different consonant blends can be easily contrasted and classified based on their sounds. For example, pictures with words that start with the phoneme /s/ may be contrasted with pictures starting with the consonant blends *sc, sk, sl, sm, sn, sp,* and *sw. S* blends are probably the easiest of the blends (because /s/ is easier to isolate and elongate) and make a good starting point. *R* blends (*br, cr, dr, fr, gr,* and *tr*) and *l* blends (*bl, cl, fl, gl,* and *sl*) are more difficult. As in all picture sorts, each column should be headed by a card with the letters being taught (*s* juxtaposed with *st*, for example). Having children write the words that were just sorted with the picture cards will provide practice and serve as a good diagnostic tool to see if children understand blends.

Picture card sorting fosters phonemic awareness. Children's books such as *Copy Me, Copycub* by Richard Edwards, *Snow!* by Christine Ford, and *Noisy Nora* by Rosemary Wells, each of which repeats words containing the same blends, can serve to introduce blends or give children practice with them.

The list of suggestions in In the Classroom 5.6 shows how word-study instruction on *r* blends such as *br, cr,* and *dr* might take place.

Word-Study Instruction on Consonant Blends

- Ask children to find *br, cr,* and *dr* words among their word-bank words. Write these words on the board. Or start by having students locate some of these words in a book.

- Illustrate the difference between a consonant-vowel-consonant (CVC) word and a consonant-consonant-vowel-consonant (CCVC) word by writing a word such as *brat* on the board and asking the children which letter you need to erase to make *bat.* Or ask which letter you need to add to *bake* to make *brake.* Or ask how to make *light* into *bright.*

- To further develop phonemic awareness of blends, have children sort picture cards by the consonant blend and its component phonemes. For example, they could write three headings on a sheet of paper (*b, r,* and *br*) like this:

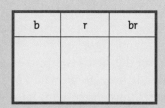

b	r	br

- Have children work with a buddy or in small groups to sort appropriate pictures, such as those depicting *bat, bed, bell, rat, room, ring, brick, bread, bridge, broom, bride,* and *brat* under the correct heading. The children might enjoy mixing up the picture cards and re-sorting them to see if they can get faster. Similarly, they can work with a buddy or in small groups to sort the pictures under the correct heading (*s* or *st* for *six, sun, saw, star, stick,* and *stairs,* for example). Or the following picture cards can be sorted under the headings *d* and *dr*: *dog, duck, dime, dress, drive, drum, drip, dream, dragon.* Or, instead of using small cards, you could do similar activities with a group of students or the whole class by using large picture cards, modeling how to place them in columns on a pocket chart.

- After the children are comfortable sorting picture cards by sounds, you can turn to connecting these sounds to letters. Have the children write *br, cr,* and *dr* on cards. As you call out a word, ask children to hold up the card with its first two letters. Or they could write down the first two letters in words you call out. Emphasize the first two sounds in words such as *drip, drive, drop, crab, crib, bring, drain,* and *brat.*

- Show children how to blend consonants, using initial blends and known short-vowel phonograms (*dr + ip = drip*). Do this with several words, pointing out that each word begins with a consonant blend (such as *br, cr,* or *dr*) and is followed by a rime.

Source: Book Buddies: Guidelines for Volunteer Tutors of Emergent and Early Readers by F. R. Johnson, M. Invernizzi, and C. Juel (1998). New York: Guilford Press.

- Now have the children write some words. Tell them that some will have the *r* and some won't. Try words such as *rag, drag, dip, drip, rat, brat, rib, crib, cab, crab, top, crop.*

- Include some sentence dictations with words that contain the onsets, rimes, and high-frequency words you have taught (*Drip, drip, went the drops of rain*). Say the sentence. Slowly pronounce each word in the sentence, and encourage children to write the words. Emphasize the sounds in the words.

- For extra blend practice, give children word parts on cards to blend together and make into words. You could also give them a card with a blend, such as *br*, and several rimes, such as *at, ag, im, ap,* and *it.* Have them work individually or in groups to make all of the words they can by combining the two parts.

Consonant Digraphs. Unlike blends, consonant digraphs behave like single consonants in that they represent one sound. Examples of consonant digraphs are *ph, ch, th, sh,* and *ng.* The study of initial consonant digraphs can be interwoven with rime study, much like that of consonant blends. The most common initial consonant digraphs are *sh, th, wh,* and *ch.* As previously described, picture sorting can be useful in drawing attention to these units. In particular, it is helpful to have children compare single initial consonants to corresponding digraphs by using picture cards. For example, you might compare pictures of *sun, sail,* and *sink* with pictures of *shoe, ship,* and *shirt.* Of course, you would head each category with the corresponding letters *s* or *sh.*

Some consonant digraphs occur at the end of the rime unit. The most common of the ending digraphs are *sh, ght, ng,* and *ck.* These ending digraphs will probably be learned as part of a high-frequency word family rather than in isolation. The *ight* word family, for example, includes *light, might, fight, sight, night, right,* and *slight.*

Learning the first few short-vowel rhyming families or the first few consonant blends may go slowly. Fortunately, most children will begin to need much less reinforcement with later families or phonics elements as they transfer their learning to new vowels and spelling patterns. However, because the first understanding of any new principle is always the hardest, you will want to provide plenty of opportunities for practice on these initial families. Once the basic alphabetic idea is understood, learning tends to progress at a much faster rate. In the Classroom 5.7 gives you an idea of what consonant digraphs your first-graders should practice.

What First-Graders Should Know

instructional routines

in the **Classroom** *5.7*

Practice with these spelling patterns will enable your first-grade students to read meaningful texts. According to the New Standards Primary Literacy Committee (1999), when leaving first grade, children should have solid knowledge of these elements of the letter-sound code:

Letter-Sound Correspondences

Most beginning consonants	*b-, c-, d-, f-, g-, h-, j-, k-, l-, m-, n-, p-, r-, s-, t-, v-, w-, y-, z-*
Ending consonants	*-b, -d, -g, -m, -n, -p, -t, -x, -ff, -ll, -ss, -zz*
Two-consonant beginning blends	*br-, cr-, dr-, fr-, gr-, pr-, tr-, sc-, sk-, sl-, sm-, sn-, st-, sw-*

Ending blends	-mp, -nd, -nk, -ng, -ft, -lt, -nt, -st, -lf
Digraphs	ch, sh, th
Short vowels	a, e, i, o, u
Long vowels with silent e at end of word	a+e, e+e, i+e, o+e, u+e (+ stands for the consonant)
Vowel digraphs	ai, ee, oa, ea
Word families ending in frequent rimes	e.g., -in, -at, -ent, -ill, -or, -un, -op, -ing
Common grammatical endings	-s, -ed, -ing (without dropping e)

A Note on Instructional Pacing. If a child is not catching on, just plowing ahead generally does not work. Taking the time to review and reteach until a word family is mastered is generally better than marching on with children not fully prepared to study the next word family. You are seeking to help your children understand the rather abstract and elusive nature of how letters and sounds relate. This understanding isn't going to emerge after just one introduction to a word family. To reach mastery, children need plenty of opportunities to see you model reading words, to engage in their own hands-on sorting of words by sound and spelling patterns, to practice writing words with target patterns, and to read text that contains words exemplifying the spelling patterns. Simply telling a child that *at* says /ăt/ doesn't mean she will get it. Teaching isn't just telling; it involves providing experiences that will foster true understanding.

Phase 3: Short Vowels, Long-Vowel Patterns, Multisyllabic Words, and Prefixes and Suffixes

The New Standards (1999) indicate that by the end of the school year second-graders should be able to read regularly spelled one- and two-syllable words and to recognize and figure out irregularly spelled words. They also should be able to recognize dipthongs, special vowel spellings, and common word endings. By the third grade, children's decoding skills should be automatic. They can then continue to learn about words—roots, inflections, suffixes, prefixes, homophones, and word families—as their vocabularies expand. To accomplish these learning goals, children need continued practice responding to short vowels, consonant blends, and digraphs. They need to compare short vowels in non-rhyming words, work with the sounds and spellings of long vowels in words, and work with multisyllabic words.

Short Vowels. In order to draw attention to the short-vowel sounds in non-rhyming words, we once again find picture cards useful. A good vowel to begin with is short *a*, contrasted with either short *o* or short *i*. Contrasting short *a* with short *e* and contrasting short *e* with short *i* are the tasks children find the most challenging and should be dealt with later. We list our suggested sequence for short-vowel contrasts here:

1. Short *a* contrasted with short *i*
2. Short *i* contrasted with short *u*
3. Short *i* contrasted with short *u* and short *a*
4. Short *e* contrasted with short *o*
5. Review of all short vowels

Reviewing letter sounds one on one provides an excellent opportunity for a teacher to note those letters and sounds the student still needs to master.

The general plan for teaching short vowels in nonrhyming words is to first sort pictures by short-vowel sounds and then sort known words. For example, a teacher can gather large picture cards of short *a* and short *i* words for use on a pocket chart. The teacher begins by putting a picture of a cat under a card with the letter *a* and says, "Cat, at, /ă/—this sound is a short *a*." The teacher repeats this with a picture of a pig, saying "Pig, ig, /ĭ/—this sound is a short *i*." The teacher continues modeling with several more pictures and then hands the children pictures to add to the pocket chart. After this group sorting activity, smaller picture cards are handed to the children to use in sorting short *a* and short *i* words with a buddy.

Now that children are concentrating on the phoneme level, another good activity is to have them use *letter cards* to make words. Blending can easily be emphasized as letter cards are put together to form words. Letter cards can be made into words on a pocket chart. As the teacher pronounces a letter, a volunteer can come up and add the letter card. For example, the teacher might say, "What letter does *big* start with?" A child would put up the letter *b*. Then the teacher might say, "What do we add to make it say /bĭĭĭ/?" The child would add the letter *i*. Finally, the teacher might say, "How do we make it say *big*?" The child would add the letter *g*. Mrs. Kee demonstrates instruction and practice on short vowels in In the Classroom 5.8.

Short-Vowel Work in the First Grade

It is December. Mrs. Kee is working with a group of early readers who are ready to focus on short vowels. They are going to practice spelling short *i* and short *a* words. The children sit around a large table. Mrs. Kee gives them each a set of letter cards and a holder for them. The holders for the letter cards are individual pocket charts. Mrs. Kee made the charts by folding a small piece of construction paper into 3 to 5 sections and stapling the bottom up to form pockets. She asks the children to spread out the letter cards in front of the holders on the table.

in the **Classroom** 5.8

Mrs. Kee asks the children to spell *big* with their letter cards. Once the word is spelled, she says, "Show me." The children hold up their individual pocket charts. Mrs. Kee has her own pocket chart, and she shares her spelling with the children. She prompts the children to correct any misspellings by repeating the word, elongating or emphasizing the misspelled phoneme.

Once all the children have spelled *big* on their pocket charts, Mrs. Kee calls out other words to spell. These words include *bag, bat, bit, fit, fat, flat, flash,* and *fish*. She lets the children work together, as needed. The hands-on work keeps their attention. As they manipulate the letters, they really see the influence of particular letters and letter combinations.

Word hunts are another useful activity for developing word knowledge, especially for the early reader who has outgrown the use of a word bank. Word hunts are literally hunts for words with specific spelling patterns. Children can hunt for words independently or in teams. They might, for example, look for short *a* and short *i* words in stories they have read or are reading. They might write lists together and meet as a class to share the lists, adding words to the word wall, other group charts, or records of favorite words in individual word-study notebooks.

Long-Vowel Patterns. Long vowels are deceptive. They are easier to perceive in words than short vowels are (compare *mad* and *made*), but they are represented by a considerable number of spelling patterns (for example, *made* and *maid*). Learning which particular long-vowel patterns are represented by which letters in which words involves a considerable amount of practice and memorization. In the Classroom 5.9 gives several examples of ways to contrast short- and long-vowel patterns. Through recognizing these differences, students come to hear and learn the sounds targeted.

Contrasting Short- and Long-Vowel Patterns

After you and your students have read and enjoyed a story or stories that contain examples of long and short *a* sounds, there are many ways to help them master short- and long-vowel patterns. Here are some examples:

- Write the words *mad* and *made* on the board. Invite a child to point to the letter in *mad* that says /ă/. Remind the children that the letter *a* often says /ă/.

  Have the children write *a* as a heading on a sheet of a paper. Now have them focus on the word *made*. Invite a child to point to the

letter in *made* that makes the long *a* sound. Ask the children to tell you the difference between *mad* and *made*. The letter *a* often has a long *a* sound when the letter *e* follows it.

Have the children write *a_e* as the second heading. Now call out various long and short *a* words, and have the children write them under the correct heading. The words might include *cape, cap, ape, make, map, skate,* and *date.*

- Have the children sort some short *a* and long *a* pictures. Have them work with a buddy or in small groups. The pictures might depict words such as *gate, cat, hat, sad, shade, game, cake, lake,* and *shake.* The children might enjoy mixing up the picture cards and re-sorting them to see if they can do it faster.

- Have the children make words with pocket charts and letter cards. For example, you can have children spell *can* and then:

  —add *e* to make *cane.*

  —make it say *cape, cap, man, mane, take, wake.*

  —continue replacing initial and final letters to make new words.

- Read another book with lots of short *a* and long *a* (CVCE) words. Have children go on a word hunt to find these words and record them on a word wall or on an individual word-study notebook page.

- Choose sentences to dictate, such as *The brave man had on a cape and a cap.* Dictate the entire sentence. Then slowly say each word in the sentence, and encourage children to write each word. Emphasize the sounds in the words.

- Encourage children to figure out "rules." Have the children work in small groups to sort word cards under the headings "short *a*" and "long *a*." They can help each other pronounce the words, decide if the word contains a short or a long *a*, and then try to come up with some spelling "rules." The sorting would look something like this:

Short *a*	Long *a*		
bat	rain	cake	tray
cat	train	plane	bay
flat	sail	plate	jay
van	pail	ape	clay
pan	jail	cape	play
trash	nail	grape	spray
cash	tail	vase	May
map	snail	gate	
rash	hail	skate	
mask	quail	blaze	
strap	pain	lake	
trap	brain	snake	
wrap	cane	hay	

Of course, there are other ways children could sort these words. You can encourage them to think of other ways and to verbalize why they sorted the words as they did. They might, for example, put all the words with the spelling pattern *ack* together, all the words with *ail,* all the words with *ate,* or even all the words that start with *s* blends.

Every time children sort words based on spelling patterns, they are attending to the fact that such patterns exist, and they are more likely to recall and use these spelling patterns to recognize and spell words (see Figure 5.12). Two helpful sources for word family lists are *Words Their Way* (2004) by Donald Bear and his colleagues and *Phonics Patterns: Onset and Rime Word Lists* (1998) by Edward Fry.

COMMON SPELLING PATTERNS FOR LONG VOWELS		OTHER VOWEL PATTERNS	
A Ate	a, a_e, ai, ay, ey, ei, eigh	Oi Oil	oi, oy
E Eat	e, y, e_e, ee, ea, ei, ie	Ou Ouch	ou, ow
I Ice	i, y, i_e, ie, igh	Ar Far	ar
O Oat	o, o_e, oa, ow, oe, ough	Er Her	er, ir, ur
U Use	u, u_e, ough	Ur Fur	ur

FIGURE 5.12

Common Spelling Patterns for Long Vowels and Other Vowel Patterns

Multisyllabic Words. As we discussed earlier in this chapter, the basic unit in speech is the syllable. All words have either one syllable or more than one syllable. As students move into more advanced reading with the demands of multisyllabic words, we want to help them realize that multisyllabic words are simply strings of syllables that contain the spelling patterns they already know. They need to examine long words to find familiar "chunks." As we have discussed, these chunks can be onsets, rimes, affixes, and root words.

Children tend to be intimidated by long words. You need to model how to approach them—how to recognize the chunks within them that children already know. Put words on the board, and think aloud as you break them into chunks. Then, after ample modeling on your part, invite children to point out the onsets, rimes, morphemes, and even vowel patterns or consonant digraphs that they spot in words. Ms. Kenney uses this technique with her second-graders in In the Classroom 5.10.

Multisyllabic Words

Because of her constant modeling of how to identify multisyllabic words, Ms. Kenney's second-grade children enjoy being word detectives. Each day, Ms. Kenney writes a multisyllabic word on the board, talks about any clues to its identity that she can find, and lists these clues on the board. Then she writes another multisyllabic word on the board and asks the children to find clues to its identity. Here are some of the words she and the children have worked with and some of the observations of different children that have helped the class figure out the words:

in the Classroom 5.10

- *chipmunk*
  Karl noticed the common rime *ip.*
  Marty said she got *unk* because she knew the word *skunk.*
  Tasha volunteered the pronunciation of the consonant digraph *ch.*

- *shameful*
  Katy said she instantly saw the affix *-ful,* meaning "full of."
  Ming said he knew the *ame* rime by heart.
  Tasha volunteered the pronunciation of the consonant digraph *sh.*

- *transit*
  Lily said she knew how to chunk it because she saw the familiar *an* and *it* units.
  Kyle added that another clue was that the letter combination *ns* doesn't start a syllable.
  Mike volunteered the pronunciation of the consonant blend *tr.*

Prefixes and Suffixes. Many multisyllabic words contain prefixes and suffixes, and teaching students to be on the lookout for these elements can be a real aid to their successfully decoding them. We have already discussed prefixes and suffixes on pages 130–131 and listed possible prefixes and suffixes to teach in Figures 5.3, 5.4, and 5.5. The routine described in In the Classroom 5.11 is a simple and straightforward way to teach them. One caution here: There are many more prefixes and suffixes than you need to or *should* teach. Choose from among the many prefixes and suffixes available only those that are fairly frequent in the material your students read.

instructional routines

in the **Classroom** **5.11**

Teaching Prefixes and Suffixes

1. Write two familiar words containing the prefix or suffix you want to teach on the board, and have students define the words. Suppose you wanted to teach the prefix *un-*. Most students know what *unhappy* and *unkind* mean, so these would be appropriate words to use as part of your instruction.

2. Underline the word part, and note its spelling. Then, if the word part is a prefix with a concrete meaning, give students the meaning or have them give its meaning if you think someone knows it. (If the word part is a suffix, it is usually best not to define it, as the abstract definitions of suffixes are often confusing.) *Un-*, of course, means "not."

3. On the board write a word that contains the word part but that students probably don't know. With *un-*, you might use the word *unreal*. Ask students to use their knowledge of *un-* and what remains when the prefix is removed (in this case, *real*) to figure out the pronunciation and meaning of the new word: *Un-* means "not," and *real* means "real." So *unreal* means "not real." (If the word part is a suffix, they will only need to figure out the pronunciation of the new word.)

4. Tell students that they are likely to see the word part fairly frequently, and that much of the time, if they lop it off the word, they'll recognize what's left (or be able to decode it) and then, if they reattach the word part, they will probably be able to pronounce the complete word and understand its meaning.

We hope that the ideas we have presented for word-study instruction will give you a good foundation on which to begin planning instruction for your emergent readers. Remember: Base any word-study instruction you design on the five principles we discussed on pages 135–137. Use your imagination, summon up your creativity, and have fun. Your enthusiasm will be contagious.

Reflect *and* Apply

5. As you have undoubtedly noticed, much word-study instruction begins with sorting picture cards for sounds and follows that activity with sorting word cards based on their spelling patterns. Explain the rationale for this basic two-step process. (Hint: Think phonemic awareness!)

6. Discuss how word cards might be sorted under the three headings *frog, toad, porch*. Explain what children might learn by

sorting the following words under these three vowel-pattern categories: *home, flock, morning, broke, storm, hope, boat, know, on, pond, rock, corn, wore, acorn, forlorn, lost, hot, wrote, note, snow, ghost, most, post, old, coast, told, gold, cold, hold, nose, rose, cove, croak, soaking, road, coach, boat, toast, float, vote, hose, smoke, block, sock, roast, stove, torch, short, spot, sport, worn, store, fork, thorn, fort, snoring, blowing, growing, snowing, blown, Joan, foam, grove, note, moaning.* If any of the words don't fit under the headers, consider adding an "oddball" category.

7. Now, consider how these same words could be sorted to reveal spelling patterns, and jot down the words you would put in several of the groupings you identify.

8. In In the Classroom 5.2 on page 145, we described how Ms. Campbell fostered beginning readers' proficiency with onsets. Get together with a classmate. Then look back at the five principles of word-study instruction listed on pages 135–136 and discuss how well her instruction matched those principles.

About Reading a Lot

In kindergarten through third grade, it is especially important for word recognition to become both accurate and fairly quick. It is critical that children read lots of text to support that process. Leveled books, books that tend to be somewhat short and can be re-read several times, are useful in the classroom to build students' reading skill.

Leveled books include books by known children's authors as well as books created specifically for reading series. These books provide practice reading words in connected text, words that contain both the letter-sound and spelling patterns children are learning, as well as practice on high-frequency words. The reading series used in many school classrooms include leveled books as part of the material. A classroom teacher needs hundreds of these books in order to be able to match a child to appropriate reading materials. One popular schema for leveled books is that developed by reading educators Irene Fountas and Gay Su Pinnell (1999). Their book contains a huge listing of leveled books (Levels A through O) that correspond to grade levels kindergarten through third grade.

The New Standards (1999) identify Level B books as appropriate for end of kindergarten, Level I books as a benchmark for the end of first grade, Level L books for the end of second grade, and Level O books for the end of third grade. Let's take a minute to look at the type of reading we expect in grades 1 through 3.

By the end of first grade, we expect children to correctly read most of the words in a Level I text like Robin Bloksberg's *The Hole in Harry's Pocket*. This text includes sentences like the following:

Harry liked to walk to the store. He liked to hop on the curb. He liked to look in all the windows and count cracks in the sidewalk.

Harry got the milk. But when he looked for his money, it was gone! What could he do?

By the end of second grade, we expect children to correctly read most of the words in a Level L text like the popular Cam Jansen mystery series by David A. Adler (text from *Cam Jansen and the Mystery of the Stolen Diamonds*):

> Eric opened his eyes. "It's no use," he said, "I'll never have a memory like yours."
> "You have to keep practicing," Cam told him. "Now try me."
> Cam looked straight ahead. She said, "Click," and then closed her eyes. Cam always said, "Click" when she wanted to remember something. She said it was the sound her mental camera made when it took a picture.

By the end of third grade, we expect children to correctly read most of the words in a Level O text like the popular Ramona series by Beverly Cleary (text from *Ramona Quimby, Age 8*):

> Ramona had reached the age of demanding accuracy from everyone, even herself. All summer, whenever a grown-up asked what grade she was in, she felt as if she were fibbing when she answered, "third," because she had not actually started third grade. Still, she could not say she was in second grade, since she had finished that grade last June. Grown-ups did not understand that summers were free from grades.

Book levels are not perfect, of course. But the above discussion gives a feel for what the benchmarks in word recognition would be at the end of grades 1 through 3. You can see that an end-of-first-grade child should be correctly reading the *Harry* text, which already contains multisyllabic words. Consider the first-grade child who enters the classroom not yet familiar with all the alphabet letters, and you can see the task ahead for the first-grade teacher. You can see why it is important that kindergarten teachers strive to make sure children arrive in first grade with not only alphabet knowledge but also the ability to apply the alphabetic principle to reading and writing very simple words.

In order to develop skilled young readers, teachers need to have a large selection of books available to be read. These books should be leveled by difficulty, linked to word-study instruction, and read and re-read until the child can accurately read at appropriate rates. Plastic tubs full of leveled books are a staple in most K–3 classrooms. The movement is from predictable texts in kindergarten to chapter books by the end of second grade.

Clearly, the first time a book is read, the teacher provides the scaffolding to help children read it. In kindergarten and early first grade, this may include highlighting some of the words, introducing key concepts, and having the children choral read the book before it is read alone or with a buddy. As children move into longer texts, re-readings are not likely to be appropriate. Rather than read *Ramona Quimby, Age 8* more than once, the child might read the whole series. The key in either case, however, is to have children read a lot in books that are fairly easy. That means selecting books that a particular child can read fluently.

English Learners

Of course, English-language learners' reading proficiency will differ hugely depending on their general proficiency in English. What is important in building their fluency is that they do a lot of reading in books they are comfortable with and can read relatively easily.

CW5.3 links to S. J. Samuels's discussion of fluency, including activities that will help you become more knowledgeable about fluency and ways to promote it in your students. (Also see the in-depth discussion of fluency presented in Chapter 6.)

Many children readily succeed at word study and become accomplished readers quite quickly. Others struggle and will need additional instruction and encouragement. The task that typically gives children the most problems in learning to read words is perceiving them as sequences of sounds—that is, acquiring phonemic awareness. To determine how readily children can do this, carefully observe them to see whether or not they can sort pictures based on onsets (*s* versus *b* versus *m* pictures), rimes (*at* versus *ig* versus *an*), and more difficult medial vowels (short *i* versus short *a*). To help children better perceive onsets and rimes, you can read nursery rhymes and stories that employ alliteration, such as *Happy Hippopotami* by Bill Martin, Jr., and *Trashy Town* by Andrea Zimmerman and David Clemesha. You can pronounce words to emphasize, elongate, and segment them into their component sounds for children. And you can help them link speech segments to writing by modeling how to do this and providing abundant writing and reading experiences for them.

You can also get a good understanding of how children are perceiving sound sequences in words, as well as their ability to link those sounds to letters, by examining their spelling. A child who consistently and accurately uses initial (or other) consonants in her writing—such as spelling *rain* as *r* or *dog* as *dg*—signals a readiness to learn specific word families or rimes. A child who spells *rain* as *b* and *dog* as *x* may need instruction about onsets. A child who spells *rain* as *rane* might benefit from sorting words with *ain, ane,* and other long *a* patterns.

Additionally, you can determine your students' needs by looking at what they do when they don't instantly recognize a word in print. First, if children are stumbling over many words, the text is probably too difficult. Children need to be able to read most of the words (say, 98 percent) of the text they work with. At this recognition rate, they can both read for meaning and enjoy reading. Their approach to the words they can't identify provides information for planning instruction. Do they guess randomly or focus on the pictures to the exclusion of the print? Do they look at initial letters? Do they look for patterns they recognize within words? Our job as teachers is to look at what our students know and plan appropriate activities to expand their word knowledge.

For children who are really struggling in first grade, there are a number of special programs available. The best known is a one-to-one tutoring program titled Reading Recovery. This program was originally developed in New Zealand by Marie Clay (1979, 1992) and adapted for use in the United States by Gay Su Pinnell (Pinnell, Fried, & Eustice, 1990). Although it has sometimes been criticized (Barnes, 1996/1997; Hiebert, 1994), if you have struggling first-graders, you may want to look at it. A somewhat similar program, but less expensive because it uses small groups rather than individualized instruction, is titled Early Intervention Reading. This program was developed and successfully implemented by Barbara Taylor and her colleagues (Taylor, Short, Frye, & Shearer, 1992). Another study (Invernizzi, Juel, & Rosemary, 1996/1997) explores the use of a tutoring program in which community volunteers tutor first- and second-graders who need help in beginning reading skills.

If you find yourself teaching students beyond the first-grade level who still need to develop basic word-study skills, you might want to consider the following programs. Elfrieda Hiebert (1996) has developed a program for third-grade children, and Taylor and her colleagues a program for second- and fourth-grade children (Taylor, Hanson, Justice-Swanson, & Watts, 1997). Lynn and Douglas Fuchs (2000) have developed and validated an ingenious peer tutoring program for improving grade 2–5 students' fluency and comprehension. Hiebert and Taylor's *Getting Reading Right from the Start* (1994) describes a number of approaches designed to help early readers who are struggling, and Patricia Cunningham and Richard Allington's *Classrooms That Work: They Can All Learn to Read and Write* (1999) is filled with practical ideas that help all students become good readers. Johnson, Invernizzi, and Juel's *Book Buddies: Guidelines for Volunteer Tutors of Emergent and Early Readers* (1998) provides very explicit instruction for word study with struggling readers.

Although most children do not have many reading skills when they enter school, you must recognize that some children do. As much as possible, you want to provide these children with books that will challenge them and expand their knowledge. In other words, you will need a considerable range of reading levels in the books you stock in your classrooms. In a typical first- or second-grade classroom, you might need to stock some reading materials that extend to the upper-grade levels.

You also need to plan many activities to which all children can respond—regardless of their current reading level. In writing words, for example, some children may successfully spell only the features that you have taught (and, after all, you can hold children accountable only for that), yet others may be able to go well beyond this and represent fuller spellings. Both groups, however, are being successful and should receive your praise, encouragement, and the next level of instruction to expand their knowledge.

Concluding Remarks

This chapter has emphasized the importance of word recognition and focused on how to help children learn to read and write words. We began by discussing why it is so important for children to learn to recognize words early on. Then we discussed the structure of spoken and written words. In the rest of the chapter, we described specific instructional techniques for teaching the emergent and early reader.

The topics in this chapter are particularly important to understand thoroughly because without the ability to read words, children will have difficulty with nearly everything else at school. Our goal is the development of the high level of literacy necessary in the 21st century. Reading, writing, being read to, discussing what is read, and thinking about what is read are all crucial to attaining present-day literacy; word study must never replace these activities. However, without competence in word recognition, attaining present-day literacy is extremely unlikely.

Extending Learning

1. Observe a first-grade classroom or, better yet, several first-grade classrooms at different times during the year. What kind of word-study instruction do you see? What kinds of texts are the children reading? How are the children progressing?

2. Meet individually with several kindergarten and first-grade children, and have them spell some words for you. Here are some possibilities: *cat, run, jump, name, goat, van, arm, stripe, little, coat, rope, back, smash,* and *light*. What can you tell from the child's spelling about what he or she knows about words? What might you plan for word-study instruction to help the child grow?

3. Meet individually with several kindergarten or first-grade children, and ask if they have a book they would like to read to you. Notice what happens as each child reads. Does the child look at the words? What happens when the child forgets a word? What insights do you have about what the children know about words? What might you do to build on their current knowledge?

For a look at word recognition in a contemporary classroom, go to Allyn & Bacon's MyLabSchool.com. In MLS Courses, click on Reading Methods, and go to MSL Video Lab. There you will find video clips about Word Recognition and Phonics in Module 2.

Children's Literature

Adler, D. (Many titles in Cam Jansen series by this author). New York: Puffin Books. This is a staple for second grade.

Benjamin, M. (1996). *Quack!* Needham Heights, MA: Pearson. This is a simple text about three little ducks. It is one of many leveled readers in the Ready-to-Read series. 8 pages.

Bloksberg, R. (1995). *The Hole in Harry's Pocket*. Houghton Mifflin's Guided Reading collection, ed. by R. Pikulski et al. New York: Houghton Mifflin. This reading series has leveled books.

Cameron, A. (1994). *The Cat Sat on the Mat*. Boston: Houghton Mifflin. Simple vocabulary is taught by following the activities of a cat. 32 pages.

Cleary, B. (Many titles in the Ramona series by this author). New York: Avon Books. This is a staple for third grade.

Edwards, R. (1999). *Copy Me, Copycub*. New York: HarperCollins. Little cub learns precious lessons about life by copying his mother, in this story full of repetitive words and phrases and consonant blends such as *spl, sw,* and *scr*. Unpaged.

Ford, C. (1999). *Snow!* New York: HarperCollins. This poetic text about the joys of winter play contains plentiful examples of consonant blends, digraphs, and rimes. 24 pages.

Grejniec, M. (1992). *What Do You Like?* New York: North-South Books. Children discover they can like the same things and still be different. 32 pages.

Hutchins, P. (1968). *Rosie's Walk*. New York: Macmillan. A hen unwittingly leads a fox into one disaster after another before arriving safely home from her walk. 32 pages.

Koch, M. (1991). *Hoot Howl Hiss*. New York: Green Willow. Different animal sounds emerge from different places. 24 pages.

Martin, B., Jr. (1992). *Happy Hippopotami*. San Diego: Harcourt Brace. In a lively rhyming story about a rollicking day at the seashore (with alliteration galore), hippos "board a beach-bound bus" and enjoy "swimming, sunning, and snacking." 32 pages.

Martin, B., Jr., & Carle, E. (1996). *Brown Bear, Brown Bear: What Do You See?* New York: Henry Holt & Company. A reissued version of this popular classic has different animals depicted in very predictable sentence structure. 24 pages.

Myers, C. (1999). *Black Cat*. New York: Scholastic. This story told in verse about the travels of an urban cat captures the rhythms of the city and answers the refrain "Black cat, black cat, we want to know / where's your home, where do you go?" 40 pages.

Robinson, F. (1996). *Who Has a Tail?* Needham Heights, MA: Pearson. This predictable text repeats *ay, ai,* and *a* consonant *e* patterns. It is one of many leveled readers in the Ready Readers series. 16 pages.

Wells, R. (1997). *Noisy Nora*. New York: Dial. Feeling neglected, Nora makes more and more noise to attract her parents' attention. 32 pages.

Zimmerman, A., & Clemesha, D. (1999). *Trashy Town*. New York: HarperCollins. This delightful tale of a trash man's job provides plentiful opportunities for pointing out alliteratives, onsets, and rimes. 28 pages.

Classroom Portrait

A Day in the Life of Jenna LeBlanc and Her First-Grade Students

Jenna LeBlanc is a first-year teacher in a first-grade class at Edgebrook Elementary School on the outskirts of Washington, DC. Her student teaching had been with older children, so she was not quite prepared for the squirmy nature of six- and seven-year-olds! Now, in mid-October, however, she believes she would never want to teach another grade. She says, "I have really seen these children emerge as readers and writers. I keep a portfolio on each child, and included in it are samples of their writing since the beginning of the school year. It's exciting to look back at these and see the progress—and to think I had something to do with it."

Jenna teaches 20 children of varied backgrounds and abilities. Most of her students come from working-class families that represent a wide range of cultures. Several of her students have parents who recently immigrated to the United States. Among her students, there are eight different languages spoken at home. None of her students have problems communicating in English. But there is a considerable range in their knowledge of English vocabulary.

Jenna tells us that, of her 20 students, three were already reading first-grade-level texts when they entered her classroom. Most of the others were not able to read conventionally and possessed quite a range of knowledge about print. Some children, for example, knew all the alphabet and some initial consonant sounds, while others had difficulty naming more than a handful of letters. All were eager to learn.

Jenna's school district uses a basal reading series that includes an anthology of children's literature and informational texts. Many of the selections are written by well-known children's authors and are grouped by theme. Within a particular theme, such as The World We Share with Animals, there might be a range of genres including predictable texts, narratives, poems, and informational texts. Every child has a copy of the anthology. The basal series also has about 200 "leveled books," which we described in Chapter 5. These leveled books range from 6 to 25 pages each. Each leveled book is a complete text. The 200 leveled books span a continuum of reading difficulty, from books with very predictable texts to ones with well-developed stories. As we discussed, these leveled books are leveled readers. That is, the vocabulary in the little books is "controlled." Leveled books provide practice in reading words with the phonics features under study. Jenna has six copies of each of the 200 leveled books.

In one corner of Jenna's classroom is the library. This inviting place contains an old sofa, pillows, a rug, a few plants, and, most of all, numerous books, magazines, and other reading materials. Many books are displayed with their covers showing, as the children are drawn to those rather than to ones with only their spines showing. Jenna frequently displays books that relate to the theme that is the focus in the basal reading anthology. In choosing books, she tries to include a wide range of reading levels to match the wide range of reading experiences among her students.

"Children do best when they feel secure," Jenna reports. "That's why routines and a daily schedule that become familiar to the children are very important." Jenna's morning schedule looks like this:

In addition to a vast selection of interesting reading materials, a classroom library should provide comfortable, inviting places to read.

8:30–8:50	Book check-in, calendar, morning message
8:50–9:30	Buddy reading/free reading
9:30–10:15	Theme-related whole-class activity
10:15–11:30	Centers: Reading, writing, and word study
11:30–11:45	Whole-class sharing of center activities
11:45	Lunch

Let's join Jenna for her morning reading/language arts period. This is a day when buddy reading occurs. Twice a week, Jenna's students participate in a schoolwide buddy reading program. Every child in the school is paired with a buddy. The buddy may be a younger or older child at the school, a community volunteer, or a teacher.

8:30—Book Check-In, Calendar, Morning Message

As children enter the classroom, they pass a bulletin board that has a chart on it with each of their names printed on an individual library pocket. Each book in the class library has a check-out pocket and a card in it with the name of the book on it. When the children leave at the end of the school day, they check out one or two books by putting the

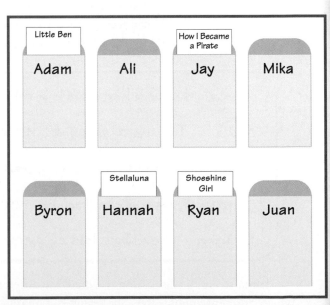

library card from the back of the book into the pocket with their name on it on the bulletin board. When they first arrive the next morning, they remove the card from the bulletin board library pocket, place it back into the book they took home, and return the book to the class library.

After checking in their books and putting their personal items in their cubbies, the children gather on a rug in front of the chalkboard and large calendar. Jenna first goes over the calendar and has them locate the date and day. The amount of time spent on this activity varies from day to day. They talk about the season, the weather, birthdays, and other special events.

Every day, Jenna prints a morning news message on the chalkboard. Jenna asks for volunteers who would like to tell what special things are happening at home, in their lives, or in the world. She writes what is said on the chalkboard under the heading *Morning News*. If there is time, she then has children share information about the books they checked out and read at home.

8:50—Buddy Reading and Free Reading

At 8:50, five community volunteers, the speech teacher, and the third-grade children appear at the door. Jenna watches the three children in her room who are the kindergarten buddies walk down the hall to that classroom. Buddy reading and tutoring begin.

Jenna loves this time. She likes to walk around and see how grown-up both the first-grade and the third-grade children appear when they work with their buddies. When needed, she is there to pitch in and help. She also enjoys the time when a buddy is absent and she has a chance to interact one on one with a student.

9:30—Theme-Related Whole-Class Activity

Jenna likes to start her theme-related work with a whole-class activity that develops the children's knowledge about the theme. The theme for the next few weeks is "animals who share the world with us." This is the first day of this theme unit. In prior conversations with us, she emphasized that she likes "to start with what children know." We see that is the case, as Jenna begins the session today by engaging the children in a discussion about animals they have seen. She makes a language chart on a large sheet of butcher paper. After a child says something, she records the child's name next to what he says. As she records their words, she often makes comments about them—such as why she used a capital letter. Here's part of the language chart:

> Jamal   I saw a horse with a policeman on it in DC!
>
> Malt   I have a gerbil at home.
>
> Kara   My dog Nick is black and white.
>
> Tyron   I saw a black-and-white zebra at the zoo.
>
> Cynara   There are lots of deer in the woods and I saw some.

Jenna steers the discussion to where the different animals were seen—to the environments in which different animals live. She brings out a large piece of butcher paper on which the class will start a wall chart. The paper is divided into sections, with the several headings printed across the top and room to the right to add additional ones, as shown below:

In the Water	On a Farm	In the Woods	In Our Homes	In the Jungle			
fish	horses	deer	dogs	monkeys			
	cows	raccoons	cats	giraffe			
		wolf					
		snake					
		owl					

Jenna starts by asking the children where the animals they have mentioned live, and she records their responses under the appropriate categories. There is some discussion about where zebras might live if they weren't in a zoo and where horses normally would be found.

Next, Jenna brings out a big book copy of *Hoot Howl Hiss* by Michelle Koch. She points to the illustrations on the cover. "Michelle Koch is not only the author, she is also the illustrator of the book," she tells the children. "The watercolor illustrations of animals are painted a lot like you paint in our class! Can you name any of the animals you see on the cover and tell where you might find them?" Jenna points to the title words as she asks which animal says *hoot*, which one *howls*, and which one goes *hiss*. They add the words *wolf, snake,* and *owl* to the In the Woods column on the wall chart. Jenna particularly emphasizes the sounds in the word *snake* as she prints the word on the chart. Jenna tells the children that when they are in the writing center, they will draw some of these animals, write about them, and paste their creations on the wall chart.

Jenna asks the children to think about where each animal mentioned in the book lives as she begins to read, "Deep in the woods, owls . . . hoot . . . ." She pauses before *hoot*, and several children correctly anticipate it. *Hoot Howl Hiss* is a short book with a very predictable structure. The illustrations help the children identify the animal words. When she finishes reading the book, Jenna asks the children about the sounds various animals make, as well as where they live.

10:15—Centers: Reading, Writing, and Word Study

There are three centers in Jenna's classroom: a reading center, a writing center, and a word-study center. Jenna generally works in direct instruction with children in the word-study center. She groups children who need similar word-level instruction there. She randomly divides the rest of her class into groups that rotate through the reading and writing centers. Most days, the children rotate through all three centers. If children finish a center activity before it is time for the next rotation, they are free to return to their desks and read from their anthologies, little books, or books from the library.

The *reading center* is the classroom library. In that center, the children can either read to a buddy or read independently. Sometimes they have assignments; sometimes they do free reading. During the animal unit, they will find lots of books about animals prominently displayed on the low table in the reading center.

Children enjoy collaborating in the writing center.

In the *writing center,* the children are going to draw and write. They can draw a picture of an animal, write its name, and then paste their paper onto the wall chart. Before they paste it, they need to discuss with one other child which environment the animal lives in and whether its name is correctly spelled. The children are encouraged to check the spellings and animal habitats by looking at books in the library center. Jenna tells us that she encourages the children to use invented spelling in free writing, but when the time comes to make the writing public, she wants the words correctly spelled. She says that she doesn't want the children to re-read incorrect spellings on a permanent basis—and she intends to make use of the wall chart throughout the unit.

Each group that comes to the *word-study center* will participate in different phonics instruction. The particular focus of the phonics instruction depends on the needs of students. One group of children is working on initial consonants, another on the consonant digraphs *ch* and *wh,* and a third group on short vowels. The basic format for each group, however, is the same. Jenna begins each group by having the children chorally read *Hoot Howl Hiss.* The focus then shifts to a word or two in that story that contains the phonics feature that is under study. The consonant digraph group, for example, will focus on the words *chirp* and *whistle.*

After locating words with the phonic features in *Hoot Howl Hiss,* Jenna extends the phonics instruction to other words. This extension often involves three activities:

- *sorting* picture or word cards (as described in Chapter 5)
- *reading* a leveled book that contains several words with the phonics features
- *writing* a dictated sentence with words that contain the target spelling pattern

Sorting. To develop phonemic awareness of initial consonant sounds, Jenna has the children do a group picture sort on a pocket chart. She calls out the name of a picture, and they help her place it under one of the word card headings *howl, lion,* and *quack.* She holds up a drawing of a hen and says "Hen, ho*wl*—hen, lion—hen, quack." The children agree that the hen picture belongs under *howl.* Then she takes out a drawing of a leg and says, "Hen, leg—lion, leg—quack, leg." The group continues in this manner with pictures of a queen, quilt, horse, and hat and pictures representing other words from *Hoot Howl Hiss.*

Reading. To provide reading practice with the newly introduced initial consonant combination *qu,* Jenna uses a leveled book entitled *Quack!* by Matthew Benjamin (1996). She gives each child a copy. "Can you read the word on the cover?" she asks. "The ducks are a good clue!" She has the children point to the letters that say /kw/ in *quack.* She tells the children that *Quack!* is about a mother duck and her three ducklings. Jenna reads the story as the children follow along, finger-pointing to the words as she says them. Then they all read it aloud together. After this re-reading, Jenna asks them to go through the book on a word hunt. They are to find all the words that start with *qu* and read them to the child sitting next to them.

There are lots of shouts of "Quack!" and "Quick!" and "Quiet!" as they locate these words in the story.

Writing. To end this word-study session, Jenna reads simple sentences and has the children write them. She will later examine what each child has written to see which children might need some extra help. She is particularly interested in their spelling of the initial consonants. She hands out a piece of lined paper and tells them to write as best they can *Ducks quack. Lions roar. I hoot.* Here's what a few children wrote:

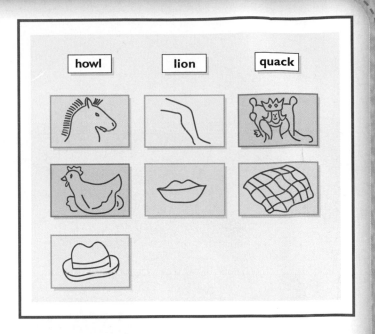

Wu	Dks quak. Lins r. I ht.
Kara	Duks quak. Lions rar. I hut.
Dustin	DS QUK LN RR I HT
Jamal	Duks quack. Lions ror. I hoot.

11:30—Whole-Class Sharing of Center Activities

The class gathers back on the rug in front of the calendar. Children bring with them any books they would like to share. Jenna begins by asking them to quack like a duck. Then she turns to the In the Water portion of the wall chart and asks if anyone put a duck up there. Several hands go up, and she has each child go over and point to his or her duck. She then asks for other children who had animals that live in the water to come up and identify their picture. There's a sea turtle and a whale among the group. Jenna does the same thing for the other categories.

With only a few minutes remaining until lunch, not everyone who has a book to share gets a chance to do so. But there's always tomorrow, and Jenna will make sure that any student who didn't get a turn today will get one the next day. Additionally, Jenna looks forward to the afternoon, when she and her students will be able to put their budding literacy skills to use in other curricular areas—science, math, social studies, art, and music.

Jenna LeBlanc always provides time for children to share their favorite books with the class.

Fluency

CLASSROOM VIGNETTE

*H*is name was Jimmy Parker, and one of us went through eight years of grade school with him. It was a small school with only one classroom for each grade level, and, therefore, the same students stayed together over the years and got to know each other really well. Jimmy had blond hair, blue eyes, and a lot of freckles. He was a popular boy and did well on the playground, originally with games like dodge ball and tetherball, and later with football and basketball. But he was not good at reading. In fact, he was terrible at it. Round robin reading was an almost daily reading activity in the school, and day after day, year after year, Jimmy would stand up and stumble with excruciating slowness through a passage in the basal reader. It was a terrible experience for Jimmy, for all of us listening, and probably for the teachers too. But concepts like automaticity, fluency, and using appropriate texts were unknown to our teachers, and so Jimmy's pain and embarrassment continued year after year.

Jimmy had not learned to read well by the time we finished grade school, and it is unlikely that he ever became a fluent reader. It is even more unlikely that he became an avid reader, a person who made reading a significant and major part of his life. It is too late to change the experiences Jimmy had, but appropriate attention to fluency can change the reading experience for many other children.

Fluency and Its Importance

Fluency is the ability to read rapidly, smoothly, without many errors, and with appropriate expression. Fluency is often thought of as an oral phenomenon, and we assess fluency by asking students to read orally. But there is also such a thing as silent reading fluency (Pikulski & Chard, 2005). When reading silently, a fluent reader reads rapidly, without stumbling over words, and with good comprehension. You cannot, of course, hear fluent silent reading, but you can recognize it because the child reads relatively rapidly, without seeming to struggle, and with good understanding of what he has read. In assisting readers to become fully competent, our goal is for them to become fluent in both oral and silent reading.

As Melanie Kuhn and Stephen Stahl (2003) explain, when considering fluency and its importance, it is useful to think in terms of children progressing through several stages of reading development, a process described by Jeanne Chall (1996). The first stage, the emergent literacy stage, occurs before formal reading instruction begins and is a period in which children begin to understand some very basic facts about reading: that print represents spoken language, that we read from left to right and from top to bottom, that words are separated by white space, that words are made up of somewhat separable sounds, and the like. Chapter 4 deals with emergent literacy. In the second stage, children begin formal reading instruction, with the emphasis being on decoding. Chapter 5 deals with this stage. In the third stage, children move from concentrating on decoding and slowly processing texts word by word to becoming automatic in their reading and thereby reading smoothly, accurately, and with expression. This third stage is discussed in this chapter. Many children enter this stage of fluency building in the early primary grades and continue to build fluency over time. It is important that their fluency increase steadily because, in the third and fourth grade, they are expected to read and learn from longer and increasingly difficult text. Other children, however, do not enter the fluency stage and begin building their fluency in the early primary grades, and these children need special help in becoming fluent readers.

In Chapter 1, when we discussed why fluency is so important, we talked about the limited processing capacity of our brains and the consequent importance of learning to automatically process words. Here we review and extend that explanation. As David LaBerge and Jay Samuels (1974) noted in their pioneering work on automaticity, the mind's capacity to process information is limited. Basically, we can attend to only one thing at a time. Reading, however, demands that we attend to at least two things. On the one hand, we need to decode the individual words; on the other hand, we need to engage in a number of cognitive processes in order to comprehend what we are reading. If too much of our limited processing capacity is taken up with decoding the individual words, we are left with no resources to comprehend what we are reading. The solution to this problem is for readers to become automatic in processing words. As defined by LaBerge and Samuels, an automatic activity is one that we can perform without conscious attention. If children can decode most of the words they encounter automatically, they will have the mental resources to comprehend what they are reading.

As LaBerge and Samuels (1974) also explain, the road to automaticity is quite straightforward. We become automatic at an activity by doing it repeatedly in non-taxing conditions. One of the best examples of an activity at which many of you reading this have attained an appropriate level of automaticity is that of driving a stick-shift car. Driving a stick-shift car requires that you push in the clutch, let up on the accelerator, shift gears, let out the clutch, and press on the accelerator—all in a very brief period of time. Moreover, it requires that you do this while simultaneously watching the traffic, looking for brake lights, looking for debris on the road, and being alert to the possibility that someone will cut in front of you or engage in some other unpredictable behavior. If you are not automatic at the various steps involved in shifting, you will not have the mental capacity to monitor the traffic and respond to what might literally be a life-or-death situation. And how do you get to be automatic at driving a stick-shift car? You do so by repeatedly practicing driving and shifting in situations in which you don't have to worry a lot about traffic—perhaps in a parking lot or on side streets. You do it again and again, and eventually it becomes second nature, requiring almost none of your mental resources.

The road to becoming automatic and fluent in reading is similar. You become automatic and fluent in reading by doing a lot of reading in non-taxing situations. Fortunately, current research and theory allow us to make much more specific recommendations. For a number of years, fluency was a largely neglected area of reading instruction. However, that changed when the National Reading Panel (National Institute of Child Health and Human Development, 2000) identified fluency as one of the five cornerstones of reading instruction. It changed even more when fluency became one of the five components of Reading First, the federal program that has strongly influenced primary-grade reading instruction. Today, fluency is a strongly recommended part of a comprehensive reading program, and the subject of current research and of several recent and upcoming books including Jean Osborn and her colleagues' *A Focus on Fluency* (Osborn, Lehr, & Hiebert, 2003), Timothy Rasinski's *The Fluent Reader* (2003), and Rasinski and his colleagues' *Fluency Instruction: Research-Based Best Practices* (Rasinski, Blachowicz, & Lems, 2006). In this chapter, we describe a number of approaches to building fluency, discuss ways of assessing fluency, consider the sorts of fluency instruction different readers need, and identify ways of matching readers with texts.

English Learners

For English-language learners who have not heard a lot of English, had many stories read to them in English, or read much English themselves, attaining fluency will be a definite challenge. This means we need to scaffold their work on fluency in every possible way.

Reflect and Apply

1. We have just given an example of an activity that some people do automatically—driving a stick-shift car. Think of an activity you do automatically, and consider how you became automatic at the activity. Talk to some classmates about automaticity, the activity that you do automatically, and how you became automatic at it. Then ask your classmates about some activities they do automatically and how they became automatic at them.

2. Think back to your elementary schooling, and see if you can remember some students who were not fluent in reading—students like Jimmy Parker, mentioned in the opening scenario. Now journal about what you think those students' attitudes toward reading were, what their attitudes toward school more generally were, and whether or not they ever became real readers. If you cannot remember any actual students, journal about some imaginary ones.

Approaches to Building Fluency

In this section of the chapter, the longest one, we describe a number of methods of helping students become more fluent. We begin with some generalizations about fluency instruction. Then, we discuss several methods of one-to-one instruction, powerful instruction to be sure but very costly in terms of teachers' time. Next, we present several methods of promoting fluency for small groups or even the entire class. Finally, we discuss the approach to fluency that is most appropriate for more able readers and that ought to be a part of all readers' activities—wide reading in interesting and enjoyable texts.

Some Generalizations About Fluency Instruction

There are a number of validated approaches to fluency instruction. Before we discuss these, however, we want to list several characteristics of the most successful approaches:

- Students read in comfortable and non-taxing situations, ones in which they are not likely to receive harsh corrections from the teacher or be embarrassed by reading poorly in front of their peers. This means situations other than round robin reading.
- There is evidence that students are generally capable of picking appropriate texts for repeated reading, ones that are neither too easy nor too difficult. Still, as we note in the section on Matching Students and Texts, ensuring that students have appropriate texts is crucial to successful fluency instruction—and to all other instruction.
- Teachers provide a good model of fluent reading for students when they first begin working on fluency and periodically after that.

- When monitoring students' oral reading, teachers balance correcting miscues with allowing students to read without too many interruptions, with the goal of having students read smoothly and fairly rapidly rather than perfectly. Too much emphasis on making no errors and too many corrections are likely to lead students to concentrate too much on accuracy.

- Students do a substantial amount of reading. In order to become more fluent, students need to actually read; they can't just pretend to read. This means that you need to build some accountability into whatever approach you use.

- In most approaches, students read orally, and they read the same material several times, often three times. However, in some approaches, students read more material but read it only once. As we stress in the section on Wide Reading in Appropriate Texts, for students whose fluency is progressing normally, silent reading may be the most appropriate road to fluency.

- Teachers chart students' progress and frequently show students (privately) this concrete evidence of their progress.

- At least when repeated reading is involved, students need to read material that presents at least a slight challenge, particularly by presenting some words that students are not already automatic with. At the same time, it is important not to make the material too challenging, as automaticity is achieved by successful engagements in non-taxing situations.

The Original Method of Repeated Reading

Having developed the theory of automaticity, Samuels (1979, 2002a, 2006) decided to search for a practical application of the theory and found one in the method of repeated reading. Samuels began by suggesting that in learning to efficiently recognize words, children go through three stages, much like those of Chall (1996) described earlier in the chapter:

- *The non-accurate stage.* At this point, students have considerable difficulty in recognizing words, do so only with considerable time and effort, and are not always accurate. If you listen to these children read aloud, you will find that they misread a number of words, stumble and read slowly, do not use appropriate expression, do not sound as though they are understanding much of what they read, and indeed do not understand much of what they read.

- *The accuracy stage.* At this stage, students are able to recognize words accurately, but doing so requires a good deal of attention, effort, and time. If you listen to these children read aloud, you will find that while they read accurately, they read slowly, haltingly, and without appropriate expression. They do not sound as though they understand what they are reading, and, in fact, many times they do not understand what they are reading.

- *The automatic stage.* At this stage, students are able to recognize words accurately and instantaneously, and doing so does not require much attention, effort, or time. If you listen to children at this stage read aloud, you will find that they read accurately, at a good pace, and with appropriate expression. They sound as though they understand what they are reading, and indeed they usually do.

Samuels next wondered at what other tasks people are slow, inaccurate, and stumbling in the beginning but eventually become fluent and automatic, and he thought of two of them—sports and music. In football, for example, a would-be offensive center may at first hike the ball over the quarterback's head, on the ground, or to his left or right. Eventually, however, the center learns to consistently hike the ball just where it needs to be, into the quarterback's outstretched hands. Moreover, the center eventually learns to accurately hike the ball while preparing to block the oncoming defensive center and carry out whatever other defensive assignments he is responsible for. Similarly, a beginning saxophone player may initially be unable to make any sound on the instrument, move to a level at which he sometimes plays the right notes and sometimes the wrong ones, progress to a level at which he accurately plays all the notes but without expression and feeling, and finally arrive a level at which he plays with feeling and grace, captivating an audience with his skill. In both cases, the route to fluency is similar: The aspiring athlete or musician repeatedly practices the task he is trying to master in non-taxing situations, gets feedback on his performance, and eventually becomes automatic and therefore fluent.

These examples provided Samuels with the inspiration for repeated reading. What he noticed was that the practice that many less-skilled readers received was very different from the practice of beginning musicians or athletes. Instead of repeatedly reading a single passage until they got it right, most less-skilled readers were faced with a new and difficult passage each day, stumbled through it without success, and were often embarrassed—like Jimmy Parker in our opening scenario—by reading poorly in front of their classmates. One could hardly imagine an approach better geared to failure. All of us need to meet with success, not failure, as we attempt to master a new skill. Samuels reasoned that if students who were relatively accurate but non-fluent in their reading could repeatedly practice reading the same passage, with each successive reading they should become more automatic and therefore fluent. Moreover, just as musicians repeatedly practice a single piece with the goal of becoming more-skilled with that piece and more skilled musicians generally, students who repeatedly read the same passage should become both more automatic and fluent in reading that passage and more automatic and fluent with other passages.

Samuels (1979) initially tested his hypothesis by providing individual repeated reading sessions for a class of mentally retarded students. The original repeated reading procedure is shown in In the Classroom 6.1. The results of this initial testing were very positive.

The Original Method of Repeated Reading

Like other methods of repeated reading, the original method is used with students who are relatively accurate in their reading but not yet automatic. This original approach involves one-to-one instruction.

- Have the student select a book that he finds interesting and enjoyable. If he selects one that you think is too hard or too easy (one that he will repeatedly stumble through or one containing exclusively or almost exclusively words he is already automatic at recognizing), help him find a more appropriate text.

instructional routines

in the Classroom 6.1

- Mark off a half dozen or so 50- to 200-word segments in the selected book. Begin with 50-word segments and gradually lengthen the segments as the student becomes increasingly able to deal with longer texts.
- Explain the nature and purpose of repeated reading to the student. He is going to read the same passage several times, trying to read it more smoothly and a bit faster each time. Note that he should not ignore comprehension but that his main goal is to read smoothly and fairly rapidly.
- Have the student read the passage aloud and chart both his speed and the number of word-recognition errors he makes.
- Then have him return to his seat and repeatedly practice reading the passage until he feels ready to read to you again. He should keep re-reading the passage, sometimes to himself at his seat and sometimes to you, until he reaches a rate of 85 words per minute. Although accuracy of word recognition is a goal, do not press the student too much for accuracy, and do not demand complete accuracy before moving on to another passage. Experience shows that too much stress on accuracy will make the student anxious and reduce his chances of meeting the rate goal.
- Once the student reaches the target rate of 85 words per minute, show him the graph of his progress, and prepare to move to another passage, probably on another day.

With each reading of a passage, reading speed increased, the number of word-recognition errors decreased, and students read with more expression. Moreover, when students went on to a new section of a book, their beginning reading speed for that section was faster than their beginning reading speed for the previous section. That is, students' performance increased on both the texts they re-read and the texts they were reading for the first time.

Figure 6.1 shows one student's progress in rate and word recognition using the original method of repeated reading on five passages. The student

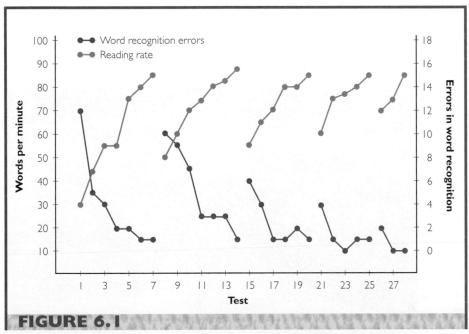

FIGURE 6.1

Progress in Reading Rate and Word Recognition for a Student Using the Original Method of Repeated Reading with Five Passages

Source: Samuels, S. Jay. (1979, January). The method of repeated readings. *The Reading Teacher, 32*(4), pp. 403–408. Used by permission.

began the new passages with tests 1, 8, 15, 21, and 25. As can be seen, as the student repeatedly read each passage, his speed (shown by the blue lines) increased and his word-recognition errors (shown by the red lines) decreased. Moreover, the student's first reading of each successive passage was faster than his first reading of the previous passages, and he made fewer word-recognition errors in his first reading of each successive reading.

The original method of repeated reading clearly does what it is supposed to—increase students' oral reading fluency. At the same time, it is costly in that it requires one-to-one instruction. In some situations, however, parents, aides, and other students may be able to monitor the procedure, making it more feasible in the classroom.

Simultaneous Repeated Reading

Simultaneous repeated reading is another one-to-one approach that has been used successfully (Heckelman, 1969). This approach is similar to the original method of repeated reading, the main difference being that the teacher or other competent reader and the student repeatedly read the passage together. The teacher (or other competent reader) originally takes the lead, reading in a strong voice, and then gradually reads in a softer and softer voice as the student takes primary responsibility. As with the original method of repeated reading, the teacher helps the student choose a book that is interesting and just a bit challenging, marks off passages of 50–200 words to read, explains the procedure and the purpose to the student, charts the student's progress in rate and perhaps word recognition, and shares the chart with the student so that he gets concrete evidence of his progress. Unlike the original method of repeated reading, simultaneous repeated reading calls for the teacher to read along with the student each time he reads the passage. The advantage of simultaneous repeated reading is that the student gets repeated models of fluent oral reading and receives sturdier scaffolding than when he is reading by himself. The disadvantage of the approach is that it is labor intensive, requiring the teacher or some other adult to participate in every reading the student does.

Repeated reading sessions help students increase their reading speed.

Echo Reading

Echo reading is yet another one-to-one approach to increasing fluency. In echo reading, the teacher or an aide reads a line and then the student reads the same line. Echo reading may or may not involve repeated reading of the same passage. That is, the teacher might read a passage once, let the student read it once, and then go on to a new passage, or they might both read the same passage several times. Echo reading provides some really sturdy scaffolding, since the teacher is repeatedly modeling just what it is the student needs to do. As Rasinski (2003) suggests, echo reading provides a good opportunity to gradually release responsibility to the student. As the student becomes more proficient, the teacher can read longer and longer passages and let him echo. Also, as the student gains proficiency, he can occasionally do the initial reading and let the teacher do the echoing. The goal, as in so much instruction, is to stretch the student a bit while providing enough support for him to succeed at the task set for him.

Tape-Assisted Repeated Reading

The three approaches described thus far have been shown to be effective and are viable options. However, all three of them are one-to-one approaches, and they thus have the disadvantage of taking a good deal of a teacher's or some other adult's time for each student. The approaches described in this and the next several sections are group or whole-class approaches, making them feasible for teachers who do not have the time for one-to-one instruction.

At about the same time that Samuels was developing his approach to repeated reading, Carol Chomsky (1978) was developing a somewhat different approach to fluency. Chomsky's approach was to tape short books. She would then have students repeatedly listen to them over a period of a week, repeatedly read them and compare their reading to the tape, and then work in a small group with her on game-like activities involving word analysis, vocabulary, writing, and discussion. The children Chomsky worked with were third-graders with adequate decoding skills but poor fluency and with negative experiences in reading and therefore negative attitudes toward reading. They were also children from homes in which books and reading were not prominent. Chomsky characterizes these children's skills and attitudes toward reading this way:

> They hated reading, avoided it whenever possible, and consistently met the many opportunities for meaningful reading, adequately provided for in a lively classroom, with a total lack of response. . . . [They] couldn't so much as read a page of simple material to me. The attempt to do so was almost painful, a word-by-word struggle, long silences, eyes eventually drifting around the room in an attempt to escape the humiliation and frustration of the all too familiar hated situation.
>
> —Carol Chomsky, Researcher and Reading Tutor

Chomsky decided that what the students needed was an opportunity to learn that reading was accessible to them and to do so in non-threatening, non-taxing, and non-embarrassing situations. And she realized that having children repeatedly listen to tapes until they had virtually memorized them and then work with her on the passage they had already mastered could provide this opportunity. She therefore got the five children she was working with tape recorders, made tapes of some short and easy books, had them read the books repeatedly over a period of a week, and then met weekly with them as a small group to work on skills, discuss what they had read, and do some writing. The program, which extended over a period of four months, produced positive results for all five students. Both their overall reading scores and their word-recognition scores went up. They read much more fluently. Equally importantly, their attitude toward reading became much more positive.

In a later investigation that involved taped reading, Michal Shany and Andrew Biemiller (1995) found that both a repeated reading approach that required teacher assistance and a tape-assisted repeated reading approach significantly improved the reading rates and reading comprehension of at-risk third- and fourth-grade children. Shany and Biemiller further found that the tape-assisted reading approach resulted in the students' doing twice as much reading as the repeated reading approach.

In the Classroom 6.2 shows an approach to tape-assisted repeated reading based on the work of Chomsky (1978), Shany and Biemiller (1995), and Osborn and her colleagues (2003).

Tape-Assisted Repeated Reading

instructional routines in the Classroom 6.2

Tape-assisted repeated reading can be done in a number of ways. Here is one approach:

- Select some books that are a bit of a challenge for the students you will be working with and that you can either get tapes of or tape yourself.

- Tell students that they will be reading the books several times in order to improve their reading and that they should choose ones that are interesting and present a bit of a challenge. Have students choose their own books, but monitor their choices and suggest other books if any are too easy or too difficult.

- Have them listen to the book or a part of it repeatedly while silently or orally reading along with the tape. Tell students they should continue listening and reading until they can read smoothly and feel they are ready to read the text to you.

- Have students read the book or passage aloud to you. Record their reading rate and the number of word-recognition errors they make. Have them talk a bit about the book and discuss it with them, both as an informal check on comprehension and as a reminder that comprehension is the goal of reading. Make charts showing their rate and number of word-recognition errors over time, and share the charts to show students their progress.

Tape-assisted repeated reading is certainly an alternative to teacher-assisted repeated reading, and it is one that requires less time on the part of the teacher or an aide. Moreover, the availability of commercial programs that employ tape-assisted repeated reading, something we discuss in the section on Commercial Fluency Programs later in this chapter, makes doing this type of reading very convenient.

English Learners

In pairing English-language learners with other students, give extra attention to pairing the English learner with a student with whom he will be comfortable reading orally. Sometimes this will mean pairing English learners with each other.

Partner Reading

Partner reading is another approach that is less demanding on teacher time. In partner reading, students who are more-capable readers pair up with students who are less-capable ones, and then the students take turns reading to each other, with the stronger reader reading each passage first and the less-strong reader reading it next. Like virtually all fluency approaches, partner reading can be used in several ways. In the Classroom 6.3 shows a slightly modified version of the procedures suggested by Osborn and her colleagues (2003).

Partner Reading

Partner Selection Procedure:

- The teacher uses fluency scores to rank-order the class from top to bottom.
- The teacher splits the class into two groups of equal size.
  Group 1: top to middle readers
  Group 2: middle to bottom readers
- The top reader in Group 1 is paired with the top reader in Group 2, and so on down the lists.

Partner Reading Procedure:

- The Group 1 reader always reads first to set the pace and ensure accuracy.
- The Group 2 reader reads, attempting to match the pace and fluency of his partner.
- The teacher closely monitors students' fluency, moving around the room to listen to each set of partners, keeping partners on track, and providing feedback as needed.

Choral Reading

Choral reading is a frequent activity in many classrooms, and it is a great way to get the whole class involved at the same time. With choral reading, the teacher chooses a selection that will lend itself particularly well to oral reading—perhaps a humorous poem from Jack Prelutsky's *It's Raining Pigs and Noodles*—and explains the importance of reading the passage smoothly, with expression, at a good rate, and accurately. Next, he reads a passage aloud as a model and then has students read it aloud in unison several times. In this way, less-fluent readers first have the scaffold of hearing the teacher read the passage, then can read the passage a few times rather quietly and perhaps lagging just a bit behind their more-skilled classmates, and finally can read louder and simultaneously with their more-skilled classmates. This is just the sort of non-taxing situation students need to develop automaticity and fluency. Primary-grade teachers often use choral reading quite a bit, but it is also appropriate for older students who need to improve their fluency; and it is likely to be an enjoyable experience for all students.

Third-grade teacher Carol Tesh points out another important benefit of choral reading.

> Coming together to read in unison throughout the day reinforces the fact that we are a team and we need to work together, whether it's in reading, in writing, on the playground, whatever.
>
> —Carol Tesh, Third-Grade Teacher (quoted in Rasinski, 2003)

Readers Theater

Readers theater refers to the well-rehearsed reading of scripts, with feeling and expression, in front of an audience (usually the class), but without the memorizing of lines, costumes, prompts, scenery, make-up, and other time-consuming and sometimes expensive features of a full-blown play performance. As an approach to building fluency, readers theater has several positive characteristics. For one thing, motivation is likely to be strong because the repeated reading that students do in order to master their parts is done under the guise of preparing for the upcoming presentation and not as a fluency exercise. For another, both more-skilled readers and less-skilled ones can participate, thus avoiding any stigma that might be associated with being in a fluency group. And for still another, more-skilled readers can be given longer and more difficult parts, while less-skilled readers are given shorter and easier parts, thus allowing all students to work at their own level. An outline for a week's work with readers theater is shown in In the Classroom 6.4.

Schedule for a Week of Readers Theater

Readers theater is the sort of activity that is best done from time to time, and a week is often an appropriate amount of time for a readers theater segment. However, with some students you may need to keep the segment shorter to maintain their attention.

- Select a script or several scripts, and make copies for each reader. If you are working with an entire class, you will probably have several different groups; they can all work with the same script, or they can work with different ones.

- *Monday:* Introduce or review the procedure, stressing the importance of students' practicing their parts so that they can do really fluent presentations. Assign parts, taking special care to assign each student only as much as he can handle.

- *Tuesday–Thursday:* Have students practice their parts. They can do so at home as well as at school. They can practice independently some of the time, but it is also important that they practice with a partner, with a group, and with you as their audience so that they get some assistance and some feedback and are prepared for their class presentation on Friday. Of course, if students do not need three days of practice or their attention begins to wane, you can shorten the practice.

- *Friday:* Have students perform their scripts for an audience, probably the class but others should certainly be welcome. Be encouraging and supportive, and make this a festive occasion.

Radio Reading

Radio reading, originally developed by Frank Greene (1979), can be thought of as a variation of readers theater. As with readers theater, the goal is to motivate students and give them an opportunity to repeatedly practice a passage so that they can read it fluently to an audience. The main difference is that with radio reading the students are motivated to practice the passage by assuming the role of professional announcers preparing to read the passage to a national audience. Another difference is that since this isn't "theater," a variety of types of texts can be used. The procedure lends itself particularly well to students working with expository texts, news stories, public service announcements, and other sorts of nonfiction announcements you might hear on the radio or television. As we have noted in earlier chapters, students need more experience than they typically get with expository texts, and so opportunities to read exposition are particularly welcome. A third difference is that with radio reading, in addition to practicing his passage before reading it to the class, each student creates one factual question and one inferential question about it, thus giving direct attention to comprehension. A plan for a radio-reading session, based on one described by Rasinski (2003), is shown in In the Classroom 6.5.

instructional routines

in the Classroom 6.5

Plan for a Radio-Reading Session

Like readers theater, radio reading is the sort of activity that is best done from time to time. Here we show the procedure as it would be completed in two days, but additional days of practice can be added if needed.

Day 1

- Select a text or several texts, and make copies for each reader. Exposition works particularly well. If you are working with an entire class, you will probably have several different groups; they can all work with the same script, or they can work with different ones.

- Stress the importance of reading fluently—accurately and with expression and feeling—making the discussion longer or shorter depending on how much you have already talked about and worked with fluency. Tell students that one group of professionals who have to be particularly careful to do fluent oral reading is radio and television announcers, and that they are to prepare for their presentations as though they were radio or TV announcers. At this point, you might show a video of a skilled announcer.

- Assign passages, giving the longer and more difficult passages to more-skilled readers, and have students begin practicing their passages. They can practice independently some of the time, but it is also important that they practice with a partner, with a group, and with you as their audience so that they get some assistance and some feedback and are prepared for their class presentations. Of course, they can practice at home too. Tell students that in addition to becoming fluent with their passages, each of them is to create one factual question and one inferential question.

Day 2

- Remind students of the importance of fluent reading and that their goal is to be as skilled as professional announcers at oral reading, and give them one last opportunity to rehearse their passages.

- Set the stage for radio reading with a microphone and an anchor desk as prompts. At some point, you may use an actual microphone that both projects to the audience and enables students to record their presentations and later listen to them.

- Have students read their passages for an audience, probably the class, but others should be welcome. Students should read their passages in order. If more than one text is being used, all of the work with one text (the steps below) should be completed before going on to the next text.

- Support students who encounter any problems in their reading, supplying unknown words or providing other help they need as unobtrusively as possible. Celebrate both good performances and efforts toward good performances.

- After each text (not each passage) is completed, have students pose their questions and discuss the answers with the class. At this time, you might also have the class summarize the text and discuss anything about it that they find particularly interesting. (Note that this step reminds students of the central purpose of reading: comprehension.)
- Have students critique their presentations, consider their progress toward becoming fluent readers, and suggest future fluency activities they might engage in.

Fluency-Oriented Oral Reading

Fluency-oriented oral reading (Kuhn, 2004/2005) is designed for use with small groups and includes elements of several other fluency approaches we have discussed—repeated reading, echo reading, partner reading, and choral reading. It also incorporates a number of features that have been shown to be productive in fluency studies: "modeling, repetition, positive feedback from instructors or peers, and opportunity for oral rendition of practiced texts" (Kuhn, 2004/2005). The procedure follows a three-day cycle, as outlined in In the Classroom 6.6.

Fluency-Oriented Oral Reading

instructional routines in the Classroom 6.6

Like readers theater and radio reading, fluency-oriented oral reading can take several days. However, unlike these other two activities, fluency-oriented oral reading is designed to be used repeatedly over some period of time, not occasionally.

Day 1
- Select an appropriate text, explain fluency-oriented oral reading and its purpose, and echo-read the text to students.
- If the text is not too long, have students choral-read the text with you.

Day 2
- Break students into pairs, and have them partner-read the entire text, with partners reading alternate pages.
- If time permits, either have students take turns reading parts of the text to their partners or have the partners again read the entire text, alternating pages.

Day 3
- Do choral reading of the text with the group.
- Invite, but do not force, students to read sections of the text aloud to the group.

Kuhn did a small study comparing fluency-oriented oral reading to wide reading, listening, and a no-treatment condition, and found that the fluency-oriented oral-reading group outperformed the listening and no-treatment groups on tests of identifying words in isolation, number of words read per minute, and quality of oral reading. However, the wide-reading group outperformed the fluency-oriented oral-reading group on a comprehension measure. As we have noted, we recommend wide reading for all students, whether or not they are engaging in other fluency-building activities.

Commercial Fluency Programs

Motivated by the same factors that gave rise to small-group and whole-class fluency instruction—the need to find fluency instruction that did not require a great deal of teacher time or the assistance of aides—several companies have developed prepackaged fluency programs. Fluency training is a rather straight-forward matter, as it is based primarily on modeling, repeated reading, and feed-back; and both taped programs and computer programs lend themselves well to providing instruction and practice incorporating these features. Several pro-grams are currently available, and with the recent emphasis on fluency, more are undoubtedly coming. Here we describe two representative programs.

Read Naturally *Masters Edition*

Read Naturally was one of the first companies to produce a fluency program. In fact, the company was founded specifically to provide fluency instruction. It produced its first program in the early 1990s. The current basic Read Naturally program is titled *Read Naturally Masters Edition* (Ihnot, 2001). The program is available in eight levels—1.0 to 8.0. Each level includes the follow-ing components:

- 24 high-interest, nonfiction stories on blackline masters
- 12 cassettes or 12 CDs of the stories
- four multiple-choice questions and one open-ended question for each story
- graphs on blackline masters, on which students chart their progress
- activities, including reading, re-reading, timing, answering questions, and graphing

The basic Read Naturally approach, which is the approach used in a lot of fluency instruction, is shown in Figure 6.2.

In addition to its *Masters Edition,* Read Naturally produces a number of other programs, including a multicultural series, a Spanish series, and assessment material. The most notable other material the company produces is probably the

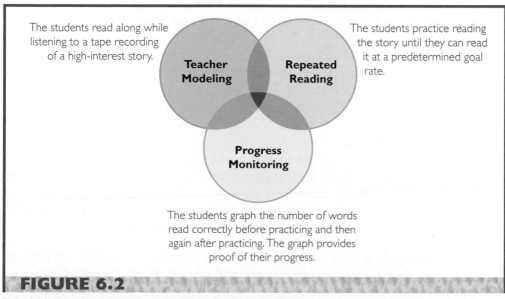

FIGURE 6.2

Read Naturally Approach to Fluency Instruction

Source: Read Naturally Rationale and Research. St. Paul, MN: Read Naturally. Copyright © Read Naturally, Inc. 2005. All rights reserved.

Read Naturally Software Edition (Ihnot, 2004). The software edition parallels the taped edition in many ways but also takes advantage of some of the functions computers make possible, such as letting students click on unknown words to get definitions, letting teachers set rate criteria, and automatically graphing students' progress.

Renaissance Learning's *Fluent Reader*

Renaissance Learning is another company that produces a computer-based fluency program. Its program, titled *Fluent Reader* (2005), is in many ways similar to the *Read Naturally Software Edition*. *Fluent Reader* includes a number of high-interest passages at varying grade levels, and a student reads using the following four-step strategy. First, the student selects a passage that is interesting and at the appropriate level and reads it once to establish his initial reading rate. Next, the student listens to the recording of the passage, sees the text on the computer, and reads along, attempting to match the professional reader's phrasing and rate. Then, the student repeatedly reads the passage aloud, recording his readings and monitoring his progress until he can read the passage accurately and fluently at a predetermined goal rate. Finally, the student takes a short comprehension quiz on the computer, and the computer generates a report on his final performance on the passage.

As we noted, these are just two of the commercial programs available, and more are undoubtedly on the way. As we also noted, fluency instruction and practice seem to be a good fit for prepackaged tape-based and computer-based programs. If you find yourself pressed for time to provide fluency training for your students who need it, you may want to consider commercial programs.

Wide Reading in Appropriate Texts

As we noted in describing the components of a comprehensive reading program in Chapter 1 and will continue to note throughout this book, wide reading is a very important part of reading instruction—for all students. Wide reading builds automaticity, vocabulary, world knowledge, and the desire to read more. One of the ways you get good at reading—in fact, one of the ways you get good at anything—is to do a lot of it. One of the ways students make reading a habit, something that is a frequent and vital part of their lives, is to read and read and read.

Wide reading is also essential for becoming fluent. Remember that the road to automaticity and hence to fluency is to practice repeatedly in situations that are interesting, enjoyable, and non-taxing; and wide reading certainly fits that description. In fact, for many children—those reading at grade level and those at or near the fluency norms for their grades—wide reading in interesting and enjoyable books is the primary road to fluency. We will say more about which students should do wide reading as their primary fluency activity and which should engage in a more direct approach to fluency instruction, as well as do wide reading, in the section of this chapter titled Choosing Among Approaches to Fluency. Jack Detmar is one teacher who recognizes the importance of both wide reading and other approaches to building fluency.

I always hate to be part of a bandwagon, but I'm afraid that these days that's just what I am. I have always been a huge supporter of the position that students need to read a lot if they are to read well, and hence wide reading has always played a big part in my classroom. However, after I began reading about the National Reading Panel's emphasis on fluency instruction, read some articles about fluency, and went to an inservice of

CW 6.1 links to both the Read Naturally Website and the Renaissance Learning Website, where additional information on their fluency programs is available.

the topic, I have come to realize that some students need more direct help with fluency than wide reading provides. We currently do as much independent silent reading in my class as we ever did, and all my students have plenty of opportunities for wide reading, but I also use more direct approaches such as repeated reading with those students who struggle with fluency.

—Jack Detmar, Second-Grade Teacher

Reflect *and* Apply

3. Choose one of the three one-to-one approaches to building fluency (the original method of repeated reading, simultaneous repeated reading, or echo reading), and describe a student with whom you would use it. Note how often you would use it and over what time period, and justify the use of the one-to-one approach with that student.

4. Choose one of the group approaches to fluency instruction (tape-assisted repeated reading, partner reading, choral reading, readers theater, radio reading, or fluency-oriented oral reading), and describe a group of students with whom you would use it. Note how often you would use it and over what time period, and explain why you would use a group approach rather than a one-to-one approach with these students.

5. Describe several students for whom independent reading will be the primary path to fluency. How often might you engage these students in fluency activities like choral reading, readers theater, and radio reading? Briefly describe your rationale for the amount of time you will spend on these activities.

Assessing Readers' Fluency

Good readers begin their road to becoming fluent in the first grade or even earlier. By the end of the second grade, they can read grade-level materials orally at something like 90 words per minute and are well on their way to becoming fluent readers. Poor readers, on the other hand, may still struggle with fluency in the upper-elementary grades and beyond. For example, sixth-graders who are at the tenth percentile in fluency still read orally at something like 90 words per minute (Hasbrouck & Tindal, 2005). Because fluency is so important and because different students need different sorts of instruction and practice with fluency, it is vital to assess the fluency of all students in the primary grades and all students whom you suspect may not be fluent readers in the upper-elementary and middle grades.

Although fluency is a straightforward concept, it has several components; if possible, each of these ought to be assessed. We say "if possible" because time may not always allow you to assess all the components of fluency, and assessing only some of them is definitely worthwhile. The components to consider are rate, accuracy, expression, and comprehension. Rate and accuracy are the first components to consider, and fortunately there is a well-established, easy, and quick procedure for doing so. The procedure, called Curriculum-Based Measurement, or CBM, was originally developed by Stanley Deno (1985). In using CBM, you simply select a grade-appropriate passage, have the student read orally for one minute, keep track of errors, and arrive at a words correct

CW 6.2 links to *Listen to Students Read Aloud: Oral Fluency,* which presents information on fourth-graders' oral fluency gathered by the National Assessment of Educational Progress and briefly considers the implications of the findings.

Some older readers still need fluency activities.

per minute (WCPM) score by subtracting the number of errors from the total number of words read. Rasinski (2003) has added a step of tallying the student's accuracy score, a useful addition. A version of CBM that incorporates Rasinski's suggestion is shown in In the Classroom 6.7.

Procedures for Measuring Rate and Accuracy

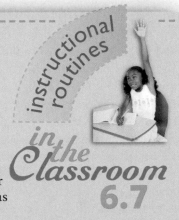

instructional routines in the Classroom 6.7

- Identify a 100- to 200-word passage at the student's grade placement.
- Ask the student to read the passage aloud in a normal way and at his normal rate for one minute. If the student hesitates on a word for two to three seconds, pronounce it for him. Tape-record his reading, and mark the point in the text that he reaches in a minute.
- Mark any uncorrected errors the student makes. Mispronunciations, substitutions, reversals, omissions, and words that you pronounce for the student after he hesitates for two to three seconds are counted as errors.
- Determine rate by counting the total number of words read correctly during the minute. For example, a student might correctly read 47 words in a minute.
- Determine accuracy by dividing the number of words read correctly by the total number of words read. For example, a student might read 50 words in a minute and make 3 errors, meaning that he has read 47 words correctly. Dividing 47 by 50 yields an accuracy score of 94 percent.

Once you have determined the student's rate and accuracy, you can compare them to the norms for rate and accuracy. Oral reading rate norms taken from the work of Jan Hasbrouck and Gerald Tindal (2005) are shown in Figure 6.3. The level of reading accuracy typically taken as indicating a student's independent reading level (the level at which he can read without assistance) is 96–100 percent, that taken as indicating a student's instructional level (the level at which he can read with some assistance) is 90–95 percent, and that taken as indicating a student's frustration level (the level at which he is likely to find similar text too challenging) is 90 percent and below (Rasinski, 2003)

Students who are markedly below the norm for their grade level, perhaps 20 percent or more below the norm, and are at the independent or instructional level with respect to accuracy are likely to profit from instruction and practice on fluency. Students whose reading shows them to be at the frustration level may need other sorts of assessments. We discuss a variety of assessments and provide assessment tools in Chapter 14, Classroom Assessment, and the *Assessments and Lesson Plans* booklet that comes with this text.

As we noted, expression, sometimes called prosody in the current literature, is another component of fluency that deserves assessment. You assess expression by listening to students read orally and making a subjective judgment about their performance. The rubric shown in Figure 6.4, which was developed and tested by The National Assessment of Educational Progress (U.S. Department of Education, 1995), has proven to be an effective and easily used tool for rating expression.

To use the scale, you simply have the child read grade-level material orally, and then you rate his reading as Level 1, 2, 3, or 4. While Level 4 is the ultimate goal, students rated at both Level 3 and Level 4 are considered fluent, while students rated at Levels 1 and 2 are not.

GRADE	FALL WCPM	WINTER WCPM	SPRING WCPM
1	—	23	53
2	51	72	89
3	71	92	107
4	94	112	123
5	110	127	139
6	127	140	150
7	128	136	150
8	133	146	151

FIGURE 6.3
Mean Oral Fluency Rates, 2005

Source: Hasbrouck, J., & Tindal, G. (2005). Oral reading fluency: 90 years of measurement (Tech. Rep. No. 33). Eugene, Oregon: University of Oregon, College of Education, Behavioral Research & Teaching. Used with permission.

CW 6.3 links to *Oral Reading Fluency: 90 Years of Measurement* by Jan Hasbrouck and Gerald Tindal (2005). This report includes both the latest fluency norms and fluency norms over a 90-year period.

Level 4	Reads primarily in larger, meaningful phrase groups. Although some regressions, repetitions, and deviations from text may be present, these do not appear to detract from the overall structure of the story. Preservation of the author's syntax is consistent. Some or most of the story is read with expressive interpretation.
Level 3	Reads primarily in three- or four-word phrase groups. Some smaller groupings may be present. However, the majority of phrasing seems appropriate and preserves the syntax of the author. Little or no expressive interpretation is present.
Level 2	Reads primarily in two-word phrases with some three- or four-word groupings. Some word-by-word reading may be present. Word groupings may seem awkward and unrelated to larger context of sentence or passage.
Level 1	Reads primarily word-by-word. Occasional two-word or three-word phrases may occur, but these are infrequent and/or they do not preserve meaningful syntax.

FIGURE 6.4
Oral Reading Fluency Scale

Source: U.S. Department of Education, National Center for Education Statistics. (1995). *Listening to Children Read Aloud, 15.* Washington, DC: GPO.

The final step in assessing fluency is to consider the student's comprehension. The most frequent method of doing so is to have students do a one-minute retell of the passage they read in one minute immediately after reading it and count the number of relevant words in their retell. Researchers (Good & Kaminski, 2002) have suggested "as a rough rule of thumb that for children whose retell is about 50% of their oral reading fluency score, their oral reading fluency score provides a good overall indication of their reading proficiency, including comprehension." On the other hand, for children whose retell score is 25 percent or less of their oral-reading fluency, their oral-reading fluency score may not be a good indication of their overall reading proficiency. Thus, for a child who correctly reads 60 words in one minute and includes 30 or more relevant words in his retell, the fluency rate of 60 is a good overall measure. However, for a child who correctly reads 60 words and includes only 15 relevant words in his retell, the fluency rate of 60 may not reflect his comprehension, comprehension may be a problem, and further assessments may be necessary. Again, information on other assessments is provided in Chapter 14 and in the *Assessments and Lesson Plans* booklet.

Once you have assessed a student's fluency, it needs to be recorded so that you can monitor the student's progress. It is generally recommended that you gather data at least three times a year. Figure 6.5 shows a form for describing all four aspects of fluency, with data entered for four second-graders' fall scores.

Each of the four students presents a different profile and will require different sorts of attention. Malcolm is doing just fine. His rate, accuracy, expression score, and retell score are all solid. He does not appear to need any special work in fluency. Jimmy, on the other hand, is doing poorly on all measures. He reads slowly, makes quite a few errors, does not read with expression, and does not demonstrate good comprehension of what he reads. He appears to need special assistance in several areas, not just fluency. Mari presents a less-even profile. Her rate is satisfactory, her accuracy is low, her expression is good, and her comprehension is a bit low. She will need further assessment, but she will probably profit from work on word recognition and vocabulary as well as fluency. Hector presents yet another profile. His rate, accuracy, and expres-

CW 6.4 links to the Dynamic Indicators of Basic Early Literacy Skills (DIBELS) Website. This non-profit organization provides a rich set of passages, other materials, and reporting services for assessing fluency and other aspects of early literacy development. It also provides a wealth of information about fluency.

Teacher							Grade	2		Year		
Student	Rate			Accuracy			Expression			Comprehension		
	F	W	S	F	W	S	F	W	S	F	W	S
Malcolm C.	50			94%			3			30		
Jimmy V.	30			77%			1			10		
Mari R.	50			86%			3			22		
Hector A.	45			94%			3			15		

FIGURE 6.5

Class Fluency Record

sion are all satisfactory, but his comprehension appears to be quite low. Further assessment is definitely in order for Hector. In the next section of this chapter, we will consider what sorts of fluency instruction these and other students should receive.

the Reading Corner

Books to Build Fluency in Developing Readers

The following list includes books that Melanie Kuhn (2004/2005) used in investigating fluency-oriented oral reading, a few newer books similar to those she used, and some Spanish-English dual-language books, which may be particularly useful with Latino English-language learners.

Barbara Bottner. *Pish and Posh* (I Can Read Book 2). HarperCollins, 2005. Wacky surprises occur when best friends Pish and Posh discover a book of fairy magic. 48 pages.

Betsy Byars. *The Golly Sisters Go West* (I Can Read Book 3). HarperTrophy, 1989. The singing, dancing Golly sisters, May-May and Rose, travel west by covered wagon, entertaining people along the way. 64 pages.

Betsy Byars. *Hooray for the Golly Sisters!* (I Can Read Book 3). HarperCollins, 1992. In these five amusing stories, May-May and Rose "cross the big river" and entertain folks with their zany variety shows. 64 pages.

Jack Gantos. *Rotten Ralph Feels Rotten*. Farrar, Straus and Giroux, 2004. When mischievous cat Ralph becomes ill after raiding garbage cans and is taken to the vet, he becomes lonesome for Sarah and makes his way home. 48 pages.

Lillian Hoban. *Arthur's Funny Money* (I Can Read Book 2). HarperTrophy, 1984. In this story, one of Hoban's many delightful tales of Arthur, his little sister Violet has a problem with math and Arthur is penniless, so they go into business and solve both problems. 64 pages.

Russell Hoban. *Bedtime for Frances*. HarperCollins, 1995. The endearing little badger Frances comes up with all sorts of delaying tactics to postpone her bedtime. 32 pages.

Arnold Lobel. *Frog and Toad Together* (I Can Read Book 2). HarperTrophy, 1979. A collection of five tales about friends Frog and Toad, each a "masterpiece of child-styled humor and sensitivity." 64 pages.

Herman Parish and Lynn Sweat. *Amelia Bedelia, Bookworm* (I Can Read Book 2). Greenwillow, 2005. When Amelia Bedelia helps out at her local library, she does everything by "the book," which, of course, gets her into a whole lot of trouble! 64 pages.

Shelley Moore Thomas. *Get Well, Good Knight* (Puffin Easy-to-Read). Puffin, 2004. When little knight's three dragon friends come down with awful colds, he sets off to find a healing potion. 48 pages.

Dual-Language Books in English and Spanish

Catherine Bruzzone. *Pupagesy Finds a Friend/Cachorrito encuentra un amigo*. Barron's Educational Series, bilingual edition, 2000. Pupagesy can't find anyone to play with until he meets a white mouse. 28 pages.

Susan Lowell. *The Three Little Pigs/Los tres pequenos jabalies*. Rising Moon Books, bilingual edition, 2004. In this southwestern retelling of *The Three Little Pigs*, three wild boars try to outsmart a hungry coyote. 32 pages.

Pat Mora. *Listen to the Desert/Oye al desierto*. Clarion, 2001. A brightly illustrated picture book that introduces readers to some of the desert sounds. 32 pages.

Pat Mora. *Uno, dos, tres/One, Two, Three*. Clarion, 2000. In this simple counting book, two little girls buy presents for their mother in a Mexican market. 48 pages.

Spanish Translations

Crockett Johnson (translated by Teresa Mlawer). *Harold y el lapiz color morado*. Rayo, 1995. In this children's classic, Harold draws his world with a purple crayon. 64 pages.

Arnold Lobel (translated by Pablo Lizcano). *Sapo y Sepo son amigos*. Alfaguara, 2003. *Frog and Toad Are Friends* is a collection of five short stories about the friendship of a frog and a toad, another children's classic. 66 pages.

Choosing Among the Approaches to Fluency

Thus far in the chapter, we have defined fluency and explained its importance, described a number of approaches to promoting fluency, and discussed ways of assessing fluency. Here we consider what sorts of approaches are likely to be appropriate for various sorts of students. To do so, it will be convenient to divide the approaches into three categories. The first category contains only one approach—wide reading. For many students, those who are making good progress in fluency and are near or above the fluency norms shown in Figure 6.3, wide reading in material they find interesting, enjoyable, and occasionally a bit challenging is *the* major road to fluency. This is the primary approach to use with Malcolm. The second category contains three approaches—choral reading, radio reading, and readers theater. All three can be used from time to time to celebrate, motivate, and improve oral reading. All students—students like Malcolm, Jimmy, Mari, and Hector—will profit from using these approaches from time to time. Remember, though, that students who are struggling will need to take smaller and less-demanding parts. The third category contains all the other approaches: the original method of repeated reading, simultaneous reading, echo reading, tape-assisted repeated reading, partner reading, fluency-oriented oral reading, and the use of commercial programs. Students who are not making adequate progress in fluency—those who are 20 percent or so below the rate norms for their grade or those who show an uneven profile across the four components of fluency for which we described assessment—are candidates for these other approaches. Mari, who seems to do well on everything but rate, clearly needs to use one or more of these approaches. Jimmy undoubtedly needs one of these approaches, but he needs other special work too. And Hector probably needs one of these approaches and may need other special work as well.

In choosing among the approaches in this third category, several matters are worth considering. First, all of them are based on sound principles and have been found to be effective. Any one of them is probably a good choice, and you should choose one or more that seem to fit you and the students you are concerned with. Second, there's no reason to limit your selection to one approach; using more than one approach provides variety and gives students some different opportunities. Third, if you have the human resources—if you have the time or have aides or parents who have the time—it is probably a good idea to use a one-to-one approach with students who are in most need of improving their fluency. Finally, if you lack the human resources to provide fluency instruction for all of your students who need it, you may want to consider commercial programs.

Matching Students and Texts

In this section of the chapter, we take up matching students and texts, something that is vital in planning fluency instruction as well as in choosing selections for all other purposes—including reading to students, doing shared reading, scaffolding reading experiences for the whole class, scaffolding reading experiences for small groups, fostering independent reading, and planning and assigning homework. There are a variety of methods of matching students and texts, but all rely on three considerations: (1) the students' reading proficiency and motivation, (2) text difficulty and accessibility, and (3) your personal and professional knowledge about your students, the books and other reading materials in your classroom, and the various purposes for which students are reading.

Assessing Students' Reading Proficiency and Motivation

Chapter 14, Classroom Assessment, and the *Assessments and Lesson Plans* booklet that accompanies this text include detailed assessment procedures and materials. Here, we describe those aspects of assessment that are particularly relevant to planning fluency instruction. Approaches to assessing students' reading proficiency and motivation range from informal teacher-based approaches to more formal text-based approaches. At the informal end of the continuum are your observations of your students and their reading. It is important to be constantly alert to how students are doing in reading and their attitudes toward reading, and one way of doing so is to be repeatedly asking questions such as these: Do students read voluntarily? Do they read when they are asked to do so? Do they seem to enjoy reading, or is it a real task for them? What sorts of books do they choose? Do they generally finish the books they choose? Do they talk about books, bring books to school, and share books with their friends? As part of these informal observations, it is useful to listen to students read, ask them a few questions, and make brief notes on their comprehension, reading rate, fluency, and attitudes. These sorts of informal observations are necessary and particularly useful for assessing attitudes and motivation, but they are only one of several approaches that should be used in concert.

Next on the informal-formal continuum come informal reading inventories, or IRIs. IRIs consist of passages that a student reads orally to a teacher. They can be used to assess the appropriateness of specific texts or levels of texts for individual students as well as to investigate areas of strength and weakness of individual students. IRIs allow you to check a student's rate and fluency as well as consider his decoding strategies, miscues, reading comprehension, sight vocabulary, and behaviors such as finger-pointing and holding the text too close.

You can construct an IRI yourself, or you can select an already-constructed IRI from several sources. To construct an IRI yourself, follow the steps shown in In the Classroom 6.8.

Constructing an Informal Reading Inventory

- Select a set of texts of increasing difficulty representative of the material you plan to use for fluency instruction, perhaps half a dozen texts in all.
- Select two passages that seem representative of the book as a whole in terms of sentence length, vocabulary, prior knowledge required, and so on. A 100- to 125-word passage is generally sufficient for beginning readers, and a 200- to 250-word passage is appropriate for higher-ability levels.
- Make sure the student feels at ease. Then introduce the passage by saying something such as "I'm going to have you read this paragraph to me, and then I'd like you to tell me about what you read."
- As the student is reading, follow along with a duplicate copy. Circle words that the student has difficulty with or omits during reading, noting in the margin any mispronunciations or

substitutions of one word for another. In addition, note any significant behaviors exhibited by the reader, such as lack of expression during reading, finger-pointing, holding the text close to the eyes, and a markedly slow or markedly rapid rate.

- After the passage has been read, check comprehension by asking the student to retell what he has read. Initially, ask the student to respond without looking back at the passage. However, if he needs to look back in order to give a satisfactory retelling, let him do so. Characterize the retelling using simple descriptions, such as "complete, coherent, and shows good understanding," "somewhat sketchy but showing basic understanding," or "sketchy and not showing much understanding." You might also want to ask a question or two, perhaps an inferential question and an application question, and record the student's success with those. Additionally, your notes should indicate whether the student needed to look back to retell the passage.

- If you are uncertain about the student's competency with this and similar texts, you can repeat the IRI with a second passage.

Obviously, an IRI can provide you with a great deal of useful information, and you will learn a lot from going through the process of constructing one. Equally obviously, constructing an IRI is a time-consuming process. Fortunately, the *Interactive Reading Assessment System-Revised* (Calfee & Hoover, 2004), which is described in Chapter 14 and included in the *Assessments and Lesson Plans* booklet, includes a set of graded passages and prompts for students' retellings of the passages. Alternatively, the commercially published *Qualitative Reading Inventory-4* (Leslie & Caldwell, 2006) contains an extensive set of graded passages. Beginning with either of these sets of passages and then perhaps adding more of your own passages is an excellent way to become knowledgeable about IRIs and incorporate them into your classroom.

At the formal end of the informal-formal continuum come commercially produced standardized reading tests such as the *Stanford Achievement Test Series* (Harcourt Educational Measurement, 2001) and *TerraNova, the Second Edition* (CTB/McGraw-Hill, 2001), which is described in Chapter 14. Tests

Standardized tests are an increasingly frequent part of today's classrooms.

such as these have the advantage of being group administered and thus take much less time than individual observations and IRIs. They yield a number of indices of performance for each student tested, including grade-level equivalents, the most important score for matching students and texts. For example, a standardized test might indicate that a particular student had a grade-level equivalent of 2.5, indicating that he scored somewhere between the average second-grader and the average third-grader on the test. Given such a score, a second- or third-grade book *may* be an appropriate text to use for fluency work. Note, however, that we emphasize the word *may*. As we note in Chapter 14, standardized tests have both strengths and weaknesses, and precisely indicating the level of text that a certain student should read for a certain purpose is not one of their strengths. Lacking other information, begin fluency instruction with a text at a student's tested grade level, and then carefully monitor the student's reading to see if that text is indeed appropriate for him. Usually, however, you will have other information gained from your observations, an IRI, or some other source and can use the standardized test score combined with this other information in initially choosing a text for the student, always monitoring the student's reading and being prepared to change texts if need be.

Assessing Text Difficulty and Accessibility

As is the case with assessing students' reading proficiency and motivation, there are various approaches to assessing text difficulty and accessibility. Those described here include using traditional readability formulas, using a list of books to which Lexile levels have been assigned, using a list of books that have been "leveled" following criteria developed by Fountas and Pinnell (1999), and considering factors that have been found to be associated with text difficulty and accessibility.

Using readability formulas, objective measures that take into account certain characteristics of a text and yield a grade-level equivalent for the text, is the traditional approach to assessing text difficulty. Such formulas generally consider two factors—a measure of vocabulary difficulty and a measure of syntactic complexity. When applied to a text, such a formula indicates that the text is written at such and such a grade level. The Fry formula (Fry, 1977) is one widely used measure. It assesses word difficulty by considering the average number of syllables in the words in a text, and it assesses syntactic complexity by a considering the average number of words per sentence in a text. For example, when applied to Marion Ripley's *Private and Confidential: A Story About Braille,* the Fry formula indicates that the book is written at approximately the second-grade level. Given this readability level, the book would appear to be appropriate for students who are reading at the second-grade level. We say "appear to be" because both estimates of text difficulty and the reading levels resulting from testing students are approximations. As we have noted, efforts to match students and texts must always be undertaken with the realization that the initial matches should be considered tentative and that you need to be continually checking on how good a match is for a particular student and be prepared to offer him another book if the first one isn't working. Nevertheless, as long as you understand that such matches are approximations, readability formulas and other approaches to assessing text difficulty can be quite useful. The procedures for using the Fry formula and a graph that is used in applying the formula are shown in In the Classroom 6.9.

ASSESSMENT

To help you select texts that are not too difficult for students, use the Directions for Decoding and Vocabulary in the *Assessments and Lesson Plans* supplement to determine students' decoding and vocabulary level. To fine-tune your assessment of a student's reading level, use the Sentence Reading and Passage Reading subtests of the Interactive Reading Assessment System (IRAS) in the *Assessments and Lesson Plans* supplement.

ASSESSMENT

To quickly assess whether or not a text is a good match for a student, have him read from the text orally. If he can read more than 100 words per minute and make fewer than five or so errors, the text is probably a good fit for him.

Using the Fry Readability Formula

1. Randomly select three 100-word samples, from the book, short story, chapter, or article that you want to assess, one from near the beginning of the selection, one from the middle, and one from near the end. For longer selections, you may want to take additional samples. In counting the 100-word samples, do count proper nouns, initials, and numerals. Count hyphenated words as one word.

2. Count the number of sentences in each 100-word sample, estimating to the nearest tenth of a sentence, and average that count.

3. Count the number of syllables in each 100-word sample, and average that count. Syllables are based on sounds, not necessarily letters. There are as many syllables in a word as there are vowel sounds. Thus, *want* has one syllable, *stopped* has one, and *wanted* has two. When counting syllables for numerals, initials, and symbols, count one syllable for each symbol. Thus, *1945* has four syllables; *IRA*, three syllables; and *&*, one syllable.

4. Find on the Fry graph the lines corresponding to the average sentence length and the average number of syllables. Go to the intersection of these two lines to get the approximate grade level of the selection. An example is given below the graph.

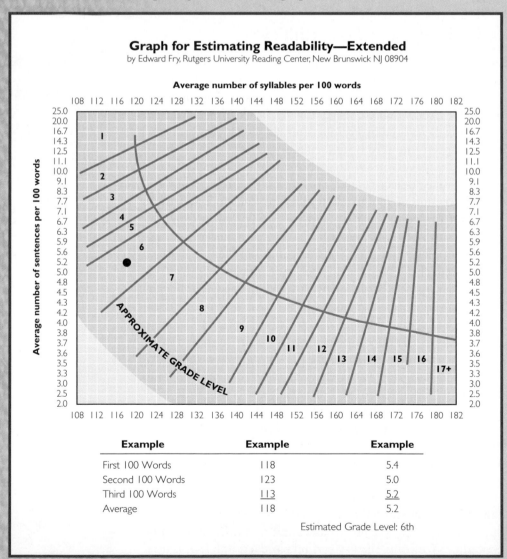

Graph for Estimating Readability—Extended
by Edward Fry, Rutgers University Reading Center, New Brunswick NJ 08904

	Example	Example	Example
First 100 Words		118	5.4
Second 100 Words		123	5.0
Third 100 Words		113	5.2
Average		118	5.2

Estimated Grade Level: 6th

Source: Fry, E. B., Polk, J. K., & Fountoukidis, D. (2000). *The Reading Teacher's Book of Lists.* Paramus, NJ: Prentice Hall.

The second text-difficulty tool we consider, the Lexile Framework for Reading, is a multipart system. The system uses a sophisticated readability formula and has a Website that includes the Lexile Book Database, showing the Lexile level of tens of thousands of books, as well as an online tool for calculating Lexile levels for texts you input. Like the Fry formula, the Lexile formula considers the factors of word difficulty and sentence complexity, although it does so in a more sophisticated way. Unlike the Fry formula and most traditional formulas, the Lexile formula yields a Lexile level, a score ranging from 200 to 1700, instead of a grade-level equivalent. Lexile levels can then be compared to students' scores on standardized tests, many of which yield Lexile levels, or they can be roughly equated with grade levels using the conversion chart shown in Figure 6.6.

LEXILE LEVELS	GRADE-LEVEL EQUIVALENTS
200L to 400L	1
300L to 500L	2
500L to 700L	3
650L to 850L	4
750L to 950L	5
850L to 1050L	6
950L to 1075L	7
1000L to 1100L	8
1050L to 1150L	9
1100L to 1200L	10
1100L to 1300L	11 and 12

FIGURE 6.6

Chart for Converting Lexile Levels to Grade-Level Equivalents

The next approach to assessing text difficulty that we discuss, the leveled books approach, was developed as a way of assessing books and ranking them for difficulty and accessibility by considering a number of factors beyond those taken into account by traditional readability formulas or by computer-based formulas such as the Lexile Framework. Irene Fountas and Gay Su Pinnell (2006) and their colleagues have examined a large number of books and placed them in levels ranging from Levels A and B (for children just beginning to read) to Level Z (for students reading at the seventh- and eighth-grade level). Among the many factors considered in Fountas and Pinnell's leveling process are the number of ideas in the book, the size of the print, the layout, the correspondence between the text and the pictures, and the sophistication and familiarity of the topics. Here, for example, are parts of the descriptions of Levels A and B books, which include books like Syd Hoff's *Barney's Horse,* and of Level M books, which include books like Jan Brett's *The Mitten.*

Levels A and B Books

Levels A and B books are very easy for young children to begin to read. Many of these books focus on a single idea or have a single story line. There is a direct correspondence between the text and the pictures, and children can easily relate the topics to their personal experience. The language, while not exactly duplicating oral language, includes naturally occurring syntactic structures. Teachers can use books at these levels to introduce children to word-by-word matching and locating known words.

Level M Books

Books in Level M are long, with lots of text per page, smaller print, and narrower word spacing. There is a wide variety of texts, but they all have complex language structures and sophisticated vocabulary. They are highly detailed and descriptive and present more abstract concepts and themes. The subtleties of these texts require more background knowledge. Many characters are involved in more complex and expanded plots; character development is a prominent feature.

CW 6.6 links to further information on the Lexile Framework for Reading, the Lexile Book Database, and the tool for calculating Lexile levels yourself.

CW 6.7 links to an online version of The Fountas and Pinnell Leveled Book List, K–8. This list is updated monthly and can be searched in a variety of ways online for a fee.

The newest list of leveled books (Fountas & Pinnell, 2006) shows approximately 16,000 titles.

Another subjective approach to assessing text difficulty is to consider the array of factors affecting difficulty discovered in recent psychological and linguistic research. This is what two of us (Graves & Graves, 2003) recently did. Although this approach does not yield a single answer, such as a grade-level equivalent, Lexile score, or Fountas and Pinnell level, it does suggest what factors to look for as you consider the appropriateness of various reading selections for your students. Here are the factors to consider:

- Vocabulary
- Sentence structure
- Length
- Elaboration
- Coherence and unity
- Text structure
- Familiarity of content and background knowledge required
- Audience appropriateness
- Quality and verve of the writing
- Interestingness

Not all of these factors are weighted equally; they are weighted differently from one book to another, and as we have noted, they do not yield a numerical score. However, considering them does help you think deeply about the match between a student or group of students and a text.

Your Personal and Professional Knowledge

At this point, we have already discussed assessing students and assessing reading materials, but in completing our consideration of matching students and texts, we want to say a bit more about each of these topics and make some comments about purposes. In considering students, it is important to go beyond the information gleaned from IRIs and standardized tests and think of each student as a person with strengths and weaknesses, likes and dislikes, favorite topics and ones that bore him, good days and bad days, successes and failures, and varying tolerance for challenges.

In considering reading materials, it is important to go beyond the grade level provided by a readability formula, the Lexile level provided by the Lexile Framework, the level assigned by the Fountas and Pinnell system, and the factors influencing text difficulty and consider the content of each book and how individual students are going to respond to that content. Is the book about salamanders you're considering for Teddy too difficult according to a readability formula but probably a great choice for Teddy because anything as slimy and snake-like as a salamander is sure to enthrall him? Is the coming of age novel you're considering for both Tammy and Ramon far too mature for almost all the other students in the class but a perfect fit for these two very mature students? Will a simple narrative set in the desert be particularly difficult for your Hmong students because they are unfamiliar with desert environments?

In addition to considering the students and the text, it is important to consider the purpose for which students are reading. As we have noted, when your purpose is to improve fluency and you are using an approach in which the students repeatedly read the same text, the text needs to be slightly challenging so that there is room for improvement across the repeated readings. Similarly, when you are working with the class or a small group, scaffolding their reading of a particular text (something we describe in detail in Chapter 8), you will generally want to use texts that are a little challenging, ones that your students can succeed at because you are assisting them. Conversely, when students are doing independent reading and do not have your assistance, they should frequently read in texts that are not a challenge, ones that they find interesting and enjoyable but not taxing. Similarly, when you are teaching a comprehension strategy, you want to use a text that is sophisticated enough to require the use of the strategy but not one where decoding is a problem, since students can hardly be expected to use a comprehension strategy if they cannot decode the text.

As we noted at the beginning of this section, matching students and texts is important for all of the reading activities students undertake. Fluency instruction and practice are no exception. Carefully matching students and texts during fluency instruction will go a long way toward ensuring that fluency instruction is effective.

Reflect *and* Apply

6. Make a copy of the Class Fluency Record shown in Figure 6.5, and make up rate, accuracy, expression, and comprehension scores for two students who show quite different profiles. Jot down the fluency activities you might provide for each of these students, and briefly justify the activities you suggest.

7. Your observations are particularly important in assessing students' motivation to read and the extent to which they need to be challenged in the fluency activities you give them. You use them, of course, in choosing activities that will be at just the right level of difficulty for particular students. Make up a brief observation form that includes half a dozen or so types of behavior you want to consider, and briefly note why each is important.

8. Identify one widely used book you estimate to be at about the second-grade level and one you estimate to be at about the fourth-grade level. Look up each book in the Lexile Book Database at www.lexile.com, and convert the Lexile level into a grade-level equivalent using the conversion chart shown in Figure 6.6. Compare your estimates to those you got using the Lexile Book Database and the conversion chart, and jot down a comment on the agreement or disagreement between the estimates.

Several sorts of diversity are particularly important in considering fluency instruction—diversity in linguistic background, in background knowledge, in reading proficiency, and in motivation and tolerance for being challenged. Here, we take up each of these in turn.

DIVERSITY IN LINGUISTIC BACKGROUND

CW 6.8 links to the Barahona Center for the Study of Books in Spanish for Children and Adolescents. Here you will find hundreds of books in Spanish and books in English about Latinos. Many of these, of course, deal with topics familiar to many Latinos, and familiar topics are a definite plus when students are working on fluency.

For English-language learners who are still struggling to learn oral English, achieving fluency in English may be a real struggle. If such students are in true bilingual reading programs, it would almost certainly be best if they could become fluent in their first language initially and then work on attaining fluency in English. However, bilingual reading program are rare and not the situation most students face. The alternative is to give English-language students just as much support as possible. One possibility is using dual-language books—books with the text in both English and the student's native language on the same page or facing pages. That way, the student can first read or hear the text in his native language and then hear it in English. Another alternative is to ensure that the student has a sufficiently easy English text, model your fluent reading of it several times, allow the student enough repetitions to truly master one passage before moving on to another, and be sure that the student is not forced to read haltingly in front of other students.

DIVERSITY IN BACKGROUND KNOWLEDGE

Many English-language learners, many minority students, and many children of poverty come to school with experiences and, therefore, background knowledge very different from those of middle-class students. It is particularly important to provide these students with texts for fluency instruction and practice that deal with topics they know something about and have some interest in. Talk to children about their experiences and interests, talk to their parents or other caregivers, and work with your school librarian and other professionals to get all students books that they will find interesting, enjoyable, and appropriate, given their experiences.

DIVERSITY IN READING PROFICIENCY

As noted at the beginning of this chapter, many more-skilled readers move easily through Chall's (1996) stages of reading development. They internalize the basic facts about reading before entering school, quickly learn decoding skills so that they can process texts word by word, achieve a significant degree of automaticity, and begin to read smoothly and accurately, with expression and with comprehension—and they do all of this with apparent ease. For these students, wide reading is the key to fluency, although choral reading, readers theater, and radio reading will also be useful for increasing their oral reading skills. Unfortunately, many less-skilled readers do not move easily through Chall's stages. They do not internalize the basic facts about reading before entering school; for them, learning to decode is a slow and not always certain process, and automaticity turns out to be an illusive goal. These students will learn to read smoothly, accurately, with expression, and with comprehension only with a good deal of direct attention to fluency instruction. These students, too, need to do wide reading in accessible, interesting, and enjoyable texts; they should have opportunities to engage in choral reading, readers theater, and radio reading. But they also need a lot of work with more direct approaches to building fluency—repeated reading, echo reading, tape-assisted repeated reading, and the like.

DIVERSITY IN MOTIVATION AND TOLERANCE FOR CHALLENGES

The more success students have experienced with reading, the more motivated they are to read and the more willing they are to accept challenges. Conversely, the less success students have had with reading, the less likely they are to be motivated to read and the fewer challenges they are likely to accept. The more problems with reading students have experienced, the more we have to work extremely hard to make fluency instruction a pleasant, non-threatening, and non-embarrassing activity. This means providing less-successful readers with texts that are not too challenging, giving them plenty of opportunities to practice in private before they read orally for you, and not putting them in situations in which they are likely to stumble through a text in front of other students. It also means that less-successful readers need to compare their current fluency achievement with their previous achievement and not with norms or with the achievement of other students in the class. With less-successful readers as with more successful ones, one of our major tasks as teachers is to continually stretch them to reach higher levels of achievement. But with less successful readers, we need to do everything possible to set realistic goals that they can and will reach.

Concluding Remarks

In this chapter, we have defined fluency and described many different procedures for assisting students in becoming fluent—the original method of repeated reading, simultaneous repeated reading, echo reading, tape-assisted repeated reading, partner reading, choral reading, readers theater, radio reading, fluency-oriented oral reading, commercial fluency programs, and wide reading. We have also discussed ways of assessing fluency, suggested criteria for choosing among the many approaches so that students get the types of fluency instruction they need, and described several tools for assessing students and assessing texts in order to match students with appropriate texts.

In recent years, fluency instruction has been identified as a critical component of a comprehensive and effective reading program. All students must reach the goal of reading fluently if they are to progress from being novices who are just learning to read to becoming actual readers who can and do read—children and later adults who read for enjoyment, for learning, to become informed citizens, to investigate topics as diverse as health and hobbies, and for the myriad of other benefits one can gain from reading. You will need to select approaches to fluency that fit your students, your teaching style, and the overall context in which you teach. But one thing is certain: Fluency instruction should be a definite part of your curriculum.

Extending Learning

1. One excellent way to understand a phenomenon is to engage in a process in which you experience it. This works particularly well with the process of becoming automatic in reading because there is a very simple way of experiencing it. Find a fairly lengthy and complex sentence, and write it backwards. Here is an example with a very short sentence: "Bob had a cow" becomes "Woc a dah boB." Once you have written out your backward sentence—and remember that it needs to be a good deal longer and more complex than the example we have given—repeatedly read it aloud from back to front (right to left) until you can read it fluently. Time each reading, and make a note of how rapidly you move toward automaticity with the reversed sentence. This is a much simpler task than the one beginning readers face, so don't think their progress toward automaticity will be nearly as rapid. Still, the task will give you a good sense of what it means to move from consciously having to think about each letter as you read to becoming automatic in processing words.

2. Get together with a teacher who is working with some students on fluency (probably a second- or third-grade teacher or possibly a teacher in a higher-grade classroom that includes struggling readers), and volunteer to help with the fluency activities for a fairly lengthy period. Two weeks is probably the minimum, and four weeks or even longer would be better. Describe the fluency activity or activities you use. Keep a log book in which you chart your student's or students' progress and keep a record of how each session goes, for you and for your student or students. Once you have completed your tutoring, write a brief summary of the experience. In the summary, include consideration of what you did, how the fluency work you engaged in was similar to or different from that described in this chapter, what your student or students gained from the activities, what you learned from them, and what you plan to do about fluency instruction in your classes.

3. Identify a widely used children's book such as Sid Fleischman's *The Whipping Boy,* and use three of the four approaches listed in this chapter to assess text difficulty and accessibility—the Fry formula, the Lexile Book Database, the levels provided by Fountas and Pinnell (2006), and the subjective approach that two of us have described (Graves & Graves, 2003). After you have used the approaches, write a fairly detailed critique of the information each yielded and its advantages and disadvantages.

mylabschool
Where the classroom comes to life!

For a look at fluency in a contemporary classroom, go to Allyn & Bacon's MyLabSchool.com. In MLS Courses, click on Reading Methods, and go to MLS Video Lab. There you will find video clips about Comprehension in Module 5.

Children's Literature

Brett, J. (1989). *The Mitten: A Ukranian Folktale*. New York: Putnam. A variety of animals are sleeping very snugly in Nicki's lost mitten—up until the bear sneezes, that is. 32 pages.

Fleischman, S. (2003). *The Whipping Boy*. New York: HarperTrophy. Prince Brat's whipping boy, the orphan Jemmy, teaches the royal heir about life and friendship when the spoiled prince flees the castle. 96 pages.

Hoff, S. (1987). *Barney's Horse*. New York: Harper & Row. Barney's horse becomes frightened by the new overhead trains he encounters in the city. 32 pages.

Prelutsky, J. (2005). *It's Raining Pigs and Noodles*. New York: HarperTrophy. This wonderful read-aloud collection of humorous poems with "impeccable rhythms and rhymes" appeals to a child's sense of humor. 160 pages.

Ripley, M. (2003). *Private and Confidential: A Story About Braille*. New York: Dial Books for Young Readers. Laura finds out that her new pen pal is nearly blind and learns to use a braille machine to write to him. 28 pages.

Vocabulary Development

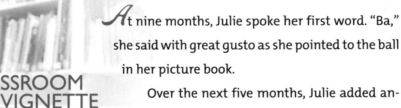

CLASSROOM VIGNETTE

*A*t nine months, Julie spoke her first word. "Ba," she said with great gusto as she pointed to the ball in her picture book.

Over the next five months, Julie added another 50 words or so to her repertoire. After that, her vocabulary grew by leaps and bounds. Everyone in her family was an avid reader, everyone read to her a lot, and everyone talked to her a lot. By the time she started school, she had an oral vocabulary of several thousand words. Was Julie an unusual five-year-old wordsmith? Not really. Julie's vocabulary development is typical of many children, but not of all children by any means.

After she began school, Julie, like many of her counterparts, began rapidly acquiring a reading vocabulary. Soon, both her reading and her oral vocabulary grew impressively. Aided by her teachers—and, of course, by the reading she did and her growing understanding of the power of words—Julie acquired the vocabulary she needed to succeed in and out of school.

As we just noted, Julie's vocabulary development is not unique. But neither is it typical of all children. Children who grow up in homes where they are seldom read to, where they are not talked to a lot, or where English is rarely or never spoken are likely to have small English vocabularies when they enter school. And having a small English vocabulary is likely to adversely affect their success in school.

Fortunately, teachers are in an enviable position. You have the unique opportunity to have a powerful effect on the vocabularies of the students you teach. Teaching vocabulary can improve students' reading comprehension, their writing, their speaking, their success in school, and their success beyond school.

The Vocabulary-Learning Task

Fortunately, since vocabulary is tremendously important to students' success, we currently know a great deal about how to create an effective vocabulary program (Baumann, Kame'enui, & Ash, 2003; Graves, 2006). Several considerations are particularly important to keep in mind as you begin planning a comprehensive and effective program: To begin, the vocabulary-learning task is enormous! Estimates of vocabulary size vary greatly, but a reasonable estimate based on a substantial body of rigorous work (Anderson & Nagy, 1992; Anglin, 1993; Hiebert, 2005; Nagy & Anderson, 1984; White, Graves, & Slater, 1990) is this: The books and other reading materials used by schoolchildren include well over 100,000 different words. The average child enters school with a very small reading vocabulary, typically consisting largely of environmental print. Once in school, however, a child's reading vocabulary is likely to soar at a rate of 3,000 to 4,000 words a year, leading to a reading vocabulary of something like 25,000 words by the time she is in the eighth grade and maybe well over 50,000 words by the end of high school (Graves, 2006).

Quite obviously, each year students learn many more words than we can teach directly. This represents a tremendous learning achievement, yet it is partially explained by the fact that students lack deep and rich meanings for many of the words they know. Instead, they often possess partial and incomplete meanings, which hinder full comprehension of reading materials that contain the words and students' confidence in using them in their speaking or writing. Isabel Beck and her colleagues (Beck, McKeown, & Omanson, 1987) have distinguished three levels of word knowledge—the *unknown, acquainted,* and *established* levels. A word at the unknown level is, as the name indicates, completely unfamiliar. The word *repel* is likely to be unknown to most third-graders. A word at the acquainted level is one whose basic meaning is recognized, but only after the student gives it some deliberate attention. The word *resident* would probably be understood by most fifth-graders but would require a moment's thought. A word at the established level is easily, rapidly, and automatically recognized. For most second-graders, the word *house* would be at the established level.

Of course, students do not need to know *all* the words they encounter in reading at the established level. They do, however, need to know most of the words they encounter at the established level because, as we noted in Chapter 1, words that are not recognized automatically will thwart the process of comprehending text. Moreover, as we just suggested, unless words are understood at the established level, students are not likely to use them in speaking and writing.

There is increasing evidence that the vocabularies of many children of poverty entering school are much smaller than those of their middle-class counterparts. There is also evidence that having a small vocabulary is a very serious detriment to success in reading. These two facts make it especially important to find ways to bolster the oral and reading vocabularies of students who enter school with limited word knowledge (Becker, 1977; Biemiller, 2001; Hart & Risley, 2003; National Reading Panel, 2000; RAND Reading Study Group, 2002; White et al., 1990). For similar reasons, bolstering the oral and reading English vocabularies of English-language learners is critically important (Nation, 2001; Schmitt, 2000; Snow, 2004).

A comprehensive and effective vocabulary program must respect these facts about children's word knowledge and how it grows, and the program we describe here does so. The program has four major thrusts. First, it provides children with frequent, extensive, and varied language experiences. Second, it includes instruction in individual words. Third, it provides students with instruction in learning words independently. Finally, it fosters word consciousness; that is, it builds students' interest in words, teaches them to value words, and gets them actively involved in building and honing their vocabularies.

Frequent, Extensive, and Varied Language Experiences

The language experiences referred to in the heading are, of course, listening, speaking, reading, and writing. What follows is a brief reminder of the importance of each of them, along with a discussion of shared storybook reading, an interactive oral-reading approach that has been shown to be very productive. Listening is the earliest to occur, with children beginning to perceive speech sounds well before their first year. Speaking comes next, with most children uttering their first word at about age 1. The most general statement that can be made about listening and speaking in the preschool years and beyond is that children need as much of both as possible. They particularly need to engage in real discussions—give-and-take conversations in which first caretakers and later teachers give young learners the opportunity to think and discuss topics of interest in an open, positive, and supportive climate. In summing up the major message of their longitudinal study showing the huge and ever-widening gap between the vocabularies of middle-class children and of many children reared in poverty, Betty Hart and Todd Risley (1995) note that "the most important difference among families was in the amount of talking that went on." Anything

Reading to children is especially effective when coupled with discussion and when students are actively involved and responding to the book being shared.

we can do to promote real discussions in school and out of school is very worthwhile.

Of course, reading to children is also very worthwhile and extremely important (Cunningham, 2005). As teachers, we should frequently read to children, model our enthusiasm for reading, and do everything we can to get parents and other caregivers involved in reading to and with their children.

While simply reading to children has been found to be effective in promoting vocabulary growth, interactive oral reading—in which an adult and a small group of children focus on and discuss words that come up in the reading—has been shown to be particularly effective (Beck & McKeown, 2004; Biemiller, 2003; De Temple & Snow, 2003; Zevenbergen & Whitehurst, 2004). Interactive oral reading is designed for primary-grade students, and it is particularly useful for students who come to school with relatively small vocabularies and therefore need special assistance to catch up with their peers. Here are some characteristics of effective interactive oral reading taken from De Temple and Snow (2003), our own experiences, and reading of the literature:

English Learners

The active, give-and-take, well-scaffolded nature of interactive oral reading makes it an excellent choice for English-language learners.

- Both the reader and the children play active roles.
- The book (or other reading selection) is read several times.
- The adult reader focuses the children's attention directly on words.
- The adult reads fluently, using an animated and lively reading style.
- The books need to be interesting and enjoyable and stretch children's thinking a bit.
- The words need to be somewhat challenging and ones children are likely to encounter in the future.

In the Classroom 7.1 shows the steps of the interactive oral-reading approach developed by Andrew Biemiller (2003).

Interactive Oral Reading as Described by Biemiller

instructional routines in the Classroom 7.1

- *Day 1.* Read the book through once, including some comprehension questions after reading it but not interrupting the reading with vocabulary instruction. (Experience has shown that children may object to interrupting the first reading of the book with vocabulary instruction.)
- *Day 2.* Re-read the book, teaching about eight words. When you come to a sentence containing a target word, stop and re-read the sentence.

  After re-reading the word, give a brief explanation. For example, after reading the sentence "It seemed like a good **solution**" in a second-grade book, pose the question "What does *solution* mean?" Then, answer your question with something like "A *solution* is an answer to a problem." Remember to keep the definitions simple, direct, and focused on the meaning of the word as it was used in the story.

  At the end of the day's instruction, review the words taught by re-reading the sentences in which they appeared and the definitions you gave.
- *Days 3 and 4.* Re-read the story two more times, teaching about eight new words each time. As on Day 2, briefly define the words as you come to them, and review all of them at the end of the reading.
- *At the end of the week.* Review all of the words taught during the week, this time using new sentences to provide some variety but giving the same definition.

One point about the use of interactive oral reading deserves special emphasis. It is, as we just noted, particularly appropriate for students who come to school with very small vocabularies. These students have a lot of catching up to do, and only sustained efforts can have the sort of effect needed. Ideally, such efforts would begin in kindergarten and continue throughout the primary grades.

Of course, once students can read, they should be reading as much as possible in a variety of materials. Wide reading is important for a host of reasons, but it is particularly important to vocabulary growth. If students learn to read something like 3,000 to 4,000 words each year, it is clear that most of the words they learn are not taught directly. With a 180-day school year, teaching 3,000 to 4,000 words would require teaching approximately 20 words each and every school day. Obviously, this does not happen. Instead, students learn many of the words that make up their vocabularies from their reading (Anderson, 1996). Thus, if we can substantially increase the amount of reading students do, we can markedly increase their vocabularies. Moreover, wide reading will foster automaticity, provide knowledge about a variety of topics and literary forms, and leave students with a habit that will make them lifelong readers.

Unfortunately, many students do very little reading, and some do almost none (Anderson, Wilson, & Fielding, 1988). Richard Allington (1977) summed up the situation nicely in his memorable plea for students to do more reading—"If they don't read much, how they ever gonna get good?" The answer is clearly that they are not. Moreover, as Allington (2001) and a number of others have noted, a substantial amount of the reading students do needs to be easy enough that they can understand and enjoy what they are reading rather than struggle to decode it.

Finally, as we now know but somehow did not know a few years ago, writing is a powerful ally and aid to reading. From the very beginning, students need to engage frequently in activities in which reading and writing are paired, and some of these paired activities should focus on words.

Reflect *and* Apply

1. Based on the growth rates we suggest, give some estimates of the size of students' reading vocabularies at the end of grades 2, 3, 4, 5, and 6. Note that because we give a range for vocabulary size at the end of first grade and a range of growth rates, a range of answers will be correct.
2. Suppose that two concerned parents, fluent in both English and Spanish, come to you and say that they really want to help their daughter build her reading vocabulary but don't know just how to do that. Assuming that you do not want to suggest they do direct teaching of words, what might you suggest they do to help their daughter build her English and Spanish vocabulary?

Teaching Individual Words

Here, we first discuss the various word-learning tasks students face and ways of identifying words to teach. Then we consider teaching procedures for each of these word-learning tasks.

Word-Learning Tasks

All word-learning tasks are not the same. They differ on matters such as how much students already know about the words to be taught, how well you want them to learn the words, and what you want them to be able to do with the words afterward. Here, we consider five tasks students face in learning words. Note that the type of learning required and the difficulty of the learning differ from task to task.

Learning a Basic Vocabulary

Many children arrive at school with substantial oral vocabularies, perhaps numbering 5,000 words. Some children raised in poverty, however, come to school with meager oral vocabularies; and, of course, some English-language learners come to school with very meager English vocabularies. For such children, building a basic oral vocabulary of the most-frequent English words and learning to read the 1,000 or so most-frequent words automatically are of utmost importance.

Learning to Read Known Words

Learning to read words that are already in their oral vocabularies is the major word-learning task of beginning readers. Words such as *surprise, stretch,* and *amaze* are ones that students might be taught to read during their first three years of school. By third or fourth grade, good readers will have learned to read virtually all the words in their oral vocabularies. However, this task will remain incomplete for many less-able readers and for some English-language learners.

Learning New Words That Represent Known Concepts

A second word-learning task students face is learning to read words that are in neither their oral nor their reading vocabularies but for which they have an available concept. For example, the word *pant* would be unknown to a number of third-graders, but almost all students have seen dogs panting and know what it is like to be out of breath. All students continue to learn words of this sort throughout their years in school, and this is one of the major word-learning tasks for intermediate-grade students. It is also a major learning task for English-language learners, who, of course, have a great number of concepts for which they do not have English words.

Learning New Words That Represent New Concepts

Another word-learning task students face, and a very demanding one, is learning to read words that are in neither their oral nor their reading vocabulary and for which they do not have an available concept. Learning the full meanings of words such as *equation, impeach,* and *mammal* is likely to require most elementary students to develop new concepts. All students continue to learn

An effective way to identify potentially difficult words is to list them on the board, point to them one by one, and have students raise their hands if they don't know a word.

words of this sort throughout their years in school and beyond. Once again, learning new concepts will be particularly important for English-language learners. Also, students whose backgrounds differ from that of the majority culture will have internalized a set of concepts that is at least somewhat different from the set internalized by students in the majority culture. Thus, words that represent known concepts for some groups of students will represent unknown concepts for other groups.

Clarifying and Enriching the Meanings of Known Words

The last word-learning task we consider here is that of clarifying and enriching the meanings of already known words. The meanings students originally attach to words are often imprecise and become fully specified only over time (Carey, 1978). For example, students initially might not recognize any difference between *brief* and *concise,* what distinguishes *cabin* from *shed,* or that the term *virtuoso* is most frequently applied to musicians. Although students will expand and enrich the meanings of the words they know as they repeatedly meet them in new and slightly different contexts, direct approaches to teaching meanings are definitely warranted.

Identifying Vocabulary to Teach

Once you have considered the word-learning tasks students face, you still have the task of selecting specific words to teach. In this section of the chapter, we recommend a two-step process in which you first get some idea of which words are likely to be unknown to your students and then follow several criteria for selecting the words to actually teach.

Three sources are useful for identifying words to teach: word lists, selections your students are reading or listening to, and the students themselves. Word lists are particularly useful for identifying a basic oral vocabulary you may want to teach to students who have not already developed such a vocabulary. The most readily available list is Edward Fry's list of the 1,000 most-frequent words (2004). Fry ranks the words individually by frequency, so the exact rank of each word is clearly shown. Another frequency list has recently been developed by Elfrieda Hiebert (2005). This list has the advantages of containing over 5,000 words and being based on newer data than is Fry's list. However, it lists words as belonging to one of several blocks rather than by individual frequency and is therefore not as fine grained as Fry's list. It is absolutely crucial that students master the most-frequent words—initially in their oral vocabularies and then in their reading vocabularies—as soon as possible, because these words make up a huge percentage of the words students will come across as they read.

The second source useful for identifying words that you might teach is the selections students are reading or listening to. English, like all natural languages, consists of a small number of frequent words and a very large number of infrequent words. Once students acquire a basic vocabulary of 1,000 to 2,000 words, the number of different words you might teach is so large that frequency does not provide much of a basis for choosing which ones to teach. At this point, using your best judgment to select vocabulary from the material students are reading and listening to becomes a better approach.

In most reading selections, you are likely to find more potentially useful vocabulary to teach than you have time to teach. In winnowing the number of words to teach, the answers to the following four questions can be helpful.

- "Is understanding the word important to understanding the selection in which it appears?" If the answer is "No," then other words are probably more important to teach.
- "Are students able to use context or structural analysis skills to discover the word's meaning?" If they can use these skills, then they should be allowed to practice them. Doing so will both help them consolidate these skills and reduce the number of words you need to teach.
- "Can working with this word be useful in furthering students' context, structural analysis, or dictionary skills?" If the answer here is "Yes," then your working with the word can serve two purposes. It can aid students in learning the word, and it can help them acquire a strategy they can use in learning other words. You might, for example, decide to teach the word *regenerate* because students need to master the prefix *re-*.
- "How useful is this word outside of the reading selection being currently taught?" The more frequently a word appears in material students read, the more important it is for them to know the word. Additionally, the more frequent a word is, the greater the chances that students will retain the word once you teach it.

Finally, the ultimate source of information about what words to teach is the students themselves. You can identify words on word lists or in upcoming selections that you think will be difficult for your students and build simple tests to find out whether or not they are difficult (see Nation, 2001 for sample tests). Of course, constructing such tests is time-consuming and certainly not something you need to do for every selection. However, several experiences of identifying words that you think will be difficult and then checking students' performance against your expectations will sharpen your general perceptions of which words are and are not likely to cause your students problems.

In addition to testing students on potentially difficult words using these traditional types of tests, you can take the opportunity to ask students which words they know. One easy way of doing this is to simply dictate words or to list words on the board and have students raise their hands if they do not know a word. This approach is quick, easy, and risk-free for students; it also gives students some responsibility for their word learning. Moreover, research (White, Slater, & Graves, 1989) indicates that students can be quite accurate in identifying words that they do and do not know.

Methods of Teaching Individual Words

How might you go about providing instruction for each of the five word-learning tasks described? As you will see, the instruction needed for some word-learning tasks is much more complex than that for others. Note too that some of these instructional methods will promote deeper levels of word knowledge than others.

Learning a Basic Vocabulary

As we have noted, building a basic vocabulary of very frequent words is crucial so that students don't repeatedly stumble over words they don't know. The first 100 words out of Fry's (2004) and Hiebert's (2005) lists account for about 50 percent of the words students will encounter as they are reading; the first 300 words, about 60 percent of the words they will encounter; and the first 1,000 words, about 70 percent of the words they will encounter. As we have also noted, while many students already have these words in their oral vocabularies, many children of poverty and many English-language learners do not. What we need to do is ensure that all student have these words in both their oral and their reading vocabularies. Interactive oral reading, which we discussed on pages 208–209, is the major approach we suggest for building a basic oral vocabulary. For building a basic reading vocabulary, we suggest that you identify ten or so words for instruction each week, define the words (unless they are function words like *the, and, of,* and the like), use them in context, and give students opportunities to contribute what they know about the words. Keep a list of words that have been taught and display them prominently in the room, perhaps pasting them to the classroom wall. After the words are initially taught, help students review and rehearse them in a variety of ways, including but not limited to those listed here:

- Point out the words and (if they are not function words) briefly define them as you are reading to students.
- Have students rapidly read the words on the wall. This can be done individually or in groups, and it is a good idea to make it a game-like activity when possible.
- Have students "cheer" the words—"*about, A-B-O-U-T, about*"—an idea suggested by Patricia Cunningham (2005).
- Students can "walk the wall"—circle the room in pairs, quizzing each other on the words as they walk, an idea suggested by Peter Dewitz (personal communication, May 2005).
- Students can listen to the words and their definitions on audiotapes.
- Students can work in pairs or larger groups teaching and testing each other on the words.
- Students can draw pictures illustrating the words and share their pictures with the class.

A word of the day recorded on a word wall not only spurs interest in words but helps build students' vocabulary.

- Students can write the new words on cards and build constantly growing individual word banks.
- Students can play games and complete puzzles with the words.
- Students can categorize the new words and relate them to other words.
- Students can engage in a number of other activities that give them opportunities to hear the words and associate them with their meanings.

Additionally, quiz students on sets of the words from time to time, give them feedback on how they are they are doing, remind them of the importance of learning these words, and talk to them about their perceptions of their progress.

Learning to Read Known Words

In learning to read known words, the basic task for the student is to associate what is unknown, the written word, with what is already known, the spoken word. To establish the association between the written and spoken forms of a word, the student needs to see the word at the same time that it is pronounced. Once this association is established, it needs to be rehearsed and strengthened so that the relationship becomes automatic. We have listed these steps to emphasize just how straightforward the process is:

Step 1. Look at the word.
Step 2. Listen to the word while looking at it.
Step 3. Rehearse that association again and again.

Each of these three steps can be accomplished in a number of ways. Students can see the word on the board, on a computer screen, or in a book that they are reading or that you are reading to them. They can hear the word when you say it, when another student says it, or when a voice simulator on a computer says it. And they can rehearse the association by seeing the word and pronouncing it a number of times, writing it, and playing games that require them to recognize printed versions of it. However, wide reading in materials that contain many repetitions of the words and that are enjoyable and easily read is by far the best way to empower students to automatically and effortlessly recognize these words whenever they see them.

Finally, one very important point to remember when teaching these words is that there is no need to teach their meanings. By definition, these are words students already know and understand when they hear them; they simply cannot read them. Time spent "teaching" students the meaning of words they already know is time wasted.

Learning New Words That Represent Known Concepts

We have found two particularly useful approaches for teaching students new words that represent known concepts. In In the Classroom 7.2, we describe them. As you will see, each requires different amounts of the teacher's time, class time, and the students' time and effort, and they are likely to yield different results. Each, however, is very appropriate for introducing a small number of potentially challenging words from a selection the class is about to read.

Two Ways to Introduce New Words Representing Known Concepts

CONTEXT PLUS USE OF THE DICTIONARY

This requires little teacher preparation time, but a fair amount of students' time.

Purpose: To provide students with a basic understanding of a word's meaning and give them practice in using the dictionary.

Procedure:

- In a handout, on a computer file, or on the chalkboard, give students a word in context. For example, for the word *excel* you could use this sentence:

  To get into the Olympics, a person must really *excel* at an Olympic sport.

- Have students read the word and the context-rich sentence and then look up the meaning of the word in a dictionary.

- Discuss the word and its meaning.

CONTEXT-RELATIONSHIP PROCEDURE

This approach (developed by Graves and Slater, in press) requires quite a bit of teacher preparation but relatively little class time.

Purpose: To provide students with both a basic understanding of a word's meaning and practice in using context to determine a word's meaning.

Procedure:

- Create a brief paragraph that uses the target word three or four times. Then follow the paragraph with a multiple-choice item that checks students' understanding of the word. A sample paragraph and multiple-choice item and the steps for presenting each word are shown here:

  conveying

  The luncheon speaker was successful in *conveying* his main ideas to the audience. They all understood what he said, and most agreed with him.

  Conveying has a more specific meaning than *talking*. *Conveying* indicates that a person is getting his or her ideas across accurately.

  Conveying means

  _____ A. putting parts together.

  _____ B. communicating a message.

  _____ C. hiding important information.

- Explain the purpose of the procedure.
- Pronounce the word to be taught.
- Read the paragraph in which the word appears.
- Read the possible definitions, and ask students to choose the best one.
- Pause to give students time to check a definition, give them the correct answer, and answer any questions they have.
- Read the word and its definition a final time.

Learning New Words That Represent New Concepts

As we have noted, learning new words that represent new concepts is often a challenging task. In the Classroom 7.3, based on a method developed by Dorothy Frayer (Frayer, Frederick, & Klausmeier, 1969), illustrates one very effective method to help students gain knowledge of new words that represent new concepts. Although the example is for primary-grade students, the procedure is appropriate for all grade levels.

Introducing New Words That Represent New Concepts

instructional routines

in the Classroom 7.3

Purpose: To introduce second-grade students to the new word *globe* and the concept of globe.

Procedure:

- Define the new concept, giving its specific attributes. For example,

  A *globe* is a spherical (ball-like) representation of a planet.

  When possible, show a model or a picture illustrating the concept.

- Distinguish between the new concept and similar but different concepts with which it might be confused. It may be appropriate to identify accidental attributes that might falsely be considered definitive attributes of the new concept. For example,

  A globe is different from a map because a map is flat. A globe is different from a contour map, a map in which mountains and other high points are raised above the general level of the map, because a contour map is not spherical.

- Give examples of the concept, and explain what makes them good examples:

  The most common globe is a globe of the earth. Globes of the earth are spherical [display a sphere or spheres such as a ball or an orange] and come in various sizes and colors. A much less common globe is a globe of another planet. A museum might have a spherical representation of Saturn.

- Give non-examples of the concept, such as a map of California or a map of how to get to a friend's house, and explain why they are not examples of the concept at hand.

- Present students with examples and non-examples of the concept, and ask them to distinguish between the two. You might include an aerial photograph of New York (non-example), a red sphere representing Mars (example), a walking map of St. Louis (non-example), and a ball-shaped model of the moon (example).

- Have students present examples and non-examples of the concept, and explain what makes them examples and non-examples. Give them feedback on their presentations.

Teaching concepts using the Frayer method will take a good deal of your time and a good deal of students' time. The method also will require considerable thought from both you and your students. However, for important concepts, the fruits of the labor will be well worth the effort, for with this method students can gain a new idea, another lens through which they can interpret the world.

Clarifying and Enriching the Meanings of Known Words

Semantic mapping and semantic feature analysis, which are illustrated in In the Classroom 7.4, are two methods of clarifying and enriching the meanings

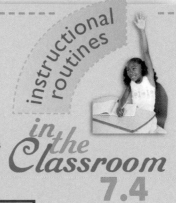

English Learners

CW 7.3 links to an extensive dictionary of Spanish-English cognates. Spanish-speaking children can draw on their knowledge of Spanish cognates—words that are spelled similarly and have similar meanings—to learn English words.

of known words. These methods, both developed by Dale Johnson (Heimlich & Pittelman, 1986; Johnson & Pearson, 1984; Pittelman, Heimlich, Berglund, & French, 1991), are also useful in preteaching unknown words to improve students' comprehension of a selection, one of the most important purposes of vocabulary instruction. They work particularly well because they focus not only on the words being taught but also on related words and on the part the words play in the selection. These two methods can also be used to teach *new* concepts—if the concepts are not too difficult and if students already have at least some information related to them.

Semantic Mapping and Semantic Feature Analysis

instructional routines in the Classroom 7.4

SEMANTIC MAPPING

Sometimes called semantic webbing, semantic mapping makes use of a graphic organizer that looks something like a spider web. Lines connect a central concept to a variety of related ideas and events. A semantic map for the word *tenement* is shown below. You and your students might create a map such as this before or after reading a social studies chapter on urban housing.

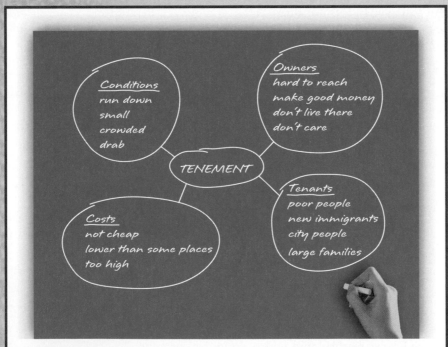

Purpose: To enrich and clarify students' existing knowledge of a concept by having them identify categories of ideas and events that relate to that concept.

Procedure:

- Put a word representing a central concept, such as *tenement*, on the chalkboard.
- Have students form groups, brainstorming as many words as they can think of related to the central concept.
- Write students' words on the chalkboard, grouped in broad categories.
- Have students name the categories and perhaps suggest additional ones.

- Discuss with students the central concept, the other words, the categories, and their inter-relationships.

SEMANTIC FEATURE ANALYSIS

This procedure employs a grid, such as the sample grid on *vehicles* shown below, which is modeled on one provided by Pittelman and her colleagues (Pittelman et al., 1991).

VEHICLES	two wheels	four wheels	more than four wheels	motor	diesel fuel	gasoline
car	−	+	−	+	−	+
bicycle	+	−	−	−	−	−
motorcycle	+	−	−	+	−	+
truck	−	+	+	+	+	−
train	−	−	+	+	+	−
skateboard	−	+	−	−	−	−
sailboat	−	−	−	−	−	−
iceboat	−	−	−	−	−	−

Purpose: To enrich and clarify students' existing knowledge of a concept by having them identify words that belong to a category, list the features of the words they have identified, and compare and contrast them using a grid.

Procedure:

- Select a category—for example, *vehicles*.
- With students' help, list words that fall into this category.
- With students' help, list the features of the items you have identified. For example, some of the features of vehicles might be two wheels, four wheels, motor, and gasoline.
- Determine which items possess and do not possess each feature. Use plus and minus signs to indicate this. Discuss these distinctions with students.
- Add more words and features. Work with students to extend the grid, particularly when making distinctions that require adding features. For example, a feature such as "operates on water" would be needed to distinguish rowboats from iceboats.
- Have students complete the grid. They can do this independently, in groups, or with your help.
- Examine and discuss the completed grid. This discussion is often the most interesting and revealing activity. For example, you would want to acknowledge that a few cars do use diesel fuel and many small trucks use gasoline.

As with many instructional activities, follow the gradual release of responsibility model (described in Chapter 2) in working with semantic feature analysis. Initially, you may need to do much of the work. Later, students can be given grids with some terms and some attributes and asked to add to both the list of related words and the list of attributes and then to fill in the pluses and minuses. Still later, after becoming proficient in working with partially completed grids that you supply, students can create grids for sets of related words that they themselves suggest.

Another level of challenge and interest can be added by including the designator *S*, meaning "sometimes," in addition to the pluses and minuses. For example, *S* might be used in the vehicle grid in the "car" row under the headings "diesel fuel" and "gasoline" because some cars do use diesel fuel. In all cases—whether or not *S* is used—there should be a good deal of discussion, for the essence of semantic feature analysis lies in the discussion.

In this part of the chapter, we have listed six approaches to teaching individual words. Note that the five approaches that deal with teaching word meanings—that is, all of them except the approach for teaching students to read known words—go well beyond simply providing students with the definition of the new word. As Steven Stahl (1998) points out, what we know about teaching individual words suggests using vocabulary instruction that "(a) includes both definitional and contextual information about each word's meaning, (b) involves children more actively in word learning, and (c) provides multiple exposures to meaningful information about the word." Although the six approaches described here are certainly enough to begin your efforts in teaching individual words, you may eventually want to add others, such as those described in *The Vocabulary Book: Learning and Instruction* (Graves, 2006).

Reflect *and* Apply

3. Consider each of the five word-learning tasks we have listed, and explain how each of them requires a different sort of learning. It would be useful to work with a classmate in doing this, but after you have discussed your response, write it out. Writing your response will force you to really think it through, and it will give you a response on paper that you can examine and evaluate.

4. Identify a group of students. Select one word that is likely to be in their oral vocabularies but that they probably don't recognize in print, one that is a new label for a known concept, one that represents a new concept, and one that they probably know but for which you would like to give them a fuller understanding. Choose an instructional procedure described in the chapter for teaching each word, create the materials you would need, and then explain how you would go about teaching each of them. If you have a few classmates available who could serve as "students," role-playing the teaching rather than explaining how you would do it would be an excellent idea.

Teaching Word-Learning Strategies

ASSESSMENT

A big part of assessing what word-learning strategies your students know and how well they use them is observing them in different situations. Observe groups and individual students while they read and write or while they are being taught by another teacher. Take notes.

As we noted at the beginning of the chapter, students learn something like 3,000 to 4,000 words each year, many more than could be directly taught. Thus, even when instruction in individual words is as frequent and rich as possible, students still need to learn much of their vocabulary independently. In this section of the chapter, we consider three strategies that students need to become independent word learners: using context clues, using word parts, and using the dictionary.

Using Context Clues

It is almost certainly the case that we learn most of the words we know from meeting them in context (Anderson & Nagy, 1992; Sternberg, 1987). No other explanation can account for students' learning 3,000 to 4,000 words each year. At the same time, gleaning a word's meaning from most contexts is not an easy task. However, wide reading exposes students to a huge number of unknown words. Given a typical amount of reading over a year's time, students with average skills in learning words from context might acquire over 1,000 words from meeting them in the context of their reading. Additionally, students learn a large number of words from oral contexts—conversations, lectures, films, and even television. Of course, students who have better-than-average skills in learning words from context will acquire more words from context than will students with only average skills.

In this section of the chapter, we discuss teaching students to use context clues—the words, phrases, and sentences that surround an unknown word and provide clues to its meaning—to learn word meanings. Teaching students to use context clues requires a significant effort on your part and on the part of your students, but research shows that it can be done (Fukkink & de Glopper, 1998), and several effective models of instruction have been described (for example, Baumann, Font, Edwards, & Boland, 2005; Graves, 2006). The approach we describe here, which we call *balanced strategies instruction* (Sales & Graves, 2005), is the approach we recommend for teaching students to use context clues, word parts, and the dictionary. It is also the approach we recommend for teaching comprehension strategies, a very important component of reading instruction and something we describe in detail in Chapter 9. In the Classroom 7.5 describes the basic components of balanced strategies instruction.

Balanced Strategies Instruction

1. *Make motivation a prime concern.* Stress how learning and using the strategy will help students with their reading and learning in school and outside of school.

2. *Use prominent visual displays.* Before teaching the strategy, as you are teaching it, and after you have taught it, use posters and the like to create interest in the upcoming instruction, highlight major features of the strategy, and remind students to continue to use it after the initial instruction.

3. *Follow the direct explanation model for the initial instruction.*
   • An explicit description of the strategy and when and how it should be used
   • Teacher and/or student modeling of the strategy in action
   • Collaborative use of the strategy in action
   • Guided practice using the strategy with gradual release of responsibility
   • Independent use of the strategy (Duke & Pearson, 2002, pp. 208–210)

4. *Provide substantial and long-term follow-up after the initial instruction.* Prompt students to use the strategy, review it periodically, and do everything possible to make it something that students internalize and use over time.

Balanced strategies instruction can be used at a variety of grade levels to teach students to use context clues. However, the ideal grades for in-depth instruction are the upper-elementary grades. In earlier grades, we would use less-formal instruction. The unit described in In the Classroom 7.6 is designed for fourth grade. A more detailed description of the approach is given in the *Assessments and Lesson Plans* booklet accompanying this text and in Graves (2006).

Teaching Context Clues

DAY 1: INTRODUCTION OF UNIT/MOTIVATION

Because learning to use context clues is a demanding and challenging task, introduce the unit with a substantial motivational activity. For example, show a film that includes a lot of clues to the setting but does not directly identify it, and ask students to use clues in the film to infer where the film takes place. Next, suggest that figuring out word meanings from context is a lot like using clues in a film to infer where it takes place.

in the Classroom 7.6

DAY 2: INTRODUCTION TO USING CONTEXT CLUES AND THE FOUR-STEP STRATEGY

Review the major points made on the first day and then introduce a strategy for figuring out the meanings of unknown words students come across as they read. The strategy entails four steps: (1) reading carefully, stopping when you come to an unknown word, (2) reading slowly from that point forward, looking for clues to the word's meaning, (3) going back and re-reading the sentences preceding the unknown word if necessary, and (4) selecting a word or phrase that seems to capture the meaning of the unknown word and substituting it for the unknown word to see if it works. After explaining the strategy, model it, explain when and where students are likely to use it, and let students try it out with some texts containing difficult words and particularly informative context clues. As students are working with the strategy, scaffold their efforts—provide additional clues as necessary, let them work in pairs if that is helpful, and answer any questions they have. At the end of the day, put up a large and colorful poster listing the steps of the strategy, and leave the poster up throughout the unit and for some time after the unit is concluded.

DAYS 3–10: ADDITIONAL INSTRUCTION, PRACTICE, ENCOURAGEMENT, INCREASED RESPONSIBILITY, AND TRANSITION TO INCREASINGLY CHALLENGING TEXTS AND TASKS

Over the next eight days, provide more detailed instruction on the four-step strategy, interrupt the hard work from time to time with games that employ the strategy, engage students in guided practice with both narrative and expository texts, have them use the strategy with a variety of authentic texts, and assist them in making plans for how they'll internalize the strategy and use it in the future. Increasingly, the students talk more and you talk less. They take more responsibility for the strategy and do more of the work, and they increasingly self-monitor and self-regulate their use of the strategy. At the same time, always be there to support students' efforts—providing encouragement, scaffolding, and feedback as needed.

Using Word Parts

While use of context clues is the most important word-learning strategy, use of word parts is a close second. As Jeremy Anglin's (1993) study of elementary students' vocabularies indicates, about half of the "new" words that students meet in their reading are related to familiar words. Once students can break words into parts, they can use their knowledge of word parts to attempt to deduce their meanings—if, of course, they understand word parts and how they function. The three types of word parts to consider are prefixes, suffixes, and non-English roots.

We have already discussed prefixes and suffixes as elements that students need to deal with as they decode words, and we provided a brief procedure for teaching them in Chapter 5. Here we consider prefixes, suffixes, and non-English roots as elements students can use in gleaning word meanings. Among these three, prefixes are the most powerful elements to teach as an aid to gleaning word meanings (see Figure 7.1).

Suffixes represent a more complex situation and present a different learning task for native English speakers than for English-language learners. As noted in Chapter 5, there are two types of suffixes: inflectional and derivational. Inflectional suffixes, the most common type, have grammatical meanings (for example, -ed, indicating the past tense) that are difficult to explain. Native English speakers already have a tacit understanding of the function of inflectional suffixes, and attempts to teach their meanings may cause confusion. English-language learners, on the other hand, do need to be taught their meanings, and we recommend using the procedure described in Chapter 5 for doing so. Derivational suffixes, most of which are less common, have abstract meanings (for example, -ence, indicating the state of being), and these too are often difficult to explain. Because many derivational suffixes are less common and difficult to explain, we recommend leaving instruction in them for the secondary grades.

Non-English roots (for example, anthro, meaning "man" and appearing in such words as anthropology, misanthrope, and philanthropy) represent a very different teaching and learning situation than do prefixes or suffixes. There are a large number of non-English roots, individual roots are not used in nearly the number of words that common prefixes are used in, they are often variously spelled and thus difficult to identify, and the relationship between the original meaning of the root and the current meaning of the English word in which it is used is often vague. For these reasons, we do not recommend systematic instruction in non-English roots at the elementary level.

A list of the prefixes sufficiently frequent to warrant teaching is shown in Figure 5.3 of Chapter 5, and In the Classroom 7.7 describes the use of balanced strategies instruction for teaching them. More details on that instruction and some additional information on teaching suffixes and non-English roots are given in the *Assessments and Lesson Plans* booklet accompanying this text and in Graves (2004b).

- There are relatively few prefixes to teach.

- They are used in a large number of words.

- They are consistently spelled.

- They appear at the beginning of words, where they are easy for students to spot.

- They generally have a clear lexical meaning that can be attached to the root word to yield a new meaning. For example, predawn means "before dawn."

FIGURE 7.1

Why Prefixes Are Particularly Worth Teaching

Teaching Prefixes

DAY 1: INTRODUCTION AND MOTIVATION

Introduce the concept of prefixes and the strategy of using prefixes to unlock the meanings of unknown words, motivate students by stressing the value of using prefixes, and give students an overview of the unit. During the four-day unit, you will teach six of the most frequent prefixes.

DAY 2: INTRODUCTION TO THE FIRST THREE PREFIXES AND THE PREFIX STRATEGY

Introduce the first three prefixes to be taught (*re-, in-,* and *un-*), and give their meanings. Describe the prefix strategy, which consists of (1) identifying and removing the prefix from the new word, (2) noting the meaning of the prefix and the meaning of the root word, and (3) combining the meaning of the prefix and the meaning of the root word to infer the meaning of the new word. Model the strategy yourself, let students try it out with your help and each other's help as needed, and have them practice using the strategy with a number of words containing the three prefixes. At this time, put up a poster that shows the prefixes you have taught and the prefix strategy.

DAY 3: REVIEWING THE PREFIX STRATEGY AND TEACHING THE REMAINING THREE PREFIXES

Review the prefix strategy, model it yourself, let several students model it, and answer any questions students have. Teach the meanings of the next three prefixes (*dis-, en-,* and *non-*), and have students practice using the strategy with a number of words containing these three new prefixes. Add the three new prefixes to the poster.

DAY 4: REVIEWING THE INFORMATION ABOUT PREFIXES, THE PREFIX STRATEGY, AND THE SIX PREFIXES TAUGHT IN THE UNIT

Review everything you have done so far, take any questions students have, and have them practice using the prefix strategy with all six prefixes you have taught.

BEYOND DAY 4: REVIEWING, PROMPTING, GUIDING STUDENTS TO INDEPENDENCE, AND TEACHING ADDITIONAL PREFIXES

From time to time, point out the prefixes you have taught when they appear in the selections students are reading, remind students of the value of using prefixes to infer word meanings, and briefly review the prefix strategy. Later in the year, teach a second set of six or so prefixes from the list in Figure 5.3, and later still teach another six or so.

Using the Dictionary

As George Miller and Patricia Gildea (1987) have convincingly demonstrated, elementary students frequently have difficulty using the dictionary to find definitions of unknown words. For example, after finding the phrase "eat out" in the definition of *erode,* one student showed her confusion in using the definition by composing the sentence *Our family erodes a lot.* Many students need help in using the dictionary effectively, and balanced strategies instruction can provide that help.

Begin by telling students that you are going to work on using the dictionary to define words, and tell them that the activity is worthwhile because using the dictionary sometimes isn't as simple as it seems. Then put some guidelines, such as those shown in Figure 7.2, on a bulletin board, and leave them up over the coming weeks.

Don't have students memorize these guidelines, but talk through them, amplifying them as necessary. For example, you should probably add to the third guideline by telling students that if they find that they still know nothing about an important word after considering context, looking for word parts, and checking the dictionary, they will probably want to ask someone about its meaning.

The remainder of the procedure continues to follow the balanced strategies instruction model. Do some modeling; demonstrate how you would look up the meaning of an unknown word. Think aloud, sharing your thinking with students as you come across the unknown word in a text. Show students how you look through a dictionary and find the word, locate the definition that seems to fit, consider all of that definition, and then mentally check to see if the meaning you chose makes sense in context. Then, gradually, let students take over the procedure and model it for you and for each other. Finally, encourage students to use the procedure when they come across unknown or vaguely known words in context, and from time to time give them opportunities to model their thinking as they use the dictionary so that you can check their proficiency and give them feedback and further instruction as needed.

In addition to learning this general approach to using a dictionary, students need to learn some things about the particular dictionary they use—what the entries for individual words contain and how they are arranged, what aids to its use the dictionary provides, and what features beyond the basic word list the dictionary includes. Much important information appears in the front

- When reading a definition, be sure to read it all, not just part of it.

- Remember that many words have more than one meaning.

- Be sure to check all the definitions the dictionary gives for a word, not just one of them.

- Decide which definition makes sense in the context in which the word is used.

- Often, the dictionary works best when you already have some idea of a word's meaning. This makes the dictionary particularly useful for checking on a word you want to use in your writing.

FIGURE 7.2

Guidelines for Looking Up Definitions in the Dictionary

A dictionary is a handy tool for readers of all ages.

matter of the dictionaries themselves, but it is very seldom read, and simply asking students to read it is hardly sufficient instruction. Thus, explicit instruction in how to use specific dictionaries is usually useful.

Reflect *and* Apply

5. In order to get a feeling for the extent to which context reveals word meanings, team up with a classmate. Each of you should independently select and photocopy a few passages of college-level material. Next, read, identify, and "white out" some difficult words in each passage. Then get together and discuss how and to what extent you can infer the deleted words' meanings from context.

6. Stop by the curriculum materials library at your university or a local public library, and examine the different levels of dictionaries found there. Note, for example, how dictionaries for younger students have fewer words, define words more simply, and are generally easier to use and therefore more appropriate for younger readers.

ASSESSMENT

Instead of writing directly on students' papers , give feedback on Post-it notes. To foster word consciousness, you could suggest more colorful word choices, such as *crimson* for *red*.

English Learners

Having English-language learners supply cognates for colorful and interesting English words the class is working with and then posting the English words and their non-English cognates on a bulletin board is one way to promote word consciousness while building English-language learners' pride in their languages.

Fostering Word Consciousness

Thus far, we have described three approaches to vocabulary development—providing frequent and extensive language experiences, teaching individual words, and teaching word-learning strategies. Here we describe a fourth approach—fostering word consciousness. Word consciousness is a disposition toward words that is both cognitive and affective. The word-conscious student knows a lot of words, and she knows them well. Equally important, she is interested in words, and she gains enjoyment and satisfaction from using them well and from seeing or hearing them used well by others. She finds words intriguing, recognizes adroit word usage when she encounters it, uses words skillfully herself, is on the lookout for new and precise words, and is responsive to the nuances of word meanings. She is also well aware of the power of words and realizes that they can be used to foster clarity and understanding or to obscure and obfuscate matters.

Fostering such attitudes is something to achieve across the elementary school years—and, of course, in the years beyond the elementary grades—and there are myriad ways to develop and nurture such positive attitudes. These include modeling and encouraging adept diction, promoting wordplay such as the use of rhymes and puns, using wordplay books and playing word games, and providing intensive and expressive instruction in vocabulary. In the Reading Corner, we list a few word books and word games. In the remainder of this section, we consider some ways of modeling and encouraging adept diction and discuss approaches to intensive and expressive instruction. For additional suggestions on developing word consciousness, see Graves (2006), Graves and Susan Watts (2002), and Judith Scott and William Nagy (2004); for a detailed discussion of some cognitive aspects of word consciousness, see Nagy and Scott (2000).

Modeling and Encouraging Adept Diction

The starting point, we believe, in encouraging and nurturing word consciousness lies in our own attitude toward words and how we project it to students.

the Reading Corner

Books About Words and Word Games

Linda Bourke. *Eye Spy: A Mysterious Alphabet*. Chronicle Books, 1994. In this exquisitely illustrated alphabet book, each letter appears with three vividly colored panels depicting a word beginning with that letter and a fourth panel that both depicts a homonym or homograph beginning with that letter and serves as a cue to the word used to represent the next letter.

Catherine Falwell. *Word Wizard*. Clarion, 1998. In this picture book, a magic spoon helps a young girl realize she can rearrange the letters in words to form new ones. She helps a lost boy get home by changing *ocean* to *canoe, shore* to *horse*, and so on.

Fred Gwynne. *A Little Pigeon Toed*. Simon & Schuster, 1988. A marvelous collection of ambiguous phrases and amusing illustrations depicting the wrong interpretations of those phrases. Other similar books by Fred Gwynne include *Chocolate Moose for Dinner*

(Windmill Books, 1976) and *The King Who Rained* (Simon & Schuster, 1970).

Richard Lederer (author) and Dave Morice (illustrator). *The Circus of Words*. Chicago Review Press, 2001. Anagrams, palindromes, spoonerisms, and more from one of the leading wordplay artists. Lederer's *Pun and Games: Jokes, Riddles, Daffynitions, Tairy Fales, Rhymes, and More Word Play for Kids* (Chicago Review Press, 1996) is another choice young readers will enjoy.

Jack Prelutsky (author) and Peter Sis (illustrator). *Scranimals*. Greenwillow, 2002. In this adventure, children set sail for Scranimal Island, where poet Prelutsky and artist Sis create a memorable cast of scranimals including Parroters, Potatods, and Ostricheetahs. Other books that show off Prelutsky's inventive wordplay include *It's Raining Pigs and Noodles* (Scholastic, 2001) and *An Ogre's Awful Day* (Scholastic, 2002).

We want children to feel that adept diction—the skillful use of words in speech and writing—is worth striving for. We want them to see that by using the right word themselves and recognizing the adept word choices authors make, they can both communicate more effectively and appreciate more fully an author's message. Various conscious efforts can promote skillful diction. One is to model adept word usage in your classroom talk, deliberately using and perhaps explaining words that at least some of your students might not yet know. Thus, in describing how you were startled by a low-flying jet on the way to school, you might tell your fourth-graders that the jet made a *thunderous* noise and point out that *thunderous* is an excellent word for describing a really loud noise because it reminds us of the great booming sound of thunder.

A simple, widely used, and very effective way of focusing students' attention on words is to include a word-of-the-day activity in daily plans. Appropriate for all ages, word-of-the-day activities can take a number of forms. In a first-grade classroom, word meaning can be linked to word recognition and general language facility by sharing with students a particular word of interest and paying special attention to the way it sounds, the way it looks, and what it means. The words of the day can be added to a bulletin board each day until, at the end of the month, the entire board is filled. Words of the day can

CW 7.4 links to Word Play: Sites That Feature Fun with Words, which lists nearly 200 sites where children can find wordplay activities.

also be acted out, used in a game of charades, or illustrated. In addition, they can be made part of a song, riddle, pun, poem, or some other form of artistic expression. Here, fifth-grade special education teacher Bette Rochman explains how she uses word-of-the-day activities in her class:

> I teach fifth-grade youngsters with learning disabilities, and one vocabulary activity I have found to be quite successful is to pair up students to be responsible for coming up with a word of the day. After our morning announcements, the student pair responsible for that day's word writes it on the board and explains to the class what it means, why they selected it, and how to use it in a sentence. Sometimes the pair selects words they aren't too sure about and says something like, "We're not sure exactly how you use this word, but when we find out, we'll let you know!" I let the students know that such partial knowledge of the word is certainly okay, as long as students set their sights on gaining fuller knowledge. Of course, students always enjoy stumping me by presenting words that are new to me as well as to their fellow students!
>
> —Bette Rochman, Fifth-Grade Special Education Teacher

Students can select words from any number of sources—books, newspapers, another classroom, their parents, and teachers, to name a few. Teachers can also suggest that students find their special words in particular sources in order to complement certain classroom activities. For example, during a unit on newspapers, the teacher might suggest that students find words in a newspaper; during a unit on weather, she might suggest that students choose "weather words." More often, however, it is worthwhile to let students find their words wherever they wish. Then they tend to view the words as their own, take greater pride in sharing them, and more readily see learning new words as an enjoyable experience.

Another occasion for focusing attention on words comes when children are reading, as sixth-grade teacher Terry Cronemeyer suggests:

> I personally love words and take every opportunity I can to point out wonderful word choices. This opportunity most often arises in conjunction with the literature children are reading. Since good authors employ appropriate and often colorful words, I will often point out to my sixth-graders particularly felicitous or interesting word choices. For example, I was sitting in on a literature circle with a group of students who were reading and discussing Russell Freedman's *Eleanor Roosevelt: A Life of Discovery* when one of the students chose to read these lines aloud, "Franklin remembered Eleanor as a skinny girl in a hopeless party dress. Now she was wearing a stylish outfit from Paris." I decided I could not resist butting in. "How could a party dress be *hopeless?*" I asked. A lively discussion then ensued that uncovered the ripples of meaning that Freedman was able to achieve by using that particular word.
>
> —Terry Cronemeyer, Sixth-Grade Teacher

Still another opportunity for recognizing and promoting adroit word usage comes from children's own writing. Thus, you might compliment a third-grader for describing banana slugs as *gigantic* and give a little recognition to a sixth-grader who noted that the odds of winning the lottery are *astronomically small.* During writing conferences, you might also encourage students to rethink word choices in an effort to make their writing more colorful and precise.

Providing Intensive and Expressive Instruction

Some very interesting and highly effective activities that can foster word consciousness have been developed and carefully researched by Isabel Beck and Margaret McKeown (1983) and by Ann Duin (Duin & Graves, 1988). The activities are quite similar, except that Beck and McKeown's goal was full and deep understanding of words, while Duin's goal was full and deep understanding of words coupled with children's using the words in writing. Developing and presenting these activities involves several steps. The first step is to select a small set of words that are semantically related. For example, a set used by Beck and McKeown—*rival, hermit, novice, virtuoso, accomplice, miser, tyrant,* and *philanthropist*—contained words that refer to people; a set used by Duin—*advocate, capability, configuration, criteria, disarray, envision, feasible, habitable, module, quest, retrieve,* and *tether*—contained words that can be used in talking about space exploration.

The next step, the central part of the instruction, is to have students work extensively and intensively with the words, spending perhaps half an hour a day over a period of a week with them and engaging in a dozen or so diverse activities with them—really getting to know them, discovering their shades of meaning and the various ways in which they can be used, and realizing what interesting companions words can be. Beck and McKeown's activities, for example, included defining the words, asking students to use them in sentences, and asking students to respond to words such as *virtuoso* and *miser* with thumbs up or thumbs down to signify approval or disapproval. Their activities also included asking which of three actions an *accomplice* would be most likely to engage in—robbing a bank by himself or herself, stealing some candy, or driving a getaway car—and asking questions such as "Could a *virtuoso* be a *rival*?" "Could a *virtuoso* be a *novice*?" and "Could a *philanthropist* be a *miser*?"

Duin's activities also began with defining the words and asking students to use them in sentences. Her other activities included asking students to discuss how *feasible* space travel might soon be, asking them how a space station could *accommodate* persons with disabilities, and asking them to write brief essays called "Space Shorts" in which they used the words in dealing with topics such as the foods that might be available in space. Reports from teachers who have used these activities indicate that students really got involved in them and did indeed become more word conscious.

The third step, which is used only if the goal includes students' using the words in their writing, is to have students write more extensive essays—using as many of the taught words as possible, playing with them, and exploring their possibilities. Students appear to really enjoy this activity. As one teacher observed, "Students who were asked to write often and to use the words in written classwork showed great involvement in their writing."

Finally, we conclude with a fourth step—directly discussing with students the word choices they make, why they make those choices, and how adroit use of words makes speech and writing more precise, more memorable, and more interesting.

Duin found that students were very successful in using the words in their writing, as this seventh-grader's essay—in which the taught words are italicized—demonstrates:

> I think the space program would be more *feasible* if we sent more than just astronauts and satellites into space. We need to send tourists and change the whole *configuration* of the space shuttle so that it could *accommodate* more people. While the tourists are in space, they could fly some of the manned-maneuvering units and *retrieve* stuff from space. They could maybe even see if our planets are *habitable* now. When the tourists would come back, they would have the *capability* of doing anything in space. They truly would be *advocates* of space. But, in order to make these special missions happen, we will need to add more *modules* onto our space station, so that we can store more equipment, supplies, food, and people!
>
> After about ten years or so we would perhaps go back to the same old thing with astronauts and satellites until we found another new idea for the space program.

My *quest*, someday, is to reach the stars. I hope to be not just an engineer, but a space engineer. We have to get more people interested since the crash. We have to try harder than ever.

—Seventh-Grade Space Exploration Fan

Obviously, this student enjoyed the instruction, learned from it, and tried to do her best—she managed to get 9 of the 13 words that were taught in the unit in her essay. To be sure, some of the usage is a bit forced, but at this point in the student's writing career that is probably just fine. She is interested in words and in using new and different words in her writing. With practice, feedback, and encouragement from thoughtful respondents to her writing—her teachers and her peers, for the most part—we expect her to become a skilled and precise word user.

Reflect *and* Apply

7. Review a recent paper you wrote, looking for the word choices you made and asking yourself if you used appropriate, powerful, and perhaps even colorful words. If you did, consider how these helped make the paper strong and effective. If you didn't, try going through the paper and changing some of the vocabulary to make it more appropriate, powerful, and perhaps colorful. Then look at your changes and consider how they affect the paper.
8. Get together with a classmate, identify a group of students, and brainstorm a set of brief and upbeat activities you might employ over a semester to foster their word consciousness.

Strengths and Challenges of DIVERSITY

Here we will consider the particular needs in vocabulary instruction for four groups—gifted learners, special students, children who had little exposure to books and reading before they came to school, and students who speak English as a second language.

With gifted students, be leery of teaching a new vocabulary-learning strategy when the student already has a perfectly good one. If a student already has a strategy for learning words from context that works well for her, there is no reason to teach her a new strategy.

With special students, be patient, and be sure they get the opportunity to work with higher-level tasks as well as less-challenging ones. You're likely to find that teaching special students vocabulary-learning strategies will take time and effort, and it may be tempting to avoid or minimize such attempts and simply teach them individual words. But don't give in to these temptations. Special students need vocabulary-learning strategies even more than more-able students.

Another approach that may be particularly useful with special students is the use of computer-aided vocabulary instruction. As Camille Blachowicz and Peter Fisher (2000) note, computer-aided vocabulary instruction has been shown to have some especially positive effects for special students. Computers can of course be useful in providing the sort of individualized instruction special students need, and they allow students to work in a relatively risk-free environment, one in which they don't have to reveal their performance to others.

Students who have not had rich experiences with language, books, and reading outside of school also deserve special consideration. As the in-depth studies of Betty Hart and Todd Risley (1995, 2003) make all too clear, some students, often those raised in poverty, do not begin school with the same vocabulary knowledge and language skills that many children with richer out-of-school literacy experiences do. These students need time, nurturing, and instruction. Like special students, they need and deserve to be taught strategies, and they need opportunities to have fun with words and to develop word awareness. They will also profit from being taught individual words, including perhaps a basic vocabulary; they may well profit from instruction and experiences designed to build their oral language skills. Andrew Biemiller (2001) has presented a powerful argument for such instruction and described several research-based instructional programs for building vocabulary and language skills.

Students who have not had rich experiences with language, books, and reading outside of school particularly need the frequent experiences of reading appropriate books that we discussed earlier. The various book lists in this text and the annotated bibliographies at the ends of the chapters will of course be useful in locating appropriate books. Additionally, you may find Catherine Barr's annotated bibliography, *Reading in Series* (1999), especially useful because it suggests whole sets of books that may catch a particular student's interest.

Finally, there is the special case of building the vocabularies of English-language learners, particularly English-language learners who have small English vocabularies. We have four suggestions. First, pair each English-language learner with a native English speaker. Have each pair frequently read together, do writing and other schoolwork together, and perhaps even do homework together. Do whatever possible to encourage out-of-class activities among the pairs.

Second, get some reading materials specifically for your English-language learners. These should include short and simple selections containing largely vocabulary students already know, selections that include some challenging vocabulary, and selections in students' native language. Also, if available, materials that include both a version in students' native language and an English version are very valuable. The short and simple selections filled with familiar English vocabulary will help students build automaticity, fluency, and confidence. Books with some challenging English vocabulary give English-language learners opportunities to build their stores of English words. Books written in their native language give students opportunities to read more sophisticated material than they could in English. Books that present the text in English and in one or more other languages give students opportunities to use their strength in their native language to learn English. Michele Salas's *A de alfabeto/A Is for Alphabet* (Spanish), Max Velthuijs's *Rah was Rah/Frog Is Frog* (Somali), and Truong Tran's *Going Home, Coming Home/Ve nha, tham que huong* (Vietnamese) are three examples of this growing genre.

Third, contact students' parents and enlist their aid. In many cases, parents' assistance will be largely in encouraging their children, in ensuring that they have a time and place to do their homework, and in seeing that they do it. Let parents know about books or homework you send home, and keep in touch with them on their children's progress. Not surprisingly, research shows that effective schools make concerted efforts to reach out to parents (Taylor, Pearson, Clark, & Walpole, 2000).

Fourth, consider some sort of systematic word study that takes place both in and out of school. Paul Nation (2001) offers a number of suggestions for such study; Biemiller's (2001) program, which we mentioned above in discussing approaches for English-speaking students who lack rich out-of-school experiences with language, is also intended for use with English-language learners.

Concluding Remarks

In this chapter, we have described the vocabulary-learning tasks students face, noted the importance of wide reading, described five word-learning tasks and ways of selecting vocabulary to teach, and presented teaching procedures appropriate for each of the five word-learning tasks. We have also suggested approaches for teaching students to use context and prefixes to unlock word meanings and ways of teaching them to use the dictionary. Finally, we have described methods of promoting word consciousness.

Summed up in this way, the task of teaching vocabulary appears to be a large one. However, no single teacher is expected to accomplish all of the various tasks of vocabulary instruction. You can choose which word-learning task is most important at a particular point in your class, which level of word knowledge you expect students to achieve with particular words, which teaching procedure or procedures will be most appropriate for the words in a particular selection your students are reading, and what specific words you wish to teach. Moreover, as we suggested earlier, not every teacher needs to take major responsibility for teaching students to use context, word parts, and the like. You and the other teachers in your school can work together to decide who will be responsible for these various teaching tasks. We believe that the discussion and teaching procedures presented here will enable you make appropriate decisions that will help your students gain rich and powerful vocabularies.

CW 7.5 links to Fostering Vocabulary Development in Elementary Classrooms, a set of slides that will help you review some of the information in this chapter and learn more about teaching vocabulary.

Rich and powerful vocabularies are of course an important part of present-day literacy. Students who have achieved the level of literacy necessary in today's world have vocabularies that enable them to be precise and even colorful in their own speech and writing, to recognize and appreciate the skillful use of words in the literary selections they read, and to understand the sometimes subtle and often crucial meanings of words in the informational reading they do.

Extending Learning

1. Throughout the chapter, we have emphasized the importance of wide reading for developing vocabulary. Your ability to promote wide reading among your students will depend heavily on getting the right books into children's hands. As one step toward becoming more skilled in selecting books for children, imagine a particular grade level and group of students, and brainstorm possible topics that would interest this group. Then, using bibliographies, library card catalogs, electronic databases, and the advice of a librarian, select half a dozen books on this topic that are likely to be of interest to your students. If the group of students you are considering includes less-skilled readers or English-language learners, be sure to include some books appropriate for these children.

2. Identify a grade level and a group of students to whom you might teach vocabulary. If at all possible, this should be an actual group of students whom you can really teach. If you are able to work with elementary students, talk to their teacher and ask her to select half a dozen or so words that she would like her students to learn. If not, select a set of words yourself. Next, identify one of the

procedures presented in the chapter that is appropriate for teaching these words, develop whatever materials you need, and prepare to do the teaching. If you haven't taught much before, it would be a good idea to rehearse with a classmate. Finally, teach the vocabulary, and then talk to students afterward to get their reaction to your instruction. If it isn't possible to work with a real class, simulate this experience using your classmates as students.

For a look at vocabulary development in a contemporary classroom, go to Allyn & Bacon's MyLabSchool.com. In MLS Courses, click on Reading Methods, and go to MLS Video Lab. There you will find video clips about Vocabulary in Module 3.

Children's Literature

BOOKS

Freedman, R. (1993). *Eleanor Roosevelt: A Life of Discovery*. New York: Scholastic. In this rich and insightful photobiography of an admirable and courageous woman, photos appear on almost every page and fill some pages. 198 pages.

Salas, M. (2003). *A de alfabeto/A Is for Alphabet*. Leon, Spain: Everest. In this Spanish/English book, each letter is presented first in Spanish and then in English. 32 pages.

Tran, T. (2003) *Going Home, Coming Home/Ve nha, tham que huong*. San Francisco: Children's Book Press. In this English/Vietnamese book, a young girl from the United States visits her grandmother in Vietnam and learns that she has a home in both countries. 31 pages.

Velthuijs, M. (2000). *Rah was Rah/Frog Is Frog*. London: Millet. In this Somali/English book, Frog at first wants to be like the other animals but then decides he is happy being himself. 28 pages.

BIBLIOGRAPHIES

Barr, C. (Ed.). 1999. *Reading in series: A selection guide to books for children*. New Providence, NJ: R. R. Bowker. This annotated bibliography lists over 800 series for children.

Book links (bimonthly from the American Library Association, 50 E. Huron St., Chicago, IL 60611). This glossy magazine features annotated bibliographies, essays, reviews, and recommendations for using literature with children from preschool through eighth grade.

CCBC choices (annually, in Spring). This annotated list of recommended children's trade books is produced by a committee of the Cooperative Children's Book Center, P.O. Box 5288, Madison, WI 53705-0288.

Children's choices (annually, in October). *The Reading Teacher*. Fiction and nonfiction books that elementary

and middle-school children have identified as some of their favorites are listed.

New books for young readers (annually, in May). Edited by Lee Galda, College of Education, University of Minnesota, this annotated list gives new trade books that have been selected for their appeal and appropriateness for children from preschool to young adult. Department of Curriculum and Instruction, 159 Pillsbury Drive S.E., Minneapolis, MN 55455

Notable children's books (annually, in March). *School Library Journal* and *Booklist*. This non-annotated list of recommended children's trade books is compiled during the American Library Association's winter meeting. Copies are available from ALA.

Notable children's trade books in the field of social studies (annually, in April/May). *Social Education*. Short reviews cover notable social studies trade books for kindergarten through eighth-grade children.

Outstanding science trade books for children (annually, in March). *Children and Science*. Short reviews cover outstanding science trade books for prekindergarten through eighth-grade children.

Stoll, D. R. (1997). *Magazines for kids and teens*. Newark, DE: International Reading Association. Easy-to-use guide lists over 200 periodicals covering almost every interest of children and teens.

Teacher's choices (annually, in November). *The Reading Teacher*. Fiction and nonfiction books teachers have identified as among their favorites for kindergarten and elementary-age students are listed.

Trelease, J. (2001). *The read-aloud handbook* (5th ed.). New York: Penguin Books. This rich source provides information on predictable books, wordless books, reference resources, picture books, short novels, novels, poetry, and anthologies.

Scaffolding Students' Comprehension of Text

CLASSROOM VIGNETTE

"*I* love to read!" Ethan exclaims. Those four words are music to any teacher's ears. If only we could hear every child we teach saying them! So how do we get that to happen?

Part of the answer lies in making reading a purposeful, successful experience for every child. Easily said, but not so easily done, given the complexities of the reading process and the complexities of our modern world, with students arriving in your classroom from vastly different backgrounds and with different interests, abilities, and needs.

However, there *are* things you can do—such as implementing in your classroom instructional frameworks and procedures that have been evolving over the years—to provide students with the support they need to develop as readers. In this chapter, we describe some of these frameworks and procedures. As you read this chapter, imagine a class full of students, *your* students. Think about how these frameworks and procedures will help ensure that all of your students' reading experiences are successful, that they will continually learn and relearn that reading is purposeful and enjoyable. If virtually every reading experience students have in your classroom is successful and fulfilling, they will almost certainly become skillful and avid readers. And you may well have the pleasure of hearing them utter that gratifying statement, "I love to read!"

Instructional Frameworks and Procedures

How do you motivate, guide, and support students in the texts they read? In this chapter, we look at five frameworks and several individual procedures designed to scaffold students' efforts in their reading and understanding of various texts, help them grow in their literacy skills, and nurture positive attitudes about reading. Three of the frameworks—the directed reading activity (DRA), the directed reading-thinking activity (DR-TA), and the scaffolded reading experience (SRE)—can be implemented with students at all grade levels. Two of the frameworks—guided reading and four blocks—are designed primarily for beginning readers in grades 1 through 3. In addition to these five frameworks, we describe several individual procedures to help students better comprehend and learn from the texts they read: story grammars, story maps, K-W-L, reading guides, discussion webs, and semantic webbing and weaving.

We begin our discussion of instructional frameworks and comprehension-building procedures by focusing on purpose, selection, and reader. All reading instruction begins by considering these critical factors.

The Roles of Purpose, Selection, and Reader in Planning a Successful Reading Experience

When we look carefully at what it means to comprehend text, three factors are always involved: the purpose or purposes for reading (why reading is being done), the selection (what is being read), and the reader (the person doing the reading)—the *why*, the *what*, and the *who*. We cannot overstate the importance and interconnectedness of these three components in planning any classroom reading experience. These critical factors should be at the forefront of your thinking whenever your students are about to read.

Purpose

Can you imagine reading something without motivation, without a purpose? As John Guthrie (Guthrie & Anderson, 1999) reminds us, "Reading is a conscious, deliberate act prompted by a plausible purpose." Purpose is what motivates us, helps focus our attention, and gives us something tangible to work toward (a goal). We read because somewhere in those combinations of symbols is something we need or want—information, escape, excitement, or knowledge, for example. This is the message we want students to get from day one and to internalize.

The Function of Purposes

Purposes serve a variety of functions in reading. First, purposes function to motivate or give a reason for reading. Such motivation is missing when a teacher merely states, "Open your science text and read Chapter 5." "Why?" a student might ask—and rightfully so. In order to motivate with a purpose for reading, the teacher might say, "What are three things you'd like to find out about earthquakes? Write those down, and then read Chapter 5 to see if the author answers those questions for you. Later, we will talk about what you learned."

In addition to motivating a person to read, purposes also determine *how* a selection is read—quickly, in order to get the gist of the text, or slowly, in order to really understand the material. Your students might give a photosynthesis experiment a quick read if their purpose is to see what materials they will need, but fully absorbing the steps in photosynthesis will take a slow and careful reading.

Having clear purposes also aids comprehension. Such purposes can serve as a cue for activating a reader's background knowledge before reading a text, suggest a plan for the reader to use while reading, and help him sort out relevant from irrelevant information.

Matching Reading Purposes with the Text and the Reader

It's important to remember that reading purposes need to match the text being read and the students who are reading. Here are some guidelines:

- *Select text-appropriate purposes.* For example, after studying about theme, an appropriate purpose for a group of second-graders reading the stories in Arnold Lobel's *Days with Frog and Toad* might be to read to discover each story's theme. On the other hand, since these characters are anthropomorphic, an inappropriate purpose would be to read the book to find out the characteristics of amphibians.
- *Select reader-appropriate purposes.* You wouldn't ask a group of beginning readers who had no experience with theme to read *Days with Frog and Toad* to discover the book's themes. You could, however, ask that same group of students to find out what the problem in each story was and how it was solved.
- *Select purposes that have significance and value and are important to the reader.* For example, if students needed to update their knowledge about fire safety, an appropriate purpose for reading an article on the subject would be to add new information to what they already know. They could make a chart that reflected both their old and their new knowledge, which they could then share with a wider audience.

- *Choose a single purpose more often than multiple purposes.* As teachers, we don't want to overload our students with so many reading purposes that they either fail at them all or are only somewhat successful at each. We'd rather they were really successful with just a few.
- *Encourage students to develop their own reading purposes.* Students need to be continually nudged and encouraged to take responsibility for their own learning, to realize what it is they need to know and how to achieve their personal goals.

Purpose is something we take for granted as adults, something that we have so internalized we don't consciously think about it as we read. However, it is an all-important factor to consider if we want students to succeed in the reading they do in our classrooms.

Selection

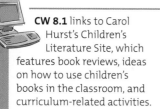

CW 8.1 links to Carol Hurst's Children's Literature Site, which features book reviews, ideas on how to use children's books in the classroom, and curriculum-related activities.

The type of text being read is inextricably intertwined with purpose. For example, if your purpose is to be entertained, you probably wouldn't choose to read your computer user's guide or the telephone book. And, although you might look to the comic pages of the newspaper to learn about current world events, it's not likely to be your primary purpose in doing so.

Types of Selections

Ideally, your students will be reading a wide range of materials. These materials should reflect a variety of cultures, should include selections that will be easy for your students and ones that will be more challenging, and should deal with an array of topics that reflect the many interests your students have. In today's classrooms, it is particularly important to have materials that reflect our multicultural society. Figure 8.1 provides a short list of authors who create books that illuminate a variety of cultures.

In addition to providing students with material reflecting different cultures, levels of difficulty, and interests, it is vital to give students opportunities to read in both narrative and expository texts and to teach them about the differences between these two types of texts and the different purposes we typically have when reading them.

English Learners

CW 8.2 links to the Celebrating Cultural Diversity Through Children's Literature Website, which provides annotated bibliographies of children's books that reflect a variety of cultures found in the United States.

Alma Flor Ada	Virginia Hamilton	Jerry Pinkney
Joseph Bruchac	Minfong Ho	Faith Ringgold
Ashley Bryan	Angela Johnson	Allen Say
Floyd Cooper	Barbara Knutson	Virginia Driving Hawk Sneve
David Diaz	Jeanne M. Lee	Gary Soto
Leo and Diane Dillon	Julius Lester	Mildred Taylor
Arthur Dorros	Patricia McKissack	Joyce Carol Thomas
Tom Feelings	Walter Dean Myers	Yoshiko Uchida
Jean Craighead George	Lensey Namioka	Mildred Pitts Walters
Paul Goble	Ifeoma Onyefulu	Lawrence Yep
Eloise Greenfield	Brian Pinkney	Ed Young

FIGURE 8.1

Authors Who Create Books Illuminating a Variety of Cultures

Narratives. Narratives, as noted earlier, are stories. Much of what students have had read to them before they go to school, much of what they read in the early grades, and much of what they see on TV or at the movies are narratives. Typical narratives reflect the temporal order of real-life events in which motives, actions, results, and reactions occur in sequence, and episodes in the main character's life are integrated by goals and subgoals. Time thus provides a natural structure for remembering episodic information. Most students enjoy narratives, and through them learn more about themselves, other places, other cultures, and the world of people generally. Narratives are also the perfect vehicle for *aesthetic* reading. As Louise Rosenblatt has explained, and as we noted in Chapter 1, the primary purpose of aesthetic reading is to experience the text—to enjoy it, to enter the world of the text and its characters, and to respond to the "associations, feelings, attitudes, and ideas" that the text prompts (Rosenblatt, 1978). Students gain much from narratives, and narratives are an important part of the literacy curriculum.

Exposition. Expository text is quite different from narrative text. It can have a variety of organizations, including, for example, list description, temporal sequence, explanation, compare/contrast, definition/example, and problem/solution (Anderson & Armbruster, 1984). Because there is no single prototypic structure for exposition and because most students don't have much experience reading exposition, many find exposition more challenging than narratives. Moreover, the purpose of reading exposition is typically quite different from that of reading narratives. In Rosenblatt's terms, exposition typically calls for *efferent* reading, or reading to gain information. Because much of the reading that students and adults do is to gain new information, assisting students in reading expository material is crucial. Preparing and guiding students in their reading of expository texts is a very important part of your task as a teacher. And preparing students to read expository text is the job of all teachers, including primary-grade teachers (Duke & Bennett-Armistead, 2003).

No two readers are the same. Each will bring a unique set of experiences, expectations, and abilities to the texts he or she reads.

To fine-tune your assessment of a student's reading level, use the Sentence Reading and Passage Reading subtests of the Interactive Reading Assessment System (IRAS) in the *Assessments and Lesson Plans* supplement.

ASSESSMENT

English Learners

Texts for English-language learners must be carefully selected. Students at the beginning stages of acquiring English respond well to stories that represent universal experiences or those common to newcomers. Selections should not require culturally specific knowledge that is not a part of their schemata.

ASSESSMENT

The Graduated Running Record in the *Assessments and Lesson Plans* supplement gives you a quick way to determine a student's reading level.

Reader

When you analyze reading material to find ways to help students successfully read it, the readers themselves will obviously be the focal point of your planning. Some considerations are the readers'

- needs and concerns,
- interests,
- strengths and weaknesses as learners, and
- background knowledge.

When you begin planning reading instruction, you will want to take all four of these factors into account. However, your students' background knowledge—what they know and have experienced—is crucial to their being able to successfully make meaning with the text.

Effective teachers, as Linda Gambrell and Susan Mazzoni (1999) remind us, assess what students already know and "*link* new ideas, skills, and competencies to prior understandings." Lamont Franklin is one such teacher. He reflects on the importance of background knowledge as it relates to a selection his fifth-graders are about to read:

> I teach fifth-graders who are average-to-poor readers living in a Midwestern city. Our social studies curriculum includes a unit on Australia, and one of the reading selections is an informational piece on the Great Barrier Reef. Although most of my students have heard of Australia and seen pictures of it in the media, they haven't been there. In fact, most have never even seen an ocean. To read this article successfully, these students will need prereading experiences that provide background information to help fill the gaps in their repertoire of concepts about Australia and about oceans, reefs, and other topics central to this piece. Also, because the reading level of the article is sixth grade, and many of my students read below sixth-grade level, I'll have to do something extra to make sure they understand it. This may include preteaching potentially difficult vocabulary and providing them with a graphic organizer that shows what topics are included and how they are organized.
>
> —Lamont Franklin, Fifth-Grade Teacher

On the other hand, if, unlike Mr. Franklin's class of Midwesterners, the class reading the selection on the Great Barrier Reef does have adequate background knowledge to successfully comprehend the text, the issue becomes one of activating those schemata (McMahon & McCormack, 1998). For example, let's say the students reading about the Great Barrier Reef are above-average readers who live in Hawaii or on the West Coast. In this case, the activities will serve to activate already existing schemata. These may include having students discuss what they know about the topic before reading it, perhaps even writing down what they know about Australia and reefs, as well as their experiences and knowledge of the ocean. After reading the article, the students might discuss new information or ideas they discovered from the reading, questions that arose while they read, and where they might find the answers to those questions.

Reflect and Apply

1. Think about the different kinds of reading you do. Do you ever read something without a purpose? Explain. Do you think it's

important for students to have a purpose for the reading they do? Why or why not?

2. Suppose you are teaching second grade and your students are going to read nonfiction books about different occupations. When you go to the library or school media center to select "occupation" books for your class, what questions will you ask yourself as you look through the books to make your selections? (For example, How difficult is the vocabulary?)

3. Suppose you are teaching fourth-graders who come from a variety of backgrounds. Your literature curriculum includes *Number the Stars* by Lois Lowry, an award-winning middle-grade novel set in Nazi-occupied Denmark. The story revolves around ten-year-old Annemarie, who, with the help of her family, helps her best friend's family escape to Sweden. Are all of your students likely to succeed in reading this selection without help from you? Why or why not?

Five Frameworks for Scaffolding Students' Reading

In this section, we describe five frameworks that have been used to organize classroom reading instruction with the purpose of guiding students into, through, and beyond the texts they read. The first three frameworks—directed reading activity (DRA), direct reading-thinking activity (DR-TA), and scaffolded reading experience (SRE)—are suitable for all grade levels. The last two—guided reading and four blocks—are appropriate for students in grades 1 through 3.

Directed Reading Activity

For decades, the directed reading activity (DRA) served as the basic lesson format for the basal reader. First described by Emmett Betts in 1946, the procedure has five steps to guide students through a reading selection. First, the students are prepared for the selection. The teacher does this by creating interest, establishing purposes, or introducing new vocabulary. During the second step, students read silently. In the third step, the teacher checks students' comprehension in a discussion. Word-recognition skills are also sometimes developed during this third step. In the fourth step, students read the selection again, this time aloud, for purposes other than those of the first silent reading. The fifth step involves postreading, follow-up activities. The five steps in DRA are listed below:

1. Readiness
2. Directed silent reading
3. Comprehension check and discussion
4. Oral reading
5. Follow-up activities

Although the procedure has been justly criticized as inviting a rigid, one-size-fits-all reading instruction approach and as being too teacher dominated,

In Phase 1 of the DR-TA, Susan Jones asks her students to make predictions about the story told in *The Best Worst Day*.

it is worth considering because it has served as the basis of so much reading instruction, quite possibly the instruction you or your parents received. Additionally, it served as the precursor of the more flexible scaffolded reading experience, which we describe later in this chapter, and the directed reading-thinking activity, which we describe next. If you want to know more about the DRA itself, *Reading Strategies and Practices*, 6th ed. (Tierney & Readence, 2005) includes both a description and an evaluation.

Directed Reading-Thinking Activity

The directed reading-thinking activity (DR-TA) developed by Russell Stauffer (1969) is a procedure that focuses on student-generated purposes. The importance of having students generate their own purposes is based on the premise that reading is a thinking process that involves the reader in using his own experiences to reconstruct the author's ideas. The teacher's role in the DR-TA is to create a situation in which this thinking process will occur.

Implementing the DR-TA for a group of students in any grade has two phases: a phase in which the teacher directs the reading-thinking process and a skill-training phase. During the first phase of the DR-TA—the directed-thinking phase—the teacher involves the reader in three steps: predicting (setting purposes), reading, and proving. The teacher encourages students to make their own predictions concerning what they are about to read, to read to discover how accurate their predictions were, and to produce the proof to verify their predictions by orally re-reading the passage that yields the answer. (See In the Classroom 8.1 for an illustration of this procedure.)

The second phase of the DR-TA—the skill-training phase—occurs after students have read a selection and have completed the directed-thinking phase. Here students reexamine the story, which might involve analyzing teacher-selected words or phrases, pictures, or diagrams. The purpose of revisiting the story is to develop students' reading-thinking abilities and other reading-related skills. This skill training might include vocabulary work, creating semantic webs or weaves, summarizing, and other postreading activities.

Phase 1 of the DR-TA

The following is an example of how to implement Phase 1 of the DR-TA with second-graders who are reading the short chapter book *The Best Worst Day* by Bonnie Graves:

- Give each student a copy of *The Best Worst Day*.
- Have the students look at the title and the picture on the cover and ask, "What do you think the story might be about?" Some possible answers: "I think something good *and* bad will happen." "I think the girl hanging on the bar is going to get hurt."
- After several students give their predictions, ask, "Which of these predictions do you agree with?" Encourage students to make several different suggestions.
- Ask students to read a segment of the story silently to see if their predictions are correct.
- Have students read passages aloud that prove or disprove their predictions.
- Proceed through the story, having students make new predictions, read silently to see if their predictions are accurate, and then read aloud the relevant passages and evaluate and revise their predictions as necessary.

instructional routines in the Classroom 8.1

Scaffolded Reading Experience

The scaffolded reading experience (SRE) is similar to the DRA and DR-TA in that it takes students through the pre-, during-, and postreading phases of the reading of a text, yet it is markedly more flexible. Its simple design can easily be implemented in any reading situation at any grade level. The SRE is based on the notion of scaffolding, which we discussed in Chapter 2. Scaffolding, you will recall, is "a process that enables a child or novice to solve a problem, carry out a task, or achieve a goal [that] would be beyond his unassisted efforts" (Wood, Bruner, & Ross, 1976). The scaffolded reading experience (Avery & Graves, 1997; Clark & Graves, 2005; Graves & Graves, 2003; Graves, Graves, & Braaten, 1996; Watts & Graves, 1997) is designed to do just that—to ensure a student's reading success in whatever he is reading, for whatever purpose.

The SRE framework takes into consideration the three all-important factors discussed at the beginning of the chapter: purpose, selection, and reader. After carefully considering a purpose, a selection, and a group of readers, the teacher develops a set of prereading, during-reading, and postreading activities that supports students in achieving their reading goals. Figure 8.2 provides a graphic presentation of the framework.

As the figure shows, the SRE has two phases: a planning phase and an implementation phase. In the planning phase, the teacher considers the following:

- *The reader:* his needs, concerns, interests, strengths, weaknesses, background knowledge—anything that might influence his success (or failure) in reading a particular selection

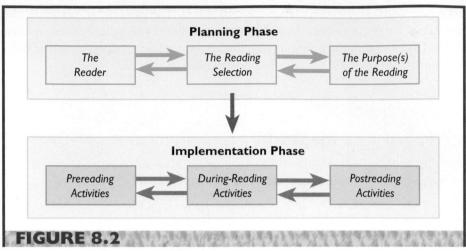

FIGURE 8.2

The Scaffolded Reading Experience

- *The selection:* its topics and themes, the background knowledge required, its organization, difficult vocabulary or other stumbling blocks, and the opportunities it presents for instruction
- *The purpose or purposes for reading:* what the reader is to gain from the reading experience. For what purposes is he reading?

As we have previously emphasized, these three factors are interrelated, and decisions made about one factor will influence and constrain the decisions made about the other two. In other words, purpose is linked to text and the students who are reading it, and students' skills and interests will largely determine which selections and purposes are appropriate for them.

In the next three sections, we discuss the three facets of the implementation phase: prereading, during-reading, and postreading activities of SREs. Then we discuss comprehensive SREs, SREs that include prereading, during-reading, and postreading activities.

Prereading Activities

Prereading activities get students ready both cognitively and affectively to read a selection. Taking time to prepare students before they read can pay big dividends in terms of their understanding what they read and finding it an enjoyable experience. Here we describe seven categories of prereading experiences.

Motivating and Setting Purposes for Reading. Motivational activities incite enthusiasm, an eagerness to discover what the written word has to offer. As Kathryn Au (1999) notes, "It is students' interest that must serve as the starting point." In other words, motivational activities will draw on the interests and concerns of the particular group doing the reading.

Activating and Building Background Knowledge. As explained in Chapter 1, having appropriate background knowledge—schemata—is absolutely crucial to understanding text. When *activating* background knowledge, you help students draw upon information they already have on a particular subject; when *building* background knowledge, you provide students with information they need to understand the text. For example, let's say a group of third-graders is going to read an expository piece on wildfires. To *activate* their prior knowledge, you might have them talk or write about what they know about fire. To *build* their background knowledge, you might draw an illustration of the fire triangle, explaining the three elements necessary for making fire, or show a video about wildfires.

Building Text-Specific Knowledge. In contrast to activities that activate or build background knowledge, activities that build *text-specific* knowledge give students information that is contained in the reading selection. Outlines and graphic organizers work well to build text-specific knowledge for expository texts. For example, before students read a chapter on waves in their science text, you might provide them with an outline or a graphic organizer like the ones shown in Figures 8.3 and 8.4.

Previews are another way of building text-specific knowledge. Previews are something like a movie trailer, providing a bit of information about the text. For informational texts, a preview might discuss topics, events, people, or places covered in the selection. For narratives, a preview might introduce the setting, characters, and perhaps a bit of the plot. Previews have been shown to be effective in facilitating comprehension with students of all ages and abilities and with English-language learners as well as with native speakers (Chen & Graves, 1996; Dole, Valencia, Greer, & Wardrop, 1991; Graves, Prenn, & Cooke, 1985).

Relating the Reading to Students' Lives. Like activating background knowledge and building text-specific knowledge, using activities that relate reading to students' lives also builds on and activates prior knowledge. In this case, however, the goal is to draw students into the text by helping them recall situations in their lives that are similar to those found in the selection.

Waves

 I. *How Do Waves Transfer Energy?*

 II. *Types of Waves*

   A. *Electromagnetic Waves*

     1. Radio Waves

     2. Higher-Frequency Waves

       a. Infrared Waves

       b. Light

       c. Ultraviolet Waves

       d. X rays and Gamma Rays

   B. *Lasers*

FIGURE 8.3
Outline of Chapter on Waves

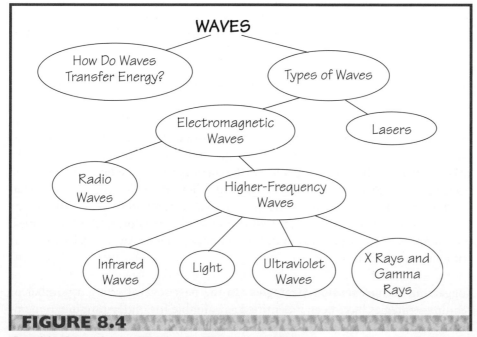

FIGURE 8.4
Graphic Organizer of Topics in Chapter on Waves

In the Classroom 8.2 shows a prereading activity that relates the reading to students' lives. It is designed to help students make connections with text through a prereading journal activity.

Prereading Activity Relating the Reading to Students' Lives

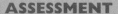

instructional routines

in the Classroom 8.2

Selection: Various biographies of Martin Luther King, Jr.

Readers: Fourth-grade students, several of whom have parents who emigrated to the United States and four of whom recently moved to the United States from Somalia. All of these fourth-graders have experienced firsthand the concept of discrimination, owing to events that occurred in their community as a result of a large influx of Somalians.

Reading purpose: To learn more about the life of Martin Luther King, Jr., and to understand and appreciate the purpose and results of his efforts to promote civil rights.

Goal of the activity: To make connections with the topics and themes found in the biographies.

Rationale: Having students write about times they felt discriminated against and later talk about them will help them better understand the concept of discrimination, a central theme in the biographies of King and a topic that has become an issue in their community. This writing will also help build an immediacy and relevancy for the biographies students will read.

Procedure: Before students begin reading biographies, ask them to write in their journals about a time in their lives when they felt that they were not treated as well as others, when they felt they were mistreated or treated unfairly. After students write, encourage them to read aloud or to discuss what they have written.

ASSESSMENT

To quickly learn which words students might need help with before they read a selection, write a list of potentially troublesome words on the board. Point to each word, and have students raise their hands if they don't know the word. Keep a tally of hands raised for each word. If the words are important to the selection's meaning and if the majority of students don't know them, spend some time on these words before students read the selection.

Preteaching Vocabulary and Concepts. Teaching selected vocabulary and concepts before students read a selection can aid them in their understanding and enjoyment of a text. Chapter 7 discussed the various sorts of word-learning tasks and instruction that facilitates that learning. Many of the procedures described in Chapter 7 can be used or modified to preteach vocabulary and concepts.

Prequestioning, Predicting, and Direction Setting. Prequestioning, predicting, and direction setting have a very similar purpose: These activities focus readers' attention on what to look for as they read, directing them to a particular aspect or several aspects of the text. With *prequestioning* activities, you and your students pose questions about the upcoming text that they would like to find answers to. In *predicting* activities, students make predictions about the text and read to find out whether their predictions are accurate. *Direction setting* reminds students about what to attend to while they read. You might say, "Read the story to find out if your predictions are correct." Other times, you might write instructions on the chalkboard, a chart, or a handout so that students can refer to them.

Suggesting Comprehension Strategies. In the past several years, a number of reading strategies have been indentified as valuable for understanding, remembering, and enjoying text (Pressley, 2000). In Chapter 9, we discuss how to teach these strategies. Once your students learn how to use these strategies, you can provide a valuable aid to their comprehension by, as part of your prereading scaffold, suggesting a strategy or strategies for students to employ while reading.

Prereading Activities: A Summary. By now, you are probably aware that the possibilities for prereading activities are almost limitless. But there is a common thread to all of them—each builds a bridge from the students to the selection, connecting what students already know to what they will learn or meet in the text. Sometimes just one brief prereading activity will be sufficient. At other times, you may want to support students' efforts by using several activities. Your prereading plans will be determined by the purposes for reading, the selection itself, and those who are reading it.

Reflect and Apply

4. In what kinds of reading situations are prereading activities likely to be unnecessary? In what situations are prereading activities essential? Why do you think relating the reading to students' lives is a useful prereading activity?
5. Do any of your college instructors engage their classes in prereading activities? If so, what are these activities? Do they help you better understand the assigned reading material? Explain.
6. What functions do prereading activities serve? Jot down as many as you can, and briefly explain how each prepares readers to comprehend and enjoy the selection they will read.

During-Reading Activities

After you have built the bridge from reader to text with prereading activities, students are ready to get into the act itself. *During-reading activities* include both things that students do themselves as they are reading and things that you do to assist them—activities that facilitate or enhance the actual reading process. Five types of during-reading activities are described here.

Silent Reading. Beyond the primary grades, most reading is carried out most efficiently by reading the words silently. Silent reading will be the most frequent during-reading activity done by middle- and upper-elementary students.

Reading to Students. Although students will generally read silently, sometimes it is appropriate for students to have material read to them. Reading aloud to your students can

- make certain texts accessible and, through intonation, stress, pauses, and inflection, give to a text meaning that their own silent reading might not (Horowitz & Freeman, 1995).
- convey your enthusiasm for information, ideas, and language and provide a model for expressive reading.
- build students' vocabularies, their knowledge of the world, their knowledge of books and many of the conventions employed in books, and—probably most importantly—their interest in reading.
- demonstrate the beauty and power of language, especially for students who struggle with reading on their own or have had little exposure to books.

Reading aloud to students is a powerful way to engage them in text and demonstrate the beauty and power of language.

Oral Reading by Students. Three popular read-aloud activities are choral reading, readers theater, and buddy reading. In *choral reading*—by using contrasts such as high and low voices, different voice combinations, sound effects, movements, gestures, or increasing and decreasing tempo—students together convey and interpret the meaning of a text. Choral reading builds confidence, fluency, and automaticity as students respond creatively to a text.

Readers theater, in which students take turns or assume roles in reading portions of text aloud, can be used effectively to interpret poetry, narratives, and even expository materials (Young & Vardell, 1993).

In *buddy reading,* two people read the same passage aloud together or take turns reading. This kind of oral reading is particularly useful for younger students, English-language learners, and those who need extra support. It also does much to boost the reading skills and self-esteem of the older child who reads with his younger buddy (Brozo, 2002; Cunningham & Allington, 1999; Friedland & Truesdell, 2004). Buddies can be two peers, cross-age students, a parent and a student, an aide and a student, or a teacher and a student.

If done in a supportive, nonthreatening way, students' read-aloud activities can enhance their interest and enjoyment of reading, improve fluency, increase vocabulary, and add to their storehouse of knowledge and concepts.

Supported Reading. Supported reading activities focus students' attention on certain ideas as they read. Particularly with exposition, it is appropriate to support students' reading, to help them focus on, understand, and learn from certain aspects of the text. Here are a few options for supporting students' reading of exposition:

- Encourage critical thinking by having students note examples of fact and opinion, make inferences, draw conclusions, or predict outcomes.
- Lead students to manipulate the text in ways that will help them better understand and retain key concepts—recording main ideas and their supporting details, outlining, summarizing, and making graphic organizers.
- Have students monitor their understanding of what they read.

Although supported reading activities are most often used to help students read expository material, they can also be employed with narratives. Supported reading activities for narratives can include the following:

- Informal writing that elicits personal responses, such as journaling or writing letters
- Reading with a partner and pausing to reflect out loud
- Using reading guides, which might include answering questions or completing charts or outlines that focus on character, plot development, point of view, or aspects of language or style

Supported reading activities should get students thinking about and manipulating the ideas and concepts in the material in a way that will help them better understand, enjoy, and remember it.

Modifying the Text. Sometimes, because of curriculum requirements or availability of texts, students will be reading selections whose length or difficulty presents too much of a challenge. In these cases, modifying—altering the original text or the medium of presentation—is a practical and powerful option. For example, if you know that a selection presents too much of a challenge to your readers, you could either read parts of the text aloud or let students listen to a recording of those parts as they silently read along. Another option is to have students read only selected portions of the text—the ones you think are most critical. This makes an otherwise impossible task feasible for your less-competent readers. A successful reading experience is always the goal, and for some students, such as those learning English, modifying the text to create a doable reading task is one more way to ensure that success.

During-Reading Activities: A Summary. As with prereading activities, there are many different kinds of during-reading activities and many ways of varying them. All during-reading activities, however, should involve students with the text as they read it in a way that best suits the students, the text, and their purposes.

Reflect *and* Apply

7. Suppose you are teaching second grade. What kinds of during-reading activities might you engage your students in, and why?
8. Briefly discuss, in writing or with a classmate, the purpose and function of supported reading activities. Discuss your personal philosophy about supported reading activities, including when they might be appropriate and when they might be inappropriate.
9. Identify a narrative or expository text you might use in the classroom. Answer the questions listed above to help you design during-reading activities for that piece.

Postreading Activities

Generally, *postreading activities* encourage students to *do* something with the material they have just read, to think—critically, logically, and creatively—about the information and ideas that emerge from their reading, to respond to what they have read, and sometimes to transform their thinking into actions.

These responses can take a variety of forms—speaking, writing, drama, creative arts, or application and outreach. Here we have categorized seven kinds of postreading activities.

Questioning. By encouraging students to think about and respond to the information and ideas in the material they have read, either orally or in writing, postreading questioning activities can promote thinking on a number of levels. They might help readers recall what they have read, show that readers understand what they read, or give readers an opportunity to apply, analyze, synthesize, evaluate, or elaborate on information and ideas. Questions might also encourage creative, interpretive, or metacognitive thinking and illustrate the various perspectives among readers. Questions can be of various kinds, but it is important that at least some of them give students the opportunity to engage in higher-level thinking (Beck & McKeown, 2001; Pearson & Duke, 2002). In the Classroom 8.3 gives some sample postreading questions for the various types of thinking.

Sample Postreading Questions for Various Types of Thinking

in the Classroom 8.3

Here are some questions that teachers might ask students after they read *Shh! We're Writing the Constitution* by Jean Fritz.

Recalling: How many delegates were supposed to attend the grand convention in 1787?

Understanding: How did the delegates keep the proceedings secret?

Applying: What are some things you might do to keep a meeting secret?

Analyzing: Why did the delegates decide to keep the proceedings secret?

Synthesizing: What do you think might have happened if the public had found out what was going on in the meetings?

Evaluating: Do you think it was a good idea to keep the meetings secret? Why or why not?

Elaborating: What do you think were the most effective features of the delegates' plan to keep the proceedings secret?

Creating: What if the delegates had decided there should be three presidents presiding over the nation instead of one? What might have happened?

Interpreting: How do you think Benjamin Franklin felt, being the oldest delegate at the convention?

Thinking metacognitively: Did you understand the author's description of the three branches of government on page 14? If you didn't, what might you do to make this explanation more clear to you?

Discussion. A large number of classroom reading experiences will include discussion—exchanging ideas out loud. The intent of discussion is to freely explore ideas, to learn something new, or to gain a different perspective by pooling the information or insights that more than one person can give. Research studies show that positive effects accrue when children engage in small-group discussions about text. These discussions enhance text recall, aesthetic response to text, and reading comprehension (Gambrell, 1996).

To become proficient in discussion, students need explicit instruction, modeling, and many opportunities for practice. Students also need feedback from

you and their peers on what has been learned in a discussion and on the process of the discussion itself.

Discussion groups can be led by the teacher or by students. They can involve the entire class, small groups, or pairs. Whatever format is used, the guidelines given in Figure 8.5 and our discussion of preparing for group work in Chapter 3 will help you implement effective discussions.

Writing. Writing has been called the twin sister of reading—a powerful way to integrate what students know with the information presented in a text, as well as to find out what they really do and don't understand. Writing is powerful because it requires a reader to actively manipulate information and ideas. As a postreading activity, writing can serve to connect information and ideas in a logical way. Writing also provides opportunities for students to extend ideas, to explore new ways of thinking, doing, and seeing—to invent, evaluate, create, and ponder. Writing is discussed at length in Chapter 12, which includes many examples that can be used as postreading activities. Figure 8.6 outlines three postreading activities that relate appropriately to the readers, selection, and purpose of reading.

Drama. As a postreading activity, drama, like writing, encourages students to extend existing meanings they have constructed with a text and to generate new ones. In the hands of a skillful, sensitive teacher, drama can become an enjoyable and highly motivating way to involve students in all of the cognitive tasks we listed at the beginning of this section—recalling, applying, analyzing, synthesizing, evaluating, and creating—through plays, skits, retelling of stories, pantomimes, and readers theater. In In the Classroom 8.4, multigrade teacher Harold Bulinski lists several examples of how he uses dramatization as a postreading activity. These illustrate only a few of the great variety of possibilities for dramatizing text.

CW 8.3 links to the Amazon and Barnes and Noble Websites, where students can write and submit book reviews, an excellent postreading writing activity.

CW 8.4 links to Children's Literature Network, where links to author Websites allow students to e-mail authors whose books they have read.

Classroom Postreading Discussion

- *Our discussions have a clear purpose.*
- *We are supportive, non-critical, and open-minded.*
- *We listen actively and show courtesy.*
- *We check the text if there is a difference of opinion.*
- *We evaluate our discussion.*

FIGURE 8.5

Sample Wall Chart of Postreading Discussion Guidelines

READERS	SELECTION	PURPOSE	APPROPRIATE POSTREADING WRITING ACTIVITY
Primary-grade students	Poem about feelings	To respond personally to the poem	Write a poem describing similar feelings that students have had.
Fourth-grade students	Numerous books on animals	To learn about the characteristics of a variety of animals and to synthesize that information	Create alphabet picture books reflecting an animal or animals of their choice.
Fifth-grade students	Chapter on electricity	To understand and remember the information presented in the text	Write summaries for each of the sections of the chapter.

FIGURE 8.6

Matching Postreading Writing Activity to Readers, Selection, and Purpose

Students' Postreading Dramatizations

- Second-graders pantomime Indian tigers while listening to Ted Lewin's informational picture book *Tiger Trek* read aloud.

- Small groups of first- through third-graders prepare a dramatization of their favorite poem in Jack Prelutsky's *Tyrannosaurus Was a Beast*.

- Two fifth-graders play the parts of Gilly and Miss Ellis, Gilly's caseworker, and dramatize the opening scene in Katherine Paterson's *The Great Gilly Hopkins*.

- Two fifth-graders, after reading a chapter on the 1960s in their social studies text, portray Martin Luther King, Jr., and Lyndon B. Johnson. They carry on a conversation posing as these two historical figures. Later, their conversation is videotaped and aired on a community cable station.

- Fourth-grade students play blood cells and dramatize the flow of blood through the circulatory system in response to a science text on the subject.

in the Classroom 8.4

ASSESSMENT

After students have read a story or part of one, asking them to retell or to pantomime the story or a scene from the story can help you assess whether or not they have understood what they have read.

Artistic and Nonverbal Activities. As the work of Howard Gardner (1993) has shown, people have multiple intelligences—a variety of ways to learn and express what they know. This category takes into account those modes of expression that are not predominantly verbal, including the visual arts, music, and dance. We also include response activities that involve the creation of media productions, visual displays, and representations.

Art, music, and dance each represent a specialized language that can be used in response to printed and spoken communication. Numerous children's books can help connect students with the arts—for example, in *To Be an Artist* by Maya Ajmera (2004), photos and text reveal how children around the world express themselves through art. In her article "Music and Children's Books," Kathleen Jacobi-Karna (1996) gives an extensive list of children's books that suggest musical possibilities. In the Reading Corner, we list 11 titles, many of which were recommended by Cheri Estes (1995) in her article "Musical Links, Part I."

In addition to responding to a selection through art, music, and dance, students can engage in other types of artistic and nonverbal activities. These include media productions, such as making audiotapes, videos, or slide shows. Or students might enjoy creating visual displays, using bulletin boards, artifacts, models, and specimens. Also, making visual representations of

the Reading Corner

Books That Invite Musical Connections

Anna Harwell Celenza. *Bach's Goldberg Variations*. Charlesbridge, 2005. This tale tells of how Bach helps out a talented young musician. CD included.

Claude Clement. *Musician from Darkness*. Little, Brown, 1990. In lyrical prose, Clement tells the story of an outsider from a primitive society who discovers the power and magic of music.

James Lincoln Collier. *The Jazz Kid*. Holt, 1994. In this story, set in Chicago in the 1920s, 12-year-old Paulie wants to become a jazz cornetist and play the Black jazz music of Louis Armstrong, King Oliver, and the New Orleans Rhythm Kings. But his prejudiced parents are against it.

Jane Cutler. *The Cello of Mr. O*. Dutton, 1999. In wartime, a man's music helps sustain a town's spirit.

Tony Johnston. *The Harmonica*. Charlesbridge, 2004. The harmonica given to him by his father helps a Polish boy survive Nazi brutality.

Robert Kraus. *Musical Max*. Simon & Schuster, 1990. Max the musical hippo drives his father and neighbors crazy with his daily practicing on every sort of instrument. One day, he loses interest and stops. But the effect is not what the complainers thought it would be.

Bill Martin, Jr. *The Maestro Plays*. Holt, 1994. The subtleties of music are introduced with rhyming text as Martin describes the way a maestro plays the music.

Metropolitan Museum of Art. *Go In and Out the Window: An Illustrated Songbook for Young People*. Holt, 1987. Art and music are brought together in this handsome volume of 61 familiar songs illustrated with works from the Metropolitan Museum of Art.

Brian Pinkney. *Max Found Two Sticks*. Simon & Schuster, 1994. A would-be drummer, Max beats on different surfaces, echoing the sounds around him. He imagines church bells, a marching band, a train. Then a real band marches by and a drummer tosses Max a pair of sticks.

Pam Munoz Ryan. *When Marian Sang: The True Recital of Marian Anderson, the Voice of the Century*. Scholastic, 2002. This book provides an introduction to the life of Marian Anderson, the first African American to perform at the Metropolitan Opera and a civil rights activist whose life and career encouraged social change.

Mildred Pitts Walter. *Ty's One-Man Band*. Four Winds, 1987. A young African American child, while playing by the pond, meets a one-legged, one-man band who brings music to the community.

information—graphs, maps, charts, trees, diagrams, and schematics—is another excellent artistic and nonverbal response activity.

Like drama activities, artistic and nonverbal activities have great potential for showing students that language can be transformed and that ideas can be seen, heard, and felt.

Application and Outreach. Each of the previously mentioned categories in one way or another reflects the idea of going beyond the text to explore other realms and other applications of information and ideas. In application and outreach endeavors, readers take the ideas and information from a text and deliberately test, use, or explore them further. Students might read a story about making ice cream or an article describing several science experiments, but it's not quite as much fun as actually following the steps and eating the ice cream or doing the experiments. The logical next step after reading about something is to try it out in the real world.

CHAPTER 8 Scaffolding Students' Comprehension of Text   *253*

Artistic and nonverbal activities, such as creating models and visual displays, provide students with the opportunity to share what they've learned as well as reinforce newly acquired knowledge.

Not only how-to books invite real-world applications, however. Fiction, nonfiction, and poetry can also spark many different kinds of personal and social action. For example, after reading Chris Van Allsburg's *Just a Dream*—in which a child dreams of a future wasted because of poor management of the environment—students might decide to write letters to state and local representatives encouraging them to support legislation to protect the environment, or they might develop an environment-related ad campaign for their school or neighborhood.

Another kind of outreach activity is for students to share their enthusiasm for books and reading outside the school doors in the form of book clubs. One such book club takes place between sixth-graders and senior citizens in Winchester, Massachusetts. The club is called the Literary Lunch Bunch; students and seniors meet to share a midday meal and discuss books (Abramson, 2002).

On their own, students will not always make the connections necessary to transfer ideas from the text to the real world. By providing activities that demonstrate such connections, you can drive home a critical aspect of the nature of good text—we should not be the same after we have read it. Our new selves contain new information and ideas that we can now use.

Reteaching. The six types of activities that we have just discussed encourage students to make logical connections between ideas and to explore new ways of thinking and of expressing themselves. Our seventh category, reteaching, is the safety net in the reading scaffold, a way to make sure students leave a reading selection with a sense of accomplishment, of a job well done.

Reteaching is often necessary when students, after reading a selection and engaging in various activities of an SRE, have not reached their reading goals. Robert Dickenson, a fifth-grade teacher, discusses his reteaching approaches:

> I sometimes find it necessary to include reteaching activities in the scaffold I build to support my students' reading experience. This happens when my students have not reached their reading goals. These reteaching activities usually consist of a retracing of the steps of a specific activity *with* students, to see what went wrong and where—for example, if students had difficulty completing a reading guide or answering postreading questions. In these cases, my reteaching might include discussing with students the problems they had and why they had them, and then reviewing the purposes and steps involved in completing the guide or answering the questions.
>
> Alternatively, reteaching sometimes involves creating a totally different activity. I do this when the original activity was a disaster—something that happens more times than I'd like to admit, even though I'm a seasoned teacher.
>
> Sometimes I have students simply repeat the original activity, approaching it with their new level of understanding. I do this when students have gained quite a bit from their reading, but a second attempt could result in greater gains. My purpose in all of these approaches—discussing the problem and then modifying the activity, creating a new activity, or repeating the original one—is to do everything possible to ensure that my students have successful and fulfilling reading experiences.
>
> —Robert Dickenson, Fifth-Grade Teacher

Postreading Activities: A Summary. Again, postreading activities help students go beyond the text and do something with the material they have read in order to help them see the relevance of reading, how it relates to their own lives and to the wider world around them. These types of activities will also help students better remember what they have read, provide them with opportunities to express themselves in a variety of ways, encourage the development of multiple intelligences, and give them opportunities to see how others interpret selections and additional opportunities to succeed. Postreading activities should involve students with ideas gleaned from text in a way that is customized to suit the text itself, the students, and their purposes.

Reflect *and* Apply

10. What purposes do postreading activities serve? Do you think you will engage your students in postreading activities for most of the reading they do in your class? Why or why not?

11. Suppose you are teaching fifth-graders who have just finished reading biographies of prominent figures in U.S. history. What sorts of postreading activities might these students engage in and why? Now, suppose you are teaching first-graders who have just read a beginning chapter book on the theme of friendship. What sorts of postreading activities might these students engage in and why?

12. Do you think it's important to engage students in application and outreach postreading activities? Why or why not?

READERS	SELECTION	PURPOSE	PREREADING ACTIVITIES	DURING-READING ACTIVITIES	POSTREADING ACTIVITIES
Fifth-graders of mixed abilities; two English-language learners	Chapter on World War II postwar years	To understand, recall, respond to, and analyze the important topics and issues in the chapter	1 Motivational 1 Preteaching concept 2 Building background knowledge 1 Suggesting strategies	1 Guided reading 1 Oral reading by teacher 1 Oral reading by students 1 Modifying the text (for English-language learners only)	1 Discussion 1 Artistic and nonverbal 1 Writing

FIGURE 8.7

Sample SRE for Fifth-Graders Reading a Chapter on World War II

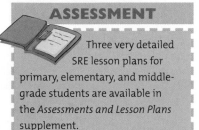

ASSESSMENT

Three very detailed SRE lesson plans for primary, elementary, and middle-grade students are available in the *Assessments and Lesson Plans* supplement.

Comprehensive SREs

In the previous three sections, we have focused on individual pre-, during-, and postreading activities. Figure 8.7 shows that these activities are interrelated—linked, one to the other, in response to the students, the selection, and the overall purpose for reading. Additionally, our *Assessments and Lesson Plans* booklet includes a very detailed SRE for Kate DiCamillo's *Because of Winn-Dixie*.

As a final word on SREs, we want to reemphasize that the purpose of an SRE is not to fill up precious reading time with a lot of activities, no matter how engaging or purposeful they might be in their own right, but rather to provide a scaffold for students to successfully build meaning from the texts that they read and do something with their newly gained knowledge and insights.

Guided Reading

Guided reading, first developed by Irene Fountas and Gay Su Pinnell (1996), is a framework for reading instruction used primarily in grades 1 through 3; however, it can be adapted to use with older students (Tierney & Readence, 2000). In guided reading, the teacher guides small groups of students in their reading of texts that offer a bit, but not too much, of a challenge for them. Regie Routman (2003) suggests that in guided reading "the teacher builds on students' strengths and supports and demonstrates whatever is necessary to move the child toward independence."

The first step in guided reading is for the teacher to select appropriate materials for students to read. A good rule of thumb is that with teacher support, students should be able to read 90 percent of the words accurately. Once the text has been selected, the students are given individual copies. The teacher briefly introduces the selection to the students, clarifying concepts or vocabulary that might prove difficult, prompting students to engage in certain reading strategies, and generally preparing the students for the reading. Next, the students read either quietly or silently while the teacher observes them, guiding them when necessary and encouraging them to use strategies to unlock meaning.

After the students have finished with the reading, they talk about what they have read, either recalling details of the selection or offering personal responses. This is a time, too, to discuss any problem solving they did during the reading. The teacher may also recommend that students revisit the text at this time to increase their fluency or may use the text to teach a skill or concept. Extending the text through postreading activities, such as those discussed with the SRE, can also be done during this portion of guided reading.

During guided reading, all students read from the same text quietly or silently while the teacher observes, guiding them to use strategies to unlock meaning. After reading, students talk about what they have read.

Another important aspect of guided reading is teacher assessment and follow-up. While students are reading and after, the teacher makes notes and keeps a record of students' progress in areas such as strategy use, fluency, self-monitoring, and correcting.

As with the SRE framework, guided reading is not meant to be the sole element of a literacy program. In contrast to the SRE, which can be implemented with any size group—whole class or small group, heterogeneous or homogeneous—guided reading is usually done in small homogeneous groups.

Four Blocks

Like guided reading, four blocks (Cunningham, Hall, & Defee, 1991, 1998) is a framework primarily for beginning reading instruction in grades 1 through 3. In contrast to guided reading, in which students are most often grouped according to reading ability, four blocks was designed to meet the needs of students reading at multiple levels by combining the major approaches to reading instruction, guided reading being one of them. Four blocks is a more comprehensive framework and, in fact, includes guided reading as one of its four blocks.

As the name implies, four blocks consists of four blocks of instruction—typically 30 to 40 minutes each—that are integrated by a theme. The four blocks are as follows:

- Guided reading
- Self-selected reading
- Working with words
- Writing

During the guided reading block, students read a variety of literature, either in basals or in trade books, that usually reflects the theme under study. The teacher's role is to teach students comprehension strategies and how to read materials that become increasingly difficult. Typically, teachers select two texts weekly, one below and one at grade level. Each book is read multiple times for different purposes to help ensure fluency.

In the self-selected reading block, students read material of their own choosing. This block generally follows the reading workshop structure we describe in Chapter 10. With early first-graders, this "reading" may include pretending to read by telling the story of a familiar book, picture-reading a book by talking about the illustrations, or reciting memorized words. Early in the year, the teacher will have demonstrated these three kinds of "reading" for the students. The self-selected reading block also includes teacher read-alouds of a wide range of materials; student-teacher conferences in which teachers make anecdotal records of student progress; and student sharing, with one or two students sharing what they are reading.

During the working-with-words block, the teacher helps students to learn to read and spell high-frequency words and to learn the visual and sound patterns of words. The learning of these patterns helps students decode and spell other words. Here are four of the suggested activities in this block:

- *Word wall.* A collection of high-frequency words are listed in alphabetical order on a wall chart. Five new words are added weekly until about 120 words are displayed; the first ten minutes of this block are spent reviewing the words.
- *Rounding up the rhymes.* After a book is read one or two times (during the guided reading block), students are encouraged to point out words that rhyme. The teacher then writes these words on index cards and places them in a pocket chart. Students identify those words with and without the same visual pattern. Those with different patterns, such as *lead* and *said,* are discarded, while those with the same patterns, such as *cake* and *bake,* are kept.
- *Making words.* In this hands-on activity, students make new words by changing the first letter of pattern words, such as changing *bad* to *dad, mad, sad,* and so on. Making words begins with short words and progresses to longer, more difficult words. (For a more complete description, see Cunningham and Cunningham, 1992.)
- *Guess the covered word.* In this activity, the teacher writes four or five sentences on the board, with one word in each covered. Students guess what the covered word is and explain their reasoning.

The fourth block is writing, which is conducted like a writing workshop, as we describe in Chapter 12.

Individual Procedures for Fostering Comprehension of Text

In this section, we describe a number of additional teacher-guided procedures that differ from the five instructional frameworks we just described in that they were designed to achieve very specific instructional goals or to focus on a particular part of reading. Some are used prior to reading, some during reading, some after reading, and some at several points in the reading process. All of them encourage active and reflective thinking and can be modified for any elementary classroom. We have divided the procedures described here into three categories:

- Procedures for narratives
- Procedures for expository texts
- Procedures appropriate for all types of texts

For a complete list and descriptions of procedures for fostering comprehension and other aspects of reading, we recommend *Reading Strategies and Practices,* 6th ed. (Tierney & Readence, 2005).

Procedures for Narratives

As we have already noted and as Rosenblatt (1978) explains at length, narratives are written primarily to entertain. Most well-written stories, whether simple or complex, have a fairly similar structure, and most children have a basic schema for this structure. Teachers can help students make this understanding explicit and give them a language for talking about stories. When teachers build on this schema, students' comprehension and enjoyment of narrative literature will be enhanced, as will their writing in this genre. Story grammars and story maps provide two ways to help students enhance their schema for stories.

Story Grammars

To identify the common elements that make up a well-developed story, several variations of story grammar have been developed (Mandler & Johnson, 1977; Thorndyke, 1977). Story grammar is similar to sentence grammar in that it attempts to explain the various components in a story and how they function. The story grammar we have found most helpful is a synthesis of those that both educational researchers and fiction writers have identified as consistent across stories. This grammar includes a *setting* with a *character* who has a problem to solve or a goal to achieve, the character's *attempts* to solve the problem or achieve the goal, the *results* of these attempts, and a *conclusion.* This conclusion illuminates the story's theme. Figure 8.8 shows these components and their relationship to one another and to the three phases of a story: beginning, development, and ending.

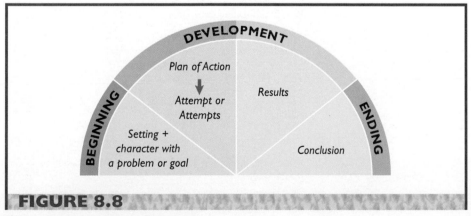

FIGURE 8.8

Representative Story Grammar

Story Maps

As described by Isabel Beck and Margaret McKeown (1981), a story map is a listing of the major events and ideas in a story, beginning at the starting point and moving through the story in sequential order. Beck and McKeown recommend that teachers create a story map to help identify the major structural elements, both explicit and implicit, in a story that students will be reading in class. Based on the map, the teacher then generates a question for the students to answer related to each major event. In the story map illustrated in Figure 8.9, you will see that the left column gives the story event and the right column the corresponding question for students to answer. These questions, when answered, constitute the essence of the story and elicit information that is central to understanding it. To create a story map, decide what the starting point for the story is, list briefly the major events in chronological order, and then write a question for each event. Students can discuss the questions before they read as a sort of preview, use them as they read to record their understanding of the story, or answer them after they read to assess their comprehension.

Story map questions can both improve students' existing schema for a story and improve their story comprehension. As Beck and McKeown note, however, story map questions are not the only questions to ask concerning reading selections. Once students understand the essence of the story, then interpretive, analytical, and creative questions are appropriate and important to pursue. For example, you might ask, "Have you ever offered to help someone as Da did? What did you offer to do? What happened?" We term such questions *extension questions* and view them as a vital part of students' response to a story.

EVENT	CORRESPONDING QUESTION
Event 1: The Chang family makes *nian-gao* for their New Year's Eve celebration.	What did the Chang family make for their New Year's Eve celebration?
Event 2: When Momma Chang starts to cut the *nian-gao,* it runs away.	What happened when Momma Chang started to cut the *nian-gao?*
Event 3: The *nian-gao* runs faster than everyone.	Why couldn't anyone catch the *nian-gao?*
Event 4: The *nian-gao* runs into an old woman and is captured.	How was the *nian-gao* finally captured?
Event 5: Da offers the family's *nian-gao* to the old woman because she hasn't eaten in two days.	Why did Da offer the family's *nian-gao* to the old woman?
Event 6: The old woman eats the entire *nian-gao* because it is so delicious and she's starving.	Why did the old woman eat the entire *nian-gao?*
Event 7: The neighbors, who have heard of their misfortune, bring food for the Changs.	Why did the neighbors bring food for the Changs?
Event 8: The neighbors won't eat the food they brought.	What wouldn't the neighbors do with the food they brought?
Event 9: All the Chang family members, except Da, offer to give their food to the neighbors.	What did all of the Chang family members, except Da, offer to do with the food?
Event 10: When Da says there is enough food for everyone, more food magically appears.	What happened when Da said there was enough food for everyone?

FIGURE 8.9

Sample Story Map for *The Runaway Rice Cake* by Ying Chang Compestine

Using the K-W-L procedure with students can help motivate and guide their reading of nonfiction texts.

Procedures for Expository Texts

As we mentioned earlier, in contrast to narratives, which are written primarily to entertain, expository texts are generally written to impart some sort of information or knowledge. We typically read them to make that information and knowledge part of our own schemata, either to use or to store for future application. That purpose alone makes reading these texts a different sort of endeavor than reading a story in which places, characters, and events unfold in our imagination. As Rosenblatt (1978) has suggested, readers take two different stances when reading—an aesthetic stance for narratives and an efferent stance for expository text. The primary purpose when reading aesthetically is not to gain information, but to experience the text. In reading efferently, however, your purpose is to locate or remember information. Therefore, with most expository texts, your attention will be focused primarily on what you will take from the reading—what information you will learn.

Successful comprehension of exposition requires skills and schemata not demanded for story reading. Expository text offers a special challenge to both teacher and student. Here we describe two procedures that are particularly useful for helping students comprehend expository material—the K-W-L procedure and reading or study guides.

K-W-L

K-W-L stands for *what do you Know? what do you Want to know?* and *what did you Learn?* The K-W-L procedure, developed by Donna Ogle (1986), is a three-part process designed to motivate and guide readers in acquiring information from expository texts; it is perhaps the best-known and most frequently used procedure for delving into expository texts. In the Classroom 8.5 illustrates how this procedure is put into practice in a California classroom with a group of fourth-graders who are reading the trade book *Earthquakes* by Seymour Simon.

Using K-W-L

After motivating students by relating the topic to their lives, fourth-grade teacher David Scott writes the title *Earthquakes* on the chalkboard. Underneath that title and to the left, he writes the heading *What Do You Know?* He then asks students to give some of the facts they know about earthquakes and jots down their responses under the heading *Earthquakes,* as shown in Figure 8.10.

Not all of the students' responses are accurate, even though during this brainstorming session Mr. Scott had asked students questions to help them consider the correctness of their statements, such as "How did you learn that?" or "How could you prove that?" Later, during the postreading discussion, he and his students will clear up the remaining misconceptions.

After Mr. Scott's students give a variety of responses, he shows them the cover illustration of *Earthquakes* and asks them to think about the kinds of information that might be included in the book. He then writes their suggestions underneath their initial responses (see Figure 8.10).

Next, Mr. Scott reminds his students that informational books such as *Earthquakes* are written to give information that we might need or want. He then asks students to think about what they would like to know about earthquakes—things they don't already know or aren't quite sure of. He records these responses in the column to the right of the *What Do You Know?* column in Figure 8.10.

On the chalkboard to the right of the previous two headings, Mr. Scott writes *What Did You Learn?* He explains to students that this is the last part of the K-W-L procedure—a procedure they can use when they read informational books and articles. He says, "You have already completed the first two steps—thinking about and writing down what you know about earthquakes and what you would like to know. The last step is to record what information you do learn."

At this point, Mr. Scott gives students their own K-W-L charts and tells them, "In the first column, record what you *know* about earthquakes; in the second column, what you *want* to know. Then, as you read, write what you *learned* in the third column." He also reminds students that not all of their questions will be answered in the text. Later, they will talk about where they might find answers to those questions.

in the *Classroom* 8.5

EARTHQUAKES

What Do You Know?	*What Do You Want to Find Out?*	*What Did You Learn?*
Can cause damage	What causes earthquakes	
Are unpredictable	How earthquakes are measured	
Are scary		
Happen in California	What places have earthquakes	
Not all are the same		
Shake the earth	What was the worst earthquake	
Don't happen at night	When most earthquakes happen	
Are getting worse		
	What we can do about earthquakes	

Categories of information that might be included:

How earthquakes happen • When they happen • What we can do about them • How much damage they do • Why they happen • Descriptions of some of the worst earthquakes

FIGURE 8.10

K-W-L

Source: Heimlich, Joan E., & Pittelman, Susan D. (1986). *Semantic Mapping: Classroom Applications.* Newark, DE: International Reading Association. Used with permission.

The K-W-L procedure is extremely useful for dealing with informational material, both in hard copy and on the Internet (Pritchard & Cartwright, 2004). The three phases of the procedure—brainstorming, establishing purposes through questioning, and finding answers to those questions—virtually guarantee that students will be actively involved in their learning. The procedure provides a scaffold to support students' own interest and inquiries.

CW 8.5 links to Teachnology. This Website will help you create a K-W-L chart to use with any subject in any topic.

Reading Guides

Reading guides are "teacher-developed devices for helping students understand instructional reading material" (Wood, Lapp, & Flood, 1992). Although reading guides, also called study guides, are sometimes useful in working with narratives, they are most often designed to help students understand and learn from expository material. These guides consist of questions and activities related to the specific texts students are reading and their purposes for reading them. Students respond to the questions or engage in the activities as they read the text. Reading guides provide a learning scaffold for students, while at the same time giving them control over their learning.

As Karen Wood and John Mateja (1983) have noted, a reading guide serves as a "tutor in print form." One such tutor in print form is a time line such as the one shown in Figure 8.11. Time lines can serve as valuable reading guides for texts that deal with events that take place over a specific period of time, such as Diane McWhorter's *A Dream of Freedom: The Civil Rights Movement from 1954 to 1968*. A time line can list dates and then ask students to name the significant event for each date and explain the reason or reasons for the event's significance. Having students complete such a guide as they read will aid them both in developing a schema for the historic events in the order in which they occurred and in practicing their critical-thinking skills.

This, of course, is only one of many types of reading guides. One teacher we know provides students with questions that encourage them to make connections between themselves and the text, similar to the Reflect and Apply questions you find throughout this text. Another teacher frequently gives students

Date	Important event or events	Why was this event important?
1954		
1955		
1957		
1960		
1961		
1962		
1963		
1964		
1965		
1966		
1968		

FIGURE 8.11

Time Line for *A Dream of Freedom: The Civil Rights Movement from 1954 to 1968* by Diane McWhorter

a handout that lists the main headings of the selection they are reading and provides space for their notes following each heading. Wood and her colleagues (1992) describe many other types of reading guides.

Procedures Appropriate for All Types of Text

We want to again note that the primary purpose for engaging students in any of the procedures we describe is to enhance their reading enjoyment, to foster understanding and learning, and to increase their competence and confidence in making meaning with texts. Some procedures are appropriate for any type of text, if adapted to reflect the specific selection, readers, and purposes involved. Here we present a few of them; we believe the discussion web and semantic webbing and weaving activities meet the criteria for engaging students with the text and developing their literacy. The discussion web and semantic webbing and weaving make use of graphic organizers and discussion to help students think about and organize ideas.

Discussion Web

CW 8.6 links to Discussion Webs in the Classroom on the Education World website. Use this link to explore lessons using the discussion web and see examples of the discussion web graphic.

The discussion web (Alvermann, 1991) uses a graphic aid to help students look at both sides of an issue raised in a text before they draw conclusions. Using this graphic aid as a guide, students meet in pairs and then in groups of four to reach consensus about the issue.

The discussion web can be used anytime students read material that raises a question that might evoke dissenting viewpoints. For example, in *Soul Moon Soup* by Lindsay Lee Johnson, Phoebe Rose decides to leave her first "real" home with her grandmother and go back to the city to live with her mother. Students might use the discussion web to decide the answer to this question: Should Phoebe Rose have left her grandmother and her new friend Ruby to make a new start with her mother in the city?

The discussion web can be modified for use across the curriculum. Suppose students have read a selection on the Civil War that discusses Stephen A. Douglas, Abraham Lincoln, and their opposing views on slavery. As a postreading activity, you might substitute the names *Douglas* and *Lincoln* for the *Yes* and *No* columns of the discussion web, write *slavery* in the box where the question usually goes, and have students discuss the two men's differing views on the issue.

Semantic Webbing and Weaving

Semantic webbing and weaving are procedures that you and your students can use together or that students can use on their own to organize ideas and graphically show their interrelatedness. Semantic webbing, or semantic mapping, was described as a vocabulary technique in Chapter 7. Its name comes from the fact that it makes use of a graphic organizer that looks like a spider web. The web connects a central topic to a variety of related ideas and events, as shown in the web on sea otters in Figure 8.12 (Heimlich & Pittelman, 1986).

Webbing can be used with students of any age before reading a selection to develop and connect a key concept in that selection to their prior knowledge. The thought processes involved in organizing concepts by making connections between them prepare the reader to make similar connec-

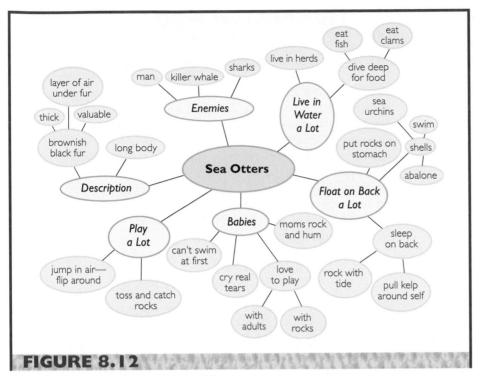

FIGURE 8.12

Sample Semantic Web on Sea Otters

tions when meeting the ideas in the text. This web, or visual display, illustrates graphically the interconnectedness of ideas. The concept or concepts that are webbed should, of course, be of central importance to the reading material.

This webbing activity can be used before, during, and after reading. Students might develop their own webs as they read a selection or after they have finished reading. Webbing can be done as a teacher-led postreading activity as well. For example, after reading the stories *Swimmy* and *Frederick the Mouse,* both by Leo Lionni, a second-grade teacher used semantic webs like the ones shown in Figure 8.13 to do a character study of the main characters in these two picture books (Calfee & Patrick, 1995). Students can be asked to justify their choices and note the page numbers of the passages that support their answers.

Like a web, a weave is also a graphic organizer, a visual display of information and how it is related. However, a weave, is very similar to a semantic feature analysis. It differs from a web by highlighting comparisons. Notice how the weave on the characters Swimmy and Frederick, shown in Figure 8.14, allows students to focus on the similarities and differences between these two characters.

Using graphic organizers such as webs and weaves supports high-level thinking and comprehension by providing a framework for focusing on important points, rather than getting lost in myriad unimportant, unrelated details. It provides a public forum for exploring the process of understanding a text, whether narrative or expository.

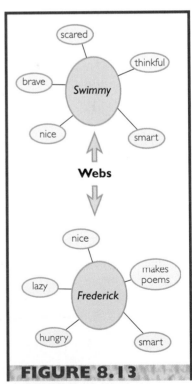

FIGURE 8.13

Sample Semantic Webs Comparing the Characters Swimmy and Frederick

	SWIMMY	FREDERICK
scared	yes	no
brave	yes	sort of
nice	yes	yes
smart	yes	yes
thinkful	yes	sort of
lazy	never	sometimes
hungry	no	yes
poet	no	yes

FIGURE 8.14

Sample Weave Comparing Swimmy and Frederick

Source: Calfee, R. C., & Patrick, C. L. (1995). *Teach Our Children Well.* Stanford: Stanford Alumni Association.

Reflect *and* Apply

13. In this section, we described the story map. Why might this procedure be helpful to use with a group of primary-grade students who are reading a folktale?
14. With what sorts of texts might the K-W-L procedure be helpful? With what sorts of texts would the K-W-L be inappropriate? These are good questions to discuss with a classmate, and your explanations of your answers are as important as the answers themselves.
15. Skim through this section, and jot down the various procedures that are described. Draw a semantic web that shows which procedures are recommended for narratives, which for expository texts, and which for both types of text.

Strengths and Challenges of DIVERSITY

We hope by now we have made the point that successful reading experiences are created by taking into account the varying needs and talents of the individual readers in your classroom. In this section, we give some suggestions for further addressing the needs of your students with diverse strengths and needs.

Virtually all of the activities described in the chapter will scaffold students' reading, and thus all are appropriate for readers who might experience difficulties. Here, we highlight some that are particularly appropriate for readers who are challenged and note a few additional techniques to use with these students.

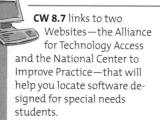

CW 8.7 links to two Websites—the Alliance for Technology Access and the National Center to Improve Practice—that will help you locate software designed for special needs students.

- Create a scaffolded reading experience with particularly strong supports during the prereading and during-reading phases.
- Provide tape recordings of the material students are reading, and have them read along silently as they listen.
- Have students who listen to a selection on tape tell about the selection in their own words. Type up their recollections in a booklet for them to read independently. This is particularly useful for English-language learners who do not yet automatically recognize common words. It is also an opportunity for more-accomplished students to pitch in and do some of the typing.
- For primary-grade students, read a selection aloud one or more times before asking them to read it silently.
- Have students read the material with a partner who is a more accomplished reader—a classmate, an aide, an older student, or a classroom volunteer parent or grandparent. The reading "buddies" can take turns reading from the text or read the text in unison.
- Provide a number of nonthreatening oral reading experiences, such as choral reading and readers theater, that give "less skilled or struggling readers support from more capable readers" (Flynn, 2004/2005, p. 361). If a selection employs a regular pattern or rhyme, have students sing or chant the text.

- Encourage students to read books at their reading level or below. Frequent reading of this kind of material will improve automaticity and confidence.
- For upper-elementary or middle-school students who read several grades below their grade level, consider using high-interest, easy-reading books, books specifically written for students reading below grade level. One of the authors and a colleague (Graves & Philippot, 2001) have described this genre.
- Encourage students to re-read material that is at their reading level or below.
- Use the reciprocal teaching strategy (Palincsar & Brown, 1985), which we describe in Chapter 11.
- When creating reading scaffolds around a particular text or texts, take into account talents other than verbal ones. Incorporate drama, art, music, movement, and other modes of expression in prereading, during-reading, and postreading endeavors.
- Show by your attitude and actions that you have total confidence that students can successfully read a selection and that you will support them in their efforts.

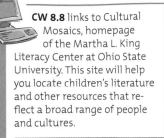

CW 8.8 links to Cultural Mosaics, homepage of the Martha L. King Literacy Center at Ohio State University. This site will help you locate children's literature and other resources that reflect a broad range of people and cultures.

Your classroom will also have its share of competent readers who read above grade level. You will want to provide for their needs, challenging and inspiring them to go further in their thinking. Here are a few suggestions:

CW 8.9 links to Making Multicultural Connections Through Trade Books, a Website designed to help teachers incorporate multicultural literature into their curriculum. The site provides an annotated bibliography of multicultural trade books indexed by title, author, cultural group, and grade level. Lesson plans are also provided for selected titles.

- Have additional reading material available that relates to the selection being read. For example, if the class is reading *Lincoln: A Photobiography* by Russell Freedman, have other biographies of Lincoln available or other biographies by Freedman.
- Provide more challenging selections as an addition or alternative to the text being read.
- Let students select their own additional reading materials related to a selection's theme, genre, or author.
- Invite students to engage in long-term, in-depth projects that relate to the material being read. For example, upper-grade students could research and read periodical and Internet literature dealing with the topics in their science text. This would provide them (and the rest of the class) with information more current than that provided in the text.
- Encourage students to create narrative or expository pieces that relate to the reading. We list a few possibilities for these sorts of writing in the Strengths and Challenges of Diversity section of Chapter 12.

As we have cautioned many times, all students, regardless of their particular needs or talents, need to explore ideas and express themselves in a variety of ways—through writing, speaking, and artistic and dramatic endeavors. We need to take care to be inclusive, not exclusive, in providing a wide variety of opportunities for students. Sometimes students who struggle with the basics or lack traditional literacy skills have been left out of enrichment activities and the growth that they can provide. We believe that all students deserve and will benefit from a range of activities and should explore as many as possible. In this way, they will make connections between what they know and what they discover in texts and will apply that new knowledge to make their lives more enjoyable, productive, and meaningful.

Concluding Remarks

This chapter has focused on teacher-led approaches and procedures that foster students' comprehension and enjoyment of the texts they read in the classroom, highlighting the possibility of offering a wide range of approaches and customizing activities in order to accommodate individual differences. The five frameworks—directed reading activity (DRA), directed reading-thinking activity (DR-TA), the scaffolded reading experience (SRE), guided reading, and four blocks—provide ways to ensure that students are successful with the texts they read and to nurture their competence and confidence as readers. And the time-tested procedures—such as K-W-L, story grammars and maps, discussion webs, and semantic webbing and weaving—that we discussed in the latter half of this chapter provide additional strategies for engaging students with the narratives and exposition they read, thereby increasing their comprehension and enjoyment of those texts.

Extending Learning

1. Choose one of the topics we have covered, such as the scaffolded reading experience, four blocks, or the DR-TA, and read more about it. Present what you learn to your instructor and classmates, emphasizing a particular aspect of it—perhaps the research and theory behind the procedure or a lesson based on it.

2. Visit an elementary school classroom, and take notes on the kinds of supports the teacher provides for students as they read a selection. Using the same selection for the same group of students, design your own plan for helping them understand and enjoy the selection. Try out your lesson on your target students, or share it with your classmates.

3. From the children's section of your library, select an expository text that you think would interest students at the age level you would like to teach. Create a scaffolded reading experience especially for those students and that text. Give your plan to a classmate to get his or her feedback. We recommend the following four books to help you select appropriate titles: *From Biography to History* edited by Catherine Barr (1998); *Kaleidoscope: A Multicultural Booklist for Grades K–8* (4th ed.) edited by Nancy Hansen-Krening, Elaine M. Aoki, and Donald T. Mizokawa (2003); *Books Kids Will Sit Still For: 3* by Judy Freeman (2006); and *Adventuring with Books: A Booklist for Pre-K–Grade 6* (13th ed.) edited by Amy A. McClure and Janice V. Kristo (2002).

For a look at scaffolding students' comprehension of text in a contemporary classroom, go to Allyn & Bacon's MyLabSchool.com. In MLS Courses, click on Reading Methods, and go to MLS Video Lab. There, you will find video clips about Comprehension in Module 5.

Children's Literature

Ajmera, M. (2005). *To Be an Artist*. Watertown, MA: Charlesbridge. Photos and text reveal how children around the world express themselves creatively through various art forms. Unpaged.

Brown, M. (1998). *Arthur's Mystery Envelope*. Boston: Little, Brown. Arthur thinks he's in trouble when the principal asks him to take home a large envelope marked CONFIDENTIAL. Audiocassette available. 58 pages.

Compestine, Y. C. (2001). *The Runaway Rice Cake*. New York: Simon & Schuster. The Chang family learns about the power of sharing during this Chinese New Year celebration. 32 pages.

DiCamillo, K. (2000). *Because of Winn-Dixie*. Cambridge, MA: Candlewick Press. This is a poignant and well-told story of a young girl's building a new life after her mother left and she and her father moved to Florida—with, of course, a little help from her dog, Winn-Dixie. 182 pages.

Duncan, A. F. (1995). *Willie Jerome*. New York: Macmillan. No one but Willie's sister appreciates his jazz trumpet playing until she finally gets their Mama to really listen to Willie play and let the music speak to her. Unpaged.

Freedman, R. (1987). *Lincoln: A Photobiography*. New York: Clarion. In photographs and text, this Newbery Award–winning book traces the life of the Civil War president. 150 pages.

Fritz, J. (1987). *Shh! We're Writing the Constitution*. New York: Scholastic. The author gives a humorous, behind-the-scenes account of how the Constitution came to be written and ratified. 64 pages.

Graves, B. (1996). *The Best Worst Day*. New York: Hyperion. In this chapter book, second-grader Lucy struggles to prove herself "best" in order to win the friendship of Maya, the new girl in class. 64 pages.

Hallworth, G. (1996). *Down by the River*. New York: Scholastic Cartwheel. This is a collection of Afro-Caribbean rhymes, games, and songs. 32 pages.

Houston, J. (1977). *Frozen Fire: A Tale of Courage*. New York: Atheneum. Determined to find his father who has been lost in a storm, a young boy and his Eskimo friend brave windstorms, starvation, and wild animals on their trek through the Canadian Arctic. 149 pages.

Johnson, L. L. (2002). *Soul Moon Soup*. Ashville, NC: Front Street. Written in free verse, this poetic chapter book tells the story of the homeless Phoebe Rose, who, after being banished by her mother to live in the country with her grandmother, learns family secrets and hopes for her mother's return. 134 pages.

Lewin, T. (1990). *Tiger Trek*. New York: Macmillan. Informative narrative tells of the preying habits of the Indian tiger and the numerous animals that live on a hunting preserve in central India. Unpaged.

Lionni, L. (1984). *Swimmy*. New York: Pantheon Books. Through teamwork and cooperation, Swimmy the fish and his friends triumph over the "big" fish. Videocassette available. 32 pages.

Lionni, L. (1985). *Frederick*. New York: Pantheon Books. Frederick, an apparently lazy mouse, has a special surprise for the mice who thought he should have been storing up supplies for the winter. Videocassette available. 32 pages.

Lobel, A. (1970). *Frog and Toad Are Friends*. New York: Harper & Row. The five stories are about the friendship of Frog and Toad and their adventures in the woods. Audio- and videocassettes available. 64 pages.

Lobel, A. (1979). *Days with Frog and Toad*. New York: Harper & Row. This classic beginning chapter book with five humorous stories stars best friends Frog and Toad and dramatizes universal truths about life and friendship. Audiotape available. 64 pages.

Lowry, L. (1989). *Number the Stars*. Boston, MA: Houghton Mifflin. In 1943 during the German occupation of Denmark, 10-year-old Annemarie learns about courage when her family shelters a Jewish family from the Nazis. Audiocassette available. 137 pages.

McWhorter, D. (2004). *A Dream of Freedom: The Civil Rights Movement from 1954 to 1968*. New York: Scholastic. In this history of the modern Civil Rights movement, the author focuses on the monumental events that occurred between 1954 (the year of *Brown v. the Board of Education*) and 1968 (the year that Dr. Martin Luther King, Jr., was assassinated). 160 pages.

Paterson, K. (1978). *The Great Gilly Hopkins*. New York: Crowell. This novel portrays feisty 11-year-old Gilly, a foster child who, in her longing to be reunited with her birth mother, schemes against all who try to befriend her. Spanish text and audiocassette available. 152 pages.

Prelutsky, J. (1988). *Tyrannosaurus Was a Beast: Dinosaur Poems*. New York: Greenwillow. Poems celebrate 14 dinosaurs in rollicking rhyme and illustration. 32 pages.

Simon, S. (1991). *Earthquakes*. New York: Morrow. This text, illustrated with colorful photos, describes how and where earthquakes occur, how they can be predicted, and the damage they cause. Unpaged.

Van Allsburg, C. (1990). *Just a Dream*. Boston: Houghton Mifflin. A young boy has a dream about the environment that causes him to wake up to his indifference. Unpaged.

Teaching Comprehension Strategies

CLASSROOM VIGNETTE

*A*s an accomplished reader with years of experience reading various types of text for a variety of purposes, you have internalized a wealth of reading strategies. Suppose, for example, you are reading an ERIC report on the Web, and you come across a mention of previewing as a prereading activity, something that rings a bell but not a loud one. In this case, perhaps you search ERIC itself for "previewing," and if that doesn't work perhaps you try searching using Google.

Or, suppose it is Saturday, and you have two tests coming up on Monday. You need to read a novel, three textbook chapters, and four journal articles. What do you do? You know you won't have time to read and study each in depth, so you must use some efficient approaches to understand and remember what you read. The novel you read quickly, skipping over lengthy descriptions and dialogue and concentrating on the basics of setting, plot, and characters. As you read, you look for recurring themes. When you finish, you might ask questions like "Why was the protagonist so driven?" and "What were the main themes?" Before you read the chapters and articles, you might think about points your instructor emphasized. While you read, you might take notes or underline material relevant to these points; after your first reading, you might re-read the sections that are most relevant to the course.

What you have done in each of these cases is to use reading strategies—deliberate plans to help you understand and recall what you read. Learning to use reading strategies is one of the most important parts of becoming an accomplished reader.

What Are Comprehension Strategies?

As defined by David Pearson and his colleagues (Pearson, Roehler, Dole, & Duffy, 1992), reading comprehension strategies are "conscious and flexible plans that readers apply and adopt to a variety of texts and tasks." Accomplished readers engage in them in order to better understand, learn from, and remember what they read. One strategy, for example, is determining what is important—that is, deciding which of the numerous concepts in any text deserve special attention. Particularly when reading informational material to gain specific knowledge on a topic, readers must determine just what it is they need to learn. In the opening scenario of the chapter, we suggested that one way you might identify the important information in a textbook is to consider which points in the chapter the instructor has emphasized. Another way would be to read the chapter introduction and summary, and still another way would be to skim through the chapter, noting what is highlighted in the headings and subheadings.

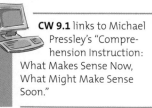

CW 9.1 links to Michael Pressley's "Comprehension Instruction: What Makes Sense Now, What Might Make Sense Soon."

As Michael Pressley (2000) has noted, and as his research with Peter Afflerbach (Pressley & Afflerbach, 1995) very clearly demonstrates, mature readers have a wide repertoire of reading strategies available, and they flexibly employ whichever strategies best fit each reading situation they encounter. This is something that all readers need to learn to do: For all students, including English-language learners and students with special educational needs, the flexible use of reading comprehension strategies leads to independence in reading. Unfortunately, research indicates that comprehension strategies instruction is not as frequent an activity as it should be (Pressley, 2006).

Characteristics of Comprehension Strategies

Here, we consider several characteristics of comprehension strategies. As the discussion will reveal, these characteristics are not absolutes but vary from one situation to another.

Strategies Are Conscious Efforts

At least when they are initially taught, the strategies discussed here are conscious efforts that you ask students to deliberately engage in. For example, after teaching students how to make inferences while reading, you will sometimes ask them to make inferences about specific aspects of material they are reading, and they will sometimes deliberately pause as they are reading and realize that they need to make an inference. With practice and experience, however, some strategies are likely to become increasingly habitual and automatic; for example, readers will frequently make inferences without realizing they are doing so. Nevertheless, even well-learned strategies can be brought to consciousness and placed under the control of the reader.

Strategies Are Flexible

Flexibility and adaptability are hallmarks of strategies. As many experts on strategy instruction have stressed, the very essence of teaching students to be strategic is teaching them that they need to use strategies in ways that are appropriate for particular situations. For example, the strategy of re-reading can be used in a variety of ways: A primary-grade student could re-read the easy chapter book *Mr. Putter & Tabby Make a Wish* by Cynthia Rylant immediately after first reading it. She also could re-read *parts* of the book immediately after first reading it, or she could re-read all of it the next day. Whether one or another of these approaches to re-reading is most useful will depend on the student, the selection she is reading, and her purpose in reading it.

Strategies Should Be Applied Only When Appropriate

Part of teaching students strategies is teaching them to apply a strategy only when it is needed. For example, the strategy we just mentioned, re-reading, is often useful. However, if a student is reading a simple story, understands it perfectly well, and is not preparing for a quiz of some sort, she does not need to re-read it for comprehension purposes (although re-reading might build her fluency and automaticity).

Strategies Are Widely Applicable

Many strategies can be used across a wide range of ages, abilities, and reading material. For example, it is appropriate for a first-grader to orally summarize a book like Elissa Haden Guest's *Iris and Walker and the Substitute Teacher* or David McPhail's *The Teddy Bear*. It is appropriate for a fifth-grader to summarize the major events in the life of the 12th-century Muslim warrior Saladin in Diane Stanley's *Saladin: Noble Prince of Islam* or those in the life of the suffragist Esther Morris in *When Esther Morris Headed West: Women, Wyoming, and the Right to Vote* by Connie Nordhielm Woolridge. It is appropriate for a graduate student to summarize the major tenets of the reader-response approach to literature as they appear in a text like Louise Rosenblatt's *The Reader, the Text, the Poem.*

Strategies Can Be Overt or Covert

Some strategies involve readers in creating some sort of observable product, while others involve mental operations that cannot be directly observed. Summarizing, for example, is a strategy that often results in a written record of what was read. Determining what is important, on the other hand, is a strategy that frequently does not result in the reader's writing down anything. When you are initially teaching a strategy, you may want students to produce an observable record of their use of the strategy so that you know that they are able to use it. However, much of the time, the strategies students use will be solely mental processes.

Reflect *and* Apply

1. For each of the five characteristics of comprehension strategies we just described, come up with a situation in which you used a comprehension strategy having that characteristic. Understanding these characteristics fully is important, so we suggest you write out your responses.

Key Comprehension Strategies

ASSESSMENT

To assess what your students know about comprehension strategies, you will need to find answers to these kinds of questions: Which comprehension strategies do the students know? Do they use them? In what contexts?

Mature readers use a wide repertoire of comprehension strategies. Fortunately, however, there is substantial agreement on the key strategies that students need to master (National Reading Panel, 2000; Pressley, 2006; RAND Reading Study Group, 2002; Sales & Graves, 2005). The key strategies we recommend are shown in the following list and discussed in the remainder of this section:

- Establishing a purpose for reading
- Using prior knowledge
- Asking and answering questions
- Making inferences
- Determining what is important
- Summarizing
- Dealing with graphic information
- Imaging and creating graphic representations
- Being metacognitive

Each of these strategies involves readers in actively constructing meaning as they read. Additionally, many of these strategies cause readers to transform ideas from one form to another or generate relationships among ideas. For example, when readers summarize, they must transform the author's text into something more concise, and when they make inferences, they must relate information in the text to information they already know.

Establishing a Purpose for Reading

One of the first things a good reader does as she approaches a text is establish a purpose for reading. What that purpose is will depend on the text, the reader, and what she needs from the text. How the reader reads—whether, for example, she takes notes, reads slowly or quickly, and re-reads—will, in turn, depend on this purpose.

Sometimes the reader's purpose is to find a specific piece of information, perhaps the score of a soccer match, a critic's opinion on a current movie, or certain facts about the brain in a trade book such as *Phineas Gage: A Gruesome but True Story About Brain Science* by John Fleischman. Sometimes the purpose is to learn everything possible from the text, perhaps in preparation for a test. Sometimes it's to simply enjoy the text, as is often the case with a novel or short story. And sometimes it's simply to fall asleep. All of these and many other purposes are totally legitimate and have their place. The goal is for the reader to identify the appropriate purpose for a particular situation and read in a way that accomplishes that purpose.

Using Prior Knowledge

When using this strategy, readers purposely bring to consciousness what they already know that relates to what they are going to read or what they are reading. Thus, they put a set of schemata into place, establishing a framework for the new information that they will encounter in the text. Let's say, for instance, that a fifth-grader is perusing the library shelf and picks up a book titled *ER Vets: Life in an Animal Emergency Room* by Donna M. Jackson. Before the student begins reading the book, she thinks about what she knows about hospital emergency rooms and veterinarians. As she thinks, she recalls times she accompanied her own dog to the vet and the time she was taken to the ER when she fell off her bike and broke her arm. But she can't really think of what kind of animals might end up in the ER or why they would have to go there. Thus, she begins to read the book with the realization that animals sometimes have life-threatening emergencies as people do, but this book is going to present something different, something she really hasn't considered before. The student is using her prior knowledge to set up expectations of what she might encounter in the text. When she reads about one of the emergency situations, she will be able to contrast it with her own emergency room experience, and making that contrast will help her both understand what she is reading and remember what she has read.

Asking and Answering Questions

Using this strategy, the reader poses questions prior to reading a selection or as she is reading the selection. Then she attempts to answer the questions while reading. Employing this strategy virtually guarantees that reading will be an active process. It also serves to focus the reader's attention. A reader who has asked a particular set of questions will be particularly attentive to the information that answers those questions.

Consider a sixth-grader preparing to read a chapter on nutrition in a health text. As the first step, she might survey the chapter and find these headings: Nutrients and the U.S. RDA, The Seven Dietary Guidelines, Shopping for Groceries, and Preventing Disease Through Proper Diet. Then, she might pose one or two questions about each heading: What are nutrients? What is the U.S.

RDA? What are the seven dietary guidelines? Do I follow them in my diet? Should I follow them? How is shopping for groceries related to nutrition? Can a proper diet prevent all disease? As she reads, the student will get answers to some of her questions, find that others are not answered in the chapter, and pose and answer additional questions. As a result of this active involvement, she is likely to learn a good deal.

Making Inferences

When they apply this strategy, readers infer meanings by using information from the text and their existing knowledge of the world, their schemata, to fill in bits of information that are not explicitly stated in the text. No text is ever fully explicit, and thus readers must constantly make inferences to understand what they are reading. By teaching students to make inferences, you are helping them learn to use their existing knowledge along with the information in the text to build meaning.

Suppose that a fifth-grader is reading a science text and learns that woodchucks build deep burrows and huddle in them in large groups during the winter. Knowing that a fair number of animals hibernate, she might infer that woodchucks hibernate in their burrows. Then, remembering that last week her teacher explained that ground temperature remains stable and fairly warm at depths greater than three or four feet, she might further infer that woodchucks make their burrows deep in order to take advantage of this warmth.

Determining What Is Important

Making use of this strategy requires that readers understand what they have read and make judgments about what is and is not important. Most texts contain much more information than a reader can focus on and learn. Consequently, determining what is important is a crucial and frequently required

Efficiently learning from informational text requires well-honed strategies.

strategy. Sometimes, texts include direct cues to what is important—overviews, headings, summaries, and the like. As seventh-grade science teacher Victor Hammel notes, it is well worth teaching students to use these aids.

> At the beginning of each year, I make it a point to go through the textbooks we will be using and talk with my students about whatever learning aids the books contain. At this time, I also model how I would use these aids. Although some students would make good use of the aids even if I didn't discuss them and model how I use them, a lot of students wouldn't. The benefit to them, as well as the time I save by helping students learn to use the aids independently, is really substantial.
>
> In addition, I check the books to see how well the aids work. For example, I look at the headings to be sure they accurately reflect the content that follows them. Sometimes textbooks aren't that well constructed, and when that's the case, I tell students. I think this is an important part of becoming a critical reader—knowing that you have to use your brain as you read and that even textbooks aren't perfect.
>
> —Victor Hammel, Seventh-Grade Teacher

We certainly agree with Mr. Hammel that such aids can be useful. In many cases, however, the text does not contain obvious clues to what is important, and students need to rely on their prior knowledge to infer just what is important in a particular selection.

For instance, while reading the short story "The Kite" in *Days with Frog and Toad* by Arnold Lobel, a first-grader might think about the most important characters and events in the story and come up with the following set of important points:

Frog is helping Toad fly a kite.

The kite doesn't fly on the first try.

Toad wants to give up, but Frog tells him to try again.

The kite doesn't fly.

Frog tells him to try a third time, and still the kite won't get off the ground.

Frog tells Toad to make one more try.

This time the kite flies.

Together, these important points constitute the essence of the story.

Summarizing

Using this strategy requires students to first determine what is important and then condense it and put it in their own words. Some years ago, Ann Brown and Jeanne Day (1983) developed and researched some very effective rules for summarizing. Slightly modified, they include the following steps:

- Delete trivial or irrelevant information.
- Delete redundant information.
- Provide a superordinate term for members of a category.
- Find and use generalizations the author has made.
- Create your own generalizations when the author has not provided them.

The earlier list of important ideas from "The Kite" constitutes a good summary of the story. By dropping less-important details and focusing on the most important aspects of the story, the student was able to understand what was taking place. An even briefer summary, focusing on the theme of the story, is also possible: Frog was trying to help Toad. By listening to Frog and doing what he said, and by continuing to try instead of quitting, Toad was able to get his kite into the air.

Dealing with Graphic Information

When they employ this strategy, readers give conscious attention to the visual information supplied by the author. Before youngsters learn to read, they are drawn to and fascinated by the visual material books offer. Teaching them when, how, and why to use the illustrations, graphs, maps, diagrams, and other visuals that accompany selections will enable them to make optimal use of the visual aids texts often provide.

History texts, for example, almost always contain maps that include a legend to the symbols they employ. Students need to learn that maps usually have legends, the kind of information legends normally contain, where legends are typically placed, and how to interpret them.

Imaging and Creating Graphic Representations

Imaging and creating graphics are likely to be particularly helpful for English learners.

Using this strategy, readers create visual representations of text, either in their minds or by reproducing them on paper or in other tangible formats. One kind of imaging occurs when readers visualize people, events, and places. Another kind of imaging consists of visually organizing key ideas in a text in a way that graphically displays their relationships. The former type of imaging is most frequently used with narrative material; the latter is most frequently used with expository text. The directions in In the Classroom 9.1 suggest how you might reinforce the imaging strategy with a group of first-graders to whom you have previously taught it. We want to stress, however, that this is a review of the strategy and not the initial instruction on the strategy. As you will see when you read our description of a validated approach to teaching strategies on pages 282–290, initial instruction on a strategy is much more robust than this review session.

Practicing Imaging with First-Graders

To give students practice in creating mental images of story characters, setting, and events as well as practice in sequencing story events, you can have them draw and sequence pictures. Here is how this might be done with Maurice Sendak's *Where the Wild Things Are*.

- Tell students that you are going to read one of your favorite stories to them, and, as you read, you want them to create pictures in their minds. Remind them of their lesson on this important reading strategy. Tell them how creating pictures in their minds of what's happening in the story—the characters and what they look like, the place where the characters are, what the characters are doing—can help them enjoy and understand the story better. Note that today they are going to practice that strategy with *Where the Wild Things Are* by Maurice Sendak. Explain that you are not going to show them the pictures as you usually do when you read them a picture book, because you want them to make up the pictures in their minds. Tell them the story is about Max, a little boy with a wonderful imagination, who, because he was naughty, was sent to bed without his supper.

instructional routines

in the Classroom 9.1

One particular form of graphic representation that students enjoy creating and that has proved very useful for them is semantic mapping. As you will recall, we discussed semantic maps in Chapters 7 and 8. In those chapters, however, we emphasized the use of maps by teachers or by teachers and students working together. Here, we are concerned with students learning to create their own semantic maps. For example, a student-constructed semantic map for a chapter on mountains in a geography text might look like the one shown in Figure 9.1.

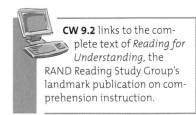

CW 9.2 links to the complete text of *Reading for Understanding,* the RAND Reading Study Group's landmark publication on comprehension instruction.

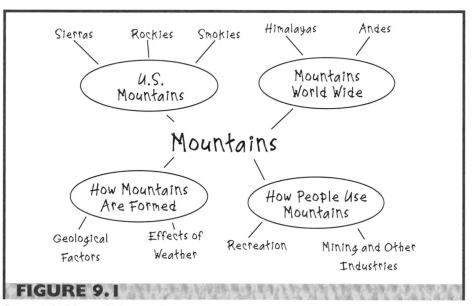

FIGURE 9.1

Semantic Map of Mountains

Being Metacognitive

As we explained in Chapter 1, good readers are metacognitive. They understand themselves as readers, the reading tasks they face, and the strategies they can employ in completing these tasks. Before reading, they consider such matters as their purpose in reading, the difficulty of the text, how much they already know about the topic of the text, and how long they have to complete the reading. During reading, they monitor their comprehension, employ fix-up strategies like re-reading if they do not understand something, and use the comprehension strategies we have just described when needed. After reading, they self-check to see if they have gotten what they want and need from the text and again use fix-up and comprehension strategies as needed. For example, realizing that the history chapter she has just read is crucial to the report she is writing, a sixth-grader might write a summary of it.

Being metacognitive is a more general strategy than the others we have discussed, and part of being metacognitive is knowing when to use other comprehension strategies. Readers who are being metacognitive are asking themselves questions like these: Am I understanding what the author is saying? What do I do if I don't understand what I am reading? What could I be doing to better understand what the author is saying? Can I do something to help me remember the material better? Which of the strategies I know should I employ here?

In helping students to be metacognitive, teachers are teaching them to be active learners who monitor their reading and take appropriate steps when they are not getting what they want and need from their reading. In helping students to be metacognitive, teachers are also encouraging them to think about the comprehension strategies they have learned and to use them when they are needed. It is extremely important that students thoroughly learn a small repertory of comprehension strategies like the nine strategies we have just described and employ them when needed (Cummins, Stewart, & Block, 2005). It is also important that students become independent, fluent, and sometimes automatic in using the strategies (Pressley, 2005). This means that after initially teaching strategies, teachers need to encourage, foster, and prompt students to use them over a considerable period of time, something sixth-grade teacher Ron Novack does in In the Classroom 9.2.

Fostering Metacognition

To foster students' metacognition and help them thoroughly internalize and fluently use the strategies you have taught, it is important to repeatedly remind them of the importance of being metacognitive and employing the repertory of strategies they have learned. This is what Mr. Novack is doing as he questions his students.

in the **Classroom** **9.2**

Mr. Novack: What does it mean to be metacognitive?

Felicity: To monitor your reading and do something when what you are reading doesn't make sense.

Doug: To think before you read something and have a good idea of why you are reading it and what you want to get out of it.

Artrell: To decide which of the comprehension strategies we know we should use in a particular situation.

Mr. Novack: What do you do when you are reading along and suddenly realize you don't understand what you're reading?

Amad: When that happens to me, I go back and read the same words again.

Mr. Novack: You mean you re-read. That's a good strategy.

Ted: If I'm reading science or social studies, or something like that, and there are words I don't know, I'll look them up or ask somebody.

Mr. Novack: You consult another source. That's a good strategy, too.

April: Sometimes it helps me to look at the pictures or maps, if there are any.

Mr. Novack: You consider any graphic information. Good.

Doug: If something isn't making sense, I'll think about something I already know and see how it fits what I'm reading.

Mr. Novack: You connect what you already know with what you're reading. Excellent strategy.

Felicity: I try to picture in my mind what I'm reading, what the author's describing. I guess I'm always drawing pictures in my mind when I read.

Mr. Novack: You're imaging, and that's another very effective comprehension strategy.

Clearly, Mr. Novack encourages his students to do whatever is necessary to arrive at a satisfactory understanding of what they are reading. This, of course, is precisely what we want to prepare students to do.

The strategies described here—establishing a purpose for reading, using prior knowledge, asking and answering questions, making inferences, determining what is important, summarizing, dealing with graphic information, imaging and creating graphic representations, and being metacognitive—will help students reach the goal of understanding and learning from what they read. In learning these strategies, students are internalizing an approach to reading and thinking that is active and reflective, an approach vital to literacy in the 21st century. Having learned this mode of reading and thinking, students will be both able and inclined to engage in a variety of reading and learning strategies in order to understand, appreciate, and learn from what they read. It should be noted that students will differ in the rate at which they learn the strategies that have been described. It is vital that all students be given sufficient time and scaffolding to thoroughly learn and internalize the strategies you teach.

It is also vital that students get a real sense of what it means to be strategic. One way to help students understand the concept of being strategic is to use children's literature that illustrates children using strategies, like those selections listed in the Reading Corner on page 282.

ASSESSMENT

Find out the conditions under which a student uses or fails to use comprehension strategies, with the assumption that success is eventually possible, of course. One part of assessment means convincing students that they can achieve.

Reflect *and* Apply

2. Identify one of the nine strategies that you use or that is similar to one you use. Then describe two or three situations in which you have used it and why it was appropriate in those situations. It would be a good idea to do this in writing.

3. Consider the nine strategies we have discussed, and identify those that are likely to be particularly useful for second-graders, for fourth-graders, and for sixth-graders. Then compare your assessments to those of a classmate.

4. One thing good readers learn to do is coordinate their use of the various strategies they know. That is, in reading a text they often use several strategies, not just one. Find a short informational text that you would like to learn something from, and read it fairly carefully. Then consider the nine strategies we have discussed, and jot down a list of those you used as you read the passage.

the Reading Corner

Books That Illustrate Strategic Behavior

Children's literature abounds with characters (real and imaginary) who strategically go about trying to achieve their goals or solve problems. These characters, who exhibit deliberately planned behavior that takes into account their unique situation, are among children's favorites in literature. Here is a small sampling.

Alma Flor Ada. *My Name Is Maria Isabel*. Atheneum, 1993. Renamed Mary by her teacher, Maria Isabel, recently arrived in the United States from Puerto Rico, finds a way to get back her own name *and* to fit in with her classmates. 57 pages.

Nan Willard Cappo. *Cheating Lessons*. Atheneum, 2002. After Bernadette suspects someone of cheating to get their high school quiz team into the state quiz bowl competition, she seeks out the cheater. 240 pages.

Louise Erdrich. *Grandmother's Pigeon*. Hyperion, 1996. After three eggs in one of Grandmother's bird nest collection miraculously hatch a breed of passenger pigeons long thought to be extinct, Grandmother's family takes matters into their own hands when visiting scientists threaten the hatchlings' freedom. 32 pages.

Dennis Brindell Fradin. *My Family Shall Be Free: The Life of Peter Still*. HarperCollins, 2001. After buying his own freedom from slavery, Peter Still heads north to earn the money to free his wife and children. 176 pages.

Rosa Guy. *The Disappearance*. Delacorte, 1979. After leaving an alcoholic mother behind in Harlem, Imamu Jones finds hope for a better life with a middle-class family in Brooklyn. Once there, he becomes involved in locating his missing sister. 246 pages.

Patricia Hermes. *Mama, Let's Dance*. Little, Brown, 1991. Eleven-year-old Mary Belle learns to cope with being in charge of her brothers and sisters when her mother leaves home. 168 pages.

Barbara Knutson. *Love and Roast Chicken: A Trickster Tale from the Andes Mountains*. Carolrhoda, 2004. In this Peruvian tale, Cuy the guinea pig uses his smarts to outwit a hungry fox and powerful farmer. 40 pages.

Gary Paulson. *Hatchet*. Bradbury, 1987. This gripping adventure story is about Brian Robeson's surviving 54 days alone in the northern Canadian wilderness. 195 pages.

Eileen Ross. *Nellie and the Bandit*. Farrar, 2005. Plucky Nellie uses her brains to repeatedly outwit the bad guys. 32 pages.

Louis Sachar. *Holes*. Farrar, Straus, and Giroux, 1998. In this Newbery Award–winning book, the ever-unlucky Stanley Yelnats, after being sent to a detention camp for a crime he didn't commit, manages to turn around four generations of family bad luck through his own resourcefulness and tenacity. 233 pages.

Marjorie Weinman Sharmat. *Nate the Great and His Mother's Monsters*. Delacorte, 1999. When his mother's treasured recipe for monster cookies disappears, Nate uses his sleuthing talents to recover it. 48 pages.

Cynthia Voight. *Homecoming*. Atheneum, 1983. After their mother abandons them in a shopping mall parking lot, 13-year-old Dicey keeps her three younger siblings fed and out of harm's way as they journey in search of a home. 312 pages.

Nancy Willard. *Shadow Story*. Harcourt, Brace & Company, 1999. Holly Go Lolly, who has played with shadows all her life, saves herself from the evil ogre Ooboo by luring him into a forest she creates with hand shadows. 32 pages.

A Powerful Approach to Teaching Strategies

The past two decades have produced a very substantial body of research and theory on teaching comprehension strategies (see, for example, Block & Pressley, 2002; Brown, Pressley, Van Meter, & Schuder, 1996; Deshler & Schumaker,

1993; Dole, Brown, & Trathen, 1996; Duffy et al., 1987; Pearson & Duke, 2002; Pressley, 2006; Reutzel, Fawson, & Smith, 2003). This research has demonstrated some very positive results. As Michael Pressley has pointed out, "The evidence is overwhelming that upper-grade elementary students can be taught to use comprehension strategies, with substantial improvements in student comprehension following such instruction" (2002a). Actually, Pressley need not have limited his claim to upper-grade students because one of the best studies—the one by Brown and her colleagues (1996)—clearly shows that children as young as second-graders can profit from strategy instruction.

The extensive body of theory and research on comprehension strategies instruction has shown two approaches to teaching strategies to be extremely effective: direct explanation of strategies (Duffy, 2002; Duffy et al., 1987; Duke & Pearson, 2002) and transactional strategies instruction (Pressley, El-Dinary, Wharton-McDonald, & Brown, 1998; Pressley, 2002a; Reutzel et al., 2003). Direct explanation is, as the name indicates, the more direct and explicit of the two. Transactional strategies instruction, on the other hand, embeds strategy instruction in the ongoing activities of the class. Here, we describe a synthesis of these two methods designed by one of us (Sales & Graves, 2005). This is a powerful approach that can be used at a variety of grade levels to give all students the strategies they need to become independent learners who are able to deal with various kinds of texts and achieve a variety of purposes as they read.

To illustrate the approach, we describe the first two days of instruction with a third-grade class working with the strategy of determining what is important. Next, we note how instruction proceeds and changes over the course of a three- or four-week unit. After that, we discuss the ways in which good strategy instruction must be constructive in nature. Finally, we note the types of transfer, review, and integrating activities that are needed to make a strategy a tool that students will really use. Although instruction will vary somewhat with different strategies, different students, and different age groups, the general plan presented is widely applicable.

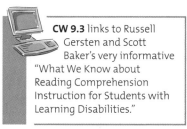

CW 9.3 links to Russell Gersten and Scott Baker's very informative "What We Know about Reading Comprehension Instruction for Students with Learning Disabilities."

English Learners

Thoroughly understanding your initial instruction on a strategy is crucial for your English-language learners. Therefore, slow down as necessary, check to be sure all students are following you, do more modeling, and reteach as necessary.

The First Day's Instruction on Determining What Is Important

The activities described in this section are those used on the first day of instruction on a new strategy. In this illustration, the students are fourth-graders, and the strategy to be taught is determining what is important. The students have had some experience with the strategy in previous grades, but this is the first time it has been formally taught. Recently, they have had difficulty sifting out less-important details and focusing on more-important ideas in their science and social studies books, and so this seems to be an opportune time for instruction in this particular strategy. The first day's instruction includes six different components.

Motivation and Interest Building (about 5 minutes)

To capture students' attention and build interest, introduce the strategy by having students guess the categories represented by various sets of words you write on the board. Choose categories and words of interest to the particular group of students being taught. We have chosen fast-food restaurants, sports that use balls, and sports that don't use balls. Write the word sets on the board underneath unlabeled umbrellas—an idea suggested by James Baumann (1986) and illustrated in Figure 9.2. Tell students that these words are examples of more-general ideas, have them guess what those more-general ideas are, and have them write these more-general ideas in the umbrellas above the sets of examples.

Teacher Explanation (about 5 minutes)

After students have determined the more-general ideas represented by several sets of examples, explain that identifying these ideas is part of a strategy you are going to teach them. At this point, ask students about the reading they have been doing in science and social studies, and discuss some of the challenges they have faced. One of the challenges that is likely to come up is that these books cover a lot of information, and it is hard to remember all of it. Explain that the strategy they will learn—determining what is important—will help them to better understand and remember what they read.

Next, explain that when they use this strategy, they should focus on the most important information and let less-important details fade into the back-

What idea covers all of these?

McDonald's	tennis	swimming
Burger King	soccer	track
Wendy's	football	gymnastics
Arby's	basketball	weightlifting
Taco Bell	broomball	archery

FIGURE 9.2

Word Sets for Motivation and Interest Building

ground. Talk about how much of the social studies and science material they read contains a great deal of information and how concentrating on only the most important information cuts down on what they need to learn and remember. Tell students that knowing how to determine what is important can make understanding and remembering what they read much easier.

Teacher Modeling (about 5 minutes)

Reveal more about how the strategy works by writing a sentence such as *Matthew Blaine, a fourth-grade student at Ridgeview Elementary School, won first prize in the Rotary Speech Contest with his essay titled "What Freedom Means to Me"* on the board. Read the sentence aloud, and model the thought processes you might go through in identifying the most important information in the sentence:

> Let's see, what is the main idea the author is communicating in this sentence? The topic seems to be Matthew Blaine. And what is the most important information about Matthew? Winning first prize sounds pretty important. [Circle the phrases *Matthew Blaine* and *won first prize in the Rotary Speech Contest* on the board.] The other information—that he's a fourth-grade student at Ridgeview Elementary School and the title of his essay—is interesting, but not as important. [Cross out *a fourth-grade student at Ridgeview Elementary School* and *with his essay titled "What Freedom Means to Me"* on the board.]

The board work used to illustrate that Matthew Blaine won the Rotary Speech Contest is the most important information in the sentence is shown here:

(Matthew Blaine,) ~~a fourth grade student at Ridgeview~~ ~~Elementary School,~~ (won first prize in the Rotary Speech Contest) ~~with his essay title "What Freedom Means to Me."~~

Once you have explained the strategy and modeled it, check to see if students were following you by asking a few students to explain the strategy and tell why it is worth knowing.

Large-Group Student Participation and Teacher Mediation (about 10 minutes)

Put a paragraph from one of the students' social studies or science texts on the overhead, and read it aloud. The paragraph should be one in which the important information stands out. The sample paragraph used here is taken from *Scaly Babies: Reptiles Growing Up* by Ginny Johnson and Judy Cutchins (p. 24):

> For many people, the word *reptile* describes an ugly, slippery, and sometimes dangerous animal. But reptiles are not slimy, and most are not dangerous. There are nearly six thousand different kinds of these scaly-skinned animals in the world today. It is true that some are large and scary-looking and a few are venomous, but most reptiles are harmless to humans. Like many wild animals, reptiles may strike or bite to defend themselves. But they rarely bother a person who has not disturbed or startled them.

Ask students what the paragraph is mainly about (reptiles). Next, ask them how they determined this (everything in the paragraph is about reptiles). Have students supply the details about reptiles that are given in the paragraph and write these on the board, as shown in Figure 9.3.

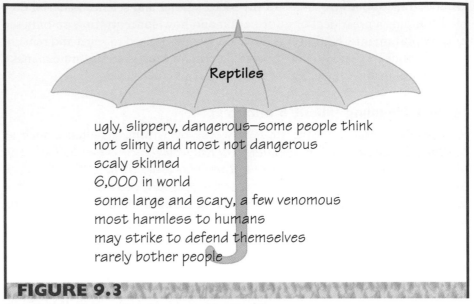

FIGURE 9.3

Details About Reptiles Suggested by Students

After you have written the details students have suggested on the board, ask them which information in the paragraph is the most important. Explain that all of these details say something about reptiles, but that one is the most general and important idea, probably the idea that the author really wants to get across. Help students determine the most important idea by asking questions such as these about each of the details: Is this the most important idea in the paragraph? Do the other ideas support this one? Do you think this is the main thing the author is trying to tell you?

After students have agreed on the most important idea (something like "although many people think reptiles are dangerous, most are not"), rewrite the chart on the board to show the most important idea with its supporting details underneath it, as shown in Figure 9.4.

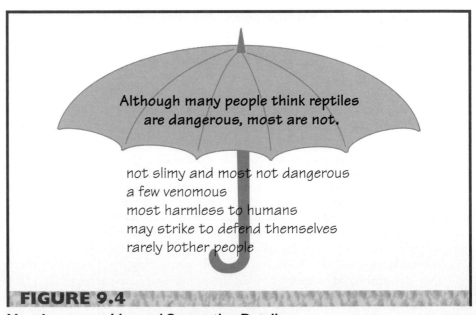

FIGURE 9.4

Most Important Idea and Supporting Details

Thus far, this introductory session has lasted about 25 minutes. In most classrooms, it would be a good idea to move to another topic at this time and continue the strategy instruction the next day.

The Second Day's Instruction on Determining What Is Important

Very briefly review the first day's lesson, again discussing what strategies in general are and what the specific strategy of determining what is important is. Motivate students by reminding them how helpful the strategy will be for understanding and remembering what they read, and model your thought processes as you determine what is important in a short text—probably the paragraph with which you ended yesterday's lesson.

More Large-Group Student Participation and Teacher Mediation (10 to 20 minutes)

Work together with students to determine the most important ideas in several additional paragraphs in the same book. Call on students to determine what is most important in each paragraph and to explain how they determined that the information they selected is the most important. On the board, create a visual display similar to the one for the first paragraph. If students seem to understand the strategy, move to the next step. If not, do some further explaining and modeling.

Cooperative Group Work (about 10 minutes)

Once large-group questioning indicates that students have a basic understanding of the strategy, they need a chance to practice it. Initially, they can practice in pairs. Remember, they are just beginning to work with the strategy, and a lot of scaffolding is appropriate. You want to ensure that students are successful and feel successful at this point. Because they have worked only with paragraph-length selections thus far, they should continue with paragraph-length selections in this practice session. Also, since the selections used thus far have been ones in which the important information stood out clearly, the practice paragraphs should also clearly reveal the important information. Two or three such paragraphs might be appropriate for this part of the lesson.

English Learners

Make sure that for group work each of your English-language learners is teamed with a competent and helpful native English speaker who can act as a co-learner and coach.

Sharing Group Work and Teacher Response and Mediation (about 10 minutes)

Once students have had an opportunity to use the strategy in pairs, they should share their work with the class. Call on pairs to present the important information they found in the passages, and discuss how they determined that this was the crucial information. Monitor their responses carefully, and provide feedback and clarification as necessary.

This would conclude the first two days of instruction and practice with the strategy. The remainder of the unit is discussed in the next section. First, however, we do want to remind you that teacher explanation, modeling, and mediation need to be carried out in a way that engages students and keeps them attentive. It is difficult to capture the flexibility and fluidity of good strategy instruction in a written text. Also, we want to note that the instructional periods will vary greatly according to the age and maturity of the students. For example, most first-graders may be able to attend to a teacher presentation for only 5 to 10 minutes, while upper-elementary students may be able to attend for 15 to 20 minutes. All of the time estimates we give are suggestions. You need to spend whatever time is necessary for your students to learn.

Overview of a Unit

A typical unit might last for three or four weeks. Although instruction should continue to include a number of the features of the first day's instruction, it should gradually change as students become increasingly competent with the strategy. Here are some of the major ways in which instruction should change.

- Subsequent instructional periods become shorter.
- Instruction becomes less concentrated each week.
- Students do more of the work.
- Texts become longer and more challenging.
- Strategies are used on authentic tasks.
- Students are encouraged to use the strategies independently.

A colorful bulletin board such as that shown in Figure 9.5 can serve as a reminder to students to use the strategies they've learned or reviewed during the year, and as a refresher on how to use them.

The Constructive Nature of Good Strategy Instruction

As we just mentioned, conveying the constructivist, interactive, flexible nature of good strategy instruction is difficult on paper, and we want to be certain that our description of strategy instruction thus far has not left some of you thinking of it as rather rigid and teacher centered. Good strategy instruction is neither rigid nor teacher centered. In Figure 9.6, we emphasize this by comparing teacher-dominated instruction to constructivist instruction.

Transfer, Review, and Integration Activities

Thus far, we have described the first two days of strategy instruction, explained how instruction changes over a three- to four-week unit on a strategy, and ex-

Frequently observe students to see how well they are internalizing the strategies that you teach.

FIGURE 9.5
Strategy Bulletin Board

amined the way in which good strategy instruction must be a constructive, interactive, and flexible process. If you were to create and present a unit based on the suggestions presented thus far, students would be well on their way to becoming effective and independent strategy users. However, in order to assist students in completing their journey toward mastery of the strategies, you will need to provide additional reviews of the strategies you teach, help students transfer their use of the strategies to all appropriate areas of learning, assist them in modifying the strategies and making them truly their own, and aid them in integrating their use of newly learned strategies with other strategies.

ASSESSMENT

Meet individually with students to discuss their strengths and the areas that need improvement. Use student work samples and your journal notes to identify their strengths and weaknesses in using comprehension strategies.

TEACHER-DOMINATED INSTRUCTION	CONSTRUCTIVIST INSTRUCTION
• The teacher lectures, and the students listen.	• The teacher and the students interact, with modeling, scaffolding, and discussion prominent.
• Children assume the role of passive, rather than active, participants.	• Children assume the role of active participants.
• It is as if the knowledge the teacher has could be transmitted directly to the students.	• It is understood that the knowledge the teacher has cannot be transmitted directly to the students.
• There is little discussion and debate.	• There is considerable discussion and debate.
• Teachers do very little on-the-spot diagnosis of individual students' understanding and progress.	• Teachers frequently make on-the-spot diagnoses of individual students' understanding and progress.
• The instruction proceeds at a predetermined rate and sequence dictated by the curriculum.	• The instruction proceeds at a rate and sequence dictated by the students' needs and progress.
• Lessons are often scripted.	• Lessons are not scripted.
• All students are expected to proceed at the same rate.	• Students are expected to proceed at their own rate.
• Skills are emphasized at the expense of understanding.	• Understanding is emphasized as strategies are developed.
• Students are rarely informed about the purposes of the strategies taught.	• Students are always informed about the purposes of the strategies taught.
• Little, if any, attention is given to developing students' self-monitoring and self-regulation skills.	• Developing students' self-monitoring and self-regulation skills is a central concern.

FIGURE 9.6

Teacher-Dominated and Constructivist Strategy Instruction

The descriptions here are modified forms of descriptions originally written by Brown and Campione (1990) and Pressley, Harris, and Marks (1992).

If students are to become permanent strategy users, their use of the newly learned strategy needs to be encouraged and nurtured beyond the initial unit of instruction. Several types of follow-up are important:

ASSESSMENT

As Michael Pressley has noted, "Active comprehension develops over months and years, not days and weeks." This means that the observations you use to assess students' use of the strategies you teach needs to extend throughout the year and, if possible, be continued by the students' teachers in the years following initial instruction.

- Providing one- or two-day formal reviews
- Conducting occasional mini-lessons
- Finding opportunities to use the strategies
- Listening to students and providing feedback
- Repeatedly providing motivation to use the strategies
- Making frequent suggestions to use the strategies
- Giving students the freedom to modify strategies and make them truly their own

Reflect *and* Apply

5. Get together with half a dozen of your classmates, pick a strategy and a grade level, and design the first two days of instruction on the strategy, with each of you creating one segment of the instruction—for example, the motivation and interest-building segment. Then, actually present the instruction to another group of your classmates.

6. Consider our description of the ways in which strategy instruction changes as you progress through a unit, and see if you can come up with some other ways in which it might change as students become more and more competent and comfortable with a strategy.

Strengths and Challenges of DIVERSITY

As we have repeatedly noted, a balanced literacy curriculum is for all students—more-accomplished readers, less-accomplished readers, students who come less prepared to school, and students who do not speak English as their native language. This is as true for comprehension strategies as it is for other parts of the curriculum; however, adjustments for individual needs will be important here as well.

With strategies, one danger is that capable readers who have already learned comprehension strategies might be both unreceptive to learning new strategies and actually confused by attempts to replace an already functional strategy with a new one. The solution here is to know your students and their capabilities well, find out what strategies they already have, check periodically to see if they view the new ones as useful, and not make them continue to learn a new strategy that just isn't working for them.

With less-proficient students, on the other hand, comprehension strategies are likely to be particularly welcome—if, that is, students see them as helpful, and the only way they will see them as helpful is if they are. You need to be especially careful to introduce them at a rate slow enough to prevent frustration yet rapid enough to avoid boredom, to give students plenty of time to apply them in class, and to deliberately structure students' work and the assessment system you use to reward their use of strategies. Over the past two decades, Donald Deshler and Jean Schumaker (1993; Schumaker & Deshler, 2003) have conducted more than a dozen studies clearly indicating that at-risk students can successfully learn to use comprehension strategies—if they are properly instructed. And over the past three decades, Irene Gaskins (2005) has run a school in which students who struggle with reading master comprehension strategies on the road to becoming strong and successful readers.

In classrooms in which English-language learners receive some instruction in their native language, it may be useful to introduce a strategy in students' native language and use it with native language material before helping students transfer its use to English material. We also need to ensure that English-language learners are not restricted to learning basic skills and have plenty of opportunities to learn complex literacy tools such as comprehension strategies (Gutiérrez, 2005).

For students from certain cultures, the group work involved in learning strategies may be particularly facilitative and particularly comfortable. With these students, you might let the group work continue for some time, gradually building in independent assignments and explaining to students that they will often need to use strategies in situations in which their classmates are not available, such as with work done at home.

Concluding Remarks

In this chapter, we focused on teaching reading comprehension strategies. Up to this point, we have

- defined comprehension strategies,
- identified nine key strategies, and
- described well-researched procedures for teaching strategies.

One very important task remains—making your decision on which strategies to teach. These strategies will, in some cases, be determined by your school's curriculum. More often, however, identifying strategies to teach will be left up to you. In this case, we have a definite recommendation: Teach a few strategies well, rather than many strategies less well. Comprehension strategies are complex procedures, and they need to be learned well if they are to be of real use to students. Teaching three or so a year and teaching students how to coordinate the use of the three you teach, as well as any strategies they have previously learned, are ambitious but very reasonable goals. We suggest that you choose strategies that your students appear ready to learn and that can be used frequently in dealing with the selections students read in your classes. Additionally, when possible, it would be a good idea to coordinate the teaching of strategies with other teachers in the school, both other teachers in the same grade and teachers in the grades above and below yours. One plan would be to extend instruction in the nine strategies we discuss here over three years, teaching three each year and continuing in subsequent years to assist students in practicing and coordinating their use of all the strategies they have learned.

Whatever strategy or strategies you teach, remember that learning the strategy itself is not the primary goal. Like word-recognition strategies, comprehension strategies are a means to an end—students' understanding of, learning from, and enjoying what they read.

Extending Learning

1. One excellent way to better understand and appreciate the nature of good comprehension strategy instruction is to observe a teacher who is doing an excellent job of it. We suggest that you locate an effective strategy instructor, observe her teaching, and afterward talk to her about it. Potential sources for locating teachers are your university instructor, your cooperating teacher, other teachers you know, and your classmates.

2. To really come to understand strategy instruction, it is useful to study quality materials used in teaching strategies. One very solid set of materials, *Making Meaning,* is published by the Developmental Studies Center, a non-profit educational organization in Berkeley, California. Versions of the program are available for kindergarten through grade 6. Get a copy of one of the *Making Meaning* teacher's manuals, study it carefully, and compare the approach suggested there to that suggested in this chapter. You will find a good deal of similarity but also some important differences. Write a brief description of the Making Meaning approach and its similarities to and differences from the approach suggested here.

CW 9.4 links to additional information on the Making Meaning program, including a sample lesson plan.

For a look at comprehension strategies in a contemporary classroom, go to Allyn & Bacon's MyLabSchool.com. In MLS Courses, click on Reading Methods, and go to MLS Video Lab. There, you will find video clips about Comprehension in Module 5.

Children's Literature

Fleischman, J. (2002). *Phineas Gage: A Gruesome but True Story About Brain Science*. Boston: Houghton Mifflin. This fascinating and admittedly gruesome book tells about Phineas Gage, who, having survived a hideous brain accident in the mid 19th century, provided doctors with valuable information about how the brain functions. 85 pages.

Guest, E. H. (2004). *Iris and Walter and the Substitute Teacher*. San Diego: Gulliver/Harcourt. When Iris's beloved teacher becomes ill, her grandfather steps in as substitute, with mixed results. 44 pages.

Jackson, D. M. (2005). *ER Vets: Life in an Animal Emergency Room*. Boston: Houghton Mifflin. A behind the scenes look at the animal-saving drama of a veterinary ER room. 96 pages.

Johnson, G., & Cutchins, J. (1988). *Scaly Babies: Reptiles Growing Up*. New York: Morrow. This informational book has four chapters of descriptive text and color photographs highlighting snakes, lizards, crocodiles, turtles, and their young. 40 pages.

Lobel, A. (1979). *Days with Frog and Toad*. New York: Harper & Row. This classic beginning chapter book with five humorous stories stars best friends Frog and Toad and dramatizes universal truths about life and friendship. Audiotape available. 64 pages.

McPhail, D. M. (2002). *The Teddy Bear*. New York: St. Martin's Press. A young boy's lost teddy bear ends up being found by a homeless old man who learns to love it as much as the boy did. 32 pages.

Rylant, C. (2005). *Mr. Putter & Tabby Make a Wish*. San Diego: Harcourt. Mr. Putter's friends, both animal and human, plan a birthday party for him. 44 pages.

Sendak, M. (1963). *Where the Wild Things Are*. New York: Harper & Row. When Max is sent to bed without his supper, he imagines a world where he is King of the "wild things." 32 pages.

Stanley, D. (2002). *Saladin: Noble Prince of Islam*. New York: Morrow. This picture book tells of the life of the 12th-century Saladin, a Muslim hero who held off the crusaders and united his people. 48 pages.

Woolridge, C. N. (2001). *When Esther Morris Headed West: Women, Wyoming, and the Right to Vote*. New York: Holiday House. This inspiring nonfiction picture book tells about the life of Esther Morris, a trailblazer for women's rights. 32 pages.

CHAPTER 10

Encouraging Independent Reading and Reader Response

CLASSROOM
VIGNETTE

"*H*ey, I read that book. It's cool!" Michael said.

"We're reading it now . . . for literature circle," Ian told him.

"Really? We read it in book club."

"Book club? What's that?"

"It's what we do in school . . . for reading. Everybody reads the same book, then we get together and talk about it. It's fun to hear what other people think about the same book. Sometimes they have the same ideas about a book, and sometimes they don't. It's kind of weird how people can read the same book and come up with lots of different ways to talk about it. Our teacher says it's because we have different experiences and those experiences make us see things differently."

"Your book club sounds a lot like our literature circle. We have some really cool discussions."

This conversation tells us a lot about these boys *and* their teachers—they very strongly value reading and responding to literature, something not all students do. How can we as educators make sure that all of our students very strongly value reading and responding to what they read? We can create classrooms that nurture independent reading and provide the time and space for students to respond to literature—two topics we discuss in this chapter.

Independent Reading

Independent reading, as we define it here, means students' selecting their own material to read for their own purposes. These purposes may include pleasure, information, insight—whatever motivates those who love reading to pick up a book. If students are to become fluent and engaged readers who constantly choose to read for knowledge and pleasure, it is crucial that they be given many opportunities to do so. Some years ago, Dixie Lee Spiegel (1981) suggested several benefits of independent reading. These are still true today. Independent reading

- develops positive attitudes toward reading.
- gives students a chance to expand their knowledge.
- provides practice in decoding strategies.
- helps develop automaticity.
- develops and expands students' vocabularies.

More recently, Richard Anderson (1996) and Anne Cunningham and Keith Stanovich (2003) have summarized research that clearly demonstrates the rich cognitive gains that come from wide reading. These include, as we noted in Chapter 7, substantial vocabulary growth (Cunningham, 2005).

Providing Time to Read

Common sense tells us that we get better at just about anything by doing more of it. Reading is no exception, and, as we just noted, research confirms this notion. In one study, for example, Anderson and his colleagues (Anderson, Wilson, & Fielding, 1988) investigated fifth-graders' activities outside of school and the relationship of those activities to reading proficiency. Not surprisingly, what they found was that those students who spent time reading books made greater strides in reading in grades 2 through 5 than those who spent their time on other activities.

How much time should be set aside each school day for students to read independently for pleasure? Based on their research, Linda Fielding and her colleagues (Fielding, Wilson, & Anderson, 1986) recommend at least an hour per week. The amount of time spent in independent reading each day can vary from 5 minutes to 30 minutes and will depend on a number of factors—how often you schedule independent pleasure reading; what other opportunities for sustained reading students have in your classroom; the likelihood that students will read outside of school; and the age, interests, and maturity of students. As a rule of thumb, we recommend beginning with 5- to 10-minute periods for primary-grade children and 15- to 20-minute periods for older students, with primary students having independent reading sessions daily and older students having them perhaps three days per week. These times can of course be increased if your curriculum and students' interest and involvement allow it. All in all, the exact amount of time is not as important as making certain that there *is* a time set aside for pleasure reading on a consistent basis.

Providing a Rich Array of Reading Material, the Incentive to Read, and a Place to Read

As mentioned in Chapter 3, providing a rich array of reading material, plenty of motivation to read it, and a comfortable and inviting place to read is crucial. This is true for all students, but it is particularly true for those who do not gravitate to reading and those whose home environment does not prompt and nurture reading. Students' reading material can come from a variety of sources—including their homes, their friends, the classroom library, classroom book clubs, the school library, and the public library. Types of selections can and should run the gamut from fiction to nonfiction, trade books, magazines, even textbooks—the choice is up to the student.

Although what children choose to read will vary considerably and come from a variety of sources, we have found it extremely important for the classroom teacher to make reading materials readily available—in fact, to make them virtually unavoidable. One absolute essential is a well-stocked classroom library, a feature lacking in all too many schools (Allington et al., 1996). If school funds will not support a classroom library, we suggest that you investigate the possibility of obtaining funds from parents or from a local business or civic group. Joining a classroom book club—a commercial club that sells paperbacks at low prices and frequently sends out class sets of attractive and enticing flyers—can be an excellent way to promote books. Commercial book clubs make it very easy for you and your students to order books. Three such clubs are Scholastic Book Clubs, Inc. (800-724-2424), Troll Book Clubs (800-654-3037), and the Trumpet Book Club (800-826-0110).

You will also want to become thoroughly acquainted with your school library and local public library and the media specialists and librarians there, and you will want to introduce your students to these resources. Regular class visits to the school library and occasional field trips to the local public library are time well spent.

In the Classroom 10.1 provides some guidelines for choosing books.

> ***English Learners***
>
> Support literacy development in students' first language by stocking your classroom library with books in their languages. Encourage students to read selections written in their first language.

Guidelines for Choosing Books for Your Classroom Library

- Find out your students' interests. The first few weeks of the year, ask students about what interests them. Jot these down in a teacher logbook (as described in Chapter 14). Then, throughout the year, record the likes and dislikes of each student and the books and other material they have enjoyed reading.

- Get recommendations from your colleagues and school media specialist. Ask your students' former teachers about what reading material has been successful with these students and your school media specialist about what is available and what she recommends for your particular group of students.

- Become familiar with the many guides to selecting reading material for children, such as the *Horn Book Guide to Children's and Young Adult Books* (2002) and *Best Books for Children: Preschool Through Grade 6* (Gillespie, 2002).

in the Classroom 10.1

Assisting Students in Selecting Material

Helping students select the right material—material that they can read, will read, will enjoy, and will profit from—is tremendously important. Moreover, this is a task that is particularly important and particularly difficult with less-able and less-avid readers, students who do not read much and are therefore less familiar with what's available and less skilled at selecting appropriate material. As you are thinking about matching students and texts—particularly matching less-proficient readers with texts they can and will read—be sure to consider the information on text difficulty we presented in Chapter 6. In the Classroom 10.2 offers some guidelines for assisting students in selecting reading material they will enjoy.

Guidelines for Helping Students Select Reading Material

- Give book and author talks. Occasionally, introduce students to new authors by telling a little about the authors, giving previews of their works, and reading excerpts from their books.
- Read from a "big book" and then make multiple copies of the "little" books available.
- Read a chapter from a novel or chapter book and then make that book available.
- Suggest that students use the "Goldilocks Principle"—choose a book that's not too hard, not too easy, but "just right."
- Invite students to give book and author talks in which they recommend books and authors they have enjoyed.
- Invite students to write previews, reviews, and testimonials and display them around the room.
- Invite guest authors to read from their work and make those works available.
- Invite your school media specialists or public librarians to talk about their favorite books and authors as well as give information on the public library's resources and how to locate materials.
- Invite other adults—parents, the principal, secretary, custodian, coach, nurse—to talk about their favorite books.

in the **Classroom 10.2**

Establishing and Maintaining an Independent Reading Program

As mentioned in Chapter 3, we recommend establishing an independent reading program in which a designated time is set aside for everyone to read. By incorporating an uninterrupted reading time into your daily routine, you will be not only contributing to students' growth in reading fluency but also sending several powerful messages. Among these are that reading books is important, that reading is something everyone can do, that reading is important to you, that children are capable of sustained thought, and that you believe they can and do comprehend what they read (McCracken & McCracken, 1978).

An inviting, well-stocked classroom library goes a long way in nurturing lifelong readers.

Encouraging Out-of-School Reading

Thus far, we have stressed the importance of in-school reading because that is the reading that you as a teacher have the most control over. However, anything you can do to encourage and support out-of-school reading is likely to be well worth your efforts. As we have said repeatedly, students need to read a lot if they are to get really good at it *and* enjoy all the cognitive benefits reading provides. As shown in Figure 10.1, students spend only about 14 percent of their time in school (Donovan, Bransford, & Pellegrino, 1999). This being the case, out-of-school reading can, and if at all possible *must,* contribute hugely to the amount of practice students get.

Getting parents involved can greatly enhance students' out-of-school reading time. One way to do this is with book bags and home/school reading logs. Book bags are simply bags made of sturdy material, such as corduroy or canvas. And book logs are small journals that fit into the bags. Students carry books to and from school in these bags. Parents and students use the logs to make comments about the books they read.

Here's how one teacher orchestrated an out-of-school reading program. Students and their parents in Roslyn Breslouer's first grade participated in a program called "We Love to Read Beary Much" (*Reading Today,* 1997):

As part of the "We Love to Read Beary Much" program, my first-graders carry books home for their parents to read

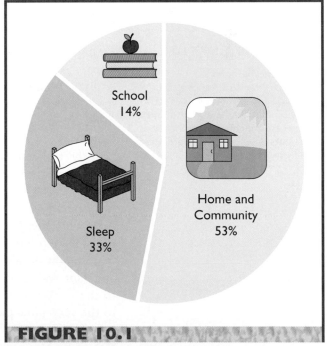

FIGURE 10.1

Students Spend Only 14 Percent of Their Time in School

Source: Donovan, M. S., Bransford, J. D., & Pellegrino, J. W. (Eds.). (1999). *How people learn: Bridging research and practice.* Washington, DC: National Academy Press.

CW 10.1 links to TeacherWeb and Eboard, two Websites that allow you to create your own teacher Webpage. At these Websites, you can post reading lists for parents and students in order to encourage out-of-school reading.

with them. Their parents sign a comment sheet, and many include notes about their reading experience. I think something as simple as sending home a book or letter on a regular basis makes a big difference. I think parents just need that personal communication.

As part of the bear theme, all students have their own bear symbol on a bear bulletin board, and they get a bear sticker for every book that a parent has signed a card for. We have a big bear named Love-a-Lot that sits on a chair in the front of the classroom. Sometimes children read to Love-a-Lot or to Ted, the troll who sits on the bear's lap.

One of the keys to the success of this program is a classroom library well stocked with paperbacks. Another important factor is keeping parents involved. To do this, I hold "We Love to Read Beary Much" parties in December, March, and June each year. These parties often draw 15 to 20 parents, who sometimes bring along grandparents, aunts and uncles, and students' younger siblings. Students recite poetry to the group of parents, who then spread out and read to their own children (and sometimes others as well). They like the idea that they can read with the children and hear the children read and recite. I also hold after-school workshops twice a year to give parents advice on how to read to children.

It's especially enjoyable to me that the program gets the parents to spend quality time with their children to read and discuss books. By the end of the year, the kids love books. Books are an integral part of their lives.

—Roslyn Breslouer, First-Grade Teacher

Although Ms. Breslouer's program used a bear theme, the children read books on every topic under the sun! The extra time spent reading not only served to increase their vocabularies and add to their general knowledge but reinforced the idea that reading is an enjoyable and worthwhile thing to do.

ASSESSMENT

Occasionally, collect students' home/school reading logs, tally the number of books students have taken home to read, and note the types of books students have chosen. This will give you an idea of not only how much and how often students read at home, but also what their interests are and what level of books they choose to read.

English Learners

Provide nonverbal opportunities for responding to literature—such as art, music, and dance. These kinds of activities give English learners opportunities to showcase their accomplishments and talents even though they are not yet fully proficient in English.

Responding to Literature

Perhaps you recall a time when your teachers asked a series of questions about a story you read. You believed there were "right" answers to those questions, and you tried your best to deliver them. Some of those questions certainly did have "right" answers. For example, if your teacher asked you to name the two main characters in "Gone with the Wiener," and you answered Homer and Gustav when they actually were Tina and Joey, your teacher might assume (rightly) that you either read a different story, didn't comprehend the story, or hadn't read the story (certainly an unlikely eventuality!). However, other kinds of questions leave room for interpretation, that personal transaction that takes place between the reader and the text. One such question is, How do you think Tina felt when Joey sent her roses? *You* might answer the question by saying that Tina felt happy because Joey remembered her birthday. However, a classmate might decide that Tina felt nervous because roses are a symbol of love and Tina was ambivalent about her own feelings for Joey. You are responding to the story one way, and your classmate is responding quite a different way to the very same piece of literature.

Reader Response

ASSESSMENT

You can assess whether or not students are responding emotionally to literature by occasionally asking students questions such as "How did it make you feel when . . . ?"

As discussed in Chapter 1, reader-response theory—much of which evolved from the extended work of Louise Rosenblatt (1938/1995, 1978)—centers on the belief that the reader is crucial to the construction of the literary experience. The reader doesn't come to the text empty, hoping to be filled, but brings meaning to the text. Reading is a transaction between the reader and the writer. Any particular reading of a text—particularly a literary text such as fiction and poetry—will produce an interpretation that reflects both the meaning intended by the author and the meaning constructed by the reader (Galda & Cullinan, 2006; Mills, Stephens, O'Keefe, & Waugh, 2004).

A number of the postreading activities we discussed in Chapter 8—for example, those involving discussion, writing, art, dance, music, and drama—promote reader response. As you recall, many of these encourage students to make personal responses to literature and give them opportunities to use a variety of modes of expression in doing so, as Galda and Graves (in press), among others, recommend. In the Classroom 10.3 illustrates how a class of third-graders might be encouraged to respond artistically after reading several books about animals.

Students' Artistic Responses After Reading About Animals

instructional routines in the Classroom 10.3

Imagine your third-grade class has just finished a unit on animals. Over a four-week period, they have read numerous fiction and nonfiction trade books. As a culminating activity, you read William Jay Smith's book of poems, *Birds and Beasts,* aloud to them.

- Divide the class into three heterogeneous groups and assign each group one of the three nonverbal expressive "languages"—art, music, or dance.

- Have each group decide which animal it will portray in its appointed "language" and brainstorm about what materials and approaches it might take. For example, the art group might suggest watercolor painting, collages, scratch boards, paper sculpture, clay modeling, and papier-mâché. After the students have brainstormed together and decided on their animal and some possibilities for depicting this animal in a visual way with the resources available, have them work individually, in subgroups, or in pairs to create their animal, using whatever medium they feel will best capture the essence of their animal.

- The music group's goal is to create an instrumental piece to depict its animal. During the brainstorming session, invite students to think about the musical resources available to them as well as the characteristics of their particular animal. Encourage them to consider rhythm and percussion instruments and those that produce melody. Some of their suggestions might include drums, cymbals, sticks, sandpaper blocks, recorders, song flutes, xylophone, bells, piano, and keyboard. After they think about what animal they are going to depict and how they might depict this animal through music, they begin working in pairs or small groups to re-create their animal through music.

- The dance group's goal is to depict its chosen animal through movement. During a brainstorming session, encourage students to offer suggestions about what body movements represent this animal. Their discussion will involve both showing and telling, with these sorts of words describing the characteristics and movements of their chosen animal—*slow, steady, heavy, swinging, head-moving, tail-swishing, clomp-clomp-clomp.* The group might decide to work together to create one dance that represents the animal or to work in pairs or subgroups.

- After their brainstorming sessions, give students an hour or so over two or three days to come up with nonverbal expressions of their chosen animals. On the fourth day, invite them to present their work. They will make their animals come to life in visual art, music, and dance, and other students can guess the animals they are depicting.

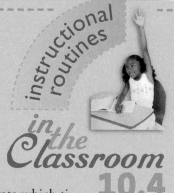

Literature Circles

A host of postreading discussion groups designed to foster reader response emerged during the 1990s. One of those was literature circles (Short & Klassen, 1993). Simply defined, *literature circles* are groups of students who come together to discuss material they have all chosen to read—a book, article, poem, etc. Before meeting to discuss what they have read, the students read silently, respond in their journals to what they have read, and use their journal responses as initial agendas for discussion (Spiegel, 1998). Discussions are student-led, and when students finish reading and discussing one selection, new groups are formed.

According to Harvey Daniels (1994), the teacher's role in literature circles is that of a facilitator or monitor, but not a participant. However, in examining "teacher talk" in literature circles, Kathy Short and colleagues (Short et al., 1999) noted that, in addition to being a facilitator, the teacher assumed the role of participant, mediator, and active listener, depending on what students talked about and the topic under discussion.

In the Classroom 10.4 describes how to set up literature circles in a fourth-grade classroom.

Establishing Literature Circles in a Fourth-Grade Classroom

instructional routines in the Classroom 10.4

- Preselect a number of books and have students look through them. For example, you might choose books by a single author such as Patricia MacLachlan and make available *Sarah, Plain and Tall; Skylark; Caleb's Story; Journey; Baby; The Facts and Fictions of Minna Pratt; Cassie Binegar;* and *Painting the Wind,* which represent a range of interests and reading skills. Or you might choose books representing a theme such as pioneer times, life in the city, families, or friendship.

- After students have had a chance to look through the books, ask students which titles they would like to read and write those titles on a sheet of butcher paper. Give a book talk or preview of each of the chosen books, telling something about the setting, the main characters, and the premise of the story. Next, ask students to write their names on the butcher paper under the titles of their first two choices.

- Place students in groups where they will be reading their first- or second-choice books. Once the groups have been formed, determine (with input from each group) how long will be spent reading the book, how many pages a day group members will read to reach that goal, when the group will meet, and how members will respond to their reading. Remind students when the next meeting of their group will be, how many pages they will need to read, and what type of response will need to be completed before their next meeting. Ask them to jot this information down in their journals.

- As students read their books, meet periodically with each group—as a participant, not as a leader—while students take turns leading the discussion, which revolves around the individual responses they have recorded in their journals.

- When the group is close to completing the book, encourage them to discuss possible postreading activities, such as those listed in the SRE framework described in Chapter 8.

- After all groups have finished reading their books and related activities, take time to evaluate the literature circle, noting things that went well and things that could use improvement.

- Form new groups with new student-selected reading material. This allows students the opportunity to work with other students and gain other perspectives.

Although In the Classroom 10.4 illustrates literature circles based on works by a single author, groups might also be organized around certain themes or topics—including topics from content areas such as science or social studies. For example, students might select books about friendship, the Civil War, or the solar system. An excellent resource for identifying theme-related books to introduce to your students is *The Complete Guide to Thematic Units: Creating the Integrated Curriculum* (Meinbach, Rothlein, & Fredericks, 2000).

Whatever their focus, literature circles put a premium on the element of student choice and on open-ended student-led discussions. These result in "critical thinking and self-reflection on the text and higher student engagement" (Galda, Ash, & Cullinan, 2000). Through discussion, students share their own understanding of what they have read, test it against what others have gleaned, and come to new insights and interpretations. As third-grader Chris puts it:

> In literature circles, everyone has a chance to give their opinion and even if you don't agree with that person, you keep on talking because you know that you will get more ideas. You aren't trying to figure out one right answer. In reading groups, when someone gave the right answer, we were done talking. In literature circles, we keep on going. We try to come up with as many different directions as possible. (Short & Klassen, 1993)

Through this synthesizing process, readers come to a deeper understanding and appreciation of the literature they read.

Three Frameworks That Promote Literature and Reader Response

Whereas literature circles are essentially groups of students who read and discuss the same piece of literature, Book Club, Book Club *Plus,* and the reading

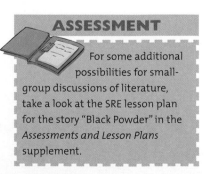

ASSESSMENT

For some additional possibilities for small-group discussions of literature, take a look at the SRE lesson plan for the story "Black Powder" in the *Assessments and Lesson Plans* supplement.

workshop are instructional frameworks that center around students' reading and personally responding to literature. While these programs have literature and reader response at their core, they have other goals and instructional objectives as well.

Book Club and Book Club *Plus*

Book Club and later Book Club *Plus* are both the result of a collaborative effort involving university-based and school-based educators (Goatley, Brock, & Raphael, 1995; McMahon, Raphael, &, Goatley, 1995; Raphael & McMahon, 1994; Raphael, Florio-Ruane, & George, 2001; Raphael et al., 2004). According to Taffy Raphael (2000), one of the creators of the Book Club and Book Club *Plus* programs, in the initial planning of the Book Club program she and her colleagues searched for a theoretical model that would foster a high degree of student engagement and also provide opportunities for literacy instruction. What they discovered was a model called the Vygotsky Space (see Figure 10.2). This model consists of two axes—the public/private axis and the social/individual axis. When these two axes intersect, four quadrants are formed.

Each of the quadrants provides opportunities for an activity or set of activities in the Book Club program. For example, quadrant 1, the public and social, is the whole-class setting where students learn literacy skills, strategies, and attitudes through teacher instruction and modeling. Quadrant 2, the social and private, represents opportunities for students to use what they have learned in quadrant 1 in the same way and for the same purposes. Working in this quadrant, third-graders might read about Gabrielle in *No Copycats Allowed!* (Graves, 1998) or fifth-graders might read about Angel in *The Same Stuff as Stars* (Paterson, 2002) and then write responses in their reading logs about times they have found themselves in new and challenging situations. Quadrant 3, the private and individual, is where students transform privately what they have learned and practiced. As Raphael notes, "By transforming what they have learned, they create something new and unique that serves their own purposes" (2000). In quadrant 4, the

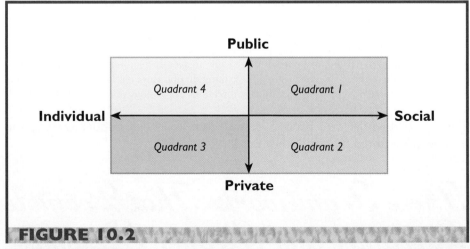

FIGURE 10.2

The Vygotsky Space

Source: Gavelek, J. R., & Raphael, T. E. (1996). "Changing Talk About Text: New Roles for Teachers and Students." *Language Arts, 73* (3), 182–192. Copyright 1996 by the National Council of Teachers of English. Reprinted by permission.

individual and public, publication of private activity occurs. It is through publication—through student writing or book club discussions—that students' learning of conventional knowledge or transformation of that knowledge is revealed.

In addition to providing opportunities for students to work within each of these four quadrants, the Book Club program provides opportunities for students to be involved in four types of activities—reading, writing, book club, and community share.

- *Reading* (10 to 20 minutes): The reading component of the Book Club program encourages students to respond aesthetically to what they read with evaluations, personal responses, comparisons to other texts, and the like. However, attention is also given to such matters as fluency, reading vocabulary, comprehension strategies, and genres of literature.
- *Writing* (10 to 15 minutes): The writing component grows out of the reading students do for the Book Club program and is designed to enhance their understanding and response to what they read. Additionally, opportunities are provided for the kind of writing that requires planning, revision, and publishing.
- *Book clubs* (5 to 20 minutes): Book clubs are the student-led discussion groups for which the program was named. One of the goals of the Book Club program is for students to develop control over book club discussions and their own ways of preparing for them (Tierney & Readence, 2000). Another goal is for students to really learn to talk about books. In the Book Club program, in contrast to literature circles, the reading material is teacher-selected. Teachers select high-quality literature based both on student interests and on various instructional objectives.
- *Community share* (5 to 20 minutes): The community share component is a time for teachers to meet with students as a whole class. Community share time can occur before or after students read a selection. If it is held prior to reading, the teacher engages students in activities that will help prepare them for reading, such as building background knowledge or discussing the structure of the upcoming selection. If it follows book club discussions, students in different book clubs might share their thoughts on their books, debate issues prompted by their reading, or talk about confusing or disturbing aspects of their book that they have not been able to resolve in their individual book clubs. Community share time might also encompass mini-lessons, which can include any one or a combination of explicit instruction, modeling, and scaffolding.

ASSESSMENT

When reporting student progress to parents, use multiple pieces of evidence. Information on students' oral reading, information on their participation in discussion, and some writing samples are three good options.

The teacher's role in any of the four quadrants and during any of the four activities can be that of instructor, modeler, scaffolder, facilitator, or participant, depending on what the students or situation requires. That is, the teacher does whatever is necessary to further students' competence.

Book Club *Plus* adds a skills-and-strategy instruction component to the Book Club program and is built around a theme for the year. For example, MariAnne George used "Our Storied Lives" as a theme for her third-grade class (Raphael, 2001). In George's classroom, the Book Club *Plus* instruction took place within three three- to eight-week units—Unit 1: "Stories of Self" Unit 2: "Family Stories" Unit 3: "Stories of Culture." The weekly instruction consisted of three consecutive days of Book Club followed by two days of a literacy block. In the literacy block, the focus is on instruction and practice of

CW 10.2 links to the Horn Book Guide, which includes more than 57,900 reviews published between 1989 and 2004, searchable by title, keyword, grade level, and more, to help you locate books for your Book Club *Plus* theme of the year.

MONDAY	TUESDAY	WEDNESDAY	THURSDAY	FRIDAY
Daily Teacher Read-Aloud				
Book Club	Book Club	Book Club	Literacy Block	Literacy Block
• Opening community share (5–15 mins.)			Guided reading groups	
• Reading (10–20 mins.)			Skills centers	
• Writing (10–20 mins.)			Internet searches	
• Book clubs (5–20 mins.)			Journaling	
• Closing community share (5–20 mins.)			Unit work/writers workshop	
Social Studies Connection				

FIGURE 10.3

A Week's Organization for Book Club *Plus* Activities

Source: Raphael, T. E. (2001). Book Club *Plus:* A Conceptual Framework to Organize Literary Instruction. *Language Arts, 79,* 159–169. Copyright 2001 by the National Council of Teachers of English. Reprinted by permission.

skills and strategies. During this block, students work in guided reading groups and skills centers where they meet with the teacher. When students are not meeting with the teacher, they work independently to practice skills and work on theme-related writing, doing Internet research, journaling, and so on. See Figure 10.3 for a week's organization.

The Book Club and Book Club *Plus* programs put quality literature at their core and provide space for teachers to teach conventional knowledge about text processing.

Reading Workshop

Like Book Club and Book Club *Plus,* the reading workshop, first developed by Nancie Atwell (1987, 1998a), structures reading time and activities to make reading the primary activity and to give students ownership of their reading. The reading workshop stresses the importance of the teacher's demonstrating and endorsing the value of reading by discussing books that he has read and what reading means to him, teaching strategies that will help students become independent readers, giving students time to read, responding to students' responses to what they read, and giving students opportunities to share their responses to what they read with others.

Since Atwell originally proposed the reading workshop, various authors have critiqued, tried out, and modified the procedure. Our suggestions have been influenced by these authors and by our experiences. The four main components of the version of the reading workshop that we suggest are listed below:

- Teacher sharing time (5–10 minutes)
- Mini-lessons (5–15 minutes)
- Self-selected reading and response (30–40 minutes)
- Students' sharing time (5–10 minutes)

During the short *teacher sharing time* that begins each session, the teacher shares some of the selections that have touched and interested him. For example, he might share the poem "Buffalo Dusk" by Carl Sandburg with his fifth-graders who are studying American history.

Sharing a self-selected book with a buddy underscores the fun and value of reading.

Next comes a short and tightly focused *mini-lesson,* a 5- to 15-minute period during which the teacher instructs the class as a whole. Early in the year, mini-lessons are likely to deal with procedural matters about conducting the reading workshop: what materials can be read, how long the reading period is, what sorts of reporting will be required, what to include in a response to a selection, what sorts of conferences will be held, and the like. Later mini-lessons can focus on whatever skill, strategy, convention, or general information is particularly relevant to what students are reading. You might teach a mini-lesson on a literary device such as foreshadowing, or you might use a mini-lesson to give students advice on how to choose books they're likely to enjoy. Mini-lessons are often motivated by student needs that the teacher has observed. For example, if quite a few students are writing summaries of what they have read and their summaries lack focus, you might review the strategy of summarizing.

Self-selected reading and response is the core of the reading workshop. On most workshop days, most students will spend 30 to 40 minutes silently reading. However, silent reading is punctuated with several other activities.

The most frequent of these other activities is journaling. As they are reading their books, students keep a dialogue journal, something we describe in Chapter 12, in which they record their reactions, questions, and musings about what they are reading. These dialogue journals typically go to the teacher, who periodically gives a personal response to each student's thoughts. Dialogue journals can also be addressed to other students, so that there is student-to-student dialogue as well as teacher-to-student and student-to-teacher dialogues.

Another activity that takes place during the self-selected reading and response time is teacher conferencing. Periodically, the teacher meets with each student to discuss his reading accomplishments and upcoming plans for reading, as well as any concerns the student has. Because teachers might have 30 students and conferences take up a fair amount of time, these conferences are typically held once a quarter or so, toward the end of the quarter.

Another possibility is student meetings. If several students discover that they are reading the same author, book, or genre, they may decide they have some things to discuss. Similarly, if the teacher learns that several students have

When conferencing with students in reading workshop, try the funnel approach described in Chapter 14. Begin with general questions that focus on a particular problem—expository writing, for example. Then move to more specific queries—supporting a main idea with details, for example.

something to share—or a common need—the teacher might schedule a small-group meeting. Whether or not the teacher is present will depend on the topic and purpose of the meeting.

Student sharing time is the last component in the reading workshop, a time when the class comes together to share the things students have been doing. As in the writing workshop, which we describe in Chapter 12, not every student shares each day. Often it works best to have students sign up in advance to share, usually two to four students per session. The most common activity involves students' talking about what they have been reading and sharing their experiences and suggestions for good reading.

In the Classroom 10.5 scenario describes the reading workshop in Kathleen Swift's sixth-grade class.

A Glimpse into a Reading Workshop in Action

For Kathleen Swift's students, the reading workshop begins with a 10- to 15-minute mini-lesson. She chooses the lesson topic according to the current needs of the class. At the beginning of the school year, the lessons center on the organization of the classroom: behavioral expectations, choosing books, checking out books, how to complete dialogue journals, grading, and earning extra points. Swift frequently introduces books and authors that she thinks the children will like. Once students know her expectations and organization, she devotes more lessons to topics such as narrative voice, point of view, author's purpose, theme, and specific reading strategies, such as focusing on important words.

When she finishes the mini-lesson lesson, students begin reading. A few students choose to sit on the cushions in the reading area. One or two pull their chairs to isolated corners of the room. Students do not use the period to look for books in the library unless they happen to finish a book during class. Swift expects everyone to come to class ready to read. A student might leave the room to read a book with a parent volunteer. This is the strategy she has developed for those few children who need the guidance of an adult to focus their attention. The adults help students find books they want to read and read aloud with them, alternating paragraphs.

From time to time, students go to the shelves to get their reading dialogue journals. They add the title of the book they just started to a list of previously read books at the back of the journal. They then turn to the correspondence section of their journal, write the date, and begin a letter to Swift. All students have to write a minimum of once every two weeks, telling Swift the title and author, sharing their opinions of their books, and relating their books to their lives in some way. Swift responds in writing to each letter, expressing her own ideas and encouraging students to try books and authors new to them. (Swift, 1993)

in the Classroom 10.5

Reading is the primary activity in the reading workshop. However, as our description makes clear, the reading workshop also includes the other language arts—writing, speaking, and listening. As mentioned on page 306, various authors have written about and experimented with reading workshops (Atwell, 1987, 1998; Orehovec & Alley, 2003; Reutzel & Cooter, 1991; Serafini, 2004; Swift, 1993; Tierney & Readence, 2000). We recommend that you read what they have to say and consider the perspectives they offer.

Reflect *and* Apply

1. Jot down a few reasons why it's important for students to do a lot of out-of-school reading as well as in-school reading. Prepare a pep talk on this subject to give to parents on "Back-to-School" night. Write out your pep talk, or give it orally in front of your classmates.

2. List as many advantages as you can for one of the approaches discussed in this chapter—literature circles, Book Club or Book Club *Plus* programs, or the reading workshop. Think also of disadvantages to these methods, and discuss the pros and cons of these ways of organizing reading with a classmate or group of classmates.

3. Identify a grade you would particularly like to teach. Then, in writing, describe the approach or approaches you would use to foster independence in reading in that class, explaining your rationale and procedure as you might describe them to parents at your first classroom open house.

Strengths and Challenges of DIVERSITY

As we have repeatedly noted, the present-day literacy curriculum is for all students—more-accomplished readers, less-accomplished readers, students who come less prepared to school, and students who do not speak English as their native language. How can teachers accommodate these needs when it comes to encouraging independent reading and reader response?

In Chapter 6, we talked about using readability formulas and other more subjective measures to determine text difficulty and to help match readers with appropriate texts. Another such subjective measure, called leveling, was first developed in New Zealand by Marie Clay (1991), who, as part of her Reading Recovery Program, needed to find books with closely spaced difficulty levels to use with at-risk first- and second-graders. As Edward Fry (2002) points out, leveling takes into consideration factors that are absent from most readability formulas, factors such as a text's content, illustrations, length, curriculum it may or may not relate to, language structure, reader's background knowledge, and format. Thinking about these factors as you choose books for your challenged readers can help you locate appropriate material for their independent, literature circle, or book club reading.

To help students select their own books for independent reading, you might try color coding, as did Benchmark School, a school that has been particularly successful in improving the reading performance of less-proficient readers. All of the books in its very large library are color coded for difficulty (Gaskins, 1994). Benchmark School requires its students, all of whom are less-proficient readers, to read a lot of books. Having the books color coded greatly simplifies the task of getting the right books to each student.

High-interest, easy-reading series books, specifically written for students who read below their grade level, can be particularly valuable for less-proficient readers (Graves & Philippot, 2001). But having well-stocked libraries is sometimes not enough. Less-proficient readers usually have to be lured

CW 10.3 links to Audio Bookshelf and Listening Library, two resources for audiobooks with multicultural themes. One way to celebrate diversity and encourage independent reading and reader response from your less-able readers is to provide audiocassettes or CDs of multicultural books.

into those libraries and connected with the texts. In the Classroom 10.6 is based on the suggestions of John Manning (1999), a former elementary teacher and former president of the International Reading Association, on how to encourage reluctant readers.

Encouraging Reluctant Readers

- Listen to your reluctant readers over a period of time to discover their interests.
- Go to the school library or media center and ask the media specialist for books that might interest your particular students.
- Examine a few of the recommended books.
- Find an opportune time to preview a couple of the books you think are most likely to interest your readers.
- Encourage your reluctant readers to go to the library and give these books a try.

in the Classroom 10.6

You also will want to provide encouragement and support to students at the other end of the spectrum, those who do read well and want to think about and discuss what they read. One way of doing this, suggested to us by Anita Meinbach, a teacher of gifted and talented students, capitalizes on that all-important out-of-school reading time. She recommends encouraging students to participate in the book groups available at many local bookstores. Here are Ms. Meinbach's comments on her school's involvement in a Grand Conversations book group, which takes place in a local bookstore once a month:

> For the past five years, I've conducted Grand Conversations at Borders Books. We invite students from several middle schools, and they all get together to discuss a predetermined book they've all read. Borders supplies the drinks and snacks. The kids run the whole show. I just show up, say "Hello," and introduce next month's selection. The idea's catching on. Two other teachers have begun this in their area of the county.
>
> —Anita Meinbach, Teacher of the Year, Miami-Dade County, 2003

Three good resources for selecting books for book group discussion in bookstores or other out-of-school locations are your school media specialist, your local library's children's librarian, and children's bookstore personnel. Say, for instance, your students are interested in reading and discussing books on the topic of family life in various time periods and locales. In a quick call to a local children's librarian, we received the following four recommendations: Eva Ibbotson's novel *The Star of Kazan*, a mystery about an adopted foundling child set in Austria and Germany in the early 20th century; *Little Cricket* by Jackie Brown, about a Hmong family's flight from Laos after the Vietnam War to a refugee camp in Thailand and eventually to Minnesota; Kerry Madden's *Gentle's Holler,* which takes place in rural North Carolina in the early 1960s; and Gennifer Choldenko's

Al Capone Does My Shirts, set on Alcatraz Island during 1935. The first two books are appropriate for readers in grades 4–6; the last two are appropriate for readers in grades 6–8.

Concluding Remarks

In this chapter, we discussed the importance of providing independent reading time, a rich array of reading materials and the incentive to read them, and an inviting place in which to read. We also suggested ways to help students select material for independent reading and to establish and maintain an independent reading program. As an adjunct to independent reading, we talked about the importance of reader response and literature circles and of discussion groups that encourage students to make personal connections with the texts they read. We emphasized the need to invite students to express their own ideas and to listen to those of other students. Finally, we presented three frameworks that promote reader response—the Book Club and Book Club *Plus* programs and the reading workshop. Each of these frameworks presents a way to organize reading time that makes reading and student response the focal point, with instruction supporting this main endeavor.

The topics presented in this chapter—encouraging independent reading and reader response—are important components of a well-balanced literacy curriculum; both are vital to helping students meet the challenging literacy demands of the 21st century.

Extending Learning

1. Imagine you are a beginning teacher in a new school and your principal tells you that the PTA will purchase 30 books for your classroom library. Select a grade you would most like to teach. Write up a brief description of that class—ages of students, ethnic backgrounds represented, and range of reading ability. Using resources such as *Promoting a Global Community Through Multicultural Literature* (Steiner, 2001) and *The Best of the Best from 60 Years of Notable Children's Books, 1940–99* (Association for Library Service to Children, 2004), select 30 books for your library.

2. Select a grade you would most like to teach. If possible, arrange to visit a classroom to observe independent reading and literature discussion groups in this grade. Take notes on what you observe. What are students reading? Do they appear to be engaged in the reading? How do they respond to their reading (in a journal, through discussion, or merely privately in their minds as they read)? Plan a reading experience for these students that will include group discussion that focuses on reader response. Let them select a book, or assign one yourself. Write your plans for this reading experience from beginning to end, including how the students will be prepared for the experience, how the reading will be done, and how the discussion will be handled. Here are some questions to think about as you develop your plan: What

will your role be? What will students' role be? How will the reading be handled? How will the discussion be handled? What will be discussed? Who will lead the discussion? How will it begin and end? How will you ensure student engagement, participation, and success? If possible, try out your plan on a group of students. If this isn't possible, present your ideas to your classmates for feedback.

Where the classroom comes to life!

For a look at independent reading in a contemporary classroom, go to Allyn & Bacon's MyLabSchool.com. In MLS Courses, click on Reading Methods, and go to MLS Video Lab. There, you will find video clips about using literature in Module 7.

Children's Literature

Brown, J. (2004). *Little Cricket*. New York: Hyperion. In the aftermath of the Vietnam War, 12-year-old Kia and her Hmong family flee from the mountains of Laos to a refugee camp in Thailand and eventually to Saint Paul, Minnesota. 252 pages.

Choldenko, G. (2004). *Al Capone Does My Shirts*. New York: G. P. Putnam's Sons. In 1935, when twelve-year-old Moose's family moves to Alcatraz Island, where guards' families were housed at that time, he has to deal not only with his strange new environment but with an autistic sister as well. 228 pages.

Graves, B. (1998). *No Copycats Allowed!* New York: Hyperion. Wanting desperately to fit in at her new school, Gabrielle tries to copy her classmates, only to learn that the best way to make friends is by being herself. 51 pages.

Ibbotson, E. (2004). *The Star of Kazan*. New York: Dutton. After 12-year-old Annika, a foundling living in late 19th-century Vienna, inherits a trunk of costume jewelry, a woman claiming to be her aristocratic mother arrives and takes her to live in a strangely decrepit mansion in Germany. 405 pages.

MacLachlan, P. (1982). *Cassie Binegar*. New York: Harper & Row. One summer, fourth-grader Cassie learns to accept change and to find her own space. 120 pages.

MacLachlan, P. (1985). *Sarah, Plain and Tall*. New York: HarperCollins. This Newbery Award–winning novel tells the story of mail-order bride Sarah from Maine and the family who long to have her stay with them on the prairie. Audio- and videotape available. 58 pages.

MacLachlan, P. (1988). *The Facts and Fictions of Minna Pratt*. New York: Harper & Row. Eleven-year-old Minna, a cello student in New York City, learns about life, love, and music through her family, her first boyfriend, and Mozart. Audiotape available. 136 pages.

MacLachlan, P. (1991) *Journey*. New York: Delacorte. This novel explores how photographs and a grandfather's love enable young Journey to come to terms with his mother's abandonment and restore a past that he feels has been erased. 83 pages.

MacLachlan, P. (1993). *Baby*. New York: Delacorte. This exquisitely crafted short novel is about a family learning to deal with the death of their own infant son after a baby girl is left on their doorstep for them to care for. 132 pages.

MacLachlan, P. (1994). *Skylark*. New York: HarperCollins. In this sequel to *Sarah, Plain and Tall*, Anna and Caleb worry that a drought on the prairie will send their new mother, Sarah, back to her home in Maine. Audio- and videotape available. 86 pages.

MacLachlan, P. (2001). *Caleb's Story*. New York: Joanna Cotler Books. Caleb narrates this sequel to *Sarah, Plain and Tall* and *Skylark* in which Jacob is reunited with his father. 128 pages.

MacLachlan, P. (2003). *Painting the Wind*. New York: Joanna Cotler Books. By observing how each of four artists paints the same island, a boy hopes to learn how to paint the wind. 40 pages.

Madden, K. (2005). *Gentle's Holler*. New York: Viking. Twelve-year-old Livy dreams of seeing the world beyond the poverty-stricken North Carolina holler where she lives with her large family in the early 1960s. 237 pages.

Paterson, K. (2002). *The Same Stuff as Stars.* New York: Clarion. When 11-year-old Angel and her younger brother are dumped at their great-grandmother's Vermont backcountry home, Angel struggles to make a new life for herself and her family. 256 pages.

Sandburg, C. (1965). Buffalo Dusk. In *Arrow Book of Poetry,* selected by Ann McGovern. New York: Scholastic. This evocative poem laments a time gone by when the great buffalo herds roamed the prairie.

Smith, W. J. (1990). *Birds and Beasts.* New York: Godine. In poetry and pictures, this volume presents a fun and satisfying, if slightly offbeat, view of 29 animals. Unpaged.

Classroom Portrait

A Day in the Life of Dolores Puente and Her Third- and Fourth-Grade Students

Dolores Puente has been teaching for eight years at Lincoln Elementary School, a K–6 school in a suburb of Los Angeles. Lincoln's students are primarily from middle- to lower-income families. About half of the students in Ms. Puente's combination third/fourth grade are of European American descent; the other half are of Hispanic, Asian, and African American descent. When we asked how she would describe her reading program, Ms. Puente thought for a moment. "You know, based on workshops the district has had on the Report of the National Reading Panel, I've changed it somewhat in the past several years. I'm more conscious of ensuring that all of my students learn crucial skills and strategies than I once was. But I still plan to do a lot with literature—I always have, and I plan to continue. I have an overall plan for teaching the literacy skills that appear in our curriculum, and I make a big effort to teach certain skills when my students find they need them in order to reach a particular goal. For example, if they are involved in projects that involve library research, I'll create lessons to help them with note taking. But I can tell you this, no matter what we're involved in—social studies, science, art—reading and writing instruction is an integral part of our day, beginning with the morning meeting and continuing to the afternoon wrap-up."

Dolores Puente realizes that teaching reading and writing cannot and should not be limited to one specified time slot in the day. Although Ms. Puente does set aside a specific amount of time each day for what she officially designates as reading—a time in which students are actively engaged in reading activities aimed directly at improving reading skills, strategies, and behaviors—this is only part of literacy learning in her classroom. Because she and her students use language throughout the school day, there are literacy opportunities from the moment students step into the classroom to the moment they leave.

Let's join Ms. Puente for a day with her third- and fourth-graders. The day is Monday, January 11. She has written the following schedule on the chalkboard.

9:00	Journal writing	11:45	Lunch
9:05	Silent reading	12:15	Read-aloud time
9:15	Morning meeting	12:35	Mathematics
9:25	News reports	1:25	Physical education
9:30	Reading	2:15	Science and health
10:30	Recess	2:50	Wrap-up
10:45	Language arts: response journals		

9:00—Journal Writing

As students arrive, they take out their journals and write their entry for the day. Ms. Puente, who believes in modeling the behavior she expects of her students, writes in her journal as well. Here is her entry for January 11:

Today we begin our unit on courage. I've been excited about this unit ever since I wrote the idea on my school calendar back in August. And I'm even more excited now because of the successful unit we had in the fall that revolved around the concept of thankfulness. What I had written on the yearly calendar was "courage"—the unifying theme for January–February. Courage to my way of thinking is a concept worth spending some time on, and January–February seems the perfect time to do it—because Martin Luther King Jr.'s birthday is in January, and February is both Black history month and a month to remember and honor past presidents. I'm looking forward to seeing how the kids will respond to this idea and what we will learn together.

As you can see from Ms. Puente's journal entry, much thought and planning occurred well before this day arrived. The idea for building activities around the central concept of courage had sprouted many months earlier. In fact, she had written it on her yearly planner back in August. Shortly after the winter holiday, Ms. Puente formulated a general goal for her literacy activities:

> To learn more about the concept of courage as displayed in the lives of people past and present from a variety of cultures as it is expressed in literature, music, art, science, and in the community, school, and families.

After formulating a general goal, she started to do some brainstorming as the second step in planning the unit's activities. She thought about her curriculum and how she could incorporate literacy activities and the theme of courage in a variety of subject areas. Here is what she jotted down in her brainstorming:

> **READING, LANGUAGE ARTS, AND SOCIAL STUDIES**
>
> Read and write biographies. Biography as a literary form or genre. Discuss various genres. Present opportunities for listening and viewing, also—tapes and films, a guest speaker. Choral reading and dramatics? Time lines? Graphic display showing what parts of the world courageous people have come from. Work on strategies of summarizing and determining what is important. Figurative language—simile and metaphor?
>
> **SCIENCE**
>
> We will be reading about the plant and animal kingdoms. Think about where courage might come in here—can plants be courageous? Animals? (Food for thought!) Present some biographies of courageous scientists, particularly those representing diverse cultures. George Washington Carver? East Indian physicist Subrahmanyan Chandrasekhar? Others? Work on strategies for gleaning information from informational books.

MATHEMATICS

Bring in biographies of mathematicians. How about engineer Mary Ross? This Cherokee woman helped launch Sally Ride into space! Continue working on strategies for solving story problems. Have students write story problems. Make books containing story problems? Put story problems on computer?

MUSIC

Songs about courage. Have students share contemporary songs that talk about courage. What about courageous musicians? Discuss when and why composers might write songs that instill or celebrate courage. Gospel music is very illustrative of this theme. Learn a gospel song that illustrates aspects of courage (ask Danika for suggestion).

PHYSICAL EDUCATION

Discuss courage for doing sports. Biographies of courageous sports figures. How about Native American long-distance runner Billy Mills? Have students read rules, directions, and daily reminders written on board. Use context cues. How about a "courage" box or "good sportsperson" box for students to write about evidence of courage or good sportsmanship?

HEALTH

We will be reading about diseases in the health text. People who have diseases need courage as well as the people who are trying to find cures. Read about Sadako and her battle with leukemia? Biographies of physicians and researchers. Work on summarizing strategy and other strategies for gleaning information from chapters in textbooks.

ART

How is courage expressed in art? Visit art museum to view selected paintings illustrating this theme? Create a classroom mural depicting our most courageous heroes? Are artists themselves courageous? What *about Hopi potter Al Qoyawayma, who switched from being a successful engineer to pursue his culture's ancient art? Children's book illustrator Filipino Jose Aruego. Chinese artist Maya Lin, who designed the Vietnam War Memorial. Does it take courage to pursue your artistic dreams? Let students pursue individual art projects if they are so inspired.*

After this brainstorming, Ms. Puente plotted her ideas on her monthly calendars, outlining her general plans for the weeks to come. Once she had her general plans outlined, she then focused on the individual weeks and days, making more detailed plans, ordering books and films, and lining up field trips and guest speakers.

Her overall plan, in the schedule in Figure 1 on pages 320–321, shows Ms. Puente's weekly plans in a bit more detail. The schedule in Figure 2 on pages 322–323 focuses even more closely on the first week of the unit. It is obvious that she has more ideas than it will be possible to implement. However, the activities that best fit her students and their mutual goals will come into focus as the days progress and her plan becomes more precise and detailed. Also, the ongoing needs and interests of her students will influence her choices of which activities to implement—plans for Tuesday will need to be altered to reflect what occurred on Monday. Ms. Puente's plans are guidelines that she knows will be shaped and reshaped day by day, minute by minute.

Let's return now to January 11, and see how Ms. Puente incorporates reading activities into every aspect of her students' day. After students finish writing in their journals, they begin silent reading.

9:05—Silent Reading

Each morning, students read silently from material of their choosing. While the students are reading this morning, Ms. Puente is reading also—an article from *The Reading Teacher*.

9:15—Morning Meeting

The morning meeting is a time to discuss daily concerns and to read and discuss the schedule for the day. Today, before the schedule is even discussed, Ms. Puente puts the outline for a courage map on the chalkboard and has students brainstorm to suggest examples of three related concepts—courageous people, courageous deeds, and other words for *courage*.

After students have given their responses, Ms. Puente explains that they will be focusing on the concept of courage for the next several weeks, thinking about how courage relates to many things they learn about and do, in school and out.

Ms. Puente asks a volunteer to transfer the responses she has written on the board onto a chart. The chart will be kept on display and new ideas added to it as the month progresses.

9:25 — News Reports

For several weeks, Ms. Puente's class has been working on giving news reports, which involve answering these questions: Who? What? When? Where? Why? How? Today, Ms. Puente will focus students' attention on the courage theme.

She begins by telling students she is going to read a newspaper article that she thinks illustrates the concept of courage and asks students to listen to see whether they agree with her. The article focuses on a single mother of five who is getting her college degree. After reading the article, Ms. Puente tells students why *she* thinks the woman shows courage and then encourages students to give their opinions.

Next, Ms. Puente displays the news report chart and shows students how she would complete it, sharing with them her thought processes as she does so.

NEWS REPORT CHART

<u>What is the report about?</u> A woman getting her college degree.

<u>Who is the report about?</u> Janet Crow, single mother of five.

<u>Where did the event take place?</u> State University, Middletown, U.S.A.

<u>When did the event take place?</u> December 23.

<u>How does this event show courage?</u> I think it takes courage to go back to school when you're older because there may not be many people your age at school and it's probably been a long time since you've had to study and take tests. Also, Janet had to give up some things for herself and her kids. She was taking a chance that getting a college education would allow her to get a better job so her kids might have more opportunities. I think that takes courage.

	WEEK 1	WEEK 2
Morning Meeting	Intro concept of courage, courage unit, and news reports on courage	Daily concerns Preview of week News reports
Reading and Language Arts **Social Studies** **Music** **Art**	Review skimming Begin "determining what is important" strategy Silent and oral reading Discuss biographies (culturally diverse) Figurative language Response journals Courage in gospel music: Learn Black National Anthem Film on Harriet Tubman	Practice "determining what is important" w/ bios Review focusing; start silent reading in bios Discuss vocab work Response journals Read aloud Maya Lin bio and "The Wall" by Eve Bunting Students plan memorial sculpture or other project Make timelines representing people in bios Research major event of time periods represented
Reading Aloud	Harriet Tubman biography	Tubman
Math	Independent and peer tutoring Group word problems Mystery word: *product*	Writing word problems Mary Ross bio Mystery word: *mathematician*
P.E. (Display bios of sports figures throughout unit)	Volleyball Context cues in directions, rules, etc.; "Courage" box	Volleyball Students write and read evaluation of group progress
Science or Health	Plant and animal kingdoms Strategies for gleaning info from informational books Ask question: Do plants and animals display courage? George W. Carver bio	Plant and animal kingdoms Strategies for remembering info (graphic organizers) Answer question: Do plants and animals display courage? Bio of monkey lady (get name)
Wrap-Up	Discuss concerns and highlights of day	Discuss concerns and highlights of day

FIGURE 1

Five-Week Plan for a Unit on Courage

Ms. Puente explains to students that their news reports for the next several weeks are to focus on courage. They can select articles from newspapers or magazines to read to the class, or they can write up a short report from TV or radio news. They can also report courageous events that take place in school or at home. As a class, they will do two things to help remember the people and events students report—complete a What, Who, Where, When, and How chart for each person and record all courageous events reported on a large sheet of butcher paper.

9:30—Reading, Language Arts, Social Studies, Music, and Art Block

After the morning meeting and news reports, Ms. Puente begins the reading, language arts, social studies, music, and art block of activities, which usually runs from 9:30 to 11:45, with a

WEEK 3	WEEK 4	WEEK 5
Daily concerns	Concerns; preview of week	Concerns; preview of week
Preview of week	Reports on courage of presidents	Reports on courage of presidents
News reports		
Finish reading bios	Continue adding to time lines	Make books or produce radio shows of bios
Motivate, explain, and model bio writing	Students write rough drafts of bios	Finish mural projects and time lines
Strategy (a writing strategy to be determined)	Students read bios aloud to groups	Read and perform bios for other classes and at nursing home
Students do prewriting for bios	Critique groups; revise bios	Trip to art museum to view portraits
Guest speaker: Native American Gary Cavanaugh	Continue mural and individual projects	Perform songs and dances
Students interview him for possible bio	Individual conferences to hear students read bios	Invite parents and others to class
Begin courage mural	Final draft of bios due Monday	Compare and contrast Native American and Asian music
Native American songs and drumming	Listen to Asian guest musician	
Tubman and Comanche chief Quanah Parker	Quanah Parker	Quanah Parker
Students find bios of mathematicians, especially those from other cultures	Independent skills work and peer tutoring	Work with other numeric bases
Mystery word: *dividend*	Einstein bio	Bio of An Wang
	Mystery word: *base*	Compose and read chart of possible careers in math
Dance	Dance	Dance
Read Billy Mills bio	Learn Asian dance	Review Native American and Asian dances
Learn Native American dance	Read diagrams	
Diseases	Diseases	Review science and health units
Review approaches to chapter reading	Re-read chapter to complete chart	Evaluations and reports
Read chapter using reading guide	Group work	
Group work	Read aloud bio on Constance Tom Noguichi	
Discuss concerns and highlights of day	Discuss concerns and highlights of day	Make drums for dances and songs

15-minute recess in the middle. Today, though, Ms. Puente is not following her usual time schedule. The activities for the morning meeting and news reports demanded extra time. Also, because the activities Ms. Puente has planned for reading and language arts require a sustained block of time, music and art will not be included in this time block today. However, if you look at her weekly planner, music activities are slated for later in the week. For their reading activity this morning, Ms. Puente and her students will discuss biographies as a special genre, review skimming as a reading strategy for selecting a biography to read in depth, and read silently for 15 minutes. Beginning tomorrow, Ms. Puente will also work with a selected group of students who need help with various skills. Language arts endeavors revolve around journal writing and social studies activities and include investigating courage as displayed in real people's lives. All of these subjects are interrelated; this interrelatedness mirrors the real world.

	MONDAY	TUESDAY
Morning Meeting	Semantic map on courage	Read and discuss daily concerns and schedule
	Explain and model news reports on courage	Explain and model second example of courage for news report
	Read and discuss daily schedule	
Reading and Language Arts	Intro bios as a genre	Motivate, explain, and model "determining what's important" strategy
Social Studies	Read snippets from bios to motivate	Group work practicing strategies with bios
Music	Review skimming strategy	Evaluate skills work and group functioning
Art	Students skim at least three books to select bio to read	
	SSR	
Recess		
Reading and Language Arts	Motivate, explain, and model response journals	Intro MLK and his colorful language—simile and metaphor
Social Studies	Distribute journals	Read excerpts from King bio
Music	Silent reading bios	Students write and illustrate own examples
Art	Write responses in journals	
Read Aloud	Harriet Tubman, Ch 1	Ch 2
Math (Mystery word for week: product)	Group work—Review steps to solve story problems (see Collier and Redmond article)	Answer math question from previous day
	Mystery word clue 1	Mystery word clue 2
	Independent work	Skills group—long division
P.E.—Volleyball	Review context cues while reading conduct reminders	Introduce "Courage" or "Sportsmanship" box
Science or Health	Review info vs. fiction	Meet with groups that want to do extra projects
	Review features of info books	Groups meet to share what they learned yesterday
	Pose courage theme—students skim and begin reading in trade books	
	Plant and animal kingdoms	
Wrap-Up	As needed	As needed

FIGURE 2

Week One of Unit on Courage

9:30—Reading: Motivating and Suggesting Strategies

To motivate her students, Ms. Puente has spent some time selecting biographies (with the help of librarians and media specialists as well as several bibliographies) that reflect her students' linguistic and cultural backgrounds, interests, and abilities. Because one of her goals is to expose students to individuals of many different cultures, her selection of biographies also reflects this.

On the chalkboard ledge and table, she has displayed numerous biographies of culturally diverse individuals. These range from picture books to lengthy chapter books.

Ms. Puente begins by telling students that all the books on display have one thing in common—each of them focuses on the life and deeds of a single individual. After that, she has students think about and discuss why a book might have been written about these people and writes students' suggestions on the board.

WEDNESDAY	THURSDAY	FRIDAY
Daily concerns and schedule	Daily concerns and schedule	Daily concerns and schedule
Form news report groups and review report model	Have one member from each group present news report in one category	Have one member from each group present news report in one category
Skills group on blending	Reading guide for practicing "determining what is important" with bios	See film on Harriet Tubman
	Evaluate activity and discuss as a class	Discuss courage
		Make chart
		a slave — (Harriet Tubman) — brave; smart — spiritual
Students share responses from journals	Courage as expressed in music	SSR in bios; meet individually with students
Silent reading in bios	Listen to recording of Black National Anthem; read lyrics; look for courage and examples of metaphor and simile; sing anthem	Students and teacher make portfolio entries
Write in journals		
Ch 3	Ch 4	Ch 5
Whole class—word problems	Students write story problems	Solve student story problems
Skills group—word problems	Skills group—long division	Skills group?
Math word clue 3	Math word clue 4	Reveal mystery word
		Treat—new math game for class
Review rules—use context cues	"Sportsmanship" box	Read "Sportsmanship" entries
		Choose sport
Film strip on classifying plants and animals	Read from George Washington Carver bio	Whole class shares journal responses
Group reading and recording in journals		Classify plants and animals as a whole-class activity
		Make chart
As needed	As needed	As needed

Next, she reads a paragraph or two from several of the biographies that she has preselected and that she knows will pique her students' interests. After reading, she reminds students that these books are called biographies—written accounts of a person's life. She writes *biography* on the board and talks about how biographies differ from other types of books. She asks students to tell about biographies they have read, note if they liked them, and explain why.

Ms. Puente explains to students that during the next five weeks they will be reading and writing biographies and will get to choose which biographies they want to read and whom they want to write a biography about. She discusses with them what they might expect to gain from biographies, why biographies are interesting and informative, and how the ideas revealed in biographies might be useful in their own lives.

To help students decide which biography they want to read, Ms. Puente suggests that a good strategy to use is skimming. She models the strategy with several of the biographies—reading the

Teachers can make a number of books available and invite students to skim these to select one to read in depth.

title and the table of contents, scanning the chapters from beginning to end, commenting on illustrations and photographs, and maybe reading a few passages aloud. Then she models the thinking she went through in trying to decide whether or not *Beyond the Myth: The Story of Joan of Arc* by Polly Schoyer Brooks was the biography she wanted to read:

> Hmm. This might be an interesting book. I like reading about heroic women. But I see that Joan of Arc lived in the 15th century, and I think I'd like to read about someone a little more modern. Also, it's kind of long and has a lot of words I don't know. I like learning new words, but it may take me too long to read if I have to stop and look up a lot of words in the dictionary, and I wouldn't want to skip too many words. I think this is a book Tara would like—and I'm going to recommend it to her— but I think I'll see what some of the other books are like.

Ms. Puente then models skimming and considers a few more books before letting students choose their own books to skim. Finally, she tells students to skim at least three books and then choose one of those to read. They will have until recess, at 10:30, to skim and get started on their reading.

10:45—Language Arts: Response Journals

The next activity, writing in and sharing response journals—which Ms. Puente has labeled in her plans under the subject language arts—is a continuation of the previous reading activity and is one the students are familiar with, having kept reading journals of various sorts since the beginning of the school year. It is also an activity students will be involved in daily until they finish reading their selected biographies.

Ms. Puente's students have made dual entries in their journals before, but because they will be doing something slightly different in these journals, she spends a little time motivating, explaining, and modeling the procedure.

"You know," Ms. Puente tells her students, "when I was reading through biographies to bring to class, I kept reading things that made me stop and think, 'Wow, that's neat,' or 'I know how she feels. I felt that way myself.' Things like that. I'll show you what I mean."

Writing personal responses in journals requires that students think about the ideas in a text and express their ideas in writing.

After that, Ms. Puente reads a sentence or two from a biography about mathematician and computer genius An Wang, to illustrate her point, and then writes the following on the board:

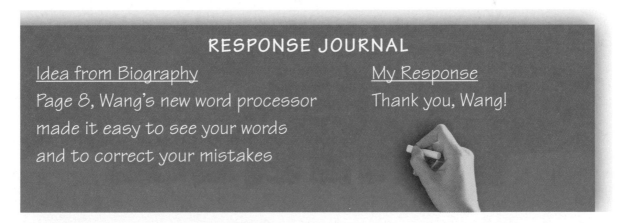

RESPONSE JOURNAL

Idea from Biography
Page 8, Wang's new word processor made it easy to see your words and to correct your mistakes

My Response
Thank you, Wang!

As Ms. Puente explains to her students, "When I read that Wang had invented the word processor, it really hit me how this man had made my job so much easier and more enjoyable. I really feel grateful to him."

Ms. Puente proceeds to describe several other types of responses she had—questions brought to mind, ideas that prompted her to make connections with her own experiences, strong feelings she had in response to certain events or ideas—and writes these on the board. After sufficient explanation and modeling, Ms. Puente tells students she wants them to use their journals similarly while reading in their biographies—to write, for example, a quotation, idea, or word on the left side of the journal page and their response to the quote, idea, or word, next to it on the right side of the page. This kind of activity encourages the generative learning we discuss in Chapter 11.

Next, Ms. Puente distributes the journals, but before students begin reading and writing in them, she makes certain that they are clear on the purpose and procedure for this activity. She assigns reading buddies to students who might need extra help with reading and writing. Buddies go to special locations designated to be conference areas—places where students are free to interact with each other without disturbing other students.

While students are reading silently and writing in their journals, Ms. Puente is reading a biography and writing in her journal. Her classroom aide (who is available every day from 10:30 to 12:00) circulates among students to offer advice and encourage students to keep on task.

Before students leave for lunch each day at 11:45, Ms. Puente asks if any of them have something they would like to share from their journals. If so, a few students read from their journals; if not, Ms. Puente shares something from hers.

12:15—Read-Aloud Time

This routine fosters quiet and rest after an active play period. It also provides students with an opportunity to hear good literature skillfully read. Today, Ms. Puente begins reading aloud from *Harriet Tubman* by George Sullivan. To preserve the atmosphere of calm that prevails at this time of day, she begins reading with only a brief introduction in which she talks about courage and how students will see many examples of courage as they listen to the biography. Before she begins reading the first chapter, she encourages them to think about and remember one example of Tubman's courage that is illustrated in the chapter.

12:35—Mathematics

Before students begin independent work and small-group instruction on a specific math skill, Ms. Puente conducts a 15-minute whole-class lesson, which includes two topics: reviewing how to solve story problems and presenting the new "mystery" math word for the week.

At the beginning of the lesson, Ms. Puente writes this problem on the board: The gym floor is 100' × 50'. How far did Matt run if he ran 10 lengths of the gym?

"Does this problem sound familiar?" she asks her students.

The students are well aware of what Ms. Puente is talking about. The week before, they had been keeping track of how many times they ran across the gym but didn't calculate how *far* they had run.

Questions to Ask When Solving Story Problems

What situation is described?

Can I describe the situation with a drawing, diagram, or mathematical sentence?

What am I trying to find out?

Do I need to combine, separate, or compare?

Are all the data given necessary?

Are the data complete?

Do I know what to do to determine the answer?

How will I know if the answer I get is reasonable?

Ms. Puente refers her class to the questions for solving word problems shown on page 326 (Collier & Redmond, 1974), and together they come up with this equation: 100' × 10' = 1,000'.

Ms. Puente challenges students with these questions: "Did Matt run more than a mile or less than a mile? How much more than a mile or less than a mile? Try and find out, and we'll discuss the answers tomorrow."

Before they begin their independent and small-group sessions, Ms. Puente shows students the first clue for the "mystery" math word for the week. The clue is $A \times B = C$. Students are not to say the word out loud but to put their written guesses with their name and the date on them in the mystery word box. Each day, Ms. Puente reports how many have correctly guessed the word and gives a new clue. At the end of the week, she reveals the mystery word, and if 90 percent of the class has guessed it, the class gets a special reward. The mystery word this week is *product*.

1:25—Physical Education

For the next few weeks, Ms. Puente's students will be learning how to play volleyball. Besides actually playing the game, they will need to learn volleyball rules and review etiquette for traveling to and from the gym. Both activities will require some reading. Because the class has recently completed a unit on using context cues to figure out unknown words, she decides to reinforce this skill in reading these rules, which are rich in context cues.

Before students go to the gym to play volleyball, Ms. Puente writes these sentences on the board:

When we walk to the gym, we need to remember that other classes are working. If we are noisy, we might d_____b them. Let's try to remember to walk q_____y.

Ms. Puente encourages her students to use context cues to figure out the unknown words. She asks students who can guess what the unknown words are to raise their hands and tells them she will know if they had the right words if they do as the sentences tell them on their walk to the gym.

After students return from the gym, Ms. Puente praises their excellent behavior and then discusses the missing words in the sentences on the board, encouraging students to explain just how they used context to determine the words and which clues in the sentences enabled them to figure out the unknown words.

2:15—Science and Health

Last week, Ms. Puente began motivating students for their unit on the plant and animal kingdoms. She decided that reading and research on these topics would best be accomplished through both group and individual work. When planning goals and activities for the unit, she also made provisions

Ms. Puente always makes sure her classroom has comfortable places for independent reading.

for those with special needs and interests. Additionally, the books Ms. Puente selected for the unit reflect the varied reading abilities of her students to ensure that all students succeed with the reading they do.

To begin, Ms. Puente reviews the special features of informational books, reminding students that informational books are written and organized differently from picture books and chapter books because their main purpose is to provide the reader with information, whereas stories are primarily meant to entertain. To illustrate what she means about communicating information being the main goal of informational books, she reads a few book titles aloud and asks students to tell what sort of information they think each book will disclose. Next, she explains that informational books often have a number of special features. These include a table of contents, headings and subheadings, introductory paragraphs and summaries, graphs, illustrations, labels, charts, maps, indexes, and glossaries. Ms. Puente points out these features in several books she has preselected for this purpose. After Ms. Puente has reviewed these features, she asks students why the author might have included them.

Next, Ms. Puente divides the class into two groups—those who want to learn more about plants and those who want to learn more about animals. Each student is to select three books to skim. Paying attention to the various features of the books—table of contents, headings and subheadings, introductory paragraphs and summaries, graphs, illustrations, labels, charts, maps, indexes, glossaries—students are to record in their informational books journal one piece of information they find interesting about each book. The next day they will meet again with their groups to share what they found. To tie in the courage theme, Ms. Puente also asks students to think about the question of whether or not plants or animals are capable of courage. They will discuss this idea as they get further into their study of the plant and animal kingdoms.

Students gather with their groups and select and skim their books, recording the title and one piece of information from each in their journals. Because students have differing interests and abilities and work at varying rates, Ms. Puente has provided for these individual needs:

- Students who need special assistance—for example, English-language learners or visually challenged students—will be assigned reading partners.
- Additional activities will challenge students who are particularly talented in various areas. Students can create a graph, either on graph paper or on the computer, indicating the number and kind of features found in the various books on their selected topic; write glossaries for those books without them and include student glossary pages in the books for other readers to use; or draw additional illustrations, charts, or maps for the various books.

■ These projects are optional and ongoing, with students working on them at their own pace. Ms. Puente will meet with students interested in pursuing these projects to explain how to do them. Any student in the class has the option of working on these projects. Students can work on them individually or in groups. Also, students might choose to work on these projects at other times of the day when their other work is completed.

2:50—Wrap-Up

About 10 or 15 minutes before the end of the day, one of Ms. Puente's students plays the class theme song on the xylophone—a simple melody the class composed at the beginning of the year. This tune gives students a sense of order and belonging—they expect it, they know what it means, and it is *their* class song. By the time the song is completed, students are in their seats and ready to review the schedule for the day, which is written on the chalkboard. Together they read and briefly talk about each subject or activity, with a student in charge of leading the discussion. During this time, students ask questions, share something they enjoyed or learned, or bring up problems they had. Problems that can't be resolved easily are tabled until there is a better time for resolution, perhaps at the next day's morning meeting time.

3:00—School Day Ends

After the students have gone, and while the day's events are still fresh in her mind, Ms. Puente begins planning for the next day. She knows this planning can't take place without first reviewing the day's activities and reflecting on what worked, what didn't work, and why. Quickly, she makes a few entries in her teacher's logbook. On Jenny's page, she writes *Used context cues to figure out several unknown words she ran across in her reading,* and on Terrell's page, *Pleased to see Terrell become extremely absorbed in Margo Sorenson's* Fight in the Fields, *a hi-lo adventure biography about Cesar Chavez. Ask him about it.* She jots down comments for a few other students and glances briefly at some of her yearly goals.

Next, as she looks at what she had planned for Tuesday, she realizes she will have to make some changes. In math, some students had a difficult time solving the word problem. Instead of taking whole-group time for another problem, she decides she will group the students who need a bit more instruction for a mini-lesson. Other students then will have more time to work independently and to tutor other students. Because her parent volunteer comes on Tuesdays from 12:25 to 1:25, the volunteer can monitor these students while Ms. Puente works with the group that needs more assistance on word problems. She jots down her plans, makes a few additional comments in her logbook, and walks to the teachers' lounge to get a well-deserved cup of coffee.

Fostering Higher-Order Thinking and Deep Understanding in Content Areas

CLASSROOM VIGNETTE

*M*ichael Pellegrini never thought he would become a primary-grade teacher. In college, he had majored in history and minored in political science, and his plan was to be a high school history teacher. Then, while he was observing elementary classrooms during his first methods course, Michael was struck by the range of understanding and reasoning skills he observed. In classrooms at every grade level, some students understood many topics deeply and were already adept and even sophisticated thinkers. They could identify a problem, investigate it thoroughly, break it into logical components, and pursue a chain of reasoning that led to valid conclusions. Unfortunately, other children in these same classrooms virtually never seemed to engage in these sorts of activities. Not only could they not identify a problem, break it into logical components, and come to understand it thoroughly, but they seemed to have no interest in doing so.

These observations led Michael to an abrupt shift in his career plans. He switched his major to elementary education and developed a particular interest in teaching higher-order thinking and fostering understanding in younger students. On graduating, he took a position as a first-grade teacher, believing that higher-order thinking and deep understanding can and should be nurtured, even in very young children. And he found his belief to be true. You can foster significant thinking and understanding at any grade level. It is critical to do so in first grade, and it continues to be critical to do so in sixth grade and beyond.

Two Roads to Competent Thinking and Learning

As both the chapter title and our opening scenario suggest, this chapter deals with two closely related topics—fostering students' higher-order thinking and fostering their deep understanding of topics. Not only are these topics closely related; they are thoroughly intertwined. Students can engage in higher-order thinking only when they think about topics they understand. The more thoroughly they understand a topic—the richer their schema for the topic—the better their higher-order thinking will be. Thus, we need to teach students how to think, and we need to give them the raw material of thinking—deep understanding of topics—that will enable them to use and hone their thinking skills.

Fostering Higher-Order Thinking

We define higher-order thinking quite broadly. A number of authorities have contributed to our understanding of the concept. They include philosophers such as Robert Ennis (1985); psychologists such as John Bransford and Ann Brown (Bransford, Brown, & Cocking, 2000), Howard Gardner (2005), Lauren Resnick (1987), and Robert Sternberg (Sternberg & Spear-Swerling, 1996; Sternberg & Grigorenko, 2004); and critical thinking proponents such as Arthur Costa (2001; Costa & Kallick, 2004). We have gleaned valuable insights from each of them. Here, we briefly define higher-order thinking and describe two taxonomies of thinking skills that we believe will guide you as you simultaneously teach content in such areas as social studies and science and develop your students' thinking ability.

After noting that higher-order thinking resists precise definition, Resnick (1987) lists some key features of higher-order thinking. Although lengthier than a typical definition, Resnick's list does an excellent job of capturing the full meaning of the concept, and we therefore present all of it here.

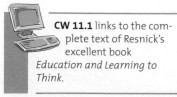

CW 11.1 links to the complete text of Resnick's excellent book *Education and Learning to Think*.

- Higher-order thinking is nonalgorithmic. That is, the path of action is not fully specified in advance.

- Higher-order thinking tends to be complex. The total path is not "visible" (mentally speaking) from any single vantage point.
- Higher-order thinking often yields multiple solutions, each with costs and benefits, rather than unique solutions.
- Higher-order thinking involves nuanced judgments and interpretation.
- Higher-order thinking involves the application of multiple criteria, which sometimes conflict with one another.
- Higher-order thinking often involves uncertainty. Not everything that bears on the task at hand is known.
- Higher-order thinking involves self-regulation of the thinking process. We do not recognize higher-order thinking in an individual when someone else calls the plays at every step.
- Higher-order thinking involves imposing meaning, finding structure in apparent disorder.
- Higher-order thinking is effortful. There is considerable mental work involved in the kinds of elaborations and judgments required.

We suggest that you keep these features clearly in mind as you work with students and repeatedly ask yourself if you are engaging students in these sorts of thinking.

As noted, one of the two roads to competent thinking and learning is to repeatedly engage students in higher-order thinking by asking higher-order questions, an approach strongly endorsed by both common sense and recent theory and research (Beck & McKeown, 2001; RAND Reading Study Group, 2002; Taylor, Pearson, Peterson, & Rodriguez, 2003). We have found two guides to types of questions particularly useful. The first of these, and the source we recommend as your major guide to asking higher-order questions, is *A Taxonomy for Learning, Teaching, and Assessing* (Anderson & Krathwohl, 2001). This is a considerably enlarged and updated version of Benjamin Bloom's *Taxonomy of Education Objectives* (1956), which has been the standard guide to types of thinking and questioning for nearly 50 years. Below is a simplified version of Anderson and Krathwohl's taxonomy. The definitions of the first six types are taken nearly verbatim from Anderson and Krathwohl. The last definition reflects a mixture of their thinking and our own.

English Learners

Sometimes people think that higher-order thinking is just for some students, but this is absolutely not the case. All students—including all English-language learners—need and deserve instruction and practice with higher-order thinking.

- *Remembering*—retrieving relevant knowledge from long-term memory
- *Understanding*—constructing meaning from instructional messages, including oral, written, and graphic communications
- *Applying*—carrying out or using a procedure in a given situation
- *Analyzing*—breaking material into its constituent parts and determining how the parts relate to one another and to an overall structure or purpose
- *Evaluating*—making judgments based on criteria and standards
- *Creating*—putting elements together to form a coherent or functional whole, reorganizing elements into a new pattern or structure
- *Being metacognitive*—being aware of one's own comprehension and being able and willing to repair comprehension breakdowns when they occur

It is not the case that all of these types of questions need to be asked about every selection students read. However, all of these questions need to be asked over time, and all need to be asked frequently. We need to be particularly careful to avoid asking only lower-level questions—those that demand only factual knowledge. Classroom observations have revealed that too many teachers fall into the trap of doing so.

Here is an example of each type of question, based on a story you know—*The Three Little Pigs:*

- *Remembering*—What did each of the three little pigs build his house from?
- *Understanding*—Why isn't straw a very good building material?
- *Applying*—Suppose you had to build a house. What material would you build it with?
- *Analyzing*—In what ways is a brick house better than a straw or stick house?
- *Evaluating*—What do you think of the first little pig's decision to build a straw house? Why do you think this?
- *Creating*—What are some things the first little pig might have done to make his house safer from the wolf?
- *Being metacognitive*—When you learned that we were going to read the story of *The Three Little Pigs,* how difficult did you think it would be? Why did you think this?

The other source that we have found particularly useful in choosing questions to ask is Robert Sternberg's work (Sternberg & Spear-Swerling, 1996) on what he calls a "triarchic theory of intelligence." The central thesis of Sternberg's theory is that there are three basic kinds of thinking: analytic, creative, and practical. He defines these three sorts of thinking as follows:

- *Analytic thinking* involves analyzing, judging, evaluating, comparing and contrasting, and examining.
- *Creative thinking* involves creating, discovering, producing, imagining, and supposing.
- *Practical thinking* involves practicing, using, applying, and implementing.

As Sternberg notes, schools typically focus on analytic thinking and largely neglect the other two sorts. This, he argues, is very unfortunate, because all three sorts of thinking are important, both in the classroom and beyond it. We strongly concur and suggest that, as you create questions and plan other activities, you frequently make it a point to include all three sorts of thinking. Here are examples representing each of Sternberg's three sorts of thinking, again based on *The Three Little Pigs.*

- *Analytic thinking*—Why isn't straw a very good building material?
- *Creative thinking*—What are some things the first little pig might have done to make his house safer from the wolf?
- *Practical thinking*—Suppose you had to build a house. What material would you build it with?

As you can see, these are three of the seven questions we used to illustrate use of Anderson and Krathwohl's taxonomy. The two systems overlap. However, we think it is useful to consider Sternberg's scheme as well as Anderson and Krathwohl's to avoid putting too much emphasis on analytic thinking, which sometimes happens in schools.

Whatever system you use to remind yourself to ask higher-order questions, the first thing to keep in mind about fostering higher-order thinking is to re-

ASSESSMENT

One method for communicating students' achievement to parents—which also requires students to use analytic, creative, and practical thinking—is a quarterly conference in which the student describes what her goals for the quarter were, shows her work, talks about her successes and shortcomings, and gives her goals for the next quarter.

English Learners

Focusing solely on analytic thinking can be particularly unproductive with English-language learners. Be sure to give students who are in the process of building their proficiency in English plenty of opportunities for creative and practical thinking.

peatedly engage students in such thinking. The second thing to keep in mind is to foster students' understanding of topics so that they have something to actively think about.

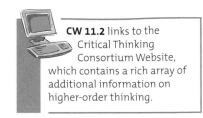

CW 11.2 links to the Critical Thinking Consortium Website, which contains a rich array of additional information on higher-order thinking.

Teaching for Understanding

Understanding enables a person "to perform in a variety of thought-demanding ways . . . [to] explain, muster evidence, find examples, generalize, apply concepts, analogize, represent in a new way, and so on" (Perkins, 1993). As David Perkins and his colleagues (Blythe, 1998; Perkins, 1992, 1993, 2004; Wiske, 1998) emphasize, to teach for understanding we must go beyond simply presenting students with information and ensure that students

- understand topics deeply,
- retain important information, and
- actively use the knowledge they gain.

The reader who has attained an understanding perspective consciously seeks understanding and uses the knowledge she gains through reading. Of course, everything we have discussed in this book thus far has understanding as an ultimate goal. But here we treat understanding as a specific goal, and there is a good deal of evidence that we should do so.

As authorities such as Resnick (1987), Perkins (1992), Fred Newmann (1996), the RAND Reading Study Group (2002), and Grant Wiggins (Wiggins & McTighe, 1998) point out, expectations of schooling and the level of knowledge and skills that our society requires have risen dramatically in recent years and will continue to rise, perhaps even more dramatically, in the future. Yet, as indicated by these same authorities, by empirical data such as those produced by the National Assessment of Education Progress (Perie, Moran, Lutkus, & Tirre, 2005), and by reports such as *The Twin Challenges of Mediocrity and Inequality* (Sum, Kirsch, & Taggart, 2002), few U.S. students are performing at the advanced levels necessary for full participation in our society. Teaching for understanding can change this.

We want to emphasize four key attributes of teaching for understanding. The first and most basic one is ours, and the remaining three are from Richard Prawat (1989):

- It takes time.
- It requires focus and coherence.
- It involves negotiation.
- It is highly analytic and diagnostic in nature.

Almost certainly the most basic fact to keep in mind as you consider teaching for understanding is that it takes time. You simply cannot develop the knowledge and attitudes necessary for students to understand topics deeply, retain important information, and actively use their knowledge without spending significant amounts of time on the topics you choose to teach. However, the time is well spent because when we don't teach for understanding, the knowledge students acquire is fragile, inert, of little or no use in solving real problems, and soon gone.

Because teaching for understanding requires more time, it also demands focus. If we are going to spend a good deal of time on something, we had

Because teaching for understanding requires negotiating meaning with students, it often takes time and a good deal of mental effort. But the reward of true understanding is worth the effort.

better be sure just what it is we are spending time on. Similarly, if we are going to spend a good deal of time on a topic, it needs to be coherent—to us as teachers and to students as learners. Thus, for example, if students are reading narratives with strong plots, such as *Lunch Money* by Andrew Clements or *Owen Foote, Mighty Scientist* by Stephanie Greene, and we are focusing on plot, it is important that both we and the students understand that we are focusing on plot, understand what plot is, and understand why we are focusing on plot.

In order to ensure coherence, we are frequently going to have to negotiate meaning with students. As we discussed in Chapter 1, the process of making meaning is a constructive one. Meaning does not simply spring from a text to the reader's head. Readers must grapple with a text, manipulate ideas, shape them, and interpret them if they are to derive significant learning from what they read. What the reader gets from reading depends heavily on the sum total of her experience and on her unique intellectual makeup. No two readers or listeners will construct exactly the same meaning from a particular text or discussion. Thus, in situations in which we want students to construct the same meaning or very similar meanings, we will often need to engage in negotiation—a give-and-take discussion in which students and their teacher talk through a topic, often re-reading a text and listening to what others say about it, attempting to understand what each person is saying, and coming to some agreement on the meaning.

This sort of negotiation is shown in the following excerpt provided by Isabel Beck and Margaret McKeown and their colleagues (Beck, McKeown, Hamilton, & Kucan, 1997, pp. 96–97), in which a teacher and several students in Pennsylvania negotiate the meaning of a fourth-grade Pennsylvania history text. The passage the group is considering is taken from Lucille Wallower and Ellen Wholey's *All About Pennsylvania* and describes some insights George Washington had about the willingness of the French to relinquish their holdings in Pennsylvania:

Washington gave the Governor's letter to the French leader. No one knew this, but Washington made a drawing of the fort. Washington saw that the French planned to make war on the English. At last, the French leader gave Washington a message for the governor. He said that the French would not leave Pennsylvania.

Teacher: So, what's the author's message here?

Kalondah: That, um, the French aren't gonna leave Pennsylvania. And they just plan to keep it.

Teacher: The French plan to keep it for themselves. What's the author say to make Kalondah think that?

Deandre: They were planning to stay, and I think that they're bound to have a war.

Teacher: Deandre said that they were bound to have a war. Hmm. What do you think gave Deandre that idea?

Kristen: Because the governor knew that, um, the French were staying because, um, I think he knew that the French wouldn't just let the English have it without having a war.

What is important to recognize here is how the teacher's prompts serve to focus the discussion, get several students involved, and help the students come to some consensus on the meaning of the passage.

Finally, teaching for understanding is both analytic and diagnostic. That is, the teacher needs to analyze students' responses in an effort to determine what they are thinking, decide whether or not there is a problem of understanding, and, if there is a problem, diagnose its nature and come up with a solution. Suppose that the social studies passage just discussed had produced these responses:

Teacher: So, what's the author's message here?

Kalondah: That, um, Washington wants to make war on the French.

Teacher: Now, why do you say that, Kalondah?

Kalondah: Well, because he made a map.

Teacher: That's true. He did make a map, and he might have made it because he wanted to make war on the French. But we don't really know that. Can anyone suggest another reason he might have made a map?

Deandre: Maybe he didn't want a war. Maybe he just thought that the French might want a war, and he wanted a map just in case, in case they made war, so he could fight back.

Teacher: Now what Deandre said is certainly possible. And what Kalondah said also makes sense. The truth is, we're not sure what Washington's plans are yet. He might want a war, or he might just want to be prepared in case the French start a war, or he might have other plans. We'll have to read further and see if we can learn more.

Here, the teacher has tried to find out what caused Kalondah to make the inference she did, how other students are interpreting the passage, and what the passage actually does and does not reveal. And the result of her analysis and diagnosis is the very reasonable conclusion that the class will need to read further to find out more about just what is going on. We believe that many discussions of text will take a form much like this, as students and teachers delve into texts and their interpretations of them in the quest for true understanding.

Reflect and Apply

1. Choose a short expository text that you might use in teaching science, health, social studies, or some other content area, and write one question illustrating each of Anderson and Krathwohl's seven levels of thinking. Then scramble those questions, give them to a classmate without indicating their levels, and ask your partner to identify the level of each. Afterward, discuss the extent to which you agree on the levels. If you don't agree perfectly, don't be concerned. The purpose of using a questioning scheme such as Anderson and Krathwohl's is to be sure you ask various types of questions, not to classify each question as this type or that type.

2. One of the key attributes of teaching for understanding is that it takes time, more time than we often allot to topics in school. Take a moment to think about a fairly difficult concept that you understand quite thoroughly. Now, think back and try to remember how you came to understand the concept—when you were first introduced to it, how you were first introduced to it, what you did to initially learn it, how you refined and extended your learning of it, and when and how you actually made use of the concept. Next, consider the total amount of time you put into mastering this difficult concept. With a classmate, share recollections of learning the concept and the time it took you to do so.

Practical Approaches to Higher-Order Thinking and Deep Understanding

ASSESSMENT

The SRE lesson plan in the *Assessments and Lesson Plans* supplement is designed to promote deep understanding. When you read the lesson, think about how you would assess its results.

Here, we describe several approaches to fostering higher-order thinking and deep understanding—teaching for understanding units, text talk and questioning the author, reciprocal teaching, and jigsaw. These approaches differ in their makeup, the sorts of understanding they foster, and the amount of time they require. Together, they provide you with a rich array of ways to develop students' understanding of the content you view as important and at the same time improve their higher-order thinking.

Teaching for Understanding Units

Several author teams have developed frameworks for instructional units that foster higher-order thinking and deep understanding. These include Fred Newmann's authentic assessment (Newmann, 1996, 2000) and Grant Wiggins and Jay McTighe's understanding by design (McTighe, Seif, & Wiggins, 2004; Wiggins & McTighe, 1998). These and other frameworks have much to offer. However, David Perkins's framework—developed with Howard Gardner, Vito Perone, and others at the Harvard Graduate School of Education's Project Zero, is both excellent and the approach most fully described (Blythe, 1998; Perkins, 1992, 2004; Perkins & Blythe, 1994; Wiske, 1998); it is the approach we describe here.

Perkins's teaching for understanding units (TFU units) typically last two to four weeks, which allows students the time needed to reach true understanding and gives them opportunities to establish links between the many concepts necessary to full understanding. These units follow a four-part framework:

- Generative topics
- Understanding goals
- Understanding performances
- Ongoing assessment

Here, we define, elaborate on, and give an example or two of each of these parts.

Generative Topics

Generative topics are central to the subject area students are studying, accessible to students, and connectable to many other topics in the same subject and in other areas. Generative topics can be concepts, themes, procedures, historical periods, theories, ideas, and the like. For example, in the field of literature, plot is a generative topic. Plot is central to the study of literature, is an important element in many types of literature and in many individual pieces of literature, and exists outside of literature as well. Historical episodes—for example, the Civil War period—basically follow a plot, as do our lives. As another example, consider the field of history. Cause and effect is a concept central to much of history, and, like the generative concept of plot, cause and effect also exists in areas outside of history. In fact, many, if not most, fields of study—science, humanities, and art, for example—deal with cause and effect. As still another example, consider the idea of beauty. Beauty is a central concept in art and literature, of course, but beauty also plays an important role in our lives and even in science. Frank Press (1984), former president of the National Academy of Sciences, once spoke of the discovery of the double helix that broke the genetic code as not only rational, but beautiful as well. Finally, consider the topic of health. Health can be considered a part of science, but it is also a subtopic of social science; there is psychological health as well as physical health. Of course, health can also be related to government—as when a powerful world leader becomes ill—and it can be related to myriad other areas, including our daily lives. Some examples of generative topics for first-graders and fifth-graders are listed in Figure 11.1.

Public library, bookstore, and children's literature Websites can lead you to literature on the topics you are exploring with the students in your classroom. For example, a quick search of the Hennepin County libraries' Website (www.hennepin.lib.mn.us), a Minneapolis-area library system that two of us use a lot, yielded 44 children's titles on the subject of "seasons of the year." At the Barnes & Noble Website (www.barnesandnoble.com), we searched books for children using the key word *seasons* and found 2,180 possibilities. The Barnes & Noble site also showed book covers and listed book reviews from sources such as the *School Library Journal* and the *Horn Book*.

Working with highly generative topics whenever possible is important because, as we have already noted, teaching for understanding takes time. If you are going to spend a good deal of time on a topic—and that's what you do when you teach for understanding—you need to carefully choose topics that are important, that connect to many other topics, and that students can access and appreciate.

English Learners

If you have English-language learners in your classroom, an additional criterion for choosing generative topics is that at least some of the topics be particularly valuable for students who are just learning English and are perhaps relatively recent immigrants.

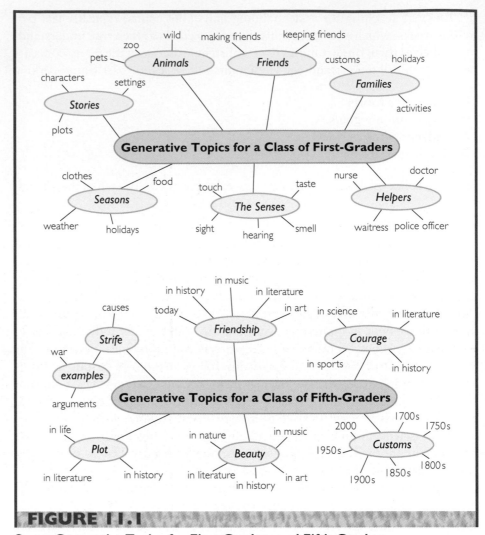

FIGURE 11.1

Some Generative Topics for First-Graders and Fifth-Graders

Understanding Goals

One problem with generative topics is that they are often too broad. The concept of beauty, for example, could be studied in any time period, in any medium, and in almost any field. Even though understanding units may last for two to four weeks, the time available is obviously not infinite, so you almost always need to select one or several parts of a broad generative topic to deal with and some specific goals to be achieved. One possible understanding goal for sixth-graders who are studying the idea of beauty might be to understand that people's idea of physical beauty has changed over time—for example, to understand that the ancient Romans' idea of beauty differed from that held by Italians during the Renaissance and from that held by Italians today. Another possible understanding goal for these sixth-graders might be to grasp that the idea of what constitutes physical beauty also differs from culture to culture and even from individual to individual.

Or consider again the generative topic of health, and assume that the students you are concerned with are in first or second grade. Obviously, first- and second-graders will be able to deal with only some aspects of health. They could, for example, understand and profit from studying some aspects of nutrition. In this case, one goal for understanding might be to have students learn the six types of food described in a contemporary food pyramid (grains, vegetables, fruits, oils, milk, and meat and beans). Another might be to understand what foods help keep them healthy. And another might be to become more knowledgeable consumers, learning at least a little about food labels and advertising.

These goals were in fact developed by a group of first- and second-grade teachers we worked with as they designed an understanding unit on nutrition (Asfeld, Schwab, Gagliardi, & Henke, 1994), and we will use their unit as an example as we discuss the remainder of Perkins's four-part format. Their understanding unit was developed for typical classes of first- or second-graders and involved children in a variety of interesting, involving, instructional, and fun activities over a period of about three weeks. An outline of the unit is shown in Figure 11.2. As the titles of the lessons suggest, the unit dealt with a variety of topics—including grains, vegetables, fruits, labels, menus, and advertising—and it involved students in a variety of activities—including listening, reading, writing, planning, and creating. This is indeed a significant set of topics and issues, and we would expect some significant learning and understanding to develop during the three-week unit. It is also a topic for which there are many children's books available. Asfeld and her colleagues relied primarily on Loreen Leedy's *The Edible Pyramid*. Newer children's books on nutrition include *Eating Well* by Lisa Trumbauer, *Eating Right* by Mary Elizabeth Salzmann, *Food Rules!* by Bill Haduch, and *Good Enough to Eat: A Kid's Guide to Food and Nutrition* by Lizzy Rockwell.

LESSON	TOPIC
1	Why Do We Need Nutrition?
2	Introduction to the Food Pyramid
3	Grains
4	Vegetables
5	Fruits
6	Oils
7	Milk
8	Meat and Beans
9	How to Read a Food Label
10	Introduction to Menu Planning
11	Menu Planning
12	Looking at Food Advertising
13	Letters to Consumers
14	Designing a Commercial
15	Conclusion

FIGURE 11.2

Lessons from a First-Grade Understanding Unit on Nutrition

Understanding Performances

In Perkins's four-part framework, students demonstrate their learning and understanding in what he calls "understanding performances." Understanding performances are student activities that require an understanding of the content you are teaching. Thus, when students complete an understanding performance, they demonstrate that they have in fact understood. During the three-week nutrition unit we have outlined, students took part in a number of understanding performances. Fairly early in the unit, they demonstrated their understanding of the six types of food in the food pyramid by classifying products presented in commercials according to their food groups. Later in the unit, they demonstrated their understanding of how foods are labeled by discussing food labels they had located. And still later, they demonstrated a very practical understanding of nutrition by developing nutritious menus. The following list shows these and some other understanding performances students engaged in:

- Classifying products presented in food commercials
- Journaling about food intake
- Discussing food labels
- Writing letters to consumers
- Dramatizing grocery store experiences
- Making a commercial focusing on nutritional values
- Developing nutritious menus

As the list shows, these children engaged in a lot of understanding performances. Also, as we just noted, they engaged in these understanding performances

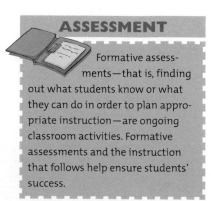

ASSESSMENT

Formative assessments—that is, finding out what students know or what they can do in order to plan appropriate instruction—are ongoing classroom activities. Formative assessments and the instruction that follows help ensure students' success.

throughout the unit; they did not wait until the end of the unit to demonstrate their understanding. This is important; students should be engaged in understanding performances throughout the period in which they are studying a topic.

Ongoing Assessment

The last part of Perkins's four-part framework, ongoing assessment, is closely related to understanding performances. Just as students should be engaged in understanding performances throughout the unit, students and teachers should be engaged in ongoing assessment throughout the unit. Of course, one of the things that teachers assess is students' understanding performances—for example, whether or not the first- or second-graders taking part in the nutrition unit can correctly classify food items in the appropriate food groups. If some of them cannot, then they need feedback and some reteaching, and they need the feedback and reteaching early on so that they do not continue through the unit with misconceptions about foods and food groups and the resulting confusion. Each of the later understanding performances in Asfeld and her colleagues' nutrition unit—journaling about food intake, discussing labels, and so on—offers additional opportunities for ongoing assessment and for feedback and reteaching, if needed. However, ongoing assessment is not limited to understanding performances. At all points in the unit and during all activities—individual conferences, small-group discussions, writing assignments, or other events—it is important to be assessing whether or not students are understanding and to be ready to assist students in reaching understanding if they are experiencing problems. As Perkins and Blythe (1994) put it, "To learn for understanding, students need criteria, feedback, and opportunities for reflection from the beginning of and throughout any sequence of instruction."

Summary Comments on Teaching for Understanding Units

Certainly, all of us want to teach for understanding. We obviously would not want to teach for misunderstanding or teach with the goal of getting students to forget whatever they have learned. Yet we know that, in too many cases, misunderstanding and forgetting take place. Teaching for understanding is hard. But we can achieve this goal by keeping clearly in mind its attributes (time, focus and coherence, negotiation, and frequent analysis and diagnosis). If we employ the four-part framework (generative topics, understanding goals, understanding performances, and ongoing assessment) in situations where it is appropriate, understanding is a goal we can reach.

Reflect *and* Apply

3. Outline a TFU unit for a particular grade level and content area, such as social studies, science, or health. Choose a generative topic, state one or more understanding goals that fall under that topic, describe at least two understanding performances that students could engage in as they participate in the unit, and explain how you could provide ongoing assessment very early in the unit and periodically throughout the remainder of it. Do this in writing, making your outline as specific and concrete as you can.

4. Get together with a classmate or colleague and make a list of what is gained and what is lost when you teach the TFU unit you outlined rather than using a more conventional—and, in all likelihood, considerably shorter—approach. After you have made the list, study it and discuss the extent to which the extra time needed for the TFU unit is worth it in terms of students' learning. TFU units can definitely be worth the time they take, but not every topic merits such an approach.

Text Talk and Questioning the Author

Text talk, developed by Isabel Beck and Margaret McKeown (Beck & McKeown, 2001; McKeown & Beck, 2003), is an interactive oral reading procedure meant to obtain the best possible learning benefits from reading aloud with kindergarten and first-grade children. Beck and McKeown were prompted to develop text talk because their classroom observations revealed that many read-aloud experiences are not as beneficial to students as they could be. During the read-alouds they observed, students tended to respond to the colorful and vivid pictures often found in children's literature rather than to the text itself. Also, students tended to respond to teachers' questions using background knowledge that was not particularly relevant to the story being read, and they often failed to attend to important ideas in the text. These same observations revealed that teachers often asked questions about specific words or facts from the text that produced only brief responses from students and that when students gave these brief answers teachers often had difficulty expanding them into more meaningful responses.

Text talk was therefore designed to get students actively involved with the major ideas in the selections being read and to teach them to respond to these major text ideas in meaningful ways. To accomplish these goals, text talk considers six aspects of instruction and deals with each in a specific way. Each of these aspects, ways of dealing with them, and solutions to potential problems are discussed in Figure 11.3.

McKeown and Beck (2003) evaluated text talk in two kindergarten and two first-grade classrooms in an urban elementary school and received strongly positive results: "The results suggest, first, that teachers were able to change their read-aloud style to carry out an approach based on interspersed open questions and follow-up scaffolding." Specifically, about 80 percent of the questions teachers asked at the beginning of the study were closed questions, but by the end of the study about 80 percent of those they asked were open questions. "Second, children responded to this read-aloud situation by producing language and expressing ideas about the stories." Specifically, at the beginning of the study students' responses averaged 2.1 words, while at the end of the study students' responses averaged 7.65 words. Obviously, this is a very substantial gain. The results certainly suggest that those of you working with kindergartners and first-graders should give text talk a try in your classrooms.

Beck and McKeown (2001) conclude their consideration of text talk with a very useful list of the concepts they believe can guide the development of more effective read-aloud experiences for children:

■ Awareness of the distinction between constructing meaning of ideas in a text and simply retrieving information from the text

English Learners

Text talk is an excellent procedure to use with English-language learners whose listening skills are superior to their reading skills.

ASPECT OF INSTRUCTION	APPROACH TAKEN IN TEXT TALK
Selecting texts	The texts you choose need to be complex and challenging enough that children have something to talk and think about. The linguistic content, rather than the pictures, needs to be primary, and the stories should follow an event structure and not simply be a series of individual topics (for example, one page about a dog, another about a cat, etc.). Jan Brett's *The Mitten* is one book that Beck and McKeown found appropriate.
Initial questions	The questions you ask need to be open ones that allow children to give full and meaningful responses rather than simply answer with a word or phrase taken from the story.
Follow-up questions	Even when you ask good open questions that should elicit full and meaningful responses, children at first tend to give perfunctory one- and two-word answers. To counter this, you need to be prepared to scaffold children's efforts by prompting them to give more elaborated responses. General follow-up prompts such as "What does that tell us about . . . ?" and "So we know . . . , but why does it say . . . ?" are likely to be helpful in eliciting further responses from students. Providing this sort of scaffolding can be a challenge, and asking good follow-up questions is something that will probably require a good deal of effort on your part.
Pictures	Generally, you present pictures to students after they have heard and responded to the text itself. This, of course, is because if they see the pictures first, children will sometimes respond to them rather than to the text.
Background knowledge	Since children have a tendency to bring in tangential background knowledge when they respond to a story, be continually on the alert for this possibility and gently coach students toward more relevant responses when they produce less relevant ones.
Vocabulary	With text talk, you vary from the typical procedure of presenting vocabulary before students deal with the story and instead present it afterward. Also, you focus on a few sophisticated words that will enrich students' vocabularies. Some words that met these criteria for Beck and McKeown were *reluctant, nuisance,* and *commotion.* In teaching the words, use one of the forms of rich instruction we describe in Chapter 7, perhaps semantic mapping.

FIGURE 11.3

Using Text Talk to Improve Read-Alouds

- Understanding the difficulty of the task children face in gaining meaning from decontextualized text
- Designing questions that encourage children to talk about and connect ideas and developing follow-up questions that scaffold, building meaning from those ideas
- Helping students to meaningfully incorporate their background knowledge and reduce the kind of surface association of knowledge that brings forth a hodgepodge of personal anecdotes
- Awareness of how pictures can draw attention away from processing the linguistic content in a text, and thus attention to the timing of the use of pictures
- Taking advantage of the sophisticated words found in trade books by using them as a source of explicit vocabulary activities

Questioning the Author (QtA) is a large-group questioning and discussion technique also developed by Beck and McKeown (Beck, McKeown, Hamilton, & Kucan, 1997; Beck et al., 1996). Unlike text talk, QtA is designed for upper-elementary-age students. It is, as Beck and McKeown explain, "an approach to text-based instruction that was designed to facilitate building under-standing of text" (Beck et al. 1997). In the Classroom 11.1 describes the QtA procedure.

Reflect *and* Apply

5. Choose a kindergarten or first-grade book appropriate for text talk. Be sure that the book is complex enough to challenge children, that the linguistic content is primary, and that the text follows an event structure. Then, plan a text talk presentation. Your plans should include (a) creating a set of open questions that deal with the major ideas of the text, (b) creating some follow-up questions to scaffold children's efforts when their initial responses are too brief, (c) deciding when and how to deal with the pictures, and (d) selecting a few sophisticated words to present after the story and identifying some powerful and interesting ways to teach them. If you can actually use your text talk lesson with children, we encourage you to do so. And if you can get a classmate or colleague to critique your lesson and your use of it, do that, too.

Reciprocal Teaching

Reciprocal teaching, developed by Annemarie Palincsar and Ann Brown (1984), is a cooperative-learning procedure in which students and a teacher work together to improve students' understanding of complex informational texts and at the same time improve students' general ability to monitor their comprehension and to learn from such texts. The procedure has been extensively researched and has produced very positive results with first-graders (Palincsar & David, 1991), sixth- and seventh-graders (Palincsar & Brown, 1984), and even college students (Fillenworth, 1995). Studies show that students who worked with reciprocal teaching increased their group participation and use of the strategies taught, learned from the passages studied, and increased their learning when reading independently. The studies also demonstrated that the procedure could be used in various settings and that students maintained the gains they achieved.

The procedure is quite simple, straightforward, and consistent with the instructional principles we discussed in Chapter 2. For example, it includes scaffolding, puts learning in students' zone of proximal development, and follows the gradual release of responsibility model.

The procedure employs four carefully selected strategies: generating questions, clarifying issues, summarizing, and making predictions. Each of these strategies serves one or more definite purposes. Questioning focuses students' attention on main ideas and provides a check on their current understanding of what they are reading. Clarifying ensures that students are actively engaged as they are reading and helps avoid confusion. Summarizing requires students to attend to the major content of the selection and determine what is important and what is not. And predicting requires students to rehearse what they have learned thus far and approach the next section of the text with some expectations of what is to come.

Initially, reciprocal teaching is teacher directed. At first, the teacher or some other experienced reader, such as a classroom aide, serves as the leader of the group, taking the primary role in carrying out the strategies and modeling them for others in the group. The leader's task includes modeling the strategies she wants the children to learn, monitoring students' learning and understanding, scaffolding their efforts, providing students with feedback, and tailoring the session to the students' existing level of competence. One central purpose of reciprocal teaching, however, is to get students actively involved in using the strategies—that is, in doing the questioning, clarifying, summarizing, and predicting themselves. Thus, from the beginning, the teacher increasingly hands over responsibility to the students in the group. As soon as possible, the teacher steps out of the leadership role, and each student in the group takes her turn as group leader. It is, in fact, when students have the leadership role that they do some of their best learning. The teacher, however, continues to monitor the group as much as possible and intervenes when necessary to keep students on track and to facilitate the discussion.

In the Classroom 11.2 shows the four steps of the procedure and very briefly illustrates the responses they might prompt for fifth-graders reading Bradley Cruxton's *Discovering the Amazon Rainforest*.

Students can use reciprocal teaching on their own.

Reciprocal Teaching

in the Classroom 11.2

The session begins with the leader reading aloud a short segment of text, typically a paragraph or so. Four steps then follow:

1. *Questioning.* Once the segment has been read, the leader or other group members generate several questions prompted by the passage just read, and members of the group answer the questions. For example, after reading the opening paragraph of Cruxton's *Discovering the Amazon Rainforest*, a student might ask, "What does a rainforest look like?" Another student might respond, "Very tall trees, lots of plants and animals, not much light under the tall tree branches."

2. *Clarifying.* If the passage or questions produce any problems or misunderstandings, the leader and other group members clarify matters. For example, in continuing to work with *Discovering the Amazon Rainforest,* a student might point out that the only plants that can grow in the rainforest are ones that can grow upward toward the light, because the branches of the giant trees act like a sun umbrella and block the light. Other members of the group might agree but then point out that some plants, such as mushrooms, don't need light.

3. *Summarizing.* After all the questions have been answered and any misunderstandings have been clarified, the leader or other group members summarize the segment: "A rainforest is a place of giant trees, lots of rain, many different kinds of plants and animals, and with little change in temperature, day to night, season to season."

4. *Predicting.* Based on the segment just read, segments that have preceded it, and the discussion thus far, the leader or other group members make predictions about the contents of the upcoming section: "I think in the next section we will learn about some of the different kinds of things—plants, animals, and people—that live in the rainforests."

The sequence of reading, questioning, clarifying, summarizing, and predicting is then repeated with subsequent sections.

In formal studies of reciprocal teaching, students have usually worked with reciprocal teaching for a 20-day period, which has been sufficient to produce the gains described earlier. To give you a more concrete indication of what those gains look like, we present a transcript of a seventh-grader's work with the procedure. In the Classroom 11.3 presents the student's discussion of several texts (taken from the work of Brown & Palincsar, 1989) and illustrates the student's progress by showing her performance on five different days.

Increasing the Questioning Ability of a Seventh-Grade Student

instructional routines

in the Classroom 11.3

DAY 1

Text: The water moccasin, somewhat longer than the copperhead, is found in the southeastern states. It lives in swampy regions. It belongs, as do also the copperhead and the rattlesnake, to a group of poisonous snakes called pit vipers. They have pits between their eyes and their nostrils which, because they are sensitive to heat, help the snakes tell when they are near a warm-blooded animal. Another name for the water moccasin is "cottonmouth." This name comes from the white lining of the snake's mouth.

Student: What is found in the southeastern snakes, also the copperhead, rattlesnakes, vipers—they have. I'm not doing this right.

Teacher: All right. Do you want to know about the pit vipers?

Student: Yeah.

Teacher: What would be a good question about the pit vipers that starts with the word *why?*

Student: (No response)

Teacher: How about, "Why are the snakes called pit vipers?"

Student: Why do they want to know that they are called pit vipers?

Teacher: Try it again.

Student: Why do they, pit vipers in a pit?

Teacher: How about, "Why do they call the snakes pit vipers?"

Student: Why do they call the snakes pit vipers?

Teacher: There you go! Good for you.

DAY 4

Text: Spinner's mate is much smaller than she, and his body is dull brown. He spends most of his time sitting at one side of her web.

Student: (No question)

Teacher: What's this paragraph about?

Student: Spinner's mate, How do spinner's mate . . .

Teacher: That's good. Keep going.

Student: How do spinner's mate is smaller than . . . How am I going to say that?

Teacher: Take your time with it. You want to ask a question about spinner's mate and what he does, beginning with the word *how.*

Student: How do they spend most of his time sitting?

Teacher: You're very close. The question would be, "How does spinner's mate spend most of his time?" Now, you ask it.

Student: How does spinner's mate spend most of his time?

DAY 7

Text: Perhaps you are wondering where the lava and other volcanic products come from. Deep within our earth there are pockets of molten rock called magma. Forced upward in part by gas pressure, this molten rock continually tries to reach the surface. Eventually—by means of cracks in the crustal rocks or some similar zone of weakness—the magma may break out of the ground. It then flows from the vent as lava, or spews skyward as dense clouds of lava particles.

Student: How does the pressure from below push the mass of hot rock against the opening? Is that it?

Teacher: Not quite. Start your question with, "What happens when?"

Student: What happens when the pressure from below pushed the mass of hot rock against the opening?

Teacher: Good for you! Good job.

DAY 11

Text: One of the most interesting of the insect-eating plants is the Venus's flytrap. This plant lives in only one small area of the world—the coastal marshes of North and South Carolina. The Venus's flytrap doesn't look unusual. Its habits, however, make it truly a plant wonder.

Student: What is the most interesting of the insect-eating plants, and where do the plants live at?

Teacher: Two excellent questions! They are both clear and important questions. Ask us one at a time now.

DAY 15

Text: Scientists also come to the South Pole to study the strange lights that glow overhead during the Antarctic night. (It's a cold and lonely world for the few hardy people who "winter over" the polar night.) These "southern lights" are caused by the Earth acting like a magnet on electrical particles in the air. They are clues that may help us understand the Earth's core and the upper edges of its blanket of air.

Student: Why do scientists come to the South Pole to study?

Teacher: Excellent question! That is what this paragraph is all about.

Source: Brown, A. L., & Palincsar, A. M. (1989). "Guided Cooperative Learning in Individual Knowledge Acquistion." In L. B. Resnick (Ed.), *Knowing, Learning, and Instruction.* Hillsdale, NJ: Lawrence Erlbaum Associates. Reprinted by permission.

As the preceding transcript illustrates, the student progressed from being unable to phrase an appropriate question to phrasing a very clear and concise one. As the student became increasingly competent, the teacher gradually turned over responsibility for generating questions to her. On day 1, the teacher had to phrase the question for the student. On day 4, she provided substantial scaffolding to assist the student in phrasing a question. On day 7, she needed to use much less scaffolding. On day 11, when the student produced two good questions, she reminded her that the procedure called for only one. And on day 15, she simply praised the student, as she was able to produce a clear, concise, and appropriate question without the teacher's assistance.

As the transcript further shows, the leader's role is crucial. Skilled leaders can keep the discussion on track, constantly assess students' strengths and weaknesses, and provide just enough scaffolding to challenge students while ensuring that they succeed. No one, of course, is better able to do this than a skilled teacher. However, aides can certainly be trained to be competent leaders, and research has shown that peer tutors can also be trained to be competent leaders (Palincsar & Brown, 1986).

Because reciprocal teaching is consistent with the principles of effective teaching, is strongly supported by research, and assists students in understanding and learning from challenging expository material, we recommend using it in your classroom as yet another procedure for fostering your students' increasingly sophisticated literacy.

ASSESSMENT

In designing classroom assessments of student performance, effectiveness and efficiency are key. Use the Tile Test and the Graduated Running Record found in the *Assessments and Lesson Plans* supplement as models to help guide you.

Reflect *and* Apply

6. Select a text that you might use in doing reciprocal teaching with a group of intermediate-grade students. We suggest that you use an expository one. Decide on a text segment to focus on, probably a paragraph or two. If the segment you choose is not at the beginning of the text, assume that the students you are working with

have already read and discussed previous segments. Now do four things: Create a question that you, as the discussion leader, might pose to a small group working with the segment. Identify and then explain an issue from the segment that might need clarification. Write a brief summary of the segment. And, before you have read further in the text, make a prediction about the contents of the next segment.

7. Choose a text that students in your college class might use with reciprocal teaching, identify a segment of that text to be dealt with at one session, and complete the activities in the previous item for college students working with that segment.

Jigsaw

Jigsaw is an easily implemented and very powerful technique that puts students in the position of becoming experts in some part of a domain and then sharing their expertise with others in the class. It is a particular type of cooperative learning, an approach which has been widely discussed and widely used and which has been shown to produce some extremely positive results in a variety of cognitive and affective areas (Johnson, Johnson, & Holubec, 1994; Slavin, 1987; Tierney & Readence, 2005). Research has demonstrated that students in cooperative groups showed superior performance in academic achievement, displayed more self-esteem, accommodated better to mainstreamed students, showed more positive attitudes toward school, and generally displayed better overall psychological health. Students in cooperative groups also displayed better interpersonal relationships; these improved interpersonal relationships held regardless of differences in ability, sex, ethnicity, or social class (Johnson & Johnson, 1989). Moreover, cooperative learning has been shown to be successful in teaching students how to resolve conflicts (Johnson & Johnson, 1996).

Jigsaw was developed and investigated by Elliot Aronson and his colleagues (Aronson & Patnoe, 1997; Aronson et al., 1978). Using the jigsaw approach, a class of 30 or so students work in five heterogeneous groups of six or so members on material that the teacher has broken into subsections for each student to work on. In the Classroom 11.4 shows the major steps of the approach.

instructional routines

in the Classroom 11.4

Steps in Using Jigsaw

1. Each student in a group learns one part of the material being studied. For example, in studying a particular state, one student in each group might investigate cities in the state, another in each group the state's agriculture, another its industries, and so on.

2. After studying her section individually, the member of each group who has studied a particular subpart of the topic gets together with the four members from other teams who have studied the same subpart.

3. The five students in each of these "expert" groups discuss their subtopic, refining their knowledge about it.

4. The experts return to their own groups and teach their classmates about their sections. Because classmates afford the only opportunity for students to learn about sections other than their own, students are necessarily interested and motivated to attend to each other's presentations.

5. Students take individual exams on all of the material, both the material they taught to others and what they learned from others.

Jigsaw, of course, must be used in a situation in which a subject can be broken into subparts for students to teach. With that single proviso, the procedure is widely applicable. One excellent use of jigsaw is in peer response to writing. In a class of 30 students, five groups of six students can each identify and become "experts" in a particular aspect of writing. Suppose, for example, that sixth-grade students were working on expository writing over a period of a month or so. One group might become experts in introductions to expository essays, focusing on such matters as the clarity of the introduction and whether it provided an adequate overview of the paper. A second group might become experts on the body of the paper, focusing on whether the body supported what was said in the introduction. A third group might deal with conclusions, focusing on the clarity of the conclusion and the extent to which it was appropriate for what was said in the body of the paper. A fourth group might become experts on transitions between paragraphs and sentence structure, looking for complete sentences and for clarity and variety in the sentences used. And a fifth group might deal with punctuation and spelling, checking to ensure that punctuation and spelling followed acceptable conventions.

Each paper written by the members of a group is then checked by all members of the group, with each member focusing on his or her specialty; it is then revised by the original writer. This procedure lets all students become authorities in at least one aspect of expository writing, provides all members of each group with substantial feedback, and is very likely to result in better second drafts than if only one student had responded to each paper.

A teacher who completed her master's degree with one of us investigated the use of jigsaw in conjunction with peer response to writing and found it very useful (Rahne, 1997). In making her concluding comments on the approach, she endorsed the procedure strongly; she also stressed that students need a lot of assistance from their teacher as they work toward becoming skilled responders to each other's papers.

Reflect *and* Apply

8. Identify a topic from a reading methods course that a class could use jigsaw with. Identify the five or six subtopics that you would assign to the expert groups, and write out the assignments for each group. Estimate the time the expert groups would need to work on their subtopics and the time the experts would need to teach what they had learned to their groups. Finally, get together with a classmate and discuss the costs and benefits of using jigsaw. Because jigsaw and other cooperative learning activities have been shown to be very effective, you might want to complete this activity as a cooperative group.

9. Complete the activity just described as it would be carried out with a class of upper-elementary or middle-grade students. Also, if you have an opportunity to actually try out jigsaw in a classroom, do so.

Strengths and Challenges of DIVERSITY

English Learners

CW 11.3 links to "Expanding Opportunities: Academic Success for Culturally and Linguistically Diverse Students," a description of effective strategies for promoting the intellectual growth of English learners and other diverse students.

Which students do you think will benefit from the various procedures presented in this chapter? We hope you answer, "All students." Teaching for understanding is a crucial part of the literacy curriculum for all students—those who like school and almost always succeed, those who do not take to school and often seem uninterested in school subjects, and those who continually try but find many school tasks challenging. All of these students need to understand what they learn in school well enough to retain important information and be able to use that information both in school and out of school, now and in the future. This being the case, we have only three more comments.

First, do not slight any students by denying them the opportunity to learn for understanding. All students will profit from participating in TFU units, participating in text talk sessions, using reciprocal teaching, and working with jigsaw.

Second, not slighting any students means attending to individual differences. In order to succeed with these understanding activities, some students will need more scaffolding and accommodation than others. Some English-language learners may benefit from using their native language in text talk sessions. Similarly, some students will benefit from listening to some of the texts used in teaching for understanding lessons. Second-grade teacher Becka Thomas talks about how audiotapes helped meet the needs of some of her special needs students:

> My group of second-graders this year, several of whom were bused from the inner city, particularly enjoyed and benefited from audiotapes that accompanied the books we read in class. Hearing the words (sometimes many times over!) seemed to help with their understanding of the concepts we were learning. One of our topics was families. In our month-long study, we looked at many facets of this concept, including family interests and activities. We discovered that B. J.'s cousin was a rap artist, that Desi's granddad was a trumpet player, and that Shana's mom was an artist—just to name a few! Luckily, I was able to find books and audiotapes that added to the children's knowledge of these activities and the diversity of families and their interests. Three of the many books and audiotapes we used were *Ben's Trumpet* by Rachel Isadora, *Bein' with You This Way* (a rap poem) by W. Nikola-Lisa, and *Art Dog* by Thacher Hurd. The classroom audiotapes were such a hit, I applied for a small grant from the PTA to purchase a few inexpensive tape recorders and multiple sets of audiotapes for the children to check out and take home. We lost only one audiotape during the entire year. What the children gained in knowledge and confidence was immeasurable.
>
> —Becka Thomas, Second-Grade Teacher

English Learners

Irene Gaskins's (2005) *Success with Struggling Readers: The Benchmark School Approach* describes a number of techniques for helping all students, including English learners who can use some extra assistance with reading.

Different students, of course, bring different stores of prior knowledge to any activity they participate in. When working with jigsaw, for example, you should strive to find subtopics that all students in each subgroup can become experts in. The situation with reciprocal teaching is similar. Even though reciprocal teaching is focused on the text, prior knowledge relevant to the text is important, and thus the texts used for reciprocal teaching need to reflect the diverse interests and knowledge bases of your students. Reciprocal teaching also requires the use of strategies—questioning, summarizing, and predicting. Some students will need instruction in these strategies; many will need a good deal of scaffolding in the discussions.

In text talk, as in reciprocal teaching, prior knowledge relevant to the text is crucial, and thus text selection is critical. Also, because text talk is a group activity, there is always the danger that more verbal, outgoing students will dominate the discussion. Finding ways to encourage and support the participation of all students is vital. It helps to first establish the sort of literate environment we described in Chapter 3—one in which students feel free to speak out in class, students support one another in class discussions, and you support students' responses by acknowledging partially correct responses or rephrasing a question to give a student another opportunity. Beyond that, you will want to be on the lookout for ways to draw in individuals who often do not participate. For example, students who lack confidence will gain it if you give them a lot of opportunities to answer questions that they can definitely answer; students who lack certain sorts of background knowledge will begin to participate more when the reading they're working with taps background knowledge familiar to them.

Third, recognize that these teaching for understanding techniques tend to center on verbal performances and that some students have strengths in other areas. Howard Gardner's insights on multiple intelligences (Baum, Viens, & Slatin, 2005; Gardner, 1993, 1999) can be particularly helpful here. In Gardner's view and that of many contemporary psychologists, the concept of intelligence as a single, objectively measured, unchangeable trait is misleading and unhelpful. Instead, Gardner argues for the existence of at least eight intelligences: linguistic (verbal), logical-mathematical, spatial, bodily kinesthetic, musical, interpersonal, intrapersonal, and naturalist.

Although individuals are likely to be particularly strong in one or more of these intelligences, each individual possesses all eight, and most people can develop each of them to a satisfactory level. Thus, subscribing to the theory of multiple intelligences does not mean identifying individuals as requiring one particular type of instruction. Instead, it means recognizing that different students have different strengths. We want to give students opportunities to use all of these intelligences at various times, including when we are teaching for understanding. Of course, allowing students to make use of their multiple intelligences is not limited to teaching for understanding activities. The curriculum offers many opportunities for these varied activities; for example, they work particularly well as postreading activities in SREs.

Concluding Remarks

This chapter has taken an in-depth look at teaching for understanding. We began the chapter by defining *understanding* and describing some key attributes of teaching for understanding—it takes time, requires focus and coherence, involves negotiation, and is highly analytic and diagnostic. Next, we described and gave examples of several specific approaches that can foster deep understanding—TFU units, text talk and questioning the author, reciprocal teaching, and jigsaw.

The approaches described in this chapter are by no means the only ways of fostering deep understanding. Many approaches described in other parts of the book can be used for this purpose. These include the general approach of fostering present-day literacy described in Chapter 1, the Frayer method described in Chapter 7, the scaffolded reading experience described in Chapter 8, teaching comprehension strategies as described in Chapter 9, and promoting independent reading as described in Chapter 10, to name only a few.

We want to note that we consider this chapter one of the most important chapters in the book. Teaching for understanding—fostering deep knowledge and giving students knowledge and skills that they will retain and that they can use in the world beyond school—must be a goal all teachers share.

Extending Learning

1. Arrange a meeting with a teacher who teaches at an elementary grade level that interests you, and discuss the notion of teaching for understanding generally. Describe one of the TFU procedures we have discussed—TFU units, text talk and questioning the author, reciprocal teaching, or jigsaw—and ask whether she uses it or a similar procedure; if so, ask about how useful and effective she has found it to be. If the teacher you talk with hasn't used the first procedure you bring up, describe each of the others and pursue the suggested line of questioning to try to identify one that the teacher is familiar with. Finally, if the teacher does use one of the procedures, ask if you can observe the class as she uses it. Then observe the class, and make some notes about how the procedure works. Of course, if you have the time and opportunity to discuss and observe more than one of the procedures, certainly do so.

2.  Meet with a class or small group of elementary students, and try out one of the teaching for understanding procedures—a TFU unit, text talk and questioning the author, reciprocal teaching, or jigsaw. This is a time-consuming activity—you have to search for a class or small group, thoroughly prepare for your teaching, do the teaching, and describe the experience. However, it can be extremely beneficial because it gets you directly involved in teaching.

(mylabschool™
Where the classroom comes to life!

> For a look at content area reading in a contemporary classroom, go to Allyn & Bacon's MyLabSchool.com. In MLS Courses, click on Reading Methods, and go to MLS Video Lab. There, you will find video clips about Content Area Reading in Module 6. Additional video clips can be found if you return to MLS Courses and click on Content Area Reading.

Children's Literature

Brett, J. (1989). *The Mitten*. New York: Putnam. This rich retelling of a Ukrainian folktale will capture the interest and imagination of many children. 32 pages.

Clements, A. (2005). *Lunch Money*. New York: Simon & Schuster. When the principal bans sixth-grader Greg Kenton from selling his handmade miniature comic books at school, he works to change school policy. 224 pages.

Cruxton, B. J. (1998). *Discovering the Amazon Rainforest*. New York: Oxford University Press. This book in the Discovery series describes the tropical rainforest of Brazil and examines plans for saving the rainforest. 64 pages.

Greene, S. (2004). *Owen Foote, Mighty Scientist*. Boston: Houghton Mifflin. Hoping to impress a popular fourth-grade science teacher, third-grader Owen Foote sets out to find the perfect idea for the school science fair. 96 pages.

Haduch, B. (2001). *Food Rules! The Stuff You Munch, Its Crunch, Its Punch, and Why You Sometimes Lose Your Lunch*. New York: Puffin. This kid-friendly book also delivers scientific information about food and nutrition. Full-color illustrations, stories, jokes, rumors, facts, and recipes add to the appeal. 106 pages.

Hurd, T. (1996). *Art Dog*. New York: HarperCollins. When the mysterious and incredibly talented Art Dog is accused of stealing a famous painting, he manages to paint his way out of a difficult situation and uncover the real criminals. Audiotape available. Unpaged.

Isadora, R. (1979). *Ben's Trumpet*. New York: Mulberry Books. Ben plays an imaginary trumpet outside the Zig Zag Club until a trumpet player opens the door to his dreams. Audiotape available. Unpaged.

Leedy, L. (1997). *The Edible Pyramid: Good Eating Every Day*. New York: Holiday House. A children's guide to diet, nutrition, and the food pyramid. 32 pages.

Nikola-Lisa, W. (1994). *Bein' with You This Way*. New York: Lee & Low. A lively playground rap song celebrates diversity. English audiotape and Spanish audiotape available. 28 pages.

Rockwell, L. (1999). *Good Enough to Eat: A Kid's Guide to Food and Nutrition*. New York: HarperCollins. In simple language and examples that will appeal to youngsters, this book on nutrition describes the six categories of nutrients needed for good health, how they work in the body, and what foods provide each. 40 pages.

Salzmann, M. E. (2004). *Eating Right*. Minneapolis: Abdo. This simple text explains the importance of eating the right quantities of nutritious foods. 23 pages.

Trumbauer, L. (2004). *Eating Well*. Mankato, MN: Capstone Press. With photographs and simple text, this easy-to-read book introduces readers to the major food groups and the nutrition they provide. 16 pages.

Wallower, L., & Wholey, E. J. (2004). *All About Pennsylvania*. Lansdale, PA: Penns Valley Publishers. A brief look at the history, geography, and prominent figures of Pennsylvania. 56 pages.

Writing and Reading

chapter outline

CLASSROOM VIGNETTE

*S*ixth-grader Derrick sits at his desk, his social studies book propped open in front of him, jotting down words in a notebook.

Bryce glances over Derrick's shoulder. "What are you doing?" he asks.

"Writing stuff."

"Why?" Bryce asks.

"So I remember it. We have a test tomorrow . . . in case you've forgotten."

In the third-grade room down the hall, Jasmine plops into a beanbag chair and starts reading a story her friend Brianna wrote. It's a story featuring the characters in a book the class just read. Next to her, Brianna giggles as she reads Jasmine's story.

Next door, second-grade teacher Maria Chavez writes on the board:

Dear Class,

We have been talking about gifts lately. I just wanted to tell you that each of you is a special gift to me. Thank you for working so hard and for being so kind to one another.

Love,

Mrs. Chavez

Each of these writers is using writing for a different purpose—for learning, for understanding, for communicating, and for just having fun with words—as this chapter will illustrate.

The Reading-Writing Connection

As you know, we write for a number of different reasons and audiences, and *how* we do it—the *process*—is different for each. But no matter what the reason, the audience, or the process, what we write is usually meant to be read, either by ourselves or by someone else. And quite obviously, anything we read has to have been written by someone. Writing and reading, as Bernice Cullinan (1993) has noted, are two sides of the same coin. Like speaking and listening, they are two complementary components of a communications process (Pearson, 1990) and depend on the same cognitive structures and strategies (Langer, 1986).

Even though this reading-writing connection might appear obvious, these two language arts have traditionally been taught as separate subjects in U.S. classrooms. Today, however, virtually all educators agree that combining reading and writing in the classroom makes a great deal of sense, both theoretically and practically. Forty years ago, John Carroll (1966) suggested that reading and writing be experienced as parallel and reciprocal processes, in much the same way that their own speaking and the speech that they hear are parallel and reciprocal to younger children. Today, researchers and practitioners alike continue to recommend that this notion be put into practice in the classroom (Atwell, 1987, 1998b; Farr, 1993; Moore, Moore, Cunningham, & Cunningham, 2003; Olson, 1996; Routman, 2003, 2005).

Throughout this chapter, we explore this reciprocal process of reading and writing, focusing on a variety of writing forms, purposes, and procedures. But before we can begin that discussion, the stage must be set. The writing classroom—what does it look, sound, and feel like?

A Positive Reading-Writing Environment

"I write because I have something important to say, and I think people need to hear it!" says Brandon, a fifth-grader. Brandon's heartfelt, if somewhat boastful, comment succinctly captures in one sentence at least three critical truths about writing that will greatly affect your own thinking about the writing opportunities you provide for students:

- Students should write for important purposes.
- What students write should be valued by themselves, by you, and by the others in your classroom community.
- Writing should function to communicate or to foster the writers' own learning, understanding, or appreciation.

If literacy is to prosper in our classrooms, we need to create an environment in which children view themselves as writers. Writers flourish in an atmosphere in which written words are used and valued and writers are encouraged to take risks and are supported in their attempts. This environment involves both the intellectual climate of the classroom and its physical attributes.

The Intellectual Climate

The intellectual climate of the ideal reading-writing classroom conveys this message: "We are all readers and writers. Together we are all learning to be better readers and writers." The intellectual climate will be reflected in the number of children seen reading and writing at any given moment and their engagement in their writing tasks. It will be reflected in the students' writing displayed throughout the room—student-made books, posters, bulletin boards. It will be reflected in the faces and voices of students meeting to read and respond to each other's writing.

A positive classroom writing environment is one in which students write often and for a variety of purposes and one in which they feel free to take risks. Writing across the curriculum provides extended opportunities for students to write, and when they do so, their comfort level increases (Spandel, 2005). Students need to be given opportunities to write without fear of criticism. One very effective way teachers can help establish this risk-taking atmosphere is to become writers themselves. Doing so helps teachers understand the arduous

Literacy prospers in classrooms in which children view themselves as writers and what they write is valued by the classroom community.

process involved in transforming thoughts into words and to appreciate what it is like to have those words evaluated.

Another important element in the intellectual climate of a classroom is the teacher's role as modeler. Writing in front of students, showing them what you are doing, and talking about what you are doing and why provides students with concrete examples of how writers work (Dyson & Freedman, 1991; Graves, 1991; Routman, 2005; Temple, Nathan, Temple, & Burris, 1993).

The Physical Environment

Students need *time* to write, a *place* to do it, and *materials* to write with. The physical environment of a productive reading-writing classroom will reflect the attitude "This is a great place to read and write!" Joanne Hindley, a teacher at the Manhattan New School, has developed this kind of environment. This is what she had to say about the writing environment of her classroom (Hindley, 1998, reprinted with permission).

> I think carefully about how the room needs to look in order to allow comfortable working space for the whole group, small-group, paired, and individual working situations. Materials need to be clearly labeled and organized so that it is easy for children to use and take care of them. This not only promotes good "housekeeping" in the small space we share, it also ensures that the room belongs to all of *us* and not just to *me*. It is much easier for 30 people to take on the responsibility of caring for our home than for one person to do it for the other 29. When something in our system is not working, we discuss the problem together, not only to discover possible solutions, but also to understand why it needs to be changed in the first place.
>
> When we as teachers think about ourselves as learners, we are able to envision what our students need in terms of support from us and from the environment. Creating an atmosphere that encourages students to interact, feel independent, and take pride in the upkeep of their classrooms is critical for everything we do throughout the year.
>
> —Joanne Hindley, Elementary Teacher

The main goal is to provide a place where students feel safe and comfortable exploring ideas on paper. In the Classroom 12.1 gives you suggestions for creating such an environment.

Guidelines for Creating a Positive Writing Environment

- Establish a predictable writing time.
- Create a writing center equipped with writing necessities—writing materials, dictionaries, a thesaurus, and books on the writer's craft.
- Provide opportunities to write throughout the day in all the subject areas for a variety of purposes and audiences.
- Become a writer yourself, and share with your students your writing and the struggles you experience in writing.
- Provide students with guidance and constructive feedback.
- Stock the classroom library with texts in a variety of genres—magazines, picture books, biographies, informational books, novels, beginning chapter books—that reflect a wide range of interests and readability levels.

in the Classroom 12.1

- Read aloud quality literature—fiction, nonfiction, and poetry.
- Model writing forms and techniques.
- Guide students to write about topics that are important to them—writing that has a genuine purpose and a real audience.
- Provide opportunities for students to share their writing with their peers and receive constructive feedback from them.
- Provide direct instruction on matters of mechanics—grammar, usage, spelling, and punctuation—and the writer's craft—dialogue, characterization, voice, engaging beginnings, and so on—as the need arises.

The Process Approach to Writing

In recent years, a particular approach to teaching writing—the process approach—has been widely explored, and evidence indicates that students in classrooms that include more elements of the process approach indeed become better writers than those in less process-oriented classrooms (Persky, Daane, & Ying, 2003). We think this evidence is convincing, and we strongly endorse the process approach as a method of teaching writing. However, a good deal of the writing students do in relation to their reading is less planned, less lengthy, less polished, and less formal than that for which the process approach is appropriate. As Gail Tompkins (1996) has pointed out, effective reading teachers give students plenty of opportunities to do both process writing and informal writing. Thus, after discussing the process approach, which can include informal types of writing such as brainstorming, listing, and semantic mapping, we will describe the nature and place of less-formal writing.

For some writing projects and in some situations, the writer goes through several stages of writing, particularly when writing formal pieces. However, not too long ago, most writing instruction gave virtually no attention to the process of writing. Fortunately, with the release of Janet Emig's (1971) study of 12th-graders' composing process and Donald Graves's (1975) observations of seven-year-old writers, educational researchers began focusing on the process involved in writing and its implications for classroom instruction. The result of this research has been a shifting of emphasis away from the end product of writing toward the process involved in the writing.

Step into a third-grade classroom for a moment, and witness this event:

Gabbie, wearing gray sweatpants, high-top sneakers, and a wide grin, is sitting in the "author's chair," reading her story "The Noise in the Laundry Chute." You are impressed that a third-grader could write so well. You notice, however, that Gabbie's face, her body language, and her whole demeanor are speaking even more eloquently than her words: "This is good. I like this and am proud of my story."

Gabbie didn't get to this moment of accomplishment and satisfaction in one quick leap but went through several stages before arriving at the author's chair to read her "finished" product. First, she engaged in *prewriting* activities, which helped her generate ideas. With the teacher acting as a recorder, the whole class had brainstormed "scary moments" together on the chalkboard.

Students like Gabbie enjoy reading aloud the stories they have written. Sharing one's work with others helps develop an awareness of audience and its importance in the writing process.

As a second prewriting activity, Gabbie did a quickwrite to let her own thoughts run free and then capture them on paper, discovering what she knew and how she felt about the frightening moments in her life. Next, her teacher had her think about the audience for her story, her purposes for writing it, and the form she would use. She decided she would write and illustrate a picture book for her younger brother and two older sisters, one that would be funny and scary at the same time.

During the next stage, *drafting,* Gabbie wrote a rough draft of her story, trying to keep her audience and purposes in mind. Gabbie went through three drafts before she felt ready to share her story with her classmates to get their feedback. When she did read her story to a small group of classmates, they responded to what she had written, giving her positive feedback on some aspects of her story and suggesting what she might think about for her next revision.

Revising the story—reviewing it in light of the comments she received from her classmates and rewriting it—was the next stage in the process. Here, Gabbie reworked her composition by adding, deleting, changing, and moving words, sentences, and even whole sections. During this stage, Gabbie's main interest was in making the story "work." Does it make sense? Is it scary *and* funny? Would her brother and sisters like it?

After Gabbie was satisfied that she had done what she could to tell the story she wanted in the way she wanted, she began *editing* the piece. Here she focused on mechanical elements such as grammar, punctuation, and spelling. This proofreading process required that Gabbie hunt word by word for errors, a different focus from that of the revising stage, in which she concentrated on the meaning she was creating. Because young writers, like Gabbie, are not usually critical readers, it can be helpful to provide suggestions for revising and editing. Teacher Marilyn Blackley (Five & Dionisio, 1999) finds an editing list, such as the one shown in Figure 12.1, helpful with her third-graders. Using a colored pencil, her third-graders work with a partner to edit their own writing.

English Learners

To help students edit their drafts, use a different colored highlighter pen for each type of writing error when marking student papers. For example, use blue for spelling and orange for punctuation. Communicating through color instead of words or symbols can be helpful for ELL and non-ELL students alike. A classroom chart indicating the meaning of the colors is a helpful reference tool.

Steps to Editing

←————————————————————————————→

THE TITLE OF MY PIECE IS _____ .

MY EDITING PARTNER WAS _____ .

I read my story to a friend to see where to **STOP** for

periods ·   _____

question marks **?**   _____

exclamation points **!**   _____

I took out extra words that I didn't need (and, then)   _____ .

I checked for capital letters

at the beginning of each sentence   _____

for the first letter of a name   _____

for the word I   _____

I circled words that may be misspelled.   _____

Example: I (plade) with my dog.

FIGURE 12.1

Form to Help Third-Graders Edit Their Writing

Source: Five, C. L., & Dionisio, M. (1999). "Revisiting the Teaching of Writing," *School Talk, 4,* 3. Copyright 1999 by the National Council of Teachers of English. Reprinted with permission.

The last stage of the process, *publishing,* involved a sharing or "celebration" of the work. To prepare her story for sharing, Gabbie keyed her story into a word processor, printed it, cut it into sections, and pasted them in the pages of a booklet. Then she drew pictures to accompany her text. Other types of publishing possibilities are discussed later in this chapter as well as in Chapter 8.

To review, the five major steps in the writing process are as follows:

- Prewriting
- Drafting
- Revising
- Editing
- Publishing

A word of caution is in order here. The description just provided gives merely the highlights of what is in reality a very complex and recursive process. Writers don't simply move lockstep from one stage to another; they repeatedly move back and forth between the processes involved in prewriting, drafting, revising, and editing, as the writing task dictates. Additionally, no two writers approach writing in exactly the same manner, and the same writer writes differently at different times. The scenario about Gabbie presented a *general characterization* of the writing process. To be sure, virtually all formal and polished writing is the product of a relatively lengthy and multifaceted process that involves thinking, drafting, and revising. However, the process itself is not always the same. Different writers, different topics, different purposes, and myriad other factors will affect the writing process.

Informal Writing

As we noted earlier, whereas formal writing represents one very important sort of writing for students to engage in, a lot of their writing in relation to their reading will not involve the process approach and thus will *not* involve prewriting, drafting, revising, editing, and publishing. Typically, a student does informal writing for his own purposes—to learn from his reading, to better understand ideas, and to explore or personally engage with what he is reading. This writing will take the form of notes, lists, diagrams, journals, summaries, and the like. Much of this writing will be a one-step process. For example, in response to her teacher's prompt "What makes you scared?" first-grader Erin writes her feelings in a journal (Figure 12.2). Fourth-grader Yuki reads a chapter in Margo Sorenson's *Tori and the Sleigh of Midnight Blue*, jots down her reaction to Tori's being asked to recite her poem at the Christmas program, and returns to these notes only as she is deciding how she wants to present her thoughts on this historical novel in her literature circle.

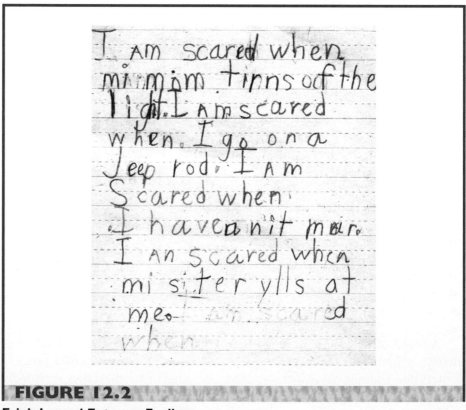

FIGURE 12.2

Erin's Journal Entry on Feelings

Sometimes, of course, informal writing will involve more than one step, as fifth-grader Twega testifies:

> I don't know why, but I can't remember very much when I read in our history book, so I take notes—lots of them—as I read. Ms. Stallman has us meet in "history circles" the day after we read a chapter to talk about what we've learned, and I don't want to sit there looking dumb with nothing to say! So I'd better be prepared. After I take these notes, I go back through them before our circle meets and underline the things I think are really important. Usually I even take my notes to the circle. After we discuss the chapter in our history circle, I sometimes make a few additions or changes in the notes. Why? Because Ms. Stallman usually tells us she is going to give us a quiz on the chapter, and I want to have the right answers!!!
>
> —Twega, Fifth-Grader

The point here is not that Erin, Yuki, or Twega illustrates *the* correct way to do informal writing; instead, the point is that there are many, many ways to do informal writing. Students need to know this and be given the freedom to explore different alternatives.

Reflect *and* Apply

1. We have discussed reading and writing as being reciprocal and parallel processes, or "two sides of the same coin." Explain what this idea means to you.
2. Think about your own writing experiences in elementary school. What did you write? For what audiences did you write? Did any of your writing take you through the various processes we talked about in this section? What sorts of informal writing did you do? At this point, jot down the types of writing elementary students might do that illustrate both the process approach and informal kinds of writing.

Some Writing Forms and Purposes

As we have already discussed, in a typical elementary classroom students will be writing for a variety of different reasons and for different audiences. Some writing—such as editorials, reports, and stories—is fairly formal and will require prewriting, drafting, revising. Other types—such as writing summaries or responding to literature in a journal—are more informal and typically don't require drafting or revising. In this section, we take a look at some of the types of writing elementary students are likely to find most useful and talk about when, why, and how each type should take place:

- Writing to learn and to understand
  —Note taking
  —Brainstorming and quickwriting
  —Semantic mapping

CW 12.1 links to Imagine That! Playing with Genre Through Newspapers and Short Stories, which asks students to condense a short story into a newspaper article and expand a newspaper article into a short story.

—Venn diagram
—K-W-L
—Journals
■ Writing to communicate
—Letters
—Biographies
—Reports
■ Imaginative writing
—Stories
—Poems

As you can see, we have divided the types into three broad categories. However, we want to stress that these categories only suggest what is *generally* the purpose or nature of the various types. We by no means intend to suggest a rigid category system or imply that the various types do not overlap in a number of ways. For example, a student could write a story or poem in her journal, a Venn diagram might constitute part of a report, and students could brainstorm topics for poems. These loosely defined categories can, however, serve as a reminder that students can profitably undertake many sorts of writing to enrich and complement reading.

Writing to Learn and to Understand

Often, we use writing as a vehicle to learn about something or to more fully understand it. When students take this stance, they are using written language to help them wrestle with information, ideas, feelings, and intuitions. Reading done in subject matter areas such as science, social studies, and literature offers rich opportunities for this kind of writing, which fosters comprehension and personal response. In this kind of writing, students are actually "thinking on paper" or perhaps on a computer screen. In other words, they are using written language to discover, clarify, refine, expand, or reflect on meaning.

James Britton and his colleagues (1975) have noted that this type of writing is closely related to talk, and Richard Vacca and Wayne Linek (Vacca & Linek, 1992) point out that such writing can serve as a catalyst for reading and studying content-area material. In fact, many of the writing-to-learn activities we discuss are often accompanied by small-group discussion centered on the topics students are writing about.

What kinds of writing can students do to help them better learn, understand, and personally respond to the information and ideas in the texts they read? To enhance their ability to "think on paper" and actively integrate new knowledge into old? To prepare them for more formal genres such as reports and stories? Note taking, brainstorming, quickwriting, semantic mapping, the Venn diagram, the K-W-L procedure, and journals are the ones we discuss in this section. You will notice that we described several of these procedures in Chapter 8 when we talked about helping students comprehend the various texts they read. Here, we focus on the writing component of these endeavors.

Note Taking

Although note taking is perhaps the most traditional of all the activities we discuss in this section, students do not pick it up naturally. To help students learn how to take notes, Regie Routman (1995) recommends using demonstration, participation, practice, and sharing in a variety of note-taking situations.

These situations include taking notes from texts, oral presentations, films, and videos. To be successful at note taking, students not only need repeated practice in the skill but also need to have it demonstrated to them again and again throughout the school year.

The sample lesson in In the Classroom 12.2 is adapted from a procedure Routman and third-grade teacher Julie Beers did with a group of third-graders who were getting ready to begin research reports on animals.

Sample Lesson on Note Taking

1. Make a transparency out of the first page of the selection students will be reading, and leave the other half of the page blank. (For example, Routman and Beers made a transparency of the page on alligators and crocodiles from *Zoo Books 2* [Wildlife Education, 1986].) This transparency will be used on an overhead projector to demonstrate note taking.

2. Slowly read the passage aloud, highlighting key phrases and important information by underlining them with a yellow marker. Verbalize the thought processes you go through in deciding what to highlight. Demonstrate to students how to turn these key phrases into notes by writing these key phrases on the right side of the transparency.

3. Demonstrate the process several times with additional pages from the text, inviting students to participate in choosing the notes to write down.

4. Have students form small groups. Give each group a photocopied page from the book they will read, a blank transparency, and two pens—a yellow highlighter and black marking pen for writing on transparencies.

5. Tell students to place the blank transparency over the article and underline key phrases and important points with the yellow marker (as they did earlier as a whole class) and then write their notes on the right side of the page with the black marking pen.

6. Invite each group to come up to the overhead projector with the completed transparency. Ask members to place it over a transparency of the text they have just read, and encourage them to discuss their notes. Give feedback and guidance on their note taking, and invite other students to give feedback as well.

instructional routines in the Classroom 12.2

In evaluating the effectiveness of this procedure, Routman offers the following suggestions for additional work on note taking:

- Have students work in pairs instead of groups, with one acting as scribe and the other giving suggestions and feedback.
- Allow students to take notes on their first reading of the material with their books open.
- Repeat note-taking sessions throughout the year, giving teaching demonstrations and working with various genres and contexts.

Brainstorming and Quickwriting

When *brainstorming,* students quickly jot down single words or short phrases that come to mind in response to a topic. For example, before a group of third-graders read Steve Parker's *It's a Frog's Life! My Story of Life in a Pond,* they brainstormed words and phrases that the word *pond* brought to mind and came up with this list:

water	frogs	pollywogs	weeds	woods	forest
ducks	green	slime	mud	turtles	ducks

English Learners

Pair English-language learners with English-speaking students. Have ELL students brainstorm on a topic while their partners write the words and phrases the ELL students suggest.

And before sixth-graders read *Sparks Fly Upward*, Carol Matas's historical novel about a Russian immigrant family in 1910 trying to adapt to a new culture and new circumstances, they wrote down words and phrases in response to the word *immigrant*. Brainstorming can be done individually, as a small-group activity, or as a whole-class activity; it can be done before or after reading. However it is done, brainstorming generally leaves students with some raw material that they will employ as they read or write.

In contrast to brainstorming, *quickwriting*—a technique popularized by Peter Elbow (1973)—is a way of very quickly getting down connected sentences and phrases on a topic without stopping to correct or analyze them. Simply stated, quickwriting is jotting down thoughts on a topic as quickly as they come to mind. Because the students are not worrying about mechanics, structure, or communicating their ideas to someone else, they are free to generate many thoughts and ideas, and they gain confidence and fluency in writing. Below is an example of a quickwrite a fifth-grade student did after reading an excerpt from *Strange Plants* by Howard Halpern and thinking aloud with a partner (Armbruster, McCarthey, & Cummins, 2005).

> I'm writing about stinging nettles. Stinging nettles have sharp needles that have asid in it, and, if you get a needle in you, you will get a read warm rash that stings and hurts very, very, very badly. It will sting for 2 hours or, if its very bad, it will last for a day or even more. I would hate to run into that plant because I've gotton poked by a needle really hard, and it hurts!

Like brainstorming, quickwriting is a strategy students can use as a prereading or postreading activity. Quickwriting before students read a text can help them relate the reading to their lives and activate and build schemata, bringing ideas from the subconscious level to the conscious level. For example, before third- or fourth-graders read any one of Joanna Cole's Magic School Bus books, they might do a quickwrite on what they know about the topic of the book—the human body, for example. Or, as a postreading activity after reading Russell Freedman's *Eleanor Roosevelt*, sixth-graders could quickwrite on what they discovered to be the most memorable moments in this biography.

Both brainstorming and quickwriting are excellent strategies for generating ideas. Students can be invited to engage in these activities before or after they read a particular text. Both can also be very effective strategies for gathering thoughts and ideas in the beginning stages of formal writing.

Semantic Mapping, the Venn Diagram, and K-W-L

Semantic mapping, the Venn diagram, and K-W-L all make use of brainstorming to some degree but take it a step or two further by organizing the brainstormed ideas in a specific way.

As we discussed in Chapter 8, in *semantic mapping* (also called clustering or webbing), words generated in brainstorming are linked to a nucleus word, which reflects a main idea. This nucleus word functions in much the same way as the main idea in an outline.

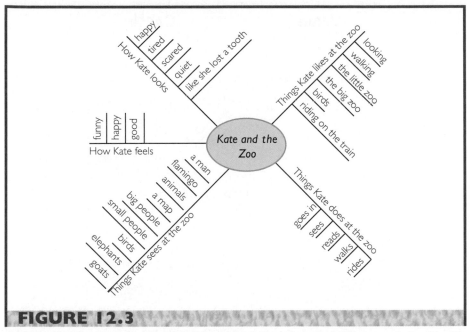

FIGURE 12.3

Semantic Map Used with First-Graders After Reading "Kate and the Zoo"

Source: Heimlich, Joan E., & Pittelman, Susan D. (1986). *Semantic Mapping: Classroom Applications.* Newark, DE: International Reading Association. Used with permission.

Semantic maps can have one nucleus idea or several and can be used with both narrative and informational texts. Students can develop them individually or as a small- or large-group activity, and they can be used either as a prereading activity to activate prior knowledge or as a postreading activity to recall and organize pertinent information (Heimlich & Pittelman, 1986). As a prereading activity, a semantic map can function to activate knowledge on a particular topic before students read a selection. As a postreading activity, semantic mapping can serve as a helpful prewriting technique preceding more formal writing such as reports, stories, or biographies. Figure 12.3 shows a semantic map developed by first-graders after reading "Kate and the Zoo," a story from a basal series.

A variation of the semantic map is the star organizer (Poindexter & Oliver, 1998/1999), which can help primary-grade students in the prewriting stages to organize their thoughts when writing a description. The framework can be used as a map for writing a paragraph describing an object. Figure 12.4 shows a star organizer for writing a paragraph about a friend.

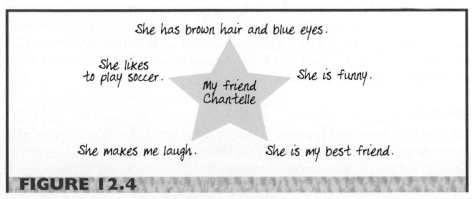

FIGURE 12.4

Star Organizer for a Five-Sentence Paragraph

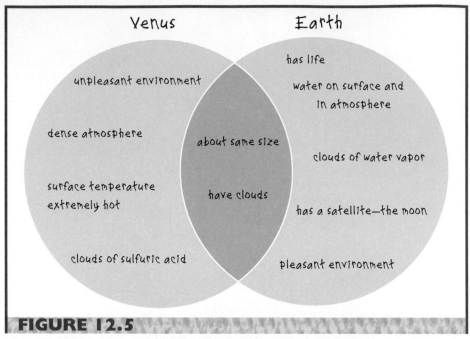

FIGURE 12.5

Venn Diagram Comparing and Contrasting Venus and Earth

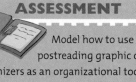

ASSESSMENT

Model how to use postreading graphic organizers as an organizational tool for writing essays. Student essays can be used to assess reading comprehension as well as essay writing skills.

Like the semantic map, the *Venn diagram* is a way to organize ideas and present them graphically. However, with the Venn diagram, two or more topics or ideas are contrasted. Consisting of circles that intersect, the diagram highlights the similarities and differences between topics. The differences are indicated by words or phrases written in the non-overlapping parts of the circles, while the similarities are written in the space created by the intersection of the circles. Figure 12.5 shows how one group of fifth-graders used the Venn diagram to compare and contrast the planets Earth and Venus after reading *The Planets in Our Solar System* by Franklyn Mansfield Branley.

The Venn diagram is a particularly effective device for students to use when reading informational texts in which two or more topics are being compared and contrasted. It can also be used to compare and contrast books that explore a similar theme or topic, such as Ann Martin's middle-grade novel *Belle Teal,* a fictional account of desegregation, with Ruby Bridges's photobiography *Through My Eyes,* a personal account of the author's own experiences with desegregation. It can also be used with characters in the same story, such as Prince Brat and Jemmy in Sid Fleischman's *The Whipping Boy* or Princess Elizabeth and Iris in Jane Resh Thomas's *The Counterfeit Princess.*

In Chapter 8, we described K-W-L as a group procedure for engaging students in the informational texts they read. However, as we illustrate here, it can also be used by individual students as a writing-to-learn tool. Figure 12.6 shows how K-W-L was used by a fourth-grader reading *The Magic School Bus on the Ocean Floor* by Joanna Cole.

Journals

Perhaps you have used journals yourself, either for personal reasons or as a learning tool in academic classes. If so, you're probably not alone, for journal writing is a widely recommended procedure. Chris Anson and Richard Beach (1995) view the journal as a genre in its own right and a "significant tool for

CW 12.2 links to Teachers of English to Speakers of Other Languages (TESOL) and Everything ESL, which provide writing ideas for your English-language learners.

What I know	What I would like to know	What I found out
The ocean is deep.	How deep is it?	Didn't find out!!!
The ocean has fish.	What kind of fish?	hermit crabs, sea urchins, jelly fish, squid, scallops—No! these are invertebrates—animals without backbones—not fish!!!
The ocean is salty.	Why is it salty?	Salt comes from the rocks! When the rocks are worn down by the water, the salt goes into the water.
The ocean has plants.	What kind of plants?	seaweed, plankton
Fish breathe under water.	How do fish breathe?	Fish have gills that can take oxygen from the water. Water flows into the fish's mouth then the gill, and out through the slits in the fish's sides.
The ocean has waves.	What makes the waves?	The wind!

FIGURE 12.6

Sample K-W-L for *The Magic School Bus on the Ocean Floor*

learning." Toby Fulwiler (1987) suggests that journaling engages the writer in a vast range of cognitive activities—observing, questioning, speculating, becoming aware of oneself, digressing, synthesizing, revising, and informing. Routman (1991) describes the journal as a "nonthreatening place to explore learnings, feelings, happenings, and language through writing" and of significant benefit to both teacher and student. Here we list some of the specific benefits Routman highlights:

- Promotes fluency in writing
- Promotes fluency in reading
- Encourages risk taking
- Provides opportunity for reflection
- Validates personal experiences and feelings
- Provides a safe, private place to write
- Promotes thinking and makes it visible
- Promotes development of written language conventions
- Provides a vehicle for evaluation
- Provides a personal record for students

> Journals can be a valuable tool for writers when used for worthwhile purposes that student writers understand and embrace.

Four types of journals—reading logs, learning logs, double-entry journals, and dialogue journals—are particularly effective for developing reading-writing connections and promoting thinking and learning.

Reading Logs. Reading logs, sometimes called response journals, are journals in which students record *personal responses* to the literature they read. Before students write in their journals, you will want to talk about some of the topics they might write about and model how you write responses in your own reading journal. In the Classroom 12.3 shows one way to introduce primary-grade students to response journals, is based on an approach used by first-grade teacher Barbara Werchadlo (Wollman-Bonilla & Werchadlo, 1995).

Introducing the Response Journal to Primary-Grade Students

- During the first week of school, read aloud a chapter a day from an engaging book such as *James and the Giant Peach* by Roald Dahl.

- For the first few days, model how to write a response by expressing a few ideas by thinking aloud. Then write a sentence on the board such as *James is very sad because his parents are gone* or *James does not like living with Aunt Sponge and Aunt Spiker.*

- When you think the children are ready, perhaps on the third day, give them their own journals. These can be made by stapling story paper (blank on the top and lined on the bottom) between manilla or cardstock covers that the children can decorate.

- Ask students to write in their journals about the story. Give them writing prompts such as "What did you like about this chapter?" or "What do you think will happen next?"

- Invite students to illustrate their responses when they have finished writing.

instructional routines

in the Classroom 12.3

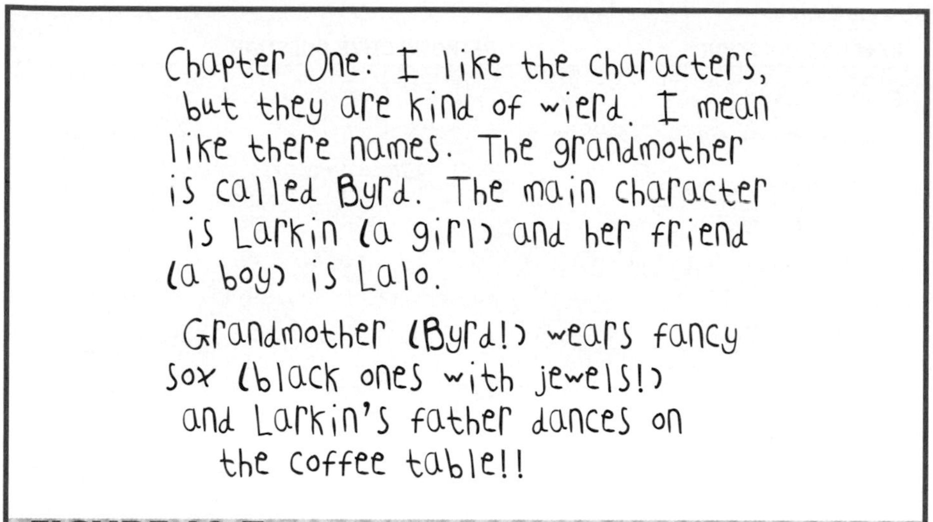

Chapter One: I like the characters,
but they are kind of wierd. I mean
like there names. The grandmother
is called Byrd. The main character
is Larkin (a girl) and her friend
(a boy) is Lalo.

Grandmother (Byrd!) wears fancy
sox (black ones with jewels!)
and Larkin's father dances on
the coffee table!!

FIGURE 12.7

Reading Log Entry

As good teachers always do, you will want to reflect on the success of the journaling activity and make adjustments if necessary. After Werchadlo's first experiences with response journals, she decided to provide more modeling of varied responses and give prompts that were even more open-ended. She did this in order to help children view journals not as a place to simply retell or predict what might happen in a text, but rather as a place to react personally. The following is a list of possible open-ended questions:

How does the story make you feel?

Does anything puzzle you? If so, explain.

Do the characters seem real to you? Why or why not?

Are you enjoying the story? Why or why not?

Are there words that you particularly like? What are they, and why do you like them?

Does anything in the story remind you of your own life?

Is anything the author says particularly meaningful to you? Why?

Figure 12.7 provides a sample entry in a fifth-grade student's reading log, written after he had read the first chapter of *Baby* by Patricia MacLachlan.

Learning Logs. In contrast to reading logs or response journals, learning logs are generally oriented to subject matter rather than personal response and are used in content areas such as science, mathematics, and social studies. They can include a variety of entries—questions to the author, summaries of the material, explanations of problems solved, or recording of observations as in an experiment. As Stephen Koziol, Brad Minnick, and Kim Riddell (1996) observe, one important function of learning logs is to enable students to select, connect, and organize knowledge in ways that allow them to better understand what they read. They have suggested three types of questions for learning logs: questions that elicit prior knowledge, questions that encourage students to interact with the text, and questions that ask students to respond retrospectively to what they have learned. Figure 12.8 shows a question and a response for each

ANTICIPATORY QUESTION	REACTIVE QUESTION	RETROSPECTIVE QUESTION
What do you want to know about the California condor?	What didn't you understand about the California condor?	What information did you learn about the California condor that was the most interesting or important?
I'd like to know why they almost became extinct.	I didn't understand why Topa Topa's parents abandoned him or why he couldn't survive on his own.	I learned that it has taken a long, long time to bring only a few more condors back. It has taken a lot of work. I hope I get to see a condor fly sometime. They're huge!

FIGURE 12.8

Three Types of Learning Log Questions and Responses

of these three types, relating to the book *California Condor: Flying Free* by Bonnie Graves.

Double-Entry Journals. Double-entry journals are two-columned journals that can be used when reading any type of text. In the left column students might write a quotation or a selected passage from the text, and in the right column their comments, questions, or responses to the quotation or passage. Or, instead of writing quotations or passages from the text in the left column, the student might write about events, characters, or settings in the left column and then make personal comments on them in the right one, as illustrated in the example in the Classroom Portrait on page 475.

Dialogue Journals. In a dialogue journal, a teacher and a student or two students carry on a written conversation over a designated period of time. As you can see from the following example, the entries in a dialogue journal look very much like informal letters. These entries are written by a fourth-grader and her teacher. They are dialoguing about a book the teacher recommended, *The Tiger Rising* by Kate DiCamillo.

Dear Mrs. G,

I'm on chapter 8 of The Tiger Rising. It's a good book so far. I'm not sure if the tiger is real or if Rob just imagined it. I can't imagine finding a caged tiger in my neighborhood!!! I wish Rob could make some friends. But I think he will, probably, I hope. What was your favorite part of the book? So far the tiger is my favorite!!

Dear Andrea,

I'm glad you like The Tiger Rising. It's interesting that you think the tiger might be imagined. I'm not going to give away if you are right or not! You'll just have to keep reading to find out, also to find out if Rob does make friends. After you finish reading, I'll tell you my favorite part. I don't want to give anything away!

The dialogue journal can be used to help students become more aware of the power of language (Mode, 1989) and of audience (Wollman-Bonilla, 2001), to help students become more comfortable about writing and more willing to write (Britton et al., 1975; Hannon, 1999), to assist students from varied backgrounds in learning to write (Fulwiler, 1987), and as a means for individualizing instruction (Werderich, 2002).

All types of journals—from reading and learning logs to double-entry and dialogue journals—can be used successfully in classrooms from kindergarten through middle school. However, a word of caution: Do not overuse them. All writing forms have a time and a place. Variety is the spice of the student writer's life. To ensure that journals are useful and not viewed by students as busywork, teacher Raymond Philippot offers some worthwhile suggestions in In the Classroom 12.4.

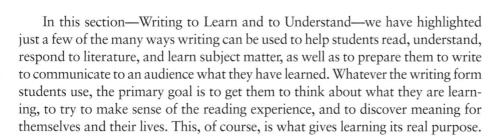

Guidelines for Journal Writing

- Read and comment on students' journal entries as often as possible. Doing so not only gives you the chance to offer encouragement and feedback but demonstrates to students that you value this activity.

- Make the purposes for journal writing explicit. Students need to know *why* they are writing in their journals and *how* it will benefit them. For example, students might be using their journals to generate ideas for an extended writing project.

- Use journals purposefully and carefully, or, as Regie Routman (2005) advises, "Make sure the writing children do in response to their reading is worth their time." Misuse or overuse could cause students to view journaling as trite, boring, or a waste of time.

instructional routines

in the **Classroom 12.4**

In this section—Writing to Learn and to Understand—we have highlighted just a few of the many ways writing can be used to help students read, understand, respond to literature, and learn subject matter, as well as to prepare them to write to communicate to an audience what they have learned. Whatever the writing form students use, the primary goal is to get them to think about what they are learning, to try to make sense of the reading experience, and to discover meaning for themselves and their lives. This, of course, is what gives learning its real purpose.

Reflect *and* Apply

3. Think about the term *writing to learn*. What does it mean to you? Discuss your response with a classmate or classmates.

4. In addition to journal writing, six other writing-to-learn activities were discussed in this section. Give an example of an appropriate reading situation for using each of these six techniques. For example, when might it be appropriate for students to take notes? To quickwrite? To use K-W-L?

Writing to Communicate

Although students do some writing primarily to learn and understand, they do other writing in order to communicate. When we talk about writing as communication, four interrelated factors are always involved—audience (who), purpose (why), content (what), and form (how). When students write to communicate, they need to be aware of these factors. Very often, it is the audience, purpose, and content that determine the form the writing will take. Three particularly useful forms to use in conjunction with reading are letters, biographies and autobiographies, and reports, which we discuss here.

Before students begin writing in any form or genre, it is critical that they read examples of the various forms they are being asked to write. As Courtney Cazden (1991) notes, "Children would not learn to speak a language they do not hear; so how do we expect them to learn the forms they do not read?"

Letters

Letters are a wonderful way to highlight the reading-writing connection. Students can write formal letters to request something, express thanks, issue a complaint, or express a point of view. They might be addressed to businesses, government employees, authors and illustrators, or other adults. Formal letters are likely to go through several stages—drafting, revising, and editing. Informal letters, however, may or may not require drafting and revision. Students who have had plenty of experience writing letters can often pen a friendly letter just once before sending it off. Students can write informal letters to classmates, friends, relatives, and pen pals; in these letters they can deal with reading-related topics such as stories, story characters, and other aspects of stories that they are particularly interested in. Teacher David Carberry has his fifth-graders write letters to first-graders, a writing task his students find particularly appealing. "The kids are very aware of taking their audience and purpose into account," Carberry says.

Students can also write simulated letters to or from fictional characters or to or from real people whom they encounter in reading true narratives or informational books. In the Classroom 12.5 provides some examples.

Writing Letters to or from People Students Read About

instructional routines

in the Classroom 12.5

- After reading a biography, invite students to write a letter to that person.
- Have students assume the role of a character in a story and write a letter to one of the other characters. For example, in the following letter, a student is assuming the persona of Miata in Gary Soto's *The Skirt* and is writing to Miata's friend Ana:

> Dear Ana,
>
> What is my mother going to say when she finds out I lost my folklorico skirt?
>
> She is going to be so mad! You've got to help me out!
>
> Your amiga,
>
> Miata

- Suggest that two students take on the roles of characters in stories and write letters to each other about novel situations those characters might face. For example, after reading Nancy Carlson's *Arnie and the New Kid,* one student might write a letter from Arnie's perspective and the other student from the perspective of Philip, the new kid in a wheelchair.

Dear Philip,

I wish they had given me a wheelchair like yours instead of these dumb crutches. Can you believe I broke my leg falling down some steps?

Your friend,
Arnie

Dear Arnie,

Sorry you broke your leg, but now I can do some things faster than you. Ha! Want to come over and play some video games?

Your friend,

Philip

One effective way to teach letter writing is to model the process, composing a letter in front of students (either on an overhead transparency or on the board) and explaining the thought processes you go through. Or you could develop a letter as a class effort—a letter to invite parents to Back-to-School Night, for example.

Posting sample letters on a bulletin board or keeping a file folder or notebook of sample letters is also helpful to students when they go to write letters on their own. Books that feature letters, such as *Dear Mr. Henshaw* by Beverly Cleary, *The Ballad of Lucy Whipple* by Karen Cushman, *Nettie's Trip South* by Ann Turner, and *Dear Papa* by Anne Ylvisaker, can provide good models of this form as well.

Biographies and Autobiographies

Biographies and autobiographies are another type of writing in which a primary purpose is to communicate—in this case, communicate some of the events in a person's life. Biographies and autobiographies are a popular genre with children because they enjoy reading about real people and because biographies and autobiographies often represent fairly easy reading, following as they do the basic narrative form children are familiar with. Biographies written expressly for young readers range from picture books such as *Dr. Martin Luther King, Jr.* and *America's Champion Swimmer: Gertrude Ederle*, both by David Adler, or *The Amazing Life of Benjamin Franklin* by James Giblin and *Revolutionary John Adams* by Cheryl Harness to in-depth portraits of noteworthy figures such as *Behind the Mask: The Life of Queen Elizabeth I* by Jane Resh Thomas, *Free to Dream: The Making of a Poet: Langston Hughes* by Audrey Osofsky, and *Pocahontas* by Joseph Bruchac. Biographers take a variety of approaches in presenting their subjects, some focusing on the historical aspects, some on the sociological aspects, and others on the internal conflicts the person faced.

After students have become familiar with the form and content of biographies through ample reading, a good place to start writing them is with a collaborative piece on a familiar subject. This should be someone they all know, perhaps a well-known figure in the school—a secretary, custodian, cafeteria worker, or principal. Once students have had some practice writing about people they know and have built some confidence in their skill with biography, they can write library-researched biographies in conjunction with the reading they do in subject matter areas—for example, biographies of historical figures, scientists, politicians, artists, sports figures, or favorite authors.

ASSESSMENT

CW 12.3 links to the "All About Me" lesson plan, helping students create a multimedia PowerPoint presentation. In addition to the traditional writing portfolios in which students' work is archived, students can make electronic portfolios using presentation software.

Reports

In general, reports represent a more challenging writing and thinking task than do biographies or letters, primarily because they usually do not follow the chronological, narrative structure children are so familiar with and because they often require students to use several sources of information. On the other hand, we are fortunate today in that an ever-increasing number of excellent models of informational writing are becoming readily available. More and more informational books and periodicals—which include everything from why animals have tails to the mechanics of spaceflight—are being written expressly for elementary-level students. Many of these informational materials are intriguing, relevant, and expertly crafted; they provide excellent models for students' own writing of reports. The Reading Corner on page 379 contains a list of a few such authors and titles.

As Shelley Harwayne (1993) so aptly states, in addition to having numerous opportunities to read the sorts of materials they are asked to write, students also need to "develop the same hunger for learning and communicating what they find out" that professional writers demonstrate. Harwayne suggests three lessons we can learn from professional nonfiction writers that we would do well to pass on to our students:

- They take learning about their subject seriously.
- They want to claim their information as their own by offering their own slant or perspective on it.
- They know their options and their audiences.

Spending time communicating these truths to students through the reading-writing opportunities you provide will pay off in their enthusiasm for writing and the quality of their products.

As defined here, reports include a range of informational writing that generally serves two purposes—to learn about a topic and to communicate that information through written language. A report can take any form—a

CW 12.4 links to the interactive ReadWriteThink Printing Press, designed to assist students in creating newspapers, brochures, flyers, and booklets. Have students explore the parts of a newspaper and then create their own class newspapers or newsletters.

"Our daily classroom newspaper is a whole-class shared writing activity and one of the best mini-lessons I have for helping children learn about the mechanics of writing. The students are actively engaged in constructing sentences about classroom projects and events in their lives. It's their newspaper and they know it." —Barbara Brunetti

the Reading Corner

Books by Exemplary Nonfiction Children's Book Authors

Science

Aliki. *Wild and Woolly Mammoths*. HarperCollins, 1998. This fascinating delineation of the woolly mammoth and the Ice Age is a "model of interesting factual writing for children" *(Horn Book)*. 32 pages.

Gail Gibbons. *Owls*. Holiday House, 2005. Author-illustrator Gibbons is an expert at depicting complicated subjects in a clear and simple style. In this book, one of her many on a variety of science-related topics, she answers questions young readers might have about owls. 32 pages.

Sandra Markle. *Outside and Inside Spiders*. Bradbury/Simon & Schuster, 1994. In a clear and energetic style, the author tells about the life of a spider, its traits and life processes. Fascinating photos. 40 pages.

Laurence Pringle. *Scorpion Man*. Macmillan, 1994. In a text accompanied by photographs taken by the subject—Gary Polis, the "scorpion man"—Pringle describes the fascinating work of this biologist and the creatures he studies. 42 pages.

Millicent Selsam. *How to Be a Nature Detective*. HarperCollins, 1995. In this text, Selsam shows readers how anyone can be a nature detective by learning to recognize clues, especially footprints, that tell which animals have been around. 32 pages.

Seymour Simon. *Winter Across America*. Hyperion, 1994. The beauty and harshness of winter, from Alaska to the southern United States, is depicted in clear prose and stunning photographs. 32 pages.

Social Studies

David A. Adler. *A Picture Book of Thurgood Marshall*. Holiday House, 1999. One of the books in Adler's Picture Book Biographies series, this title re-creates the life history of the first African American to serve as a judge on the United States Supreme Court. 32 pages.

Russell Freedman. *The Voice That Challenged a Nation: Marian Anderson and the Struggle for Equal Rights*. Clarion Books, 2004. In this chronicle of the acclaimed singer's life—with a special emphasis on the historic 1939 Easter concert at the Lincoln Memorial—Freedman illustrates how a person's life is molded by its historical and cultural context. 128 pages.

Jean Fritz. *Harriet Beecher Stowe and the Beecher Preachers*. Putnam, 1998. This book tells of the life and times of the mid-19th-century woman, born into a celebrated family of preachers, who wrote America's first protest novel, *Uncle Tom's Cabin*. 144 pages.

James Cross Giblin. *Good Brother, Bad Brother: The Story of Edwin Booth and John Wilkes Booth*. Clarion, 2005. In an engaging narrative, Giblin intertwines the tale of the two Booth brothers with accounts of their families, friends, the Civil War, and 19th-century theater. 256 pages.

Patricia C. McKissack and Frederick McKissack. *Christmas in the Big House, Christmas in the Quarters*. Scholastic, 1994. The authors depict the last Christmas in Virginia before the Civil War and the fears and dreams of both Blacks and Whites. 80 pages.

Milton Meltzer. *Hear That Train Whistle Blow! How the Railroad Changed the World*. Random House, 2005. In this nonfiction text, illustrated with numerous archival photographs, Meltzer presents the myriad ways in which the railroad affected almost every aspect of modern civilization. 176 pages.

paragraph on table manners, a picture book on penguins (Figure 12.9), a page or two on pandas, or a multimedia research report on natural disasters. Figure 12.10 provides a few recommendations for nurturing students' enthusiasm for and adeptness with report writing.

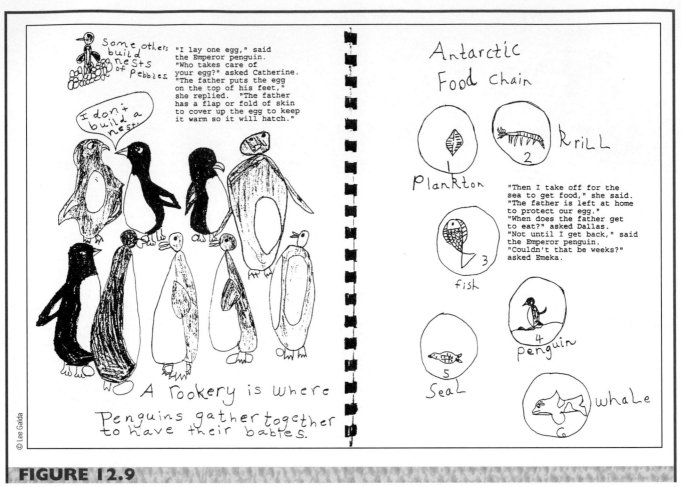

FIGURE 12.9

Sample Page from a Third Grade's Collaboratively Written Book About Penguins

Source: Literature and the Child by Lee Galda and Bea Cullinan, copyright © 2006. Reprinted by permission of Lee Galda.

Imaginative Writing

In addition to writing to learn and writing to communicate, students deserve and will profit from opportunities to do some imaginative writing in conjunction with the literature and content-area texts they read. With imaginative writing, the writer's intent is more to entertain, evoke feelings, or stimulate imaginative thinking than it is to inform. Such writing should include not just stories and poems, but also creative and expressive forms such as play scripts, song lyrics, and riddles, as well as writing that challenges students to think imaginatively about math concepts, as In the Classroom 12.6 illustrates.

Writing Imaginative Mathematics Scenarios and Questions

1. On a chalkboard or overhead projector, display a mathematical word problem. For example, let's say students have just read the following problem in their math book or found a similar situation described in a trade book they have read:

Brad saw a garage sale sign that read: "Baseball cards—cheap!" He fished in his pocket and found two dimes, a nickel, and five pennies. At the garage sale, he discovered cards at two prices: Perfect cards = ten cents. Imperfect cards = five cents.

2. Have students read through the problem and discuss the kinds of questions they might develop out of the situation. As a whole class, work through a variety of examples, including the following.

What is the largest number of cards Brad could buy? The largest number of perfect cards? What is the largest number of perfect cards Brad can buy if he also buys imperfect cards? If Brad purchases one perfect card, how many imperfect cards can he buy? What did Brad buy if he spent all his money? What did Brad buy if he had a dime left?

3. As a whole-class shared writing activity, compose another mathematical situation and questions to go with it.

4. When students are ready to work on their own, have them form groups and write similar word problems and imaginative questions about these mathematical situations.

5. Have students exchange their word problems and questions with another group. Make sure students work through their own word problems and questions to confirm that they are doable before giving them to another group of students to read and answer.

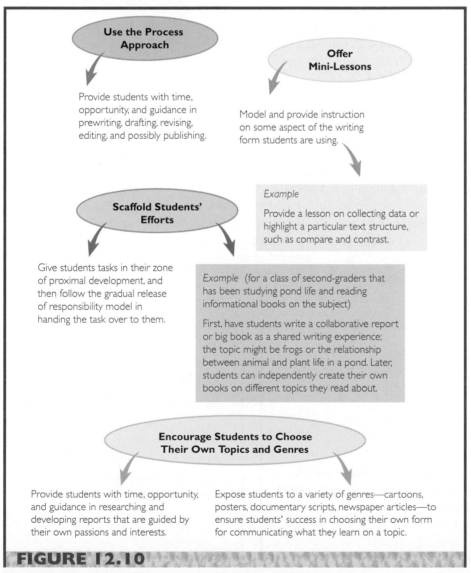

Use the Process Approach

Provide students with time, opportunity, and guidance in prewriting, drafting, revising, editing, and possibly publishing.

Offer Mini-Lessons

Model and provide instruction on some aspect of the writing form students are using.

Example

Provide a lesson on collecting data or highlight a particular text structure, such as compare and contrast.

Scaffold Students' Efforts

Give students tasks in their zone of proximal development, and then follow the gradual release of responsibility model in handing the task over to them.

Example (for a class of second-graders that has been studying pond life and reading informational books on the subject)

First, have students write a collaborative report or big book as a shared writing experience; the topic might be frogs or the relationship between animal and plant life in a pond. Later, students can independently create their own books on different topics they read about.

Encourage Students to Choose Their Own Topics and Genres

Provide students with time, opportunity, and guidance in researching and developing reports that are guided by their own passions and interests.

Expose students to a variety of genres—cartoons, posters, documentary scripts, newspaper articles—to ensure students' success in choosing their own form for communicating what they learn on a topic.

FIGURE 12.10

Nurturing Students' Adeptness with Report Writing

Fiction

Writing fiction provides opportunities for students to express themselves in creative ways and to explore a topic by giving their imaginations free rein. For example, at Beauvoir, the National Cathedral Elementary School in Washington, D.C., first-graders wrote and recorded their own stories about "If I Was a Sled Dog" as part of their study of the Inuit Indians, and second-graders wrote German folktales after reading and listening to stories by the Brothers Grimm (*Reading Today,* 2005). Fifth- and sixth-graders in Anchorage, Alaska, created their own imaginary creatures and wrote about them after a unit on how various species adapt to their environment. Their teacher, Diann Stone, had them select an environment with which they were familiar—in this case, their own neighborhoods—and create a creature who would dwell in that environment. Along with drawing a map of the creature's environment, students wrote a fictional report that included what this creature would look like, what it would eat, and what its habits would be.

The create-a-creature project was the culmination of a unit on animal habitats, adaptation, and survival. Ms. Stone's students had done extensive reading and study on the subject (which included a number of field trips to wildlife habitats). Ms. Stone also had sufficiently prepared the students to tackle all the cognitive tasks required in this project before they began. She also supported their efforts while they gathered their data, made their maps, created their creatures, and wrote about them. In other words, she built a sturdy scaffold to make certain that they were successful through the beginning, middle, and culmination of their efforts.

Poetry

Poetry can be written in response to anything children read. For example, after reading about the Gold Rush, students could write poetry about some aspect of that particular slice of U.S. history. After reading about the weather, they could write a cloud poem, as second-grader Lucy did (Figure 12.11). Or they could write either jump rope rhymes after reading Afiodelia Scruggs's *Jump Rope Magic* or a variation of the Japanese tanka on the horse, as fourth-grader Julie did (Figure 12.12), after reading several of Marguerite Henry's horse stories. You will find wonderful examples of poetry on almost any subject imaginable to read to your students, which will inspire them to express themselves in this special form as well.

Nimbostratus
by Lucy Hooper, second grade

Yuckey!
Nasty!
Dismal!
Nimbostratus clouds
are like a witch's huge black
hat with spiders' webs all over it.
Dismal!
Dreary!

FIGURE 12.11
Student Poetry Sample

HORSES
by Julie Graves, fourth grade

Swift, gallant
great flowing manes
and large flying tales
beautiful!

FIGURE 12.12
Student Poetry Sample

Writing Poems Around a Theme

- Read aloud to students several poems that relate to a theme or unit of study, such as weather.
- Choose a particular poem to concentrate on, such as "A Week of Weather" by Lee Bennett Hopkins, and talk about the words the poet chose to describe the weather.
- Have students perform the poem as a choral reading.
- Together, as a shared writing activity, write a poem that reflects the week's weather in your town.

An intrinsic feature of each of the types of writing we have discussed in this section and the previous one is that it is meant to be read. The writer creates a letter, biography, report, story, or poem with an audience and purpose in mind—to inform, entertain, persuade, evoke feelings, or tickle or challenge the imagination. As you read to your students, occasionally ask them to identify the intended audience (Olness, 2005) and purpose. Additionally, as with any writing students do, sufficient scaffolding must be provided before students begin the writing and when students are actually using the writing processes. Careful motivation, preparation, modeling, encouragement, coaching, and feedback are *crucial* to success.

Reflect *and* Apply

5. Think of a piece of writing you have done recently, and briefly answer these four questions about it: Who was the audience? What was your purpose? What was the content? What form did you use?
6. Think of a piece of writing you have done for which you went through several stages before you finished the piece. Briefly describe the process you went through. Compare your process with that described on pages 361–364.
7. If you wanted to ensure that your students were successful in writing reports on a topic they had been reading about, what steps would you take to guide them to success? Be as specific as possible in your explanation.

The Writing Workshop

Simply stated, a writing workshop is a designated time during the school day when children write on topics of their own choosing, for their own purposes. This writing may take place several times a week or, in some classrooms, every day and is done by students individually or collaboratively. As Charles Temple and his colleagues (Temple, Nathan, Temple, & Burris, 1993) point out, the writing workshop provides a setting in which children's "own interest in life, coupled with their desire to express themselves," motivates them to write. Additionally, it provides a predictable structure and routine in which students feel comfortable

English Learners

For writing assignments, write key words students will need and place a picture next to each word. Pictures can be sketched, taken from computer graphics, or cut from magazines. Store these word-picture pages in a binder for students' future reference.

taking risks, "collaborate with their peers, and take control of their own learning" (Hindley, 1998).

Over the past 25 years, educators have discovered that when students know they will have a chunk of time to write, a time in which they will be actively involved in writing for reasons that are important to them, they really develop as writers. Donald Graves (1991) suggests that it takes at least three hours a week for this habit of mind to take hold, where students are "rehearsing off stage" what they will write about. The writing workshop—a concept developed by Nancie Atwell (1987, 1998b) and a number of other teachers and researchers—is designed to provide your writers with that sort of time.

In the writing workshop, both teacher and student have equally important roles. The teacher's role is that of facilitator, coach, and guide—someone who establishes a community of writers who interact and support one another through all the phases of the writing process. The student's role is to write and encourage and support other writers.

A typical writing workshop has a number of key components and activities, with student writing at the core, as shown in Figure 12.13. Instruction takes place through mini-lessons, demonstrations, and shared writing activi-

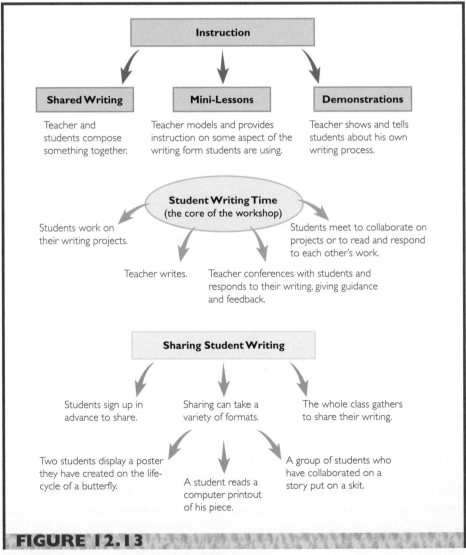

FIGURE 12.13

Key Components of the Writing Workshop

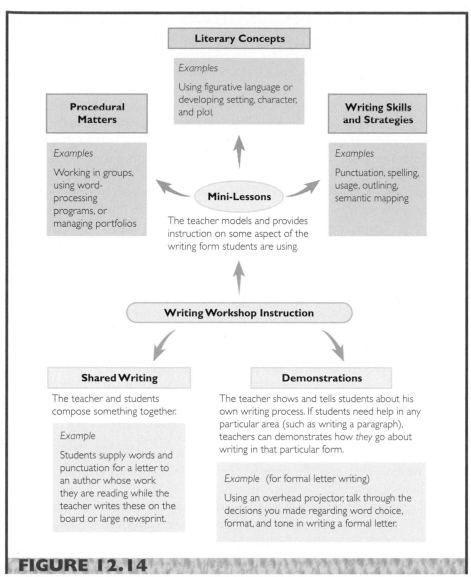

Literary Concepts

Examples

Using figurative language or developing setting, character, and plot

Procedural Matters

Examples

Working in groups, using word-processing programs, or managing portfolios

Mini-Lessons

The teacher models and provides instruction on some aspect of the writing form students are using.

Writing Skills and Strategies

Examples

Punctuation, spelling, usage, outlining, semantic mapping

Writing Workshop Instruction

Shared Writing

The teacher and students compose something together.

Example

Students supply words and punctuation for a letter to an author whose work they are reading while the teacher writes these on the board or large newsprint.

Demonstrations

The teacher shows and tells students about his own writing process. If students need help in any particular area (such as writing a paragraph), teachers can demonstrates how *they* go about writing in that particular form.

Example (for formal letter writing)

Using an overhead projector, talk through the decisions you made regarding word choice, format, and tone in writing a formal letter.

FIGURE 12.14

Three Types of Writing Workshop Instruction—Mini-Lessons, Shared Writing, and Demonstrations

ties, as shown in Figure 12.14. These activities usually occur before students begin their own writing in the workshop setting.

The writing workshop, coupled with the wide reading that provides students with both content and form for their writing and frequent opportunities to discuss their reading and their writing, can be one important component of a rich and nurturing literate environment.

Responding to Students' Writing

To grow as readers and writers, students need to receive feedback on their writing and what it reveals about their reading. In Chapter 14, we will deal with assessment more generally and talk about how to evaluate students' reading-writing abilities. Here, we present a handful of suggestions on how to respond to students' writing in ways that will help them evaluate their own success at achieving their writing goals.

English Learners

To assess your English-language learners' writing skills, ask students to write about a friend, family member, or pet. If they are unable to write anything, encourage them to draw a picture. Help them label their pictures in both English and their first language.

- *Be positive.* Emphasize what works in a piece more frequently than what doesn't—"Wow, you really got my attention with that great opening sentence!" Recall the emphasis we placed on success in Chapter 3, and realize that writing is for most of us (teachers and students alike) an area in which we are very vulnerable to criticism.

- *Respond to only some of what students write.* Students don't need your feedback on everything they write. In many cases, they will profit from feedback from their peers. They will also profit from their own self-criticism and can use that self-criticism to decide what writing they want you to look at.

- *Respond to only a few matters at any one time.* It is simply a waste of your time and energy to respond to many things at once. Students will attend to only a limited number of comments.

- *Comment primarily on works in progress rather than final drafts.* Comments after a final draft is completed get very little attention.

- *Give feedback during brief conferences with students on their works in progress* (Graves, 1996). A typical conference between a teacher-writer and a student-writer might begin with "Tell me about your piece" or "How is it coming?"

- *Observe students as they write.* Asking questions or making statements can lead students to solve their own writing dilemmas.

- *Deal with content first and mechanics later.* It is not that mechanics are unimportant, but the content of students' writing should take priority, especially as it reflects and promotes students' proficiency in reading.

- *Praise correct spelling, but also encourage invented spelling* (especially with primary-grade writers). If your student's goal is to have someone else read his writing, then spelling is an important means to that end, and correct spelling is something to strive for.

- *Make peer response an integral and frequent part of your reading and writing program.* There is probably no better way to learn something than to teach it—which is part of what peer reviewers are doing. However, students must be taught how to be effective peer respondents. They need to be taught both the general principles for responding to a person's writing and the specific writing elements they will be responding to—content, coherence, transitions, form, dialogue, and so on. Having checklists showing the specific criteria is often useful, so that students know what to look for. In his book *Writer to Writer: How to Conference Young Authors*, Tommy Tomason (1998) gives practical suggestions on how to teach students to have peer conferences.

Finally, in addition to following these suggestions for responding to students' writing, like virtually all current writers on writing, we recommend that you have students keep portfolios of their writing—ongoing and cumulative records and examples of their work. Items to be included can be selected by both you and your students. A major strength of these portfolios is that students can use them to evaluate their work and growth as writers. You and the students can use these portfolios as a tool for evaluating their writing and deciding where future efforts might be directed, sharing with parents, and determining and agreeing on grades. Portfolios are discussed in detail in Chapter 14, and ideas about what students can choose to put in their portfolios are provided.

Celebrating students' writing is an important part of the writing process.

Publishing and Celebrating Writing

There is something universal in the appeal of a book, with good-quality paper and a hard cover. And sometimes good paper and a hard cover will be just the right format for kids' published works. However, charts, posters, articles, and radio or TV scripts can also be "published."

Publishing means making a work available to some "public" audience. This audience might be the writer's classmates, students in another class, the entire school, a broader audience such as readers of a newspaper or magazine, or perhaps even an e-mail audience. Publishing highlights the importance of considering an audience while writing, and writing intended for publication is usually the result of the full writing process—brainstorming, drafting, revising, and editing. Although the larger audiences just mentioned are certainly possibilities, in many cases publishing will be accomplished simply by posting the work in the classroom. Whatever audience it reaches, published work is generally produced with the aid of word processors, spell checkers, computerized dictionaries and thesauruses, and, in some cases, desktop publishing programs.

One such publishing program is the Panther Paw Press, with which children's original works can be published as bound books. This is a school-based publishing program and is built on the efforts of students, teachers, parents, and school principals (Chihak, 1999). Another highly successful publishing effort is that of Cheri Cooke's seventh-grade reading classes. Each year, they produce a bound volume of reviews of their favorite books (Cooke & Graves, 1995). Lauretta Beecher's second-graders celebrate their writing in yet another way. They host a party and invite parents and other adults in the school to listen to their stories and poems.

Reflect and Apply

8. Identify a grade level at which you would like to teach, and consider for a moment the mini-lesson component of the writing workshop. Name some topics you might choose to cover early in the year, some you might choose to cover in the middle of the year, and some you might choose to cover late in the year. Now consider what surprises you might find in your students' writing and how these would affect your plan.

9. We listed nine suggestions for responding to students' writing. Rank these in order from those that you think are most important to those that you think are least important, and ask a classmate to do the same. Then get together and discuss the similarities and differences in your rankings, trying particularly to understand any large differences and what those differences suggest about your views of writing instruction.

Strengths and Challenges of DIVERSITY

CW 12.5 links to Inspiration, software that can help some of your more sophisticated students organize ideas for writing or for any other purpose, and to Kidspiration, software that can be used similarly by less sophisticated and younger children.

With writing, as with any other curricular area we have discussed, one of the most effective ways to meet the needs of different students is to differentiate the curriculum. For example, let's say that after a class of fourth-graders has completed a unit in which students have been reading self-selected books on the theme of courage, you want them to respond to what they read by writing on the topic. Students who struggle with writing can enjoy success by dictating "courage stories" to an adult, who then transcribes them. Students who are skilled in writing in a language other than English might write in that language in this situation. Verbally talented students can be challenged to write a researched biography on a courageous person whom they admire.

Modifying writing tasks to address needs and talents is another approach. The form illustrated in Figure 12.15, which is based on suggestions by Susan Winebrenner (1992), can be used as a guide and reminder as you individualize writing activities. Of course, it is neither possible nor desirable to individualize writing activities all of the time, but it is something you can do some of the time, and the individual success it fosters is certainly worth the effort.

Students who find writing a challenge, who speak and write in a dialect other than standard English, or whose native language is not English may profit from extra support. The following suggestions offer such students help with writing tasks; some were recommended by Robin Scarcella (1996), director of the ESL program at the University of California at Irvine.

- Keep directions simple, and check to be sure students understand them.
- Have a model of the completed writing task available.
- Demonstrate or model the writing activity.
- Guide the students through the activity.
- Have needed writing supplies readily available.
- Teach students to use a simple word processor.
- Provide feedback that is both comprehensible and constructive.
- Show respect for students' home languages and cultures.

A writing activity that shows respect for students' home languages and cultures encourages students to write stories, songs, or customs from their

STUDENT'S NAME	PURPOSE OF THE ACTIVITY	ALTERNATIVE ACTIVITIES FOR THE STUDENT
Jason DeWitt	Synthesize, recall, and apply information in science chapter on the water cycle.	Develop a way to teach the water cycle to a group of first- and second-graders—perhaps a picture book.
Jennifer Wong	Synthesize, recall, and apply information in science chapter on the water cycle.	Research and write about a question the chapter brought to mind or left unanswered—perhaps an "I search" paper.
Eric Sanders	Synthesize, recall, and apply information in science chapter on the water cycle.	Listen to tape of chapter, then tell important information learned to an aide, who writes what Eric dictates. Eric then reads back what he "wrote."

FIGURE 12.15

Sample Guide for Individualizing Writing Activities

home cultures or in their own languages (Canney, Kennedy, Schroeder, & Miles, 1999). *Salsa Stories* by Lulu Delacre, in which characters from several South American countries tell stories of their customs and holiday traditions, would be a good read-aloud springboard and model for this writing activity. Should students be allowed to write in their own dialects as well as their home languages? As educator Lisa Delpit (1988) has eloquently argued, students of color need and deserve to become adept at writing in standard English, and teachers need to assist them in doing so. However, in some situations, such as writing stories that are based on the writer's personal experiences and are a reflection of his cultural heritage, dialect is definitely appropriate. Two questions can serve to guide both you and your students with regard to whether or not dialect is appropriate and effective in a piece of writing: What is the purpose for writing? Who is the audience?

Some approaches to writing are especially appropriate for very skillful writers. One activity we have found particularly useful and well received by skillful developing writers is creating narratives or expository pieces related to their reading. In the Classroom 12.8 lists some possibilities (Graves & Graves, 2003).

CW 12.6 links to Co-Writer, a software program that can help writers who have difficulty with grammar and sentence structure. This program aids students in composing sentences by predicting words that follow logically within the context of the sentence.

Activities to Challenge Skillful Writers

- Select a scene from a book, and rewrite it to show what might happen if a character did something differently.
- Write an alternative ending to a story.
- Write a sequel or a prequel to a story.
- Present the events of a text in newspaper format.
- Rewrite a contemporary story as a fairy tale.

in the Classroom 12.8

Of course, less-skilled writers can also profit from some of these activities, but remember that less-skilled writers will need sufficient scaffolding to be successful with them.

Another activity particularly suited to gifted writers is participating in writing contests. Submitting writing to contests can be highly motivating, as it provides students with an authentic goal and audience. Magazines, organizations, and state and county fairs all sponsor writing competitions. A listing of writing contests can be found in the *Children's Writer's and Illustrator's Market* (Buening, 2006) in the section titled Young Writers and Illustrators.

Concluding Remarks

The value of developing a literate environment and establishing a curriculum to help students grow as writers in concert with their reading has been the overriding theme of this chapter. That means providing a classroom atmosphere, both physical and intellectual, that is safe and nurturing as well as inviting, fun, and challenging. It means providing opportunities to write for real purposes and for real audiences, purposes that include writing to learn for yourself and writing to communicate with someone else. It means providing students with opportunities to improve their writing and thinking skills through all sorts of writing—informal writing, such as brainstorming, quickwriting, and journaling, as well as formal writing, such as reports and storybooks that require the process approach. It means giving students every benefit possible—providing daily time to write, publishing their works, and giving them constructive feedback. In short, your reading-writing environment and curriculum will help and inspire students to write more often and more effectively. It will encourage them to use writing as a thinking tool to learn more about themselves and their world and as a communicative tool to share their knowledge, feelings, and insights with others, both of which are essential for living successfully in today's world.

Extending Learning

1. Get together with several classmates and develop a set of interview questions that you can use with teachers to learn how they use writing in conjunction with reading in their classrooms. Limit yourselves to five or six questions that can be answered rather briefly. For example, you might ask how often their students write in conjunction with the reading they're doing. Once the questionnaire has been developed, try it out first on one teacher, and modify it as necessary. Then, each person in the group can interview two teachers and record their answers. Finally, get together with your classmates, share the results of your interviews, and discuss to what extent the writing you learned about is consistent with the principles and techniques recommended in this chapter. After your group meeting, you might consider presenting the results of your project to your university class.

2. Observe the reading and language arts periods of an elementary class for at least one week (two weeks, if possible), and keep a detailed record of the writing the students do. Then, as a writing-to-learn activity for yourself, write a description of the class and the teacher, the writing you observed in the one- or two-week period, and the extent to which the writing you observed is and is not like that recommended in this chapter. Next, write an evaluative statement on the quality of the writing activities you observed and the extent to which they seem to support and extend the reading experiences students had during the period. Finally, if you believe that what you observed could be modified to better support and extend students' reading, briefly describe the modifications you would suggest.

mylabschool
Where the classroom comes to life!

For a look at the writing-reading connection in a contemporary classroom, go to Allyn & Bacon's MyLabSchool.com. In MLS Courses, click on Reading Methods, and go to MLS Video Lab. There, you will find video clips about Writing and Reading Connections in Module 4. Additional videos may be found if you return to MLS Courses and click on Language Arts.

Children's Literature

Adler, D. A. (2001). *Dr. Martin Luther King, Jr.* New York: Holiday House. This short biography tells the story of Dr. Martin Luther King, Jr.—his life, his accomplishments in the civil rights movement, and his impact on U.S. history. 32 pages.

Adler, D. A. (2005). *America's Champion Swimmer: Gertrude Ederle.* San Diego: Gulliver Books. This picture-book biography covers the life of Gertrude Ederle, highlighting her world-record-breaking, long-distance swims in the late 1920s, when women were thought to be "the weaker sex." 32 pages.

Branley, F. M. (1998). *The Planets in Our Solar System.* New York: HarperCollins. Part of the Let's Read and Find Out series, this book takes a quick look at the nine planets in our solar system using photographs and color illustrations. 32 pages.

Bridges, R. (1999). *Through My Eyes.* New York: Scholastic. In this photobiography, Ruby Bridges recounts the story of her involvement, as a six-year-old, in the integration of her school in New Orleans in 1960. 63 pages.

Bruchac, J. (2005). *Pocahontas.* San Diego: Harcourt. Although the book is a historical novel, not a true biography, Bruchac goes to great lengths to present a historically accurate depiction of the relationship between the Virginia colonists and the Powhatans as seen through the eyes of Captain John Smith and the 11-year-old daughter of the Powhatan chief. 192 pages.

Carlson, N. (1990). *Arnie and the New Kid.* New York: Puffin. In this picture book, Arnie begins to better understand the new kid in a wheelchair after he falls and becomes temporarily disabled himself. Unpaged.

Cleary, B. (1983). *Dear Mr. Henshaw.* New York: Morrow. In this Newbery Medal book, 10-year-old Leigh writes letters to his favorite author that help him to cope with his parents' divorce and a new school and to find his place in the world. Audiotape and filmstrip available. 134 pages.

Cole, J. (1989). *The Magic School Bus Inside the Human Body.* Ms. Frizzle takes her class via the magic bus inside the human body to look at how the body parts work. Spanish tape available. 40 pages.

Cole, J. (1992). *The Magic School Bus on the Ocean Floor.* Ms. Frizzle takes her class to the ocean floor aboard the magic school bus where they learn firsthand the mysteries of underwater life. Spanish tape available. 40 pages.

Cushman, K. (1996). *The Ballad of Lucy Whipple.* New York: Clarion. While stuck in a California gold-mining town with her adventurous mother and siblings, Lucy pours out her heart and frustrations in a series of letters written to the folks she left behind in Massachusetts, where she longs to return. 195 pages.

Dahl, R. (1961). *James and the Giant Peach.* New York: Scholastic. Young James experiences madcap adventures as he enters a peach as big as a house and encounters new friends. Audiotape available. 128 pages.

Delacre, L. (2000). *Salsa Stories.* New York: Scholastic. In a notebook Carmen Teresa receives as a holiday present, guests fill the pages with their colorful stories from a variety of Latin American countries. 144 pages.

DiCamillo, K. (2001). *The Tiger Rising.* Cambridge, MA: Candlewick. After Rob's mother dies and he and his father move to rural Florida to get their lives back together, Rob finds a way to come to terms with his mother's death through the help of a friend and a tiger. 116 pages.

Fleischman, S. (1986). *The Whipping Boy.* New York: Greenwillow. In this Newbery Medal book, Prince Brat and his whipping boy, Jemmy, run away from the palace, end up trading identities, and have many adventures together. Audiotape available. 90 pages.

Freedman, R. (1993). *Eleanor Roosevelt: A Life of Discovery.* New York: Clarion. This photobiography portrays the first wife of a president to carve out an influential career of her own. 198 pages.

Giblin, J. C. (2006). *The Amazing Life of Benjamin Franklin.* New York: Scholastic. In a concise, readable style, this biography presents a realistic, unsentimental portrait of the famous inventor, statesman, and diplomat, including his contributions and his challenges. 48 pages.

Graves, B. (2002). *California Condor: Flying Free.* Des Moines, IA: Perfection. Through the story of the capture of TopaTopa, the first California condor in the condor recovery program, the reader learns facts about this endangered bird and efforts to save it from extinction. 62 pages.

Halpern, M. (2002). *Strange Plants.* Washington, DC: National Geographic Educational Service. From the Windows on Literacy series, this brief text discusses meat-eating plants. 24 pages.

Harness, C. (2006). *Revolutionary John Adams.* Washington, DC: National Geographic Children's Books. This appealing and informative book is about the life and contributions of the second president of the United States, John Adams, who is often overshadowed by the more colorful Washington and Jefferson. 48 pages.

Hopkins, L. B. (Ed.). (1995). *Weather: Poems for All Seasons.* New York: HarperCollins. This collection of poems by well-known as well as lesser-known poets describes various weather conditions. 64 pages.

MacLachlan, P. (1993). *Baby.* New York: Delacorte. This exquisitely crafted short novel tells of a family learning to deal with the death of their own infant son after a baby girl is left on their doorstep for them to care for. 132 pages.

Martin, A. (2001). *Belle Teal.* New York: Scholastic. In 1962, fifth-grader Belle Teal faces the challenges of sticking up for Black students in her newly desegregated school in Coker Creek, Tennessee, as well as sorting out problems at home. 214 pages.

Matas, C. (2002). *Sparks Fly Upward.* Boston: Houghton Mifflin. In 1910, 12-year-old Rebecca and her Russian immigrant family try to adjust to a new culture while maintaining their traditions and faith. 192 pages.

Osofsky, A. (1996). *Free to Dream: The Making of a Poet: Langston Hughes.* New York: Lothrop, Lee, and Shepard. This is a biography of the Harlem poet who gave a voice to the African American experience in America. 112 pages.

Parker, S. (1999). *It's a Frog's Life! My Story of Life in a Pond.* Pleasantville, NY: Reader's Digest Children's Publishing. This is a look at the busy life of an English pond from a frog's viewpoint. 32 pages.

Scruggs, A. (2000). *Jump Rope Magic.* New York: Blue Sky Press. Shameka and her crew, who love to skip rope to the music of the jump-rope beat, make even Mean Miss Minnie a believer in "jump rope magic." David Diaz's colorful illustrations add to the warmth and fun. 40 pages.

Sorenson, M. (2002). *Tori and the Sleigh of Midnight Blue.* Fargo: North Dakota State University. After her beloved Papa dies during the Depression in North Dakota, 11-year-old Tori, an aspiring writer, tries to keep her life from changing. 123 pages.

Soto, G. (1992). *The Skirt.* New York: Delacorte. After fourth-grader Miata accidentally leaves her folklorico skirt on the bus, she tries desperately to get it back before her parents find out. 74 pages.

Thomas, J. R. (1998). *Behind the Mask: The Life of Queen Elizabeth I.* Boston: Clarion. This biography of Elizabeth I, daughter of Henry VIII and Anne Boleyn, describes how she takes a personal misfortune and turns it around to make a difference in the world. 196 pages.

Thomas, J. R. (2005). *The Counterfeit Princess.* Boston: Clarion Books. This book is set in 16th-century England, as the young King Edward nears death and various factions vie for control of the throne. Fifteen-year-old Iris, who is trained as a spy for Princess Elizabeth, acts as the princess's double in an effort to save the country from the Duke of Northumberland. 176 pages.

Turner, A. (1987). *Nettie's Trip South.* New York: Macmillan. Based on the actual diary of the author's great-grandmother, this picture book tells about the cruel realities a 10-year-old girl encounters when she visits Richmond, Virginia, and witnesses a slave auction. 32 pages.

Wildlife Education. (1984). *Zoo Books 2: Alligators and Crocodiles*. San Diego: Wildlife Education. This series of books depicts a variety of zoo animals.

Ylvisaker, A. (2002). *Dear Papa*. Cambridge, MA: Candlewick. One year after her father's death in 1942, nine-year-old Isabelle begins writing him letters, which are interspersed with letters to other family members, relating important events in her life and how she feels about them. 184 pages.

Reading Instruction for English-Language Learners

chapter outline

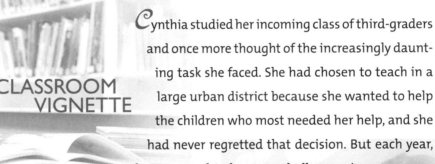

CLASSROOM VIGNETTE

*C*ynthia studied her incoming class of third-graders and once more thought of the increasingly daunting task she faced. She had chosen to teach in a large urban district because she wanted to help the children who most needed her help, and she had never regretted that decision. But each year, there seemed to be more challenges, including meeting Reading First requirements, preparing students for the ever-increasing and ever-more-critical testing the state did annually, and working with more and more students who did not speak English as their first language.

The latter challenge, working with English-language learners, was for her the most daunting one. She had completed a teacher education program in the Midwest a decade ago, where no attention had been given to working with children who did not speak English as their first language. This year, almost 30 percent of her students were English learners. A few of them spoke no English. Two of them had not had any sort of formal schooling. Others had received excellent instruction in their homeland schools and could read and write very well in their native languages.

What could she do? Her task, she knew, was to lead all of her English learners as well as her students who spoke English as their native language toward a level of literacy that would enable them to succeed in school and beyond. She knew a lot about good teaching, and she was convinced that good teaching is effective with all students. But she was constantly on the lookout for approaches that would prove particularly effective for English learners.

Learning to Read English as a Second Language in the United States

Here, we first comment on the challenges Cynthia and many other teachers face in fostering reading achievement in English-language learners and then briefly describe the historical and contemporary U.S. landscape within which English learners must learn to read English.

Fostering Reading Achievement in English-Language Learners

As Cynthia realizes, fostering reading achievement in English-language learners is a significant challenge. Yet as Cynthia and many other educators are increasingly realizing (Vaughan, 2005), good teaching is effective with all students. All students, including English learners, will benefit from both the more traditional instructional practices and the instructional practices motivated by constructivist and sociocultural theories that we recommended in Chapter 2.

This is not to say that using effective instructional practices is all that we can do for English learners. There are many more things we can do, and in the section of this chapter on instructional principles, we list several sets of suggestions specific to English learners. However, following the general principles of effective instruction summarized in In the Classrooms 13.1 and 13.2 is the starting point for instructing all students.

Traditional Instructional Principles

- Focus on academically relevant tasks—that is, on important topics, skills, and strategies that students really need to master.

- Employ active teaching. Know your subject well, be the instructional leader in your classroom, and actively convey to students the content to be learned in presentations, discussions, and demonstration.

- Foster active learning. Give students opportunities to manipulate and grapple with the material they are learning.

instructional routines in the **Classroom 13.1**

- Distinguish between instruction and practice. Instruction consists of teaching students knowledge, skills, and strategies. Practice consists of asking students to use the knowledge, skills, and strategies that they have already been taught.
- Provide sufficient and timely feedback. Whenever possible, respond to students' work with immediate and specific feedback.
- Teach for transfer. Transfer seldom occurs automatically. If we want students to use what they have learned in one context in a new context, we need to show them how to do so.

Instructional Principles Motivated by Constructivist and Sociocultural Theories

instructional routines in the Classroom 13.2

- Scaffold students' efforts. Provide students with the temporary support they need to complete tasks they could not complete independently.
- Provide instruction in students' zone of proximal development. Instruct students at a level that challenges them but allows them to achieve with effort and with your assistance.
- Use the gradual release of responsibility model. Begin instruction on difficult topics by initially doing much of the work yourself; then, over time, give students increasing responsibility for the work until eventually they are doing all of it.
- Use cognitive modeling. Think aloud for students, demonstrating the thinking you employ as you complete a task that you are teaching them to do.
- Use direct explanation. In teaching strategies, (1) give students a description of the strategy and when, how, and why it should be used, (2) model it, (3) work along with students as they use the strategy, (4) gradually give students increased responsibility for using the strategy, and (5) have students use the strategy independently.
- Ensure that students contextualize, review, and practice what is learned. Real learning takes time, effort, and a lot of practice.
- Teach for understanding. Teach in such a way that students understand topics fully, remember important information, and actively use what they have learned.

The U.S. Landscape

As noted in the U.S. Department of Education's *The Conditions of Education 2005* (Wirt et al., 2005), the number of school-age children speaking a language other than English at home grew from 3.8 million in 1979 to 9.9 million in 2003. During this same period of time, the number of children speaking English with some difficulty increased from 1.3 million to 2.9 million. This huge increase in the number of English learners has had a tremendous impact on U.S. schools; while the overall number of school-age children increased by 19 percent from 1979 to 2003, the number of children who spoke English with some difficulty increased by 124 percent (Wirt et al., 2005).

Data cited by Kamil and Bernhardt (2004) indicate that the vast majority of these children—almost three-quarters of them—speak Spanish; no other language is spoken by more than 4 percent of the remainder of the students, whose languages include Vietnamese, Hmong, Cantonese, Cambodian, Korean, and a number of Native American languages. While English learners can be found

Immigrants, many of whom speak languages other than English, have long been a part of the U.S. scene.

in the vast majority of large schools, their distribution across the United States is uneven. The percentages of school-age children who speak a language other than English at home range from 31 percent in the West to 10 percent in the South, with 19 percent in the Northeast and 16 percent in the Midwest (Wirt et al., 2005).

The most recent National Association of Educational Progress (NAEP) report (Perie, Grigg, & Donahue, 2005) presents some data comparing performance of English-language learners to that of non-English-language learners. The NAEP reports students' performance in terms of three achievement levels—basic, proficient, and advanced. The lowest level, the basic level, is defined as denoting "partial mastery of prerequisite knowledge and skills that are fundamental for proficient work at each grade." According to the most recent NAEP report, only 27 percent of ELL fourth-graders scored at or above the basic level, while 66 percent of non-ELL fourth-graders scored at or above the basic level. Thus, over twice as many non-ELL students as ELL students succeeded at this level.

U.S. schools have always been populated with children from diverse linguistic backgrounds, and teachers have had to confront the challenges of linguistic diversity for many years. One estimate suggests a total of 42 percent of all public school teachers have at least one English-language learner in their classes (Olson & Goldstein, 1997).

The apparently opposing forces of the home language and English have been at issue since the birth of the United States. Benjamin Franklin, John Adams, and Noah Webster, for example, all argued that a common language was a key element in promoting social unity (Simpson, 1986). Indeed, throughout the development of the U.S. public school system during the 19th and early 20th centuries, the concept of one people/one language was central (Higham, 1988). The world wars, particularly World War I and its aftermath, marked by southern and eastern European immigration, solidified this belief in the minds of many Americans.

Yet other Americans have always viewed ethnic pride as a hallmark of American freedom and the suppression of language and culture as contradicting the American spirit. They argue that the strength of America lies in the diversity of culture, beliefs, and perspectives of persons who flock to America seeking a better life (Tollefson, 1995). This tolerance for diversity is certainly reflected in the most recently published large-scale study of reading instruction for English learners, Robert Slavin and Alan Cheung's "A Synthesis of Research on Language of Reading Instruction for English Language Learners" (2005). It is also the position that will undoubtedly be reflected in the upcoming report of The National Literacy Panel (August & Shanahan, in press), an even more comprehensive review of the literature on reading instruction for English learners.

CW 13.1 links to Dave's ESL Cafe, which includes material for teachers, students, and all those interested in promoting English learners' achievement.

Some Challenges of Learning to Read in a Second Language

Most immigrant families become English-dominant in less than two generations, so why is there anything to be concerned about? We know that the children in our classrooms will more than likely become speakers of English. Isn't it a simple case of waiting until this happens? The answer is no! Research indicates that it takes English-language learners at least five years to reach the oral skill level of their English-speaking peers (Cummins, 2001). Waiting five years to begin reading instruction would mean that many ELL children would be adolescents before we started them on literacy learning. This would be educationally and morally absurd. We know that all children need to begin literacy learning as early as possible in order to become effective literacy users. What, then, does every teacher need to understand about what having a first oral language means in relation to learning a second language and learning to read in that language? We will discuss this question first in terms of the challenges faced by learners, then in terms of the challenges faced by teachers, and finally in terms of the light that research can shed on these challenges.

Before we do so, however, we will introduce some linguistic terms and concepts (see Figure 13.1 on page 400). Some of these terms and concepts are probably familiar to you and some probably are not, but at this point it is crucial that you become familiar with all of those listed here.

Challenges Faced by English-Language Learners

As we pointed out in Chapters 4 and 5, the oral language that children bring to school is a terrific starting point for literacy learning. English-speaking children have internalized an extraordinary amount of language by the time they come to school—about 75 percent of all the syntax and morphology they will ever acquire. Effective literacy teaching is rooted in understanding how children use what they already know about oral language as they learn to deal with printed language.

Like their English-speaking classmates, English-language learners come to U.S. schools with a considerable amount of language knowledge. They too possess nearly all of the structure and morphology they will need to become fluent speakers. The difference, though, is that they are on the road to becoming

Syntax refers to the ways in which words combine to form sentences. The syntax of an English sentence is most often a subject followed by a verb followed by an object, as in *I see the man*. An unacceptable combination in English would be *I the man I see* because the syntax of English requires the verb to follow the subject in most cases.

Morphology refers to ways that words are built through adding parts. *Man*, for example, is an individual word and one morpheme. We can add the morpheme *-ly* to form *manly*, a new word that contains two morphemes. Different languages have different morphological systems for word building.

Inflections are special types of morphemes. The addition of *-s* on many words indicates plural in English. We add *-ed* to regular verbs to indicate past tense and *-er* to indicate the comparative. Inflections do not change the type of the word they are attached to (verbs remain verbs and nouns remain nouns).

The **lexicon** of a language is the body of words that make up the language. There are hundreds of thousands of words in the English lexicon. The English lexicon is made up of a very small set of frequently used words and a very large set of infrequently used words.

Orthography refers to writing systems. English, Spanish, French, German, and Finnish all use Roman letters and hence have Roman orthography. Russian uses a different alphabet, the Cyrillic alphabet, and hence has Cyrillic orthography.

FIGURE 13.1

Some Key Linguistic Terms

fluent speakers of a language that is not typically used for either instruction or assessment in U.S. schools. It is not that English-language learners come to school with a language deficit. They come with a lack of knowledge of the particular language that is used in the schools they will be attending—English. This presents several significant challenges.

There is a surface-level mismatch between the child's language and the language of the school. Children who speak a language other than English will approach learning to read with the best strategy they have—matching the oral language they know with the written language they see. This, however, presents them with an enormous challenge: *The oral language they know and the written language they must learn will have differing degrees of overlap.*

In addition to this surface-level mismatch, there are less obvious and in some ways deeper differences between English-speaking children raised in the United States and some non-English-speaking children raised in other settings. As we pointed out in Chapters 4 and 5, most children who have grown up in the United States have internalized a number of concepts relevant to learning to read. These concepts, of course, may or may not be well developed, and some children certainly have more extensive and richer preschool literacy experiences than other children. Nevertheless, regardless of their background, an English-language print experience surrounds virtually all students who grow up in the United States; they generally know that print signals a relationship to meaning.

The situation is quite different for some students who were not raised in the United States. Some children come from cultures that are not literate. Print, reading, and the many experiences that surround print and reading have never been part of their world. These children must learn what print actually is and how it functions. This brings us to a second challenge: *They have yet to develop the rich and varied schemata that many children internalize from growing up in a literate culture.*

Quite a different situation exists for other students. Many children come from cultures with rich literacy heritages (children from Arab nations and India, for example), but those literacy heritages may have produced quite different understandings about print and how it functions. This brings us to a third challenge: *The rich and varied schemata about literacy that they internalized from growing up in their culture may need to be altered.*

Like their English-speaking classmates, English-language learners will exhibit different degrees of skills, intelligences, and motivations. As with all children in our classrooms, we see the array of talents that they demonstrate each day. We often assume that the more verbal children are the more able learners and that the very social children are the more cooperative and interested learners. However, English-language learners frequently come from cultures that do not value a great deal of verbal behavior from children, perceiving it to be rude. Moreover, and perhaps more important, English-language learners frequently cannot express what they do in fact know. This brings us to a fourth challenge—really a pair of them: *The verbal abilities of children may not match what they actually know, and they may be reticent to express themselves verbally in class.*

Challenges Faced by Teachers

Like children who must learn to read in a second language, teachers who strive to assist English-language learners in becoming competent readers face significant challenges. How can we bridge the gap between students who have five or six years of oral language development that is directly relevant to the literacy task at hand and students whose oral language development is only indirectly relevant to the literacy task at hand? Three particularly important challenges confront us here.

First, the extra processing steps needed by English-language learners make the instructional task doubly difficult. In many cases, these children have the concepts necessary to understand a text, but they use sounds and words that do not match the print. *We as teachers must prepare students to succeed at this difficult matching task by building their oral English skills.*

Second, as Figure 13.2 illustrates, speakers of different languages will have varying amounts of processing to do as they move from the language they know to the language they are learning. The Spanish-speaking child needs to go from the Spanish *gato* to the English *cat,* two words that show some distinct print overlap. But what of the child who has to go from the Vietnamese *mão* to *cat?* The task for the Vietnamese-speaking child is considerably more difficult because none of the letters overlap with those of the English word. *We as teachers must prepare for success both those students whose language overlaps a lot with English and those whose language overlaps very little with English.*

As daunting as these instructional issues are, they pale in comparison with the third challenge—dealing with the potential mismatch between children's conceptual understanding and their verbal abilities in English. Figure 13.3 illustrates this mismatch. As Juan's thoughts reveal, he definitely learned some things from the field trip, but he is unable to verbalize his understanding. As a result, the teacher mistakenly believes that he learned nothing from the trip and thus grossly underestimates his understanding. Most unfortunatly, this inaccurate assessment is quite likely to influence the teacher's future work with

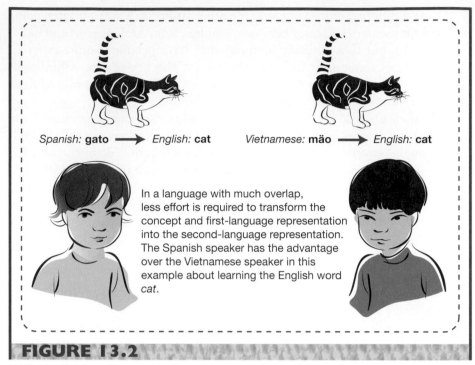

FIGURE 13.2

Differential Amounts of Print Overlap in Languages

Juan. Her developing schema for Juan is that he does not understand, and the teacher is very likely to interpret many of Juan's future actions in light of this schema. *We as teachers must work to build ELL students' conceptual understanding and also realize that they may sometimes be unable to verbalize the conceptual understanding they actually possess.*

What Light Does Research Shed on These Challenges?

Prompted by the huge increase in English learners in U.S. schools, a good deal of research has focused on how to best help non-native speakers of English develop their English literacy skills. A number of reviews provide excellent summaries of this research. In one of them, Jill Fitzgerald (1995) focuses on instructional issues. In another, Diane August and Kenji Hakuta (1998) review the research located by a national committee investigating instruction for language-minority children. In a third review, Elizabeth Bernhardt (2000) gives a general account of issues in second-language reading for students of various ages. In still another, Georgia Garcia (2000) deals with the problems of young, mostly bilingual students who are learning to read English. In a fifth report, Russell Gersten and Scott Baker (2000) focus on instructional issues. In a sixth report, Robert Slavin and Alan Cheung (2005) concentrate on the effects of the language or languages that are used for instruction. And, in a report that will be published shortly, Diane August and Timothy Shanahan (in press) present the result of research reviewed by The National Literacy Panel on Language Minority Children and Youth.

We can, of course, learn about many important dimensions of reading in a second language from research. Here, we focus on several of the most immediate dimensions: the importance of language knowledge, the importance of literacy in the first language, cross-language influences, and cross-cultural influences.

FIGURE 13.3

Mismatch Between What a Student Knows and What He Says in Response to a Teacher's Question

The Importance of Language Knowledge

There is no question that, when doing tasks in a second language, the more the learner knows about the structure and lexicon of the language, the better. Research has indicated that at least 30 percent of the process of second-language reading involves grammatical and lexical knowledge (Bernhardt & Kamil, 1995; Brisbois, 1995; Hulstijn, 1991). This finding suggests that facilitating language development is crucial. Simply put, the more English words ELL students know and the more English sentence structures they learn, the better off they will be.

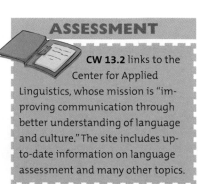

ASSESSMENT

CW 13.2 links to the Center for Applied Linguistics, whose mission is "improving communication through better understanding of language and culture." The site includes up-to-date information on language assessment and many other topics.

It is critical, however, to place this finding in the context of this fact: Second-language acquisition is developmental in nature. That is, learning a second language is more like learning a first language than different from it. Neither providing direct instruction in forms before students exhibit developmental readiness nor teaching forms out of context will lead to functional proficiency in a second language, any more than it does in a first language. ESL teacher James Garcia stresses the importance of recognizing this developmental sequence:

> Whenever I am working with English-language learners, I remind myself that they will follow certain sequences in their learning of English, regardless of what I do. For example, verbs with -*ing* forms will appear early in their spoken language; inflections, such as the third-person singular -*s*, will appear quite late, if they ever appear. Similarly, learning to deal with forming negatives is a process of first learning the negation words and attaching them externally to sentences; internal negation develops over time. The development of question forms and the creation of relative clauses also proceed over time. They are not "not there" one day and then "there" the next, no matter how much instruction I provide.
>
> —James Garcia, ESL Teacher

In order for this developmental growth to occur, the learner must experience many examples of language use. How can the learner know what is more sophisticated unless she hears it or sees it? In like manner, the influence of peers—the desire to be part of the group—is enormous. This desire compels the learner to take on the linguistic characteristics present in the environment. The more rapidly these dynamics take hold, the higher the second-language literacy achievement. Bilingual teacher Margaret Thayer suggests one powerful way to foster interactions between English-language learners and native-English speakers—establishing a buddy system:

> One of the most successful things we have done in our classroom is to set up a buddy system in which we deliberately pair our native English speakers with our English-language learners. We do this at the beginning of the year or whenever an English-language learner enters the class, and from that time on, the two students do many things together. They work as a pair doing in-class assignments, talk about what they have read, and work together on homework. Of course, in many cases, the native speaker serves more often as the tutor and the English-language learner as the learner. But whenever possible, we try to get the English-language learner in the teacher's role. Often, for example, the English-language learner teaches his English-speaking buddy some things about his language or culture. And, in many cases, the pairing doesn't end at the school. Buddies often visit each other's homes, share holidays, and pal around together. As I said, the buddy system has been a real success. Also, it does not take up a lot of the teacher's time, always an important consideration when you have lots of kids who need your assistance.
>
> —Margaret Thayer, Bilingual Teacher

The Importance of Literacy in the First Language

Unquestionably, there is a strong relationship between literacy skills in a first language and literacy skills in a second. Research indicates that about 20 percent of the process of reading in a second language is predictable on the basis of the level of first-language literacy (Bernhardt & Kamil, 1995; Brisbois, 1995; Hulstijn, 1991). In other words, the more knowledge of reading and understanding of literacy a student has in her first language, the better her knowledge and understanding will be of a second. Even when children are literate in a language that has little or no overlap with English, the mere fact that they are already literate really helps them. Why is this the case?

Attaining literacy means having developed a set of strategies for coping with written materials. Literate children understand that print represents meaning and that there are purposes for reading. They have already begun to develop many of the proficiencies described throughout this book.

The most challenged English-language learner is one who has no first-language literacy. This type of learner is in double jeopardy—she has to learn the language, and she has to learn what literacy is about.

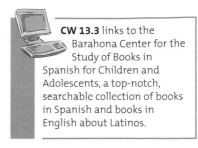

CW 13.3 links to the Barahona Center for the Study of Books in Spanish for Children and Adolescents, a top-notch, searchable collection of books in Spanish and books in English about Latinos.

Cross-Language Influences

How a person processes a second language is influenced by her processing of the first language (Bernhardt, 1991). English, for example, tends toward subject-verb-object word order, as in *The man sees the dog*. Other languages, such as German, have more flexible word order; it is the inflectional system that indicates who is seeing what. While *man* and *dog* in a German-language sentence may be in the same order as in an English sentence, the inflectional system might indicate that the man is being seen by the dog. *Der Mann sieht den Hund, Den Hund sieht der Mann, Der Hund sieht den Mann,* and *Den Mann sieht der Hund* are all possibilities in German. Subject-object-verb languages, such as Chinese, will represent the word order as *The man the dog sees*.

Because of the linguistic transfer from language to language, readers will assume that the word order they are used to will be used in the language they are learning. The comprehension challenges that such cross-language influences present are daunting.

Cross-Cultural Influences

There is no question that second-language readers employ background knowledge. This is consistent with what you have learned throughout this book about all learners. Unfortunately, in some cases the background knowledge an English-language learner brings to a text is absolutely irrelevant, and in other cases it is simply inconsistent with the knowledge assumed by the text. Such situations, of course, create serious challenges for English-language learners.

One study forcefully demonstrating the influence of background knowledge was conducted by Margaret Steffenson and her colleagues (Steffenson, Joag-Dev, & Anderson, 1979). Readers were asked to read passages about weddings—from their own culture and another culture. Even though they had no language problems, the readers recalled the passages in a way that was consistent with the way in which weddings were conducted in their own culture. They took the language at hand and reconfigured it in a way that made sense within their own framework. This is an absolutely critical issue in the second-language literacy process. Learners both read and write within the framework that is most familiar to them—their linguistic and cultural framework. They need to learn to break with these patterns in order to develop literacy abilities in English. Sixth-grade teacher Susan Chen comments on being alert to cross-cultural differences:

> I'm always on the lookout for concepts and ideas that my Hmong students are likely to interpret somewhat differently than my Anglo students or points at which my Hmong students are likely to have had somewhat different experiences that they can share with other students. For example, whenever we talk about U.S. holidays such as Martin Luther King, Jr., Day or Labor Day, I make it a point to ask my Hmong

students to talk about some of their holidays and what they celebrate. Or, if we are talking about farms and most of my students are thinking of the huge farms that exist in California and the Midwest today, I ask my Hmong students to describe the small family farms that they have known or have learned about from their parents and other grown-ups. This leaves both my Anglo students and my Hmong students knowing more than they would have without the other group's contributions. It also avoids confusion, such as that which develops when both groups are considering farms but one group is thinking of huge corporate farms and the other group is thinking of small plots of land.

—Susan Chen, Sixth-Grade Teacher

Reflect *and* Apply

1. Listen carefully to the radio or television or examine several magazines or newspapers. What kinds of attitudes toward non-native speakers of English do you find in these media?
2. Imagine a 10-year-old student who has just arrived in the United States after growing up in Iraq. Brainstorm a list of just a few of the myriad topics familiar to virtually all 10-year-olds who grew up in the United States but probably unfamiliar to this student from Iraq. Now brainstorm a list of a few topics you expect are familiar to 10-year-olds who grew up in Iraq but probably unfamiliar to U.S. students.

Instructional Principles

We now turn to practical application of the information we have discussed in the earlier sections of the chapter. Your own situation will, of course, be unique. You may have a class in which only one language other than English is spoken, or you may have a class in which several different languages are spoken. You may have only one or two non-native speakers in your classroom, or you may have many. Whatever your specific situation, the following guidelines and principles will lead you to ask appropriate questions and work toward effective classroom instruction.

As a cardinal rule, note that it is important that you remember everything you know about first-language reading when you are teaching reading to English-language learners. Most of the principles and practices will work as they do for children who speak English as natives. Some of them, of course, will have to be adapted. But very few will have to be discarded altogether. In the next three sections of the chapter, we present three sets of instructional suggestions. The first is from Lisa Delpit, and the second is a version of Michael Kamil and Elizabeth Bernhardt's (2004) recommendations. The third set is from various sources.

Delpit's Principles for Working with Poor Urban Children

Lisa Delpit (1995) has presented a set of principles for working with poor urban children. While many English-language learners are urban and poor, many are not. However, much of what Delpit suggests applies to all children. Here, we discuss and interpret those of Delpit's principles that we see as most important for working with English learners.

English Learners

CW 13.4 links to the Internet TESL Journal, an excellent source of lessons, teaching techniques, and articles useful in working with English learners.

Demand Critical Thinking

Often, we fall into the trap of thinking that students who speak a different language are not as bright as other students. Consequently, we often reason that they cannot handle critical thinking. No judgment could be more debilitating to students' growth. The goals of a high level of literacy and the literacy curriculum that we outlined in Chapter 1 and have discussed throughout this book are just as appropriate for English-language learners as they are for any other students. For example, the goal of deep understanding and the approaches to teaching for deep understanding that we described in Chapter 11—such as text talk and questioning the author—are absolutely crucial to second-language learners.

Ensure Access to the Basic Skills, Conventions, and Strategies Essential to Success in U.S. Education

We sometimes begin teaching non-native speakers with less emphasis on skills than middle-class children typically receive. This will not work! We are not suggesting that you teach only basic skills. As we just noted, a high level of literacy is the goal. But do remember that although not all children come to school with the same skills, all students need to master the building blocks that lead to literacy. As a teacher, you want to be certain that your students acquire whatever skills they need to be successful in school and in later life, something Timothy Hayden, a third-grade teacher, makes a conscious effort to do:

> One thing I really try to work on with my Puerto Rican students is mastery of basic skills, such as standard usage and spelling, while still giving them plenty of chances to do critical thinking. This is a tough decision to make because I know that in many cases my kids know more than their English skills show, and so in some sense I'm slowing them down to work on the basics. Yet I also know that if they can't read when they leave school, or use poor grammar or spelling when they're looking for a job, they

Creating an "I can do it!" attitude in second-language learners and conveying to them that you as their teacher hold an "I can help you do it!" attitude are crucial.

won't get very far. That's why I feel that I have to balance attention to basics with attention to higher-level stuff.

—Timothy Hayden, Third-Grade Teacher

Empower Students to Challenge Racist Views of Their Competence and Worthiness

Racism and classism often extend to children who are non-native speakers of English. You must support your English-language learners' egos and help them build the sort of self-worth that will lead them to persevere when they encounter challenges. As we discussed in Chapter 2, all students need the support and skills that will enable them to meet challenges, be successful, and realize that success is something under their control. Creating an "I can do it!" attitude in your English-language learners and conveying to them that you as their teacher hold an "I can help you do it!" attitude are crucial. Providing reading experiences such as the kind sixth-grade teacher Ann Beecher does in In the Classroom 13.3 will promote positive attitudes.

Using the Shared Reading Experience in a Sixth-Grade ESL Class

Ann Beecher teaches sixth grade in a public school in a Los Angeles suburb. The majority of the students in her ESL class speak Spanish as their primary language, with a sprinkling of students speaking a variety of other languages. Ms. Beecher has found that the shared reading experience—students and teacher reading aloud together—is a highly effective technique for developing confidence and building on students' skills in reading and speaking English. "My English-language learners are often reticent to risk being wrong or making mistakes when it comes to speaking or reading in English," Ms. Beecher says. "So I need to think of ways to create a safe environment that will support their learning. One of those ways is the shared reading experience. It's a risk-free way for them to use oral language." Here are the steps Ms. Beecher usually follows in preparing a shared reading experience:

in the Classroom 13.3

- *Choose a selection.* Ms. Beecher most frequently uses poetry, perhaps a poem from Shel Silverstein's *Falling Up* (1996) or a poem from their literature text. "One of the class favorites is 'The Shark' by John Ciardi. They enjoy reciting the colorful words Ciardi uses to describe the shark, such as *gulper, ripper, snatcher, grabber.*" Ms. Beecher occasionally uses a very short piece of prose, also something from their literature text. "The key is choosing something that will engage students, something that they will really enjoy and can relate to," Ms. Beecher says. "One of the values of using the shared reading experience is that the students are reading 'at grade' materials. This is a big boost to their confidence. It gives them a real sense of accomplishment."

- *Set up an overhead projector, and make copies of the selection for each student.*

- *Prepare and motivate students for the selection.* "This usually takes very little effort," Ms. Beecher says. "When the kids see the overhead projector, they know it means we're going to read something together. It's one of their favorite things we do. Like singing or reciting jazz chants, they enjoy the rhythm of the language and the community experience of speaking the same words together."

- *With expression and enthusiasm, read through the selection once or twice, and then invite students to read along in unison.*

- *Focus on a particular reading skill or strategy.* "If we are reading rhyming poetry, usually I will circle the rhyming words on the overhead and have students do the same on their copies. I will talk about certain words and check for students' understanding. Also, sometimes when

I first read the piece through, I will stop occasionally and have students predict what will happen next."

- *Follow up the reading with a variety of activities*—art (illustrating the shark *gulping, ripping, snatching, grabbing,* for example), writing, or evaluating: "How did we do? Did you like the piece? Why? What did you like about it? Is there anything we should do differently next time? What's your favorite new word you learned?"

Recognize and Build on Strengths

The importance of building on students' strengths is such a truism, repeated so often, that it does not have a great deal of meaning for many of us. How, indeed, does one "build on a strength"? If you do not go beyond what a student already knows and can do, you run the risk of boring that child and losing her for the real tasks of learning that are to follow. Building on strength means that you should *begin* with what she can do best and work toward those things that she does not know or does not do well. Again, many of the principles from Chapter 3 and elsewhere in the book are very applicable. Ensure that students take on challenges they can meet and experience a steady diet of success by scaffolding their efforts as they move from the known to the new. Then gradually release responsibility to the students themselves as their competence and confidence grow. For some students, this will mean a lot of scaffolding and a very gradual handing over of responsibility. Others may readily accept challenges and thrive on them.

Use Familiar Metaphors and Experiences from the Children's World

Using metaphors and experiences from the children's world is another thing good teachers do instinctively. We know the importance of background knowledge. As Delpit suggests, instead of insisting that all children have the same background knowledge at the beginning, deal with the students' knowledge and background and use that as the basis of teaching. For example, if you are teaching about the destructive power of tornadoes and have Vietnamese children in your class, you can use their knowledge of the awesome power of typhoons as a bridge to understanding the power of tornadoes.

Create a Sense of Family and Caring

ESL teacher Lillian Colon-Vila (1997) knows how crucial it is that all students feel that they are a valuable part of the class and will be supported in their efforts by both the teacher and the other students in the class:

> To welcome my ESL students, I always begin the semester by telling a story. It's usually a simple one to welcome them to the United States and particularly to my classroom. Because I use the students' names and their native countries, I invent the stories on the spur of the moment. I use puppets, pictures, flash cards, or the chalkboard to draw pictures as I go along.
>
> I make it a point to share my own first day of school, too—how I stuttered, mispronounced the teacher's name, and wished for the floor to swallow me. The students laugh and relate to my experience. The iceberg between us breaks, and I can begin to teach.
>
> —Lillian Colon-Vila, ESL Multigrade Teacher

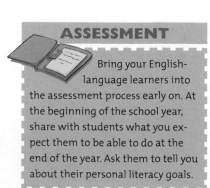

ASSESSMENT

Bring your English-language learners into the assessment process early on. At the beginning of the school year, share with students what you expect them to be able to do at the end of the year. Ask them to tell you about their personal literacy goals.

In the terminology we used earlier in the book, your classroom must be a literate environment for *all* students.

Monitor and Assess Needs, and Then Address Them with a Wealth of Diverse Strategies

Effective teaching cannot be done without careful assessment and evaluation of what students know and learn. Teachers need to be vigilant and prepared to discontinue teaching techniques that prove inappropriate for some students. Students can often benefit from a different teaching strategy when the one initially attempted did not work. Such choices require careful reasoning based on data gathered in assessing the students. As we emphasize in Chapter 14, assessment does not simply mean formal assessment. You will need to use a wide range of techniques to gauge students' strengths and weakness and then create ways to build on their strengths. These techniques are likely to include the use of formal tests, but they will also include talking to students, carefully observing them as they work at school tasks, and seeking insights from parents and others in your students' home communities. Figure 13.4 illustrates how a drawing can show a student's understanding of a story.

Honor and Respect Children's Home Cultures

It would be difficult to imagine anything seemingly easier than honoring and respecting children's home cultures, but unfortunately honor and respect are too often lacking in classrooms. Knowledge that has been gained in children's home cultures constitutes a strength that can be brought into the classroom and used as the basis for learning to read about all manner of ideas and topics. Besides, changing children's cultural orientations and allegiances is not really an option. Children come to school having spent a huge amount of time within their cultures and their families, and once they begin school, they will continue to spend far more time at home than in the classroom. You cannot win against such odds. It is just not possible to instill in children a totally different culture in a few hours a day—it may even be impossible to do so in a lifetime. Your goal must be to support students' attempts to maintain their cultural identities and to support their becoming successful in the mainstream culture represented by the school. One small step toward doing this might be

FIGURE 13.4

Maria's Drawing of *Island of the Blue Dolphins* by Scott O'Dell (1960) Reveals Her Understanding of the Story

taken during the birthday celebrations. Inviting English-language learners to share their birthday traditions with the class gives status to those traditions and adds to other students' store of knowledge about different cultures.

Another and more significant step toward demonstrating and fostering respect for children's home cultures is to provide students with literature that accurately and fairly represents a variety of cultures, as does Hispanic literature such as *Cinco de mayo* by Linda Lowery, *Julio's Magic* by Arthur Dorros, and *Napí* by Antonio Ramírez.

Reflect *and* Apply

3. Think about attitudes toward English-language learners that you have observed. Have you encountered attitudes that might negatively influence the ways in which teachers interact with students? How might you guard against allowing those attitudes to negatively affect your classroom style?

4. Consider your own family traditions. Can you think of any holiday celebrations you and your family enjoy that are not widely observed? Do you think they are any less valuable because they are not more widely observed? How might you use these holiday celebrations when you are teaching students?

Kamil and Bernhardt's Techniques for Working with English-Language Learners in Typical Classrooms

Michael Kamil and Elizabeth Bernhardt (2004) have developed a set of techniques specifically for working with English learners. Here, we present a slightly modified and shortened version of their recommendations. Like Kamil and Bernhardt, we have placed these techniques in an order reflecting their utility; thus, you should probably attempt to implement these principles in the order given. If you do this, you will probably have a good deal more success than if you simply select one or another of the principles from the list.

Take Advantage of the 20 Percent Rule

Remember that, although languages are different, there is considerable transfer between them. As indicated in the first part of this chapter, research suggests that the overlap between languages can be as much as 20 percent. Thus, your task in teaching literacy in a second language is far easier than if there were little or no overlap. You do not have to start at the beginning with English-language learners; rather, you can consider yourself as being one-fifth of the way to success.

Figure 13.5 shows the 20 percent rule in action. In this graphic display of generation of electricity, there are 17 Spanish words used. Three of the words—*natural, vapor,* and *magma*—are identical to the equivalent terms in English. Another seven words—*turbina, generador, uso, energía, geotérmica, producir,* and *electricidad*—are almost identical and certainly recognizable. This simple example illustrates the overlap between English and Spanish and reminds us that children do possess substantial information that they can draw on for reading second-language texts.

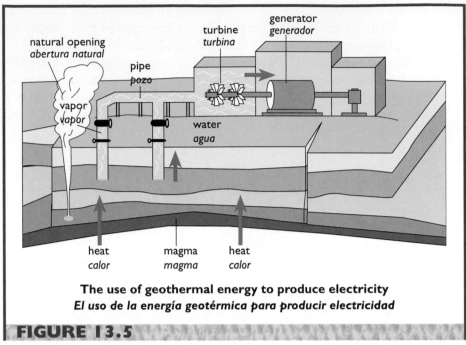

natural opening
abertura natural

vapor
vapor

pipe
pozo

turbine
turbina

generator
generador

water
agua

heat
calor

magma
magma

heat
calor

The use of geothermal energy to produce electricity
El uso de la energía geotérmica para producir electricidad

FIGURE 13.5

Graphic Display of Overlap Between Spanish and English Vocabulary

Source: Ciencias by Mallision, Mallision, Smallwood, & Valentino. Copyright © 1985 by Silver Burdett Ginn, Simon & Schuster Elementary. Used by permission.

CW 13.5 links to Pacific Resources for Education and Learning, whose vision is "a world where all children and communities are literate and healthy—global participants, grounded in and enriched by their cultures." The site includes a number of resources related to working with English learners.

Of course, as we all know, there is never a free lunch, and this rule holds true for the 20 percent dividend. The percentage will be different for each language. In some languages, the overlap may be greater than 20 percent, and in others, less.

When students in your classroom have some native-language literacy and are able to work with content, have them conduct Internet searches on topics you are covering in current events. For example, major new geologic discoveries, such as finding the bones of an ancient mammal, are often reported in *Weekly Reader* or in books that children naturally gravitate to; such findings are almost always discussed in the Internet press. Have your students read something about these findings in their native-language press and report on any differences between reports in English and what they have read. Such an activity reinforces using their first language to support their learning of the second. It also enhances their critical thinking skills by asking them to compare and contrast information presented in an array of sources and boosts their self-esteem by demonstrating to their peers that bilingualism actually provides greater access to information than monolingualism does.

Give English-Language Learners and Yourself Plenty of Time

It is important to remember that children who do not speak English as a native language will, in all likelihood, not be as automatic as native speakers at completing any English-language task, including, of course, reading. Figure 13.6 provides an example of the very different amounts of time it would take students reading at three different rates to complete a typical intermediate-grade book, in this case Gary Soto's *The Skirt*. If children are reading a longer book, something like Kazumi Yumoto's *The Spring Tone,* the amounts of time needed vary even more: To complete this book, Maria would need only about an hour, Carlos would need about two hours, and Chen would need over five and one-

STUDENT	READING RATE (WORDS PER MINUTE)	CHAPTER ONE (1,000 WORDS)	WHOLE BOOK (8,000 WORDS)
Maria	250	4 minutes	32 minutes
Carlos	150	7 minutes	53 minutes
Chen	50	20 minutes	2 hours, 40 minutes

FIGURE 13.6

Times Required for Three Students, with Varying Reading Rates, to Read Gary Soto's *The Skirt*

half hours. The instructional implication of these illustrations is straightforward: Provide English-language learners with extra time to complete the linguistic tasks you ask them to do.

Following this simple suggestion can minimize what is perhaps the greatest difficulty teachers face in multilanguage classrooms. The question, of course, is how you can provide this extra time, and we have several suggestions. Students who need the time can be given opportunities to complete their work as part of free-choice activities. Or they might be allowed to take home work that isn't completed during class. Or you might give students the questions you will ask ahead of time during reading lessons, being sure to give *all* students sufficient time to do the reading and thinking necessary to answer them. Still another option is to shorten some of the selections students are asked to read by summarizing parts of them. In the Classroom 13.4, for example, includes a summary of the first half of Pegi Deiz Shea's *The Whispering Cloth: A Refugee's Story.*

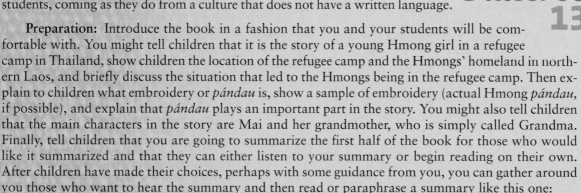

Summarizing Part of a Selection

The Whispering Cloth: A Refugee's Story is a touching story of a young Hmong girl, Mai, who learns to create embroidered tapestries—*pándau,* in the Hmong language—while in a refugee camp in Thailand. The book is beautifully illustrated with both watercolors and reproductions of the *pándau* Mai created. Although the book is not a long read for students who read fluently, for students beginning to read English it constitutes a formidable task. Summarizing the first half of the book would simplify that task considerably, particularly for Hmong students, coming as they do from a culture that does not have a written language.

Preparation: Introduce the book in a fashion that you and your students will be comfortable with. You might tell children that it is the story of a young Hmong girl in a refugee camp in Thailand, show children the location of the refugee camp and the Hmongs' homeland in northern Laos, and briefly discuss the situation that led to the Hmongs being in the refugee camp. Then explain to children what embroidery or *pándau* is, show a sample of embroidery (actual Hmong *pándau,* if possible), and explain that *pándau* plays an important part in the story. You might also tell children that the main characters in the story are Mai and her grandmother, who is simply called Grandma. Finally, tell children that you are going to summarize the first half of the book for those who would like it summarized and that they can either listen to your summary or begin reading on their own. After children have made their choices, perhaps with some guidance from you, you can gather around you those who want to hear the summary and then read or paraphrase a summary like this one:

As *The Whispering Cloth* opens, we learn that Mai lives in a refugee camp with her grandmother and that Mai can remember little of her life outside of the camp. She knows, though, that many people leave the refugee camp and some of them go to America, and it seems that she would like to go there too. Partly to give her something to do and partly to provide the family with some income, Grandma teaches Mai to make *pándau*. Mai learns very quickly and is soon very good at making this beautiful "flowery cloth." One day, Mai begins to work on a *pándau* in which she tells a story that is filling her head with thoughts.

Then introduce the reading as follows:

As you read the rest of the book, you will see pictures of the *pándau* that Mai stitched. Now read the rest of the book to see the *pándau* and what it meant to Mai and her Grandma, and what they decided to do with it.

To be an effective teacher of language-minority students, you also need to give yourself extra time, particularly when making day-to-day informal assessments of their progress. You will have to train yourself to perceive their progress in different ways, since that progress will not look or sound the same as progress for native speakers. The extra moments to think through whether you have made the right instructional decision for a second-language child will pay off in the end both for the child and for your self-confidence as a teacher.

Use the Rosetta Stone Technique

We have all heard about the wonder of the Rosetta Stone. This tremendous discovery, shown in Figure 13.7, contains the same text in Egyptian hieroglyphics, Egyptian demotic script, and several ancient Greek languages. The discovery of the Rosetta Stone allowed linguists to decipher Egyptian hieroglyphics,

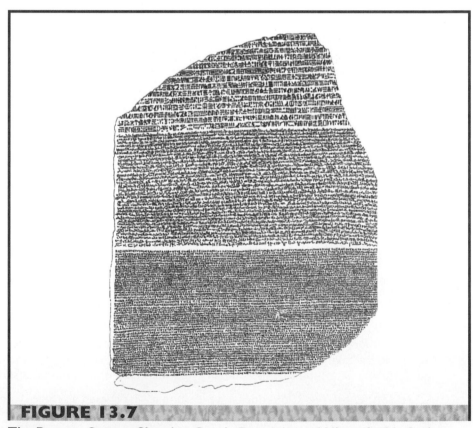

FIGURE 13.7

The Rosetta Stone—Showing Greek, Demotic, and Hieroglyphic Scripts

which they did not know how to read, based on their knowledge of ancient Greek, which they could read.

One useful vocabulary technique for working with a class that includes English-language learners is based on this approach. If you make a chart of everyday English words in one column, your students who speak other languages can contribute the equivalent words from each of their languages in other columns. Alternatively, your English-language learners might periodically bring in a word from their native language, put it on the chart, and solicit the equivalent English word and words in other languages represented in your class. Or, as you encounter words in a content lesson, you could use them as the entries in the Rosetta chart and have students add the equivalent words from their languages.

Whatever the specific source of words you put on the chart, be certain to practice pronouncing both non-English and English words with the non-native speakers, as well as with the entire class. In this way, all students will be able to do well at some parts of the task. Also, not only will your students for whom English is a native language begin to learn some vocabulary in another language; they will also begin to appreciate the difficulties other students are having. And they will be able to see that English-language learners know a great deal that they do not know.

Involve Parents, Siblings, and Other Speakers of the Children's Languages

Often, parents, siblings, or other relatives can help in translating between the native language and English, or vice versa. Sometimes all it takes is a bridge between languages to get children started. Translating the first page or so of a text they have begun to read or making a graphic organizer of what they are going to read, such as that shown in Figure 13.8, can be extremely helpful

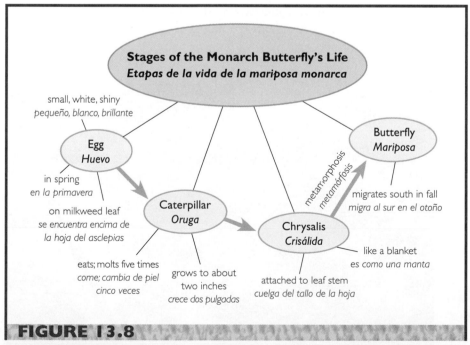

FIGURE 13.8

Graphic Organizer in English and Spanish for a Section of Lynn Rosenblatt's *Monarch Magic!*

for young learners. Moreover, such a bridge can work both ways. As students become more proficient in English, many times they assume the role of translator for parents who are not quite as proficient. This will give students a reason for wanting to learn more English and may encourage the parents to learn more English as well. In addition, as students become increasingly competent in English, they will be motivated to become still more competent.

Siblings can sometimes be particularly helpful in the classroom. Older brothers or sisters who may be reluctant to participate in their own class because they are not as proficient as their first-language classmates may work extremely well with their younger brothers or sisters. An added bonus here is that, when tutoring these younger students, the older siblings may very well realize that they know more English than they thought and consequently be encouraged to attempt to read when they would have otherwise been reluctant to do so.

Use All the Available People Resources

As we have pointed out several times, tutoring can be a useful technique in a host of literacy learning contexts. For learning to read in a second language, it may have particular benefits. Of course, one great benefit will accrue if you are fortunate enough to have older students who speak the same languages as your students and are somewhat more proficient in reading English than your students are. Again, sometimes the older students may realize that they know more English than they thought and be encouraged to attempt more challenging reading tasks themselves. They may also be motivated to learn more because they begin to realize what they do not know yet or because they wish to do a better job in helping the younger students.

Of course, students who are the same age as the tutees but have somewhat more advanced English reading skills can also serve as classroom tutors. And as is the case with cross-age tutors, peer tutors are likely to benefit from the teaching they do. As we have noted before, the research strongly demonstrates that students tutoring other students is a true win-win situation in which both

Parents or other volunteers who speak the English learners' language can be a huge help in your classroom.

tutor and tutee benefit markedly (Cohen, Kulic, & Kulic, 1982). Finally, students are not the only people resources that may be of help in your classroom. Aides, volunteers, college students preparing to be teachers, and sometimes even administrators and maintenance personnel can perform a variety of helpful tasks with English-language learners.

In Assessing Students, Give Them the Freedom to Choose the Language in Which to Respond

Research tells us that students often demonstrate greater abilities when they are given the option of responding in the language in which they feel most comfortable. This is particularly true, of course, when the text is in English and the students are not fluent in English.

Although allowing students to respond in their native language is a very easy thing for you as an instructor to do, it can pay big dividends. In addition to demonstrating better understanding when using the language of their choice, students may also be able to remember more of what they have learned in their native language. Also, students' language preference may vary for different reading materials. For example, a reading passage about a student's native country might be best responded to in the student's native language. In reading a passage about American history, however, a student might choose to use English. The key is to allow the student to choose the appropriate language in which to respond.

One thing that concerns some teachers about this technique is that they feel they will not be able to understand and assess what the students wrote or said. However, even if you cannot understand the language the student chooses, all is not lost. The easiest way to handle the situation is to have the student respond in her native language and *then* have her do the translation into English. Note the terrific practice this gives the student. She is, in effect, using the language-experience approach—writing down her own words and then translating them. Note also that allowing students the time to do this is one way of providing the extra time we have recommended. Alternatively, if the student cannot read what she wrote back to you or translate it into English later, you might obtain the assistance of a sibling, parent, or other speaker of the language to do the translating.

In addition to giving students the opportunity to respond in the language they choose, you can sometimes give them the opportunity to read in the language of their choice. Bilingual books, a growing set of children's books in which the same book contains both English and another language, make providing this option very convenient. A small sample of the books in this growing genre is shown in The Reading Corner on page 418. If you, aides, parent volunteers, or other volunteers speak the home languages of your students, you have still other opportunities to tap their native-language skills. You can give directions for classroom work and homework in both English and the students' native languages. This can be a huge help to students in doing their class work, and it can be a tremendous help to parents in assisting their children with homework.

Because there is a great deal of transfer between languages, it is probably the case that students who do not speak English fluently can often do far more than many teachers suspect. As we have already noted, many children have some literacy abilities in their native language. These abilities allow children to develop their own strategies for learning to read in a second language, particularly when the second language is similar to their native language in its

ASSESSMENT

CW 13.6 links to Assessing ELL Students. This site focuses on how students can show what they know in different ways, not just with paper and pencil.

the Reading Corner

Books Available in Bilingual Formats

Books with text in two languages, usually on facing pages, provide an outstanding opportunity for English learners to practice reading in both their own language and English. Moreover, the text in their stronger language acts as a scaffold for reading the text in their weaker language. The books listed below are a sample of the many books available. Searching sites such as Amazon.com with the terms *bilingual books* and *dual-language books* will yield hundreds more. Additionally, for locating books for Spanish-speaking students, Isabel Schon's *Recommended Books in Spanish for Children and Young Adults: 1991–1995* (1996), *Recommended Books in Spanish for Children and Young Adults: 1996 through 1999* (2001), and *Recommended Books in Spanish for Children and Young Adults: 2000 through 2004* (2004) and Schon and Sarah Berkin's *Introducción a la literatura infantil y juvenil* (1996) are extremely valuable.

George Ancona. *The Piñata Maker/El penatero*. Harcourt, 1994. With full-color photos and text in both Spanish and English, this book provides a glimpse into the art of piñata making. 40 pages. Excerpt:

When the glue is dry, he pastes metallic paper to the point of each cone, the *pico*, so they will glitter.

Cuando se seca el engrudo, pega papel metalico a la punta de cada cono, o al pico, para que reluzcan.

Rebecca T. Anonuevo. *Ang Mahiyaing Manok (The Shy Rooster)*. Pan Asia Publications, 2000. In this English/Filipino book, a shy young rooster who cannot crow as well or as loud as the other roosters proves his worth. 32 pages.

Eileen Browne. *Handa's Surprise* (Somali-English Bilingual Edition). Mantra Publishing, 1999. In this African tale, Handa puts delicious fruits in a basket to take to her friend in another village and passes several animals who find the fruit very inviting. 24 pages.

Fred Burstein. *The Dancer/La bailarina*. Bradbury, 1993. As a father accompanies his daughter to her ballet lesson, the sights they encounter—a horse, a flower, a fish, and more—are given in English, Spanish, and Japanese. 32 pages.

Lois Ehlert. *Moon Rope/Un lazo a la luna*. Harcourt, 1992. In this adaptation of a Peruvian folktale, Fox and Mole try to climb to the moon on a rope woven of grass. 32 pages.

Juan Ramon Jimenez. *Platero y yo/Platero and I*. Clarion, 1994. Short vignettes, evocatively illustrated with woodcuts, tell of the rambles of a man and his donkey around the countryside in Andalusia, Spain. 42 pages.

Robert Kraus and Debby Chen. *The Making of Monkey King*. Pan Asian Publications, 1998. This first book in the Adventures of Monkey King series, a fantasy about the adventures of a hero magically born from a rock who sets out to find the secret of immortality, is available as a bilingual text in English and Spanish, Chinese, Vietnamese, or Hmong. 34 pages.

Diana Dávila Martinez and Gabriela Baeza Ventura (Translator). *A School Named for Someone Like Me/Una escuela con un nombre como el mio* (Bilingual Edition). Pinata Books, 2004. This inspiring biography chronicles the life of Jaime Dávila, a role model and a hero in his Hispanic neighborhood in Houston. 63 pages.

Pat Mora. *Listen to the Desert/Oye al desierto*. Clarion, 1994. In this informational book, author and artist portray the sounds and sights of the desert. 32 pages.

Roser Ros. *Musicians of Bremen/Los músicos de Bremen* (Spanish-English Bilingual Edition). Chronicle Books, 2005. Retold in both Spanish and English, the universally loved story will delight early readers and older learners alike. 32 pages.

Jessica Souhami. *Rama and the Demon King: An Ancient Tale from India* (Punjabi-English Bilingual Edition). Chronicle Books, 2005. This ancient tale of Prince Rama relates his demon-killing adventures in the forest after being exiled for 14 years by his father, the king. 36 pages.

orthography, sound system, or other linguistic features. Again, be careful never to underestimate the cognitive abilities of children who do not speak English as their native language.

Use Informational Texts as a Significant Part of Instruction

Informational texts are not often used in our schools for reading instruction, and this can have serious consequences (Duke, 2004). We strongly recommend that you use informational texts with English-language learners for three reasons. First, students can read informational texts to find out things that they can use in their lives outside of the classroom. This may be a greater motivation to learn to read in English than anything else you can do. It will give students a reason to work as hard as they can to understand texts in English. The task can be as simple as reading a recipe for making chocolate chip cookies or as complex as reading a science article on hibernation. Being able to read informational texts may also contribute to the stature of a child, as the new skill can be taken home and used to help others in her family.

Second, it is possible to find informational texts dealing with topics that English-language learners have a lot of background knowledge about and that do not demand background knowledge specific to U.S. culture or to English, such as Taro Gomi's very simple picture book *Spring Is Here = Llególa primavera* or Gail Gibbons's *Dinosaur Discoveries*. Knowledge of basic facts about common animals, for example, is independent of the language and culture in which those facts were learned. Conversely, in stories written for U.S. children, there is often a good deal of cultural knowledge assumed that some English-language learners may not have.

Third, informational text can expand opportunities for home-school connections (Duke & Purcell-Gates, 2003). Some parents, older siblings, and relatives of English learners seldom have the time to read fiction and may not have much interest in reading fiction. These same people, however, may welcome opportunities to work with their children in reading and understanding newspapers, magazines, and other nonfiction texts that deal with real-world topics. As we noted earlier in this chapter, involving parents, siblings, and other speakers of students' native languages can be a huge benefit for all parties.

A note of clarification is needed here. We are not advocating the elimination of narrative texts from the reading curriculum. We are, however, recommending that exposition be used as a focus, rather than as a secondary choice, in reading instruction. In one study (Kamil & Lane, 1997), approximately 50 percent of reading instruction in first grade employed expository text, while the remaining 50 percent employed narrative text. This seems like a reasonable balance of these two different and important text types. Of course, some books—for example, Bonnie Graves's *The Whooping Crane*—both tell a story and provide a good deal of information on a topic.

One important thing to keep in mind when giving English learners informational texts is not to require them to learn large bodies of new knowledge in English. Another thing to keep in mind is to be sure to provide English learners with sufficient instructional assistance when they are expected to learn from informational English texts. In other words, provide students with plenty of scaffolding. Attempts to require English learners to learn large amounts of new information by reading English texts and attempts to require them to learn without sufficient scaffolding are simply invitations to failure.

Remember, too, that it is often not necessary for students to read the entire selection in informational texts, as it typically is with narratives. If you identify the critical information in a text and have students read only what is relevant to the task at hand, you can simplify the reading task considerably and enable students to complete the reading in a reasonable amount of time.

In addition to the teaching suggestions and the descriptions of informational books provided throughout this book, Nell Duke and Susan Bennett-Armistead's *Reading and Writing Informational Text in the Primary Grades* (2003), Rosemary Bamford and Janice Kristo's *Making Facts Come Alive* (1998), and Eileen Burke and Susan Glazer's *Using Nonfiction in the Classroom* (1994) provide a number of useful teaching ideas as well as bibliographies of informational books.

Use Alternative Assessment Strategies

Another way to lessen the burden on students who are not yet fully proficient in English is to give them opportunities to use some of the multiple intelligences that Howard Gardner (1993) has described and that we briefly described in Chapter 11. For example, drama, which we discuss in some detail in Chapter 8, is often an effective means for getting English-language learners to develop oral language skills, and those oral skills will be useful bridges to comprehending written text. Art and music, which we also consider in Chapter 8, are also useful. Not only will you find that students can develop their literacy skills by using these diverse modes of expression, but you may often be able to better understand their intended meaning when they use them.

For example, if a child is allowed to draw a picture to illustrate a written assignment, as Maria did in Figure 13.4, you may be able to assess informally what the student meant to write, even if it is not clear from her text. This information will help you determine what the child needs to know about the language. You will not have to assume, for example, that the child did not know how to write, read, or understand *any* of the content of the lesson.

Additional Suggestions for Working with English-Language Learners

In addition to Delpit (1995) and to Kamil and Bernhardt (2004), a number of other authorities have suggested ways in which teachers and schools can assist English learners. In this section, we briefly present those suggestions that we believe to be the most compelling and the most practical in In the Classrooms 13.5, 13.6, 13.7, and 13.8.

Gersten and Baker's Suggestions for Working with English-Language Learners

In gathering the following suggestions, Russell Gersten and Scott Baker (2000) took an interesting and powerful approach: They first reviewed the literature on instruction for English learners; then they conducted a series of meetings with educators from across the United States to determine what these professionals had found to be effective practices. Gersten and Baker grouped their results under several headings. Here are their major findings.

in the **Classroom 13.5**

Immersion in Content and Direct Teaching of Language Skills

- Immerse English learners in the rich content that all students need to master. However, do not rely on rich immersion in content as the sole approach. Instruction is also important.

- Directly teach language skills, and correct children's language use when appropriate. This includes teaching grammar and formal usage. To succeed in school and beyond, students need to speak English well.

- Develop students' proficiency and fluency in English using academic content that students have previously studied. Once students have some understanding of a particular content, teaching English language skills will be more productive.
- Teach new academic content in a way that puts learning demands first and language demands second.

Oral Language Use

- Involve students in extended discourse about academic topics as well as briefer responses to specific questions about academic content. Successful learners need both general knowledge and specific knowledge.
- Include significant opportunities for natural and informal oral language use, but not as a substitute for more formal language experiences.

Approaches to Effective Instruction

- Build and use vocabulary as a curricular anchor. Vocabulary is crucial to understanding content and to becoming proficient in English. Increasing English learners' vocabularies should be one of your major goals.
- Use visuals to reinforce concepts and vocabulary. Visuals are helpful to all students, but they are particularly helpful to students who have yet to achieve sophisticated verbal skills in English.
- Make use of cooperative learning and peer tutoring.
- Use students' native language strategically.
- "Modulate" cognitive and language demands to fit your English-language learners. The principal way to assist learners in meeting the reading demands they face is to scaffold their efforts, something we discussed in detail in Chapter 8 and something one of us and a colleague discuss in even greater detail in *Scaffolding Reading Experiences for English-Language Learners* (Fitzgerald & Graves, 2004).
- Use approaches that have proven highly effective for native speakers. For example, provide explicit instruction, make sure students receive sufficient time on task, foster active engagement, and give frequent and clear feedback.

Jiménez's Recommendations for Working with Latino and Latina Students

Robert Jiménez (2000) is specifically concerned with Latina/Latino students and bases his suggestions on the performance of Latina/Latino teachers. Like Gersten and Baker, Jiménez groups his suggestions under several headings.

in the **Classroom 13.6**

Language Use

- Use both languages when and where they are needed. Use Spanish to explain concepts that might be difficult in English, use Spanish to validate the worth of Spanish and to build solidarity with students, use English to help students build their English skills, and directly teach English.
- Validate Spanish speakers' language by providing students with Spanish-language texts, inviting Spanish-speaking volunteers into the classroom, encouraging the use of Spanish during cooperative learning, and learning and using Spanish vocabulary.

Instructional Practices

- Use a variety of approaches including more traditional and more current ones. These might include sheltered English instruction, cooperative learning, and writing in content areas.
- Provide a challenging and demanding curriculum, and demand high student performance.

- Emphasize vocabulary instruction.
- Use active teaching techniques.
- Provide specific instructional support to help students transfer information and skills they learned in Spanish to English-language contexts and tasks.

Attitudes Toward Latino/Latina Students and Parents

- Hold students to high-level achievement, and reject a deficit view of minority students.
- Take a positive view toward both students and parents; treat parents with respect, reach out to them through activities like home visits and participating in community activities, and involve them in their children's literacy learning.

Short and Echevarria's SIOP Model

This set of recommendations comes from Deborah Short and Jana Echevarria (2004–2005). Short and Echevarria's recommendations were developed over the course of a seven-year research project that produced the Sheltered Instruction Observation Protocol (SIOP) model (Echevarria, Vogt, & Short, 2004). The SIOP model is specifically designed to promote English learners' academic literacy in content areas. Here is a brief list of their recommendations.

- Identify the language demands of the content course.
- Plan language objectives for all lessons, and make them explicit to students.
- Emphasize academic vocabulary development.
- Activate and strengthen background knowledge.
- Promote oral interaction and extended academic talk.
- Review vocabulary and content concepts.
- Give students feedback on language use in class.

in the **Classroom 13.7**

AERA's Recommendations

The final set of recommendations we present here was developed by the American Educational Research Association (AERA, 2004), the major educational research association in the United States. Like several of the other sets we have presented, AERA's recommendations are grouped under several headings.

Word Recognition

- Emphasize decoding skill early. Like other children, English learners can learn to decode words relatively quickly—in two years or so.
- Provide systematic training in phonemic awareness.
- Give students lots of practice reading.
- Provide explicit instruction in phonics.
- Use frequent in-class assessment to find out where students need assistance, and then provide that assistance.

in the **Classroom 13.8**

Comprehension

- Allot a substantial period of time to building sophisticated language skills. Comprehending and producing academic language and acquiring a rich and powerful vocabulary is likely to take at least five years.
- Engage students in substantive reading, writing, and discussion on academic topics.
- Provide in-depth instruction in both oral and reading vocabulary, and be sure to teach a significant number of words using powerful approaches.
- Provide instruction in learning from text.
- Provide comprehension strategy instruction.

Extensive Learning Time

- Provide more time during each year by means such as extending the school day and school year.
- Provide this extended time over a number of years.

If you compare the six sets of principles we have presented—those of Delpit, Kamil and Bernhardt, Gersten and Baker, Jiménez, Short and Echevarria, and AERA—you will find a good deal of overlap. This is good news. We deliberately included the overlapping recommendations to show how much agreement there is on how to assist English learners. Another piece of good news is that many of these recommendations are easily to implemented by typical teachers in typical classrooms. We encourage you to make use of as many of these recommendations as you can in your classroom.

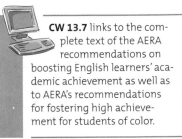
CW 13.7 links to the complete text of the AERA recommendations on boosting English learners' academic achievement as well as to AERA's recommendations for fostering high achievement for students of color.

Reflect *and* Apply

5. Think about reading activities that are not specific to a particular language. For example, the process of using a table of contents in a book is the same, regardless of the language used. What other reading tasks are similar across different languages?
6. Create your own Rosetta Stone chart, with words or phrases that you know in English and in one or two other languages. For example, you might already know that *mesa* is the Spanish word for "table." If you cannot construct much of a chart by yourself, get together with classmates who speak other languages and create a chart together.

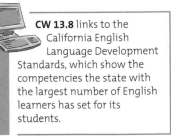
CW 13.8 links to the California English Language Development Standards, which show the competencies the state with the largest number of English learners has set for its students.

Concluding Remarks

In this chapter, we have outlined some of the history of English-language learning in this country, noted some of the linguistic challenges that English-language learners and teachers face, and described a number of instructional approaches for dealing with English-language learners. In concluding the chapter, we want to emphasize three points.

First, with English-language learners, as with all children, it is not merely low-level literacy or the rudiments of literacy that we must assist students in reaching. The goal is full literacy in English—the ability to use the English language as a vehicle for thinking, for problem solving, and for communicating—in other words, the ability to use English in a way that makes possible full and productive participation in our society.

Second, vocabulary instruction was stressed in five of the six sets of suggestions we discussed on pages 406–423. Vocabulary is increasingly recognized as absolutely crucial to English learners (August, 2005). Take advantage of the many techniques for vocabulary instruction described in Chapter 7. Also, you may want to consider the fuller discussion of vocabulary learning and instruction one of us presents in *The Vocabulary Book* (Graves, 2006).

Finally, the task of assisting non-English-speaking children in reaching the goal of English literacy for the 21st century is difficult. Yet it is a task we can accomplish and one we must aim for; the ultimate rewards for our society will be among the greatest we could imagine.

Extending Learning

1. Visit a school that enrolls English-language learners. You might volunteer to work with some students whose first language is not English. If you cannot find such a school, many social service agencies, religious organizations, and other nonprofit groups have programs that target reading for English-language learners. Volunteering to work in these settings, or even simply observing, will allow you to see how the principles in this chapter play out in real life.

2.  Study the instructional recommendations made on pages 406–423. There are over 40 of them, many more than you can implement at one time. Identify half a dozen or so that you see as particularly useful and as steps that you definitely could take in your present or future classroom. Explain in writing why you selected each of these recommendations and in what order you are likely to implement them.

mylabschool
Where the classroom comes to life!

For a look at working with English learners in a contemporary classroom, go to Allyn & Bacon's MyLabSchool.com. In MLS Courses, click on Reading Methods, and go to MLS Video Lab. There, you will find video clips about Diversity and Special Needs in Module 9. Additional videos may be found if you return to MLS Courses and click on ESL.

Children's Literature

CHILDREN'S BOOKS

Ciardi, J. (1975). "The Shark." In *Fast and Slow: Poems by John Ciardi*. Boston: Houghton Mifflin. This poem provides a colorful and engaging description of a shark. 1 page.

Dorros, A. (2005). *Julio's Magic*. New York: HarperCollins. Julio, a young woodcarver in a rural Mexican village, helps his elderly mentor complete a set of beautiful carvings to enter in a wood-carving competition. 32 pages.

Gibbons, G. (2005). *Dinosaur Discoveries* New York: Holiday House. In simple language, Gibbons provides details of the most recent theories about the history of dinosaurs, along with amazing facts about dinosaur discoveries. 33 pages.

Gomi, T. (2006). *Spring Is Here = Llegó la primavera* San Francisco: Chronicle Books. In this colorful, dual-language picture book, a winsome calf provides the backdrop for the story line, which follows the cycle of the seasons from one spring to the next. In spare text, the author conveys the underlying themes of renewal and growth. 34 pages.

Graves, B. (1997). *The Whooping Crane*. Des Moines, IA: Perfection Learning. While on an airplane ride from Texas to Maryland, a young girl sits next to a biologist transporting a whooping crane chick to the Patuxent Wildlife Research Center and learns about this endangered species. 64 pages.

Lowery, L. (2005). *Cinco de mayo*. Minneapolis: Lerner. This colorful book honors the joyful holiday that celebrates Mexico's victory over the French army at the Battle of Pueblo in 1862. 48 pages.

O'Dell, S. (1960). *Island of the Blue Dolphins*. Boston: Houghton Mifflin. By using her wits and the resources at hand, a young Indian girl survives alone on an island for several years. Newbery Medal winner. Audio- and videotapes available. Spanish text also available. 154 pages.

Ramírez, A. (2004). *Napí*. Toronto: Groundwood Books. A Mazateca girl, who lives beside a river in Oaxaca, describes her home and village at different times of the day. 32 pages.

Rosenblatt, L. (1998). *Monarch Magic!* Charlotte, VT: Williamson Publishing Co. Simple text and colorful photographs depict the life cycle of a monarch butterfly, from egg to caterpillar to chrysalis to butterfly. Includes 40 butterfly activities. 96 pages.

Shea, P. D. (1995). *The Whispering Cloth: A Refugee's Story*. Honesdale, PA: Boyd Mills Press. A young Hmong girl in a Thai refugee camp creates a *pándau* (embroidered tapestry) that tells her own story. Includes glossary. Illustrated by A. Riggio, with reproductions of *pándau* by Y. Yang. 32 pages.

Silverstein, S. (1996). *Falling Up*. New York: Scholastic. This book includes over 100 poems and drawings by this favorite author. 171 pages.

Soto, G. (1994). *The Skirt*. New York: Bantam-Doubleday. When Miata leaves the skirt she is to wear for the folklorico dance performance on the school bus, she must use all her wits to get it back before her parents find out. Illustrated by Eric Velasquez. Audiotape available. 74 pages.

Yumoto, K. (1999). *The Spring Tone*. New York: Farrar Straus Giroux. Resenting the changes in her life and resisting growing up, Tomomi joins her younger brother in taking revenge against the neighbors with whom her family is battling. 166 pages.

BIBLIOGRAPHY

Schon, I. (2004). *Recommended books in Spanish for children and young adults: 2000 through 2004*. Lanham, MD: Scarecrow Press. Schon's newest bibliography of books in Spanish presents critical annotations for over 1,300 books.

Schon, I. (2001). *Recommended books in Spanish for children and young adults: 1996 through 1999*. Lanham, MD: Scarecrow Press. This is an excellent bibliography of books in Spanish.

Schon, I. (1996). *Recommended books in Spanish for children and young adults: 1991–1995*. Lanham, MD: Scarecrow Press. This, too, is an excellent bibliography of books in Spanish.

Schon, I., & Berkin, S. C. (1996). *Introducción a la literatura infantile y juvenil*. Newark, DE: International Reading Association. (Available only in Spanish.) This is an excellent resource for Spanish-speaking teachers.

CHAPTER 14

Classroom Assessment

by Kathleen M. Wilson and Robert C. Calfee

chapter outline

CLASSROOM
VIGNETTE

The Test: 10:00 a.m., Friday morning, early May. Carol Aiken tinkles a small bell and says, "Put away your books; sharpen your pencils. Time for the reading test. Put your name at the top. Fill every circle. No talking." A few groans, a couple of questions, but by 10:05 a.m. the 32 fifth-graders hunch in silence over test packets, filling in answers. Ms. Aiken roams the classroom, patting a shoulder, cautioning a student with roving eyes, reminding students to recheck their answers, warning when five minutes are left. At 11:05 a.m. she says, "Time is up. Pass in your tests—Robert, right now!" The test is finished.

The Project: A month before, in early April. Ms. Aiken's students return from lunch for science. "Today is the A-team report on Mars. Eduardo, you're in charge. Bring up your group to tell us about your project." Eduardo and three classmates tape sheets of butcher paper with the headings *Place in the Solar System, Physical Characteristics,* and *Building a Habitat* on the front wall. Each sheet is a collage of graphics, photos, notes from Websites. For 40 minutes, the group describes the Red Planet. Then they add their sheets to a huge "Planets" display being prepared for Parents' Night. Ms. Aiken prompts each group for accuracy and encourages them to check with the class for understanding. But mostly she watches the class for reactions, interest, and attention. She jots brief notes in the logbook on her lap.

The Report Card: Fast forward to June, with only two more weeks left in the school year. It's midafternoon, the students are gone, and Ms. Aiken is preparing for the end-of-school-year parent conferences. Phillippa's mother enters the room with her daughter. They greet Ms. Aiken, Phillippa retrieves her portfolio, and the gangly 11-year-old begins her report. "When I started this year, I really wanted to concentrate on history. I don't know why; it just seemed interesting. I'm African American, and there's lots of prejudice, so I wanted to study about civil rights." For ten minutes, Phillippa discusses her year's work, noting strengths and limitations. "I really worked hard this year, and I'm really happy with the paper I did on Coretta Scott King. It's three pages long, and I checked the spelling and punctuation. And I think the computer art work is really great." Ms. Aiken draws the mother into the conversation and then offers her own evaluation. Phillippa is making solid progress. The report card will contain no surprises.

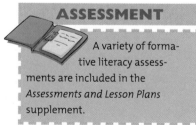

ASSESSMENT

A variety of formative literacy assessments are included in the *Assessments and Lesson Plans* supplement.

Our Perspective on Assessment

These three scenarios span the range of methods available to the classroom teacher for appraising student learning. Figure 14.1 shows the continuum from the formative activities that you will use in the classroom to monitor student learning to the summative events represented by the externally mandated standardized tests familiar to all of us. Formative assessment refers to focused and ongoing evaluations, like the scores on pop quizzes. Summative tests come at the end of a course of study, when students become accountable for their achievement. Formative assessments guide instruction; summative tests evaluate achievement (Bloom, Hastings, & Madaus, 1971; Bloom, Madaus, & Hastings, 1981). Figure 14.1 shows the extremes of this continuum; there are clearly many variations between these endpoints.

In the chapter, we first describe our perspectives on assessment. Next, we examine teacher-based strategies for classroom assessment, in which your role is to carry out practical research on student learning. Then we look at the place of standardized tests in formal appraisal of student learning.

An Emphasis on Inquiry

We have chosen, in this chapter, to emphasize the left-hand side of the spectrum shown in Figure 14.1—teacher-based assessment—for three reasons. First,

	FORMATIVE ASSESSMENT DESIGNED FOR INSTRUCTION	SUMMATIVE ASSESSMENT DESIGNED FOR ACCOUNTABILITY
Purpose and Source	Designed by teachers for classroom decisions	Designed by experts for policy makers
	Several sources of information	Stand-alone, single indicator
	Strong link to curriculum and instruction	Independent of curriculum and instruction
Criteria	Valid for guiding instruction	Predictive validity to other tests
	Profile reliability—strengths and weaknesses	Total test reliability—one score
	Sensitive to changes in performance	Stable over time and situations
Pragmatics	Judgmental, quick turnaround, flexible	Objective, cost- and time-efficient, standardized
	Performance-based "real" task	Multiple-choice "school" task
	Continuously, as needed	Once or sometimes twice per year

FIGURE 14.1

Comparison of Assessment for Instruction and Assessment for Accountability

the teacher's role in standardized testing is often limited to management and reporting. To be sure, teachers do have important responsibilities for managing, interpreting, and applying standardized tests. But administrators select the tests, manuals tell how to give them, and publishers score them and return results and interpretations. Reading series often include worksheets and end-of-unit tests that resemble standardized tests, but neither demand much input from the teacher.

The second reason for focusing on teacher-based assessment is that these techniques require considerable knowledge, skill, and professional judgment. You may know teachers who rely on routine lessons they prepared long ago and stay with the same material year after year. This approach can't prepare today's and tomorrow's students for a changing world and is not in accord with the view of reading and writing presented in this book.

This leads to the third reason for emphasizing teacher-based assessment: Authentic assessment of present-day literacy can never be completely "standardized." While prepackaged tests provide a rough index of reading and writing achievement, the classroom teacher can most adequately monitor students' ability to use language to think and communicate. Knowing that a student is at the 50th percentile in reading comprehension doesn't tell you what the student can and can't do. Picking the right answer to a multiple-choice question is less reflective of literacy than being able to explain the shift in the relationship between Charlotte (a spider) and Wilbur (a pig) over the course of E. B. White's *Charlotte's Web*.

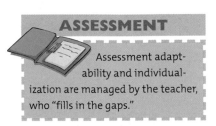

ASSESSMENT

Assessment adaptability and individualization are managed by the teacher, who "fills in the gaps."

Three Themes of Assessment

Three themes of assessment run through this chapter. First is the notion of *assessment as inquiry*. It is easy to build a test that fails students; it is much more difficult to find ways to discover what students know and can do. Developing this sensitivity requires the teacher to act as a researcher, creating situations that support success and provide a starting point for instruction.

A second theme is *development*. As an elementary teacher, you may deal with children from kindergarten through sixth grade, from 4-year-olds to 13-year-olds, from preschoolers to adolescents. You may set your sights on a particular grade or age, but even if you succeed in this endeavor (and new teachers don't usually have a say), developmental levels within any class are likely to span two or more years. Students are not identical peas in a pod, and assessment must adapt to individual differences.

The third theme is *progress monitoring*. Teacher-based assessment builds on a rich array of data sources, including observations, class discussions, and intuitive judgments, as well as more formal assignments and quizzes. As September moves toward June, you must judge both learning and accomplishment. You must come up with a "bottom line"—a number, a score, or a grade. How much has the student grown? How well can the student perform various tasks expected at a particular grade level? Surveys show that elementary teachers don't like to grade students. Their "success" orientation leads them to "accentuate the positive." But parents and other clients need and deserve information about progress and accomplishment. In this case, progress refers to students' growth and learning; accomplishment measures student achievement against a standard. If teachers don't supply the information, then someone else will, probably by using standardized tests. We think that teachers can be trusted to assess student learning—indeed, for the kind of assessment described in this book, others must rely on you and your colleagues!

Balanced Assessment

Figure 14.1 laid out the spectrum of assessment strategies: more objective or subjective, more formal or informal, more prepackaged or judgment-based. In your role as a classroom teacher, you confront the practical question of how to achieve a balance that makes effective use of this full range of strategies.

Some educators question whether standardized tests have any place in today's schools (Calkins, Montgomery, Santman, & Falk, 1998; Johnston, 1990; Mitchell, 1992; Wiggins, 1993; Wiggins & McTighe, 1998). Although these tests have limitations, they also have strengths. Problems arise when they are misused or overused. Public information about student achievement frequently depends solely on what students do in an hour or two on multiple-choice items that tap knowledge and skills quite unlike those required for their regular classwork. Imagine the plight of a seven-year-old, accustomed to working on "real" problems with adequate time and resources and being able to ask questions when confused. Then comes the day of the test. The teacher calls the class to attention: "Put away your books, sharpen your pencils, be quiet, no questions."

Teachers typically prepare their students for tests; indeed, this preparation can become the entire reading program. But standardized testing measures only part of what students know and are able to do. The curriculum is more than a preplanned scope-and-sequence chart, and instruction is more than transmission of knowledge from teacher to student. Assessment is more than guessing the best answer to a simple question, and performance is complex and interactive. The student's response is important, but the process is also important.

The rest of this chapter explores the broad spectrum of assessment activities, suggesting how to use a variety of methods to explore reading and writing and how to make sound instructional decisions throughout the school year. Genuine balance requires the classroom teacher to move across the spectrum,

---

ASSESSMENT

The classroom teacher monitors both progress and accomplishment. Standardized tests are generally limited to accomplishment, and only a small "slice" at that.

---

from portfolios to multiple-choice tests. The *Assessments and Lesson Plans* supplement that accompanies this text contains more information on these tests.

Teacher-Based Strategies

In this section, we describe classroom assessments designed to inform teachers' instructional practice, helping them meet the needs of individual students and the class as a whole. The following questions outline several factors central to conducting teacher-based assessment:

- What does the teacher need to know, week by week, and why?
- What about students? What feedback do they need, and when?
- What about parents? How can you connect them with their children's learning?
- What about other teachers? How can you operate as a team to set benchmark assessments?
- What about the principal? When and how can the principal become involved in assessment?

Features of Contemporary Assessment Methods

Classroom assessment has changed dramatically in recent years, reflecting a larger movement described as performance-based assessment, portfolios, or exhibitions (Harp, 1991; Hart, 1994; Herman, Aschbacher, & Winters, 1992; O'Malley & Pierce, 1996; Phye, 1996; Strickland & Strickland, 2000; Wiggins, 1993). Several features distinguish these methods, which support teaching for understanding as described in Chapter 9.

- Student *production* is more important than recognition. Students must show that they can do more than pick the right answer. They have to construct something on their own.
- *Projects* are more important than items. The preference is for depth over breadth, and the emphasis is on validity rather than reliability.
- The teacher's *informed opinion* is more important than mechanized scoring. Professional judgment replaces the ever-popular Scantron machine.

In the Classroom 14.1 illustrates these concepts.

ASSESSMENT

At the beginning of the school year, the teacher's task is to find out what students know and can do, as well as what "turns them on." This job requires assessment. By year's end, the job has switched to measuring accomplishment, which increasingly relies on mandated testing.

The Roots Project

Ms. King's 30 third- and fourth-graders vary in backgrounds, interests, and achievement levels. Some receive a "free lunch" (the family is poor), several have been labeled as learning disabled, and the eight fourth-graders in the class were candidates for retention.

In September and early October, Ms. King organizes each week around "little lessons," based on a short text or a familiar topic. For example, to find out what students know about the concepts of character and plot, she conducts a "movie review," in which students talk about favorite summer movies. To determine what they know about informational text, she arranges a "news report," in which they discuss selected newspaper articles on current events, from which

in the Classroom 14.1

they prepare oral reports. Students also compile personal journals, doing free writing (Monday) and writing on assigned topics (Wednesday and Thursday). Work samples (individual and group) are posted around the room. By mid-October, Ms. King's logbook contains entries about each student's proficiencies, predilections, and problems in reading and writing.

For the post-Halloween parent conferences, Ms. King prepares a one-page synopsis about each student, drawing on her logbook notes and student journals to review the student's status in literature, science, social studies, citizenship, art/music, and physical education. Asked about the place of reading and writing in this mix, Ms. King's response is short and simple: "We work on reading and writing all day long."

Suddenly, it's early April. Ms. King gathers the class. "We don't have much time left," she tells the group. "It's time for our 'big' project. This spring, our project is Roots—your family history, your own book to keep!"

The Roots project is Ms. King's culminating assignment. It lasts almost six weeks. The project generates an authentic product but also provides summative assessments of student achievement. The project proceeds in several phases. Students first view selections from the *Roots* television series, available on videocassette. Next, they talk about the story line and then, as prologues to their own books, prepare reports on the selections they viewed. For Ms. King, this exercise provides the opportunity to assess students' proficiency in the basic concepts of character, plot, setting, and theme.

In the second phase, students analyze several autobiographies and biographies—from the autobiographical *Little House on the Prairie* books by Laura Ingalls Wilder to several trade book biographies of Martin Luther King, Jr. They review their family's past, making notes and collecting data. A wall chart serves to display the results—interviews, Bibles and genealogies, letters and photo albums. The tasks are both individual and collaborative; in her logbook, Ms. King records contributions from specific students and group participation.

In the final phase, each student designs and constructs a Roots book. These are lengthy pieces, 20 pages or more; some are handwritten, some computer-assisted. Each book includes a title page, table of contents, dedication ("To my parents, without whom this report would not be possible"), thematic overview (the *Roots* story), research on the student's family, and a "Forward to the Future" piece, where the children imagine themselves at their high school graduation. Each book includes writing, artwork, graphics, and artifacts.

English Learners

When considering home-school connections across the variety of families in today's world, you should take into account cultures, language, and family makeup.

With the Roots project, Ms. King's third- and fourth-grade students demonstrate critical reading and writing skills and strategies they have learned in class. Ms. King has assigned a task that is both relevant and authentic—two factors that can motivate students to do their best work. In the project wrap-up in May, you can see several significant outcomes. First, every student has completed the Roots project with distinction. All have created artistic works of high quality. Second, they don't see these as mere homework assignments; they are proud of their accomplishments, which they plan to "keep forever." They are eager to explain how they approached the project and what they learned. Third, the students display a strong sense of audience. They see themselves as the primary audience, which is why they plan to keep the books forever, but they also comment on parents' and relatives' reactions. Every classroom visitor becomes an audience member. Finally—and especially important—they express a sense of rich fulfillment.

The Roots Project and Assessment

The linkages among student learning, curriculum, and instruction appear seamless in this example. A conversation with Ms. King offers insights into how the project serves as assessment. Roots was an experiment. She had assigned projects before, but these had been fairly short and prescriptive. She admits that the Roots activity went far beyond what she had originally intended, both in time and in effort. She had expected to stretch her students, but was genuinely surprised by their accomplishments. In planning and carrying out the assessment, she played the role of a researcher: She developed a design, tried some innovative methods, collected data, and reflected on the results. This case conveys several themes.

- *Assessment is integrative.* The Roots project yields a wealth of information about reading and writing, as well as research skills. Product and process cover the entire curriculum—formal (literacy, literature, social studies, art) and informal (initiative, cooperation, persistence). The casual observer may experience a collage, but Ms. King can identify distinctive elements.

- *Assessment builds on meaningful tasks.* The students aren't taking a test; they are working on a project, solving a problem, doing something that matters. Motivation and challenge stimulate achievement. It is easy to set up conditions where many students do poorly; creating a situation that promotes success is more difficult.

- *Assessment emphasizes both top-level competence and performance skills.* For Ms. King, the most critical achievements are "top-level"—understanding overall passage structure, an awareness of audience, a sense of thematic coherence. Her notes also cover the "micro-skills" of spelling, grammar, neatness, and even aesthetics. The final products are all polished, but students differ in the guidance they need to make revisions and complete the job. Ms. King has noted these variations, which she shares with students and parents.

- *Assessment is purposeful for all involved.* Ms. King describes each task, from the year's beginning to its end, in ways that make sense to both students and parents. She explains her September assessments: "I'm going to be checking what each of you can do and where you need help." She connects each lesson with the next job: "We are studying dinosaurs, and you will need to divide long words like *tyrannosaurus* into syllables. The key is to look for vowels." By the time they begin the Roots project, students have learned that classroom activities have a purpose, which motivates them to do their best.

- *Assessment emphasizes explanation.* Students must be able to present their work and show their capacity to describe what they are doing and why and how they are doing it. Right answers need right reasons to count. Ms. King encourages group activities in planning, reviewing, and presenting because they promote active discussion. She teaches students technical vocabularies that help them communicate with one another. An interesting story requires character development. It needs a problem that is resolved across several episodes. In creating stories of their past, present, and future, students use these terms to explain their efforts and to help one another.

- *Assessment is scaffolded.* Just as you can and should support students' reading of individual selections, you can and should undergird their efforts on larger projects. The aim is for every student to produce an exceptional book, but some require more support than others in moving ahead with the project, in their approach to the task, in their ability to sustain the effort, and in their willingness to assist others and to seek out assistance. Ms. King makes sure that support is available, from her and from others such

ASSESSMENT

Assessing fluency versus application and skill versus transfer is too narrow a view. Instruction is more far-reaching when students get quality opportunities to transfer their skills and apply them in a variety of situations.

as other students, parents, and volunteers. Her logbook captures these facets of student performance.

■ *Assessment is guided by developmental standards.* Ms. King's guideposts are as clear in her mind as a scope-and-sequence chart. Her assessments may not produce numbers, but they refer to growth and to relative strengths and weaknesses. For instance, here are her comments about one of her students, Sam:

> Sam's oral language skills are exceptional, and he works hard on topics that interest him: science, computers, and games. He has made great progress in his writing and spelling but still lacks fluency with mechanics. Unless he is really excited about a project, he is sloppy with the details. He is better with exposition than narrative. Stories bore him, but his "rockets" report shows that he can do top-flight work. He sometimes behaves immaturely for a fourth-grader and does not listen well. He is impatient with "boring" tasks like documenting or summarizing.
>
> This year, he has learned a lot about the importance of working on assignments that don't have an immediate payoff. He stayed with his Roots biography, even though he became distracted halfway through. At the beginning of the year, he would have dropped it or done a sloppy job. He came to me and explained that he was stuck and wanted to start over. He had lost a page of notes and didn't want to redo them. I asked him to spend a day thinking over his choices and talking about them with his project buddy. The next morning, Sam had written down his choices and explained why he had decided to stay with his first plan. This episode is an important sign of growth.

Ms. King prepares similar comments for each student, which she attaches to the district's report card. She finds that parents value these comments as highly as the official grades. They were also excited about the Roots project, because it showed what their children could really do.

Some Answers to Our Opening Questions

Ms. King's Roots project offers answers to the questions posed at the beginning of this section, which we now address one by one.

What Does the Teacher Need to Know, Week by Week, and Why?

Ms. King's answer to the question of what the teacher needs to know changes throughout the school year. At year's beginning, her assessments are formative. They are frequent, focused, and individual. She assigns mini-tasks that inform her about students' skills and interests. By midyear, she switches to larger tasks, giving students more responsibility for their own learning and for self-assessment. By year's end, her assessments become summative. To what degree and in what ways can students demonstrate mastery of external standards mandated by the district and the state? She looks at the quality of the projects but attends to process as well as product, to the way students handle problems as well as the solutions they manage to come up with, and to collaborative contributions as well as individual accomplishments.

What About Students?

What feedback do students need, and when? Ms. King brings students into the feedback loop early and often, explicitly but gently, individually and as a class. She begins the year by telling students what she expects by year's end. She makes

it clear that reading and writing are high on her list, along with skills in speaking and in attentive listening. By late fall, she has spent time with individual students, reviewing what she sees as strengths and areas for improvement. She keeps less-detailed records than she did earlier, relying more on student work and brief journal notes. At midyear, students are appraising their own work. By the end of the Roots project, they have become their own toughest critics.

What About Parents?

Ms. King relies on three methods to connect parents with their children's achievements. The first is home-school communication. She assigns homework regularly. Weekly newsletters explain assignments and suggest how parents can help their students. She tailors assignments to individual needs. Every student receives the same basic assignment, but she jots down individualized notes on the newsletter for each student's parents. The child who handles basic spelling and punctuation but seldom experiments with unfamiliar words might carry home this note: "For the Dinosaurs report, have Pete think up more interesting words. His vocabulary is rich, but he doesn't use it much in writing. Encourage him to use wild and crazy adjectives and verbs." The second connection is the quarterly conference. Students conduct this event, describing their goals for the quarter, displaying their portfolio of work, discussing successes and shortcomings, and laying out goals for the next quarter. The final home-school connection takes place at the open house night at year's end, where student projects serve as the centerpiece.

Connect your classroom open house to different languages and cultures by incorporating multiple dimensions, including art and graphics along with texts. A picture is worth a thousand words.

What About Other Teachers?

Ms. King collaborates with the other third- and fourth-grade teachers in her school. At the grade-level meeting before the school year starts, the team reviews state and district standards. Woven throughout the plans for instructional activities are benchmark assessments for monitoring student progress and problems during the year. Results from these assessments guide the team's instructional discussions and decisions. The team also decides to carry out an integrated project featuring a different theme for each class as a summative assessment. The projects are an experiment. Although each class will be pursuing different activities, the teachers are convinced that they will be able to determine the degree to which students have met grade-level standards.

What About the Principal?

Ms. King's discussions of student progress with the principal are based on notes from her daily log and student work samples. The plan for multiple formative assessments during the year and the final summative assessment allows Ms. King to demonstrate student learning—to provide the principal with concrete evidence of growth in reading and writing skills and strategies. The principal has the job of combining this classroom-based information with the standardized test results to build profiles of student progress.

A Final Word on the Roots Project

Numerous features in this scenario link with literacy outcomes described in earlier chapters. Ms. King has a substantial impact on her students. She often depends on intuition and experience but can explain her methods if asked. She relies less on standardized tests but prepares her students to deal with them. She understands assessment concepts like reliability and validity and has her own way of interpreting them. Her experience, conviction, and success with students allow her to practice her "art" in a special way. The next section of this chapter describes assessment as inquiry, telling the story behind the story.

ASSESSMENT

By designing a read-write assessment, you can see if your students are able to transfer the skills they have learned when doing projects like the Roots project. You can find a model in the *Assessments and Lesson Plans* supplement.

Reflect *and* Apply

1. It is spring; you have moved to a new neighborhood and are looking for a teaching position. The personnel director invites you to visit several schools. The district has a reputation for supporting thematic projects and reading-writing portfolios. One item on your list is the district's assessment policy. What do you look for in classrooms and discuss with colleagues about the potential of projects and portfolios for assessing student achievement?
2. You and a fellow teacher would like to complement the report card with a narrative based on a final project. You have collected several examples, and although the plan will take work, you are convinced it's worth a try. You have five minutes to explain your plans to the school board, enough time to make three points. What will they be? How will your answer depend on the grade you teach?

Assessment as Inquiry

This part of the chapter, building on the concept of the teacher as a practical researcher, describes how the teacher assesses students' development of literacy through a process of professional inquiry. The idea has a long history (Calfee & Hiebert, 1991; Cronbach, 1960; Hiebert & Calfee, 1992; Paris et al., 1992; Stephens & Story, 2000). In 1960, for example, researcher Lee Cronbach recommended assessments based on careful observations, multiple

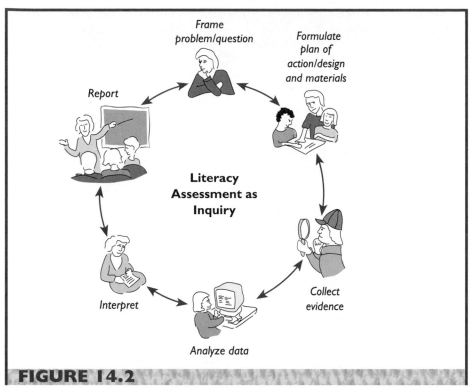

FIGURE 14.2

Literacy Assessment as a Process of Inquiry

methods and measures, and integrated information, a list found in research textbooks and diagrammed in Figure 14.2. The process begins with framing the question, which then leads to designing a plan of action. Next comes the task of collecting and analyzing data, followed by interpreting, or making sense of, the findings. Finally, action is taken on the results—reporting and making decisions. The process is more a collection of activities than a sequence of stages, more a roller-coaster than an elevator, and thus the arrows in the figure are bidirectional. In the following sections, we discuss each element, linking Ms. King's classroom with new cases along the way, to show how assessment becomes an integral part of instruction in the literacy curriculum.

Framing the Problem: What Is the Question?

At the beginning of each school year, the primary question for the classroom teacher seems simple enough: What do the students already know? At year's end, the question is similar: What have the students learned? Along the way, questions become more dynamic: How are students responding to various instructional activities? Who is getting it? Who is not? The foundation for these questions is the curriculum. For Ms. King, the curriculum means much more than getting through the textbook. She begins by reviewing goals for the school year. Having taught several grades, she has a good idea of what students need to know and do by the end of the school year. She is familiar with the learning standards the school district has prepared, statements describing student performance at certain mileposts, including the middle elementary grades. Figure 14.3 shows samples from the *New Standards* program, a national program at the University of Pittsburgh, which developed curriculum-based assessments used by many states and districts as models. Ms. King is not exactly

The student reads at least twenty-five books.... The quality and complexity of materials to be read are illustrated in the sample reading list ... [and] should include traditional and contemporary literature....

The student reads and comprehends at least four books ... about one issue ... by a single author ... or in one genre and produces evidence of reading that:

- makes and supports ... assertions about the text;
- supports assertions with ... evidence;
- draws texts together to compare and contrast ...;
- makes perceptive and well-developed connections;
- evaluates writing strategies and ... the author's craft.

The student reads aloud, accurately (in the range of 85–90%), familiar material of the quality and complexity illustrated in the sample reading list, and in a way that makes meaning clear to listeners by:

- self-correcting when subsequent reading indicates an earlier miscue;
- using a range of cueing systems, e.g., phonics and context clues ...;
- reading with a rhythm, flow, and meter that sound like everyday speech.

The student produces [four types of writing]:

... a report [that] engages the reader ... develops a controlling idea ... creates an organizing structure....

... a response to literature [that] advances and supports a judgment ... demonstrates an understanding ... provides closure....

... a narrative account [that] ... establishes a situation, plot, point of view, setting, and conflict ... creates organizing structure....

... a narrative procedure [that] ... provides a guide to action ... makes use of appropriate writing strategies....

FIGURE 14.3

Elementary School Performance Description—English-Language Arts— from the *New Standards* Program

Source: Used by permission. *New Standards: Performance Standards: Volume I, Elementary School.* National Center on Education and the Economy and the University of Pittsburgh. 1997. All rights reserved.

sure when or how the district decided on these standards, but in her view it is the classroom teacher's responsibility to interpret learning goals. She sees the standards as starting points, minimum achievements, and emphasizes understanding and communication more than the basics.

Ms. King's thoughts about summative, bottom-line outcomes shape many of her assessment questions. Her entering third-graders vary considerably in their knowledge and abilities, and so her initial questions center around the students themselves: What will this group of students be like? What are their past experiences? What do they know? What can they do? What do they like? How do they get along together? Some of her questions are linked to curriculum outcomes: Where is each student in relation to year-end standards? Other questions relate to immediate instructional plans: What activities will help this diverse collection of students attain the goals? Finally come questions about program effectiveness: How can I discover what works and what doesn't this year?

Using such questions as a model, you should frame them in your own language. Classroom assessment is applied action research (Calfee, 2000; Hiebert & Calfee, 1992; Patterson, Santa, & Smith, 1993; Shea, Murray, & Harlin,

2005). The strategies and methods for action research are the same as for other research, but as a teacher you don't have the luxuries of unlimited time and resources available to most researchers and so your research questions must be focused and timely.

Consider the tension between developing instruction for individual students and developing instruction for the class as a whole. Suppose that September's activities suggest that some of your sixth-graders can't write and aren't interested. One strategy would be to form a group of low achievers and assign them to practice basic skills, while arranging for the more-accomplished students to engage in creative writing exercises. With the average learners, you must manage three groups, but you are providing individualized programs based on the assessment results. Or are you? Your attention is divided three ways, students are immersed in different learning paths, and every day individuals must live with their status in the classroom. The year-end standards remain the same for everyone, which means that the low achievers face certain failure.

An alternative strategy starts with a common set of experiences that are tailored and scaffolded around individual differences. For instance, imagine a series of small-scale writing activities throughout the year around holiday topics. These projects will engage students' interest, but will they support skill learning? To make the situation more problematic, suppose three students enter in November, recent arrivals from Cambodia with limited English. How can you meet their needs, while attending to the rest of the class? Helping them learn academic English will take a lot of work. Should you work with them separately or immerse them in the classroom? Their linguistic heritage offers opportunities to enrich the classroom experiences for the other students. The challenge is to discover ways to connect the new arrivals with the classroom community, despite barriers of language and culture. Sixth-graders are likely to pick up "practical" English fairly quickly, given the chance. How might the holiday theme fit into this picture? Thanksgiving, Christmas, and Valentine's Day might be totally unknown to these youngsters. And their holidays may be equally foreign to you. By Googling "Cambodian celebrations," you learn that the Water Festival is celebrated for three days in November and features processions of brightly decorated boats pulled by costumed oarsmen. The Khmer New Year comes in April, another three-day celebration that combines religious ceremonies, the giving of gifts, and a time for boys and girls to get together for dates. Every culture has holidays—you can move from the casual to the academic by studying differences in music, art, drama, customs, and so on.

Here is an even more challenging situation. When you meet with your new first-grade class, you discover that you have been assigned students whose primary languages include Spanish, Cantonese, Tagalog, Croatian, Farsi, and Hindi. All speak some English, but (unlike many sixth-graders) these students tend to be shy and withdrawn.

You know a little Spanish, but that's it. You can't and shouldn't administer diagnostic tests to these students. How can you find out what they know? Your goal is the same as for the other students—by the time spring arrives, they should be able to handle most elements of the Tile Test (in the *Assessments and Lesson Plans* supplement) to demonstrate their phonics skills and knowledge. At the beginning of the year, think about situations that will engage them in language and literacy activities that will allow you to observe their behavior, including language. You may not understand everything they say, but you can capture glimpses of what they can do and under what conditions they can do it. For everyone in the class, but especially these children, you can create

ASSESSMENT

Achievement testing generally measures all students on a single scale. Classroom assessments offer you the opportunity to explore students' strengths and weaknesses more carefully. You can take into account variations in students' interests, between boys and girls, and in language and culture.

literacy play stations with letter blocks, alphabet and picture books, tape recorders, and perhaps even video playbacks. The idea is to elicit speech by whatever means possible, to model at every opportunity, and to monitor and record the results. Again, the situations are designed for the class as a whole, but support and observations are tailored to the individual.

In a diverse society like ours, teachers need to know more about language and culture than ever before. The assessment task can be quite a challenge if you try to handle the variations by yourself. It helps when school faculty work as a team. You may call upon specialists when they are available, but you can also profit by sharing resources and information with colleagues. Ask a fellow teacher to observe one of your lessons, focusing on a particularly puzzling student. Colleagues will include globetrotters who have spent time in other countries and other individuals who are themselves first- or second-generation Americans. These colleagues can provide valuable help in understanding the varied cultural behaviors of your English-language learners. Conversations with parents can also provide insights into students' language and literacy abilities.

Designing a Plan of Action

A design is a refinement of the original question, a plan for arranging conditions and deciding what to assess. You often begin with hypotheses, or "hunches," and then move on to creating situations to explore these hypotheses, as Kiko Furakawa does in In the Classroom 14.2. Being open to alternatives is important; don't deceive yourself by deciding on an answer and then setting up a situation to prove it.

Vocabulary Assessment in the Third Grade

in the Classroom 14.2

It is the beginning of the school year, and Ms. Furakawa, a second-year teacher, is thinking about ways to assess her third-graders' vocabulary skills. She knows that in order to comprehend and compose, students need to be proficient in using vocabulary strategies—what they need is not a random accumulation of words, but a mastery of concepts, collections of ideas, and words as keys to communication. She has found that students often seem to struggle to find words to express their ideas. Many fall back on informal and commonplace terms. For example, they may say, "What I think about atmosphere is that it's about air and storms and stuff like that."

Ms. Furakawa jots down a "starter" question: What do the students *really* know? Her hunch is that students know only the words that they use, but she decides that this idea is wrong—they surely know more words than they actually use! She asks the other third-grade teacher for advice, and he recommends the vocabulary section of the Iowa Test of Basic Skills (ITBS; Hoover, Hieronymus, Frisbie, & Dunbar, 1996) for a quick vocabulary check. (See Kame'enui, Simmons, & Cornachione, 2001, for an annotated list of published assessment instruments.)

Next, she decides to spend a little time with a few students who appear to have particular problems; they say hardly anything in class discussions. For example, Sam scores at a grade level of 1.2 on the ITBS vocabulary test, two grades below expectation. Sam seldom volunteers during classroom discussions, simply shrugging his shoulders. She decides to explore an alternative hypothesis: Sam actually has a substantial vocabulary (most nine-year-olds do), but his storehouse of words is not tapped in typical school tests and formal talk. What might be the keys to his storehouse?

The design problem in this case calls for Ms. Furakawa to imagine other ways to bring out Sam's vocabulary. He may lack the full range and depth of concepts expected in third grade. He clearly needs to learn how to express himself more effectively. But what is there to build upon so that Ms. Furakawa can help him most effectively, assuming that he knows more than he appears to on the surface?

Designing an assessment often means planning mini-experiments for observing performance under different conditions. Ms. Furakawa decides to check out three possibilities: (1) Sam can recognize words that he may not use spontaneously; (2) he may be able to talk about words that he doesn't appear to know; or (3) he may be able to use context to figure out the meaning of unfamiliar words.

What happens when Sam is asked to make choices about the meaning of more or less familiar words? "Sam, which of these words best describes the pizza we had for lunch today [slight pause between each word and the next]: scrumptious, bedraggled, succulent, delectable, ambrosial, good, yummy?"

What happens when he is asked to explain a word's meaning in different ways? "Sam, what is a diamond? Do you know anyone who has a diamond? What does it look like? Which best describes a diamond—a ring, a jewel, a star? Can you think of another way the word *diamond* is used? What about a diamond in baseball? Is it a catcher's mitt, someone on the team, or the way the playing field is laid out?"

When and how does Sam use context to figure out the meaning of a novel word? Suppose Sam is given these sentences: "The bones from pterosaurs, a giant aerial reptile that terrorized other beasts during the Jurassic Age, have been found throughout the western United States" and "A flying reptile with a body as big as a horse, the pterosaur swooped down on other small beasts and carried them away to his mountain hideaway." What clues can Sam use to understand the meaning of pterosaur?

Ms. Furakawa's design, shown in Figure 14.4, begins with easy tasks, moves to tougher ones, and adds support as needed. A *clean* assessment investigates student performance when conditions are optimal. Everyone fails under some circumstances. By finding a way to help Sam show that he knows something about *diamonds* and *reptiles,* Ms. Furakawa has a more valid assessment of Sam's capacities and can target instruction for Sam and for other students.

DEPTH OF WORD KNOWLEDGE	CHARACTERISTICS	MEANING ASSESSMENT	STRATEGY ASSESSMENT
Can recognize word (listening/reading)	"Has something to do with . . . ." (identify picture)	IRAS vocabulary "Does *glad* mean *sad,* or *nervous,* or *happy*?"	"How did you know?" Immediate recall Scaffolded recall
Can define word	"It means . . . ."	IRAS vocabulary "What does *scrumptious* mean?"	"I figured it out from the text."
Can understand word in context (listening/reading)	"It is talking about a kind of . . . ."	"What does that word mean in this sentence/passage?"	"I know what the parts of the word mean" (*dis-* = not; *like* = enjoy; *-ed* = past tense).
Can use word in appropriate contexts (speaking/writing)	"You have to use *tyrant* here."	Writing samples Oral presentations Fill-in-the-blank exercise "What would be a different word for *sat*?"	
Knows multiple meanings of word	"It can mean _____ or _____."	"Tell me all the meanings of *grow*."	
Can use word in multiple contexts to mean different things (speaking/writing)	"A run earned in baseball; a run in your stockings; to move quickly."	How many different ways can you use the word *run*?"	

FIGURE 14.4

Vocabulary Assessment Design from the Interactive Reading Assessment System (IRAS)

Note: See the *Assessments and Lesson Plans* supplement.

Sam is only one student. What about the others? The answer is that in-depth assessment allows you to enhance your understanding of student learning by studying particular cases, which you can apply in the classroom turmoil. You must often collect information on the fly, switching your attention for a few moments to Sam, then to Deborah and a few other students, taking advantage of naturally occurring variations in classroom situations. On occasion, you may ask a specific question of Sam to check out a hunch or assign him a particular task to see how he does. You cannot give huge amounts of individual attention to every student—nor do you need to. But what you learn from studying Sam will help you know how to assess from moment to moment. You are learning to "kid-watch."

Planning an assessment design is a matter of making choices. Should you work with groups or individuals? Group testing brings to mind paper-and-pencil tasks, but there are other possibilities. Individual assessment offers greater latitude but is costly and poses problems in class management. Is the assessment oral or written? Does the task require production or recognition? For example, you can ask students to write a sentence about petroleum or pick the correct answer *(oil)* from four choices. The first task requires more effort from both student and teacher but offers more information.

Time is an important consideration in assessment design. Most schools begin in September and end in June. You have nine months to make something happen. How will your assessment plan vary over the months? How will you adjust the plan as you learn more and puzzles emerge?

Time should also capture development. The September focus of a kindergarten teacher will be quite different from that of the teacher with a combined fourth-fifth-grade class. In kindergarten classes, you can study individual children to discover their interests and find out what they know about letters, sounds, words, sentences, books. Clay's (1993) concepts-about-print assessment provides a helpful model for teacher-made questions to discover what emergent readers know about print and books. For example, a kindergartner can be asked about directionality with such questions as "Where is the front of the book?" and "Where is the top of the page?" He can also be asked function questions such as "Where do I begin to read on this page?" and questions about boundaries such as "Underline one word. Where does it start? Where does it end?" The focus is not on the "right" answer, but on how the student handles the question. Year-end achievements should be gauged with a greater margin of tolerance in the early grades. Your major task is to move children from the broad spectrum of entry levels toward the academic demands of the next grade.

For a teacher of upper-grade students, choices become more constrained. You must quickly learn how close your students are to handling middle-school demands. You can't spend September casually engaging in discussions with students about interests and backgrounds. Given a combination of fourth- and fifth-graders, you are likely to have both a larger class and greater diversity than your kindergarten colleague. Your plan of action requires focus and efficiency. The basic strategy is the same: Explore conditions under which a student succeeds or fails but assume that success is possible. Motivation is especially critical in the later grades. After several years of failure, students may have learned that they cannot learn. Assessment may mean finding ways to convince students that they can succeed. Skill and will are both important, for setting learning conditions and for deciding what evidence best informs you about students' abilities and achievements.

Your design should allow you to evaluate various hypotheses. You can proceed "on the fly," as in the example of Sam. You should also consider predesigned instruments like informal reading inventories (IRIs). These assessments, which are individually administered, include graded lists of words along with short graded narratives and expository passages. The teacher records and analyzes students' reading miscues to determine instructional reading levels.

The Interactive Reading Assessment System (IRAS; Calfee, 1999) in the *Assessments and Lesson Plans* supplement illustrates the IRI strategy. Some or all of the components may be administered, depending on what information you need. IRAS begins with a selection of letters from the alphabet to measure a student's understanding of sound-symbol relationships. Next are graded word lists, which assess both word-recognition skills and vocabulary levels. Lists of synthetic words allow you to diagnose decoding and spelling abilities. These lists cover each of the three layers of English orthography: the Anglo-Saxon layer (common patterns like *cat*), the Latin layer (patterns like *protracted* and *transportable*), and the Greek layer (*television* and *telekinetic*). Graded sets of related sentences assess students' ability to read connected text where context may be an aid when reading unknown words within a passage. The sentence sets guide you in selecting passages, both stories and reports, to check out comprehension skills. Along the way, metalinguistic questions reveal students' thinking processes as they perform different tasks: "Why is *fab* said differently than *fabe*?" As noted above, you can use only those parts of IRAS that you need for a particular purpose, but you can also use it as a "shell" for developing your own assessments.

> **ASSESSMENT**
>
> Most informal reading inventories focus on reading fluency, which is an important indicator. IRAS is designed to capture a broad range of the components that go into skilled reading, including metacognitive responses.

Collecting Evidence

The collection process is a practical enterprise with lots of options. At the beginning of the chapter, we discussed the broad continuum of assessment options, from informal tasks to formal methods. Here, we focus on midrange methods that provide the most informative strategies for classroom applications: observing, discussing and questioning, interviewing, student work samples, scoring rubrics, and traditional, teacher-made tests. These strategies overlap with good teaching practice, and instruction and assessment often intertwine.

Observing

The best information about student learning often comes from looking and listening, or kid watching (Goodman, Goodman, & Hood, 1989). (For more information on observing, see Johnson, Kress, & Pikulski, 1987; Johnston, 1992; and Owocki & Goodman, 2002.) This job is easier said than done. Until you know how to look and listen, it can be hard to both instruct and observe. The classroom may seem a blooming, buzzing confusion. How can you make sense of student responses as you teach? What do you look for? How do you find out what's really happening in students' heads? The following questions offer a framework for looking and listening:

- Who are the students? How many are there? How are groups organized? Which students stand out, and why?
- Who are the adults? How many are there? What are their roles and status? Who are they working with?
- What is going on? What is each group doing—reading, writing, talking, completing worksheets?

- Who is instructing, and how? Is it a teacher, aide, tutor? Is the instructor talking, asking questions, managing, facilitating, observing?
- What is the instructional content? What is the subject matter? What skills and activities seem central? What is the focus? What materials and supports are present?
- How are the students responding? Are they attentive? Productive? Interested and engaged? What is their level of performance? Of social interaction?
- How is the time being used? Does the lesson introduce new material? Is time provided for guided practice or to use previously introduced skills in new ways? Are class management problems handled?

These questions serve as a solid starting point, but let us offer a couple of cautions. First, you probably can't simultaneously monitor all seven questions for all students, and so for a particular observation you should pick a focus. Select those facets and students that fit a particular situation, and place everything else in the background. A clear purpose allows you to "zoom in," setting the stage for action research. For instance, you might study how a particular student handles different situations with varying amounts of support. How does Sam handle vocabulary in whole-class activities versus small groups? How does he do with and without a helping hand? On topics that are more or less interesting to him? When he is talking or writing? Focusing on Sam and his vocabulary situation makes the job possible. And, as noted earlier, what you learn about Sam can inform you about other students as well.

Second, it is hard to observe while you are teaching. You can remedy this problem in a couple of ways. First, practice observing. Study your class while they are taught by someone else—a colleague, a student teacher, maybe even the principal. Even brief looks give you a different perspective on students, a chance to see how individuals respond to the classroom ebb and flow. "David never seems to join the discussion. I placed him at the front on the reading rug so that I could watch him. Now I see that he is totally distracted by the posters that I tacked underneath the chalkboard! I should move David or the posters."

One of the most informative strategies for collecting data is interviewing students and recording what you hear and observe.

Another way to find time for observation is to build it into your teaching. You can organize group activities and individual assignments to allow you time to look at learning. It is tempting to use these occasions to work with students with special needs or to respond to questions on homework papers. But sometimes, rather than talk, you might stop, look, and listen. Also, becoming generally more familiar with other classrooms and students will enable you to gain more from your formal and informal observations.

While observing your class, don't limit your attention to academic work. You can informally assess students' motivation for reading or writing by listening to what they say and watching how they approach a challenging but doable task. For example, when Jim and Nancy begin the task of writing about life in a covered wagon on the Oregon Trail without hesitation, they are demonstrating a high level of self-efficacy for this writing task. Their teacher, Mr. Edwards, has given them multiple opportunities during the year to brainstorm a topic and then organize their ideas in a topical web. They have been taught to use an index to locate additional information for their web in the library books on display in the classroom. When the teacher comments on the quality of their reports, the students attribute success to their decision to work hard this quarter to become better writers and improve their report card grades in writing.

Mr. Edwards: You both created wonderful descriptions of life on the Oregon Trail for the pioneers. You used interesting adjectives and verbs that helped me imagine what the people were doing and what the land looked like as I read what you wrote. You also organized all of the information well, and that made it easy to understand what you wanted your readers to know.

Nancy: I remembered when you told us that writing was more interesting when you used words that are really accurate and can paint a picture in the reader's mind. Reading the books about life back then helped me to know what words to use.

Jim: I remembered that, too. I decided to use some of the writing strategies you taught us, like using a web to plan how I would organize what I wanted to write about and thinking about my audience. Nancy and I talked about how much interesting stuff we found about the Oregon Trail, and we decided to try our best to get an "A" on this writing assignment. And I'm happy it worked!

When Dave, on the other hand, hears the assignment, he spends the next few minutes in avoidant behaviors. He rummages through his backpack for a pencil, bothers the student next to him, and so on. Earlier, when the class was asked to read silently about the Westward Movement, he flipped dispiritedly through the history book—he wasn't especially interested in the topic. It seemed to Dave that he always had trouble understanding history. He thinks, "How can I handle the writing assignment when I know nothing about the topic? My writing scores are always low, so what's the point in trying? Mr. Edwards is always asking me to write about things that I can't understand and don't like."

These scenarios challenge Mr. Edwards to analyze his students' self-efficacy (or confidence) and to respond to students' motivation as well as their performance. When he praises the quality of Jim's and Nancy's reports, their comments lead him to think that they attribute their success on this assignment to their own efforts—just the type of attribution he wants his class to make.

Dave's behavior may seem resistant; he "just doesn't care." By checking with him about his perceptions of the situation, Mr. Edwards may find that Dave's attributions emphasize external factors like the difficulty of the task, the irrelevance of the assignment, or other factors that he cannot control—the luck of the draw. Redirecting the assignment to connect with Dave's interests may open the way to help him understand that his efforts can make a difference. Observing on the fly can capture behaviors that are the starting point for more detailed inquiry.

Discussing and Questioning

New teachers generally anticipate engaging students in active discussions and are then frustrated by the lack of participation. Students either say nothing or go completely wild, leading the teacher to resort to lecturing as a control mechanism. The result is to shut down an important opportunity for assessment. Student talk, when well planned and managed, offers important opportunities to study student thinking.

One way to foster meaningful discussion is the knowledge-as-design approach developed by David Perkins (1994). Perkins suggests that exploration of many topics can be organized around the following questions:

- What is the relevance of the topic?
- What is the structure of the topic?
- What are examples of the topic?
- What are positives and negatives of the topic?

The idea is not to use these questions only in guiding discussion, but to give them away to the students for their personal use. The knowledge-as-design strategy offers students a scaffold for participation and an opportunity, individually and collectively, to think deeply about a topic and voice a variety of opinions while still keeping the discussion on track.

Much can also be learned from the methods of successful questioners. Socrates, a philosopher of ancient Greece, would pose a single question that engaged his students for hours. The idea is that the question might be as important as the answer! Modern-day versions of the Socratic approach turn up in unlikely places, such as Oprah Winfrey's television talk show and Ann Landers's newspaper columns. In these exchanges, rich dialogues depend on three elements: why the questioner is asking the question, what kind of question is asked, and how the questioner handles the responses (Dillon, 1988).

1. *Why are you asking the question?* In school, most questions are designed to find out whether the student knows what the teacher already knows. Outside school, a question is usually a genuine effort by one person to learn something from someone else. Students may be startled when classroom discussion takes this turn and be reluctant to respond. They have learned that school questions have a right answer, and the teacher knows what it is. "Real" questions seldom have one right answer.

2. *What kinds of questions lead to rich discussions?* It's useful to think about the kind of answer you have in mind. Questions that lead to yes-no answers do not yield much dialogue unless asking "Why?" is a natural follow-up. The same is true for questions that call for specific answers. Broad questions can be quite simple. While you are reading a story, for instance, a natural question at a critical juncture is "What do you think will hap-

pen next?" Starting with broad questions and then exploring the responses can promote rich discussion. We introduce the funnel approach in the following section on interviewing.

3. *How can you extend student responses to more fully reveal their thinking?* Again, keep it simple: "Gee, that sounds interesting—say more." Several boys in a Hawaiian classroom, after reading about volcanoes in their science book, are building a soda-vinegar model. The teacher asks, "Do you really think that if you dig really deep you'll find melted rock?" The boys mull it over, and decide "No, it can't be!" The teacher continues, "You know, Oahu [their island] was once a volcano." Disbelief registers on their faces, but then one boy mentions that his father told him that the lava rocks in their yard were from old volcanoes. It becomes clear to the teacher that the students "understood" the text at one level but had not connected it with their personal experience. The teacher now questions them about the soda-vinegar activity. This model is a popular activity in elementary classrooms, but misleads students about how volcanoes really operate.

Interviewing

Talking with students can take many forms. Sometimes, you spend time with individual students, not in an on-the-fly casual conversation or a formal assessment, but in one- or two-minute sessions around a particular question with a particular student. The funnel approach, illustrated below in In the Classroom 14.3, is an efficient strategy for collecting both broad and focused information during an exchange. The key is to prepare yourself in advance with a collection of models, such as those of the funnel approach (What does *lonely* mean? Does it mean to be afraid, to miss your friends, or to want to smile?). IRAS provides several models of this approach.

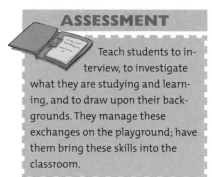

ASSESSMENT

Teach students to interview, to investigate what they are studying and learning, and to draw upon their backgrounds. They manage these exchanges on the playground; have them bring these skills into the classroom.

The Funnel Approach

The funnel approach begins with general queries and moves toward specific questions. Second-grader Martha has problems with story comprehension and can't seem to identify with characters. After reading *Nate the Great* by Marjorie Weinman Sharmat, a simple detective story that tells how Nate finds his friend Annie's lost picture, Martha expresses neither empathy nor interest. Here is the teacher's one-minute interview using the funnel approach.

in the **Classroom 14.3**

Teacher: Martha, what do you remember about *Nate the Great?* What can you tell me about what the characters were feeling?

Martha: I dunno. I guess I like the way Nate feels good when he helps Annie find her picture.

Teacher: How do you think Nate feels when Annie tells him on the phone about her missing picture?

Martha: Happy, because he likes to solve mysteries and call himself "Nate the Great"! And Annie feels sad and mad, 'cause I think she really liked that picture.

Teacher: Very nice! What does the story tell you about why Annie likes the picture?

Notice how the teacher starts with a broad question designed to reconnect Martha to an earlier discussion about the story. She focuses Martha's understanding of the characters' feelings. "Why" and

"How do you know that" questions delve into students' reasoning and explore their capacity to reflect and make inferences. Whatever Martha's answers, the teacher will learn something from this exchange, which she will jot in her logbook.

Student Work Samples: Performances and Portfolios

During a typical school day, students produce a lot of paperwork. Some products (for example, worksheets) serve for practice, the work of a moment, and are seldom worth keeping. As noted earlier, today's assessment methods are more likely to emphasize authentic performance and showing one's work. Students assemble portfolios for writing and mathematics, science and social studies (Farr & Tone, 1994; Tierney, Carter, & Desai, 1991). These collections, like Ms. King's Roots project, take shape as major activities representing significant amounts of time, engaging the creative impulse, and reflecting meaningful personal investment.

A writing portfolio can show a student's progression from early ruminations about a task to final publication. The read-write-cycle model (the CLAS-Plus Assessment model) in Figure 14.5 (Calfee & Wilson, 2004) provides effective support for portfolio projects for students in the mid-elementary

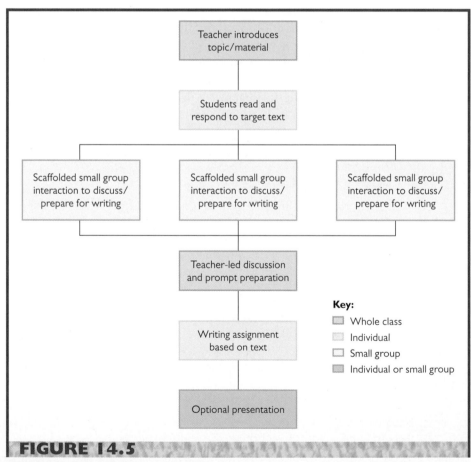

FIGURE 14.5

CLAS-Plus Model of Assessment

Source: Calfee, R. C., & Wilson, K. M. (2004). "A classroom-based writing assessment framework." In C. A. Stone, E. R. Silliman, B. J. Ehren, & K. Apel (Eds.), Handbook of language and literacy: Development and disorders (pp. 583–599). Copyright 2004. Reprinted with permission of The Guilford Press.

grades and beyond. The aim is to guide instruction, but the activities also reveal students' abilities to translate prior experiences and topical reading into a well-developed written text, with ongoing support along the way.

Work samples assess both product and process through a series of stages. In the *develop* stage, students brainstorm together, sharing what they already know about the topic. They then read stories, articles, books, or Web pages to research the topic further and to study texts that offer models for writing. In the *draft* stage, their ideas coalesce into the beginnings of an essay. During the *review* stage, students conference with peers for feedback and suggestions on their drafts. During the *revision* stage, choices are made about incorporating suggestions and modifying the original draft. The students work on grammar and mechanics in the *polishing* stage. The essays are now ready for the *publication* stage, where their work becomes public. The final result can be judged as a product, but the process reveals student learning and can help inform instruction. The read-write-cycle model applies to both narrative and expository text. The flexible framework allows the teacher to employ the model with any genre.

Portfolios often include captions, brief comments by the teacher reflecting on the work and pointing out strengths and areas for improvement. Post-its allow the teacher to provide feedback and instructional guidance without marking up the original. Students can add their own Post-it captions, putting themselves into the assessment loop.

Scoring Rubrics

What is the best way to score papers? The answer is the *rubric,* a scoring guide something like a letter grade but without the letters and with instructions about the meaning of each level on the scale. Figure 14.6 shows a rubric for evaluating primary-grade writing. Later in the chapter, we present a rubric for intermediate-grade reading. Rubric systems include benchmarks, or samples, at each level, along with an explanation of why the work received a particular grade.

Figure 14.7 shows a six-level format for writing in the elementary grades. A rating is provided for five dimensions—length, coherence, grammar/mechanics, vocabulary, and spelling—each of which is important in a well-written composition. A separate score for each dimension allows teachers and students to identify specific strengths and areas that need attention.

ASSESSMENT

Portfolios can easily become "trash bins" if you aren't careful. It often helps to design a system around a working portfolio, in which students store lots of their work, and one or more presentation portfolios for finished products.

CW 14.1 links you to the federally funded Northwest Regional Education Laboratory, which provides a variety of downloadable reading and writing assessment rubrics, such as the 6 + 1 Traits Scoring Guide.

ASSESSMENT

Tests often have an aura of secrecy, while assessments tend to be much more open. For example, you can introduce writing rubrics to students at the beginning of the year and encourage them to apply the rubrics to self-review and peer assessment.

Exceptional	Sparkles! Vocabulary uses descriptive words. Creates suspense or surprise. Aware of audience. Strong personal voice. Emotion transmitted. Clincher at end.
Commendable	Clear beginning, middle, and end. Strong story sense. Mostly conventional spelling. Passage flows. Supporting detail.
Adequate	Listing of events. Phonetic spelling. Catalog of facts. Train of thought. Sense of beginning and end, but lost in details.
Some Evidence	Complete thought. Coherent but weak. Inventive spelling.
Little Evidence	Minimal fluency. Off topic. No story line or train of thought. Repetitive.
Minimal Evidence	No meaning in print. Random letters with pictures.

FIGURE 14.6
Rubric for Evaluating Primary-Grade Writing

SCORE	LENGTH*	COHERENCE	GRAMMAR/MECHANICS
6	3–5 pages, or 176 or more words	• Writer provides overall links/transitions; examples and descriptions are presented logically. • States main topic and supports it with details and examples • Shifts topics smoothly; easy to follow and logical.	• Makes few, if any, errors in grammar and punctuation. • Utilizes appropriate variety of sentence structures, including phrases and clauses.
5	1–2 pages, or 86–175 words	• Shows ease and facility in expressing ideas. • Writing flows smoothly and naturally and is understandable. • Generally focused on topic • Provides description, elaboration, evidence, and/or support. • Writer provides overall links, but transitions may not always be smooth; ideas/reasons are clear and logical.	• Uses some variation in sentence structure, including phrases and clauses. • Minimal errors may be present as complex structures are explored. • Has few run-ons or fragmented sentences.
4	¾ page, or 61–85 words	• Provides descriptions, elaboration, evidence and/or support. • Information or examples may be in a list-like form (no tying together of ideas). • Addresses the topic without wavering. • Writing is generally understandable and coherent, but lacks complete control. • Focus may shift and be somewhat difficult to follow.	• Shows clear sentence sense. • May display variety in sentences. • Makes minimal or no errors in punctuation. • Has few, if any, run-ons or fragmented sentences.
3	4 sentences/½ page, or 36–60 words	• Addresses the topic. • Includes little description, elaboration, evidence, or support. • May include rambling sentences or lists with no elaboration. • Vague and/or confusing	• Uses simple repetitive sentences. • May include fragments and run-ons. • Makes some errors in punctuation and grammar, which do not impede reading.
2	2–3 sentences/¼ page, or 11–35 words	• Addresses the topic minimally. • May wander off topic. • Fragmented expression of ideas	• Uses simple sentence structure or phrases with many fragments and/or run-ons. • Makes errors that are highly evident and interfere with reading.
1	1 sentence or less, or 0–10 words	• Generally unintelligible or unrelated • Copied from the board or another student	• Unintelligible due to grammar or punctuation • Copied from the board or another student

FIGURE 14.7

Read-Write-Cycle Assessment Rubric

*Grade-level-appropriate paper, margins, and penmanship; no skipping of lines.

**Most Anglo-Saxon words can stand alone and be affixed. Affixes are often prepositional: *over-, under-, in-, for-*. Common suffixes include *-ed, -er, -ing, -ly, -hood, -ness*.

VOCABULARY	SPELLING
• Shows substantial use of complex Romance Language Layer words. • Uses lexical variety. • Uses precision in dealing with topic. • Uses Latin and Greek roots and affixes.	<u>Complex Conventional</u> • Shows substantial evidence of attempting complex words with few errors (polysyllabic words, prefixes and suffixes, Latin and Greek roots and affixes) • Shows command of vowels in polysyllabic words. • Shows mastery of conventional spellings for familiar 1- to 2-syllable words.
• Shows some evidence of complex but familiar Romance Language Layer words. • Shows limited variety and reliance on relatively common words(national). • Uses Latin (and Greek) roots and affixes. • Uses precise and/or rich language (*no ordinary friend, compassionate*).	<u>Conventional</u> • Has command of long/short vowel contrast. • Makes few errors. • Uses polysyllabic words with few or no errors.
• Uses a substantial number of familiar polysyllabic words (*interesting, understand*), including compounds. • Shows noticeably increased precision (*friendly* for *nice*).	<u>Phonetic Appropriate</u> • Is beginning to show long/short vowel contrast. • Uses short vowels accurately. • May have other vowel errors (e.g., digraphs). • Reversals may be present (especially in blends and *r/l* patterns). • Polysyllabic words (including compounds), if present, include vowels.
• Uses 1- to 2-syllable words, most frequently with little variety or precision. • May include compounds and Anglo-Saxon** affixation (prepositions, comparatives: *under-, -er, -est*) • May include descriptive words.	<u>Phonological</u> • Uses short vowels accurately. • Represents each sound with very few omissions. • Reversals may be present (especially in blends or *r/l* patterns. • Easily readable
• Frequently uses one-syllable (CVC) and basic sight words. • Uses short "safe," commonplace words, • Uses simplistic and/or imprecise language.	<u>Beginning Phonological</u> • Can identify consonants. • Includes vowels, but frequently the selection is incorrect. • Omits sounds (*sitr = sister*). • Readable with minimal effort
• Most words are difficult to interpret. • Uses few words and/or limits words to those provided by the teacher. • Uses incorrect and/or ineffective language.	<u>Alphabetic, Prephonetic</u> • Uses letters. • Consonants may represent some sounds. • Omits most vowels. • May or may not spell sight words conventionally. • Unreadable or readable with considerable effort

| | LEVEL OF PROFICIENCY | | |
STANDARD	Exemplary	Proficient	Developing
Making Sense of a Story	Thoroughly understands complex stories	Understands most stories including some complex ones	Has limited and literal understanding of simple stories
	Connects personal experiences to characters and themes	Makes some connections of personal experiences to characters and situations	Extracts meaning but with little personal connection
	Has multiple perspectives across stories	Has different perspectives on a story	Describes events, people, and places factually
Using Tools and Strategies in Reading	Masterfully uses several strategies to deepen understanding	Uses various strategies to understand story	Has limited range of strategies
	Makes sophisticated analyses of plot and theme	Uses re-reading and rethinking to support understanding	Uses some re-reading to support understanding

FIGURE 14.8

Sample Rubrics for Intermediate-Grade Literacy Standards

The rubric system also provides information about reading comprehension (see Figure 14.8). For example, if a student's book report on Colin Powell is poorly written but shows an understanding of the content, then content and coherence will be high but other dimensions will be low. Doesn't this approach mix reading and writing? The answer is "Yes, but it doesn't matter." Until we develop a mental probe that allows us to tell about a person's internal thoughts, we have to rely on indirect measures. Multiple-choice tests also depend on much more than reading; as we shall see later, they require strategies, motivation, and background knowledge. Asking a student to discuss a passage is probably the most direct method for gauging comprehension but is impractical for a class of 35 students. To assess reading through writing, you look for different features in a composition.

Models for Teacher-Made Tests

Thus far, we have emphasized performance assessments, but you will also need to rely on traditional tests when appropriate. Nitko (1996) and Stiggins (1994) both describe procedures for the development of various types of teacher-made tests, ranging from multiple-choice instruments to short-answer techniques. For children in the early grades, informal reading inventories (Farr & Carey, 1986) and running records (Clay, 1993; Goodman, Goodman, & Hood, 1989) offer a useful middle ground between standardized methods and completely open-ended approaches.

In the latter approaches, students read aloud passages of increasing difficulty until they reach a frustration level (too many miscues or too much time). For example, in the Developmental Reading Assessment (DRA; Beaver, 1997), the student moves through a series of "little books" of increasing difficulty. As the student reads, the teacher records the student's oral reading errors (omissions and substitutions) along with hesitations, repetitions, and self-corrections. This process provides a performance level, along with information about reading strategies and error patterns. These methods focus on oral reading fluency, but you can also have students discuss their understanding of the passage and explain their word-attack strategies. These methods require considerable time, and so you should use them sparingly, generally as supplements to ongoing observations and along with results from formal tests like the Wide Range Achievement Test (WRAT; Wilkinson, 1995) or the Woodcock-Johnson III Tests of Achievement (Woodcock, McGrew, & Mather, 2001).

CW 14.2 links to the Dynamic Indicators of Basic Early Literacy Skills (DIBELS), which includes a free, downloadable series of graded fluency assessments.

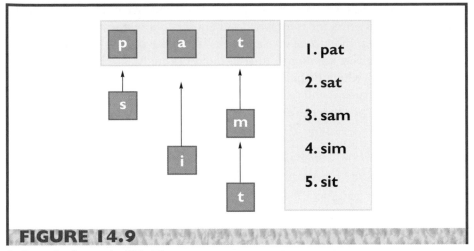

FIGURE 14.9

A Sample from the Tile Test

Finding ways to adapt these techniques to meet classroom needs is the key. In the *Assessments and Lesson Plans* supplement, the Tile Test (Calfee, 1999) and the Graduated Running Record provide models that you can use as is or as templates. The Tile Test (see Figure 14.9), designed for primary-grade children, uses letter and word tiles in short, engaging activities to quickly assess letter knowledge, sound-symbol relationship, articulation, decoding/spelling abilities, metaphonic understanding, and skill at reading simple sentences. With letter tiles, children who have yet to master paper and pencil can demonstrate what they know about spelling—and the activity can be fun. As shown in Figure 14.9, the student plays a Scrabble-like game, beginning with *pat* and changing one letter at a time to make *sat, sam,* and so on. To assess metalinguistic processes, students are asked along the way to explain their decoding/spelling strategies.

The Graduated Running Record (GRR; see Figure 14.10) can be used throughout the elementary grades to measure fluency (reading rate, prosody/

	First Home
Mid-First Grade	What made this a good place for a mother, father, and chil-
End of First Grade	dren to work and play? Many children who were living on
	this land a very long time ago slept at night in little huts.
Second Grade	These small houses were made with reeds or branches and
	had places carefully made of stones for cooking the food the
Third Grade	family found. Early each morning, the hard-working people
	living together in the tiny village were ready to walk to dif-
Fourth Grade	ferent places looking for special foods. After gathering a va-
	riety of edible acorns and seeds using woven reed baskets,
	the women and girls of the settlement mashed the mounds
Fifth Grade	of nuts into meal. Several men traveling by particular routes
	into the wilderness hunted the plentiful small prey such as
	squirrels, rabbits, and birds with nets, curved throwing
Sixth Grade	sticks, or bows and arrows. Other adults rowed large
	wooden boats protected with tar to neighboring island set-
	tlements to trade for unique and nourishing sources of pro-
	tein to expand their seafood diet.

FIGURE 14.10

The Graduated Running Record

phrasing, stress, and intonation). In addition, you can also determine students' understanding of semantic, syntactic, and grapho-phonemic cuing systems by analyzing miscues. In place of leveled books like those used in the DRA (which can take a significant amount of time to move through), GRR relies on a single paragraph in which difficulty gradually increases with each sentence. At some point, the student will reach his reading level. The tester then finishes the passage, asking the student to retell the story in order to determine his comprehension skill.

Analyzing and Summarizing the Data: The Teacher Logbook

It is late September. You probably know a little about your class, partly from discussions with the previous teacher and from spring testing and partly from classroom observations. You will need to organize this information into a coherent portrait for parent conferences and for fine-tuning instructional plans for the rest of the fall. You will face similar tasks throughout the year. The school day has limited hours, and you must choose how to spend them. Students differ, and you must decide how to meet individual needs, how to organize students, and how to plan activities. You need to think about what you know and how to communicate it to others.

Analyzing and summarizing need not mean a sudden shift in the assessment process. You don't stop collecting evidence to begin analysis; the process is ongoing and interactive. Throughout September, you have formed individual portraits. But now, you need to shift your emphasis, to think about the class as a whole and how to structure the course ahead. It is time to assemble the evidence so that you can decide what it means and how to use it, for your own purposes and for feedback to others.

Teachers use a variety of strategies to handle these tasks. Some rely on basal management systems, while others keep narrative journals. In In the Classroom 14.1, about Ms. King and the Roots project, we referred on several occasions to her logbook. In this section, we offer a more detailed example of the logbook approach to maintaining assessment records. The teacher logbook, a sample from which is shown in Figure 14.11, is a practical method for organizing assessment data (Calfee, 2000; Calfee & Perfumo, 1993).

The logbook is arranged in three segments: a summary of student performance, journal judgments of student achievement, and a curriculum-planning record. You work with the logbook from back to front—that is, from Section III to Section I. Your first task, before school begins, is to review your curriculum plans, especially those for the fall quarter. These plans are laid out at the back of the logbook, much like a road map. Here is where you make notes about how you will start the year, learn about your class, and establish end-of-grade expectations. You need to review your options for materials and activities; a change in the textbook series, a new collection of trade books, a conference with the librarian will all influence your curriculum plans.

Your main job will be to review and refine a small number of critical curriculum outcomes as your focus for the year. You can't teach everything. With state and local standards as the reference point, what will be your emphasis? What will your students know by year's end? How will you judge the quality of their accomplishments?

Story comprehension and composition, for example, are built around four critical outcomes (Lukens, 1990): character, plot, setting, and theme. For kinder-

FIGURE 14.11

A Sample from a Teacher Logbook

Teacher: *Ms. King* School: *Lakeview Elementary*

Year: *2005–2006* Grade: *2*

Section I: Student Summary

| | Reading/Writing/Language | | | Math |
	Vocab	Narrative	Expos Skills	Addition
Able, J	+ + +	+ +	+ + +	+ +
"		"	"	"	"
"		"	"	"	"
Matthews, K	+ +	+ +	– –	+ + +
"		"	"	"	"
"		"	"	"	"
Zetter, B	+ +	+ + +	+ +	+ +

Karen Matthews is an avid reader as long as a book fits with her interests. She prefers stories and will attempt difficult pieces (The Trolls and Shadows) if they capture her imagination. She seldom selects nonfiction books. Her oral reports are well prepared, and she puts herself into the delivery. She has written only a limited amount; her personal journal contains only brief notes, as do her other reports. She is capable but hesitates to do anything that is not perfect on the first draft. Karen is very capable and has shown growth this year but needs to explore and expand her reading and writing activities.

Section II: Journal Notes

Week of January 15. Worked on nonfiction reading. Students could choose from new selections I laid out in the classroom library with science, geography, and historical events. Jeff Able, who has shown little interest in reading thus far, came to life when he saw the books on space. Now I know how to grab him. Karen Matthews, who has been doing well, asked if she could re-read Shadows and described the new collection as "boring."

Section III: Curriculum Plans   *January 20, 2005*

The new state standards emphasize informational reading and writing beginning in third grade, and I want to explore them with my second-graders. They appear to be doing quite well, and I can give them a head start. Story comprehension will stay on my agenda, of course. . . .

I suspect that boys will enjoy informational topics, but girls may be another matter. Check with Thelma (the librarian) on recent acquisitions. Orr's nature books have great graphics—I can bring in more science while dealing with the emphasis on reading.

gartners, understanding the moral of a simple fable is a reasonable goal. By third grade, students should be able to identify thematic issues in works such as E. B. White's *Charlotte's Web*, and to express the personal meaning of such stories. Sixth-graders should be able to appreciate the themes that link related stories, and to incorporate these themes in their compositions. Like *Charlotte's Web*, Katherine Paterson's *Bridge to Terabithia* tells how two characters are at first at odds but then develop a deep friendship that eventually ends in tragedy. *Charlotte's*

Web follows a spider and a pig from mutual disgust to intense affection, and eventually to Charlotte's death. In *Bridge to Terabithia,* the characters are a preadolescent boy and girl, and the tragedy is sudden and unpredictable. The competent sixth-grader will appreciate the parallels and can explore the theme—the abiding importance of genuine friendship—using real-world experiences.

The logbook lays out selected curriculum strands like those sketched above. Assessments allow you to locate each student on each strand. For example, in Ms. King's third-/fourth-grade combination, one student is struggling with the task of describing how Wilbur and Charlotte change from the beginning to the end of the story, while another can relate these changes to his own personal experience by composing a personal narrative about his emerging friendship with his new stepbrother.

The curriculum-planning section in Section III at the end of the logbook provides the place for you to record your planning activities. It is placed at the back because it is your section; it is for your analysis and reflection, not day by day but long term, not set in stone but constantly changing. It is not a collection of daily lesson plans for the principal, but a foundation for analysis: Where is the class headed? Where are they at present? How am I changing in my development as a teacher?

The middle of the logbook, Section II, provides journal space to record evidence about student performance observations, informal assessments of student activities and projects, and questions requiring further thought and action on your part. These notes may comment on students' portfolios, along with more formal assessments. They include brief jottings, notes based on student discussions, pointers to other information, and ponderings about individual students. Before school starts, you will enter preliminary information about the students. During September, a time of ongoing and intense formative assessment, the pages will fill quickly.

Beginning teachers often keep written notes, but seldom do they view these as research. In fact, journal notes offer a valuable record for reflection and action. An empty sheet in Section II warns that the student has slipped from sight. A long list of books read but no evidence of written work is a reminder to encourage the student to put his thoughts on paper. The logbook provides a record and a prompt for genuine individualization.

Finally, Section I includes information about individual students for official analysis and summative assessment. The class list runs down the left-hand column; curriculum strands are along the top. Although this section comes at the end of the process, you open it first for parent conferences, to review student progress, and to discuss students and the class with colleagues and the principal. The entries summarize your judgments of individual student performance for each strand, based on rubrics for each task that describe your interpretation of test scores, observations, and interviews. A question mark indicates uncertainty. For example, suppose Samantha shows little interest in writing; her journal contains a few brief sentences, obtained under duress: "Satrdy we went to Grat Amrica. I went on the Wav." But when you overhear her talk with a friend about the trip to the amusement park, she shares a great deal more information. She clearly has greater command of language than appears in her written work. Analysis leads to action. How can you provide conditions that will elicit the best that she can do? She prefers talking to writing and is impatient with the mechanics. For now, you enter a question mark under expository writing, a puzzlement to share with her parents and for you to explore in the weeks ahead.

The logbook helps you keep track of students' learning over the school year and pinpoint areas where you need to focus instruction. Analysis means com-

ASSESSMENT

Practice with feedback is the key to effective learning. Classroom assessments can be used for grades but, more importantly, can provide students with a running record of how they are doing and how they can improve.

bining information from many sources to create individual portraits and collective images over time. For instance, an example using the format shown in Figure 14.11 combines rubrics and other classroom performance measures with standardized scores. At the individual level, Edward scores at a 4.0 grade level on standardized tests, reads voraciously, and completes assigned writing tasks. His papers are longer than average, the mechanical details earn a 5 on length and a 6 for grammar/mechanics on the read-write-cycle rubric in Figure 14.7. But in both writing and group discussions, he reacts to thematic issues like a first-grader—at a superficial level (a coherence score of 3). He chooses short, simple books for free reading and races through them at breakneck speed. He retains the literal information but shows little depth of understanding. Reading seems a retreat into himself. He is small for his age and young for his cohort and has few friends. Perhaps he needs a better audience for sharing his ideas. Participating in a literature circle group may be just what he needs. The other members of the group will model higher-order thinking about the books they read and discuss. He will be given a role and will have to dig deeper than a surface-level understanding of the books to carry out that role. Checking entries in the logbook a few months later, we read that Edward is an eager contributor to his literature circle discussions. His inferences are right on target, showing increased depth of understanding. More evidence indicating that he is developing his reading skills is the obvious pleasure he showed as he read two Newbery Award winners.

Interpreting: Making Sense of the Results

Interpretation gives meaning to evidence and shapes generalizations that lead to action. Interpretation goes beyond concrete data to broader meanings. But inquiry does not travel in a straight line. As noted at the end of the previous section, interpretation is embedded in the questions, the design, and the evidence. You review a student's profile and develop a hunch, which leads you to look again at the data, and so on. Interpretation requires reflection, which means time and occasion to ponder the evidence. Pondering often works best when you also have opportunities to consult with colleagues.

Interpretation faces two challenges—consistency and persuasiveness, which are akin to reliability and validity. Reliability asks "Is the evidence dependable?" while validity asks "Can the evidence answer your question?" Standardized tests, covered later in this chapter, establish reliability and validity through statistics. Teacher-based assessment handles the issues through argument and debate. In the Classroom 14.4 shows a first-year teacher learning how to give meaning to evidence, to shape generalizations that lead to action.

ASSESSMENT

Interpreting is hard work. One of its purposes is to allow you to reflect on your teaching and student learning. Another purpose is to prepare for parent conferences, where thoughtful feedback can make a big difference.

Interpreting Evidence in the Sixth Grade

Jennifer Coombs, a new sixth-grade teacher, is assigned at the last minute to a school in a low-income, urban neighborhood. The previous teacher, Mr. Milton, has taken a health leave. His notes and the principal's comments suggest that the students have limited experience and poor language skills. Working from Mr. Milton's lesson plans, Ms. Coombs greets her new class. The morning goes fine. After lunch, she starts social studies with a discussion of the U.S. Constitution.

in the
Classroom
14.4

Ms. Coombs: Today, we're going to study the U.S. Constitution. Who can tell me something about the Constitution?

What does Ms. Coomb's experience reveal about the students? Several alternatives are consistent with the evidence but call for different courses of action:

- The students are not used to open-ended questions in school and don't understand strategies like brainstorming.
- They feel uneasy with a new teacher and don't want to seem foolish.
- They know something about how government works but don't know the official vocabulary.
- They really don't know much about the government and have a limited vocabulary.
- They really don't know much about government and don't care very much about the topic.

How can Ms. Coombs further evaluate these interpretations? As we noted earlier, inquiry is not a straight-line process. Validating an interpretation often calls for experimentation—for changing conditions and collecting new data, as we can see in In the Classroom 14.5.

Collecting More Evidence

Ms. Coombs decides to check whether students simply lack discussion strategies and are uneasy with open-ended questions. She plans a discussion for the following day around the topic of weather. The Constitution may be unfamiliar, but students surely know something about weather.

Ms. Coombs: Let's spend a little time talking about the weather. What comes to mind when you think about this topic?

Students: [Silence.]

[Ms. Coombs realizes this evidence suggests that something is at work other than lack of knowledge, and she makes a strategic move by offering some simple "starters."

Ms. Coombs: [Points toward the window.] What is it like today?

Student: Cloudy?

Ms. Coombs: Right! What was it like yesterday?

Student: Cold.

Ms. Coombs: OK. These are useful weather words! What about weather in other places—who knows something about the Florida hurricanes?

in the
Classroom
14.5

By the lesson's end, Ms. Coombs has collected considerable evidence about conditions that engage this particular group of students in discussion. She is forming some ideas about how to approach more abstract topics like U.S. government. If her interpretation had stopped with the first lesson, she might have decided to teach basic skills. Now, she is more inclined to focus neither on government nor on skills, but on developing a sense of classroom community.

Assessments like these may appear subjective, and they are; they depend on informed judgment. How can teachers assure critics about the trustworthiness of such complex judgments, especially when the outcome is assessment of individual students? One approach is to triangulate, to use multiple sources of evidence. You gather one piece of evidence from students' oral reading, another from class discussion, and still another from writing. Triangulation provides evidence of consistency, the keystone of reliability (Fetterman, 1998), but also ensures validity. Another answer depends on professional interaction. In Great Britain, teachers rely on "moderation" (Harlen, 1994), in which teacher teams review samples of student work, presenting and defending their interpretations to the group.

Ms. Coombs is still learning about interpretative processes. She is early in her career, with little time to consult with colleagues, who are as busy as she is. But she is on the right path—she is inclined to experiment and to persist, not a bad beginning for the first week of school.

Reporting and Decision Making

Now we move to the final stage of the inquiry process. You have gathered evidence about student achievement and are satisfied with its consistency and substance. What to do next? Inquiry-based assessment serves little purpose unless it leads to action, bringing the inquiry cycle full circle. To guide action, it often helps to gather your thoughts in written form (reports), so that you can see what you think and weigh various alternatives (decisions).

Reports (as in report cards) may bring to mind grades, which are traditionally associated with testing. We will offer a few thoughts about this topic and then look at reports from a different perspective. Grading on the A-to-F scale is familiar to most of us. Many schools now use performance levels, which they link to standards (Marzano, 2000; Nitko, 1996). Whatever the label, reports focus on competition (norm-referenced, grading on the curve) or preset limits (criterion-referenced, 90+ means an A). The goal is to summarize a complex portrait in a single index. Teachers view student achievement as a complex mix of effort and accomplishment. Joan's end-of-year compositions weren't as polished as Susan's, but Joan entered fourth grade barely able to finish a complete sentence while Susan was a budding author. No wonder traditional grades frustrate both teachers and students.

Standards-based tests, a new version of criterion-referenced testing, offer an alternative to grading. Standards lay out what students should be able to do in a particular area at a particular grade level, using descriptions like those in Figure 14.8. Rubrics (see also Figure 14.6) assign students to performance levels by combining information from a collection of work products. You will encounter labels like "Proficient: Meets the Standard," "Accomplished: Exceeds the Standard," and "Fails to Meet the Standard." On the surface, this approach looks different from traditional grading, but for practical purposes the two are much the same. They provide little guidance for instructional decisions; the teacher can place students in achievement groups or tracks, or the school can decide to retain a failing student or place him in a remedial program.

Grades and other summative judgments serve as important indicators at significant mileposts, as students move through the grades. The transition from elementary to middle school marks a major change for a youngster, a time for a clear signal about his level of accomplishment. Even at these points, it makes sense to provide a richer portrait of strengths and areas of need. The logbook provides one model along these lines; other approaches include the portfolios and narrative reports described earlier. All of these techniques call for weaving evidence from student work into an account that lays out a student's progress and accomplishments across the achievement spectrum. The idea is to create a portrait that provides feedback to the student about past efforts, but also offers guidance about future choices and decisions, for both student and teacher.

Preparing narratives or case studies for individual students may seem costly in time and effort, and you should probably focus on a small number of students at the outset. Teachers in the United States are driven by an action orientation, and slowing down to reflect on the past and think about the future may seem strange at first. This practice is fairly commonplace in other countries, including Great Britain, Australia, and Japan, where students are typically brought into the process. Once you have conducted a few such reviews, the blend of reporting and decision making is likely to "click" for you.

Decision making means creating alternatives and making choices. In the earlier In the Classroom, Ms. Coombs decided to take time to teach discussion around everyday topics before turning to more demanding content. But textbooks cover enormous amounts of content, and talking about the weather might mean slighting the Louisiana Purchase. Teachers feel enormous pressure to "finish the book." Our recommendation, consistent with the idea of teaching for understanding presented in Chapter 9, is to use assessment to help you decide when to slow down to solve a problem. Taking time to reflect on student performance can be particularly important at the beginning of the year. Reflection is difficult work; putting your thoughts on paper can help you in this task and makes it possible to compare notes with other teachers.

Reflect *and* Apply

This matrix sets the stage for the following questions:

	Grades K–2	Grades 3–4	Grades 5–7
September			
December			
March			
May			

3. As you move through the matrix, how do the six stages of inquiry-based assessment apply? What is their relative importance? What are the special problems? How do you maintain contact with colleagues, students, and parents?

4. You and two other teachers have discussed the inquiry model and are planning for the coming school year. You meet to finalize

arrangements, and one partner raises concerns. What about students with special needs? Your school has a full-inclusion policy, and he will have two learning-disabled students in his fourth-grade class. What about combination grades? He is a new teacher and may have a third-/fourth-grade combination class. What about mobility? As a new teacher, he may have to deal with mid-year entrants. As the experienced team member, how would you handle these issues from an assessment perspective? How would your advice change for younger or older students?

5. The other partner, also newer than you, has better news. She will have two top-of-the-line computers in her classroom. She will also have an aide because her class is three students over the contract limit. She has visited most of the families on her class list (she has incredible energy), and several parents have volunteered to help in the classroom. But she is worried about class size and the range of student differences (she will have a third-/fourth-grade combination class). What are your recommendations about how she can take advantage of her resources to handle the assessment tasks throughout the year? How would your advice change for younger or older students?

Test-Based Strategies

Suppose you could survey hundreds of elementary classrooms with a gadget that buzzed whenever it detected a "reading test." What would you find? When does it happen? What does it look like? Why do people do it? In the United States, the picture is pretty clear. First, you would see a lot of testing embedded in the basal reading systems described in Chapter 2. These systems all provide worksheets and end-of-unit tests for formative appraisal of student progress. Second, in May you would find most school districts administering the annual standardized test of reading achievement for summative assessment. These tests are scored during the summer, and results are reported in local newspapers in the fall. This section describes these types of tests, tells you how to use the information, and suggests how to prepare your students for the task.

Basal Reader Tests

As we noted in Chapter 2, basal readers are in flux, but all are planned around the scope-and-sequence chart, a road map of specific objectives laid out in a predefined order (Chambliss & Calfee, 1998). The text is divided into units (several stories lasting a month or so) and lessons (one or two stories that typically last a week). Each lesson includes several objectives, basic building blocks that range from fine-grained tasks ("vowel *a* with silent *e*") to broad goals ("character analysis"). Each objective moves through a sequence of instruction, practice, and testing.

Basal lessons follow a fairly standard format across grades and series. The teacher begins the lesson with a vocabulary task. For example, he might write the following words on the board: *changes, autumn,* and *seasons.* Then he asks students to pronounce each word, tell what it means, and use it in a sentence. The teacher next prepares students for the story and guides them as they read

Most states now require standardized tests in several subjects, including reading.

it. In the primary grades, each student reads aloud a sentence or two; older students read the story silently. The teacher asks questions from the manual to check story understanding. As the week progresses, students practice objectives by completing worksheet assignments.

Assessment is woven throughout these activities, in responses to teacher questions, in demonstrations of oral reading skills, and in worksheet performance. The teacher has many opportunities to judge student performance and understanding. Oral reading fluency and skill in answering questions are key indicators (Cazden, 2001). The student struggling with a new sentence needs attention. So, too, does the student who shrugs his shoulders when asked "What is the cat's name?" Teachers may not record the details, but they keep mental notes.

Basal systems offer other indicators of student performance. Workbooks address practical problems and keep students busy. They also offer practice on test-like activities. Each worksheet covers a single objective and can be scored by a classroom aide or parent. The scores serve mostly to provide feedback to students and parents, but teachers also keep track.

Basals also include end-of-unit tests to measure student progress. These tests, usually given every four to six weeks, closely mirror standardized tests. They employ the multiple-choice format, are administered to the entire class, and are scored according to the manual. The results can affect decisions about student placement and progress. Students who are considerably ahead of or behind the middle of the class are assigned to high or low groups. All students go through the same materials (at least as much of them as they get to), but the pacing of activities depends on group assignment. Low-achieving groups spend more time on remedial worksheets, and high-achieving groups on enrichment exercises. Low groups tend to fall behind in coverage; by the end of sixth grade, they may be doing fourth-grade work and are likely to be considered for referral to special education.

Assuming that you are required to use worksheets and end-of-unit tests, what can you make of the information? These measures provide a narrow view of students' abilities to think and communicate. But standardized tests are gatekeepers, and so all students need to learn how to deal with these devices. We therefore suggest that you approach worksheets not as things to do but as problems to solve. Sixth-grade teacher Peter Stahl puts the perspective in plain language:

> As much as we may like it to be so, we just can't get away from the "assessment" worksheet. So why not approach it in a positive way, in a way that empowers students, that helps them with both skills and attitudes? Many times before my struggling, remedial students approach the end-of-the-unit tests in the basal our district requires, I ask them questions such as "What does the person who made this page want you to do?" "Do you see any traps and tricks?" "Where are they?" "Look at question 5. How could you help someone having trouble understand that problem?" Obviously, these assessment worksheets were not designed for this problem-solving purpose, but the possibility is there, and I take advantage of it when I can.
>
> —Peter Stahl, Sixth-Grade Teacher

By approaching worksheets and like activities in a similar spirit, you can prepare your students to handle similar situations in life. But don't rely on these instruments as the sole basis for making major decisions about either students or programs. Doing so would be unethical (AERA/APA/NEA, 1985; AFT/NCME/NEA, 1990).

Standardized Tests

You are well educated, and so you know about tests. You have been there—college admissions, teacher certification, driver's license, CPR certification. In the modern world, the multiple-choice test is a fact of life. These instruments will be around for a while because they are cheap and efficient, offer a simple bottom line, and are "scientific" (Airaisan, 1994; Baumann, 1988; Nitko, 1996; Popham, 1999; Stiggins, 1994). They meet high standards of design and reliability. Test publishers publish technical manuals with detailed information about the standardization procedures, student samples, and lots of statistics. You can find detailed information in many sources; *A Teacher's Guide to Standardized Reading Tests* by Lucy Calkins and her colleagues (Calkins et al., 1998) is one source of useful advice.

Standardized tests fall into two broad categories, as shown in Figure 14.12: criterion-referenced and norm-referenced. Criterion-referenced tests include the basal tests described earlier, along with tests designed by school districts for local achievement monitoring. The principle guiding these tests is that the student must meet a preset performance level. The class takes a ten-item test on vowels; students who are correct on nine items have "mastered" the objective and "meet the standard." Students who fall below the criterion are assigned additional practice on the objective until they attain a passing score.

ASSESSMENT

Test scores are often used to identify students with achievement problems for special programs like retention or summer school. In almost all these situations, teacher recommendations are also considered, offering you a role in the decision. This is especially important when you have information about the student's background and the balance between the student's progress and accomplishment.

NORM-REFERENCED SCORING	CRITERION-REFERENCED SCORING
Performance Is Compared with Scores of Others	*Performance Is Compared to an Absolute Standard*
• Once the test is developed, it is administered to a norm group, and then each student's performance is described by how he ranks in comparison to the group.	• The test is developed with a goal in mind (students must read at a rate of 150 words per minute), or a fixed standard is assigned (80% of the answers must be correct).
Scores Represent a Norm Group	*Scores Represent a Standard*
• Percentile. The percentile gives the percentage of students whose scores fall below the particular student's score. If a student scores in the 60th percentile, then he outperforms 60% of the students in the norm group.	• Pass-fail. The score either meets or exceeds the preset value.
• Grade-level equivalent (GLE). The average performance of students at a given grade is used to convert a score into a comparative indicator. If a student scores at the average level for all students leaving third grade, he is given a GLE of 3.9, meaning "end of third-grade performance."	• Mastery of learning objective. In this approach, often linked to a curriculum sequence, students, by a given grade level, are expected to achieve a specific outcome. For instance, by the end of kindergarten, students should know all letter names, numbers 1–10, colors, and "common" words.
• Grading on the curve. In this common practice, grades are assigned based on the distribution within a particular class on a particular test. The teacher decides that the top 15% of the scores will receive A, and so on.	• Advanced, proficient, basic. This variation on pass-fail, similar to regular grades but not on a curve, is used by many state and federal assessment programs.

FIGURE 14.12

Norm-Referenced and Criterion-Referenced Scoring

Norm-referenced tests measure individual student standing relative to others—"grading on the curve" (Nitko, 1996). Percentile scores show how many other students rank above or below a particular individual. Someone at the 50th percentile falls right in the middle; a person at the 99th percentile has performed better than 99 percent of those in the norming sample. Stanines sort students much as percentiles do, but in ranges from 1 to 9. Normal-curve equivalents are another variation on percentiles. Scale scores place students on a statistical "growth curve," which lets you know how a student is doing on a developmental learning pathway. The grade-level equivalent, or GLE, also reports growth scores. The third-grader who scores 3.8 at the end of the year is doing about as expected; a score of 3.0, on the other hand, means that the student reads like an entering third-grader and so is in trouble. Assessment experts worry that GLEs can be misinterpreted (Nitko, 1996), but teachers still rely on GLEs because the concept makes sense to them and serves practical purposes. GLEs are most problematic at the extremes. A beginning third-grader with a score of 8.0 can't really handle Dickens's *A Tale of Two Cities*. He may be able to read most of the words in the novel but is unlikely to get much out of it and certainly will not understand the nuances of the narrative. In the middle ranges of a grade, the GLE provides a reasonable indicator of reading achievement.

As a teacher, you will almost certainly receive reports about your students' performance on standardized tests. Whatever the indicator—GLE, percentile, stanine, scale score—the challenge is to use this information along with that from other sources to make informed judgments about student progress. Standardized tests are most accurate for students who know the "school game." Those who are unfamiliar with the cultural and linguistic traditions assumed by test makers may perform poorly, even though they are learning a lot. Later in this section, we discuss two ways in which you can help these students: through the use of test-taking strategies and motivation.

Students	Scores	Reading		Lang		Math		Total Score
Abby, Karen DOB: 2/26/83	**NP**	41		36		67		59
	NS	4		4		6		5
	GE	4.9		4.7		8.4		7.7
	NCE	39		42		60		55
	SS	702		723		758		748
Kramer, Martin DOB: 8/22/83	**NP**	55		18		35		40
	NS	5		3		4		5
	GE	7.7		3.3		5.8		6.1
	NCE	53		31		41		42
	SS	741		699		738		736
Zhang, Louisa A. DOB: 8/07/83	**NP**	89		71		75		79
	NS	7		6		6		7
	GE	11.7		9.5		9.6		10.1
	NCE	77		60		64		67
	SS	786		758		766		767
Class Summary Number of Students = 26	**MDNP**	60.0		37.2		68.2		52.0
	MNS	6.0		4.5		6.8		5.3
	GME	8.8		5.1		8.8		7.3
	MNCE	55.0		43.8		60.4		51.8
	MSS	750		724		759		742

NP: NATIONAL PERCENTILE   **MDNP:** MEDIAN NATIONAL PERCENTILE
NS: NATIONAL STANINE   **MNS:** MEDIAN NATIONAL STANINE
GE: GRADE EQUIVALENT   **GME:** GRADE MEAN EQUIVALENT
NCE: NORMAL CURVE EQUIVALENT   **MNCE:** MEAN NORMAL CURVE EQUIVALENT
SS: SCALE SCORE   **MSS:** MEAN SCALE SCORE

Terra Nova

TEACHER: JONES
GRADE 6

Purpose:
The class record sheet serves as a permanent record of test results for students in a class or other specified group. It is most often kept in the classroom for easy access by the teacher. It also provides summary data or average scores for the group as a whole. The reports lists up to six scores, chosen by the local test coordinator, for each test section and total score. The result may be used to evaluate individual and group achievement compared to the nation, determine overall performance, and identify areas of strength and weakness.

FIGURE 14.13

Simulated Class Record from the Terra Nova Test

Source: CTB/McGraw-Hill, *Terra Nova*. Reprinted with slight modifications by permission of McGraw-Hill Companies, Inc.

How can you learn to "read" the test reports? Figure 14.13 shows a simulated class record for the Terra Nova test, a popular instrument developed by the California Test Bureau (1996). The printout appears in your box in the fall sometime after school has started. You probably experience number shock, no matter how experienced you may be. Here are a few words of advice:

■ Pick one or two indicators to review. Percentiles and grade equivalents often serve as practical starting points, if taken with a grain of salt. The percentile is a national index, which means that your class and students are being compared with students throughout the nation. If you teach in a middle-class neighborhood in the Midwest, you should expect that your class will score around the 50th percentile and perform at grade level. If you work in a more privileged community or an urban ghetto, you should probably consider the setting—not to expect more or less of your students, but to take into account the challenges that you confront.
■ Start with summaries, and then look for patterns. The example in the figure presents scores for Reading, Language, and Math. These scores are

correlated, which means that performance levels tend to be similar across tests. The Total Score for each student provides an overall achievement index; Karen is about average, Martin has some problems, and Louisa is excelling. But patterns add important complexity. Reading and Math for the class are substantially above national averages, while Language is noticeably below. Karen did much better on the Math test than on the Reading and Language tests. What might this mean?

■ Use other sources of information to develop portraits of student achievement. The report may be six months out of date. The numbers look very precise, but they are actually based on a limited amount of information: a 40-item, multiple-choice test administered at the end of the school year. Test publishers are the first to caution against overreliance on a single indicator.

How can the classroom teacher make the best use of the scores? First, recognize their strengths. They are reliable (Nitko, 1996). The consistency emphasized by testing experts and administrators should be reflected in your classroom assessments. Practically speaking, reliability means that students are ranked much the same across a collection of scores. Suppose you line up a group of students based on their scores on two reading tests. If the rankings are different, which test should you trust? Taking the average doesn't help; if one of your students scored at the top of the class one day and handed in a blank test the next week, should you conclude that he is an "average" student? Probably not. In general, student performance is likely to be about the same on one standardized test as on another standardized test.

Standardized tests are predictive. The question is, what do you do with the prediction? An entering kindergartner's knowledge of the alphabet predicts reading achievement in later grades. Will you improve kindergartners' reading simply by teaching the alphabet? No. Teaching kindergartners the alphabet makes sense for several reasons, but it does not guarantee high levels of reading achievement in the later grades. Here is where information from other sources can be especially critical. Reading means more than picking the right answer on a multiple-choice test. What does the following statement mean: "Martin scored at the 40th percentile at the end of sixth grade"? Here are some possibilities:

1. Martin will score around the 40th percentile on other reading tests.
2. Martin will score at the 40th percentile at the end of seventh grade.
3. Martin will have problems with sixth-grade science textbooks.
4. Martin will have trouble reading the sports section of the newspaper.
5. Martin should be in special education or given remedial tutoring.

Standardized tests do an excellent job when it comes to making predictions like those in the first two entries. They are less trustworthy with respect to the other items on the list. The challenge to you as the classroom teacher is to do something to help Martin begin to move up through the ranks. Other evidence may show that Martin has skills and knowledge not tapped by the standardized test. What if he is helping other students with computer writing assignments? The bottom line is that standardized test scores can fill in one piece of the puzzle, but you shouldn't rely on them too much.

Preparing Students for Standardized Tests

The previous section cautioned against overreliance on standardized tests. This section offers suggestions about how you can help your students do their best on these instruments, so that you can use the results with confidence. How can you prepare your students for the tests without compromising validity? "Teaching to the test" may improve scores, but scores may no longer mean what they are supposed to mean. When your car runs low on gas, you can fiddle with the gas gauge to make it show "full," but you will eventually run out of gas.

The first word of advice is to connect the test situation with the best learning in your classroom. Testing can be a shock. *First Grade Takes a Test* by Miriam Cohen (1983) delightfully describes young children's thoughts on their first encounter with a test. The excerpt in Figure 14.14 shows George's thoughtfulness but lack of test-taking savvy. The message is clear: The children are suddenly alone, the task is mysterious, and the activity is disconnected from classroom routines. Students' answers, right or wrong, cannot be trusted to tell you what they know and can do. How can you improve this state of affairs?

The second word of advice is to help students see the test as a problem to be solved strategically and thoughtfully, a process that is consistent with best learning. What does strategic preparation look like? Here are three suggestions for handling the testing game that work from kindergarten through graduate school, for all kinds of tests.

The first suggestion centers on the big picture. Why am I taking this test? What will happen if I fail? Who will find out how I did? On your driving test, you had ideas about purpose and audience. You were taking the test so that you could get a driver's license. Your test was checked by a computer program that accepted one right answer for each question. If you failed, you studied some more and re-took the test.

Ask fourth-graders similar questions about school tests, and you will be amazed at the answers. They don't know why they are being tested. They don't

George looked at the test. It said:

Rabbits eat
☐ lettuce ☐ dog food
☐ sandwiches

He raised his hand.

"Rabbits have to eat carrots, or their teeth will get too long and stick into them," he said. The teacher nodded and smiled, but she put her finger to her lips. George carefully drew in a carrot so the test people would know.

FIGURE 14.14

Excerpt from *First Grade Takes a Test* by Miriam Cohen

Source: First Grade Takes a Test by Miriam Cohen. Illustrated by Lillian Hoban. Text copyright © 1980 by Miriam Cohen. Illustration copyright © by Lillian Hoban. By permission of Greenwillow Books, a division of William Morrow & Company, Inc.

know the rules of the game—"Is it all right to guess?" They worry that they will fail, whatever that means. Test scores may be used to retain students, but publishers caution against this practice. So find out what your students think about tests, and set the record straight. This need not mean generating a cavalier attitude of "These tests don't matter for me," but rather creating an understanding that "These tests matter for all of us!" It means ensuring clarity and honesty about the consequences.

The second suggestion centers around test instructions, which aim to help but can be a hindrance. Standardized tests "script" the teacher: "Read the following instructions." During the test, you can't explain. You can't answer questions. You can't help. But before the students take the test, you can do some things that will help. You can teach students to listen carefully and actively. You can tell them the testing vocabulary. You can practice "following instructions," as in In the Classroom 14.6.

Using "Simon Says" to Practice Test Taking

The district's benchmark reading tests are scheduled for next week. To prepare his second-graders to follow directions, George Westbelle takes the students through the game of Simon Says. He tells the class that they are going to be taking a test and they will need to listen carefully. He reviews the rules for Simon Says—do it only if "Simon says." He then hands out paper and pencil to each student.

Mr. W: Simon says, "Pick up your pencil." [Students all raise their pencils.]

Mr. W: Simon says, "Write your name on the top of your paper." [Students all fill in their names.]

Mr. W: Write the name on the bottom of your paper. [Several students start to write.]

Mr. W: Whoops! Simon didn't say! [A round of giggles.]

Mr. W: Simon says, "Turn your paper over." [Brief hesitation, and then a rustle of papers.]

Mr. W: Write your name on the back of your paper. [Again, several students start writing.]

Mr. W: Whoops! Gotcha again! Simon didn't say!

Mr. Westbelle keeps the sessions short and snappy, focusing on tasks like those the students will perform during test taking. He offers a word of warning about the technique: "If the game is too close to the test day, students may expect you to say 'Simon says' before each test direction!"

in the Classroom **14.6**

ASSESSMENT

"Test prep" is often assigned by administrators. The problem is generally not the materials, but the way they are used. Rote repetition is boring, and it seldom helps students who are having problems. They need to "talk out" their problems, which is often hard for them to do.

Most standardized tests provide practice sets. It's generally more helpful to use these practice sets to discuss test-taking strategies rather than for rote practice. Preparing students to deal with test instructions works best when you combine practice with "talking it through." Here is how you can use worksheets to help with both parts of this strategy. First, build a practice test using worksheet material, including directions, a short passage, and test items, as illustrated in Figure 14.15. Choose sample items that allow students to try out particular test-taking strategies. The bracketed entries in the figure are not on the students' sheets but suggest questions to raise during the discussion.

Next, read the instructions, and start the test. Give students a limited amount of time to finish the page (two minutes is about right for the page in

THINK ABOUT IT! Taking a reading comprehension test is a tough job. You should always **study the questions** before you try to pick an answer. What do you need to know? Do you need to read the passage? Do the question and the answers raise any alarms? Think about these things while you take this practice test. You will have two minutes to complete it. Ready—turn over the page and begin.

Quickly read through these instructions:

> It is easy to make butter. First you need a jar and some *heavy* cream. Fill the jar partway with cream. Then shake it for about 20 minutes. Soon the cream will start to get lumpy. Stop when most of the cream turns into *lumps*. You will find that the lumps are butter.
> Take the lumps out of the jar, and wash them with cold water. Mix a little salt with the lumps, and pat them together. Leave the butter in a cool place overnight. In the morning, the butter will be hard and ready to eat.

Now answer the questions:

Which word rhymes with *lumps*?

- cream
- leaves
- bumps
- butter

[You don't have to read anything in the passage to answer this question. Why not?]

Which word means the same as *heavy*?

- large
- thick
- strong
- bulky

[Answering this question depends completely on carefully studying the passage. Why?]

What does the passage tell you to do after you have finished making the butter?

- Put the lumps on toast in the morning.
- Throw away the lumps.
- Shake the lumps for 20 minutes.
- Salt the lumps and put them in a cool place.

[You have to read the passage, which tells you exactly what to do.]

If you forget to refrigerate the butter after you have made it, then

- mix it with some more salt.
- eat it as soon as you can.
- it will be soft and not good to eat.
- melt it in a pan and then cool it down.

[The passage doesn't really answer this question but gives you a clue about the right answer. What do you think it is?]

FIGURE 14.15

A Brief Practice Test

Figure 14.15). Even when there is no preset time limit, students always feel pressed for time, and they need to learn how to deal with this issue. When the time is up, score the test by tallying the answers on an overhead, and discuss the experience. What was easy? What was hard? What was confusing? What did it feel like? Here is where the bracketed questions come in. Such discussions allow students to internalize a variety of test-taking strategies, so that they become more comfortable and competent when facing the real thing.

The third suggestion highlights time and stress. As noted above, there is never enough time. Students have only so much energy, and the school day has only so many hours. Most tests do not penalize incorrect choices, and so the best advice is "Finish the test!" Advise students that, when uncertain, they should pick the best-looking answer and then go to the next item. Older students may "tick" items about which they are uncertain and return to these if they have time. The main message: Don't skip and don't fret.

Time pressure is part of stress, but, as you know, there is more to it. To manage stress, students must first be aware of it. Imagine a class about ten

English Learners

For ELL students, the instructions, including writing prompts, often pose a greater challenge than the actual task. For example, instructions that call for predicting the outcome require careful translation for Spanish-language students. *Predict* is from Latin, while *outcome* is an Anglo-Saxon compound.

minutes into a test: wrinkled brows, fingers tight around pencils, bodies hunched over desks. It looks painful, but the students may not realize the extent of their agony. Learning to monitor stress is the first step in managing it. Here again, talking about the situation gives students permission to think about it and to come up with techniques of their own: "Put your pencil down, relax your shoulders, think nice thoughts."

Ben Franklin wrote, "We must indeed all hang together, or, most assuredly, we shall hang separately!" Competition may be a reasonable goal in high school—who will be valedictorian, receive the highest SAT scores, and so on. In the elementary grades, testing can become a community event. Here are fourth-grade teacher William Settlemeyer's thoughts on the matter:

> I try to build team spirit around the test event for my fourth-graders. Seldom do standardized tests mean a lot for individual students in the elementary grades. The better the class does as a whole, the better the school looks! That's what I try to sell.
>
> How do I translate this idea into practice? First of all, I make it clear to students that they are not really competing with one another. I encourage them: "Do your personal best. That's what really counts. That's what you should strive for." Second, I encourage them to support one another before the test—"Hey, good luck! I know you will do great." And after the test—"I bet you aced that puppy!" Third, I involve parents. I advise them to talk with their children in the days before the test, make sure they get a good night's sleep and a solid breakfast on the day of the test, and talk with them about the test once it is over.
>
> —William Settlemeyer, Fourth-Grade Teacher

What does the advice in this section have to do specifically with reading assessment? Not a whole lot, it might appear. We mentioned neither content nor skills. Nothing about vowel digraphs, analogies, or main ideas. These objectives are important, but reading tests are only partly about reading. To excel on a sixth-grade science test, students should bone up on electricity, astronomy, geology, and so on. Success on a sixth-grade math test depends on familiarity with fractions. But studying *The Diary of Anne Frank* does not guarantee that students will do well on a sixth-grade reading test. Memorizing Latin and Greek prefixes may help a little on a reading test, but don't count on it.

That is why we recommend a strategic approach to reading tests. You can help your students by emphasizing fluent decoding and techniques for searching a passage for specific information. Students should be alert for key words and concepts like *words, stories,* and *reports.* But the most effective preparation is to back away from the details, carefully study the questions, and strategize about how you will approach the task. Such preparation helps with all sorts of tests, from reading readiness to college admission.

Finally, what should you do when the class has finished the test? The usual approach is to put the experience behind you, and forget it until the following year. But testing is an important event for students, and you should consider dealing with the aftermath and what can be learned from the event. You can develop your own "after-the-test" plan. Publishers handle scoring and reporting, which means that neither you nor your students will learn the results of the May test until September. But you can deal with the experience as soon as the test is over. Ask your students about their reactions. How did they do? How did they feel? What would they have done differently? Celebrate the event! Let students know you're proud of their efforts! Knowing that they all did their best is important in its own right.

Reflect and Apply

6. You are serving on a school committee to review standardized tests for the district. The committee is looking at six tests, and you can pick one of the following three assignments: teacher manual and instructions, student test materials, or technical manual (reliability, validity, and other technical features). Which assignment would you prefer, and why?

7. It is March, and your district requires that third-graders take a standardized reading test in May. As a third-grade teacher, how would you prepare your students for this assessment? You have decided to begin test preparation in April and so have a month to plan. You want to keep test preparation to a minimum, except as it meshes with your curriculum. What will be your strategies and timelines?

8. Your school places great emphasis on standardized test scores. All students in first through sixth grades will be tested in three weeks. Students in your fifth-/sixth-grade combo class have talked about testing for the past week. From their memories of previous grades, they are planning a skit to help first-graders with the tests. The first-grade teacher is enthusiastic about the idea. The principal calls you in; he has heard about the plan and is interested in what you are doing. How is the skit going to help your students? How will you explain the activity?

Concluding Remarks

Assessing reading, writing, and language is a tough job that calls for professional judgment. Effective assessment requires information from a broad range of sources, including standardized tests, classroom portfolios, informal observations, and student conversations. There is no substitute for the teacher's ongoing inquiries into student growth and accomplishment, which are essential for adapting instruction to individual needs.

This chapter has emphasized the interrelatedness of curriculum, instruction, and assessment. The examples have highlighted the academic dimension of schooling, but it's important to keep other dimensions in mind as well, including students' interests, motivation, social interactions, and efficacy. This advice fits with the inclinations of most elementary teachers. They have a success orientation and aspire to academic success for every student, but they also value the traits of self-directedness and self-confidence.

Assessment captures the research side of the schooling endeavor, whether you are approaching classroom assessments or preparing for standardized tests. The inquiry approach involves asking the right questions, formulating a clear view of learning goals, determining the current status of the students, and deciding on a course of action. Once the stage is set at the beginning of the school year, the process is continuous, an ongoing series of mini-experiments designed to inform you and your students about progress. Feedback is easy to handle when all is going well, but you also need to be honest with students about both limitations and strengths. The long-term prospects for genuine success are greater for all involved when you are candid with students, their parents, school administrators, and (of course) yourself. The ultimate aim of literacy assessment is to provide the ongoing guidance you need to guide each student to the highest possible level of present-day literacy.

Extending Learning

There is no substitute for involving yourself directly in assessment activities and the inquiry process. The three following exercises are designed to "get you into it."

1. Visit a school or district office, and talk with the people in charge about testing policies and practices. What tests are used? At what grades? Why? What happens to the results? After you have located the information, study a couple of standardized tests and printouts of the results for a class or two. Think about what you can learn from these documents. Once you have digested the information, discuss your impressions with a principal, a teacher, and a couple of upper-grade students.

2. Informally assess the reading and writing knowledge and skills of a student. You will find several assessment models in the annotated bibliography and the *Assessments and Lesson Plans* supplement, but the simplest approach may be to find a few short passages, read them yourself to think about what it would mean to understand them, and compose an effective summary of the material, all as a basis for discussing the passage with the student. Your assessment should cover performance: How well can the student read? Respond? React? Equally important are "think-aloud" questions that ask the student to describe how he is approaching the task and attitudinal questions about motivation and efficacy.

3. Locate two teachers who appear to differ in experiences and assignments and ask them about their assessment policies. In a brief interview, explore various facets of their inquiry process. How do they plan the assessment year? What methods do they use to measure student progress and accomplishment? How do they use standardized test results? How do they communicate with students? Parents? Teachers? Whom do they rely on for consultation? How do they handle assessment of special students? Once you have finished the interviews, think about what you have learned. If, in a few years, a new teacher approached you to ask about this topic, how would you prepare for the session?

mylabschool™
Where the classroom comes to life!

For a look at reading assessment in a contemporary classroom, go to Allyn & Bacon's MyLabSchool.com. In MLS Courses, click on Reading Methods, and go to MLS Video Lab. There you will find video clips about Assessment in Module 8.

Children's Literature

Cohen, M. (1983). *First Grade Takes a Test*. New York: Dell. Not a typical piece of literature, this little book tells a worthwhile story for children and adults about the challenges of standardized tests. 32 pages. Illustrated.

Dahl, R. (1988). *Matilda*. New York: Viking. Matilda uses her mental powers to rid her school of the evil, child-hating Miss Trunchbull and restore her beloved teacher Miss Honey to financial security. 240 pages.

Haseley, D. (1991). *Shadows*. New York: Farrar, Straus, & Giroux. A *New York Times* review recommends this book as "strong and appealing, tightly written and fast moving, perfect for reluctant readers as well as those who love good books." 74 pages. Illustrated.

Paterson, K. (1977). *Bridge to Terabithia*. New York: Crowell. This tale of an enchanted place, which a boy and girl create from their emerging friendship, ends tragically, but the author's skill in handling this tension earned a Newbery Award. 128 pages. Illustrated.

Perkins, L. R. (2005). *Criss Cross*. New York: Greenwillow Books. This novel explores the universal emotionso f adolescence, as teenagers in a small town in the 1960s search for the meaning of life and love. 337 pages.

Scieszka, J. (1989). *The True Story of the Three Little Pigs*. New York: Viking. The wolf gives his version of what really happened in his encounters with the three little pigs. 32 pages.

Sharmat, M. W. (1972). *Nate the Great*. New York: Dell. When Annie's newly painted picture of her dog Fang is missing, she calls on Nate to help her find it. 64 pages.

Sobol, D. J. (2005). *Encyclopedia Borwn and the Case of hte Jumping Frogs*. New York: Yearling. Encyclopedia Brown solves ten new mysteries with the help of his partner, Sally Kimball, the prettiest and toughest girl in the fifth grade. 80 pages.

Sperry, A. (1960). Call It Courage. New York: Macmillan. This is the story of Mafutu, a young island boy who overcomes his fear of the sea and proves his courage to himself and his tribe. Audiotape and Spanish text available. 95 pages.

White, E. B. (1952). *Charlotte's Web*. New York: Harper. A widely recognized classic of children's literature, this story of an empathic spider and the runt of a pig litter appeals to a wide array of readers. This Newbery Honor story offers many opportunities for assessing students' understanding of thematic issues. 184 pages.

Classroom Portrait

A Day in the Life of David Carberry and His Fifth- and Sixth-Grade Students

David Carberry has been teaching fifth- and sixth-graders at Oak Grove Intermediate School for ten years. Oak Grove, which includes grades 4–6, is located in a southern suburb of Minneapolis. Most of the children at Oak Grove come from middle-income families; the majority are European Americans, with a sprinkling of Asian Americans, Native Americans, and African Americans.

David works in a team with three other teachers, which is fairly typical of many upper-elementary classrooms. Before the school year begins, the team meets to make program decisions and to discuss matters such as scheduling and curricular responsibilities. The four classrooms in David's team are made up of approximately 15 fifth-grade students and 15 sixth-grade students each. When the sixth-graders move on to junior high school, 15 fifth-grade students take their place, so students are with the same homeroom teacher for two years.

When we asked David to describe the literacy program he and his colleagues have developed, this is what he had to say:

> The literacy program we have developed over the years reflects the unique challenge we face as upper-elementary teachers. Differences in reading ability are extreme in students in grades 5 and 6. For example, one of my students, 11-year-old Kelly, reads at an 11th-grade level and devours John Grisham novels during her free reading period. Tommy, also 11 years old, struggles with anything beyond second-grade materials. He finds it difficult to read even short, episodic stories. This disparity presents a critical question for me and my teammates: How do we meet the needs of students, given such a huge range of ability? Given that current thinking in elementary instruction is to move away from ability grouping of students toward whole-group and flexible group instruction, meeting the needs of the students becomes even more challenging. My team has developed a plan we think best meets the needs of our students.

On the following pages, David describes in his own words his team's plan for organizing the fifth-/sixth-grade curriculum to emphasize reading and writing instruction throughout the school day.

Every district has a list of goals and objectives or learning outcomes. At the beginning of, during, and following the school year, my colleagues and I sit down and figure out what to teach. Our team looks for connections within all the language arts and within broad themes as well. As a starting point, we choose a broad theme that will connect all the students' learning experiences to a rich schema. The theme we choose is determined by a number of factors, including appropriateness of topic, access to resources, our own talents and failings, and district outcomes. Typically, we choose three themes over the course of the year.

Although each day has a particular focus for instruction, I have found it useful to teach content that will serve the students in a variety of settings throughout the school year. Over the years, I have become more and more convinced that the teaching of comprehension strategies makes for more powerful readers. I choose strategies that are flexible and widely applicable. I will ask the students to use them in their content area classes and when using self-selected materials, as well as in my class. My suggestion to a beginning teacher—or any teacher—is to develop a small number of them (perhaps three) throughout the year. I have found periodically returning to a strategy to be particularly helpful to students. (A number of helpful comprehension strategies are noted in Chapter 9.)

At the beginning of the year, I note several strategies I think would be helpful for my students. One of my favorites is teaching students to create story maps (see Chapter 8). Although the use of story maps is presented as a teacher-led procedure in this book, I teach students to make their own story maps and in this way give them a tool that they can use independently to improve their understanding of any selection they are reading. My first goal is to teach the strategy in such a way that all students will learn, regardless of their reading level. For this reason, I choose content that is familiar to all students and that they do not need to read. For example, I may ask them to recall the story "Little Red Riding Hood" as a text to use in doing their first story mapping. I let students know that they will be learning a strategy designed to help them understand what they are reading and that they will be using it throughout the school year and beyond. Then I model the activity in a large-group setting. I begin by working with students to compose a "T" graphic similar to this one:

Important events	Mapping questions
Red begins her journey to Grandmother's house.	Where is Red Riding Hood going?
Red encounters a wolf.	Who does Red meet along the trail?
The Hunter slays the wolf, releasing Grandma.	How does the story end?

I ask the students to assist me in completing the map. Because students do not have to read a text to construct the map, they can learn to map regardless of their reading proficiency. After creating their first simple map, I use a read-aloud for the next one; again, my interest is minimizing the effect of reading ability as a critical factor in acquiring the strategy. I've found picture books to be an excellent vehicle for this, as they are nonthreatening to the listener—short, full of illustrations, and appealing.

Following whole-group instruction, small groups work with picture books in cooperative groups. One member of the group is responsible for an oral reading. The group as a whole is responsible for developing a story map. Each group checks with me for feedback, and following my okay (signified by a scrawled set of initials), groups may exchange their story maps with other groups working through different books. Now the students have learned a strategy that may be applied to a variety of texts; have had an opportunity to integrate reading, writing, listening, and speaking; and have provided curriculum for a real audience (other groups). One student's map for *The True Story of the Three Little Pigs* by Jon Scieszka is shown in the figure.

Of course, it takes a great deal of time to introduce a comprehension strategy such as creating story maps. Even so, the time is well spent. Having learned the strategy, students have a tool to attack just about any narrative.

Two aspects of our team approach are particularly important to our use of a language arts block and our literature-based orientation. First, the language arts block provides time for focusing on and interrelating all of the language arts. Second, an important aspect of literature-based instruction is its advocacy of both flexible grouping and student self-selection of reading materials. In my classroom, we use a "book wheel"

Name: Silipanh, L.

Title of book: The True Story of the Three Little Pigs

Author of book: Jon Scieszka

On the left side of the page, list important events in the story (choose between 3 and 12 events). On the right side, write a question for each event to create a **story map**. Story maps help readers understand what they are reading.

1. The wolf was sick and wanted a cup of sugar.	1. Why did the wolf go to the pigs' houses?
2. The wolf sneezed and blew down the first pig's house.	2. What happened when the wolf got to the first pig's house?
3. The wolf ate the first pig.	3. What happened after the wolf blew down the first pig's house?
4. The wolf sneezed and blew down the second pig's house.	4. What happened when the wolf got to the second pig's house?
5. The wolf ate the second pig.	5. What happened after the wolf blew down the second pig's house?
6. The wolf went to the third pig's house and sneezed, but nothing happened.	6. What happened when the wolf got to the third pig's house?
7. The police came and thought the wolf was trying to blow down the pig's house.	7. What did the police think when they saw the wolf at the pig's house?
8. The police took the wolf to jail.	8. What happened to the wolf?

(like the one shown in the figure) to meet individual needs and interests. The students use this graphic organizer to ensure that they respond to a variety of genres. The students may read individually or in self-selected groups. They respond to the texts in a variety of ways, sometimes determined by the instructor and sometimes determined by the students. The book wheel is designed to encourage broad reading and the meeting of individual needs.

A literature-based approach is particularly attractive to fifth- and sixth-grade students. Meeting to discuss what they read in literature circles, described in Chapter 10, helps students develop rich, engaging schemata. The students really get into a piece of writing when they are sharing the experience with others. I find it easy to model and be enthusiastic about appropriate literature circle behaviors, as I am able to relate my own experiences in a book club. Literature circles and other literature-based approaches encourage deep understanding of texts. The circles have an advantage over whole-group instruction

"Each group checks with me for feedback, and following my okay, groups may exchange their story maps with other groups working through different books." —David Carberry

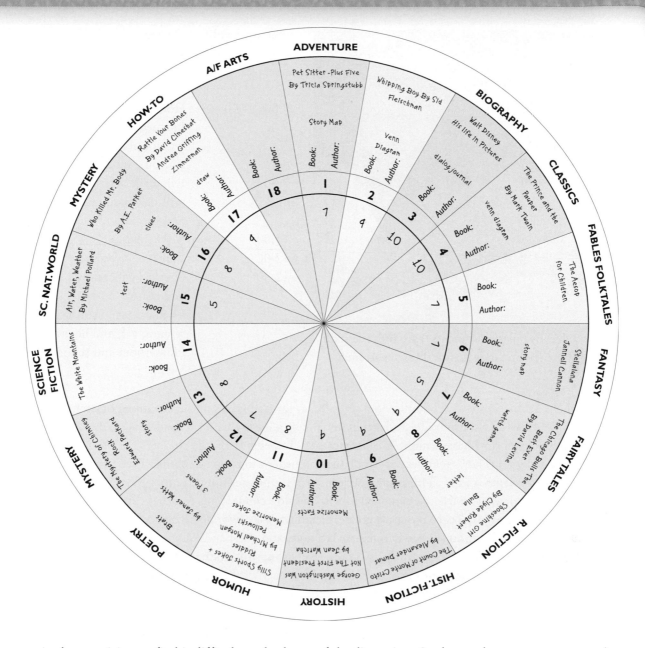

in that participants find it difficult to check out of the discussion. Students who are eye-to-eye and knee-to-knee and responsible for developing meaning have a greater chance of experiencing the "aha" phenomenon—gaining a perspective that they hadn't considered before. An additional advantage to literature-based approaches is that students are able to self-select their groups. The teacher, for example, may select four texts, differing in length, type of characters, and so forth, that all relate to a broad, general theme. Emily may be ready for Lynne Rae Perkins's *Criss Cross,* a complex Newbery Medal–winning story, while James may prefer a book made up of short, easy-to-read episodic stories like Donald Sobol's *Encyclopedia Brown and the Case of the Jumping Frogs.* Allowing student choice increases the likelihood that students will read an engaging book at their level of reading competence.

There are four important features in our organization of time, curriculum content, space, and students. First is the concept of the homeroom, second is scheduling large blocks of time for students to be in one place with one teacher, third is centering instruction around a broad theme, and fourth is selecting reading comprehension strategies and procedures to teach throughout the year

As David has noted, by the time students reach fifth and sixth grades, some students can tackle texts written for an adult audience.

that are flexible and broadly applicable. Here is what our typical schedule looks like:

9:00–11:00	Homeroom
9:00	Independent silent reading, journal writing
9:20	Morning meeting
9:30	Language arts: reading, writing, listening, and speaking
11:00	Mathematics
12:00	Lunch and recess
12:30	Physical education and music
1:30	Themes: social studies, science, art, and health
3:00	Homeroom and school logs

As the schedule shows, each homeroom stays intact for two hours in the beginning of each day. For example, fifth- and sixth-grade students in my homeroom stay with me from 9:00 to 11:00.

Large blocks of time have a number of advantages. To begin with, the students have less downtime between classes. They spend less time moving from room to room. Lengthier time periods also allow for greater depth and breadth of instruction. We have greater opportunities to go into detail on a given topic, or we can use the extended time to develop connections to other curricular areas. Another advantage of large time blocks is greater flexibility for everyone involved, making it easier to schedule special education services, computer lab time, and guest speakers.

After homeroom, students separate into grade-level groups for mathematics, music, and physical education. Heterogeneous groups made up from each of the four classrooms within our team comprise the classes for instruction in social studies, science, art, and health.

9:00—Independent Silent Reading, Journal Writing

Homeroom begins with one of two different activities—independent silent reading or journal writing, which I alternate throughout the school year. Having a structured activity ready for the students helps them warm up for school and establishes a healthy working culture for the classroom.

Independent Silent Reading

Independent silent reading (which was discussed in Chapter 10) is an important part of any elementary-level reading curriculum. I've found it helpful to ask the students to have their books out and ready to read the moment class begins. I think it is good practice to feature sustained reading of student-selected texts as a primary feature of the classroom, rather than an adjunct to the "real work" of the day. If students are asked to do silent reading only when their other assignments are done, this almost guarantees that the least-successful students will get the least amount of time to read independently and the least opportunity to develop fluent, success-oriented reading practice. My students are especially interested in a pre-set quiet reading time, as this gives them time to complete their book wheel, which is part of the independent reading program I require.

Journal Writing

I have tried all sorts of journal writing, both structured and nonstructured. I have responded at length to students' writing and have enjoyed it, although it is terrifically time-consuming. However, having students write to a real audience is powerfully motivating. Lately, I have found it particularly productive to have students share their writing thoughts with two or three others. I may suggest a topic for a journal entry, or the students may choose their own. The small group that develops as a result of this journaling activity is asked to respond to what each member of the group writes. Conversations between students develop in print, similar to what happens in dialogue journals (see Chapter 12). I like to introduce this activity by modeling my own journal writing and students' responses, sharing these on an overhead projector. The figure shows two journal entries by students who were reading *Matilda*, by Roald Dahl.

4/14   Kaj—So far I think this book is very interest, but it is kind of hard to believe that a four year old could read books like Oliver Twist, Kim, & Animal Farm & actually understand what she is reading.

J. R.

I think that your right Justin, because it is amazing that she read books that thick and that fast. It also is amazing that she understands the books that she is reading when she goes to the library every afternoon.

K. L.

4/15   Kaj—I think it is hilarious how Matilda put glue in her Dad's hat, it was also pretty good how she put the parrot up the chimney & her parents thought it was a ghost. I'm surprised when she didn't cry when her father tore the pages out of the library book.

Justin—I think that you are right it is pretty hilarious, you were also right that the book is different than the movie that I saw. I like the part where Matilda slams the door on her dad.

K. L.

Working in small groups not only provides students with a real audience but also allows me to give feedback quickly and efficiently. To give this feedback, I ask each group of three or four students to come up to my desk, where I respond orally to their writing.

9:20—Morning Meeting

Just about every teacher I know sets aside time during the beginning of the day to do the routine chores that are part of every classroom. Here, we talk about the day's schedule, important dates, current events, and the like. The time required for our morning meeting varies day by day. It is common practice in my classroom to use this time to assign ad hoc student committees designed to solve problems. For instance, we may have a party coming up. Following a list of guidelines, a student committee is formed to submit their written recommendations as to treats, activities, and the like. A committee may be responsible for cleaning and putting fresh water in the iguana cage or figuring out a way to get homework to absent students. In almost all cases, students are asked to submit a written plan, which I will review. These authentic language arts experiences allow students to have an impact on their world, and they really work well with fifth- and sixth-graders.

9:30—Language Arts: Reading, Writing, Listening, and Speaking

What might a typical day of instruction look like in the language arts, considering that the students have acquired the story-mapping comprehension strategy and we are investigating the sea as a theme?

Because of the purpose I have in mind—having students explore another aspect of our sea theme—a selection in the basal appeals to me. The selection is taken from *Call It Courage,* Armstrong Perry's Newbery Medal–winning story about a shipwrecked boy searching for courage. Purpose and selection, of course, are two of the three factors of the scaffolded reading experience (which was described in Chapter 8). The third is taking into account the readers. So, next, I consider how to make the selection accessible for all my students: What sort of scaffold will I build for them to ensure their success in reading this piece?

I begin developing a reading scaffold by thinking of my prereading activities, asking myself what sort of background knowledge will be required for the students to understand the story. One advantage of using a story out of a basal text (which is usually highly illustrated) is that all students have access to a powerful cue—illustration. Illustrations are one way to tap into the students' existing schemata. I ask them to look at the pictures and to write predictions of what they expect will happen in the story. The illustration for *Call It Courage* shows the character Mafatu on a beach, apparently making something out of bamboo. He appears to be alone, but for a seagull and a dog. Students might predict that he is alone on an island and that he is intent on building a shelter, which they will later find to be the case. Analyzing illustrations is also a helpful way to introduce semantic mapping to further activate background knowledge. Besides activating background knowledge, mapping serves an additional purpose. Inevitably, important vocabulary will surface; or you, as the instructor, can make it surface. My colleagues and I have found that the key in vocabulary instruction is picking out several critical terms or concepts (three is a good number) and giving the students repeated exposure to them, using a variety of techniques. Students need to hear and use critical vocabulary in a variety of contexts.

At this point in the instruction, the students have activated their background knowledge through illustrations and a semantic map. And because they have had previous experience in creating a story map as a comprehension strategy, they are ready to go. Right? Perhaps not. I have to ask myself whether all of my students will be able to successfully read the text, given its length and difficulty. If the answer is no, I need to provide additional scaffolding. I have found that reading the text aloud is the easiest way to make it more accessible. A read-aloud provides additional scaffolding and shortens the amount students will be responsible for. Finally, I often provide written instructions—whether on the board or in a handout—including a checking-for-understanding feature. The assignment might read like this:

> *I am interested in whether you can apply story mapping as a strategy for your reading of the selection taken from Call It Courage. Remember, comprehension strategies are designed to help you understand what you read. Note important events, and the question that goes along with each. Look over pages 232–236, and pick out three events. Then, write out one appropriate question about each of the three events, and come see me with your questions. When we meet, we'll talk about those questions and about your choosing the dozen most important events of the story and developing an appropriate question for each of them.*

Notice that the entire class is engaged in this activity, and individual accountability and opportunities for teacher feedback are built in as well. Following the activity, the students discuss their choices in small groups and try to come up with a common core of 12 important events. Again, there is an implicit appeal here for integrating language arts—students are reading, writing, speaking, and listening. Furthermore, now that the students have demonstrated facility in creating story maps, each is able to use this strategy with his own content. Students are able to use the procedure to take notes, to test others, and to generate discussion questions.

David often pairs up English-language learners with a buddy when an assignment, such as developing a story map, proves to be too much of a challenge.

11:00—Mathematics

As I said earlier, our team is made up of four classrooms, each serving two grade levels. My teammates and I are always looking for ways to connect with our theme. For example, I know through team meetings that the science teacher will be using whales to illustrate content in a unit on oceanography. I have an opportunity to illustrate mathematics in an engaging way, which will enrich their understanding of our theme, by having my students make cutout re-creations of whales. In doing so, the students work from a pattern, grid out an image, and convert their numbers, using the concept of scale in creating paper or chalk models. In a variety of ways, my students will develop a better sense of number and demonstrate facility in the use of ratios and estimation, while further developing a rich and engaging schema that will serve them in other content areas.

12:00—Lunch and Recess

The themes here are eating and playing!

12:30—Physical Education and Music

Our district uses specialists to teach these two content areas. The students alternate classes each day. I can't always integrate physical education and music with common themes, as these teachers have their own scope and sequence. Integration requires meeting with these teachers to plan our curricular content together, which, although it is a challenge, I occasionally do with music. For example, a music teacher developed a score for a play that my classroom was working on.

1:30—Themes: Social Studies, Science, Art, and Health

As I mentioned earlier, my team—Nancy Eller, Troy Miller, and Suzy Neet—uses a thematic approach to interrelate our classes. Our goal is to find a way to connect the disciplines of science, social studies, art, and health, given available curricular materials, district outcomes, and teacher expertise. Nancy's area of expertise is social studies, Troy's is science, and Suzy's is health.

Social Studies

Nancy has a pretty good background in ancient civilizations. For the present unit, she's going to focus on the Roman Empire's movement throughout the Mediterranean region. She plans to focus in part on trade routes, commerce, and the transmission of Greco-Roman culture throughout the Mediterranean. (Social studies requires a good deal of expository reading by the students, which is particularly difficult. It would be appropriate for all team members to use a comprehension procedure—for instance, K-W-L, which was discussed in Chapter 8—in the language arts setting.)

Science

Troy has decided to do a unit on oceanography. The content fits with our district outcomes in that he will explore relationships between a marine environment and all sorts of creatures. There are a bunch of opportunities to connect with mathematics, including graphing the ocean floor via echo sounding and determining the speed of sound in various environments.

Art

I'm responsible for art instruction. Our art instruction includes teaching students to use lines in a variety of ways. Students are asked to use contour drawing and abstract and impressionist techniques to represent the world. I've found that still photographs of marine creatures taken from various periodicals serve as good prompts for drawing. In the past, my classroom has drawn huge murals, made up of both living and nonliving things in an ocean environment, as a culminating activity.

Health

Connecting health to other content areas has always been a stretch for our team. Suzy has agreed to do health the past several years. Sometimes she is able to make connections, but in this case the topic of the sea fails to inspire her. As her colleagues are at a loss to make thematic connections between health and the sea, she will be out of the loop this time around. She will likely have greater success when we pursue other themes—challenges, for example.

In trying to find connections between theme and subject areas, we have learned something that Sean Walmsley (1996, p. 54) stresses: "Don't try to integrate every subject area into every theme." Sometimes there are important connections, and sometimes not. We try to concentrate on connections that really make sense. Walmsley offers some other tips about theme teaching that I'd like to pass along:

- When you teach a theme, tuck the skills inside it.
- Balance teacher-generated and student-generated themes.
- Avoid cutesy treatment of themes.
- Draw themes from a variety of arenas—concepts, content areas, current events, people, the calendar.
- Make sure your themes are the right size.
- Approach year-long and schoolwide themes with caution.
- Bump up your own knowledge of the themes you're preparing.
- Teach a theme twice (to different groups of students) to recoup your investment in it.
- Borrow theme ideas from others.

Although writing thematic units can be hard work and time-consuming, we have found the process of planning together to be fruitful and stimulating and the results rewarding. Resources such as *The Complete Guide to Thematic Units* (Meinbach, Rothlein, & Fredericks, 2000), which provides 20 comprehensive units that can be adapted to fit any classroom, can help you with valuable and time-saving information on teaching strategies and books to use.

3:00—Homeroom and School Logs

All of our students have school logs. At the end of each day, I ask students to write down what happened over the course of the day. The purpose of the activity is to give them an opportunity to reflect on learning, to have a written record to communicate to parents, and to note any assignments or other tasks that will be due. This can be difficult unless you really make it a vital part of your classroom culture.

Afterword

The classroom portraits of Jenna LeBlanc, Dolores Puente, and David Carberry illustrate only three of the many possible ways literacy instruction might be implemented in similar elementary school class-rooms. You, of course, will develop a unique program of your own to fit the needs and interests of the particular group of students and the school and community in which you teach.

There is a song from a Broadway musical with lines that go something like "Bit by bit, putting it together, we can make a work of art." Although the lyricist is alluding to a musical production, in many ways a teacher, along with his or her students, plays every role in the ongoing production of classroom instruction—playwright, producer, actor, audience, and critic. What they produce together, with the help of many stagehands and with hard work, energy, commitment, laughter, and sometimes tears, is a work of art whose value is measured by the degree to which the lives of those who had a hand in its creation are enriched and empowered.

We wish you a great deal of success and satisfaction as you pursue a career that we believe is sec-ond to none in its potential to have an impact on individual lives, which in turn will affect the lives of others. We close with the words of the great French novelist Gustave Flaubert, which were written in the mid-19th century but are still true as we begin the 21st century:

Read in order to live.

With all best wishes,

Michael Graves
Connie Juel
Bonnie Graves

References

Abramson, M. (2002). Lunch special. *Book, 24,* 34–35.

Adams, M. J. (1990). *Beginning to read: Thinking and learning about print.* Cambridge, MA: MIT Press.

Airasian, P. (1994). *Classroom assessment.* New York: McGraw-Hill.

Allington, R., Guice, S., Michelson, N., Baker, K., & Li, S. (1996). Literature-based curricula in high-poverty schools. In M. F. Graves, P. van den Broek, & B. M. Taylor (Eds.), *The first R: Every child's right to read* (pp. 73–96). New York: Teachers College Press.

Allington, R. L. (1977). If they don't read much, how they ever gonna get good? *Journal of Reading, 21,* 57–61.

Allington, R. L. (1983). The reading instruction provided readers of different abilities. *Elementary School Journal, 83,* 548–559.

Allington, R. L. (1984). Oral reading. In P. D. Pearson, R. Barr, M. L. Kamil, & P. B. Mosenthal (Eds.), *Handbook of reading research* (vol. 1, pp. 829–864). New York: Longman.

Allington, R. L. (2001). *What really matters for struggling readers: Designing research-based programs.* New York: Longman.

Allington, R. L. (2002). *Big brother and the national reading curriculum: How ideology trumped evidence.* Portsmouth, NH: Heinemann.

Allington, R. L. (2005). The other five "pillars" of effective reading instruction. *Reading Today, 22*(5), 3.

Alvermann, D. (1991). The discussion web: A graphic aid for learning across the curriculum. *The Reading Teacher, 45,* 92–99.

American Educational Research Association. (2004). English language learners: Boosting academic achievement. *Research Points: Essential Information for Educational Policy, 2*(1), 1–4. Washington, DC: Author. Available at http://www.aera.net/publications/?id=314.

American Educational Research Association (AERA), American Psychological Association (APA), & National Education Association (NEA). (1985). *Standards for educational and psychological testing.* Washington, DC: Author.

American Educator. (1995, Summer). *Learning to read: Schooling's first mission* (Special Issue). Washington, DC: American Federation of Teachers.

American Educator. (1998, Spring/Summer). *The unique power of reading and how to unleash it* (Special Issue). Washington, DC: American Federation of Teachers.

American Federation of Teachers. (1999). *Teaching reading is rocket science: What expert teachers of reading should know and be able to do.* Washington, DC: Author.

American Federation of Teachers (AFT), National Council on Measurement in Education (NCME), & National Education Association (NEA). (1990). Standards for teacher competence in educational assessment of students. *Educational Measurement: Issues and Practice, 9*(4), 30–32.

American Guidance Service. (1987). Woodcock-Johnson reading mastery test. Cinole Pines, MN: Author.

Ames, C. (1992). Classroom: Goal, structures, and student motivation. *Journal of Educational Psychology, 84,* 261–271.

Anderson, L. W., & Krathwohl, D. R. (2001). *A taxonomy for learning, teaching, and assessing: A revision of Bloom's Taxonomy of Educational Objectives.* New York: Longman.

Anderson, R. C. (1996). Research foundations to support wide reading. In V. Greaney (Ed.), *Promoting reading in developing countries* (pp. 55–77). Newark, DE: International Reading Association.

Anderson, R. C., Hiebert, E. F., Scott, J. A., & Wilkinson, I. A. G. (1985). *Becoming a nation of readers.* Washington, DC: National Institute of Education.

Anderson, R. C., & Nagy, W. E. (1992). The vocabulary conundrum. *American Educator,* Winter, 14–18, 44–47.

Anderson, R. C., & Pearson, P. D. (1984). A schema-theoretic view of basic processes in reading. In P. D. Pearson (Ed.), *Handbook of reading research* (pp. 255–291). White Plains, NY: Longman.

Anderson, R. C., Wilson, P., & Fielding, L. (1988). Growth in reading and how children spend their time outside of school. *Reading Research Quarterly, 23,* 285–303.

Anderson, T. H., & Armbruster, B. B. (1984). Content area textbooks. In R. C. Anderson, J. Osborn, & R. J. Tierney (Eds.), *Learning to read in American schools* (pp. 193–226). Hillsdale, NJ: Erlbaum.

Anglin, J. M. (1993). Vocabulary development: A morphological analysis. *Monographs of the Society for Research in Child Development, 58* (10, Serial No. 238).

Anson, C. M., & Beach, R. (1995). *Journals in the classroom: Writing to learn.* Norwood, MA: Christopher-Gordon.

Armbruster, B. B., McCarthy, S. J., & Cummins, S. (2005). Writing to learn in elementary classrooms. In R. Indrisano & J. R. Paratore (Eds.), *Learning to write, writing to learn: Theory and research in practice* (pp. 71–96). Newark, DE: International Reading Association.

Aronson, E., Blaney, N., Stephan, C., Sikes, J., & Snapp, M. (1978). *The jigsaw classroom.* Newbury Park, CA: Sage.

Aronson, E., & Patnoe, S. (1997). *The jigsaw classroom: Building cooperation in the classroom.* New York: Longman.

Asfeld, S. T., Schwab, J., Gagliardi, S., & Henke, M. A. (1994). *Nutrition: The good way to health.* Unpublished manuscript.

Association for Library Service to Children (2004). *The best of the best from 60 years of notable children's books, 1940–99.* Chicago, IL: American Library Association.

Atwell, N. (1987). *In the middle: Writing, reading, and learning with adolescents.* Portsmouth, NH: Heinemann.

Atwell, N. (1998a). *In the middle: New understandings about writing, reading, and learning* (2nd ed.). Portsmouth, NH: Boyton/Cook.

Atwell, N. (1998b). *In the middle: Writing, reading, and learning with adolescents* (2nd ed.). Portsmouth, NH: Heinemann.

Au, K. H. (1993). *Literacy instruction in multicultural settings.* New York: Harcourt, Brace, Jovanovich.

Au, K. H. (1999). Foreword. In J. T. Guthrie & D. E. Alvermann (Eds.), *Engaged reading: Processes, practices, and policy implications* (pp. 17–45). New York: Teachers College Press.

Au, K. H., & Mason, J. M. (1983). Cultural congruence in classroom participation structures: Achieving a balance of rights. *Discourse Processes, 6,* 145–167.

August, D. (2005, October). *Building vocabulary in English-language learners.* Paper presented at the 3rd Guy Bond Memorial Conference on Reading, Minneapolis, MN.

August, D., & Hakuta, K. (1998). *Educating language-minority children.* Washington, DC: National Academy Press.

August, D., & Shanahan, J. (Eds.). (in press). *Report of the National Literacy Panel on Language Minority Children and Youth: Acquiring literacy in a second language.* Mahwah, NJ: Erlbaum.

Avery, P. G., & Graves, M. F. (1997). Scaffolding young learners' reading of social studies texts. *Social Studies and the Young Learner, 9*(4), 10–14.

Bamford, R. A., & Kristo, J. V. (1998). *Making facts come alive: Choosing quality nonfiction literature K–8.* Norwood, MA: Christopher-Gordon.

Barnes, B. L. (1996/1997). But teacher you went right on: A perspective on Reading Recovery. *The Reading Teacher, 50,* 284–292.

Barr, C. (Ed.). (1998). *From biography to history.* New Providence, NJ: R. R. Bowker.

Baum, S., Viens, J., & Slatin, B. (2005). *Multiple intelligences in the elementary classroom: A teacher's toolkit.* New York: Teachers College Press,

Baumann, J. F. (1986). The direct instruction of main idea comprehension ability. In J. F. Baumann (Ed.), *Teaching main idea comprehension* (pp. 133–178). Newark, DE: International Reading Association.

Baumann, J. F. (1988). *Reading assessment: An instructional decision-making perspective.* Columbus, OH: Merrill Publishing.

Baumann, J. F., Font, G., Edwards, E. C., & Boland, E. (2005). In E. H. Hiebert & M. Kamil (Eds.), *Teaching and learning vocabulary: Bringing research to practice* (pp. 179–205). Mahwah, NJ: Erlbaum.

Baumann, J. F., Kame'enui, E. J., & Ash, G. E. (2003). Research on vocabulary instruction: Voltaire redux. In J. Flood, D. Lapp, J. R. Squire, & J. M. Jensen (Eds.), *Handbook on research on teaching the English language arts* (2nd ed., pp. 752–785). Mahwah, NJ: Erlbaum.

Beach, R. W. (1993). *A teacher's introduction to reader-response theories.* Urbana, IL: National Council of Teachers of English.

Bear, D. R., Invernizzi, M., Templeton, S., & Johnston, F. (2004). *Words their way: Word study for phonics, vocabulary, and spelling instruction* (3rd ed.). Upper Saddle River, NJ: Merrill.

Beaver, J. (1997). *Developmental reading assessment.* Parsippany, NJ: Pearson Learning Group.

Beck, I. L., & McKeown, M. G. (1981). Developing questions that promote comprehension: The story map. *Language Arts, 58,* 913–918.

Beck, I. L., & McKeown, M. G. (1983). Learning words well. A program to enhance vocabulary and comprehension. *The Reading Teacher, 36,* 622–625.

Beck, I. L., & McKeown, M. G. (2001). Text talk: Capturing the benefits of read-aloud experiences for young children. *The Reading Teacher, 55,* 10–20.

Beck, I. L., & McKeown, M. G. (2004). *Increasing young children's oral vocabulary repertoires through rich and focused instruction.* Unpublished paper. University of

Pittsburgh, Learning Research and Development Center.

Beck, I. L., McKeown, M. G., Hamilton, R., & Kucan, L. (1997). *Questioning the author: An approach for enhancing student engagement with text.* Newark, DE: International Reading Association.

Beck, I. L., McKeown, M. G., Hamilton, R., & Kucan, L. (1998). Getting at the meaning: How to help students unpack difficult text. *American Educator, 22*(1–2), 66–71, 85.

Beck, I. L., McKeown, M. G., & Kucan, L. (2002). *Bringing words to life: Robust vocabulary instruction.* New York: Guilford Press

Beck, I. L., McKeown, M. G., & Omanson, R. C. (1987). The effects and uses of diverse vocabulary instructional techniques. In M. G. McKeown & M. E. Curtis (Eds.), *The nature of vocabulary acquisition* (pp. 147–163). Hillsdale, NJ: Sage.

Beck, I. L., McKeown, M. G., Worthy, J., Sandora, C. A., & Kucan, L. (1996). Questioning the author: A year-long classroom implementation to engage students with text. *Elementary School Journal, 96,* 385–414.

Becker, W. (1977). Teaching reading and language to the disadvantaged: What we have learned from field research. *Harvard Educational Review, 47,* 518–543.

Berliner, D., & Biddle, B. (1995). *The manufactured crisis.* White Plains, NY: Longman.

Berliner, D.C. (1979). Tempus educare. In P. L. Peterson & H. J. Walberg (Eds.), *Research on teaching: Concepts, findings, and implications* (pp. 120– 135). Berkeley, CA: McCutchan.

Bernhardt, E. (1991). *Reading development in a second language.* Norwood, NJ: Ablex.

Bernhardt, E. (2000). Second language reading as a case study of reading scholarship in the twentieth century. In M. Kamil, P. Mosenthal, P. Pearson, & R. Barr (Eds.), *Handbook of reading research* (vol. 3, pp. 791–812). Mahwah, NJ: Erlbaum.

Bernhardt, E. B., & Kamil, M. (1995). Interpreting relationships between L1 and L2 reading: Consolidating the linguistic threshold and the linguistic interdependence hypotheses. *Applied Linguistics, 16,* 15–34.

Berninger, V. W. (1995). Has the phonological recoding model of reading acquisition and reading disability led us astray? *Issues in Education: Contributions from Education and Psychology, 1,* 59–63.

Berninger, V. W., Yates, C., & Lester, R. (1991). Multiple orthographic codes in reading and writing acquisition. *Reading and Writing Quarterly: An Interdisciplinary Journal, 3,* 115–149.

Betts, E. A. (1946). *Foundations of reading instruction.* New York: American Book.

Biemiller, A. (2001). Teaching vocabulary: Early, direct, and sequential. *American Educator, 25*(1), 24–28, 47.

Biemiller, A. (2003, April). *Teaching vocabulary to kindergarten to grade two children.* Paper presented at the annual meeting of the American Educational Research Association, Chicago.

Bissex, G. L. (1980). *Gnys at wrk: A child learns to read and write.* Cambridge, MA: Harvard University Press.

Blachowicz, C. L. Z., & Fisher, P. (2000). Vocabulary instruction. In M. Kamil, P. Mosenthal, P. D. Pearson, & R. Barr (Eds.), *Handbook of reading research* (vol. 3, pp. 503–523). New York: Longman.

Block, C. C., & Pressley, M. (Eds.). (2002). *Comprehension instruction: Research-based best practices.* New York: Guilford Press.

Bloodgood, J. R. (1999). What's in a name? The role of name writing in children's literacy acquisition. *Reading Research Quarterly, 34,* 342–367.

Bloom, B. S., Englehart, M. D., Furst, E. J., Hill, W. H., & Krathwohl, D. R. (1956). *The taxonomy of educational objectives. Handbook I: Cognitive domain.* New York: David McKay.

Bloom, B. S., Hastings, J. T., & Madaus, G. F. (1971). *Handbook of formative and summative evaluation of student learning.* New York: McGraw-Hill.

Bloom, B. S., Madaus, G. F., & Hastings, J. T. (1981). *Evaluation to improve learning.* New York: McGraw-Hill.

Blythe, T. (1998). *The teaching for understanding guide.* San Francisco, CA: Jossey-Bass.

Boaler, J. (2002). *Experiencing school mathematics.* Mahwah, NJ: Erlbaum.

Bogner, K., Raphael, L., & Pressley, M. (2002). How grade 1 teachers motivate literate activity by their students. *Scientific Studies in Reading, 6,* 135–165.

Bond, G. L., & Dykstra, R. (1967/1997). The cooperative research program in first-grade reading instruction. *Reading Research Quarterly, 2*(4), 1–142. (Reprinted in *Reading Research Quarterly, 31.*)

Bransford, J. D., Brown, A. L., & Cocking, R. R. (Eds.). (2000). *How people learn: Brain, mind, experience, and school* (expanded edition). Washington, DC: National Academy Press.

Bransford, J. D., & Schwartz, D. L. (1999). Rethinking transfer: A simple proposal with multiple implications. *Review of Research in Education,* 61–100.

Brisbois, J. (1995). Connections between first- and second-language reading. *Journal of Reading Behavior, 27,* 565–584.

Britton, J. N., Burgess, T., Martin, N., McLeod, A., & Rosen, H. (1975). *The development of writing abilities.* New York: Macmillan.

Brophy, J. (1986). Teacher influences on student achievement. *American Psychologist, 41,* 1069–1077.

Brophy, J. (1987). Socializing students' motivation to learn. In M. L. Maehr & D. A. Kleiber (Eds.),

Advances in motivation and achievement: Enhancing motivation (vol. 5, pp. 181–210). Greenwich, CT: JAI Press.

Brophy, J. (2000). Beyond balance: Goal awareness, developmental progressions, tailoring to the context, and supports for teachers in ideal reading and literacy programs. In B. M. Taylor, M. F. Graves, & P. van den Broek (Eds.), *Reading for meaning: Fostering comprehension in the middle grades* (pp. 170–192). New York: Teachers College Press.

Brophy, J. (2004). *Motivating students to learn* (2nd ed.). Mahwah, NJ: Erlbaum.

Brown, A. L., & Campione, J. C. (1990). Interactive learning environments and the teaching of mathematics and science. In M. Gardner, J. G. Greeno, F. Reif, A. H. Schoenfeld, A. diSessa, & E. Stage (Eds.), *Toward a scientific practice of science education*. Hillsdale, NJ: Erlbaum.

Brown, A. L., & Day, J. D. (1983). Macrorules for summarizing text: The development of expertise. *Journal of Verbal Learning and Verbal Behavior, 22,* 1–14.

Brown, A. L., & Palincsar, A. M. (1989). Guided cooperative learning in individual knowledge acquisition. In L. B. Resnick (Ed.), *Knowing, learning, and instruction*. Hillsdale, NJ: Erlbaum.

Brown, J. S., Collins, A., & Duguid, P. (1989). Situated cognition and the culture of learning. *Educational Researcher, 18*(1), 32–42.

Brown, R., Pressley, M., Van Meter, P., & Schuder, T. (1996). A quasi-experimental validation of transactional strategies instruction with low-achieving second-grade readers. *Journal of Educational Psychology, 88,* 18–37.

Brozo, W. G. (2002). *To be a boy, to be a reader*. Newark, DE: International Reading Association.

Bruck, M., & Treiman, R. (1992). Learning to pronounce words: The limitations of analogies. *Reading Research Quarterly, 27,* 375–388.

Buening, A. P. (2006). *Children's writer's and illustrator's market*. Cincinnati, OH: Writers Digest Books.

Burke, E. M., & Glazer, S. M. (1994). *Using nonfiction in the classroom*. New York: Scholastic.

Burns, M. S., Griffin, P., & Snow, C. E. (1999). *Starting out right: A guide to promoting children's reading success*. Washington, DC: National Academy Press.

Calfee, R. C. (1999). *Interactive reading assessment system–Revised (IRAS–R)*. Unpublished.

Calfee, R. C. (2000). Writing portfolios: Activity, assessment, authenticity. In R. Indrisano & J. R. Squire (Eds.), *Theoretical models and processes of writing* (pp. 278–304). Newark, DE: International Reading Association.

Calfee, R. C., & Calfee, K. H. (1976). Reading and mathematics observation system (RAMOS/II) (rev.). Unpublished manuscript, Stanford, CA.

Calfee, R. C., & Drum, P. A. (1986). Research on teaching reading. In M. C. Wittrock (Ed.), *Handbook of research on teaching* (3rd ed., pp. 804–849). New York: Macmillan.

Calfee, R. C., & Hiebert, E. H. (1991). Classroom assessment of reading. In R. Barr, M. Kamil, P. Mosenthal, & P. D. Pearson (Eds.), *Handbook of research on reading* (2nd ed., pp. 281–309). New York: Longman.

Calfee, R. C., & Hoover, K. (2004). The interactive reading assessment system—revised. In K. Wilson, R. C. Calfee, M. F. Graves, & G. Trainin, *Assessments and lesson plans for Teaching Reading in the 21st Century* (3rd ed.). Boston: Allyn & Bacon.

Calfee, R. C., & Patrick, C. L. (1995). *Teach our children well*. Stanford, CA: Stanford Alumni Association.

Calfee, R. C., & Perfumo, P. (1993). Student portfolios: Opportunities for a revolution in assessment. *Journal of Reading, 36,* 532–537.

Calfee, R. C., & Wilson, K. M. (2004). Assessment frameworks for composition. In B. Ehren & K. Apel (Eds.), *Handbook of language and literacy development and disorders*. New York: Guilford Press.

California Test Bureau. (1996). *Terra Nova*. Monterey, CA: Author.

Calkins, L. M., Montgomery, K., Santman, D., & Falk, B. (1998). *A teacher's guide to standardized achievement tests: Knowledge is power*. Portsmouth, NH: Heinemann.

Campbell, J. R., Hombo, C. M., & Mazzeo, J. (2000). *NAEP 1999 trends in academic progress: Three decades of student performance*. Washington, DC: U.S. Department of Education.

Canney, G. F., Kennedy, T. R., Schroeder, M., & Miles, S. (1999). Instructional strategies for K–12 Limited English Proficiency (LEP) students in the regular classroom. *The Reading Teacher, 52*(5), 540–544.

Carey, S. (1978). Child as word learner. In M. Halle, J. Bresnan, & G. Miller (Eds.), *Linguistic theory and psychological reality* (pp. 347–389). Cambridge, UK: Cambridge University Press.

Carroll, J. B. (1966). Some neglected relationships in reading and language. *Elementary English, 43,* 577–582.

Cazden, C. (2001). *Classroom discourse* (2nd ed.). Portsmouth, NH: Heinemann.

Cazden, C. B. (1991). Contemporary issues and future directions: Active learners and active teachers. In J. Flood, J. M. Jensen, D. Lapp, & J. R. Squire (Eds.), *Handbook of research on teaching the English language arts* (pp. 418–422). New York: Guilford Press.

Center for Educational Policy. (2005). *From the capital to the classroom: Year 3 of the No Child Left Behind*

Act. Washington, DC: Author. Available at http://www.cep-dc.org/.

Chall, J. S. (1967). *Learning to read: The great debate.* New York: McGraw-Hill.

Chall, J. S. (1996). *Stages of reading development* (2nd ed.). Fort Worth, TX: Harcourt-Brace.

Chambliss, M. J., & Calfee, R. C. (1998). *Textbooks for learning: Nurturing children's minds.* Oxford, UK: Blackwell.

Chen, H-C., & Graves, M. F. (1996). Effects of previewing and providing background knowledge on Taiwanese college students' comprehension of American short stories. *TESOL Quarterly, 29,* 663–686.

Chihak, J. (1999). Success is in the details: Publishing to validate elementary school authors. *Language Arts, 96*(6), 491–498.

Chomsky, C. (1978). When you still can't read in third grade: After decoding, what? In S. J. Samuels (Ed.), *What research has to say about reading instruction* (pp. 13–30). Newark, DE: International Reading Association.

Clark, K. F., & Graves, M. F. (2005). Scaffolding students' comprehension of text. *The Reading Teacher, 56,* 570–580.

Clay, M. (1991). *Becoming literate: The construction of inner control.* Portsmouth, NH: Heinemann.

Clay, M. (1993). *An observation study of early literacy achievement.* Portsmouth, NH: Heinemann.

Clay, M. M. (1979). *The early detection of reading difficulties.* Portsmouth, NH: Heinemann.

Clay, M. M. (1992) *Reading Recovery: A guidebook for teachers in training.* Portsmouth, NH: Heinemann.

Cobb, L. (1835). *The North American reader.* New York: B and S Collins.

Cohen, E. (1994). *Designing group work: Strategies for heterogeneous classrooms.* New York: Teachers College Press.

Cohen, P., Kulic, J., & Kulic, C. L. (1982). Educational outcomes of tutoring: A meta-analysis of findings. *American Educational Research Journal, 19,* 237–248.

Collier, C. C., & Redmond, L. A. (1974). Are you teaching kids to read mathematics? *The Reading Teacher, 5,* 804–808.

Colon-Vila, L. (1997, February). Storytelling in an ESL classroom. *Teaching K–8,* 48.

Cooke, C. L., & Graves, M. F. (1995). Writing for an audience—for fun. *Middle School Journal, 26*(3), 31–37.

Costa, A. L. (2001). *Developing minds. A resource book for teaching thinking.* Washington, DC: Association for Supervision and Curriculum Development.

Costa, A. L., & Kallick, B. (2004). Launching self-directed learners. *Educational Leadership, 62*(1), 51–55.

Cremin, L. A. (1990). *Popular education and its discontents.* New York: Harper & Row.

Cronbach, L. J. (1960). *Essentials of psychological testing* (3rd ed.). New York: Harper & Row.

Csikszentmihalyi, M. (1990). *Flow: The psychology of optimal experience.* New York: Harper & Row.

CTB/McGraw-Hill. (2001). *Terra Nova, the second edition.* Monterey, CA: Author.

Cullinan, B. (1993). *Pen in hand: Children become writers.* Newark, DE: International Reading Association.

Cummins, C., Stewart, M. T., & Block, C. C. (2005). Teaching several metacognitive strategies together increases students' independent metacognition. In S. E. Israel, C. C. Block, K. L. Bauserman, & K Kinnucan-Welsch (Eds.), *Metacognition in literacy learning* (pp. 277–298). Mahwah, NJ: Erlbaum.

Cummins, J. (2001). *Negotiating identities: Education for empowerment in a diverse society* (2nd ed.). Los Angeles: California Association for Bilingual Education.

Cunningham, A., & Stanovich, K. (2003). Reading matters: How reading English influences cognition. In J. Flood, D. Lapp, J. R. Squire, & J. M. Jensen (Eds.), *Handbook of research on teaching the English language arts* (pp. 666–675). Mahwah, NJ: Erlbaum.

Cunningham, A. E. (2005). Vocabulary growth through independent reading and reading aloud to children. In E. H. Hiebert & M. L. Kamil (Eds.), *Teaching and learning vocabulary: Bringing research to practice* (pp. 45–68). Mahwah, NJ: Erlbaum.

Cunningham, P. (2005, June). *What good is phonics if they don't use it?* Paper presented at the 2005 Minnesota Reading First Summer Literacy Institute, Minneapolis, MN.

Cunningham, P. M., & Allington, R. L. (1999). *Classrooms that work: They can all learn to read and write* (2nd ed.). New York: Longman.

Cunningham, P. M., & Cunningham, J. W. (1992). Making words: Enhancing the invented spelling-decoding connection. *The Reading Teacher, 46,* 106–115.

Cunningham, P. M., Hall, D. P., & Defee, M. (1991). Nonability-grouped, multilevel instruction: A year in a first-grade classroom. *The Reading Teacher, 44,* 566–571.

Cunningham, P. M., Hall, D. P., & Defee, M. (1998). Nonability-grouped, multilevel instruction: Eight years later. *The Reading Teacher, 51,* 652–664.

Daniels, H. (1994). *Literature circles: Voice and choice in the student-centered classroom.* New York: Stenhouse.

De Temple, J., & Snow, C. E. (2003). Learning words from books. In A. van Kleeck, S. A. Stahl, and E. B. Bauer (Eds.), *On reading books to children* (pp. 16–36). Mahwah, NJ: Erlbaum.

Delpit, L. D. (1988). The second dialogue: Power and pedagogy in educating other people's children. *Harvard Educational Review, 58,* 280–298.

Delpit, L. D. (1995). *Other people's children: Cultural conflict in the classroom.* New York: The New Press.

Deno, S. (1985). Curriculum-based measurement: The emerging alternative. *Exceptional Children, 52,* 219–232.

Deshler, D. D., & Schumaker, J. B. (1993). Skills mastery by at-risk students: Not a simple matter. *Elementary School Journal, 94,* 153–167.

Developmental Studies Center. (2004–2005). *Making meaning.* Berkeley, CA: Author.

Diller, D. (1999). Opening the dialogue: Using culture as a tool in teaching young African American children. *Reading Teacher, 52,* 820–828.

Dillon, J. T. (1988). *Questioning and teaching: A manual of practice.* New York: Teachers College Press.

Dole, J. A., Brown, K. J., & Trathen, W. (1996). The effects of strategy instruction on the comprehension performance of at-risk students. *Reading Research Quarterly, 31,* 62–88.

Dole, J. A., Valencia, S. W., Greer, E. A., & Wardrop, J. L. (1991). Effects of two types of prereading instruction on the comprehension of narrative and expository text. *Reading Research Quarterly, 26,* 142–159.

Dolezal, S. E., Welsh, L. M., Pressley, M., & Vincent, M. (2003). How do grade 3 teachers motivate their students? *Elementary School Journal, 103,* 239–267.

Donovan, M. S., Bransford, J. D., & Pellegrino, J. W. (Eds.). (1999). *How people learn: Bridging research and practice.* Washington, DC: National Academy Press.

Duffy, G. G. (2002). The case for direct explanation of strategies. In C. C. Block & M. Pressley (Eds.), *Comprehension instruction: Research-based best practices* (pp. 28–41). New York: Guilford Press.

Duffy, G. G., & Roehler, L. R. (1982). Commentary: The illusion of instruction. *Reading Research Quarterly, 17,* 438–445.

Duffy, G. G., Roehler, L. R., Meloth, M., Vavrus, L., Book, C., Putnam, J., & Wesselman, R. (1986). The relationship between explicit verbal explanation during reading skill instruction and student awareness and achievement: A story of reading teacher effects. *Reading Research Quarterly, 21,* 237–252.

Duffy, G. G., Roehler, L. R., Sivan, E., Rackliffe, G., Book, C., Meloth, M., Vavrus, L. G., Wesselman, R., Putnam, J., & Bassiri, D. (1987). Effects of explaining the reasoning associated with using reading strategies. *Reading Research Quarterly, 22,* 347–368.

Duin, A. H., & Graves, M. F. (1988). Teaching vocabulary as a writing prompt. *Journal of Reading, 22,* 204–212.

Duke, N. K. (2004). The case for informational text. *Educational Leadership, 61*(6), 40–44.

Duke, N. K., & Bennett-Armistead, V. S. (2003). *Reading and writing informational text in the primary grades: Research-based practices.* New York: Scholastic.

Duke, N. K., & Pearson, P. D. (2002). Effective practices for developing reading comprehension. In A. E. Farstrup & S. J. Samuels (Eds.), *What research has to say about reading instruction* (3rd ed., pp. 205–242). Newark, DE: International Reading Association.

Duke, N. K., & Purcell-Gates, V. (2003). Genres at home and at school: Bridging the known to the new. *The Reading Teacher, 57,* 30–37.

Dyson, A. H., & Freedman, S. W. (1991). Writing. In J. Flood, J. M. Jensen, D. Lapp, & J. R. Squire (Eds.), *Handbook of research on teaching the English language arts* (pp. 754–774). New York: Guilford Press.

Echevarria, J., Vogt, M. E., & Short, D. (2004). *Making content comprehensible to English learners: The SIOP model.* Boston: Allyn & Bacon.

Ehri, L. C., & Robbins, C. (1992). Beginners need some decoding skill to read words by analogy. *Reading Research Quarterly, 27,* 13–26.

Elbow, P. (1973). *Writing without teachers.* Oxford, England: Oxford University Press.

Emig, J. (1971). *The composing process of twelfth graders.* Urbana, IL: National Council of Teachers of English.

Ennis, R. (1985). A logical basis for measuring critical thinking skills. *Educational Leadership, 43*(2), 44–48.

Estes, C. (1995). Musical links: Part I. *Book Links, 4,* 48–52.

Farr, R. (1993). Writing in response to reading: A process approach to literary assessment. In B. E. Cullinan (Ed.), *Pen in hand: Children become writers* (pp. 64–79). Newark, DE: International Reading Association.

Farr, R., & Carey, R. F. (1986). *Reading: What can be measured?* (2nd ed.). Newark, DE: International Reading Association.

Farr, R., & Tone, B. (1994). *Portfolios and performance assessment.* San Antonio, TX: Harcourt Brace.

Fetterman, D. M. (1998). *Ethnography step by step* (2nd ed.). Newbury Park, CA: Sage.

Fielding, L. G., Wilson, P. D., & Anderson, R. C. (1986). A new focus on free reading: The role of trade books in reading instruction. In T. E. Raphael (Ed.), *The contexts of school-based literacy* (pp. 149–160). New York: Random House.

Fillenworth, L. I. (1995). *Using reciprocal teaching to help at-risk college freshmen study.* Unpublished doctoral dissertation, University of Minnesota.

Fitzgerald, J. (1995). English-as-a-second-language reading instruction in the United States: A research review. *Journal of Reading Behavior, 27,* 115–152.

Fitzgerald, J., & Graves, M. F. (2004). *Scaffolding reading experiences for English-language learners.* Norwood, MA: Christopher-Gordon.

Five, C. L., & Dionisio, M. (1999). Revisiting the teaching of writing. *School Talk, 4*(4), 5.

Flavel, J. (1976). Metacognitive aspects of problem solving. In L. B. Resnick (Ed.), *The nature of intelligence* (pp. 231–235). Hillsdale, NJ: Erlbaum.

Flesch, R. (1955). *Why Johnny can't read—and what you can do about it.* New York: Harper.

Flynn, R. M. (2004/2005). Curriculum-based readers theatre: Setting the stage for reading and retention. *The Reading Teacher, 58*(4), 361.

Forsythe, S. J. (1995). It worked! Readers Theatre in second grade. *Reading Teacher, 49*(3), pp. 264–265.

Fountas, I. C., & Pinnell, G. S. (1996). *Guided reading: Good first teaching for all children.* Portsmouth, NH: Heinemann.

Fountas, I. C., & Pinnell, G. S. (1999). *Matching books to readers.* Portsmouth, NH: Heinemann.

Fountas, I. C., & Pinnnell, G. S. (2006). *Leveled books, K–8: Matching texts to readers for effective teaching.* Portsmouth, NH: Heinemann.

Frayer, D. A., Frederick, W. D., & Klausmeier, H. J. (1969). *A schema for testing the level of concept mastery.* Working paper no. 16. Madison, WI: Wisconsin Research and Development Center for Cognitive Learning.

Freeman, J. (1995). *More books kids will sit still for: A read-aloud guide.* New Providence, NJ: R. R. Bowker.

Friedland, E. S., & Truesdell, K. S. (2004). Kids reading together: Ensuring the success of a buddy reading program. *The Reading Teacher, 58*(1), 76–79.

Fry, E. (1977), Fry's readability graph: Clarifications, validity, and extension to level 17. *Journal of Reading, 21,* 242–252.

Fry, E. (2002). Readability versus leveling. *The Reading Teacher, 56,* 286–291.

Fry, E. B. (2004). *The vocabulary teacher's book of lists.* San Francisco: Jossey-Bass.

Fry, E. B., Polk, J. K., & Fountoukidis, D. (2000). *The reading teacher's book of lists.* Paramus, NJ: Prentice Hall.

Fry, E. F. (1998). *Phonics patterns: Onset and rhyme word lists* (4th ed.). Laguna Beach, CA: Laguna Beach Educational Books.

Fuchs, L. S., & Fuchs, D. (2000). Building students' capacity to work productively during peer-assisted reading activities. In B. M. Taylor, M. F. Graves, & P. van den Broek (Eds.), *Reading for meaning: Fostering comprehension in the middle grades* (pp. 95–114). New York: Teachers College Press.

Fukkink, R. G., & de Glopper, K. (1998). Effects of instruction in deriving word meanings from context: A meta-analysis. *Review of Educational Research, 68,* 450–469.

Fulwiler, T. (Ed.). (1987). *The journal book.* Portsmouth, NH: Boyton/Cook.

Galda, L. (1998). Mirrors and windows: Reading as transformation. In T. Raphael & K. Au (Eds.), *Literature-based instruction: Reshaping the curriculum.* Norwood, NJ: Christopher Gordon.

Galda, L., Ash, G. E., & Cullinan, B. E. (2000). Children's literature. In M. Kamil, P. Mosenthal, P. D. Pearson, & R. Barr (Eds.), *Handbook of reading research* (vol. 3, pp. 361–379). Mahwah, NJ: Erlbaum.

Galda, L., & Cullinan, B. E. (in press). *Literature and the child* (6th ed.). Belmont, CA: Wadsworth.

Galda, L., & Graves, M. F. (2007). *Reading and responding in the middle grades: Approaches for all classrooms.* Boston: Allyn & Bacon.

Gambrell, L. B. (1996). What research reveals about discussion. In L. B. Gambrell & J. F. Almasi (Eds.), *Lively discussions! Fostering engaged reading* (pp. 25–38). Newark, DE: International Reading Association.

Gambrell, L. B., & Mazzoni, S. A. (1999). Principles of best practice: Finding the common ground. In L. B. Gambrell, L. M. Morrow, S. B. Neuman, & M. Pressley (Eds.), *Best practices in literacy instruction* (pp. 11–21). New York: Guilford Press.

Garcia, G. (2000). Bilingual children's reading. In M. Kamil, P. Mosenthal, P. Pearson, & R. Barr (Eds.), *Handbook of reading research* (vol. 3, pp. 813–834). Mahwah, NJ: Erlbaum.

Gardner, H. (1985). *The mind's new science.* New York: Basic Books.

Gardner, H. (1993). *Multiple intelligences: The theory in practice.* New York: Basic Books.

Gardner, H. (1999). *Intelligence reframed: Multiple intelligences for the 21st century.* New York: Basic Books.

Gardner, H. (2005). *Development and education of the mind: The selected works of Howard Gardner.* London: Routledge.

Gaskins, I. W. (1994). Creating optimum learning environments. Is membership in the whole language community necessary? In F. Lehr & J. Osborn (Eds.), *Reading, language, and literacy: Instruction for the twenty-first century* (pp. 115–130). Hillsdale, NJ: Erlbaum.

Gaskins, I. W. (2005). *Success with struggling readers: The Benchmark School approach.* New York: Guilford Press.

Gaskins, I. W., Ehri, L. C., Cress, C., O'Hara, C., & Donnelly, K. (1996/1997). Procedures for word learning: Making discoveries about words. *The Reading Teacher, 50,* 312–327.

Gavelek, J. R., & Raphael, T. E. (1996). Changing talk about text: New roles for teachers and students. *Language Arts, 73*(3), 182–192.

Gergen, K. J. (1985). The social constructionist movement in modern psychology. *American Psychologist, 40,* 266–275.

Gersten, R., & Baker, S. (2000). What we know about effective instructional practices for English-language learners. *Exceptional Children, 66,* 454–470.

Gillespie, J. T. (2002). *Best books for children: Preschool through grade 6.* Westport, CT: Bowker-Greenwood.

Goatley, V. J., Brock, C. H., & Raphael, T. E. (1995). Diverse learners participating in regular education "Book Clubs." *Reading Research Quarterly, 30,* 352–380.

Good, R. H., & Kaminski, R. A. (Eds.). (2002). *Dynamic indicators of basic early literacy skills* (6th ed.). Eugene, OR: Institute for the Development of Educational Achievement. Available at http://dibels.uoregon.edu/.

Good, T., & Brophy, J. (2003). *Looking into classrooms* (9th ed.). Boston: Allyn & Bacon.

Goodman, K. (1970). Behind the eye: What happens in reading. In K. S. Goodman & O. S. Niles (Eds.), *Reading: Process and program* (pp. 1–38). Urbana, IL: National Council of Teachers of English.

Goodman, K. (1986). *What's whole in whole language?* Portsmouth, NH: Heinemann.

Goodman, K. (2005). Making sense of written language: A lifelong journey. *Journal of Literacy Research, 37,* 1–24.

Goodman, K. S., Goodman, Y. M., & Hood, W. J. (1989). *The whole language evaluation book.* Portsmouth, NH: Heinemann.

Goodman, Y. (1978). Kidwatching: An alternative to testing. *Journal of National Elementary School Principals, 57*(4), 22–27.

Gordon, E. W. (2004). Closing the gap: High achievement for students of color. *Research Points, 2*(3), 1–4. Available at http://www.aera.net/publications/?id=314.

Goswami, U., & Bryant, P. (1992). Rhyme, analogy, and children's reading. In P. B. Gough, L. C. Ehri, & R. Treiman (Eds.), *Reading acquisition* (pp. 49–63). Hillsdale, NJ: Erlbaum.

Goswami, U., & Mead, F. (1992). Onset and rime awareness and analogies in reading. *Reading Research Quarterly, 27,* 153–162.

Graves, D. H. (1975). An examination of the writing processes of seven-year-old children. *Research in the Teaching of English, 9,* 227–241.

Graves, D. H. (1991). *Writing: Teachers and children at work.* Portsmouth, NH: Heinemann.

Graves, D. H. (1996, April). Spot the lifetime writers. *Instructor,* 27.

Graves, M. F. (1998, October/November). Beyond balance. *Reading Today,* 16.

Graves, M. F. (2000). A vocabulary program to complement and bolster a middle-grade comprehension program. In B. M. Taylor, M. F. Graves, & P. van den Broek (Eds.), *Reading for meaning: Fostering comprehension in the middle grades* (pp. 116–135). New York: Teachers College Press.

Graves, M. F. (2004a). Theories and constructs that have made a significant difference in adolescent literacy—but that have the potential to produce still more positive benefits. In T. Jetton & J. A. Dole (Eds.), *Adolescent literacy research and practice* (pp. 433–452). New York: Guilford Press.

Graves, M. F. (2004b). Teaching prefixes: As good as it gets? In J. F. Baumann & E. B. Kame'enui (Eds.), *Vocabulary instruction: Research to practice* (pp. 81–99). New York: Guilford Press.

Graves, M. F. (2006). *The vocabulary book: Learning and instruction.* New York: Teachers College Press.

Graves, M. F., & Dykstra, R. (1997). Contextualizing the first-grade studies: What is the best way to teach children to read? *Reading Research Quarterly, 32,* 342–344.

Graves, M. F., & Graves, B. B. (2003). *Scaffolding reading experiences: Designs for student success* (2nd ed.). Norwood, MA: Christopher-Gordon.

Graves, M. F., Graves, B. B., & Braaten, S. (1996). Scaffolded reading experiences: Bridges to reading success. *Educational Leadership, 53,* 14–16.

Graves, M. F., & Philippot, R. A. (2001). High interest–easy reading book series. In B. E. Cullinan & D. G. Person (Eds.), *The encyclopedia of children's literature.* New York: Continuum.

Graves, M. F., Prenn, M. C., & Cooke, C. L. (1985). The coming attraction: Previewing short stories to increase comprehension. *Journal of Reading, 28,* 594–598.

Graves, M. F., & Slater, W. H. (in press). Vocabulary instruction in content areas. In D. Lapp, J. Flood, & N. Farnan (Eds.), *Content area reading and learning: Instructional strategies* (3rd ed.). Mahwah, NJ: Erlbaum.

Graves, M. F., & Watts, S. M. (2002). The place of word consciousness in a research-based vocabulary program. In S. J. Samuels & A. E. Farstrup (Eds.), *What research has to say about reading instruction* (3rd ed., pp. 140–165). Newark, DE: International Reading Association.

Greene, F. (1979). Radio reading. In C. Pennock (Ed.), *Reading comprehension at four linguistic levels* (pp. 104–107). Newark, DE: International Reading Association.

Guthrie, J., & Wigfield, A. (2000). Engagement and motivation in reading. In M. Kamil, P. Mosenthal, P. D.

Pearson, and R. Barr (Eds.), *Handbook of reading research* (vol. 3, pp. 403–424). Mahwah, NJ: Erlbaum.

Guthrie, J. T., & Anderson, E. (1999). Engagement in reading: Processes of motivated, strategic, knowledgeable, social readers. In J. T. Guthrie & D. E. Alvermann (Eds.), *Engaged reading: Processes, practices, and policy implications* (pp. 17–45). New York: Teachers College Press.

Gutierrez, C. D. (2005). The persistence of inequity: English-language learners and educational reform. In J. Flood & P. L. Anders (Eds.), *Literacy development of students in urban schools: Research and policy* (pp. 288–304). Newark, DE: International Reading Association.

Hannon, J. (1999). Talking back: Kindergarten dialogue journals. *The Reading Teacher, 53*(3), 200–203.

Hansen-Krening, N., Aoki, E. M., & Mizokawa, D. T. (Eds.). (2003). *Kaleidoscope: A multicultural booklist for grades K–8* (4th ed.). Champaign-Urbana, IL: National Council of Teachers of English.

Harcourt Educational Measurement. (2001). *Stanford Achievement Test Series* (10th ed.). San Antonio, TX: Author.

Harlen, W. (Ed.). (1994). *Enhancing quality in assessment.* London: Paul Chapman.

Harp, B. (1991). *Assessment and evaluation in whole language programs.* Norwood, MA: Christopher-Gordon.

Hart, B., & Risley, T. R. (1995). *Meaningful differences in the everyday experiences of young American children.* Baltimore: Paul H. Brooks Publishing.

Hart, B., & Risley, T. R. (2003, Spring). The early catastrophe: The 30 million word gap. *American Educator, 27*(1), 4–9.

Hart, D. (1994). *Authentic assessment: A handbook for educators.* Menlo Park, CA: Addison-Wesley.

Harwayne, S. (1993). Chuzpah and the nonfiction writer. In B. E. Cullinan (Ed.), *Pen in hand: Children become writers* (pp. 19–35). Newark, DE: International Reading Association.

Hasbrouck, J., & Tindal, G. (2005). *Oral reading fluency: 90 years of measurement* (Tech. Rep. No. 33). Eugene, Oregon: University of Oregon, College of Education, Behavioral Research and Teaching. Available at http://brt.uoregon.edu/tech_reports.htm.

Heath, S. B. (1983). *Ways with words: Language, life, and work in communities and classrooms.* Cambridge, MA: Cambridge University Press.

Heckelman, R. G. (1969). A neurological-impress method of remedial-reading instruction. *Academic Therapy Quarterly, 4,* 277–282.

Heimlich, J. E., & Pittelman, S. D. (1986). *Semantic mapping: Classroom applications.* Newark, DE: International Reading Association.

Henderson, E. (1981). *Learning to read and spell: The child's knowledge of words.* DeKalb, IL: Northern Illinois Press.

Henderson, E. H. (1990). *Teaching spelling* (2nd ed.). Boston, MA: Houghton Mifflin.

Herman, J. L., Aschbacher, P. R., & Winters, L. (1992). *A practical guide to alternative assessment.* Alexandria, VA: Association for Supervision and Curriculum Development.

Hiebert, E. H. (1994). Reading Recovery in the United States: What difference does it make to an age cohort? *Educational Researcher, 23*(9), 15–25.

Hiebert, E. H. (1996). Creating and sustaining a love of literature and the ability to read it. In M. F. Graves, P. van den Broek, & B. M. Taylor (Eds.), *The first R: Every child's right to read* (pp. 15–36). New York: Teachers College Press.

Hiebert, E. H. (2005). In pursuit of an effective, efficient vocabulary program. In E. H. Hiebert & M. Kamil (Eds.), *Teaching and learning vocabulary: Bringing research to practice* (pp. 243–263). Mahwah, NJ: Erlbaum.

Hiebert, E. H., & Calfee, R. C. (1992). Assessment of literacy: From standardized tests to performances and portfolios. In A. E. Farstrup & S. J. Samuels (Eds.), *What research says about reading instruction* (pp. 70–100). Newark, DE: International Reading Association.

Hiebert, E. H., Pearson, P. D., Taylor, B. M., Richardson, V., & Paris, S. G. (1998). *Every child a reader: Applying reading research in the classroom.* Ann Arbor, MI: Center for the Improvement of Early Reading Achievement.

Hiebert, E. H., & Taylor, B. M. (Eds.). (1994). *Getting reading right from the start: Effective early literacy interventions.* Boston: Allyn & Bacon.

Higham, J. (1988). *Strangers in the land: Patterns of American nativism, 1860–1925.* New Brunswick, NJ: Rutgers University Press.

Hindley, J. (1998). The workshop environment. *School Talk, 3*(4), 4.

Hoover, H. D., Hieronymus, A. N., Frisbie, D. A., & Dunbar, S. B. (1996). *Iowa Test of Basic Skills, Form M.* Itasca, IL: Riverside.

Horn Book guide to children's and young adult books. (2002). Boston, MA: Horn Book.

Horowitz, R., & Freeman, S. H. (1995). Robots versus spaceships: The role of discussion in kindergartners' and second graders' preferences for science text. *The Reading Teacher, 49,* 30–40.

Hulstijn, J. (1991). How is reading in a second language related to reading in a first language? *AILA Review, 8,* 5–15.

Ihnot, C. (2001). *Read naturally master edition.* Saint Paul, MN: Read Naturally.

Ihnot, C. (2002). *Read naturally rationale and research.* Saint Paul, MN: Read Naturally.

Ihnot, C. (2004). *Read naturally software edition* (Version 2.0). Saint Paul, MN: Read Naturally.

International Reading Association. (1997). *The role of phonics in reading instruction.* Newark, DE: Author.

Invernizzi, M., Juel, C., & Rosemary, C. A. (1996/1997). A community volunteer tutorial that works. *The Reading Teacher, 50,* 304–311.

Jacobi-Karna, K. (1996). Music and children's books. *The Reading Teacher, 49*(3), 265–269.

Jiménez, R. T. (2000). Literacy lessons derived from the instruction of six Latina/Latino teachers. In B. M. Taylor, M. F. Graves, & P. van den Broek (Eds.), *Reading for meaning: Fostering comprehension in the middle grades* (pp. 152–169). New York: Teachers College Press.

Johnson, D. D., & Pearson, P. D. (1984). *Teaching reading vocabulary* (2nd ed.). New York: Holt, Rinehart & Winston.

Johnson, D. W., & Johnson, R. T. (1989). *Cooperation and competition: Theory and research.* Edina, MN: Interaction Book Company.

Johnson, D. W., & Johnson, R. T. (1996). Conflict resolution and peer mediation programs in elementary and secondary schools: A review of the research. *Review of Educational Research, 66,* 459–506.

Johnson, D. W., & Johnson, R. T. (2002). Teaching students to resolve their own and their schoolmates' conflicts. *Counseling and Human Development, 34*(6), 1–12.

Johnson, D. W., Johnson, R. T., & Holubec, E. J. (1987). *Structuring cooperative learning: Lesson plans for teachers.* Edina, MN: Interaction Book Company.

Johnson, D. W., Johnson, R. T., & Holubec, E. J. (1994). *The new circles of learning: Cooperation in the classroom.* Alexandria, VA: Association for Supervision and Curriculum Development.

Johnson, F. R., Invernizzi, M., & Juel, C. (1998). *Book buddies: Guidelines for volunteer tutors of emergent and early readers.* New York: Guilford Press.

Johnson, M. S., Kress, R. A., & Pikulski, J. J. (1987). *Informal reading inventories.* Newark, DE: International Reading Association.

Johnston, P. H. (1990). Steps toward a more naturalistic approach to the assessment of the reading process. In J. Algina & S. Legg (Eds.), *Cognitive assessment of language and mathematics outcomes* (pp. 92–143). Norwood, NJ: Ablex.

Johnston, P. H. (1992). *Constructive evaluation of literate activity.* New York: Longman.

Johnston, P. H., & Winograd, P. N. (1985). Passive failure in reading. *Journal of Reading Behavior, 17,* 279–301.

Juel, C. (1988). Learning to read and write: A longitudinal study of fifty-four children from first through fourth grade. *Journal of Educational Psychology, 80,* 437–447.

Juel, C. (1990). Effects of reading group assignment on reading development in first and second grade. *Journal of Reading Behavior, 22,* 223–254.

Juel, C. (1994). *Learning to read and write in one elementary school.* New York: Springer-Verlag.

Juel, C. (2005). The impact of early school experiences on initial reading. In D. K. Dickinson & S. B. Neuman (Eds.), *Handbook of early literacy research* (vol. 2, pp. 410–426). New York: Guilford Press.

Juel, C., Griffith, P. L., & Gough, P. B. (1986). Acquisition of literacy: A longitudinal study of children in first and second grade. *Journal of Educational Psychology, 78,* 243–255.

Juel, C., & Minden-Cupp, C. (2000). Learning to read words: Linguistic units and instructional strategies. *Reading Research Quarterly, 35,* 458–492.

Juel, C., & Roper/Schneider, D. (1985) The influence of basal readers on first grade reading. *Reading Research Quarterly, 18,* 306–327.

Just, M. A., & Carpenter, P. H. (1980). A theory of reading: From eye fixations to comprehension. *Psychological Review, 87,* 329–354.

Kame'enui, E., Simmons, D., & Cornachione, C. (2001). *A practical guide to reading assessments.* Eugene: University of Oregon, National Center to Improve the Tools of Educators.

Kamil, M. L., & Bernhardt, E. B. (2004). Reading instruction for English-language learners. In M. F. Graves, C. Juel, & B. B. Graves, *Teaching reading in the 21st century* (3rd ed., pp. 496–541). Boston: Allyn & Bacon.

Kamil, M. L., & Lane, D. (1997). *Using informational text for first-grade reading instruction.* Paper presented at the annual meeting of the National Reading Conference.

Kirsch, I., & Jungeblut, A. (1986). *Literacy: Profiles of America's young adults.* Princeton, NJ: National Assessment of Educational Progress, Educational Testing Service.

Knapp, M. S., & Associates. (1995). *Teaching for meaning in high-poverty classrooms.* New York: Teachers College Press.

Koziol, S. M., Minnick, J. B., & Riddell, K. (1996). *Journals for active learning: A two-day workshop module for primary teachers in Bosnia.* Pittsburgh, PA: University of Pittsburgh International Institute for Studies in Education.

Krashen, S. (2004). False claims about literacy development. *Educational Leadership, 61*(6), 18–21.

Kuhn, M. (2004/2005). Helping students become accurate, expressive readers: Fluency instruction for small groups. *The Reading Teacher, 58,* 338–344.

Kuhn, M. R., & Stahl, S. A. (2003). Fluency: A review of developmental and remedial practices. *Journal of Educational Psychology, 95,* 3–21. An earlier version is available at http://www.ciera.org/library/reports/inquiry-2/.

Kurlanski, M. (1997). *Cod: A history of the fish that changed the world.* New York: Walker and Company.

Kurlanski, M. (2002). *Salt: A world history.* New York: Walker and Company.

LaBerge, D., & Samuels, S. J. (1974). Toward a theory of automatic information processing in reading. *Cognitive Psychology, 6,* 293–323.

Langer, J. (1986). *Children reading and writing.* Norwood, NJ: Ablex.

Leslie, L., & Caldwell, J. (2006). *Qualitative Reading Inventory–4.* New York: Longman.

Lukens, R. J. (1990). *A critical handbook of children's literature* (4th ed.). Oxford, OH: Scott, Foresman.

Lundberg, I. (1984, August). Learning to read. *School Research Newsletter,* National Board of Education in Sweden.

Maclean, M., Bryant, P., & Bradley, L. (1988). Rhymes, nursery rhymes, and reading in early childhood. In K. E. Stanovich (Ed.), *Children's reading and the development of phonological awareness* (pp. 11–37). Detroit, MI: Wayne State University Press.

Maehr, M., & Midgley, C. (1996). *Transforming school cultures.* Boulder, CO: Westview Press.

Mandler, J., & Johnson, N. (1977). Remembrance of things parsed: Story structure and recall. *Cognitive Psychology, 9,* 111–151.

Mann, H. (1944/1965). Method of teaching young children on their first entering school. In N. B. Smith (Ed.), *American reading instruction* (2nd ed., p. 117). Newark, DE: International Reading Association. (Original work published in 1884.)

Manning, J. M. (1999, September 15). Remarks made in an interview on the Minneapolis Public Radio *Midmorning* program. Minneapolis, MN: MPR.

Mansukhani, P. (2002). The explorers' club: The sky is no limit for learning. *Language Arts, 80,* 31–39.

Marshall, J. (2000). Response to literature. In M. Kamil, P. Mosenthal, P. D. Pearson, & R. Barr (Eds.), *Handbook of reading research* (vol. 3). Mahwah, NJ: Erlbaum.

Marzano, R. J. (2000). *Transforming classroom grading.* Alexandria, VA: Association for Supervision and Curriculum Development (ASCD).

McClure, A. A., Harrison, P., & Reed, S. (1990). *Sunrises and songs: Reading and writing poetry in an elementary classroom.* Portsmouth, NH: Heinemann.

McClure, A. A., & Kristo, J. V. (Eds.). (2002). *Adventuring with books: A booklist for pre-K–grade 6* (13th ed.). Champaign-Urbana, IL: National Council of Teachers of English.

McConkie, G. W., & Zola, D. (1981). Language constraints and the functional stimulus in reading. In A. M. Lesgold & C. A. Perfetti (Eds.), *Interactive processes in reading* (pp. 155–175). Hillsdale, NJ: Erlbaum.

McCracken, R. A., & McCracken, M. J. (1978). Modeling is the key to sustained reading. *The Reading Teacher, 31,* 406–408.

McKeown, M. G., & Beck, I. L. (2003). Taking advantage of read-alouds to help children make sense of decontextualized language. In A. van Kleeck, S. A. Stahl, & E. B. Bauer (Eds.), *On reading books to young children* (pp. 159–176). Mahwah, NJ: Erlbaum.

McMahon, M. M., & McCormack, B. B. (1998). To think and act like a scientist: Learning disciplinary knowledge. In C. R. Hynd (Ed.), *Learning from text across conceptual domains* (pp. 227–262). Mahwah, NJ: Erlbaum.

McMahon, S. I., Raphael, T. E., & Goatley, V. J. (1995). Changing the context for classroom reading instruction: The Book Club project. In J. Brophy (Ed.), *Advances in research on teaching* (vol. 5, pp. 123–166). Greenwich, CT: JAI Press.

McTighe, J., Seif, E., & Wiggins, G. (2004). You can teach for meaning. *Educational Leadership, 62*(1), pp. 26–30.

Meinbach, A. M., Rothlein, L., & Fredericks, A. D. (2000). *The complete guide to thematic units: Creating the integrated curriculum* (2nd ed.). Norwood, MA: Christopher-Gordon.

Miller, G. A., & Gildea, P. M. (1987). How children learn words. *Scientific American, 257*(3), 94–99.

Mills, H., Stephens, D., O'Keefe, T., & Waugh, J. R. (2004). Theory in practice: The legacy of Louise Rosenblatt. *Language Arts, 82,* 47–55.

Mitchell, R. (1992). *Testing for learning: How new approaches to evaluation can improve American schools.* New York: Free Press.

Mode, B. A. (1989). Dialogue journal writing. *The Reading Teacher, 42,* 568–571.

Moll, L. C. (1992). Literacy research in community classrooms: A socio-cultural approach. In R. Beach, J. L. Green, M. S. Kamil, & T. Shanahan (Eds.), *Multidisciplinary perspectives on literacy research* (pp. 211–244). Urbana, IL: National Council of Teachers of English.

Moore, D. W., Moore, S. A., Cunningham, P. M., & Cunningham, J. W. (2003). *Developing readers and writers in the content areas K–12.* Boston: Allyn & Bacon.

Mullis, I. V. S., Martin, M. O., Gonzales, E. J., & Kennedy, A. M. (2003). *PIRLS 2001 international report*. Boston: International Study Center, Boston College.

Nagy, W. E., & Anderson, R. C. (1984). How many words are there in printed school English? *Reading Research Quarterly, 19,* 304–330.

Nagy, W. E., & Scott, J. A. (2000). Vocabulary processes. In M. Kamil, P. Mosenthal, P. D. Pearson, & R. Barr (Eds.), *Handbook of reading research* (vol. 3, pp. 269–284). Mahwah, NJ: Erlbaum.

Nation, I. S. P. (2001). *Learning vocabulary in another language*. Cambridge, England: Cambridge University Press.

National Center on Education and the Economy. (1997). *New standards: Performance standards. Volume 1: Elementary schools*. Pittsburgh, PA: University of Pittsburgh.

National Council of Teachers of English and International Reading Association. (1996). *Standards for the English language arts*. Urbana, IL: Author.

National Council of Teachers of English (NCTE) Commission on Reading. (2004). *On reading, learning to read, and effective reading instruction*. Retrieved December 2005 from http://www.ncte.org/about/over/positions/category/read/118620.htm.

National Reading Panel. (2000). *Report of the National Reading Panel: Teaching children to read*. Bethesda, MD: National Institute of Child Health and Human Development.

National Research Council. (2004). *Engaging schools: Fostering high school students' motivation to learn*. Washington, DC: National Academies Press.

New Standards Primary Literacy Committee. (1999). *Reading and writing grade by grade*. Pittsburgh: National Center on Education and the University of Pittsburgh. Available online at www.ncee.org.

Newmann, F. N. (1996). *Authentic achievement: Restructuring schools for intellectual quality*. San Francisco: Jossey-Bass.

Newmann, F. N. (2000). Authentic intellectual work: What and why? *Research/Practice, 8*(1), 15–20.

Nitko, A. J. (1996). *Educational assessment of students* (2nd ed.). Englewood Cliffs, NJ: Merrill.

No Child Left Behind Act of 2001. (2002). Public Law 107–110. 115 Stat, 1425.

Noddings, N. (2003). *Happiness and education*. Cambridge, England: Cambridge University Press.

Ogle, D. (1986). K-W-L: A teaching model that develops active reading of expository text. *The Reading Teacher, 39,* 564–570.

Olness, R. (2005). *Using literature to enhance writing instruction: A guide for K–5 teachers*. Newark, DE: International Reading Association.

Olson, C. B. (1996). Strategies for interacting with text. In C. B. Olson (Ed.), *Practical ideas for teaching writing as a process at the elementary and middle school levels*. (rev. ed., pp. 231–235). Sacramento: California Department of Education.

Olson, J. F., & Goldstein, A. A. (1997). *The inclusion of students with disabilities and limited English proficient students in large-scale assessments: A summary of recent progress*. Washington, DC: National Center for Education Statistics (ED).

O'Malley, J. M., & Pierce, L. V. (1996). *Authentic assessment for English language learners: Practical approaches for teachers*. New York: Addison-Wesley.

Orehovec, B. & Alley, M. (2003). *Revisiting the reading workshop: Management, mini-lessons, and strategies*. New York: Scholastic.

Osborn, J., Lehr, F., & Hiebert, E. H. (2003). *A focus on fluency*. Honolulu: Pacific Resources for Education and Learning.

Owocki, G., & Goodman, Y. M. (2002). *Kidwatching: Documenting children's literacy development*. Portsmouth, NH: Heinemann.

Palincsar, A. M., & Brown, A. L. (1984). Reciprocal teaching of comprehension and monitoring activities. *Cognition and Instruction, 1*(2), 117–175.

Palincsar, A. M., & Brown, A. (1985). Reciprocal teaching: A means to a meaningful end. In J. Osborn, P. T. Wilson, & R. C. Anderson (Eds.), *Reading education: Foundations for a literate America* (pp. 299–310). Lexington, MA: DC Heath.

Palincsar, A. M., & Brown, A. L. (1986). Interactive teaching to promote independent learning from text. *The Reading Teacher, 39,* 771–777.

Palincsar, A. M., & David, Y. M. (1991). Promoting literacy through classroom dialogue. In E. Hiebert (Ed.), *Literacy for a diverse society: Perspectives, programs, and policies*. New York: Teachers College Press.

Paris, S. G., Calfee, R. C., Filby, N., Hiebert, E. H., Pearson, P. D., Valencia, S. W., & Wolf, K. P. (1992). A framework for authentic literacy assessment. *The Reading Teacher, 46,* 88–98.

Patterson, L., Santa, C. M., & Smith, K. (1993). *Teachers as researchers: Reflection and action*. Newark, DE: International Reading Association.

Pearson, P. D. (1990). Foreword. In T. Shanahan (Ed.), *Reading and writing together: New perspectives for the classroom* (pp. v–vi). Norwood, MA: Christopher-Gordon.

Pearson, P. D. (2000). Reading in the twentieth century. In T. L. Good (Ed.), *American education: Yesterday, today, and tomorrow* (pp. 152–208). Chicago: National Society for the Study of Education.

Pearson, P. D., & Duke, N. K. (2002). Comprehension instruction in the primary grades. In C. C. Block & M. Pressley (Eds.), *Comprehension instruction: Research-*

based practices (pp. 247–258). New York: Guilford Press.

Pearson, P. D., & Gallagher, M. C. (1983). The instruction of reading comprehension. *Contemporary Educational Psychology, 8,* 317–344.

Pearson, P. D., Roehler, L. R., Dole, J. A., & Duffy, G. G. (1992). Developing expertise in reading comprehension. In S. J. Samuels & A. E. Farstrup (Eds.), *What research has to say about reading instruction* (2nd ed., pp. 145–199). Newark, DE: International Reading Association.

Perie, M., Grigg, W., & Donahue, P. (2005). *The nation's report card: Reading 2005.* Washington, DC: U.S. Department of Education.

Perie, M., Moran, R., Lutkus, A.D., & Tirre, W. (2005). *NAEP 2004 trends in academic progress: Three decades of student performance in reading and mathematics.* Washington, DC: U.S. Department of Education.

Perkins, D. (1992). *Smart schools: From training memories to educating minds.* New York: The Free Press.

Perkins, D. (1993). Making education relevant: Teaching and learning for understanding. *New Jersey Educational Association Review,* October, 10–18.

Perkins, D. (1994). *Knowledge as design: A handbook for critical and creative discussion across the curriculum.* Pacific Grove, CA: Critical Thinking Press.

Perkins, D. (2004). Knowledge alive. *Educational Leadership, 62*(1), 14–18.

Perkins, D., & Blythe, T. (1994). Putting understanding up front. *Educational Leadership, 51*(5), 4–7.

Persky, H. R., Daane, M. C., & Ying, J. (2003). *The nation's report card: Writing 2002.* Washington, DC: U.S. Department of Education.

Phillips, D. C. (Ed.). (2000). *Constructivism in education.* Chicago: National Society for the Study of Education.

Phye, G. D. (Ed.). (1996). *Handbook of classroom assessment.* Orlando, FL: Academic Press.

Pierce, K. M. (Ed.). (2000). *Adventuring with books: A booklist for pre-K–grade 6.* Champaign-Urbana, IL: National Council of Teachers of English.

Pikulski, J. J., & Chard, D. J. (2005). Fluency: Bridge between decoding and reading comprehension. *The Reading Teacher, 58,* 510–519.

Pinnell, G. S., Fried, M. D., & Eustice, R. M. (1990). Reading Recovery: Learning how to make a difference. *The Reading Teacher, 43,* 282–295.

Pittelman, S. D., Heimlich, J. E., Berglund, R. L., & French, M. P. (1991). *Semantic feature analysis: Classroom applications.* Newark, DE: International Reading Association.

Poindexter, C., & Oliver, I. (1998/1999). Navigating the writing process: Strategies for young children. *The Reading Teacher, 52*(4), 420–423.

Popham, W. J. (1999). *Classroom assessment: What teachers need to know* (2nd ed.). Boston: Allyn & Bacon.

Prawat, R. S. (1989). Teaching for understanding: Three key attributes. *Teaching and Teacher Education, 5,* 315–328.

Press, F. (1984, May 30). Address given at the annual commencement convocation, School of Graduate Studies, Case Western Reserve University, Cleveland, OH.

Pressley, M. (2000). What should comprehension instruction be the instruction of? In M. Kamil, P. Mosenthal, P. D. Pearson, & R. Barr (Eds.), *Handbook of reading research* (vol. 3, pp. 545–561). Mahwah, NJ: Erlbaum.

Pressley, M. (2002). Comprehension strategies instruction: A turn-of-the-century status report. In C. C. Block & M. Pressley (Eds.), *Comprehension instruction: Research-based best practices* (pp. 11–27). New York: Guilford Press.

Pressley, M. (2005). Final reflections—Metacognition in literacy learning: Then, now, and in the future. In S. E. Israel, C. C. Block, K. L. Bauserman, & K. Kinnucan-Welsch (Eds.), *Metacognition in literacy learning* (pp. 391–411). Mahwah, NJ: Erlbaum.

Pressley, M. (2006). *Reading instruction that works: The case for balanced teaching* (3rd ed.). New York: Guilford.

Pressley, M., & Afflerbach, P. (1995). *Verbal protocols of reading: The nature of constructively responsive reading.* Hillsdale, NJ: Erlbaum.

Pressley, M., Allington, R. L., Wharton-McDonald, R., Block, C. C., & Morrow, L. M. (2001). *Learning to read: Lessons from exemplary first-grade classrooms.* New York: Guilford Press.

Pressley, M., Dolezal, S. E., Raphael, L., Mohan, L., Bogner, K., & Roehrig, A. (2003). *Motivating primary grade students.* New York: Guilford Press.

Pressley, M., El-Dinary, P. B., Wharton-McDonald, R., & Brown, R. (1998). Transactional instruction of comprehension strategies in the elementary grades. In D. H. Schunk & B. J. Zimmerman (Eds.), *Self-regulated learning: From teaching to self-reflective practice* (pp. 42–56). New York: Guilford Press.

Pressley, M., Harris, K. R., & Marks, M. B. (1992). But good strategy instructors are constructivists! *Educational Psychology Review, 4,* 3–31.

Pritchard, A. & Cartwright, V. (2004). Transforming what they read: Helping eleven-year-olds engage with internet information. *Literacy, 38*(1), 26.

Purcell-Gates, V. (1989). What oral/written language differences can tell us about beginning instruction. *The Reading Teacher, 42,* 290–294.

Rahne, D. S. (1997). *Beyond the case for cooperative learning: Comparing the jigsaw and peer-response methods.* Unpublished master's thesis, University of Minnesota.

RAND Reading Study Group. (2002). *Reading for understanding: Toward an R&D program in reading comprehension.* Santa Monica, CA: Rand Education. Also available at http://www.rand.org/multi/achievement-forall/reading.

Raphael, T. E. (2000). Balancing literature and instruction: Lessons from the Book Club project. In B. M. Taylor, M. F. Graves, & P. van den Broek (Eds.), *Reading for meaning: Fostering comprehension in the middle grades* (pp. 70–94). New York: Teachers College Press.

Raphael, T. E., Florio-Ruane, S., & George, M. (2001). Book Club *Plus:* A conceptual framework to organize literacy instruction. *Language Arts, 79,* 159–169.

Raphael, T. E., Florio-Ruane, S., George, M. A., Hasty, N. L., & Highfield, K. (2004). *Book Club Plus! A literacy framework for the primary grades.* Laurence, MA: Small Planet Communications.

Raphael, T. E., & McMahon, S. I. (1994). Book Club: An alternative framework for reading instruction. *The Reading Teacher, 48,* 102–116.

Rasinski, T., Blachowicz, C. L. Z., & Lems, K. (Eds.). (in press). *Teaching reading fluency: Meeting the needs of all readers.* New York: Guilford Press.

Rasinski, T. V. (2003). *The fluent reader: Oral reading strategies for building word recognition, fluency, and comprehension.* New York: Scholastic.

Reading Today. (1997, February/March). Program gets parents, students to love reading "beary" much. Newark, DE: International Reading Association.

Reading Today. (2005, April/May). Wordsmiths: Helping students develop as writers. Newark, DE: International Reading Association.

Renaissance Learning. (2005). *Fluent reader.* Wisconsin Rapids, WI: Author.

Resnick, L. B. (1987). *Education and learning to think.* Washington, DC: National Academy Press.

Reutzel, D. R., & Cooter, R. B. (1991). Organizing for effective instruction: The reading workshop. *The Reading Teacher, 44,* 548–554.

Reutzel, D. R., Fawson, P. C., & Smith, J. A. (2003, December). *Teaching comprehension strategies using information texts.* Paper presented at the annual meeting of the National Reading Conference, Scottsdale, AZ.

Rinsky, L. A. (1993). *Teaching word recognition skills.* Scottsdale, AZ: Gorsuch Scarisbrick.

Rosenblatt, L. (1978). *The reader, the text, the poem: The transactional theory of the literary work.* Carbondale, IL: Southern Illinois Press.

Rosenblatt, L. M. (1938/1995). *Literature as exploration.* New York: Modern Language Association.

Routman, R. (1995). *Invitations: Changing as teachers and learners K–12.* Portsmouth, NH: Heinemann.

Routman, R. (2003). *Reading essentials: The specifics you need to teach reading well.* Portsmouth, NH: Heinemann.

Routman, R. (2005). *Writing essentials: Raising expectations and results while simplifying teaching.* Portsmouth, NH: Heinemann.

Rumelhart, D. E. (1977). Toward an interactive model of reading. In S. Dornic (Ed.), *Attention and performance* (vol. 6, pp. 573–603). Hillsdale, NJ: Erlbaum.

Rumelhart, D. E. (1980). Schemata: The building blocks of cognition. In R. J. Spiro, B.C. Bruce, & W. F. Brewer (Eds.), *Theoretical issues in reading comprehension* (pp. 33–58). Hillsdale, NJ: Erlbaum.

Sales, G. H., & Graves, M. F. (2005). *Teaching comprehension strategies.* Minneapolis, MN: Seward Incorporated.

Sampson, M. B., Sampson, M. B., & Linek, W. (1994/1995). Circle of questions. *The Reading Teacher, 48,* 364–365.

Samuels, S. J. (1979). The method of repeated reading. *The Reading Teacher, 32,* 403–408.

Samuels, S. J. (2002a). Reading fluency: Its development and assessment. In S. J. Samuels & A. E. Farstrup (Eds.), *What research has to say about reading instruction* (3rd ed., pp. 166–183). Newark, DE: International Reading Association.

Samuels, S. J. (2002b). *Building reading fluency.* Retrieved 2003 from http://education.umn.edu/CI/MREA/Fluency/fluencyMODtoc.html.

Samuels, S. J. (in press). Reading fluency: Its past, present, and future. In T. Rasinski, C. L. Z. Blachowicz, & K. Lems (Eds.), *Teaching reading fluency: Meeting the needs of all readers.* New York: Guilford Press.

Scarcella, R. C. (1996). English learners and writing: Responding to linguistic diversity. In C. B. Olson (Ed.), *Practical ideas for teaching writing as a process at the elementary school and middle school levels* (pp. 97–103). Sacramento, CA: California State Department of Education.

Schlesinger, A. M., Jr. (1986). *The cycles of American history.* Boston: Houghton Mifflin.

Schmitt, N. (2000). *Vocabulary in language teaching.* Cambridge, England: Cambridge University Press.

Schon, I., & Berkin, S. C. (1996). *Introducción a la literatura infantil y juvenil.* Newark, DE: International Reading Association. (Available only in Spanish.)

Schumaker, J. B., & Deshler, D. D. (2003). Can students with LD become competent writers? *Learning Disability Quarterly, 26,* 129–141.

Schunk, D. H., & Zimmerman, B. J. (Eds.). (1998). *Self-regulated learning: From teaching to self-reflective practice.* New York: Guilford Press.

Scott, J. A., & Nagy, W. E. (2004). Developing word consciousness. In J. F. Baumann & E. J. Kame'enui (Eds.), *Vocabulary instruction: Research to practice* (pp. 201–217). New York: Guilford Press.

Searle, J. R. (1993). Rationality and realism: What is at stake? *Daedalus, 122*(4), 55–83.

Serafini, F. (2004). *Lessons in comprehension: Explicit instruction in the reading workshop.* Portsmouth, NH: Heinemann.

Shany, M. T., & Biemiller, A. (1995). Assisted reading practice: Effects on performance of poor readers in grades 3 and 4. *Reading Research Quarterly, 30,* 382–395.

Share, D. L., Jorm, A. F., Maclean, R., & Matthews, R. (1984). Sources of individual differences in reading achievement. *Journal of Educational Psychology, 76,* 1309–1324.

Shea, M., Murray, R., & Harlin, R. (2005). *Drowning in data: How to collect, organize, and document student performance.* Portsmouth NH: Heinemann.

Short, D., & Echevarria, J. (2004–2005). Teacher skills to support English language learners. *Educational Leadership, 62*(4), 8–13.

Short, K., Kaufman, G., Kaser, L. H., Kahn, L. H., & Crawford, K. M. (1999). "Teacher-watching": Examining teacher talk in literature circles. *Language Arts, 76,* 377–385.

Short, K. G., & Klassen, C. (1993). Literature circles: Hearing children's voices. In B. E. Cullinan (Ed.), *Children's voices: Talk in the classroom* (pp. 66–85). Newark, DE: International Reading Association.

Simpson, D. (1986). *The politics of American English, 1776–1850.* New York: Oxford University Press.

Slavin, R. E. (1987). *Cooperative learning: Student teams* (2nd ed.). Washington, DC: National Education Association.

Slavin, R. E., & Cheung, A. (2005). A synthesis of research on language of reading instruction for English language learners. *Review of Educational Research, 75,* 247–284.

Smith, F. (1971). *Understanding reading. A psycholinguistic analysis of reading and learning to read.* New York: Holt, Rinehart & Winston.

Smith, N. B. (2002). *American reading instruction* (special edition). Newark, DE: International Reading Association.

Snow, C. E. (Ed.). (2004, Winter). English language learners: Boosting academic achievement. *Research Points: Essential Information for Educational Policy, 2,* 1–4. Available at http://www.area.net.

Snow, C. E., Burns, M. S., & Griffin, P. (1998). *Preventing reading difficulties in young children.* Washington, DC: National Academy Press.

Spandel, V. (2005). *The 9 rights of every writer: A guide for teachers.* Portsmouth, NH: Heinemann.

Spiegel, D. L. (1981). *Reading for pleasure: Guidelines.* Newark, DE: International Reading Association.

Spiegel, D. L. (1998). Reader response approaches and the growth of readers. *Language Arts, 76,* 41–56.

Stahl, S. A. (1998). Four questions about vocabulary knowledge and reading and some answers. In C. R. Hynd (Ed.), *Learning from text across conceptual domains* (pp. 73–94). Mahwah, NJ: Erlbaum.

Stanovich, K. E. (1991a). Changing models of reading and reading acquisition. In L. Rieben & C. A. Perfetti (Eds.), *Learning to read* (pp. 19–31). Hillsdale, NJ: Erlbaum.

Stanovich, K. E. (1991b). Word recognition: Changing perspectives. In R. Barr, M. L. Kamil, P. B. Mosenthal, & P. D. Pearson (Eds.), *Handbook of reading research* (vol. 2, pp. 418–452). New York: Longman.

Stanovich, K. E. (1992). Speculations on the causes and consequences of individual differences in early reading acquisition. In P. B. Gough, L. C. Ehri, & R. Treiman (Eds.), *Reading acquisition* (pp. 307–342). Hillsdale, NJ: Erlbaum.

Stanovich, K. E. (1994). Constructivism in reading education. *Journal of Special Education, 28,* 259–274.

Stauffer, R. G. (1969). *Directing reading maturity as a cognitive process.* New York: Harper & Row.

Steffenson, M. S., Joag-Dev, C., & Anderson, R. C. (1979). A cross-cultural perspective on reading comprehension. *Reading Research Quarterly, 15,* 10–29.

Steiner, S. F. (2001). *Promoting a global community through multicultural children's literature.* Portsmouth, NH: Teacher Ideas Press.

Stephens, D., & Story, J. (2000). *Assessment as inquiry: Learning the hypothesis-test process.* Urbana, IL: NCTE.

Sternberg, R. J. (1987). Most vocabulary is learned from context. In M. G. McKeown & M. E. Curtis (Eds.), *The nature of vocabulary acquisition* (pp. 89–105). Hillsdale, NJ: Erlbaum.

Sternberg, R. J., & Grigorenko, E. L. (2004). Intelligence in the classroom. *Theory into Practice, 43,* 274–280.

Sternberg, R. J., & Spear-Sperling, L. S. (1996). *Teaching for thinking.* Washington, DC: American Psychological Association.

Stiggins, R. J. (1994). *Student-centered classroom assessment.* New York: Merrill.

Stipek, D. (2002). *Motivation to learn: Integrating theory and practice* (4th ed.). Boston: Allyn & Bacon.

Strickland, K., & Strickland, J. (2000). *Making assessment elementary.* Portsmouth, NH: Heinemann.

Sulzby, E., & Teale, W. (1996). Emergent literacy. In R. Barr, M. Kamil, P. B. Mosenthal, & P. D. Pearson

(Eds.), *Handbook of reading research* (vol. 2, pp. 727–758). New York: Longman.

Sum, A., Kirsch, I., & Taggart, R. (2002). *The twin challenges of mediocrity and inequality: Literacy in the U.S. from an international perspective.* Princeton, NJ: Educational Testing Service.

Swift, K. (1993). Try reading workshop in your classroom. *The Reading Teacher, 46,* 366–371.

Taylor, B. M., Hanson, B. E., Justice-Swanson, K., & Watts, S. M. (1997). Helping struggling readers: Linking small-group intervention with cross-age tutoring. *The Reading Teacher, 51,* 196–209.

Taylor, B. M., Pearson, P. D., Clark, K., & Walpole, S. (2000). Effective schools and accomplished teachers: Lessons about primary-grade reading instruction in low-income schools. *Elementary School Journal, 101,* 121–165.

Taylor, B. M., Pearson, P. D., Peterson, D. S., & Rodriguez, M. C. (2003). Reading growth in high-poverty classrooms. *Elementary School Journal, 104,* 3–28.

Taylor, B. M., Pressley, M., & Pearson, P. D. (2002). Research-supported characteristics of schools and teachers that promote reading achievement. In B. M. Taylor & P. D. Pearson (Eds.), *Teaching reading: Effective schools, accomplished teachers* (pp. 361–373). Mahwah, NJ: Erlbaum.

Taylor, B. M., Short, R. A., Frye, B. J., & Shearer, B. A. (1992). Classroom teachers prevent reading failure among low-achieving first-grade children. *The Reading Teacher, 45,* 592–597.

Taylor, B. T., Pearson, P. D., Peterson, D. S., & Rodriguez, M. C. (2003). Reading growth in high-poverty classrooms. *Elementary School Journal, 104,* 3–28.

Taylor, B. T., Pearson, P. D., Peterson, D. S., & Rodriguez, M. C. (2005). The CIERA school change framework. *Reading Research Quarterly, 40,* 40–69.

Temple, C., Nathan, R., Temple, F., & Burris, N. A. (1993). *The beginnings of writing* (3rd ed.). Boston: Allyn & Bacon.

Thomason, T. (1998). *Writer to writer: How to conference young authors.* Norwood, MA: Christopher-Gordon.

Thorndyke, P. (1977). Cognitive structures in comprehension and memory of narrative discourse. *Cognitive Psychology, 9,* 97–110.

Tierney R. J., Carter, M. A., & Desai, L. E. (1991). *Portfolio assessment in the reading-writing classroom.* Norwood, MA: Christopher-Gordon.

Tierney, R. J., & Readence, J. E. (2000). *Reading strategies: A compendium* (5th ed.). Boston: Allyn & Bacon.

Tierney, R. J. & Readence, J. E. (2005). *Reading strategies and practices: A compendium* (6th ed.). Boston: Allyn & Bacon.

Tollefson, J. W. (1995). Introduction: Language policy, power, and inequality. In J. W. Tollefson (Ed.), *Power and inequality in language education.* Cambridge, England: Cambridge University Press.

Tompkins, G. E. (1996). Becoming an effective teacher of reading. *WSRA Journal, 13*(2), 1–7.

Torgesen, J. K. (1998). Catch them before they fall. *American Educator, 22*(1–2), 32–39.

Treiman, R. (1992). The role of intrasyllabic units in learning to read and spell. In P. B. Gough, L. C. Ehri, & R. Treiman (Eds.), *Reading acquisition* (pp. 65–106). Hillsdale, NJ: Erlbaum.

Trelease, J. (1995). *The new read-aloud handbook* (4th ed.). New York: Penguin Books.

U.S. Department of Education. (1995). *Listening to children read aloud.* Washington, DC: Author. Available at http://nces.ed.gov/pubs95/web/95762.asp.

Vacca, R., & Linek, W. M. (1992). Writing to learn. In J. W. Irwin & M. A. Doyle (Eds.), *Reading/writing connections: Learning from research* (pp. 145–159). Newark, DE: International Reading Association.

Vandervelden, M. C., & Siegel, L. S. (1995). Phonological recoding and phoneme awareness in early literacy: A developmental approach. *Reading Research Quarterly, 30,* 854–875.

Vaughan, S. (2005, October). *A three-tier model for preventing and remediating reading difficulties: Response to intervention.* Paper presented at the 3rd Guy Bond Memorial Conference on Reading, Minneapolis, MN.

von Glaserfeld, E. (1984). An introduction to radical constructivism. In P. Watzlawick (Ed.), *The invented reality* (pp. 17–40). New York: W. W. Norton.

Vygotsky, L. S. (1978). *Mind in society: The development of higher psychological processes.* Cambridge, MA: Harvard University Press.

Walmsley, S. A. (1996, August). Ten ways to improve your theme teaching. *The Instructor,* 54–60.

Watts, S. M., & Graves, M. F. (1997). Fostering middle school students' understanding of challenging texts. *Middle School Journal, 29*(1), 45–51.

Werderich, D. E. (2002). Individualized responses: Using journal letters as a vehicle for differentiated reading instruction. *Journal of Adolescent and Adult Literacy, 45*(8), 746–754.

Wertsch, J. V. (1998). *Mind as action.* New York: Oxford University Press.

Wharton-McDonald, R., Pressley, M., & Hampston, J. M. (1998). Literacy instruction in nine first-grade classrooms: Teacher characteristics and student achievement. *Elementary School Journal, 99,* 101–128.

White, T. G., Graves, M. F., & Slater, W. H. (1990). Growth of reading vocabulary in diverse elementary schools: Decoding and word meaning. *Journal of Educational Psychology, 82*(2), 281–290.

White, T. G., Slater, W. H., & Graves, M. F. (1989). Yes/no method of vocabulary assessment: Valid for whom and useful for what? In S. McCormick & V. Zutel (Eds.), *Cognitive and social perspectives for literacy research and instruction.* Chicago IL: National Reading Conference.

White, T. G., Sowell, J., & Yanagihara, A. (1989). Teaching elementary students to use word-part clues. *The Reading Teacher, 44,* 302–307.

Whitehead, A. N. (1929). *The aims of education and other essays.* New York: Macmillan.

Whitehurst, G. J., Arnold, D. S., Epstein, J. N., Angell, A. L., Smith, M., & Fischel, J. E. (1994). A picture book reading intervention in day care and home for children from low-income families. *Developmental Psychology, 30,* 697–699.

Wiencek, J. E. (1996). Planning, initiating, and sustaining literature discussion groups: The teacher's role. In L. B. Gambrell & J. F. Almasi (Eds.), *Lively discussions! Fostering engaged reading* (pp. 208–223). Newark, DE: International Reading Association.

Wigfield, A., & Eccles, J. S. (2002). *Development of achievement motivation.* San Diego: Academic Press.

Wiggins, G., & McTighe, J. (1998). *The understanding by design handbook.* Alexandria, VA: Association for Supervision and Curriculum Development.

Wiggins, G. P. (1993). *Assessing student performance.* San Francisco: Jossey-Bass.

Wilkinson, G. S. (1995). *Wide-Range Achievement Test 3.* Wilmington, DE: Jastak.

Winebrenner, S. (1992, September). Meeting the needs of your high-ability students. *Instructor,* 60–63.

Wirt, J., Choy, S., Rooney, P., Hussar, W., Kridl, B., & Livingston, A. (2005). *The Conditions of Education 2005.* Washington, DC: U.S. Department of Education.

Wise, B. W. (1992). Whole words and decoding for short-term learning: Comparisons on a "talking-computer" system. *Child Psychology, 54,* 147–167.

Wise, B. W., Olson, R. K., & Trieman, R. (1990). Subsyllabic units in computerized reading instruction. Onset-rime versus postvowel segmentation. *Journal of Experimental Child Psychology, 49,* 1–19.

Wiske, M. S. (Ed.). (1998). *Teaching for understanding: Linking research with practice.* San Francisco: Jossey-Bass.

Wittrock, M. (1986). Students' thought processes. In M. C. Wittrock (Ed.), *Handbook of research on teaching* (3rd ed., pp. 297–314). New York: Macmillan.

Wollman-Bonilla, J. E. (2001). Can first-grade writers demonstrate audience awareness? *Reading Research Quarterly, 36*(2), 184–201

Wollman-Bonilla, J. E., & Werchadlo, B. (1995). Literature response journals in a first-grade classroom. *Language Arts, 72*(8), 562–570.

Wood, D. J., Bruner, J. S., & Ross, G. (1976). The role of tutoring in problem-solving. *Journal of Child Psychology and Psychiatry, 17*(2), 89–100.

Wood, K. D., Lapp, D., & Flood, J. (1992). *Guiding readers through text: A review of study guides.* Newark, DE: International Reading Association.

Wood, K. D., & Mateja, J. A. (1983). Adapting secondary-level strategies for use in elementary classrooms. *The Reading Teacher, 36,* 492–496.

Woodcock, R. W., McGrew, K. S., & Mather, N. (2001). *Woodcock-Johnson III Tests of Achievement.* Itasca, IL: Riverside Publishing.

Wylie, R. E., & Durrell, D. D. (1970). Teaching vowels through phonograms. *Elementary English, 47,* 787–791.

Yokota, J. (Ed.). (2001). *Kaleidoscope: A multicultural booklist for grades K–8* (2nd ed.). Champaign-Urbana, IL: National Council of Teachers of English.

Young, T. A., & Vardell, S. (1993). Weaving readers theatre and nonfiction into the curriculum. *The Reading Teacher, 46,* 396–406.

Zevenbergen, A. A., & Whitehurst, G. J. (2004). Dialogic reading: A shared picture book reading intervention for preschoolers. In A. V. Kleeck, S. A. Stahl, & E. B. Bauer (Eds.), *On reading books to children: Parents and teachers* (pp. 177–200). Mahwah, NJ: Erlbaum.

Photo Credits

Chapter 10

294 © Jonathan Nourok/PhotoEdit
299 © Will Faller
303 © Tannen Maury/The Image Works
307 © Brian Smith

Classroom Portrait

314 © Lindfors Photography
324 © Lindfors Photography
325 © Lindfors Photography
328 © Lindfors Photography

Chapter 11

330 © Dennis MacDonald/PhotoEdit
336 © Will Faller
346 © Will Faller

Chapter 12

356 © Peter Hvizdak/The Image Works
359 © Brian Smith
362 © Lindfors Photography
372 © Will Faller
378 Courtesy of the author
387 © Will Hart

Chapter 13

394 © Robin Sachs/PhotoEdit
398 © Bettmann/CORBIS
407 © Michael Newman/PhotoEdit
416 © Nancy Richmond/The Image Works

Chapter 14

426 © Bob Daemmrich/The Image Works
435 © Bob Daemmrich/The Image Works
444 © Pearson Education
462 © Tony Freeman/PhotoEdit

Classroom Portrait

474 Courtesy of the author
476 Courtesy of the author
478 © Will Hart
481 © Lawrence Migdale Pix

Name Index

Cronbach, L. J., 436
Cronemeyer, T., 228
Cronin, D., 107
Cruxton, B., 346, 347
Cruxton, B. J., 355
Csikszentmihalyi, M., 69
CTB/McGraw-Hill, 194, 465
Cullinan, B., 358
Cullinan, B. E., 63, 64, 301, 303, 380
Cummings, M., 3
Cummins, C., 280
Cummins, J., 399
Cummins, S., 368
Cunningham, A., 296
Cunningham, A. E., 208, 296
Cunningham, J. W., 258, 358
Cunningham, P., 214
Cunningham, P. M., 162, 248, 257, 358
Cushman, K., 377, 392
Cutchins, J., 285, 293
Cutler, J., 253

Daane, M. C., 361
Dahl, R., 372, 392, 473, 479
Daniels, H., 302
David, Y. M., 345
Day, J. D., 277
de Glopper, K., 221
De Temple, J., 208
Defee, M., 257
Delacre, L., 389, 392
Delpit, L. D., 25, 406, 409, 420
Demarest, C., 142
Deno, S., 187
Desai, L. E., 448
Deshler, D. D., 282, 291
Detmar, J., 186–187
Dewitz, P., 64, 214
DiCamillo, K., 1, 27, 256, 269, 374, 392
Dickenson, R., 255
Diller, D., 50
Dillon, J. T., 446
Dionisio, M., 362, 363
Dole, J. A., 21, 245, 272, 283
Dolezal, S. E., 49, 76, 85
Dolphin, L., 22, 27
Donahue, P., 398
Donovan, M. S., 299
Dooley, N., 65
Dorros, A., 411, 425
Duffy, G. G., 21, 33, 40, 272, 283
Duguid, P., 41
Duin, A. H., 228, 229
Duke, N. K., 40, 221, 239, 250, 283, 419, 420

Dunbar, S. B., 440
Duncan, A. F., 269
Durrell, D. D., 146
Dykstra, R., 42, 45, 134
Dyson, A. H., 360

Eccles, J. S., xxvii
Echevarria, J., 422
Edwards, E. C., 221
Edwards, R., 151, 163
Ehlert, L., 107, 318
Ehri, L. C., 95, 100, 144, 146
El-Dinary, P. B., 283
Elbow, P., 368
Eller, N., 482
Emig, J., 361
Ennis, R., 332
Erdrich, L., 282
Estes, C., 252
Eustice, R. M., 161

Falk, B., 430
Farr, R., 358, 448, 452
Fawson, P. C., 283
Feelings, M., 107
Fetterman, D. M., 459
Fielding, L., 59, 209, 296
Fillenworth, L. I., 345
Fisher, P., 230
Fitzgerald, J., 402, 421
Fitzhugh, J., 33
Five, C. L., 362, 363
Flake, S., 3
Flake, S. G., 27
Flaubert, G., 484
Flavel, J., 11
Flawell, C., 227
Fleischman, J., 275, 293
Fleischman, S., 202, 203, 370, 392
Flesch, R., 45
Fleshman, S., 202
Flicker, M. L., 58
Flood, J., 263
Florio-Ruane, S., 304
Flynn, R. M., 266
Font, G., 221
Forbes, E., 23, 27
Ford, C., 151, 163
Forsythe, S. J., 248
Fountas, I. C., 12, 159, 195, 197, 198, 202, 256

Kulic, C. L., 417
Kulic, J., 417
Kurlansky, M., 73

LaBerge, D., 9, 173
Lane, D., 419
Langer, J., 358
Lapp, D., 263
LeBlanc, J., 164–169, 484
Lederer, R., 227
Leedy, L., 341, 355
Lehr, F., 173
Lems, K., 173
Leslie, L., 194
Lester, R., 147
Lewin, T., 252, 269
Linek, W., 69, 70
Linek, W. M., 366
Lionni, L., 265, 269
Livingston, M. C., 107
Lizcano, P., 191
Lobel, A., 12, 93, 121, 191, 237, 269, 277, 293
Lord, B. B., 27
Lowell, S., 191
Lowery, L., 31, 241, 269, 411, 425
Lukens, R. J., 454
Lundberg, I., 127
Lutkus, A. D., 14, 335

MacLachlan, P., 302, 312, 373, 392
Maclean, M., 94
Maclean, R., 92
Madaus, G. F., 428
Madden, K., 310, 312
Maehr, M., 76
Mandler, J., 259
Mann, H., 44
Manning, J. M., 310
Mansukhani, P., 250
Maras, C., 392
Markle, S., 31, 379
Marks, M. B., 290
Marshall, J., 7, 90, 104, 121
Martin, A., 370, 392
Martin, B., Jr., 144, 161, 163, 253
Martin, M. O., 15
Martinez, C., 108, 109
Martinez, D. D., 418
Marzano, R. J., 459
Marzollo, J., 142

Mason, J. M., 50
Masters, N., 78–79
Matas, C., 358
Mateja, J. A., 263
Mather, N., 452
Matthews, R., 92
Mazzoni, S. A., 240
McCarthy, S. J., 368
McClure, A. A., 66, 268
McClure, A., 66
McConkie, G. W., 126
McCormack, B. B., 240
McCracken, M. J., 298
McCracken, R. A., 298
McDonald, A., 38, 53
McGrew, K. S., 452
McKeown, M. G., 206, 208, 228, 229, 250, 260, 333, 336, 343, 344
McKissack, F., 379
McKissack, P. C., 379
McMahon, M. M., 240
McMahon, P., 65
McMahon, S. I., 304
McMillan, B., 107
McPhail, D., 273
McPhail, D. M., 293
McTighe, J., 335, 338, 430
McWhorter, D., 263, 269
Mead, F., 146
Meinbach, A., 310
Meinbach, A. M., 303, 483
Meloth, M., 40
Meltzer, M., 279
Meyers, C., 140
Midgley, C., 76
Miles, S., 389
Miller, G. A., 224
Miller, T., 482
Miller-Lachmann, L., 64
Mills, H., 301
Minden-Cupp, C., 141, 144, 146
Minnick, J. B., 373
Mitchell, R., 430
Mizokawa, D. T., 268
Mlawer, T., 191
Mode, B. A., 374
Moll, L. C., 76
Montgomery, K., 430
Moore, D. W., 358
Moore, S. A., 358
Mora, P., 191, 418
Moran, R., 14, 335
Morice, D., 227
Morris, A., 107
Morris, E., 274
Morrow, L. M., 4, 59
Mullis, I. V. S., 15
Murray, R., 438

Musgrove, M., 142
Myers, C., 163

N

Nagy, W. E., 206, 220, 226
Nathan, R., 360, 383
Nation, I. S. P., 207, 213, 231
National Center on Education and the Economy, 438
National Council of Teachers of English (NCTE), xxvii, 18, 64
National Council of Teachers of English and International Reading Association, 17, 18
National Council on Measurement in Education (NCME), 463
National Education Association (NEA), 463
National Institute of Child Health and Human Development, 173
National Reading Panel, xxvii, 18, 47, 95, 134, 207, 274
National Research Council, xxvii, 47, 56, 72, 76
Neet, S., 482, 483
New Standards Primacy Literacy Committee, 100, 152, 153, 159
Newmann, F. N., 335, 338
Nikola-Lisa, W., 355
Nitko, A. J., 452, 459, 463, 464, 466
No Child Left Behind Act of 2001, xxvii, 19
Noddings, N., 72
Novack, R., 280–281

O

O'Dell, H., 144–145
O'Dell, S., 410, 425
O'Keefe, T., 301
O'Malley, J. M., 431
Ogle, D., 261
Oliver, I., 369
Olness, R., 383
Olson, C. B., 358
Olson, J. F., 398
Olson, R. K., 147
Omanson, R. C., 206
Oppenheim, S. L., 65
Orehovec, B., 308
Osborn, J., 173, 180, 181
Osofsky, A., 377, 392
Owocki, G., 443

P

Palincsar, A. M., 267, 345, 347, 349
Parish, H., 191
Park, B., 87
Parker, S., 57, 87, 367, 392
Paterson, K., 252, 269, 304, 313, 455, 473
Patnoe, S., 42, 75, 350
Patrick, C. L., 6, 265, 266
Patterson, L., 438
Paul, A. W., 142
Paulson, G., 282
Pearson, P. D., 5, 19, 21, 30, 37, 40, 43, 45, 59, 73, 218, 221, 231, 250, 272, 283, 333
Pellegrini, M., 331
Pellegrino, J. W., 299
Perfumo, P., 454
Perie, M., 14, 335, 398
Perkins, A. R., 64
Perkins, D., 16, 41, 335, 338, 342, 446
Perkins, L. R., 473, 477
Perone, V., 338
Perry, A., 480
Persky, H. R., 361
Peterson, D. S., 19, 30, 73, 333
Pfeffer, W., 31
Philippot, R., 375
Philippot, R. A., 267, 309
Phillips, D. C., 5
Phye, G. D., 431
Pierce, L. V., 431
Pikulski, J. J., 10, 20, 172, 443
Pinkney, B., 253
Pinnell, G. S., 12, 159, 161, 195, 197, 198, 202, 256
Pittelman, S. D., 218, 219, 264, 265, 369
Poindexter, C., 369
Polk, J. K., 196
Pomerantz, C., 118, 121
Popham, W. J., 463
Prawat, R. S., 335
Prelutsky, J., 66, 181, 203, 227, 252, 269
Prenn, M. C., 245
Press, F., 339
Pressley, M., xxvii, 19, 30, 48, 49, 56, 57, 59, 69, 76, 77, 78, 85, 246, 272, 274, 280, 282, 283, 290
Pringle, L., 31, 379
Pritchard, A., 263
Puente, D., 314–329, 484
Putnam, J., 40

R

Rahne, D. S., 351
Ramirez, A., 411, 425

Stahl, P. 463
Stahl, S. A., 172, 220
Stan, S., 64
Stanley, D., 273, 293
Stanovich, K., 296
Stanovich, K. E., 6, 7, 126
Stauffer, R. G., 242
Steffenson, M. S., 405
Steiner, S. F., 311
Stephens, D., 301, 436
Sternberg, R. J., 220, 332, 334
Stewart, M. T., 280
Stiggins, R. J., 452, 463
Stipek, D., 76
Story, J., 436
Strickland, J., 431
Strickland, K., 431
Sullivan, G., 326
Sulzby, E., 90
Sum, A., 335
Sun, C. F., 6, 27
Sweat, L., 191
Swift, K., 308

T

Tafuri, N., 91, 121
Taggart, R., 335
Tatham, B., 75, 87
Taylor, B. M., 30, 161, 162, 231
Taylor, B. T., 19, 69, 73, 333
Teale, W., 90
Temple, C., 360, 383
Temple, F., 360, 383
Templeton, S., 136
Tesh, C., 181
Thayer, M., 404
Thimmesh, C., 75
Thomas, B., 352
Thomas, J. R., 370, 377, 392
Thomas, S. M., 191
Thorndyke, P., 259
Thornhill, J., 142
Tierney, R. J., 42, 242, 256, 259, 305, 308, 350, 448
Timmesh, C., 87
Tindal, G., 187, 189
Tirre, W., 14, 335
Tollefson, J. W., 399
Tomason, T., 386
Tomlinson, C. M., 64
Tompkins, G. E., 361
Tone, B., 448
Torgesen, J. K., 117
Tran, T., 231, 233
Trapani, I., 47
Trathen, W., 283

Treiman, R., 95, 144, 146, 147
Trelease, J., 111
Truesdell, K. S., 248
Trumbauer, L., 341, 355
Turner, A., 377, 392
Turner, P., 31

U

U.S. Department of Education, 189, 397

V

Vacca, R., 366
Valencia, S. W., 245
Van Allsburg, C., 254, 269
Van Leeuwen, J., 12
Van Meter, P., 282
Vandervelden, M. C., 95, 146
Vardell, S., 248
Vaughan, S., 396
Vavrus, L., 40
Velthuijs, M., 231, 233
Ventura, G. B., 418
Viens, J., 353
Vincent, M., 49, 77
Vogt, M. E., 422
Voight, C., 282
von Glaserfeld, E., 5, 6
Vygotsky, L. S., 7, 36

W

Wallower, L., 336, 355
Walmsley, S. A., 483
Walpole, S., 231
Walter, M. P., 253
Wardrop, J. L., 245
Waters, K., 107
Watts, S. M., 162, 226, 243
Waugh, J. R., 301
Weatherford, C. B., 31
Wells, R., 151, 163
Welsh, L. M., 49, 76
Werchadlo, B., 372, 373
Werderich, D. E., 375
Wertsch, J. V., 7
Wesselman, R., 40
Westbelle, G., 468
Weston, M., 46
Wharton-McDonald, R., 49, 283

Subject Index

Comprehension
    active awareness of, 13
    as assessment of fluency, 190
    definition of, 9
    direct explanation and, 40
    federal programs promoting, 47–48
    as goal of word study, 137
    metacognition and, 11–12
    purpose, selection, and reader and, 236–240
    rubric system and, 452
    scaffolding of, 21
    strategies for teaching. *See* Comprehension
        strategies
    in whole-language and literature-based approaches, 46
Comprehension strategies
    appropriate for all texts, 264–266
    assessment of, 274, 281, 288, 290
    characteristics of, 273–274
    constructivism in, 288, 290
    definition of, 272
    for English learners, 291, 423
    for expository texts, 261–264
    key types of, 274–281
    modification of, 291
    for narratives, 259–260
    in prereading activities, 246–247
    teaching of, 282–290
Computer-aided vocabulary instruction, 231
Concepts, learning, 211–212, 246
Concepts-about-print assessment, 442
Concepts of Print Test, 94
Conditions of Education 2005, The (U.S. Dept. of
        Education), 397
Conferences
    parent, 432, 435
    quarterly student, 334, 435
    on student writing, 386
Conflicts, cooperative learning and, 74
Conjunctions, as function words, 126
Consonant(s), 128–129, 133
    final, 149
    initial, 145
Consonant blends, 150–152
Consonant-consonant-vowel-consonant (CCVC) struc-
        ture, 151
Consonant digraphs, 152, 153
Consonant-vowel-consonant (CVC) structure, 129, 144,
        151
Constructivism, 5–6
    in comprehension strategies, 288, 290
    instructional practices and, 35–42, 397
Content words, 126
Context clues
    in reading game rules, 327
    in vocabulary development, 220–222
Context-relationship procedure, 216
Contexts, authentic, 40, 41
Contextualized meaning, 40–41, 125–126

Conventions of print, 106
Cooperative learning
    benefits of, 74–75
    definition of, 41–42
    for English learners, 421
    jigsaw technique in, 350
    in story problems, 82
    as teaching strategy, 287
Copy Me, Copycub (Edwards), 151
Counterfeit Princess, The (Thomas), 370
Cowboy ABC, The (Demarest), 142
Creative thinking, 334
Criss Cross (Perkins), 477
Criterion-referenced tests, 459, 463, 464
Critical responses, informational books for, 31, 33
Critical thinking, by English learners, 407
Cross-cultural influences, on literacy, 405
Cultural authenticity, 63
Cultures. *See also* Diversity; English learners
    books illustrating, 65, 238
    making connections to students', 75–76, 410–411
    variety of literacy heritages in, 401
    writing activities around, 388–389
Current events, as reading opportunity, 104
Curriculum
    differentiating, 388
    federal role in, 47–48
    literacy, 18–23
    logbook planning for, 454, 456
    strands of, 456
Curriculum-based assessment, 437
Curriculum-Based Measurement (CBM), 187–188
CVC, 129, 144, 151

D

Daily schedule
    case study of, 112–117, 164–169
    as reading opportunity, 104
Dan the Flying Man (Cowley), 114
Dance, as postreading activity, 301
Dancer/La bailarina, The (Browne), 418
Days with Frog and Toad (Lobel), 237, 277
Dear Mr. Henshaw (Cleary), 377
Dear Papa (Ylvisaker), 377
Decision making, in assessment, 459–460
Decoding, 32, 172
    assessing skills in, 443
    in English learners, 422
Decontextualized meaning, 126
Deliberately Heterogeneous Groups, 81
Delpit's principles, 406–411
Demonstrations, in writing workshop, 384–385
Derivational suffix, 130, 131
Developmental Reading Assessment, 452
Developmental standards, in assessment, 434

high-frequency, 135, 138, 144, 212
making new, 150, 258
multisyllabic, 133, 157
root, 130, 131, 223
sight, 138
sources of, 228
student knowledge of, 206, 210–213
synthetic, 443
Words Their Way (Bear), 156
Workbooks, 462, 463
Worlds Apart (Johnson), 75
WRAT, 452
Writer to Writer: How to Conference Young Authors
    (Tomason), 386
Writers, challenging skillful, 389
Writing
    as aid to reading, 210
    assessment rubrics for, 449–452
    brainstorming in, 367–368
    classroom environment for, 359–361
    to communicate, 375–379
    as component of Book Club, 305
    across the curriculum, 359
    in emergent literacy, 106–110

feedback on, 385–386
imaginative, 380–383
informal, 364–365
invented, 98–99
to learn and understand, 366–375
peer response to, 351, 386
as postreading activity, 251, 252
process approach to, 46, 361–364
publishing, 387
responding to, 385–386
time for, 384
Venn diagrams in, 370
Writing center, 168, 360
Writing contests, 390
Writing portfolio, 386, 448–449
Writing workshop, 383–385

Z

Zone of proximal development, 36–37, 397
Zoo Books 2, 367